Fay, Bernard, 1893-
Bernard Fay's Franklin, the apostle of modern times. Boston, Little, Brown, and Co., 1929.
xvi, 547 p. front., plates, ports., maps (part fold.) facsims. 24cm.
The English version was prepared by Bravig Imbs. cf. Pref.
Bibliography: p. [517]-533.

1. Franklin, Benjamin, 1706-1790. I. Imbs, Bravig, tr. II. Title: Franklin, the apostle of modern times.

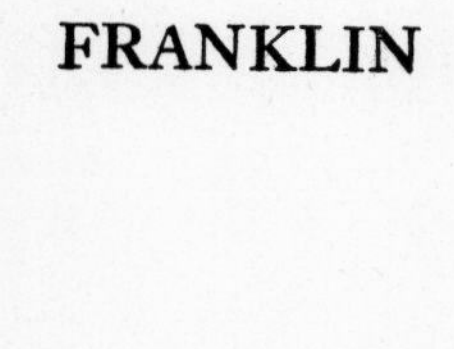

FRANKLIN

PORTRAIT OF FRANKLIN MADE IN FRANCE

BERNARD FAŸ's

FRANKLIN,

THE APOSTLE OF MODERN TIMES.

With Illustrations.

BOSTON:

Published by LITTLE, BROWN, AND COMPANY, MCMXXIX

Published November, 1929
Reprinted November, 1929
Reprinted December, 1929

PRINTED IN THE UNITED STATES OF AMERICA

PREFACE

When Franklin was living in France, he claimed that his face was as familiar there as the moon. This was no exaggeration: innumerable prints and engravings pictured the Patriarch everywhere; columns in the newspapers were devoted to his activities, and historians wrote about him constantly.

They have continued to do so ever since — at least in America. Few great men have been honored with more biographies than he. Some of them are excellent: Parton's huge work, "Life and Times of Benjamin Franklin", is of an inexhaustible erudition; Paul Leicester Ford's "The Many-Sided Franklin" is incomparably precise, but the latest biography "Franklin, the First Civilized American", by Mr. Phillips Russell is rather comical.

Why, then, write a new book on Franklin? Simply, because in the last six years I have spent in research, I have discovered innumerable documents unknown to former biographers — between six hundred to nine hundred unpublished letters, for example, which throw new light on the Doctor's life. They have cleared up many obscure points: his religious and moral attitude, his Masonic rôle, his political and diplomatic activity, and the loves of his later years.

Some have called Franklin Christian, others, Atheist. Both judgments are equally unjust. These documents of Franklin's private life enable me to show that he was a follower of the seventeenth-century English Pythagoreans. He believed in metempsychosis, and in a supreme Deity, who was surrounded with innumerable inferior gods, with Christ for one of His prophets. He garnered these ideas during his boyhood in the curious society of anti-clerical radicals, doctors, shopkeepers, tavern-keepers and journalists, which he and his brother, James, frequented (1720–23).

Franklin's successes and setbacks, his principles and opinions cannot be followed or understood, unless his Masonic career, with all its implications, is carefully studied. He never could have formed a middle-class political party in Pennsylvania, nor had himself accepted by the British Government, nor — and most important — could he have been able to win over Vergennes and Louis XVI to America's side, had it not been for the invaluable support of his Masonic brothers. I have attempted in this book to give a complete and continuous history of Franklin's Masonic career, and it is the first time that such an attempt has been made.

The unpublished documents at my disposal gave an entirely different sense to Franklin's political activity. Its nationalistic character disappears, and the fact that Franklin's policies were based on a haunting ideal of an empire becomes more and more evident. Earl Loudoun's diaries, now in the Huntington Library, clear up the mystery of Franklin's brusque departure for England, and reveal the great hopes he entertained on his voyage. The Franklin-Galloway correspondence at the Mason Library enables us to follow day by day his incomparable diplomacy between the crafty Penns, and haughty King and the mercenary Parliament. It also includes the extraordinary letter to Pitt in which Franklin denounced the Privy Council of the King as being a pack of rascals. This revealing document has been hitherto unknown and offers a brilliant example of Franklin's infinite cunning.

Thanks to the archives of the Ministry of Foreign Affairs in France, and the Public Record Office in London, we can at length realize the difficulties that Franklin had to surmount before he inveigled France into the Revolutionary War. He was surrounded with spies. Some of his best friends, and American advisers, such as Bancroft, were paid by England. His colleague, Ralph Izard, who had been sent over by Congress, almost succeeded, by a last minute maneuver, in hindering the signing of the Franco-American treaty. Izard also kept

London in touch with what was going on. Some Frenchmen dabbled in treason, too, those who were suspected the least, the Philosophers, who were, besides, most friendly to Franklin. But they were so fond of peace they kept up a continual correspondence with London! Franklin's success is well known, but the obstacles he had to overcome before he triumphed have been less emphasized.

As to Franklin's sentimental life, its richness has already been hinted at, and there was so much to discover! Mr. Roelker's archives give us details on Franklin's love for Katy Ray, the pretty Rhode Island girl, whom he kept from marrying a handsome Spaniard. (In after years, to thank Franklin, she sent him sugar plums.) Thanks to the papers of the Guestiers and Mun families, we learn of Franklin's courtship (at the age of 75), of Madame Helvétius, who had been pretty and who was still attractive; of his plan to marry his grandson, Temple, to a charming, wealthy French girl, Mademoiselle Brillon; and how Temple rascally repaid his efforts by presenting him with an illegitimate great-grandson, and causing a lovely blue-eyed Frenchwoman to grieve.

The innumerable facts that I have gathered together here for the first time, bring us closer to Franklin and show him to be more picturesque, more in contrast to the background of his epoch, the eighteenth century. This biography is neither local nor national, but is the story of one of the great leaders of men in the eighteenth century. Thus, one can judge and estimate his immense influence, which was also varied, as he dominated the political, scientific and philosophic world of his time. But of all his titles to glory, the most outstanding one is that he was the first bourgeois in the world.

In this eighteenth century which attempted to do away with aristocracy, and to orient itself to the domination of the middle-class, Franklin was the great precursor, the great example. He defined the principles of the bourgeois in his works, and made his life a pattern to follow. He exemplified it by Poor Richard and this was why the entire universe submitted to his influence. To understand the amplitude and importance of this influence,

Franklin had to be considered from an international standpoint, and his activity in science, politics, religion and philosophy had to be fully studied.

A work of such great scope could not have been accomplished without the aid and support of the very many generous persons who, by their erudition, criticism, and acquirements, rendered me such inestimable services. Mr. Mason's collection, the richest in the world, was opened to me, and I am especially indebted to him and his librarian, Mr. George Edward, for their invaluable suggestions. Mr. G. S. Eddy, whose Franklinian erudition is profound, furnished me with the most precious part of my bibliography, and offered solutions to such prickly problems as Franklin's territorial speculations, the Hutchinson affair, the Gargaz affair, etc. In several cases, I have simply used the facts he gave me, or permitted me to collect, though, of course, I alone am responsible for my conclusions and my method.

I wish also to thank the National Library of France — in particular, M. de La Roncière, M. Lailler and their colleagues for their innumerable kind services; the administration of the British Museum, the Public Library of New York, the Imperial Library of Berlin, the Royal Library of Stockholm, the Royal Archives of Denmark, the Boston Public Library, the Massachusetts Historical Society, the American Antiquarian Society, the New York Historical Society, the Morgan Library of New York, Dr. Rosenbach, etc.

I must single out, for my especial gratitude, Mr. Franklin Bache, a direct descendant of Franklin, who allowed me to make use of his extraordinary collection; the American Philosophical Society, and the Historical Society of Pennsylvania (at Philadelphia) whose archives were opened to me with unstinted generosity.

The burden of my work was considerably lightened by my special study of the collection in the Huntington Library of Pasadena, and I derived much benefit from the erudition of its director, Mr. Farrand, as well as from the amiable assistance of the Librarian, Mr. Bliss, the Keeper of Manuscripts, Mr. Hazelden, and the Keeper of Printed Books, Mr. Shad.

Professor Laski of the School of Economics in London and his secretary, Mrs. Turin, greatly facilitated my researches and gave me many precious suggestions.

At Philadelphia, Miss Cherry, a graduate student of the University of Pennsylvania, offered invaluable practical assistance. Finally, I wish especially to thank Mr. Bravig Imbs, who prepared the English version of this book with friendly zeal and his customary talent.

I should have to add many more names to this list, were I to give a complete account of all those who have encouraged me and indirectly bettered my work. I have not forgotten them, but I fear it would seem presumptuous on my part to present this book to the public with so great a company of friends. I only hope that, once published, it may win as much good will as it has already enjoyed in manuscript.

BERNARD FAŸ.

PARIS.
June, 1929.

CONTENTS

ILLUSTRATIONS

listening to the Devil who whispers to him: "Thee shall be my Agent, BEN, for all my realms." On the left a group of Quakers with their big hats are discussing their chances of winning the election. On the right the other friends of Franklin, *Associators* and *Junto*, come to his rescue. In the center is shown the City Hall where the balloting took place. In 1764 the tide was turned against Franklin, who was beaten principally because of the hostility of the democracy. Note that Franklin is shown bareheaded in this cartoon and in the other two. It shows that this habit of his had impressed his contemporaries. See page 197, and also pages 13, 198, 200, 207, 310.

Franklin and the Pennsylvania politicians described by a contemporary cartoon. Franklin says: "Fight Dog, Fight Bear, I am contented if I but get the Government." He is getting the money and holding the bag, while his Quaker friends are smoking and scheming with the Devil. One of them, Pemberton, is very busy with an Indian girl. The cartoon was drawn in 1764, but gives a good idea of the political situation in Pennsylvania from 1750 to 1770. See pages 213–216, and also pages 112, 234–236, 251, 307, 308.

Franklin is shown holding a paper on which is written: "Resolves, ye Proprietaries are knave and tyrant." He is handing it to a Quaker (easy to recognize because of his big hat) who is riding on a Scotch-Irish man and leading a blindfolded German by a rope. On the German an Indian is riding. The package carried by the Indian bears two letters: I. P. (Indian Presents) because it seemed highly shocking to the Proprietary Party to have to make gifts to the Indians, and it was, on the contrary, one of the essential features of the Quaker policy followed by Franklin. See pages 256–257, 277–280, 304–306.

Portrait made by Mason Chamberlin. Print made in France after 1776. It shows Franklin as he was between 1755 and 1775, with his wig and the rather elegant way of dressing he had adopted in England. (Compare with the simplicity of his dress in France, as shown in the Carmontelle drawing.) Through the window one sees a thunderstorm and a lightning rod. In the room behind Franklin is his library, and next to him, on his right, the famous electric bell he had invented and put in his Philadelphia home. It rang when the electricity was passing through it, and during Franklin's stay in England Deborah was so scared to hear it ring day and night that it had to be dismantled. See page 271, and also pages 227, 231, 341, 344, 351–354.

in France in 1788 to celebrate the French-American Alliance. It was sold in the streets for a few cents. It is the only one actually known and is for the first time reproduced with permission of the Bibliothèque Nationale, where it is preserved in the Hennin collection. See pages 438–439, 480–481.

View of the Seine and Paris from Franklin's Terrace at Passy 454

In the foreground are small Passy houses, a typical French garden of the time, on the Seine the ferryboat which bothered Franklin and Benny Bache so much when they went to swim in the river precisely at that place. Near to the ferryboat is the scaffold (on which a few years later so many of Franklin's friends were going to be hanged by the crowd). In the sky a beautiful balloon, such as were made then, with the initials of the King: two interlaced L's. On the other bank of the Seine, from left to right, are to be seen the Invalides (Home for the Old Soldiers), the two towers of Notre Dame, the two towers of Saint Sulpice, one of them then in process of being repaired. Drawing made in 1783 apropos of the balloon experiments in La Muette and Passy. See pages 454–469, 479, 483.

Emblematical Portrait of Franklin 512

Diogenes with his lantern is holding the portrait of Franklin. (It is the portrait of Franklin by Van Loo.) He is glad to have found at last a MAN. Behind him a bird flies, after having escaped from a cage, and on a pike a liberty cap is raised. A book, probably the laws of Pennsylvania, is open. In front of Franklin and Diogenes are to be seen some carrots, commemorating Diogenes' and Franklin's frugality, a broken yoke, evoking Franklin's triumph over English despotism, and an eagle spreading thunder on a map of North America, as a symbol of Franklin's emancipating influence in the New World. A Latin inscription announces: "Nations! Stop and wonder: Diogenes has found a man." This print was made and presented to Franklin in July, 1780. See pages 468, 480–481, 512, 515.

MAPS

The Town of Boston During Franklin's Youth . 7
Philadelphia and Parts Adjacent, 1750 111
London, 1767 261
Paris and Environs, 1781 403
Passy and Auteuil 453

BOOK ONE

THE REARING OF AN XVIIITH CENTURY RADICAL

I

The month of January, 1706, in the distant colony of New England was a bitter one, and the little city of Boston, squeezed between the Atlantic and the marshes, had all it could do to resist the storms and the rigorous cold. The weather was very disagreeable with its brusque alternations of intense frosts, hurricanes, snow and thaws; the last part of December was one continual tempest. At the beginning of January, the weather improved slightly and there were a few mild hours, but, starting on the fourteenth, the cold struck in again with a blizzard, bringing back suffering and danger. John Coleburn of Dedham lost himself in the snow and his corpse was found near Roxbury. In the taverns where men got together to drink rum they hardly spoke about anything but the precautions they had to take in driving their ox-carts and sleighs over the snowy countryside, when they were looking for firewood, or carrying provisions to the farms of the interior.

Then, too, they gossiped a little about their neighbors. A son had just been born to Josiah Franklin, the tallow-chandler at the Sign of the Blue Ball, on Milk Street, — a big boy named Benjamin. He was born on the sixth, a Sunday, so of course he would be lucky. He would be a good Christian, too, and a good Whig; his parents had had him baptized immediately in the neighboring church, Old South, thus making one more Presbyterian for the city. And the drinkers laughed in whispering that Old Josiah wasn't leading such a dull life; his wife was pretty and he wasn't losing his time, fourteen children already. And no doubt they wouldn't be all. Well, such families would provide soldiers for Queen Anne and her great general, Marlborough. They would be needed with all those men killed now in Flanders, Germany and America, and with all the epidemics that had swept the country. For the moment, there were more than enough people, but in 1703 nearly three hundred persons had died of smallpox.

Life wasn't easy with such three enemies as the Winter, the French and the Devil. Ever since the Puritans, Children of God and Preservers of Holy Tradition, had gained the desert and founded their pious colony in distant America, these three enemies had persisted against them. The Puritans had never confessed themselves conquered, but, in spite of the vigilance of their pastors, the Devil was always prowling around the pious people and their dwellings. In 1692, hadn't he come to attack them directly and in person by loosing those horrible witches whom the virtuous Mr. Mather denounced and had put to death? With a little courage and firmness, the Devil had been vanquished, a few executions had sufficed, and the People of God, after some hours of anguish, had found their peace once more. But the Devil hadn't given up, after all; now he employed devices and ruses less direct.

The city grew, it became a kind of capital, and some even said it included four thousand houses and eighteen thousand inhabitants. No doubt they exaggerated, but really to remain pure in this port filled with sailors, young exiled craftsmen, outlaws, merchants from all countries, and Negro slaves, was not always easy, and the Devil had his due. How many young men were enticed and carried away by the sailors who never gave them up, how many little children were born five or six months after their parents' marriage, and how many times men left home to warm themselves on winter evenings at the tavern and returned, late and drunk, to beat their wives!

No doubt there remained some good customs and apostles. No doubt the Sabbath was still enforced by the law and one could not, under pain of the most severe punishments, either walk about, swim or travel on Sunday. The faithful had, besides their sermons on Sunday, the "lectures" on Thursday, when their devoted pastors informed them of God's word. And these latter, no doubt, let no occasion such as catastrophes, national or royal anniversaries, or public executions, slip

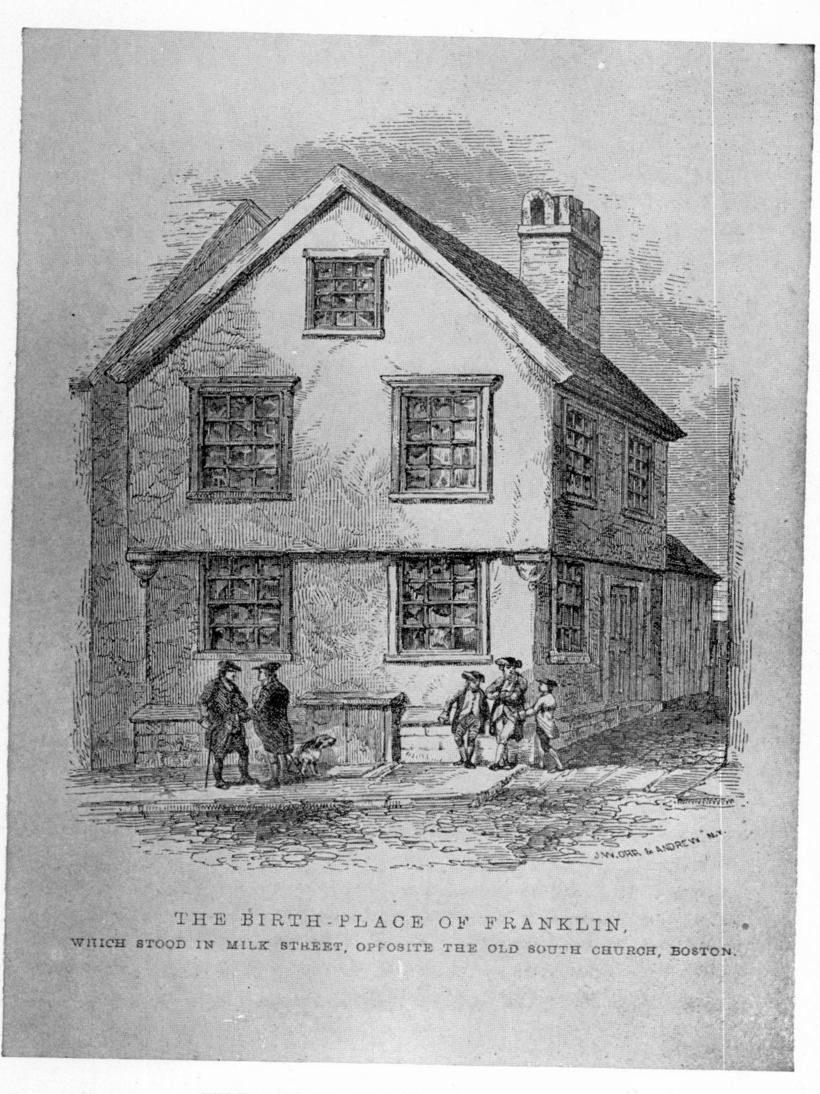

THE BIRTH-PLACE OF FRANKLIN,
WHICH STOOD IN MILK STREET, OPPOSITE THE OLD SOUTH CHURCH, BOSTON.

THE BIRTH–PLACE OF FRANKLIN

by without commenting on them in the pulpit or accompanying them with a sermon. Some of them were well attended, in particular those which were pronounced before the executions. But also what backsliding in the city and in the entire colony! Since the king had changed the charter, it sufficed to be rich to vote; a prospective citizen no longer had to undergo a public conversion, or prove that he was a member of the Calvinist Church. The king delegated his authority to a governor chosen by himself and not by the pious Christians. Massachusetts had no longer a government elected by unaided devotees, but it was submitted to the influence of rich men, merchants, ungodly and indifferent. Even the college, this Harvard, founded to educate pastors and to be a sanctuary of pure religion, forsook its traditions more and more. The young men drank every day, and sang often, even on Sunday. The most strict and pious pastors had been rejected and the presidency refused to the venerable Mr. Mather. A layman, Mr. Leverett, was going to direct this institution, formerly so holy.

Was it surprising that God should punish New England for its infidelity? That He should unloose Indians and French against them? Had he not once armed the Philistines against the guilty Israelites in the same way? And every Sunday, every Thursday, in the pulpits of New England, along with pressing invitations to become converted, violent invectives were hurled against Louis XIV, this "detestable old tyrant, this persecutor of God, this new Nebuchadnezzar, surrounded by his courtesans, his illegitimate children, the glorification of his sins and the pagan pomp of Catholic civilization." His death was predicted and his defeats celebrated, as on the twenty-fourth of January, 1706, when the governor ordered a great thanksgiving festival in honor of Marlborough's victories in Flanders. However, the people still trembled a little from fear. Canada was so close and the French privateers so often laid hold on the English vessels.

In 1707 they went to see a fair-sized fleet brought together in the harbor of Boston for the purpose of attacking the French.

Preparations and defense were necessary. They could never forget that danger was always pressing. The people hoped for victory; Louis was growing old, and all of Europe, including the Empire, Holland, Portugal, Savoy and England, were armed against him, endeavoring to wrest Spain from his grasp, a country he wanted to give to his grandson, as well as the world scepter he also sought for him.

But he was always feared and his court remained the center of the civilized world. What stories were told about the luxury of the court, its unheard-of bursts of debauchery! From far off it was vaguely fascinating and those who saw it closely and without illusion were dazzled.

The Duc de Saint Simon Pair de France, an exact observer, and not very favorable to his king, noted in his diary for the first weeks of 1706:

> I do not know whether the misfortunes of the year just ended and the great enterprises being planned for the coming one, have not but inclined the King to the pleasures of winter as a policy to cheer his realm and show his enemies how slightly he is disturbed by their prosperity. However it came about, we were surprised to hear him announce that, beginning the first day of the year up to Lent, there would be balls held at Marly at all his appearances there. At the same time he named the men and women to dance at them and said that he would be well pleased if impromptu balls should be given at Versailles in honor of Madame la Duchesse de Bourgogne. Also many balls were given for him and there were masquerades at Marly from time to time. One day the King even desired that the oldest and most serious men of his court, here at Marly, as well as the women, attend the ball, masked: he, himself, in order to do away with all exception and all restraint, came and remained throughout with a robe of gauze over his garments.

The glory of the King of France was so sparkling that he had to veil it in order not to blind his subjects. Even in the midst of trials and clouds it shone at a distance, symbol of absolute monarchy, of the divine right of kings, of Catholicism, of classic Greek art, of pagan elegance, of all this aristocratic old Roman Europe, which Boston, new and far-away, hated and feared.

The Town of Boston during Franklin's youth, from the map of Captain Bonner (1722). According to Bonner the city had then "Streets 42, Lanes 36, Alleys 22, Houses near 3000, 1000 Brick, rest Timber; Near 12000 People."

A. The Old Church, 1630, the oldest in Boston.

B. The Old North Church, 1650.

C. The Old South Church, 1669, the one in which Franklin was baptized, and where as a boy he often heard Cotton Mather preach.

D. The Baptist Church, 1680.

E. The Church of England, 1688.

F. Brattle Street Church, 1699.

G. The Quaker Meeting, [illegible].

K. The French Church, [illegible].

L. The New North Church, [illegible].

a. The Town House. The shop of [illegible] and the Tavern of Richard Hall were in King Street near the Town House. The shop of James Franklin and the printing press of [illegible] were near it in Queen Street, on the other side of Cornhill. The jail was in Queen Street, [illegible].

b. The Governor's House.

c. The South Grammar School.

d. Alms House.

e. Bridewell.

× The house of Josiah Franklin opposite the Old South Church. Franklin was born in this house in 1706 and lived there until [illegible].

+ The house and shop of Josiah Franklin, at the sign of the Blue Ball, where the Franklin family lived after 1712.

The Town of Boston during Franklin's youth, from the map of Captain Bonner (1722). According to Bonner the city had then: "Streets 42, Lanes 36, Alleys 22. Houses near 3,000. 1,000 Brick, rest Timber. Near 12,000 People."

A. The Old Church, 1630, the oldest in Boston.

B. The Old North Church, 1650.

C. The Old South Church, 1660, the one in which Franklin was baptized, and where as a boy he often heard Cotton Mather speak.

D. The Baptist Church, 1680.

E. The Church of England, 1688.

F. Brattle Street Church. 1699.

G. The Quaker Meeting. 1710.

K. The French Church. 1716.

L. The New North Church. 1721.

a. The Town House. The shop of Checkley and the Tavern of Richard Hall were in King Street near the Town House. The shop of James Franklin and the printing press of the *New England Courant* were near by in Queen Street, on the other side of the Cornhill. The jail was in Queen Street, next door.

b. The Governor's House.

c. The South Grammar School.

g. Alm's House.

h. Bridewell.

× The house of Josiah Franklin opposite the Old South Church. Franklin was born in this house in 1706 and lived there until 1712.

+ The house and shop of Josiah Franklin, at the ensign of the Blue Ball, where the Franklin family lived after 1712.

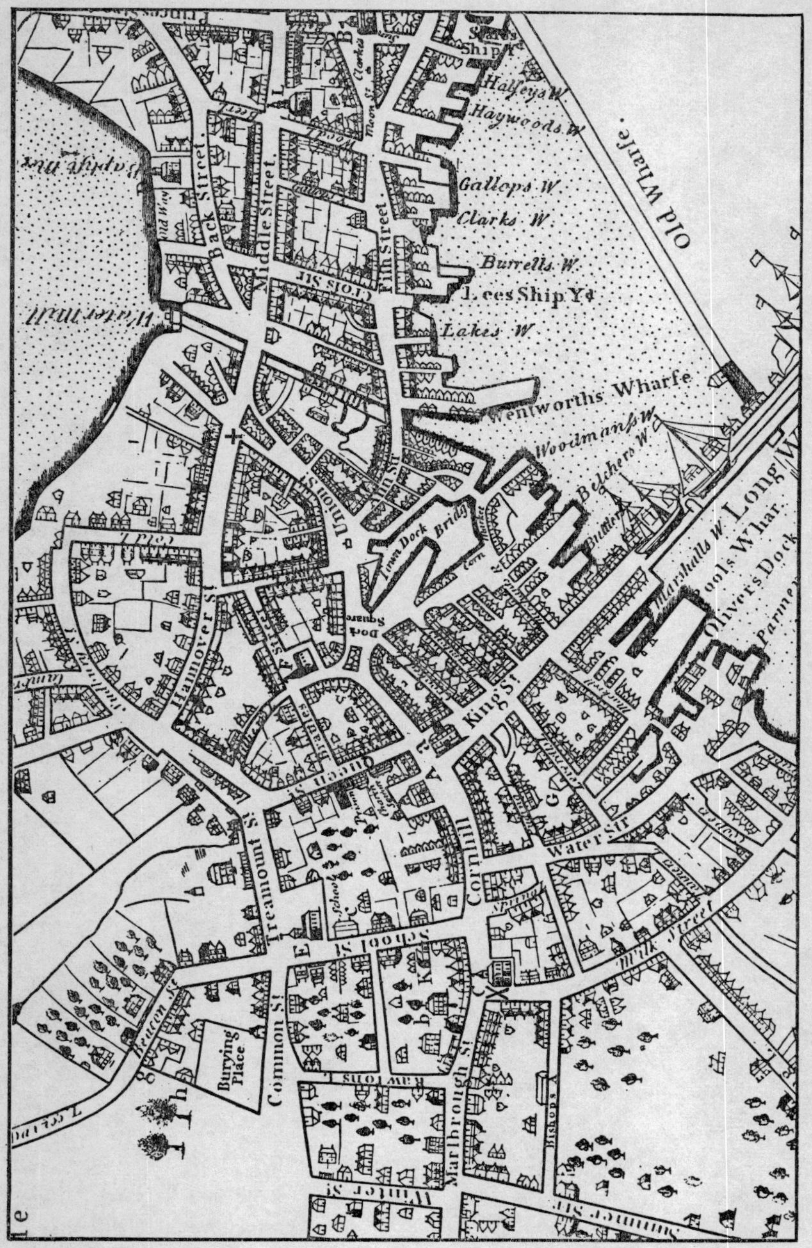

Halfeys W.
Haywoods W.
Old Wharfe.
Gallops W.
Clarks W.
Burrells W.
Lees Ship Yd
Lakes W.
Wentworths Wharfe
Woodmans W.
Belchers W.
Long W.
Marshalls W.
Pools Whar.
Oliver's Dock
Back Street
Middle Street
Fish Street
Cross St
Union St
Dock Square
Hannover St
King St
Queen St
Cornhill
Water Str
Milk Street
School St
Treamount St
Common St
Burying Place
Marlbrough St
Winter St
Summer Str
Beacon St

II

There was not a more convinced Whig nor a more fervent Protestant in Boston than Josiah Franklin, tallow-chandler of Milk Street. He was a strong, energetic and skillful man who raised his numerous family with firmness and happiness. Although he had arrived but a few years before, he had acquired an estimable position in the commerce of the city. The family belonged, really, to the lower middle-class, characteristic peasants of Renaissance England. The Franklins had long been blacksmiths and farmers in their village of Ecton, Northamptonshire (one of the counties of central England). They had become Protestants early, at a time when it was not always without danger to admit belonging to the reformed religion. There was still to be seen in their house the large Bible fastened under the seat of a taboret, to be used at critical periods. When the seat was lifted, the Bible was turned up to the light and services were held around this strange pulpit which shut up instantly, hiding the Forbidden Book when the neighbors uttered the cry agreed upon to announce the arrival of soldiers. One of the Franklin brothers had become a solicitor and a considerable citizen in the community, but the others scarcely distinguished themselves except by their honesty, the dexterity of their fingers, their intelligence and industry. Of the nine children, three had adopted the trade of dyer, — John, Josiah and Benjamin. All three were established at Banbury in Oxfordshire and were married there. The most tender intimacy united Josiah and Benjamin, both of them strong-headed and both of whom had abandoned the Church of England to join the dissenters. But King Charles II, who reigned then, looked with disfavor upon the independent sectarians and Josiah, rather than drag through a difficult and dangerous life in England, came to establish himself at Boston, with his wife and three children. He left behind him Benjamin, who could hardly manage to make a fortune in England in spite of his active mind, and who was not at all happy in his home despite his good disposition. He lost his wife and all but one of his ten children. To console himself, he read the Bible, a great many sermons, some ancient philosophers, and sent letters in verse to his brother.

Josiah had not wasted his time. He established himself immediately (1685), quit the trade of dyer which was too refined for such a new city, and became a maker and seller of candles, which was a suitable trade for a city with long winters and dark taverns, and for a man blessed by heaven with a very numerous family, to help him fill the candle molds, dip the meshes and make deliveries at the various houses. Family and candles had prospered: almost every year a new child was born; after Elizabeth (1678), Samuel (1681); after Samuel, Hannah (1683); after Hannah, Josiah (1685) (the voyage not having retarded the zeal of the father and mother); after Josiah, Joseph (1688); but after Joseph, Mrs. Franklin died. Josiah remarried without delay, after less than nine months had passed. His new wife was Abiah Folger, the daughter of Peter Folger of Nantucket, where the Folger family was respected for its honor, size, taciturnity and its spirit of liberalism. Abiah Folger Franklin was as good a mother as was Josiah's first wife. She had ten children; John (1690), Peter (1692), Mary (1694), James (1697), Sarah (1699), Ebenezer (1701), Thomas (1703), Benjamin (1706), Lydia (1708), and Jane (1712), the last of all, prettiest and the favorite of her parents and her brothers.

All this little world swarmed in the house on Milk Street, which the family left in 1712 for a home on Union Street. There had been some setbacks; three children had died at an early age, another had left home very young, attracted by the invincible fascination of the sea or the sailors. But the others remained close to their parents, a clamorous band, healthy and quarrelsome, which the father held with firm discipline and instructed in common sense. He did not have to give them all the worldly wisdom, subtle and refined logic, extensive understanding and artistic tastes which properly belonged to the upper classes, brought up by teachers under French influences. The Bible, some good preachers, the rules he had heard in his parents' house, their remarks and those of the friends often invited to come and share their frugal repasts, — such was the substance of this instruction. Josiah developed in his children, first, religious sense, then common sense, then a taste for work and for simplicity. Food and drink were unimportant. He taught them to despise luxury and to detest frills. He sang sometimes, having a pleasant voice, and played a few simple and popular tunes on the violin. This plebeian took pride only in his rectitude and his simplicity.

His manual skill was unusual and valuable in a city where there was a lack of machinery; his intellectual ability, which was above the average and which the Puritans appreciated, gave him a very worthy position, but he knew well that he could never be one of the great ones of this world. Between the old families, established for more than sixty years, the Clergy who maintained social preëminence, and the merchants who owed their newly acquired importance to their riches, a newcomer, not at all rich and knowing no Latin or Hebrew or fine manners, was destined to obscurity. But he was not at all unhappy. He was well thought of in the neighborhood, and for the present his position, his fortune, his wife, sufficed for him. For the future his children would be his triumph.

In New England at the commencement of the eighteenth century the difficulty was not at all in placing children, but, on the contrary, in keeping them. Everything lured them away; the boys were drawn by the sea, by commerce, by the excitement of pushing inland. The girls in these regions, where there were more men than women, were asked in marriage continually, especially when they were strong and pretty like the Franklin girls, Jane in particular. The only means of keeping the children was to give them a good trade which would attach them to the soil or to the city. Josiah Franklin set himself to do this.

Of all his sons he preferred his tenth, Sunday's child, Benjamin, a tiny fellow, plump and broad-backed, with bright eyes and a round face, who very soon showed especial intelligence. Everything that went on around him impressed him and interested him.

And during these years Boston certainly had lessons and sights to offer to a little boy. While across the Atlantic Louis XIV fought against the whole of Europe and his armies yielded under the blows of the Duke of Marlborough, losing Spanish Flanders bit by bit in such battles as Ramillies and Oudenarde, and the fortresses of northern France surrendered one by one, in America the struggle continued doubtful and equal.

Boston had seen, in 1711, the great fleet of Sir Howenden Walker with its fifteen warships and its forty transports carrying five thousand English soldiers. In New England they had even formed two regiments to bear down upon the French and attack them at Quebec. But all had been in vain. Nothing had been accomplished and danger was always at the door.

God vented His wrath on His elected. The same year a great fire destroyed a hundred houses and deprived one hundred and ten families of their shelter. In 1714 an epidemic ravaged the city, followed by a summer of intolerable heat and a scarcity of wheat. Pious people lifted up their heads and from the height of the pulpit the old and venerable Increase Mather consoled his flock by announcing the death of "that wicked old persecutor of God's people, Lewis the Fourteenth."

But the child played in front of his father's store, admiring the gold-braided uniforms, circling the officers and listening to all remarks. He revealed already a rapid and ironic intelligence. At five years of age he was already reading the Bible, at seven he knew how to write. He was courageous, active and clever, rather than firm in his principles. His father laughed one day to hear himself advised by the young Benjamin to lose less time in giving the daily blessing, to replace it with a great general blessing pronounced once for all on the cupboard of provisions. He admired his son's courage without blaming him when he saw him fight in the dust with his little comrades, whom he never spared the finishing blow, or swim in the river or the sea where he trained them and guided them. He rejoiced to see him take charge in the games and the expeditions.

However, he found it necessary to show anger sometimes. The day Benjamin, who was amusing himself catching the small fish left in pools of water on the beaches by the low tide, had the idea of fetching stones from a house under construction to use in building a little dike which would make it possible for his playmates to catch fish without wetting their feet, Josiah Franklin had to teach him the meaning of the seventh commandment. This caused a memorable scene.

Another day when Benjamin had been given several pennies, he devoted them to the purchase of a trifling whistle, rude and without value but which made a great deal of noise and split the heads of his parents.

They laughed at him: "So you give ten pennies for a whistle worth but two!"

Benjamin, struck dumb by this revelation, was never to forget it. The sense of the value of money, like the respect for private property, was to remain engraved in his character. Sometimes he was to neglect a little the first, the sixth, the eighth, and some say the tenth commandment, but from then on no one found anything to say to him on the subject of the seventh commandment. Perhaps it is for this reason that the eighteenth century and posterity have found him so bourgeois. Rather than against him, the accusation should be made against his father and the whistle, of which the strident and mocking sound rang in his ears all his life.

After these first lessons his father decided to make a great man of his son. In Boston the most simple means to this was to make him a minister. Benjamin was destined for the pulpit and in preparation for this he was sent to a school where he was taught Latin, arithmetic and other useful knowledge. He made rapid progress there, except in arithmetic which presented nothing concrete to this realistic mind, determined not to be taken in again by whistles. Were not the truly valuable arts at the beginning of the eighteenth century rhetoric, poetry, the ancient tongues and logic which opened all circles to you and placed you among the great of the earth, while figures were but a vain play for solitary philosophers? Kings and ladies had their poets, not their geometricians. The child's instinct, turned always toward practical things, guided him surely in this direction. He and his father understood one another well: Benjamin was to become an up-to-date middle-class man, adapted to his surroundings, his time and his circumstances. Such common sense caused his father to take the child out of the classical school in which he had first been placed and to send him to George Brownell's school, which was devoted to the teaching of writing and arithmetic and which had a good reputation in Boston. Josiah Franklin, in looking around him, had noticed that the service of the Lord carried with it some of its old-time honor but that it required an expensive education, well beyond the means of a candle merchant's son. Besides, he had ascertained that this holy profession did not always provide for the physical necessities, in spite of the glory it implied and the erudition it called for. How many of the young men with bachelor's degrees from Harvard went out with holes in their shoes to preach in rural communities, leading a miserable life in a crude village or ending sadly in a dark shop, keeping accounts for rich and ignorant merchants! Without money, science and virtue could not go far. Let all that go by!

The town was growing. Everybody wanted to buy and sell. With his good sense, politeness and cunning, little Benjamin would make a good merchant. His father took him out of Mr. Brownell's school to make him his helper and apprentice at home and to prepare him for a candle-maker's career. He had been in school about two years, and that was enough. Furthermore, he had learned little there, for he had not had sufficient Latin to do him any good and he didn't like arithmetic well enough to turn it to any account. His two years of instruction resulted only in his admirable handwriting, strong, dignified and precise; exact, as it should be for a plebeian who wrote to be understood, but also imposing, the proper attribute of a free man.

There was also the taste for reading which lasted as long as Benjamin lived. From the beginning he found time to satisfy it, for the candle trade left him some leisure during the summer and did not occupy all the long winter evenings. His father, proud of Benjamin's intelligence, let him read in peace. The real difficulty was in finding books. Josiah Franklin had little besides sermons or tracts of Protestant theology, full of attacks upon infidels, Catholics and libertines, and surcharged with apostrophes, exclamation points and italics. Benjamin read them at first with surprise, a certain pride and a vague pleasure, for he had the pugnacious spirit of the Franklins, but soon these monotonous and confused polemics wearied him. He tried some stories, liking those best which were moral and sensible, as Bunyan's "Pilgrim's Progress", or those which were true, like the ones he found in R. Burton's historical works.

Better still, he liked moralistic tales, tinged with ancient philosophy, like Plutarch's "Lives", the common nourishment of all the great men of the eighteenth century who found there, in a restful and easy style worthy of a village preacher, grandiose and picturesque allusions to the antiquity they doted on. The good Plutarch, at the crossroads of antiquity and Protestantism, offered the apprentice all that most interested him, — sound maxims, striking examples, curious narratives. He had neither that logical rigidity nor that uncompromising taste for formal beauty which rendered so many classical authors inaccessible to the ponderous spirits of those days.

And Benjamin was definitely of his own time. No doubt he wanted to find in books something about which to dream, but above all something to think about and, most essentially, some practical rules and incentives to action. Soon he adopted as his favorites two works which, while they were prosaic and lacked grandeur, were savory and useful: Daniel Defoe's "Essay on Projects" and "Essays to do Good" by Cotton Mather. These two works belonged to the great mass of books which came along just after the Revolution and which expressed the desires, hopes, and preoccupations of the middle classes then emboldened by success and a sense of their power. They cared nothing for world systems, planets, or sentimental or mystic heroes. They wanted an author, like Defoe, to show them how new banks might be established, how roads might be built, or how insurance companies and mutual benefit societies for seamen and their widows might be organized. Such projects were worthy of consideration, since they led to practical or useful acts. Benjamin could not read enough about them.

But he appreciated no less Cotton Mather's book, for the author was the most violent and traditional of the preachers in Boston, a man who knew how to combine a remarkable practical sense with his effusions, ecstasies and fits of temper. Mather wished to do good. He had the soul of a Salvation Army colonel. Coöperation, social service, religious and moral teachings, relief of the needy, — such were his themes and his aims. Mather conversed with angels such as one he described: "whose face shone like the noonday sun. His features were as those of a man, and beardless; his head was encircled by a splendid tiara; on his shoulders were wings; his garments were white and shining, his robes reached to his ankles; and about his loins was a belt not unlike the girdles of the peoples of the East." And the angels told him his books would be a success in America and even in Europe. For as early as in the eighteenth century the angels of America made an effort to announce material blessings, and Mather, inspired but positive, wished to spread them afar.

He was indefatigable. All occasions were fit for good purposes. He expelled demons in causing witches to be hanged, he took advantage of executions in order to deliver long and terrible sermons to the frightened and excited population. He went still further, using science as well as the Bible, and his conversations with the Holy Ghost, to convert and serve his brethren whose lives were in peril. His "efforts to do good" anticipated the organization of Y.M.C.A. huts for soldiers and accounted for the diverse means he used in bringing young people together in order to teach them to convert one another and to render the same service to their neighbors. A man who established and spread such organizations rendered an incalculable service to his district, he said, not unmindful of the predictions his angels had made. He wished these predictions to materialize without delay, and he worked hard to bring this about.

Benjamin had heard Cotton Mather preach, and had more than once delivered candles to him, admiring his study filled with books, so he read reverently his "Essays to do Good." He had a strong desire to work, to create. All around him and within him that powerful urge was growing. And the severe New England seasons, with long rigorous winters, brusque springs, torrid and humid summers, clear autumns sparkling with cold and purple colors, — even the growth of the town, with new buildings springing up everywhere, and the prosperity and joy over the peace of 1713, proclaimed solemnly by George of Hanover as King of England in September, 1714, heightened that feeling. The streets were illumined on that occasion and Jonathan Belcher gave a large celebration. Activity reigned everywhere. The new South Church was begun in 1715 and the building was finished in 1729. After considerable discussion, the first lighthouse was built. A splendid company of firemen, imposing with their sparkling brass axes, was organized. Luxury slipped into town, now that security was established, and soon after peace was declared a French professor installed himself there. Merchants of all lands made their appearance.

Nearly every week there was news from England, except during the winter months, and this news filled the hearts of the good American Whigs with joy. When it was learned in August, 1717, that the pretender, James Stuart, had been defeated, all the town was exuberant and every one took part in the thanksgiving celebration which was decreed. The child could only yield to hope and desire, since everything turned him in that direction. But above all, the climate soothed and exalted him. This son of an immigrant received in his veins the harsh invitation to life tendered by the American seasons, which killed the weakest and toughened the rest. After the rainy and hot summer of 1715 came the severe cold of December in the same year. The winter of 1717–1718 was so terrible that men and beasts died frozen upon the roads, in the barns and even in the houses.

The child that winter sat long hours watching the fire in the fireplace and dreaming. His destiny did not satisfy him. He could not resign himself to such a modest and monotonous rôle. The life in his father's shop became intolerable. He thought of his brother, Josiah, who had been away so long and he remembered the excursions he had made with his band of friends along the sea, the long hours passed in the water, rolling in the waves or watching the ships from distant ports come sailing in. He had need of action and liberty. All the affection his father, or his uncle Benjamin, now established in Boston, gave him no longer satisfied him. When he saw them quarreling among themselves, he thought of the tender letters they wrote when the Atlantic separated them, and this led him to reflect on the advantages of absence. The value of work and eulogies of the liberty his parents had come to this far country to seek had been repeated to him continually. Should he not also sacrifice everything to gain liberty and to accomplish his work? He was eager to do something and above all to do good.

His father followed in the glances of the child the dangerous reveries that had cost him one son. He was aware of this danger and of the character of his family. He knew that by occupying Benjamin's body and his activity he might appease his spirit. So he made it a point to take him with him around the town and to show him the workmen of all sorts busy at their trades. He saw that this interested the boy, distracted him, and won him over, but he tried in vain to discover which of all those trades the boy preferred. Benjamin seemed to be pleased with one as well as the other and not to be carried away with any. It was thought that he might be made a cutler and might enter as an apprentice at his cousin Samuel's home. But Samuel loved money too well. He wished to be paid for taking an apprentice. He forgot that a Franklin was too wise to make such a mistake, and Benjamin did not go to his cousin Samuel's house.

This turned out well, for he had need of a trade more intriguing and adventurous than that of cutler. A life far richer and more difficult was necessary for him. Suddenly Josiah hit upon just the right idea.

III

This time, without having to leave Boston or to look outside of his family, Benjamin found the adventures he desired and work which was to his taste. His brother, James, had just returned from England where he had finished his apprenticeship as a printer. He had absorbed the new ways of thinking and acting while in London, and had come back full of ambition and audacity. James was a real Franklin, strong, plebeian, full of life and quarrelsome. He had spirit and possessed unshakable Whig principles. His language was colorful, and though the way he spoke of women seemed scarcely courteous to some, he couldn't be reproached for not interesting himself enough in them.

Besides, he was very young. Aged only twenty, he was going to set up a printing press in Boston and had brought back from England all the equipment he needed. His announcements were issued immediately and made known that he would print linens and calicos as well as pamphlets.

Yet all this business lumped together wouldn't furnish him with his daily three square meals as there were already ten bookshops and printers in Boston. No more establishments were needed for a little city where there was scarcely anything to print but a few official notices, religious brochures, sermons, some popular almanacs, and, once in a great while, a commercial announcement: an escaped slave, a stallion, an adulteress. Business was scanty. But in spite of this, one sensed that the people had a lively desire to be informed, and to hear local and national issues discussed, so that they would be able to form opinions on what was happening.

Theocracy, established in time past by the Puritans, had been dethroned. The ministers still maintained a distinguished rank but they governed no longer; the city and the colony were administered by the representatives of the king and a commercial aristocracy. However, certain of the ministers hadn't given up hope of regaining their power, and the Mather family, above all Cotton Mather, aspired to continue the holy combat. He didn't realize that the hordes of new immigrants ceaselessly arriving in Boston were ambitious, avid men, impatient of authority.

These newcomers demanded their place in the city, but, not daring to conduct an attack against the new leaders, tried to make themselves valuable to the latter by crushing the clergy, stripping the ministers of whatever authority they still possessed. In doing this they were only following the example of what was happening in England, where the licentiousness of morals and freedom of speech had attained its height.

London was now under the full sway of the Deists, who were continuing the movement begun at the time of the Renaissance and the Reform, a century and a half before, leading it to its extreme limits, using the same arguments against Protestantism and the Church of England that the latter had employed in their time against Catholicism. This critical attitude, which Protestantism had taken against Catholicism, was now being taken against Christianity. The same sharp reasoning of an exacting logic, the same irony, the same indignation.

The English Protestant tradition was being well followed and even exaggerated. The radicals were strong Whigs, extremely patriotic. The Revolution, the victories over the French, the glorious peace of 1713, had made this attitude popular. It was definitely opposed to all that Louis XIV loved and had imposed on the high society of Europe. The French monarchy had maintained the divine right of kings, the superiority of Catholicism and of Greco-Roman art with its descendant, French art; in a word, Louis XIV admired all that was ancient, all that which had received the consecration of time.

Indeed, the triumph of Louis XIV and of his poets, artists, and philosophers, was to have given Europe for the first time, that which it had so long sought: a culture, founded on Christianity, but harmoniously continuing the most ancient intel-

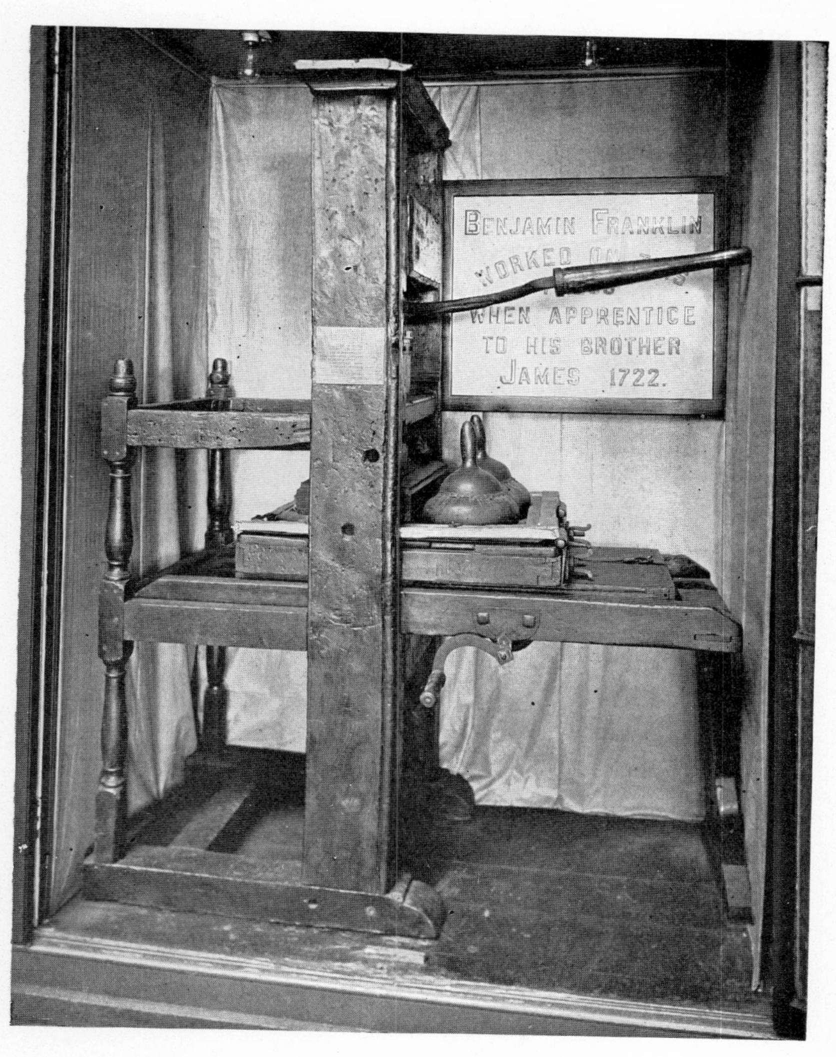

FRANKLIN'S PRINTING PRESS

lectual traditions of Greece and Rome. This social masterpiece, dreamed of by the tenth, twelfth, and fifteenth centuries, had at last been realized by the seventeenth century in France. And Louis XIV had imposed this classical culture on all the high classes of Europe, who were at once hostile and admiring.

At the time of the famous quarrel between the ancients and the moderns, that puerile discussion of frenzied artists who claimed that the ancient Greeks were uneven, or rather, that the moderns had done better, the entire official French world declared its preference for the past and, as before, vaunted only the Roman poets of the Golden Age; nothing had been created so well as in the past, in the youth of humanity. All that which had been founded in a very ancient time: religions, aristocracies, states, literatures, possessed a superior perfection. And Europe in admiration had accepted this verdict.

Not England, however, whose hardy people had continued their crusade in favor of a modern world, new, independent, proud of its newness. Of course, there were adherents to the other cause — the Stuarts had tried to imitate the Bourbons — but the national feeling was directed towards the future, to liberty and common rights; and the Hanoverian dynasty was its symbol.

James Franklin, who had read the various theological, literary and political discussions in England (aired for the most part in the *London Courant*), was all ready to lead this crusade in Massachusetts. But he needed a weapon.

A newspaper was what he needed. He had seen enough of them in London to realize how powerful a gazette was in the hands of the dissatisfied. Thanks to it, one could organize a party. Here was a truth which would certainly have been difficult to grasp for any one living in America, in the thinly sown and scattered colonies, but for one who had lived at the beginning of the eighteenth century in London, with its dense, noisy, nervous crowds, it was easy to understand. These human masses were not organized, they had no other way of expressing their feelings or of making their force felt than by sudden, brutal explosions. Ordinarily, these outbursts didn't accomplish very much, but the popular leaders thus succeeded in displaying their own talents and bringing the demands of the mob to the attention of the public and the government.

Certainly, there were some dangers for them: prison, the pillory, eventually worse punishments. There were difficulties also. One had to speak very loudly in order to be heard, and very simply and intensely so as to be understood. Such insults as "Calumniator" or "Vile Pamphleteer" were to be accepted as commonplace and a good deal of audacity was needed. Finally, some slogan had to be invented and a favorable state of excitement created. No one could hope to be a popular leader or to have a lively newspaper if he could not succeed in over-exciting his readers.

In New England, however, this was not an easy thing to do, for outside of wars, earthquakes, storms and epidemics, floods and Indians, the first colonists feared only the Devil and, of course, their wives. They were not always content with their leaders or their government, and protested in their town meetings, but they were so scattered over the immense territory they could not arrive at a general understanding.

Thus the government, the rich men, and the clergy, who controlled Boston — that center of roads, news and food stores — were all powerful. But a strong newspaper, managed like the radical English papers, established in the city, could bother them very much. James Franklin would group all the weak and dissatisfied around him, who, now scattered, would thus find themselves suddenly united and formidable.

A newspaper in 1717 didn't amount to much. Those of Europe had just started to be organized and the governments were beginning to realize their importance. The French king had given a royal privilege to the *Gazette de France* which permitted no news to appear that had not been censored or suggested by the government; no other informative newspaper was allowed to be printed in the country.

The newspapers of the time very clearly reflected the tendencies and preoccupations of the ruling classes. The *Gazette de France* spoke of wars, of court news, of the illnesses, births and deaths of kings, princes, dukes, and monsters, for all these were "remarkable events." Diplomatic items took up a good deal of room. Nothing else was of much interest to either the journalists or the public. The other periodicals, in particular, the *Mercure de France*, were literary, publishing poems, essays, criticism, but never discussions, speeches or advertisements.

On the contrary, in England, the economic and political life held first place. Though the accounts of Parliament were forbidden to be published it was so arranged that they were spoken of and discussed, nevertheless. Discussion invaded everything. The largest newspapers were the most violent, and journalists were very much in the public eye. The freedom of the press was loudly proclaimed, if not respected, permitting the journalists to make a name for themselves and sometimes to secure monetary gains at the expense of their enemies.

America was not so far advanced. For a long time in New England the sermons of the ministers were the only newspaper. The ministers were for the most part cultivated men, receiving English newspapers, official news and letters from their friends and parents in Europe. They discussed the world's happenings in the pulpit for the benefit of their flocks.

Sometimes their information was not quite exact, Increase Mather preaching on the death of Louis XIV when the latter was still quite alive. But the monarch died shortly afterwards as the Holy Ghost hadn't abandoned his faithful servant. Thus the pulpit in Massachusetts sometimes resembled a political rostrum, a fact which certainly would have shocked a French Catholic used to the prudent, classical sermons of his clergy who so carefully avoided politics. As long as the ministers played the rôle of gazetteers they exercised a great influence over the faithful and they were loath to lose this power. They did not look with any great favor on the newspapers which had begun to compete with them.

Really, the American journalists did not find themselves at first in the most favorable circumstances. The country was immense and was inhabited by only four hundred thousand persons. It was not easy to reach the readers or to send the paper to them, yet this was the first essential condition of success. So it was natural at this time and under these circumstances, that all the journalists of the new world were postmasters.

The first newspaper in America was founded and published by John Campbell, the postmaster of Boston, a man who was poorly informed and rather thick-headed (1704). His position permitted him to send his newspaper to the subscribers without any expense to himself. He printed about three hundred copies and his newspaper was a weekly. It mostly included reports taken from the English papers, often a year old, some official announcements, news brought by boat and two or three advertisements. It was not printed for people interested in politics but for those who were preoccupied with the economic side of life. Sometimes, though, this old newspaper printed long extracts from sermons or philosophical treatises.

But the news was certainly stale and the sermons that were published were terribly boring. When Campbell lost his place as postmaster the subscribers were so weary of his sheet that his successor, William Brocker, didn't hesitate to start a new one, the *Boston Gazette*, which was better printed, more interesting and livelier. He intrusted the care of printing it to the happy James Franklin. At last the young man's hour had come (December 17, 1717).

But, alas, the opportunity was only a mirage. A short while later it was learned that the nomination of Brocker, suggested by the colonial postmaster-general, had not been ratified by the director-general at London and that Philip Musgrave would be the postmaster of Boston. Brocker didn't resist. He resigned his office and gave up the gazette to Musgrave. He knew very well that one couldn't struggle against a postmaster. Hadn't he written himself that the subscribers of Campbell, since the latter had given up his work at the post-office, "had been prevented from having their newspaper sent them by the post. . . ." Thus Musgrave took the *Boston Gazette* in hand and left James Franklin for Kneeland.

The young printer was heart-broken. He had made the

greatest efforts to arrange for the printing of the *Boston Gazette*, involving much expense which was now unnecessary. Neither he, nor his family who had aided him, were rich. It was a hard blow. Still worse, his opportunity had disappeared. He was extremely irritated, for he knew he had talents which were lacking in Musgrave and Campbell, and which would have made the success of the gazette.

Doubtless, in order to send the newspaper about, it was useful to be a postmaster. But that wasn't all. Certain qualities were needed to edit an amusing gazette which the greater number of printers at that time, business men first and foremost, didn't possess.

James Franklin was a strong young man and brilliant in his brutality. He knew very well that in editing a newspaper one had to be amusing. He had seen how this was managed in England and so he knew the ways of making a newspaper exciting and diverting. For one thing, it was absolutely necessary to utilize the book stalls and the taverns. The latter were veritable institutions with scarcely any resemblance to our modern cafés and cabarets.

In a city like Boston, where the weather was so variable, the best precaution against epidemics and chills was to drink strong liquors. Rum played a large part in the life of the eighteenth-century Bostonian, especially since Boston manufactured rum for all the southern colonies and the English West Indies. Rum was also sold in good measure on the spot. Of course, there were all kinds of qualities; the clients of North Carolina even complained one year that the Boston rum gave them "dry belly ache with a loss of the use of their limbs." This was very likely, but, at least, you got your money's worth.

In the taverns and "coffees" of Boston you would meet captains and sailors who would give you news and tell their tales of distant lands, carry letters and sell your merchandise in the four corners of the world. There you would also find the latest books come from Europe and engravings and maps for sale. But mostly you would see those groups of faithful drinkers who united regularly around the thick tables to combat the dampness of the air, the cold of winter, the heat of summer and the general sadness of the times. They would discuss political events, local issues, and indeed, touched a little on most subjects, whether they were important or not.

Naturally, the Boston taverns received and sheltered more than one doubtful personage, sometimes adventurous and picturesque, who had been tossed from pillar to post. There were officers without troops or commissions, merchants who had lost their money, professors who had lost their students, captains who had lost their boats, exiled Jacobeans, French Huguenots fleeing from their country and Hollanders on the lookout for a good bargain. No policeman prowled around outside; you could talk and drink as you pleased. And it would be easy to gather a group of clever men together there, capable of editing articles and writing amusing stories that would liven up a newspaper.

The "coffee" of Richard Hall near the Town House was one of the most famous in Boston. Hall was broad-minded and allowed his customers every liberty. Besides, a certain John Checkley, writer, librarian and apothecary, was his neighbor and friend. Checkley was also something of a doctor, was suspected of belonging to the High Church and of being a Jacobean (he had edited "Choice Dialogues" attacking Calvinism). Still more serious accusations were whispered against him; Cotton Mather considered him as a faithful servant of the Devil, a traitor to his king, a Tory, and an infamous blasphemer, but he was educated, intelligent, wrote fluently, and attracted many customers to his shop, "at the sign of the Crown and Blue Gate, against the town house."

In this bookshop and at Hall's Tavern a little group of daring spirits united. The most brilliant and audacious of these was, doubtless, Doctor Douglass, born in 1691 at Gilford, Scotland. He had studied at the universities of Paris, Leyden, and had taken his degrees at Edinburgh. He spoke French, Dutch, Latin and Greek and was the only doctor in America provided with a doctor's diploma. Douglass had a restless temperament and traveled a good deal. In 1716 he visited Boston, then took a trip to the West Indies but returned to establish himself in the city of the Puritans where already fourteen druggists and several practitioners took care of the public health. Douglass, because of his curious, active mind, his strict scientific training, his avowed radicalism, his opposition to the clergy and his colorful language, was a sensation, attracting the attention of every one, and the sympathy of those who were dissatisfied. The intellectuals admired him for his erudition, for he had studied medicine thoroughly, knew botany, and was a scholar in history, politics, religion and political economy. He could even foretell the weather without the need of instruments. In short, the doctor was a personage.

James Franklin became acquainted with him and his coterie at the moment he was so irritated against Musgrave and so disgruntled by his misfortune. He needed some support and this group attracted him. The doctor and his friends consoled him and encouraged his ambition. Because of his London experience, the young printer recognized the intellectual value of these men and understood their ideas.

James Franklin was in accord with the popular cynical attitude, the radical and Deistical tendencies of the time, and like his newly found companions, was anxious to see the world adapt itself to his frame of mind. Besides, as he was the son of Josiah Franklin, the esteemed and respected candle-maker, whom the clergy held in high consideration and whom the merchants of the city strongly appreciated, he wished to break away and be heard on his own merits. James, himself, had some relations with the Mathers through one of their nephews, but it was just this family that he most wished to attack. No one was more in the public view in Boston than Cotton Mather, no one symbolized more clearly the ancient theocracy, and no one of the Puritans was more affected and ridiculous than he.

A favorable occasion presented itself. At this date a great discussion was in progress throughout the world: should inoculation be used to combat smallpox or was this proceeding more dangerous than useful? Inoculation was known and had been experimented with for some time in the regions of the Near East, especially in Turkey. But how or why inoculation was a protection was not understood and those who could not accept an idea which they could not first analyze and understand, were naturally hostile to it. Inoculation was neither scientific nor official, because it could not be explained. Many years were needed to change this attitude. The majority of doctors and savants repudiated the treatment, even made fun of it.

Inoculation was said to have come from Thessaly, the traditional country of witches, and some woman had thence brought it to the shores of the Caspian Sea. At the end of the seventeenth century it had made its way to Constantinople, where an Englishwoman, Lady Mary Montagu, wife of the English Ambassador to Constantinople, heard of it and became an enthusiastic convert. She brought the discovery back to London (1719) where it was experimented with and discussed.

The proceedings of the Royal Scientific Society of London at this time include a study on inoculation as it was practiced in the Levant by Tymonius and Pilermus (Numbers 339 and 377). Several educated men of Boston received these same accounts, among them Douglass and Mather, but the two men reacted oppositely to the new idea; Mather, always exalted, intense and desiring to do good, became an enthusiastic partisan of it immediately, while Douglass, with his solid scientific culture, thought that inoculation, coming from a backward and superstitious country, was ridiculous and absurd. Whatever doubts he may have had disappeared completely when he learned that Mather had taken up the cause with avidity.

Mysterious and terrible signs were seen in the sky on the eleventh of December, 1719, and pious people said they presaged pestilence and hard times for Boston. By direct inspiration of the Holy Ghost, Cotton Mather preached a terrifying sermon in 1720, predicting all sorts of misfortunes and punishments for the corrupted city. Some months later his prophecy was realized, and in May, 1721, the *Boston News Letter* announced that smallpox had made its appearance in the city, eight persons having been infected.

The epidemic raged during the entire summer, the entire

winter, and up to the springtime of 1722, the tired and terrified city being engaged all the while in a violent struggle between the inoculators and the anti-inoculators. The Mathers tried out the treatment immediately. With the aid of one of the best doctors of the city, they set themselves to inoculating patients, starting June 17, 1721, two months after it had been tried for the first time in England, two years before the French experiments, and four years before the German and Russian doctors made their first tentative trials.

In less than six months the Mathers and their friends had inoculated more than 250 persons. As a whole, the results were good enough: out of 286 inoculated only six died, while out of the 5759 who had not been inoculated, 844 died. But this inexplicable fashion of curing a disease by giving it to you displeased the logical and scientific mind of Douglass and horrified the general populace.

Two camps were formed, the ministers who supported inoculation and the "liberals" who attacked this fantastic practice. James Franklin's little group attacked inoculation with redoubled blows in the *Boston Gazette*, and then in the new newspaper which Franklin had founded at this timely occasion. "The chief design of the *New England Courant*," Checkley wrote in an article which appeared August 21, 1721, "is to oppose the doubtful and dangerous practice of inoculating the small pox."

The battle was public and violent. A club was founded, "The Society of Physicians Anti-Inoculator", with Checkley as president and Hall's Tavern as a general meeting place. The members of this club swore, above all, to abuse Mather. Thus, both groups appealed to mob passion, gathering strength as they continued their attacks, and creating fear, anger and jealousy.

Lawrence Dalhonde, "by order of the selectmen", published a statement in which he affirmed that twenty-five years before he had seen inoculation tried out by the French army in Italy and that the results were deplorable. As this was an official publication it stirred up great animosity in the crowd and

Mather found himself in the midst of a battle. Checkley, then Douglass, attacked him in every number of the *Courant*, James Franklin turned on him in derision, and phrases like the following were common in his columns: "Most of the Ministers are for it and it induces me to think it is from the Devil," to which was added this adroit ending, quite conforming to the method and attack of the English Deists, who never exposed themselves completely: "for he often makes use of good men as instruments to obtrude his delusions on the world."

Finally, to tease Mather more effectively, the "Courantiers", as they were called, affirmed that he had no right to his title of Member of the Royal Scientific Society. They even posted the official list of the members of the Royal Scientific Society in Hall's Tavern and the name of Mather was not included; (he had been regularly elected but was not yet considered as really being a member; for this he had still to go to London and there be officially received by the Society).

This plausible and calumnious accusation caused a lot of gossip and irritated Mather intensely. Douglass continued to stir up the people's anger against Mather in the *Courant* and he succeeded so well that one early morning at two o'clock a hand grenade was thrown into Mather's house where a sick minister was lodged at the time, on the eve of being inoculated. An insulting note was attached to the explosive: "Damn you, I will inoculate you with this, with a pox to you," but fortunately, as Mather said, "The merciful providence of GOD so ordered it that the Granado passing through the window had by the iron in the middle of the Casement such a turn given to it that in falling on the floor the fired wild fire in the fuse was silently shaken out some distance from the shell and burned out upon the floor without firing the granado."

Mather was furious, and with a group of churchmen, partisans of inoculation, answered his enemies in a violent pamphlet: "A vindication of the Ministers of Boston from the Abuses and Scandals lately cast upon them." There was nothing bothersome about this attack to James Franklin and he could laugh at it, but the measures that the Government began to employ in silencing the affair endangered the newspaper seriously. Should the situation become more critical, the printer saw no other resource than to utilize the most discreet, the most brilliant and the most daring of his collaborators, his apprentice and brother, Benjamin.

At the moment that James was fearing for the existence of his newspaper, Benjamin had already spent four years in the store and press-room. He had been practically compelled to enter the business by his father who thus wished to hinder him from sailing away, and who thought that by utilizing the boy's taste for reading and books the trend of his imagination might be changed.

Benjamin hesitated a long time. He had such a great desire for adventure, such an intense need for action. Life was repellent in this too narrow city, so close to the wide sea, and it was only by weakness that he yielded to his father's will. He submitted also to the attraction which his brother exercised over him. James knew London, life and women, and Benjamin admired him for this. Finally, it wasn't displeasing to be the apprentice in a store where he would also be the brother of the proprietor. So without much worry he signed a curious contract in which he promised his brother: "His lawful commands everywhere [to] gladly do," to stay with him until his twenty-second year, "to serve him faithfully, to keep his secrets." The contract restricted him still further in the following clause: "Taverns, inns, or alehouses, he shall not haunt. At cards, dice, tables or any other unlawful game he shall not play. Matrimony he shall not contract."

In return, James promised to teach him his art: "Finding and allowing unto the said apprentice meat, drink, washing, lodging, and all other necessaries during the said term." Benjamin was not to receive any salary except during the last year and Josiah paid James ten pounds in British money as recompense for the cares he was to lavish on his brother. This contract, in due good form, was analogous to those which were signed by other apprentices of the time, and Benjamin didn't feel slighted.

Nevertheless, he wasn't any too happy; how often he must have dreamed of escaping his long servitude and making a little money! But he was not unaware of the fourth page of his brother's newspaper, where the list of runaway slaves and apprentices appeared regularly, announcing handsome rewards to those who found them, brought them back and denounced them. On the other hand, America was huge, and the runaways, who desired liberty insatiably, were swift-footed. Still, they often died of hunger in the wilderness, were scalped by the Indians or seized by the French. These stories, which the apprentices whispered among themselves, set Benjamin thinking. Young but prudent, he meditated a long time before making any decision, applying his resourceful mind to his two great problems: how to escape and how to secure some money.

The latter was solved without much trouble. Among the books which Franklin had read were some which had struck his imagination by their strange style, their extravagances, and the practical ideas that they also contained. Written by a certain Tryon, merchant of London, who called himself a "student in physics", these little treatises inspired him with the most pure Pythagorean doctrines. The good Tryon, who knew how to make his fortune, hadn't broken off completely with the good Lord of the English, but was pantheistical, as were a great many men in the universities of Great Britain where the Renaissance and the Reformation had left such curious intellectual backwaters.

Tryon believed in metempsychosis, the spirituality of animals, fought for vegetarianism and published books which included adages on frugality and piety, recipes for simple dishes, and paragraphs on the respect due to the souls of rabbits. These little books had taken a place in the libraries of the good bourgeois Bostonians. They were so practical. They informed you of so many useful cures and at the same time included such solid truths and such judicious maxims.

"THE WAY TO SAVE WEALTH" was the title of one of his books and its summary included:

I. How a man may live well and plentifully for two pence a day.

II. Directions to make Shoe leather and other leather last much longer than usual. . . .
VII. To cure all sorts of wounds whatever by a poultice only.
VIII. To make several sorts of Powder for the Hair. . . .
XI. To brew good Liquor without malt.
XII. To make Coffee of Horsebeans. . . .
XIV. To know whether gold or silver coins be good.
XV. To cure consumption a new way. With divers other Extraordinary Experiments, Rarities and Curious Innovations.

Such a list was already alluring and gave but a hint of the treasures you would find inside: there were recipes "To make silver clean", "To take Fowls", "How to Catch Eels" — with calf's liver pounded in a bale of hay — while "To cure deafness" the following prescription was given: "Put into your ear of your own urine warm, this often. This is an extraordinary thing I am told." One was also told how "To gather fish together", "How to cure Chilblains, Dimness of the eyes, to destroy all sorts of vermin, to kill weasels"; and to kill frogs, "bruise goat, sheep, or oxgall by the water side and the frogs will all come together." A few more excerpts will give an idea of the good Tryon's resources and of the attraction he could exert over the eighteenth-century Bostonians.

To hinder the nightmare from Riding horses; take a flint and make a hole in it, and put a string through it, and hang it by the manger, or about the beast's neck, and it will prevent the nightmare. . . . To Cure an Ague, write these following words in Parchment, it must be writ triangularly, and wear it about your neck. 'Tis said one Cured about 100 with it.

ABRACADABRA
ABRACADABR
ABRACADAB
ABRACADA
ABRACAD
ABRACA
ABRAC
ABRA
ABR
AB
A

To cure the biting of a mad dog write in a piece of paper these words, Rebus, Rubus, Epilepscum, give it to the party or Beast bitten, or cat, in Bread. This never fails.

In these curious books Benjamin found sovereign formulas, but those he appreciated the most were the most practical. He read with pleasure that beds had to be kept clean, that they had to be aired and the sheets changed, for bedbugs and cockroaches multiplied in the filth of old beds. He approved of such maxims as: "The first step to wisdom is to know thyself, the consummation of it, to know God thy creator." "Be clean, observe proper times of eating, viz 8 or 9 in the morning and 3 or 4 afternoon."

The boy who knew his own quarrelsome nature and that of his family read with interest:

Rules of Health and Abstinency for all young People and other of the Cholerick complexion to observe. Such as are dignified with this Cholerick nature, whose Face burns brisk and lively, ought especially to refrain heady drinks, which heats the blood and irritates the original Fire which do powerfully inflame the property of Venus, and sets open her gates. Let no sweet drinks come into your bellies. . . . Refrain eating of eggs and rich Broths. Flower and Water, Flower and Milk, Flower and Milk and Water, prepared as we have taught in the Good Housewife made a Doctor are excellent foods.

Benjamin found much to glean in these pages. He learned that he should "Take example from wise men, not from Fools." "Be your own Cook and trust not a blind man to prepare your Food." "Be able to give a reason for all you do, for Tradition is a blind guide." "Say not in your Heart, that my Grandfather and Father and Mother did so and so, and I believe they were as wise as you, and therefore I will do so too, for such Sayings are to men of stubborn and incurable Folly. . . ." "Water is the most kindly and natural Drink especially for all young People."

Thus, preaching, advising and discussing, the good Tryon attempted to save his young readers from perdition and lead them to salvation by vegetarianism. And in his long "Treatise of cleaness in meats and Drinks, of the preparation of food", he summed up his views in a decisive argument: "Flesh is naturally the most unclean of all food, it being of a gross phlegmatick nature; and if care be not taken and order and temperance observed in the Eater it generates abundance of crude and noxious humours." To eat meat was dangerous. Worse, it was a crime, for animals had souls, and in eating their flesh the souls suffered.

And Tryon, as practical as he was mystical, entitled another one of his works: "Wisdom's Dictates; or Aphorisms and Rules, Physical, Moral and Divine; For preserving the *Health* of the *Body*, and the *Peace* of the *Mind*, fit to be REGARDED and PRACTICED by all that would enjoy the Blessings of the present and Future World.

To which is added:

A BILL OF FARE

of

SEVENTY FIVE NOBLE DISHES OF EXCELLENT FOOD, far exceeding those made of Fish or Flesh, which Banquet I present to the Sons of wisdom, or such as shall decline that depraved Custom of Eating Flesh and Blood."

Here was a lot to think about for an apprentice twelve-year-old, eager to be free, imbued with the spirit of economy, and very anxious to earn a few shillings for himself. In the school of his master, Tryon, Benjamin learned that he should give up meat and live on clear broth. So he proposed a change to his brother which would be advantageous to both of them. James, who was not yet married and who ate heartily, took his meals with his workmen at a neighbor's house, where he paid board. Benjamin offered to withdraw from this arrangement and board himself if his brother would give him the half of the money which he laid aside for his daily meals. James, like a good Franklin, found the idea excellent, so Benjamin feasted on his broth in the deserted workshop while the others ate their roast beef and drank their cider. By doing this he gained a lot of time for reading and enough money to buy books, for out of the sum his brother gave him he only spent half for his nourishment — vegetables and flour didn't cost much in Boston then, and there was plenty of water.

Nor did he lose his standing with the other apprentices by this procedure. Already he was judged ingenious, he looked wise, and James was not long in discovering these qualities in him, as well as finding that the boy had a certain naïve talent for poetry. Of course, Benjamin didn't possess a fine style, but in provincial and distant Boston, where many men knew how to read but where very few had culture, this puerile talent of Benjamin's was worth money.

At this time, people were very fond of popular ballads, half legend, half story, as the people of our day like the modern special editions. All great or moving events were commemorated in a ballad, easy to recall and amusing to recite in the long evenings. The crowds were pleased and touched by these ballads, which also sold so well and which were outside of the censor's regulations.

There was a popular saying to the effect that France in the eighteenth century was an absolute monarchy moderated by songs. Boston, more free, did not employ its songs for the same purpose; they served more to describe notable events than to criticize the Government.

When the guardian of the new lighthouse was drowned with his two daughters in December, 1718, Benjamin wrote a ballad on this tragic happening and then cried it down the streets and in the squares. The ballad was such a success that the brothers, delighted, decided to produce others.

Benjamin composed a song on the death of Captain Blackbeard, the great pirate, killed in November, 1717, by Lieutenant Maynard, after a terrible combat. Blackbeard was notorious, as he had terrorized navigation and all maritime commerce along the Virginian and Carolinian coasts for many years. The governor of North Carolina had been his accomplice. Benjamin found pleasure in recounting these happenings, as they nourished his childish dreams, swelled his pride and compensated his need of emotion.

James didn't take notice of this, charmed, if not by the talents of his brother, at least by the golden results of the enterprise. But the father saw more clearly and showed his son Benjamin to what dangers he was exposing himself. Poetry was not a good business in New England for it didn't pay enough and besides, as Josiah said frankly, these two ballads were pitiable specimens. Benjamin, with his rare common sense, realized that his father was right.

That he was easy to persuade was very typical of him and of Boston too. Under the same circumstances, Horace, Ronsard, Boileau and Marlowe had chosen the opposite road, had revolted against the paternal will. At Rome and in France, poetry was a dangerous but respected *métier;* in Boston, no one accepted the frivolous, pagan point of view of the French and their classical school. Benjamin Franklin of Boston could only hope to be a prose writer.

Still he had to be a writer. But he knew so little. This first attempt had excited him and awakened a lively desire for literary glory. Why should he repress such a worthy ambition? Every one around him praised and encouraged him.

It was beautiful to begin life in a city that was growing and developing. The first signs of industry could already be seen. A colony of Scotch-Irish had just arrived, bringing the spinning wheels which they used along with them. Every one in Boston was interested from the beginning. A committee was organized to start a school of spinning in order that the children of the city might learn the craft. Public experiments were held on the Common and the school was founded. In 1721, "a great linen wheel exhibition was held on the Common where all classes met and vied with each other in skill. It attracted a great concourse of people from town and country." Was this not a certain gauge of development for Boston?

The spinning-wheel exhibition must have interested the serious and practical Benjamin, but he did not disregard pleasures more suitable to his age and which were more likely to stimulate his imagination. It was exciting to see the lion which Captain Arthur Savage showed in Boston, solemnly announcing that there was, "Never one before in America." The entry fee, which a Negro took at the door, was rather high — six pence — but the lion was worth it. Besides, the animal was so soon to be shipped off to London. With the spinners, the lion, smallpox and pirates, some fires, festivals and storms, inoculation and Cotton Mather, life in Boston couldn't exactly be called dull.

On the contrary, serious people thought it was far too gay. The young ladies of the town behaved in a most unseemly fashion. They talked about anything, even inoculation. And in the evening you would see them slipping out of their homes, disappearing into the dark streets, into the orchards and shadowy parks, or hiding in wait under the silent trees of the Common.

> The young girls — said the well-informed *New England Courant* — spend the evening and half the night in search after, or in company with apprentice boys, young merchants, etc. They rise in the morning at about nine or ten of clock, and having tucked their hair under their nightcap, and given a sleepy scowl or two at the glass they are ready for their breakfast, which great work being over they retire to their chambers, dress themselves till twelve and approve themselves in the glass till one. After dinner they frisk away to some known place of rendez-vous, where (at night) every Jack has his Jill, and every Jill has her Jack.

Benjamin, himself, knew these nights of spring and summer in Boston and described them with precision. One evening after a walk he wrote:

> I met a crowd of Tarpolins and their Doxies, link'd to each other by the arms, who ran (by their own Account) after the rate of *six Knots an Hour*, and bent their Course towards the *Common*. Their eager and amorous Emotions of Body, occasion'd by taking their Mistresses *in Tow*, they call'd *Wild Steerage:* and as a Pair of them happen'd to trip and come to the Ground the Company were call'd upon to *bring to*, for *Jack* and *Betty* were *founder'd.* But this Fleet were not less comical or irregular in their Progress than a Company of Females I soon after came up with, who, by throwing their Heads to the Right and Left, at every boy who pass'd by them, I concluded came out with

no other Design than to revive the Spirit of Love in Disappointed Batchelors, and expose themselves to Sale to the first Bidder.

The apparent result, according to the conclusions of Benjamin, was to encourage the leather and shoe business, which has flourished in Boston ever since.

Among men of business the *Shoemakers*, and other Dealers in Leather, are doubly oblig'd to them, inasmuch as they exceedingly promote the Consumption of their Ware: and I have heard of a *Shoemaker*, who being as'k by a noted Rambler, *Whether he could tell how long her shoes would last;* very prettily answer'd, *That he knew how many Days she might wear them, but not how many Nights; because they were then put to a more violent and irregular service than when she employ'd her self in the common affair of her house.*

These pretty girls were always sure of finding devoted apprentices who would sympathize with their disappointments and wear of their shoes, but they also ran some risks, as is proven by the sad adventures of Marie Powell, Abigail Thurston and Esther Ray, who were publicly whipped in 1718 "for being nightwalkers."

IV

BENJAMIN FRANKLIN was no saint, but as the nights of Boston from 1718 to 1724 were very dark and have long since been forgotten, only a faint echo of his youthful escapades remains; he was discreet then, as throughout his whole life, and the names of his loves have been swept down the river of time with many other memories; only the flame of his desire has remained bright and clear. His early writings show us this. They are freed of Puritan morality, of almost all the principles his father thought were fundamental, and are oriented to other principles and a code of ethics he had created for himself.

To embark on his great adventure, Benjamin had no help but himself, a friend and a few books. Though he liked to swim, fish, box and court in company with his friends, he preferred solitude for his intellectual work and quiet reflection. This desire for tranquillity was imperious and stayed with him till the end of his life. He was not one of those who must talk a great deal in order to think a little; on the contrary, he was always looking for a retired place where he could meditate, write and reflect in peace.

Due to the régime he owed to Tryon he found this calm in the workshop of the *New England Courant* when he stayed alone at noon to drink his broth while the others devoured their roast beef at the boarding house. He also worked in the evening.

The offices of the *Courant* were convenient as they included a little library of philosophical, religious, historical and fiction books for the use of the contributors. Its contents give an idea of what was considered "classic" in those times: Latin, French and English books scattered pell-mell, Pliny's "Natural History", Josephus' "Life of Aristotle", volumes of French and Roman history, H. Moll's "Geography", "Athenian Oracles", "The British Apollo", Heylin's "Cosmography and Sum of Theology", "A History of New England" by C. Mather, Oldmixon's "History of the American Colonies", the works of Virgil, Shakespeare, St. Augustine, Tillotson, bound copies of the *Spectator*, "The Turkish Spy", "The Guardian", "The Art of Thinking", "The Art of Speaking", etc.

Out of this strange collection Benjamin chose those books which he thought would be useful to him in the future and devoted all his leisure time to studying and reading. His acquaintance with apprentices in book sellers' shops enabled him to secure what other books he needed and, finally, one of the friends of the *Courant*, a Mr. Adam, opened his library to him and there Benjamin was well supplied. Doubtless, these books would not have meant so much to him had not some inner need compelled him then to create his own language and style of writing.

Benjamin was very intimate with another apprentice, Collins, who had a lively mind and expressed himself more facilely than he. Following the fashion of the age, the two boys were extremely fond of discussion, held long private debates on every subject, and, of course, talked a lot about women. Franklin was not long in realizing that Collins was superior to him in reasoning and that if he wished to beat him he would have to acquire a better technique of argument. This led him to further meditation and reading.

The classics, which were so much read in France and to which the English middle class were indifferent, Franklin put resolutely to one side. In the beginning, his prayer book of literature was the third volume of Steele and Addison's *Spectator*, which he had come across by accident. With his carefully saved pence he finally bought a copy and studied in it daily. His method was intense and strict, for he was determined to know English thoroughly.

He read every one of the articles which made up the *Spectator*, wrote an analysis of them and then tried to rewrite them completely without looking at the book. This proceeding showed him his failings. He saw that his vocabulary was too limited and that he did not know enough about phrasing.

To remedy these two faults he set himself to re-writing the *Spectator* in verse and then transcribing the verses back again into prose in such a way that it resembled the original as much as possible. This task, fervently accomplished, gave results and Franklin soon learned to express himself in a practical, simple and forceful style. It was eminently suitable for what he had to say and adapted to the expression of his precise observations, ironical allusions and logical arguments, but as a vehicle for poetry or the technical exposition of pure science and abstract philosophy it was inadequate.

Here was a serious lack which a boy of another rank and temperament would have bitterly regretted. Benjamin did not even take notice of it for he was never interested in anything outside his proper field of action. His exact and fluent prose always permitted him to say simply and clearly what he thought and this sufficed.

As a matter of fact, Franklin felt himself handicapped by a more serious fault: the lack of logic and solidity in reasoning. So to train his mind, he set himself to scientific studies which up to now he had scorned: Locke's book on "Human Understanding", and "The Art of Thinking of Port Royal", which he found in the library of the *Courant*.

The latter book was dry but precise, summing up in a rather simple but honest fashion the rules of logic elaborated by the Greek and Roman philosophers and later perfected by Descartes. It was a hard, virile and formidable work. Locke was better adapted to his Anglo-Saxon mind, for his book was less formal and made a more direct appeal to common sense.

These two books freed his mind from the more rigorous forms of thought to which he had hitherto been accustomed, and aided him in his understanding of science and its technical methods. But even if he had become absorbed in some long abstract treatises demonstrating the nicest subtleties of mathematics, he would not have been touched, for Franklin only accepted the simple and realistic aspect of things and adapted his whole life to this attitude.

Then he took up the most popular books he could find in

Boston, the "Manuels" of Seller and Shermy on navigation which contained chapters on geometry, and the work of Cook on arithmetic. These books constituted all his intellectual equipment in the beginning but he studied them with the same intensity and comprehension he had employed with the *Spectator*.

In this way he really succeeded in understanding the basic principles of science. His method was not accidental, but calculated, and at the same time he was studying science he applied it to sports, particularly swimming. He had found a little illustrated book on swimming, by a certain Thevenot, translated from the French, and though he was already an expert swimmer he was soon busy in copying all the strokes described in its thirty-nine chapters:

> To swim with the head erect towards heaven, How to turn in the water, The turn called ringing the bell, To swim neither on back nor belly, To swim on the belly holding both your hands still, To carry the left leg in the right hand, To show both feet out of water, To swim having the legs tied together, To sit in the water, To cut the nails of the toes in the water, To show out of the water four parts of the body, To swim holding up one leg, To swim holding up the hand, To boot oneself in the water, The leap of the goat.

Finally, there was not one of these tricks, not one of these bizarre strokes which Benjamin could not execute. The English translator had said in his preface:

> Several little machines might be found very diverting in swimming to promote expedition, and make the motions of one single man in the water swifter than any boat; Contrivances of thin small planes of wood with valves or otherwise small hinges fastened to the legs might be very serviceable to that end, and perform the part of fish fins.

Benjamin thereupon made paddles for his hands and feet but he soon found that these tired him more than they served him. He preferred to be drawn effortlessly across a river by means of a flying kite.

Thus, in literature, science and sport, Franklin, provided with a few books, had been able to create practicable and unforgettable formulas which he used to infinite profit during his whole life and in the midst of a century which pushed intellectual and sentimental refinement to such extremes.

While other ambitious young men of the time, unsure and dissatisfied, gave themselves up to pleasure, the wise Franklin kept his physical freshness, his logical clarity, and developed a greater ease in his simple, supple and persuasive prose. Though the personal discipline he had adopted was elementary, he was faithful to its tenets, whereas other great men of the time preached doctrines they were unable to follow. This precocious self-discipline was an essential characteristic of the young Benjamin and he practiced it until the end of his life.

Franklin was to become a revolutionary who desired changes, but never a rebel or an anarchist. He detested disorder and had no faith in violence. However, at this time he was becoming conscious of himself and began to struggle against his naturally quarrelsome temperament. Under the influence of Xenophon's "Memorables" he learned to apply the Socratic method, that art of discussing without contradicting, of persuading without opposing, of avoiding all violence in language and mental attitude; he was soon able to convince by questions, dominate an adversary by his doubts, and, finally, by affecting hesitancy and an apparent ignorance, became invincible to any argument. Such a procedure exactly suited his nature, strong but opposed to brutality, his evangelistic taste, and his instinct of reserve.

Benjamin had now come to the time when a moral crisis was unavoidable; pagan doctrines which were overwhelming the century and which he had formerly held at a distance began to occupy his mind and touch his sensibility. The sermons he had read by the dozen in his father's house, began to irritate him instead of calming him. The good Tryon, with all his candor and effusive piety, had already instructed him to respect the souls of animals and the spiritual quality of the earth which he called "Nature." Indeed, he said in his book "Wisdom's Dictates":

> The more men imitate nature the nearer they come to their first state of innocency, and thereby obtain Health of Body and vigor of

mind. An example of this we have in all Animals and Birds who continue in that pure law they were made in, and placed under, how healthy most of them are when men do not render them otherwise by Oppression and Disorders.

Here was a new language for a child nourished on the strict and pious words of Calvin. And soon other impressions were added unto these. Benjamin had left his father's store and now he heard James' friends talking and blaspheming all day long. He also read the works of the great Deists, Collins and Shaftesbury, curious minds, as mystic as they were negative. How could he have resisted their doctrine and their style, now that he no longer had the example, the company, and conversation of his father to restrain him, now that he had lost his habit of attending church? At first he had regretted not going there, but he felt he could not spare the time from his reading, and, as the Sundays went on, he became more and more impervious to the call of the pealing Sabbath bells.

It is doubtful that even his father could have kept him from taking up Deism. The example of his family clearly showed Benjamin the holiness of revolt against ecclesiastical authority, and his favorite author, the pious John Bunyan, had taught him that a meeting with the Holy Ghost only occurred after a personal and individual search. Collins and Shaftesbury had gone beyond this but they still spoke of the spirit, wrote rhapsodically and were not without piety.

A story is told of Shaftesbury that, one day in speaking of religion with a friend, he concluded that all wise men have the same religion. A good woman, sewing near them, heard this comforting statement, but vaguely grasping that it was not at all clear, begged Shaftesbury to tell her what marvelous religion this was. The quick philosopher answered her politely, "Wise men never tell, Madam."

Franklin was becoming one of these wise men; he was swollen up with divinity though he never defined it; much less, he thought like all the unbelievers of the day, who did not cease to inveigh sarcastically against the Church, ministers and creeds.

The antinomy between reason and holy revelation was brutally made clear to him by these philosophers and by his companions. Like them, he had chosen reason, but more than they he had kept a hold on a simple natural belief; he always remained faithful to that religion which the sun and beasts of the earth continually proclaim and for which the human soul is eternally seeking. He enjoyed a freedom which was not tainted with the destructive ardor of his brother but which sufficed to base a commonness of thought between them.

Yet the relations between the brothers were more heated than suave. James held the upper hand and knew how to order a little more than Benjamin liked. Often the apprentice wanted to complain but he felt too great an admiration of his patron and elder brother to do so; when he stood before him he didn't dare to move. James was so dominating, so audacious and eloquent in the midst of this brilliant and eager group of friends: Checkley, Douglass, Adam and the others who aided him in writing and editing his newspaper. Benjamin, among all these intelligent and active men, soon caught the fever that animated them all, — the desire to appear in print.

The *Courant* first appeared in August, 1721, and during the early months of 1722 Benjamin had already begun to develop his startling plan. He knew very well what the *Courant* wished to accomplish and he had read enough of the contemporary authors to be able to imitate them, to succeed in employing their light sarcastic tone and being at the same time amusing and moral, cruel and patriotic. So he wrote little articles, signing them "Silence Dogood" as he didn't want to run the risk of being discovered, humiliated, and turned down because of his youth. Besides, a little mystery added to the charm of his writings and gave them more weight. The articles were slipped regularly under the door of the printer who always found them the morning after, to his great surprise.

Mrs. Silence Dogood was the amazing invention of a boy who hadn't forgotten Cotton Mather and his "Essays to do Good." But Mather, the great enemy of the *Courant*, though he was the leading minister of Boston, was also a "Garrulous Dogood."

THE New-England Courant.

[Nº 80

From Monday February 4. to Monday February 11. 1723.

The late Publiſher of this Paper, finding ſo many Inconveniencies would ariſe by his carrying the Manuſcripts and publick News to be ſupervis'd by the Secretary, as to render his carrying it on unprofitable, has intirely dropt the Undertaking. The preſent Publiſher having receiv'd the following Piece, deſires the Readers to accept of it as a Preface to what they may hereafter meet with in this Paper.

Non ego mordaci diſtrinxi Carmine quenquam,
Nulla venenato Litera onſta Joco eſt.

LONG has the Preſs groaned in bringing forth an hateful, but numerous Brood of Party Pamphlets, malicious Scribbles, and Billingſgate Ribaldry. The Rancour and bitterneſs it has unhappily infuſed into Mens minds, and to what a Degree it has ſowred and leaven'd the Tempers of Perſons formerly eſteemed ſome of the moſt ſweet and affable, is too well known here, to need any further Proof or Repreſentation of the Matter.

No generous and impartial Perſon then can blame the preſent Undertaking, which is deſigned purely for the Diverſion and Merriment of the Reader. Pieces of Pleaſancy and Mirth have a ſecret Charm in them to allay the Heats and Tumors of our Spirits, and to make a Man forget his reſtleſs Reſentments. They have a ſtrange Power to tune the harſh Diſorders of the Soul, and reduce us to a ſerene and placid State of Mind.

The main Deſign of this Weekly Paper will be to entertain the Town with the moſt comical and diverting Incidents of Humane Life, which in ſo large a Place as *Boſton*, will not fail of a univerſal Exemplification: Nor ſhall we be wanting to fill up theſe Papers with a grateful Interſperſion of more ſerious Morals, which may be drawn from the moſt ludicrous and odd Parts of Life.

As for the Author, that is the next Queſtion. But tho' we profeſs our ſelves ready to oblige the ingenious and courteous Reader with moſt Sorts of Intelligence, yet here we beg a Reſerve. Nor will it be of any Manner of Advantage either to them or to the Writers, that their Names ſhould be publiſhed; and therefore in this Matter we deſire the Favour of you to ſuffer us to hold our Tongues: Which tho' at this Time of Day it may ſound like a very uncommon Requeſt, yet it proceeds from the very Hearts of your Humble Servants.

By this Time the Reader perceives that more than one are engaged in the preſent Undertaking. Yet is there one Perſon, an Inhabitant of this Town of *Boſton*, whom we honour as a Doctor in the Chair, or a perpetual Dictator.

The Society had deſign'd to preſent the Publick with his Effigies, but that the Limner, to whom he was preſented for a Draught of his Countenance, deſcryed (and this he is ready to offer upon Oath) Nineteen Features in his Face, more than ever he beheld in any Humane Viſage before; which ſo raiſed the Price of his Picture, that our Maſter himſelf forbid the Extravagance of coming up to it. And then beſides, the Limner objected a Schiſm in his Face, which ſplits it from his Forehead in a ſtrait Line down to his Chin, in ſuch ſort, that Mr. Painter proteſts it is a double Face, and he'll have *Four Pounds* for the Pourtraiture. However, tho' this double Face has ſpoilt us of a pretty Picture, yet we all rejoiced to ſee old *Janus* in our Company.

There is no Man in *Boſton* better qualified than old *Janus* for a *Couranteer*, or if you pleaſe, an *Obſervator*, being a Man of ſuch remarkable *Opticks*, as to look two ways at once.

As for his Morals, he is a chearly Chiſtian, as the Country Phraſe expreſſes it. A Man of good Temper, courteous Deportment, ſound Judgment; a mortal Hater of Nonſenſe, Foppery, Formality, and endleſs Ceremony.

As for his Club, they aim at no greater Happineſs or Honour, than the Publick be made to know, that it is the utmoſt of their Ambition to attend upon and do all imaginable good Offices to good Old *Janus* the Couranteer, who is and always will be the Readers humble Servant.

P. S. Gentle Readers, we deſign never to let a Paper paſs without a Latin Motto if we can poſſibly pick one up, which carries a Charm in it to the Vulgar, and the learned admire the pleaſure of Conſtruing. We ſhould have obliged the World with a Greek ſcrap or two, but the Printer has no Types, and therefore we intreat the candid Reader not to impute the defect to our Ignorance, for our Doctor can ſay all the *Greek* Letters by heart.

His Majeſty's Speech to the Parliament, October 11. tho' already publiſh'd, may perhaps be new to many of our Country Readers; we ſhall therefore inſert it in this Day's Paper.

His MAJESTY's moſt Gracious SPEECH to both Houſes of Parliament, on Thurſday *October* 11. 1722.

My Lords and Gentlemen,

I Am ſorry to find my ſelf obliged, at the Opening of this Parliament, to acquaint you, That a dangerous Conſpiracy has been for ſome time formed, and is ſtill carrying on againſt my Perſon and Government, in Favour of a Popiſh Pretender.

The Diſcoveries I have made here, the Informations I have received from my Miniſters abroad, and the Intelligences I have had from the Powers in Alliance with me, and indeed from moſt parts of Europe, have given me moſt ample and current Proofs of this wicked Deſign.

The Conſpirators have, by their Emiſſaries, made the ſtrongeſt Inſtances for Aſſiſtance from Foreign Powers, but were diſappointed in their Expectations: However, confiding in their Numbers, and not diſcouraged by their former ill Succeſs, they reſolved once more, upon their own ſtrength, to attempt the ſubverſion of my Government.

To this End they provided conſiderable Sums of Money, engaged great Numbers of Officers from abroad, ſecured large Quantities of Arms and Ammunition, and thought themſelves in ſuch Readineſs, that had not the Conſpiracy been timely diſcovered, we ſhould, without doubt, before now have ſeen the whole Nation, and particularly the City of London, involved in Blood and Confuſion.

The Care I have taken has, by the Bleſſing of God, hitherto prevented the Execution of their trayterous Projects. The Troops have been incamped all this Summer; ſix Regiments (though very neceſſary for the Security of that Kingdom) have been brought over from *Ireland*, The States General have given me aſſurances that they would keep a conſiderable Body of Forces in readineſs to [illegible]

THE *NEW ENGLAND COURANT* OF FEBRUARY 11, 1723

The personage invented by Benjamin was a woman, in order that her observations might be all the more cutting to the ridiculous Mather.

Mrs. Silence Dogood, the modest and sensible widow of a country parson, was going to have a good time informing an important gossip the art of doing good. Mrs. Dogood would not be original but she would be sympathetic from the very beginning, clever in her simplicity and well informed on the ways of the world. She would also follow the prevailing fashions of London in thought and literary style.

Thomas Gordon, one of the Whig writers much in view in his time, began his series of humorous letters in the *London Journal* by an autobiography: "Having set up for a weekly wit it is expedient like others of that class who have gone before me that I give the town some true and faithful history of myself. . . ."

In the same way Mrs. Dogood wrote:

> Sir, it may not be improper in the first Place to inform your Readers that I intend once a Fortnight to present them, by the help of this Paper, with a short Epistle, which I presume will add somewhat to their Entertainment. And since it is observed that the Generality of People now-a-days are unwilling either to commend or dispraise what they read until they are in some measure informed who or what the Author of it is, whether he be *poor* or *rich*, *old* or *young*, a *scollar* or a *Leather Apron Man*, etc., and give their Opinion of the Performance, according to the Knowledge which they have of the Author's circumstances, it may not be amiss to begin with a short Account of my past Life and present Condition, that the Reader may not be at a loss to judge whether or no my Lucubrations are worth his reading.

The article, written in this dignified and modest style, so filled with serious conclusions and sly humor, delighted James Franklin and his friends. Curious, they wondered what man in the city could have written such a masterpiece of wise fooling, as no woman in Boston was known to be capable of writing so well. But the pages of this unknown handwriting were placed under the door of the printing shop at night and no one could guess whose it was.

The young apprentice in his corner listened avidly to the praises which were heaped on Mrs. Dogood. Perhaps the note which the editors of the *Courant* inserted at the end of the first article was set up by himself:

As the favour of Mrs. Dogood's Correspondence is acknowledged by the Publisher of this Paper, lest any of her Letters should miscarry, he desires they may for the future be deliver'd at his Printing House, or at the Blue Ball in Union Square, and no Questions shall be ask'd of the Bearer.

The polite and flattering acknowledgment was not so simple as it appeared, for in encouraging Mrs. Dogood and promising her discretion, it would eventually be a means of discovering her identity. But she knew the character of James Franklin far too well to be deceived, and continued sending her letters to him in the same way and with the same mystery. In all, fourteen appeared in the *Courant*, one every two weeks, between April 4, 1722, and September 24, 1722, except in numbers nine, ten, eleven and twelve.

This first intellectual and moral crusade of Benjamin Franklin merits detailed examination, for in spite of his youth he was already in possession of those methods which he practiced all his life and the principles he did not cease to defend up to his very death. The lad of sixteen took an intense pleasure in impersonating a shrewd, middle-aged widow, expressing his feelings and ideas in words proper to the virtuous wife of a Whig minister. To this he also brought to bear his veritable gift for the theater and a sharp sense of the comical. Indeed, Benjamin Franklin was born to be a humorous author and an actor, but the world was the only stage on which he ever played, for Bostonian customs and principles would never have permitted his appearance on any other.

His acting was always excellent, full of life and sincere, and what some later criticized in him as duplicity was only the natural result of his rare ability to impersonate characters and act his life as a varied and none too serious comedy.

Of course, Mrs. Dogood was a serious, dignified woman, but she had wit. Her first three letters, written as an introduction for the benefit of the good townsfolk of Boston, show this. She had a smile and a bow for every one and was as willing to receive criticism as to give it. Her character once established, Mrs. Dogood began her campaigning in earnest and showed her power.

She was a good mother; her first thought was for her young Master Dogood, so her attack was begun against Harvard. The college was no longer under Mather's hand; it was beginning to liberate itself completely from clerical domination, but it was still a citadel of conservatism and open only to the wealthy.

Young men in New England were divided into two classes at this time, the "Scollars" and the "Leather Aprons." Mrs. Dogood was strong in her defense of the latter and ridiculed the "Scollars." By doing so she was following Thomas Gordon who had bitterly criticized Oxford in the *London Journal:* "Having by my loyalty and sobriety and *pernicious Reason* scandalized the University and merited expulsion from thence . . ." — continuing for a long time in the same vein.

Mrs. Dogood wrote with a like intention and also added the observations of a virtuous New England woman, shocked and angered by the corruption, bad manners and general insolence of the young men of Harvard. Everybody knew that the General Court which had appropriated thirty-five hundred pounds for the erection of a huge building, Massachusetts Hall, had also been obliged to pass acts to control the extravagances of Commencement Day, forbidding the preparation or provision of "Plumb Cake, Roasted, Boyled or Baked Meates or Pyes of any kind." The "Scollars" were expressly prohibited from keeping in their lockers "any distylled Lyqyours or any composition therewith", under the penalty of a twenty-shilling fine and the forfeiture of the drinks. Other acts were passed against "the excesses, Immoralities and Disorders of the Commencements", and the Overseers had asked the Corporation to "restrain unsuitable and unseasonable dancing in the College", and "the great disturbance occasioned by tumultuous and indecent noyses."

The ill use that wealthy young gentlemen made of their college years was known to every one and Mrs. Dogood accused them of being unable to ascend "the Throne of Learning", as "the work proving troublesome and difficult to most of them they withdrew their hands from the plow and contented themselves to sit at the foot with Madam Idleness and her Maid Ignorance." Further, she contended that parents sent their sons to Harvard simply because they were rich and for no other reason; these boys lived in idleness and received their degree because they paid poorer ones to help them.

Her observations on the students of theology were no less acrid. "In the Temple of Theology," she wrote, "I saw nothing worth mentioning except the ambitious and fraudulent Contrivances of Plagius."

This article made a great sensation in Boston and other newspapers took up their cudgels. On May 28, the *Boston Gazette* of Boston published a letter answering Mrs. Dogood, signed, John Harvard. His counter-attacks were forceful. "Sir," he wrote, "desire Courante to no more to put upon Plagius for fear of hurting himself. I am a Person that have occasion to look into a pretty large number of books a year, which makes me capable of discovering the shameful thefts of Couranto himself," and he continued, showing that the writers of the *Courant* drew largely from the *Guardian*, the *Tatler* and the *Spectator* for the contents of their articles. He ended by aiming a direct blow at Mrs. Dogood.

Is not Couranto a fine Rhetorician and a correct writer when he says in his last but one, "Now I observed that the whole tribe who entered into the Temple with me began to climb the Throne but the work proving troublesome and difficult to most of them *they withdrew their hands* from the plow." Friend, who ever heard of ent'ring a Temple and ascending the Magnificent steps of a Throne with a Plough in his hand! O rare Allegory! Well done, Rustic Couranto! This may cause matter of speculation.

No doubt, Mrs. Dogood was hurt by this unkind attack on her style and the neat expression she had lifted from "Pilgrim's Progress", but she hid her chagrin and wisely made no reply. She wrote once more about the "empty skull" of Harvard men, but in the following numbers of the *Courant* she showed herself more amenable, and disposed to discuss more general topics: the character of the weaker sex, the danger of fashionable dress and the inferior quality of poetry in New England.

In all her articles Mrs. Dogood showed herself to be a faithful disciple of the *Spectator*, displaying her wit and irony to advantage, while their tone was in agreeable contrast to the other columns of the *Courant*. James Franklin and his friends wrote with strength and violence but with little grace and devoted themselves to attacking the rich and powerful. They gave themselves up to the task with abandon, much to the satisfaction of their readers (the number of which seemed to be increasing) but to the irritation of governmental officials who had begun to be annoyed.

Inoculation was a dead issue now but the fight against the clergy was far from finished. The governor might have let this go by but he was displeased to see a sarcastic attack on the slowness of his administration. The *Courant* had printed a letter on June 11, dated from Newport, where a pirate ship had been sighted off Block Island, and its anonymous author had written: "we are advised from Boston, that the government of Massachusetts are fitting out a ship (The Flying Horse) to go after the Pirates, to be commanded by Captain Peter Papillon, and 'tis thought he will sail some time this month, wind and weather permitting."

Furious at this impertinence, the Council summoned James Franklin. The young printer took a haughty attitude which annoyed the officials even more, refusing to divulge the name of the audacious letter writer and so was sent to jail, where he stayed a full month.

Benjamin was also forced to appear, but not wishing to reveal the author's identity any more than his brother, alleged that his contract obliged him "his master faithfully serve, his secrets keep." His good appearance and modesty, his youth and this last argument merited the indulgence of the court and he was sent back without punishment.

The apprentice took advantage of the occasion and with the aid of his brother's friends, continued the *Courant* and pleaded eloquently for his freedom. All the little quarrels were forgotten now and there only remained two Franklins fighting for liberty and their daily bread.

Benjamin attacked the Council by quoting the Magna Carta and in every way possible denounced the irregularities of his brother's prosecution. Moreover, he succeeded and won the sympathetic support of another newspaper, the *Philadelphia Mercury*, which published an indignant article in favor of James Franklin. But in 1722 a press campaign had no effect on the Government. Nor were the some hundreds of readers of the newspapers at all willing to fight for their editors. James Franklin was in jail and had to yield. He was not liberated until after he had sent the Council a letter of very humble excuses and an imploring petition.

A still greater danger menaced on July 5, 1722, when the Chamber of Representatives of Massachusetts debated a proposal to censure James Franklin. He was to put down one hundred pounds sterling as a guarantee of his good conduct and promise to show each issue to the secretary of the government before publishing it. Thus he would be hindered from attacking the Church, Governor and Government.

After a sharp discussion the proposal was rejected and the editors of the *Courant*, in announcing their triumph, gloated perhaps more than was wise. Mrs. Dogood, herself, carried away by fraternal zeal, reprinted an article by Thomas Gordon in the *London Journal* which developed this principle: "Without freedom of Thought, there can be no such Thing as Wisdom; and no such Thing as publick liberty without Freedom of Speech."

The following week she quoted again from the same author and the same newspaper, citing very strong paragraphs against "Hypocrits" and in particular, "State Hypocrits", whom she quite demolished.

Thus the two brothers were intimately united in the same undertaking and menaced by the same dangers. Benjamin, no longer fearful, conscious of his success and of the service he had rendered his brother, at last revealed himself as the author of Mrs. Dogood's letters. The fundamental principles of the two brothers were the same and they worked in active collaboration. Benjamin's methods, however, were different. Though he was still very young, he had more control of himself than James and more reserve. His articles were more carefully written, more indirect, and contained no personal attacks. Benjamin knew how to mix light, amusing observations in serious discussion without falling into burlesque, and he avoided bitterness.

After his first indignant thrusts against the Government, and when the suit against his brother was somewhat forgotten, he resumed his habitual moderation. In August, 1722, he published an article taken almost textually from Defoe's "Essays on Projects", suggesting a system of insurance to aid widows. The following week he elaborated the idea in a comical fashion, proposing insurance for old maids. Then he wrote two picturesque letters, describing the life and customs of Boston with its drunkards, "nightwalkers", and lovers. The tenor of these letters was free, sometimes a little too free, but the goal was moral and no one but hypocrites could have found anything to say against them.

His last article, far from displeasing the ministers of Boston and their pious flocks, could not but have charmed them, as it was an attack against some Connecticut ministers who had traitorously joined the Church of England. However, the article also showed that Morals were more important and more necessary to Humanity than Religion and expressed the conviction that a too great enthusiasm for the Church and pure Dogma was lamentable.

Mrs. Dogood, having accomplished her task, ceased writing, and no one could persuade her to resume her letters. The *Courant* published this article in December, 1722, to no effect:

Mrs. Dogood, I greatly wonder why you have so soon done exercising your gifts and hid your Talent in a Napkin. You told us at first that you intended to favour the Public with a speculation once a fortnight, but how comes it to pass that you have laid aside so good a design. Why have you so soon withdrawn your hands of the Plough (with which you taxed some of the scholars) and grown weary of doing good?

Is your commonplace wit all exhausted, your stock of matter all spent? We thought you were well stored with that by your striking your first blow at the College. You say (No. 2) that you have an excellent faculty of observing and reproving the faults of others, and are the vices of the Time all mended? Is not there whoring, drinking, swearing, lying, gaming, cheating, and oppression, and many other sins prevailing in the Land? Can you observe no faults in others (or yourself) to reprove? Or are you married and removed to some distant clime that we hear nothing from you? Are you (as the Prophet supposed Baal, that sottish Deity) asleep or on a Journey and cannot write? Or has the sleep of unexorable, unrelenting Death procur'd your silence? and if so you ought to have told us of it and appointed your successor. But if you are still in being and design to amuse the Publick any more, proceeding your usual course; or if not let us know it, that some other hand may take up your pen.

Your friend,
HUGO GRIM

ADVERTISEMENT

If any Person or Persons will give a true account of Mrs. Silence Dogood, whether dead or alive, married or unmarried, in town or country, that so (if living) she may be spoken with or letters convey'd to her, they shall have thanks for their Pains.

Mrs. Dogood didn't respond to this touching letter. She had died a natural death as Benjamin had nothing left to write about, and her death was also violent, as James was jealous.

James Franklin was neither very pious nor very modest. Benjamin had launched himself into a literary career under his very eyes, already gaining a reputation as a writer and philosopher while he, the eldest, the proprietor, had only succeeded in getting himself put in prison and harvesting trouble on every side. He looked enviously at his brother, so precocious and brilliant, and felt that Benjamin had had an unfairly advantageous start.

The events of the year 1722 with its work of collaboration on the *Courant* had hastened Benjamin's development exceedingly. Mrs. Dogood had been for him not only a means of making himself known but also a device to perfect his style and try himself out on the public.

Thus, at the beginning, his style had something infantile about it; the simple dignity tended to be childish however carefully he ornamented it according to the fashionable rhetoric of the time. In her first letter Mrs. Dogood said:

> At the time of my Birth my parents were on Ship board in their Way from London to N. England. My Entrance into this troublesome World was attended with the Death of my Father, a Misfortune which tho' I was not then capable of knowing I shall never be able to forget; for, as he, poor Man, stood upon the deck rejoycing at my Birth, a merciless Wave enter'd the Ship and in one Moment carry'd him beyond Reprieve. Thus was the first Day which I saw, the last that was seen by my Father; and thus was my disconsolate Mother at once made both a Parent and a Widow.

The somewhat slow and heavy grace of this style pales before the lusty vivacity that Benjamin later learned to employ and which is everywhere evident in the last pages of Mrs. Dogood's correspondence. For example, this paragraph:

> As the Effects of Liquor are various, so are the Characters given to its Devourers. It argues some Shame in the Drunkards themselves, in that they have invented numberless Words and Phrases to cover their Folly, whose proper Significations are harmless, or have no Signification at all. They are seldom known to be drunk, tho' they are very often boozy, cogey, tipsey, fow'd, merry, mellow, fuddl'd, groatable, Confoundedly cut, See two a Moons, are Among the Philistines, In a very good Humour, See the Sun, or, The Sun has shone upon them, they Clip the King's English, are Almost Froze, Feavourish, in their Altitudes, Pretty well enter'd, etc.

V

This series of articles, certainly the most brilliant that the *New England Courant* had published, displayed Benjamin's sharp sense of observation, his firm style, and above all, a capacity for reasoning far beyond his age. Indeed, they reveal his veritable cult for Reason, and his high respect for Morality. He saw the latter as a result of applying wisdom and logic, a code to control pleasure and instinctive desires. He said this clearly in his article on drunkards. "But after all it must be considered that no Pleasure can give satisfaction or prove advantageous to a reasonable Mind, which is not attended with the Restraints of Reason."

From now on Benjamin was a Deist, vowed to the cult of Reason and Liberty. Theology he considered as a mortal enemy, while Religion was an instrument that was sometimes useful but always dangerous. It was useful when designed to improve the conduct of man but it was hateful when its power was applied to support tyranny and superstition.

Ardently Whig and devoted with all his heart to new ideas, Benjamin was certainly the brother of James. But he was superior to him in the use of irony, logic and anecdote. Every one thought so, even the two brothers themselves, and this stimulated the vanity of Benjamin and caused James chagrin.

Besides, James had more than one objection against his cumbersome apprentice, for in spite of Benjamin's conversion to the Socratic attitude, he still remained headstrong, quarrelsome and cocksure of himself. Sometimes James, tired of their endless discussions, took recourse to blows, the better to impress his ideas on his younger brother. Benjamin, less strong and not so developed as James, was thus reduced to silence but was not persuaded or calmed.

More than once their quarrels finished with their father as

arbiter. Though wishing to keep an equal balance between the two, Josiah was often more apt to take the side of Benjamin and James went off angrier than before. The peace of the family suffered.

Benjamin was annoyed. It displeased him to waste his time this way, fighting with his brother, and his situation as apprentice was a burden to him. While James was in prison he had taken charge of the store, the printing shop and the newspaper, and things hadn't gone any the worse for that. Benjamin was proud of this exploit and it inflamed his desire to command. His instinct for leadership was profound and irresistible though it did not exclude any other characteristic normal in a young man. He enjoyed himself among the girls and loved women all his life, but no woman, however charming she was, could completely capture his mind and imagination. And though he was a great amateur of science and devoted many hours to philosophy and literature, he never considered them as an ultimate goal. He loved politics, too, and the struggle of commerce, but he never considered his enterprises in these fields, picturesque and intoxicating as they were, as ends in themselves. Nothing could satisfy him entirely but the feeling that he was serving men by leading them.

His natural characteristics forced him to be a chief, but neither as a conqueror nor as a Don Quixote. Franklin had a sharp sense of the real, the present and the possible. He worked in the daylight and never pretended to undertake anything that was not possible to accomplish. He was no dupe of his pleasures or his imagination and so was equally indifferent to penny whistles and chimæras.

The situation of the *New England Courant* was daily becoming more and more delicate. James had not been at all intimidated by his stay in prison and continued his audacious and impertinent attacks against the Church and Government. In the issue of January 14, 1723, the *Courant* published a particularly brutal article against "religious knaves" where it was stated that "villanies acted under the cloak of religion are the most execrable."

This was too much. Immediately the General Court named a committee of three to investigate this affair. Three days later the committee proposed to the Court that "James Franklin be strictly forbidden by this Court to print or publish the *New England Courant*, or any other pamphlet or paper of the like nature, except it be first supervised by the Secretary of this Province."

This measure was approved and James Franklin had the choice of either suspending his newspaper or allowing it to be expurgated by men who had sworn that nothing shocking or amusing would be left in its pages. In this desperate situation James had recourse to a desperate decision and begged his brother to take over the responsibility of the newspaper. The *Courant* was from then on printed "under the name of Benjamin Franklin." It was the end of January, 1723, and Benjamin was just seventeen.

This solution was the only one possible, except that of confessing defeat, but it was not agreeable to either of the brothers. James, already annoyed by the vanity of his brother, was obliged to put him once more to the fore. Moreover, he had to tear up Benjamin's contract for fear of being accused of employing a too obvious subterfuge. An apprentice couldn't edit a newspaper.

As a matter of fact, after James had thrown the first contract into the fire, he drew up another secretly which put Benjamin back in his subordinate place. But a mysterious contract that had to be hidden could not exert much importance, and so James found himself in a very false position opposite his brother.

On the other hand, Benjamin found it repellent to advocate the cause of his brother so publicly and to indorse all the opinions and wordy quarrels which James was pleased to instigate in the *Courant*. After all, Benjamin was an humble, little-known apprentice, scarcely compromised, and at the beginning of his career. He had everything to lose by becoming a target of reprobation in Boston where the ministers and the rich remained the masters of the Government, situations and money. To risk his future without hope of great financial gain, without any real authority to exercise, was a too heroic renunciation for a young man of seventeen years who had nothing of the ascetic in him and whose brother had been a little too free with his fisticuffs.

But here was an adventure and Benjamin was too young to give it up. He would never know how to refuse very well. How strongly he felt the attraction of an exciting struggle and the joy of action!

No sooner said than done. "Couranto" was substituted for Janus, the charming mythical symbol of the two collaborating brothers. With its double visage, Janus turned a gay and juvenile face to the Boston public, that of Benjamin, while in the shadow it concealed another face with a bitter, brutal expression, that of James, always present, always hidden behind.

In presenting the new *Courant* to the public, Benjamin wrote an editorial preface in which he announced a very different program from that which James had first claimed to follow.

"The main Design of this Weekly Paper will be to entertain the Town with the most Topical and diverting incidents of Human Life, which in so large a Place as Boston will not fail of a universal Exemplification", and the editor's morals were defined as ". . . clearly Christian as the Country Phrase expresses it. A man of good temper, courteous Deportment, sound judgment, a mortal Hater of Nonsense, Foppery, Formality, and Endless Ceremony."

If such a program had been followed faithfully, the *Courant* would have been guaranteed a brilliant and tranquil career. But it is not easy to be amusing and witty without being wounding and biting. The *Courant* began to attack its old enemies again very shortly.

James, embittered by his defeat and his humiliation, could not wait until the combat was renewed, and Benjamin let himself be persuaded to do so by the enthusiasm of his companions. One after another, the *Courant* attacked the principles which were considered as the pillars of peace and order in the province.

Some weeks after the change of editors the newspaper started up once more against the ministers in saying: "Tho they are the Best of Men, yet they are but Men at the best, and by consequence subject to like Frailties and Passions as other Men." (Voltaire said a few years later, "Priests are not what the silly people think they are.") Janus concluded, however, that the sins of the Clergy could be covered, for "Charity covers a multitude of Sins. Besides when you abuse the Clergy you do not consult your own Interest for you may be sure they will improve their influence to the uttermost to suppress your paper." A rather pointed compliment. On February 18, the principle of heredity was assailed in an article certainly written by the younger Franklin:

Honour Friend, properly ascends and not descends, yet the Hat when the Head is uncover'd descends and therefore there can be no Honour in it. Besides Honor was from the Beginning but Hats are an invention of a late Time and consequently true Honour standeth not therein. In old Time it was no disrespect for Men and Women to be call'd by their own Names; Adam was never called Master Adam, we never read of Noah Squire, Lot Knight and Baronet, nor the Right Honourable Abraham, Viscount Messoppotomia, Baron of Canaan . . .

But these discussions of principle, vigorous as they were, were not enough to satisfy the verve of Janus. Consequently, at the same time, the *Courant* attacked one of its former contributors, Captain Taylor, who was guilty of having publicly refused to admit the authorship of several articles attributed to him. Insults were exchanged. Janus even turned against the governor who, after many and various difficulties with the good people of the province, had quit Boston in a very irritated state of mind. The *Courant* suggested that two delegates be sent from the province to England to refute the opinions of the governor.

At length, insatiably desiring still more enemies, the *Courant* undertook a controversy with the other newspapers of the city and turned them upside down with ridicule. Truly it wasn't very hard to do. The *News Letter* was naïve and poorly armed to defend itself.

In February, 1723, a tidal wave devastated the port and flooded a part of Boston, so the *News Letter* gave this scientific explanation for the benefit of its readers: "The many great wharves which since the last overflowing tide have been run out into the harbour and fill'd so great a part of the barrier methinks contributed something not unconsiderable to the riot of the water-power."

The *New England Courant* couldn't let such a chance go by and soon the city was highly amused at the expense of the oldest newspaper of America. The *Courant* suggested that the tidal wave had been caused by the many dikes recently constructed in Holland and that the Deluge was probably the result of the numerous docks men had built at that time. The poor *News Letter* was so piqued and humiliated that readers were bored for several months after with a scientific chronicle, "The History of Nature Among Us", which submitted social, physical, scientific, theological and rational hypotheses on the origin of tidal waves.

In June a new quarrel broke out between the two newspapers, apropos of an insulting poem published in the *Courant* against the Church of England, which was making such headway throughout Connecticut and even in Boston. The verses were supposedly written by an old Mr. Fitch whose family was strongly attached to the Church of England and they were printed under his name. The Fitch family was at first annoyed, then furious. Ebenezer Fitch took up the pen for the honor of his house and Janus as quickly answered him. "All Men," wrote Mr. Fitch, "must think him Animated beyond common sense into gross nonsense." He treated Janus as a "small curr" and finally declared, "You must have in the cavity of your calabash a viscid Juice."

At the same time that the *Courant* was quarreling with Fitch and the *News Letter* about the Church of England, the editor started a new quarrel with the Pope as a subject. The *News Letter* had announced that the Pope was ill. So the *Courant* came forth the following week (June 17, 1723) with this little editorial:

This account of a complication of distempers in the Pope gives us a melancholy Prospect of the affairs of Europe; and that his Holyness is pretty well in order as to his gutts, his legs, his teeth and his pulse, he still complains of a pain in his foot, which undoubtedly affects his toes; and we all know that the Honour and happiness of a great number of Catholics depends on the sound health of his Holiness's great toe, which by this Account, I am afraid, is not in a kissing condition.

This somewhat gross maneuver was adroit in such an ardently Protestant and anti-papist city as Boston. The *Courant's* attacks against the Anglicans and the Catholics won the favor of the populace and of many bourgeois. At this time, Protestantism was much more a means of attacking the Church than of worshiping God.

Many who had rallied to the Reformed Church had done so merely to satisfy their instinct for revolution and their need for liberty. They thought that the reform was the first step to a new era and that the *Courant* was not impious but, on the contrary, faithful to the essential traditions of Protestantism. And they could not but appreciate and admire the words that Benjamin Franklin put into the mouth of Abigail Twitterfield, a poor young girl who complained in the *Courant* against the ministers of the city and their sermons on the "sin of barrenness." She protested it was unjust to be insulted "with the bitter names of drysticks, sapless trees, unfruitful Vines, etc. Job. 24–21", and concluded, "Upon the whole . . . if ministers would deliver nothing but the plain substantial Truths of the Gospels they would best magnify their office and edify their hearers."

VI

THE verve and irony of Benjamin were present in all these articles and controversies but his lassitude and discontent were also beginning to show. He was tiring of all this noise and these bitter quarrels. The personal attacks against Fitch and Taylor had highly displeased the city, the attention of the public began to wane and the necessity of daring a little more each time to retain the subscribers and hold the interest of the readers in suspense wearied him still more.

Benjamin also sensed that many people were disturbed about the young men of Boston. In February, 1723, several of them who had been refused entrance to the dancing school of a Mr. Gatchell decided to enter by force and broke the windows. The affair was not allowed to go by without punishing the offenders. They were brought before a Justice of the Peace and judged in the hearing of a huge crowd on Monday, March 3, 1723. Everybody in Boston began to think that the young men drank too heavily, went out in the evenings too often, and swore to excess. Something had to be done to remedy the situation.

All this was disagreeable to an ambitious seventeen-year-old boy of mature intelligence who was anxious to do good in the world. Before long he would not be taken seriously in Boston and the long period of waiting before he would be finally accepted would certainly be humiliating.

Benjamin thought that James had gone too far. James had made his situation impossible and did not even seem grateful for the many services Benjamin had rendered. On the contrary, he became more and more jealous, more and more brutal.

Where could Benjamin find support? Assuredly, Josiah Franklin was a good father and proud of his young son, but he could not favor him too openly as he was the one to maintain discipline in the family. Benjamin, who was meditating an open break, couldn't count on him. He had few friends since he had taken up his intense reading and studying, uncommon among the lads of his class, and his difficult adventures with his brother had forced him to isolate himself.

There only remained his great friend, Collins, who devoured books like himself and who had an open mind, thanks to the rationalistic propaganda of Benjamin. After Benjamin had looked for work among the other printers of Boston and found that James had taken care to warn them in advance, thus closing all the shops of the city to him, Benjamin realized he could count only on the resources of his imagination and the devotion of Collins. His brother would not dare to have him prosecuted or use the secret contract against him, and would never allow him to secure a decent place in the printing shop. To establish himself independently in Boston was, of course, out of the question.

To be himself and to become a leader he would have to leave the city. It was a kind of treason but there was nothing else to do. Didn't James often justify his actions in the name of "Liberty" ? And hadn't he rendered many services for which he would never be payed? God was nothing but a distant image for him then and morality a personal interest. At last nothing held him back. He would leave.

However, an opportunity to escape was lacking, so he bided his time. The end of winter passed, warm spring and summer glided softly over the trees of tranquil Boston. Now and then some one would throw hot coals wrapped in a piece of calico into his neighbor's house and there would be an exciting fire, or an old lady was put into the pillory to have her ears cut as a punishment for counterfeiting money. In July, a well-known old Negress, Ma Carlington, died and "On Thursday night she was magnificently interred at the North Burying Place, the (velvet) Pall being supported by 6 blacks of the first rank and her funeral attended by 270 more of the same colour."

In August the death of Increase Mather marked a new milestone in the decline of the clerical aristocracy, and towards the end of that month there was a great deal of talk about the Indians. John Quittamog, an old redskin of one hundred and twelve years, was solemnly received by Judge Sewall and Judge Dudley, who both treated him with much honor. At the same time, delegates of eight Indian nations with their wives and children arrived in Boston and were housed in the capacious mansion of Judge Wainwright, overlooking the Common.

The Indians impassively attended conferences at the General Assembly of the province, local curiosities and novelties were shown to them, among which was a new gun made with "one Barrel and one lock" by John Pimmin of Anne Street.

Wherever the Indians went a crowd gathered around them. They attracted public attention to such a degree that Benjamin was quite free to prepare for his escape. He arranged with Collins to sell some of his books, find a boat willing to take him and get a little money together. Collins succeeded in persuading the captain of a little sloop from New York to take Benjamin along, saying that his friend, whose name he withheld, was a poor boy beleaguered by a furious woman who was forcing him to marry her.

The good captain, touched by the recital of this painful predicament, promised to embark the boy discreetly. From then on everything was ready. The sloop only awaited a fair wind.

Still, Benjamin had to proceed with great caution. The Indians fortunately made enough noise to deafen and stun the town. Towards the middle of September,

> the said delegates had an Ox given to them . . . which they killed with bow and arrows and in the Evening a fire was made in the common and a Kettle hung over it in which part of the said Ox was boil'd where they danced in their own manner, in presence of some of our principal Gentlemen and also some thousands of spectators.

Their jamboree lasted late into the night and while the Indians capered and gesticulated around the fire before the eyes of the dumfounded Bostonians, Benjamin finished his preparations. A few days later, at the same time as the Mohawks were departing from Boston in the midst of the noisy plaudits of the crowd, the apprentice silently slipped away to the sloop, which was restlessly tugging at its ropes, steered for the sea and New York.

Benjamin was seventeen years old and was already leaving his family and his past. He knew no one, either on board the ship, or in the rest of the world. But he knew what he wanted, was conscious of his physical force, of his endurance, of the vivacity of his mind and the ardor of his ambition.

On September 30, James Franklin inserted this notice in the *Courant:* "James Franklin, Printer in Queen Street, wants a likely lad for an apprentice."

But he could search all over Boston and New England and he would never find a boy so "likely" as the one who had just left him and whom he had lost forever.

VII

As the sloop traced the coastline slowly, Benjamin, crouched on the deck, watched the sailors at their tasks and thought of his future. No more would he have to fear the Government which had so harassed him, the bigots he had scandalized, the family he had abandoned. A new life had begun which would be his own, which he would direct as he willed.

He renounced all his childish prejudices and the discipline he had imposed on himself. From now on he would do as he pleased and to celebrate his liberty he broke the only strict rule he had kept faithfully for two years, — he ate fish. Of all his early religious enthusiasms, mystical researches and plans for reform, there only remained this prohibition of meat and fish, a left-over from his studies in the books of the good Tryon.

The boat rocked gently in the calm of the warm afternoon in late September, and the sailors, to divert themselves, fished for cod and then cooked their catch on the deck. The salt air had sharpened Benjamin's appetite and the savory odor rising from the pots rapidly became irresistible. He remembered how he had loved to eat cod when he was small and having seen that the sailors in cleaning the fish had thrown out many tiny ones which the cod had swallowed, he reasoned that he had the right to eat cod if they in turn devoured their own kind. So Benjamin, with full moral satisfaction, celebrated his escape by a feast on codfish.

He was by no means as free as he thought. But he was going to become so. To run away in 1723 was really to free oneself. Little Jean Jacques Rousseau had not lost sight of the walls of Geneva when he became a Catholic, abandoning Calvinism, while François Arouet de Voltaire, scarcely outside the gates of Paris, began to satirize his king and the Jesuits who had reared him.

The social and political order was strict and restrained in the eighteenth century for those who stayed in one place, but it was proportionately loose and inoperative for those who traveled. The various governments which had had their origin in feudalism derived their powers from the soil and could only exert them on the people who stayed with the soil. The only international control which had survived the Roman Empire was the Catholic Church, with its universal language, dogmas, and system of morality. But the Church had been weakened and disarmed by the Reform.

As yet no centralized nation existed, though England was in the process of becoming one. The thousands of tiny civilizations which made up the universe of the eighteenth century existed side by side, isolated the one from the other by differences in language and the difficulties of communication. They differed extremely; language, customs, polite manners, the style of wigs and coat tails — all these changed every thirty miles. The variety was delightful to a traveler, and to go from Paris to Marseilles was like participating in a fantastic Venetian carnival.

And this carnival imposed no obligation on the sightseer. It was for him to enjoy. There were no police to bother about, no annoying passports and visas. "Travelers tell fine tales", was certainly a proverb of the eighteenth century. As travelers were so few they were always received with curiosity, avidity and an attentive hospitality which the old customs still imposed.

Beggars, sailors, merchants and great lords were the ones who traveled in those gracious times, both classes outside the common law, the former because they were poor and the latter because they could afford to indulge their desires. Travelers formed a class apart and their sovereign rights were recognized as compensating for the fatigue and danger of their journeys. There were few routes, few conveyances, few good boats, but many cutthroats, bad roads and real pirates. If you could escape such misfortunes, however, you gained prestige and were accepted everywhere; if you were adroit you could even make a fortune.

Thus, the eighteenth century was familiar with a society of travelers, one might almost say a corporation, whose sole business was never to stay in one place for long, and there were some who made veritable careers of this kind. A wide-awake and handsome lad, coming out of the forests of Germany, from the most obscure of Polish ghettoes, from the most squalid ports of the Levant or the most rustic of Russian villages, often ended his travels by frequenting nobles and eventually becoming one of them. The son of a street sweeper could die the son of a king if he had first been stripped by robbers, or led into slavery by the Turks or denounced by the Inquisition.

There were many such shooting stars in the sky of Europe between 1720 and 1790: Le Comte de Saint Germain, who was said to be the son of the Queen of Spain by a Transylvanian prince or a Polish Jew, and who charmed Madame de Pompadour, and "grew" diamonds before your eyes; and Casanova de Seingalt, who had come up from nowhere, who elated the most beautiful women of Europe by telling them of debauchery and the greatest lords of the world by instructing them in magic and wisdom, and finally, the famous Cagliostro who claimed never to have been born and that he would never die, who had spoken with Christ and who delighted the fine minds of France with his red jacket and yellow vest and his elixir of long life.

Jean Jacques Rousseau was a little apart from this group but, nevertheless, of the same brotherhood. He was the conscience of the eighteenth century and its faithful mirror. By turns he was a student, botanist, musician, teacher, lackey, diplomat, secretary, encyclopedist, Catholic, Parisian, Genevan, martyr, philosopher and saint. In traveling he lost his children, his wisdom and even his mind, but he won the greatest glory of the eighteenth century and he found it pleasing to call on duchesses.

Benjamin was later to cross his path, when both he and Rousseau were near the end of their travels. But they would never know or understand each other. The Puritan apprentice had his own way of traveling and it did not coincide in the least with that of his European colleagues. They had to suffer incarnations which would not have been to his taste.

To become a success, an adventurer had to be something of a lackey, a rascal and a magician, but above all a magician.

When Benjamin Franklin left Boston he was already a printer and always remained one. His *métier* was a protection for him and thanks to it he never descended as low as Rousseau, Casanova or Cagliostro, but it also hindered him from climbing as quickly as they and kept him from really entering the international aristocracy which permitted no taint of commerce among its members. For all that he was drunk with the joy of being free and seeing the world, Benjamin was seriously preoccupied at the same time. He wanted to be a successful printer.

After three days at sea Benjamin finally disembarked at New York and his first act ashore was to visit William Bradford, the printer, a clever and strong-minded man. But Bradford had nothing to offer him and advised him instead to go to Philadelphia, as his son Andrew, who had a printing establishment there, had just lost his master workman, Aquila Rose. In spite of his hankering for the sea and all the magnificent adventures it promised, Benjamin, true to his common sense, took the old man's advice and decided to push on as far as this new city, Philadelphia, the city of Quakers and of brotherly love.

He left New York without much regret. He had felt bewildered there, out of his element. He was used to the businesslike city of Boston and to living among the economical, quarrelsome and shrewd people of the middle class. New York, in spite of its small size — seven thousand inhabitants — had already the air of a luxurious capital and seemed hostile to him. This was a result of the founders, the Dutch, who had imported their way of easy living from Europe. The great patroons, who possessed the land, lived in the environs like feudal lords.

Finally, because of its location, New York was absolutely the center of English administration, of the naval and military organization of the colonies; its streets were filled with officials, soldiers and travelers, the kind of men which Boston, more independent and eccentric, but rarely received.

Life in New York was more civilized than in any city of New

England. Refinement was evident in the streets, which were paved in cobblestones and lined with brick houses; in the fine clothes of the passers-by; in the way you were greeted and served at the taverns; and in the homes, improved by all sorts of modern inventions, particularly forks, which were not generally employed throughout America until much later.

After four days of rest, and walking up and down the streets of the city, the apprentice set out on his travels once more but with very light baggage. He sent his trunk by sea and made his own way to Pennsylvania through New Jersey, as he was in a hurry and that was the shortest route. Every event of this picturesque and rapid journey was engraved in Benjamin's mind, he was so delighted with seeing the world for the first time and feeling the sensation of flight. Whatever happened pleased him, whether it was pleasing or no, simply because it had happened and because he was seventeen years old in a new world.

It was wonderful to cross the Hudson in a leaky wherry, even if a storm did tear the sails down and set the boat adrift all night with only an ignorant old sailor and a drunken Dutchman for company. The latter had a pretty edition of "Pilgrim's Progress" in his pocket and once reeled into the water. Benjamin caught a fever that night also, but it didn't matter; recalling what the good Tryon had said on the subject, he drank quarts of water and soon cured himself.

At Amboy there still remained fifty miles to go before he would reach Burlington. There he would take a boat once more which would land him in Philadelphia in a few hours. Though he was a good walker, his long trip of three days must have been tiresome, and ever since the storm which had soaked him, he felt dirty. His appearance was so unkempt he feared that he would be taken for one of those runaway servants advertised on the fourth page of his brother's newspaper.

But Benjamin had been born on a Sunday, life was kind to him and he was young. He was well received at the little inn where he slept for the first evening. The next day, refreshed, he made a long stretch of his journey and reached Burlington the day following. There he bought some gingerbread from an old lady whom he never forgot, and learned at the docks, to his chagrin, that the boat for Philadelphia had just left and that there would not be another for three days. He went back to the old lady who gave him a plate of ox-cheek in return for a pot of ale. She invited him to lodge with her until the boat should come and urged him to establish himself in Burlington instead.

But going to the docks again that evening he saw a boat coming down and, by good fortune, going on to Philadelphia. He embarked, and as the calm night fell, the passengers and sailors talked pleasantly of the city which they would soon attain. As there was no wind, the sailors set themselves to rowing and Benjamin lent a hand as he wanted so much to arrive. They rowed so long that some of the company were sure they had passed the city, and persuaded the sailors to stop for the night. Groping their way up a side creek, they landed and made a fire of some old fence rails. Benjamin spent the night under the stars, crouched by the fire, which vaguely colored the near-by forest.

It was quiet there by the river and in this country, scarcely cleared. Not many years past, William Penn, fleeing from Europe, its religious disputes and wars, had come to establish his ideal colony here (1688) where fraternity, liberty of conscience and peace would flourish. He had chosen the great forest which separated the province of New York from the Southern colonies, Maryland, Virginia and the Carolinas. Then he opened it to all the persecuted people of the world, welcoming all who arrived, and made treaties with the Indians instead of taking their grounds.

Dutch Dissenters, Rhinelanders, French Huguenots and many other persecuted people heard his call and the colony began to be populated. Already the city had seven thousand inhabitants. But the streets were still bordered with trees and none were paved, the houses were built of wood and brick. Rich farms began to cut into the thick forests all around where the Indians lingered, coming now and then into the city, and deer, bears and wolves were still shot at the city's gates.

Franklin must have heard their howling that cool peaceful night of autumn which preceded his entry into Philadelphia. But nature never interested him deeply though he felt purified by its contact.

About nine the following morning Benjamin entered the city where he was to play such an important rôle. He was hungry and dirty and the work clothes he had worn from Boston were in disorder. He had stuffed the large side pockets with his shirts and stockings. One Dutch dollar was all the money he had left and people stared at him when he went by. Boys shook with laughter and the serious townsfolk gazed after him with ill favor.

Benjamin first wished to buy bread and was surprised at its low price. Here *was* the land of milk and honey. After walking in the streets a while he entered the meetinghouse of the Quakers and fell asleep during their prayers. Some one woke him up when the meeting was over and he then started to look for a lodging place. He was directed to the "Crooked Billet" in Water Street and there he dined and spent the night.

Early the next morning he started to look for work. He had to hurry. He sensed that he was suspiciously regarded on every hand and he had no money. Benjamin went directly to Bradford's and there found old William Bradford again, for the latter had come down on horseback to visit his son. Benjamin made the son's acquaintance immediately but unfortunately, Andrew Bradford, whose shop enjoyed an excellent reputation in Philadelphia, could not give the newcomer any work. He offered to lodge him, however, until he should have something to do and advised him to see Keimer, a queer fellow, recently arrived, who was going to set up a printing shop and bookstore in the near future.

The old Bradford went along with Benjamin to see this Keimer and a comical scene followed, for, not knowing who the old man was, Keimer confided all his projects to him.

Benjamin was amused by the interview and it gave him an idea of what the future of the printing business in Philadelphia would be with two such rivals, the older one tricky and gruff, the new one naïve and awkward. He thought there would be eventually a place for himself.

Keimer took on Benjamin immediately, as his press needed regaining and he had no workmen. This nervous little man was one of the bizarre characters who had been attracted to Philadelphia by the liberalism of Penn, and whom the practical Quakers were already encouraging to move on elsewhere. Keimer had come from France where he had given himself up to diverse religious practices, and now, established in Philadelphia, he adhered to a strange cult of his own, not cutting his beard because Moses was supposed to have said, "Thou shalt not mar the corners of thy beard." He observed Saturday as his Sabbath and was susceptible to convulsions and mysterious delirium which strongly interested Benjamin.

Nevertheless, Keimer was a heavy eater, a poor printer, and a commonplace merchant who had learned little from his experience with men. He would have tricked his customers had he been capable. Benjamin enjoyed the company of this grotesque person whose conversation reminded him of certain familiar passages in the books of the good Tryon. To flatter Keimer's mania for religion and to make fun of him at the same time, Benjamin discussed Socratically with him. He succeeded so well that the printer was full of respect for his cleverness and proposed that the two of them found a sect, Keimer charging himself with formulating the dogmas and Benjamin with the speechifying. Benjamin agreed on condition that Keimer incorporate the Pythagorean doctrine concerning food, — that meat would be forbidden. This was a cruel condition for Keimer, and not without sarcastic inference. The printer could not keep it and the proposition ended in a banquet of roast pork which he devoured all by himself; this time Benjamin did not found a religion.

As he was well paid, was not overworked and could study what he pleased, this city delighted Benjamin, and he did not complain about his situation or regret Boston. He lodged now in the home of Mrs. Read who had a pleasant daughter with pretty ways, so the evenings were not too long. A circle of friends was formed, made up for the most part of employees in shops; they were all more or less cultivated, fluent in speech and very ambitious. The names of three are preserved: the pious Watson, Osborn the disputer, and the poet, Ralph. They gathered together every evening and on Sundays to discuss the affairs of the world, problems in metaphysics and to work on their respective literary styles.

Though Franklin was the least talkative and the least brilliant of the four, his mind dominated all the others. He spoke haltingly, often struggling for a word, and could not make a speech. The Socratic method had become too strong a habit with him. His poems were flat and his prose modest. The three others, on the contrary, wrote flamboyant elegies, and Ralph especially prided himself on his lyrical gift. Nevertheless, Benjamin was their leader for that was his birthright; he had the most daring ideas and the most subtle ways of advancing them. He scandalized Watson but delighted Ralph. All four of them got along very well together and gave each other a rendezvous in the Beyond in order to settle their religious and theological discussions in that place by more efficacious proofs.

Franklin wisely kept himself, however, from making a parade of his heterodox opinions. He wished to make a place for himself in Philadelphia and did not want to be absorbed or isolated by party quarrels as he had been in Boston. Being a foreigner he was enabled to remain outside of the disputes which were already agitating the colony. Much friction existed between the Assembly elected by the people, the Governor chosen by the Penn family, and the council also elected by the people, principally due to rivalries for influence and authority.

In spite of the care which William Penn had lavished on the constitution to make it liberal, offering full freedom of conscience and — as far as possible — freedom of action, the opposition between the Quaker and Anglican elements was sharp. Since the Penn family had renounced the doctrines of the founder in favor of Anglicism, many Quakers regarded the administration with ill favor. And there were various other causes for discontent in the very mixed population of this colony.

The great number of Rhenish immigrants, vulgar, uncultured, and incapable of speaking English (more than fifty thousand before 1722), troubled the educated Anglo-Saxons. A grave economic crisis was at hand, money was lacking; many people had left the city and those who remained were discontented. However, there was no organized radical group as in Boston or New England. The doctrine of the Quakers, who were in the majority, was on the whole vague and tolerant, not calculated to stir up violent disputes.

At least, there wasn't any of that vehement apostolic enthusiasm for discussion which Presbyterianism seems to have implanted wherever it flourished in the eighteenth century. The Independents, Dissenters and Presbyterians had a disinterested but eager passion for controversy; they had an intense fondness for theology with its definitions and its difficulties, although it forbade them to stir up violent discussions. The Quakers, more serene and commercial, spread an intellectual and sentimental atmosphere around them which was very peaceful. Franklin enjoyed it and wisely remained outside of quarrels.

Being a foreigner was an advantage in more ways than one. While he was working one day at the printing shop with Keimer, two gentlemen stopped at the door, and Keimer, proud to have such aristocratic customers, rushed out to greet them and ask what they desired. He learned with bewilderment that the gentlemen were William Keith, the governor of Pennsylvania and his aide-de-camp, Colonel French, and that they had not come to see him or his dirty shop, but the young Benjamin Franklin. He was even more astounded when he saw his apprentice leave between the two men and sit down to a table with them at a neighboring tavern before a bottle of Madeira.

William Keith was a man of wit, goodness and imagination. Besides being of distinguished birth he possessed an agreeable personality, a taste for life and a sincere love of the people. He was highly cultured, wrote charmingly and knew how to make himself sympathetic to every one. With so many qualities he should have been a great man and even a good governor, but he had no solid judgment and seemed pursued by misfortune. He was born under an unlucky star, of an old impoverished Scotch family, which, like the Penns, were so imprudent as not to betray the cause in which they believed, one of those errors that men and destiny never seem to pardon. William Keith was noticed by the Penns (who were also more or less Jacobite), however, and they sent him to Pennsylvania.

He first came to America as a general inspector of the customs, Southern Division; then in 1716 he was named governor of Pennsylvania, in which capacity he showed himself to be an enlightened administrator, knowing how to please the people whom he treated humanly, the Indians whom he dealt with justly, the Quakers he esteemed, and the Government in London. He encouraged immigration, had paper money printed to avoid the economical crisis, fought against slavery which he attempted to discourage by putting a tax on slaves, and managed to pass some laws and measures with the approval of the Assembly which were in general very successful.

Keith could have been the Solon of his new colony had not his worldly manners, lively and audacious wit, his love of adventure and his Deism put him in opposition to certain influential men of the city, among them James Logan, a very distinguished Quaker, an erudite and rich man who had been the former secretary of Penn, and who was a member of the Council. This Council believed it had the right to control all that went on in Pennsylvania and was in direct correspondence with Hanna Penn, the most important person of the proprietary family. In order to distract himself from these annoyances and difficulties Keith sometimes visited his capital as Haroun al Raschid used to do, curious to see picturesque incidents, books and new faces, especially when the faces were fresh and agreeable.

One day, when he was at Newcastle on the Delaware, and was talking with the captain of a ship recently come from New England he first learned of the little Boston apprentice. This man, Holmes, had just married a sister of Benjamin's, and while passing in the vicinity of Philadelphia had heard that the young man was there. He wrote him, insisting that he return to Boston.

Benjamin answered that he did not wish to return, giving such good reasons and writing in such a precise, dignified, and clear manner, that the brother-in-law was persuaded against his will and charmed at the same time. Holmes, talking with the governor over a few glasses of Spanish wine, praised this clever, hard-headed, young runaway and showed him the letter. Keith decided to become acquainted with a boy who could express himself so well.

Benjamin profited greatly. It was the first time he had intimately associated with a man of the world. He was just old enough to be impressed by good manners and at this time it was easy for him to adapt himself to them. Moreover, Keith had the good grace to let the apprentice see that he pleased him. At first the governor amused himself, making Benjamin talk and listening to his stories; then he decided to do business with him. Keith had divined fairly well the future of Pennsylvania and of Philadelphia, where he wished to establish himself permanently, and dreamed of making use of this clever boy to found a printing shop where he would be master, where he could print his own writings and the books of others that he enjoyed. It would be a printing shop that would serve the colony better than that of the rigid Bradford or the silly Keimer.

Talking, planning, imagining, the apprentice and the governor found that they agreed perfectly, and in spring the affair was decided. Keith sent Benjamin to Boston to ask his father for financial aid. Holmes promised to support the proposition and Keith wrote a long, exact and flattering letter which he confided to the boy.

So the apprentice left that very April for New England and entered there triumphantly. Decidedly, he couldn't complain of his adventures. Instead of being a sort of slave, submitting to the double discipline of his family and a revengeful master, open to the reprobation of influential men (as he would have been had he continued living in Boston), he was now a well-paid workman in the service of a grotesque person who amused him (and whom he was almost duping, for he had not warned him that he was planning to set up a rival printing shop), a friend of the governor's, esteemed by the men of the government, and basking in the favor of the most charming Pennsylvania girls.

He jingled money in his pockets, wore a fine new suit of clothes, had linen in his bundle, and a watch and chain in his waistcoat. He had a brilliant proposition in mind and the future seemed glowing. Benjamin returned to Boston to liquidate his departure honorably, not to make an honorable reparation or to renounce his past. From now on he was going to be a foreigner in New England, though he would always love the city of his childhood.

His parents received him kindly. They had had no news of him since his departure and the return of the prodigal in fine clothes delighted them. Their only thought was to pardon him and later to give him their full permission to leave once more. Benjamin showed his letter, and aided by Holmes, who had come up in the meanwhile, tried to persuade his father to advance him enough money to set up a printing shop. But Josiah wouldn't be convinced; he felt there was something suspicious about the proposition. The governor's friendship for his son flattered him more than it pleased him and wasn't in the least an assurance for his money. Besides, Benjamin was only eighteen and the idea of establishing a third printing shop in a city of eight thousand inhabitants wasn't very promising.

Josiah had already given too much to James whose business was not coming along at all. The *Courant* had caused him a thousand annoyances but the *Courant* could not even have existed had it not been for these controversies. Josiah gave Benjamin his benediction, advice and affection, but no money. He told him to come back when he was twenty-one. And Benjamin saw there was no use in insisting. He borrowed a few guineas from a friend and prepared to leave once more.

He had two other visits to make in Boston, however, one to his brother and one to the Mathers. He wished to know how he stood with James, how his brother's business was coming on and to see if there were not a way to leave Boston in good grace, instead of passing for a reprobate. No doubt this would have been Josiah's wish also.

The visit to James went off badly. James was working in his printing shop and was nervous for he felt his establishment was losing ground. He had no way of keeping up the *Courant* to the tone of its early days; the supply of such sharp controversies in a little city like Boston was bound to disappear. He was engaged in a war of wear and tear and sooner or later would have to give in. Benjamin's absence had become all the more marked with the slow estrangement of nearly all the contributors of the *Courant*.

When James saw his brother reappear in the shop he had traitorously quitted seven months before, dressed like a dandy, jingling money in his pockets and pulling out his watch to dumfound the workmen, he was so furious he had to exercise all his will power to keep from knocking him down.

Benjamin had failed him sadly by fleeing, by abandoning him in the midst of the combat and breaking his agreement. He had failed him again by coming this way to snap his fingers at him when he was in his printing shop, working with his men, not even having taken the trouble to ask his pardon before. It was all over between them. The two brothers separated with a look that boded no good and their father could not change the situation. The Franklins were a pugnacious family.

However, the meeting with James made the visit to Cotton Mather easier. For a long time, ever since his early adventures with the *Courant*, the virtuous and wily churchmen had attempted to separate the two brothers. When they met Benjamin on the streets, running his errands and selling papers, they told him he would come to a bad end if he continued to serve the Devil.

He never answered but merely shrugged his shoulders. Now he reflected. The *Courant* had often been more wrong than right. After all, inoculation wasn't so bad as it was painted. In England it was being used more and more. The Royal Family practiced it and it had become the fashion. The doctors who had attacked inoculation, using the *Courant* for a blind, were not so sure of their facts.

Besides, all these insulting attacks against the powerful men of the city, entrenched in impregnable positions, could only serve to irritate them, not to dethrone them, and were more exciting than useful. On the whole, this visit was in the nature of a courteous apology. Mather construed it so, was amiable, and told Benjamin there had been no misunderstanding. When he conducted him to the door, ceremoniously and amicably, he warned him of a low beam which barred the passageway and obliged him to bend down. Apropos of this he said, "You are young and have the world before you. STOOP as you go through it and you will miss many hard thumps."

Thus, Benjamin made his peace with the aristocracy of New England and he never forgot that word of Cotton Mather's. It often came to his mind in hard and difficult hours, now like a wise and encouraging saying, now like a vague menace. Many years later John Adams was to make Franklin realize its meaning utterly. Benjamin was to bend down before the men of New England more than once.

For the moment he was completely enjoying his pardon and the thought of leaving. He saw again his friend Collins who was now employed at the post-office. Collins was so overwhelmed by Benjamin's success he decided to try the career of an adventurer also.

On his way back to Philadelphia, Benjamin passed by Newport once more and there he visited his brother John, who had been his playmate in their father's shop. The two of them passed some agreeable hours together. He saw John's neighbors and friends, in particular a Mr. Vernon, who had some money due him in Pennsylvania and who begged Benjamin to secure and retain it for him until he should write him in what currency to send it.

On board the ship for New York he escaped the tempting charms of two too pretty ladies, thanks to the protection and advice of a matronly Quakeress who warned him. She was right, for the girls were arrested on arriving in New York for being thieves. Benjamin, on the contrary, was invited to see Governor Burnet of New York, a curious, erudite man who had heard the captain speak of a young passenger who traveled with many books. This was a flattering and pleasant interview for Benjamin. He had risen out of the rank and file and felt his superiority with a kind of drunkenness.

The return to Philadelphia was no less agreeable. Keith fêted him and didn't want him to abandon their fine projects for so little a thing as Josiah Franklin's disapproval. At the moment the governor was overwhelmed with innumerable annoyances and this dream and youthful adventure diverted him. Hanna Penn, pushed on by Logan, already his deadly enemy, was meditating his ruin and gave threatening signs. He still hoped to save himself; he felt he was popular and so he swaggered to hide his troubles. Benjamin pleased him, amused him. He urged him to leave for England, where he could finish his education as a printer, learn the style of the day, and procure the machinery and accessories necessary to set up a printing shop. The idea was wise from every point of view; Franklin, already a good workman, could only gain by following it, and it would be advantageous for him to get in touch with the London style as, after all, the colonies imitated the mother country as much as they could in everything.

Being a young writer also, this voyage would enrich his mind with an experience that America could not furnish. Moreover, the governor promised to attend to writing letters of introduction and to secure money for the purchase of machinery.

Benjamin lived in the secret excitement of these projects, for he told no one about them, and many envied his friendship with the governor. The friends who surrounded him added still more to his joy. Ralph, Osborn, Watson and he had become inseparable. But Ralph interested him above all, because of his irony, literary talent, and the audacity of thought he had inspired in him.

Collins was also with him but their friendship was dying. Deism, which Benjamin had taught to Collins, had taken such a firm hold on him that, though he was formerly a good lad, he now went to extremes. He drank too much and had no scruples. When they were stopping in New York Collins had been drunk most of the time. He continued to drink, shamelessly borrowing Benjamin's money, or rather Vernon's money, which Benjamin had cashed and should have kept carefully.

This little rascality was not very serious, really, for Benjamin was sure of being able, sooner or later, to make enough money to reimburse Vernon, but it was embarrassing and disgraceful. He repented this later with more sincerity and contrition than graver though nobler faults could have caused him.

For the moment, he was simply weary of Collins and had many quarrels with him. One day, in particular, when they were out rowboating he threw Collins into the water, as Collins had threatened to hit him; Benjamin refused to let him come on board until he had swum a little too much to his liking. Their friendship died thus in the Delaware, and shortly after, Collins left to be a tutor in the Bahamas, from whence he never returned.

Benjamin didn't care much. His heart was busy elsewhere. He was courting Miss Read, who was now fatherless. He would even have married her if Mrs. Read had thought they were old enough, and if he hadn't been so distracted by his fine projects and the other attractive offers of life.

But the time for the departure of the ship which made the annual voyage between London and Philadelphia had arrived. Keith, more and more preoccupied, but always pleasant to his young friend, continued to encourage him in the dreams he didn't have the courage to destroy, or the power to make true. Benjamin didn't know that the governor, overwhelmed with debts in America and England, his influence lost with the Penn family, suspected for a long while of being a Jacobite, was no longer in a position to help him.

Benjamin left with a light heart, intoxicated with his illusions and delighted that his friend Ralph had decided at the last moment to accompany him and make a business voyage in England, leaving his wife and child behind in the lurch.

The autumn was lovely; Deborah wept but kisses consoled her, and Benjamin promised to write and to return. Everything was arranged pleasantly on board, the two young men being given the excellent cabin reserved for Hamilton, a rich lawyer of Philadelphia, who had been detained in Pennsylvania by an unexpected and lucrative affair.

In the hubbub of the last few days, Benjamin couldn't get to see Keith, who was overburdened with work and absorbed by his correspondence which was to be decisive for him and which he was sending on to England to defend himself against Logan. But the governor had his compliments sent to the young man, saying in addition that the letters of recommendation and credit would be sent on board before the boat left Newcastle on the Pennsylvania side.

When Franklin saw Keith's voluminous mail bag he was told that the letters were all tied together with the correspondence of his friend and that he shouldn't be troubled. The captain promised to sort out those which were meant for him before arriving in England.

Benjamin left gayly, enjoying his good cabin, good company and the excellent provisions that had been sent in advance for Mr. Hamilton. One year in Philadelphia had brought him more pleasure, excitement and realization than seventeen years in Boston.

He told himself that London would teach him important and surprising lessons and looked forward with a happy curiosity to the long winter crossing, dangerous and swept with tempests. However, the day of departure was clear and fair, and Benjamin stood at the stern, now gazing back to America, now out to the open sea, and he smiled. Was it not a good omen that the boat should be called, *London Hope?*

VIII

A WINTER crossing on that sullen and difficult sea, the North Atlantic, in one of those slight packet boats of the eighteenth century was a slow affair. Tempests constantly set the boat off its course and the oil lamp, hung from the middle of the ceiling, marked the movements of the sea, now fast, now slow, and swung alarmingly. Storms were followed by interminable days of boredom, when cards lost their charm and draughts, though it took more time, was tiresome too. The nights were insufferably long and fatiguing, for the food was wretched and sleep impossible. There were dark hours too, when the ship would veer from its course; every one became ill at ease and annoyed. But bright days dawned as well, when the sky was filled with light and the port did not seem distant. All during the long voyage there was really little to do but talk and exchange stories.

The passengers soon learned to know Benjamin Franklin, for in storm or calm he was always the same: sober, polite, speaking little, keeping his troubles to himself and lightening the burdens of others with the charm of his presence. Every one liked him, from the captain down to the meanest sailor, and a good Quaker merchant, Mr. Denham, wise and ponderous, took an interest in him and drew him out slowly in kindly conversation.

The thought of danger and the alternate feelings of hope and discouragement kept the passengers in suspense up to the end of their trip. Tempests swept them even in the English Channel, taking a toll of several ships. But at last, on Christmas Eve, when every one's patience was exhausted, the *London Hope* arrived at Gravesend and the passengers soon entered the English capital, their former sufferings almost forgotten with the glowing prospect of a warm fire and a good glass of grog before them.

A journalist of the time has thus described the powerful impression of fear and admiration which luxurious London exerted over visitors from the country or the colonies:

London is certainly the greatest city upon Earth, at least there is nothing like it in Devonshire: but our beer is infinitely better than theirs, which is as black as Bull's Blood, and as thick as Mustard. Everything is shamefully dear there, you pay half a crown, or 3 shillings for a Chicken; which with us would not yield above a groat or 5 pence. . . . You see a great number of coaches standing in the street ready to be hired; and they carry a beggar for his money as soon as a Lord or sooner. . . . These coaches are very convenient if they were not so confoundedly dear; but if one of them carries you but 3 doors he will have a shilling. . . .

The houses here are all built of brick and for the most part, one house holds several families so fond are people of living in London, notwithstanding the badness of the Drink. There are also hireling chairs; they are covered with black leather, and brass nails; they have fine sash windows and a sash door, and fine silk Curtains, and rare soft Cushions; one of them is carried by 2 short fellows; with no heels to their shoes: they use 2 long poles, and pace along with wonderful expedition. These chairs too are devilish dear.

There are houses here call'd Chocolate Houses, cover'd all over with Sconces and Looking Glasses. Hither Gentlemen, who have nothing to do but to dress themselves, repair to show their fine clothes . . . ; or if they do anything else it is only to swear, and take snuff, or to play Dice, and then all the while they play, they are constantly damning themselves. . . . There is a fine river running by London full of ships and boats; one of these boats will carry you for 6 pence, and some of them for 5 pence a great way; and it would be very pleasant if it were not for the abuse and ugly language you meet with; for the people upon the water will affront you to your teeth and call you a hundred names. There is a street in London call'd Drury Lane, which is a very scandalous place, being for the most part inhabited by filthy lewd women; and yet it is frequented by great men and grave citizens; it is therefore no wonder these Shameless Jades wear fine Cloaths and good Watches. . . .

The bad beer, the widespread luxury, swear words and courtesans, — all these struck the traveler entering London. Benjamin, accompanied by Ralph, who had lived in London, was not long in remarking these salient details and was amazed at the atmosphere of the city.

Here was no virtuous cloak to cover the evils of civilization as in Boston, no aristocracy as in New York, no bourgeois prudence as in Philadelphia, and vice flaunted itself in clear daylight. The immorality of the eighteenth century was so manifest in London that not even a St. Anthony could have ignored it. There was nothing of St. Anthony in Benjamin, however, and he didn't turn away from London. His experience in this city was to be a curious and decisive one.

His introduction to English life was brutal and surprising. It was rather like a catastrophe. Shortly after having taken lodgings at a tavern, Benjamin opened his satchel, took the precious letters which Captain Annis had sorted out for him, and then left to deliver them, hoping to find a hearty welcome and support at their several destinations.

First, he went to a certain printing house, having a letter addressed to the master there, and he gave it to that gentleman, quite believing it had been written by Keith. The printer opened the letter, saying he did not know Keith, and then having read it, coolly handed it back to Benjamin, saying that it was from a certain Riddleston whom he considered a rascal. Benjamin then went to a well-known stationer, but it was the same story all over again.

Franklin was disconcerted and now carefully read all the letters which Annis had given him. He found that not one of them had come from Keith. They were only letters which had been intrusted to him to insure their safe delivery. Thus, Franklin found himself in London without aid or money, infamously treated by the one person he had thought his most powerful and brilliant friend. Such trickery he found very immoral.

Once his moment of anger and stupor had passed, he turned to the only person he knew in London, and in whom he had confidence, the good Quaker, Denham, and told him of his misfortune, asking his advice. Denham didn't like Keith, as was the case with the majority of the distinguished Quakers and friends of the Penns; they reproached him for his easy manners, his audacity, independence, Deism and what was later called his democratic spirit.

Denham painted a very black picture of the governor to Benjamin, affirming that he had no credit, wisdom or honesty, and this was some consolation. Furthermore, Benjamin showed him the letters which had come into his hands by chance and they proved that Riddleston, a knavish lawyer of Philadelphia, and Keith were laying a snare for Hamilton. Hamilton was a friend of Denham's and belonged to that party of powerful men opposed to Keith. Benjamin knew that Riddleston was a rascal, as he had cheated the father of his fiancée, and so he put these incriminating letters into the hands of Hamilton, when that gentleman next came to England. They became formidable weapons against Keith and Riddleston. Thus Benjamin made the most of his misfortune and the governor was soon punished.

Benjamin's action placed him in the heart of the Quaker party and gave him the firm friendship of Denham and Hamilton, extremely influential men who were to help him out greatly in his Pennsylvania career. In 1724, Benjamin had defined good as an agreeable utility, so that his action was moral and would never have to be added to his list of errors.

Letters always played an important part in the life of Franklin, and not only because he was once Postmaster-general of America. The problem of the privacy of correspondence always interested his curious intelligence, and, though he solved it boldly, it was not always with the approval of his contemporaries.

For the moment, however, every one was on his side. Keith fell to ruin rapidly, losing his governorship in 1726, as the Penns no longer wanted him. His popularity secured him a place in the Assembly by public vote but he had to return to England as his affairs were in bad shape. He spent a year in prison there for debt and then did nothing after that. He had been found wanting.

But Benjamin was out of work, had no English friends and

no definite plans. Moreover, Ralph, this brilliant and gifted boy who had become his bosom companion, told him that he had come to London to establish himself there, and that he had not the slightest idea of sending for his wife and child, as he was tired of them. His sole ambition was to be a genius and hold a high place in English letters. Benjamin, who had abandoned his fiancée in Philadelphia, was nevertheless troubled by Ralph's conduct and was doubtful that the latter could make his living by writing verses. Unfortunately, Ralph had to live on the money of his friend while he was awaiting the development of his genius. The costly crossing, ten pounds at this time, had exhausted his own resources.

Ralph, who had utter confidence in himself, attempted to borrow money from his English parents, but they were poor and did not care to aid him. He decided then to enter the theater, but Wilkes, the great actor, dissuaded him; following this, he thought it would be a good idea to write a periodical pamphlet something like the *Spectator*, but publishers were not interested. He got along much better by staying on with Benjamin, who, charmed by his easy manners, his eloquence and natural amiability, supplied him his wants until a young milliner, in a neighboring apartment, also delighted by the poet's good looks and generous heart, decided to do as much for him.

Ralph found he had chosen one of the most popular careers of the eighteenth century. Benjamin hesitated a little, however, before following him. He had the same ideas as Ralph, but not the same temperament. Although he had not a penny to his name, he had a strong body and was only eighteen — anything was possible for such a young man in early eighteenth-century London. He could have devoted himself to intrigues, to the sea, to adventures, had he still the taste for them. But from childhood his inherent sense of discipline had restrained him and now he turned instinctively to his craft and an orderly life.

The vague and brilliant indolence that the young Rousseau indulged in would not have contented him any more than the aimless and intermittent intrigues of Casanova. He had a need for order and that feeling of solidity which comes from spending one's energy heartily and healthfully in a tiresome, practical job.

So he entered the workshop of one of the greatest English printers, Palmer's, located at Bartholomew Close and employing fifty men. From the very beginning, Benjamin was paid a guinea a week, for if he were not an exceptionally skilled workman he was vigorous and hard-working and knew his craft. Out of this salary he paid three shillings and a half for his room and meals. A good number of his fellow workmen were to become prosperous proprietors.

These high wages and this milieu of intelligent workmen are explained by the great prosperity of the publishing business in England at an epoch when the victorious wars, the extension of the colonies and of commerce had given a formidable impulsion to all industries of luxury.

The high society of England was very rich, and the printers profited by this particularly, for, following the Renaissance, books and newspapers, as well as other creations of the mind, were the most suitable and necessary prerequisites of a model gentleman. The three great luxuries for an eighteenth-century man of the world were a pretty mistress, a handsome carriage, and a well-stocked library.

This was not the only reason for the prosperity of publishers, as the liberty of the press, insured by the Revolution and guaranteed by the Government, was another inexhaustible source of money for them. Already there were three daily newspapers, the leading ones of the world, ten tri-weeklies, and five weeklies; the *St. James Chronicle*, a strong Conservative organ, had just been founded, and two others were established in the course of the year 1723. Whether their circulation was large or small they were all profitable and sold well, and between 1731 and 1740 Prime Minister Robert Walpole spent fifty thousand pounds to "guide" and "enlighten" this very free press.

Furthermore, as all European printing was controlled by strict governmental censors (save in Holland, and Holland couldn't meet the demands), England supplied the Continent with all the obscene and irreligious books it desired, thus creating an enormous and profitable commerce, as collectors were always willing to pay high prices for such wares. Now and again printers were arrested for publications of this kind, as on March 25, but most of the time they escaped without bother. Thus, even at the respectable Palmer's, Franklin worked on books which would have led their author and printer to the stake anywhere else in the world.

Nothing could be done about it; a formidable tide of Deism and materialism had swept over England. It had been announced, and prepared for in advance, by the attacks against Catholicism, by the revolutions which had broken the sway of the Church over the higher classes, and it had been strengthened still more by the exciting and exotic luxury which had invaded the wealthy homes of the nation. It is not surprising that the most fashionable and representative book of the moment was Mandeville's curious and brutal "Fable of the Bees."

By his little book and the charm of his conversation, this Dutchman, Mandeville, who played the ambiguous rôle of doctor, business man and brilliant talker in London, had charmed such important personages as Lord Macclesfield and had become the center of a club which met at the Tavern. He attracted universal attention. There was no end of editions and translations of his work, following its publication in 1705, and the edition of 1723 which contained an added essay, "On Charity", stirred up much indignation and was answered by several writers, among them Richard Fiddes, J. Dennis (in 1724), William Law and Francis Hutcheson (in 1725).

Mandeville compared humanity to a beehive, showing man to be dominated by his passions and forced to act only because of them. Passions should not be damned, he said, they should be praised and encouraged. Ambition, greediness, concupiscence, far from ruining humanity, serve it, as they are forces to make men work, producing wealth and general happiness. The more there is moral disorder in a country the more active production takes place, and the nation prospers. He concluded that like a beehive,

> There every part was full of vice,
> Yet the whole mass a paradise.

All this led to the logical conclusion that the poor are poor because they are lazy. Mandeville expressed his ideas in a simple, rude style with no poetical feeling or refinement, but with a picturesque frankness that was pleasing and well suited to a lecture he published in 1725: "A Conference about Whoring."

The printers, journeymen and apprentices discussed these pamphlets among themselves as they worked on them, and also spoke with customers who came to the shop, curious to see how the arms of intellectual warfare were prepared. A kind of fraternity was thus established, for the printer was still considered a magician at this time, a man who took thoughts, which had heretofore been imprisoned in a single mind, and distributed them all over the world. He was the accomplice of all audacious books (provided they would attract attention and sell); naturally, he defended the liberty of the press and his place in the social world forced him necessarily to propagate new ideas.

Nevertheless, materialism did not have full sway over the printing shops. The corporations of the Middle Ages still retained an influence; a kind of mysticism, more or less sincere, prevailed among the workmen. Franklin had to be initiated into one of these "chapels" with all its secret rites and mummeries. They resembled the organizations of Free Masonry (which had been limited up to 1717 to a corporation of actual masons) and did not have much in common with Christianity.

Rather, the "chapels" concentrated the elements of pagan mysticism taken from the various Greek and Oriental philosophers, and mixed them up with Christian dogmas, deprived of their primitive meanings. Equality was considered as an immediate reality, not as a tenet of spiritual order. The religion of the "chapels" also included the mysterious heritage of the Deists, who publicly preached against Christianity in favor of rationalism, practiced a secret language and propagated strange cults: Pythagoreanism with the good Tryon, Platonism with Shaftesbury, Pantheism and Druidism with Toland (who moreover enhanced his writings with such titles as "Adæisidæmon", "Tetradymus", "Clidorophorus", "Hypatia", "Mangoneutes", "Pantheisticon") and Tindal advanced a natural and mystical religion as old as creation.

Arguments clashed. For every Deistical book there were a flock of Christian books in answer, and the presses rumbled while the workmen hustled about, excited by this battle of wits. Benjamin, like the others, yielded to the attraction of this avalanche of words, but more than the others, he understood. His quick and exact mind enabled him to grasp the meaning as he set the type, even forced him to do so.

By chance he set up Wollaston's work, "A Dissertation on Natural Religion" in which this good defender of the Church of England attempted to prove that the process of reason and the evidences of nature lead us directly to believe in God and the immortality of the soul. Wishing to rob the Deists of their most powerful weapon, logic, which had made so many unbelievers, he wrote his book like a treatise of geometry, heaping up an immense mass of indigestible erudition, and beginning with this essential principle, "The base of all religion is the difference between the acts of men, be they good, bad or indifferent."

After reading this phrase the young man could not keep himself from answering and soon published a refutation, his one catechism, a pretty little treatise of materialistic Pantheism, written also in a geometric style. For this work, his first and only treatise on philosophic theory, he referred largely to his own memories, desiring rather to be clear and irrefutable than to be new and startling. He utilized more than one argument of Anthony Collins ("A Philosophic Inquiry Concerning Human Liberty"), like him opposing liberty and necessity, and going even further. Collins showed man to be dominated by a spiritual necessity, the attraction of pleasure, saying that "Morality or Virtue consists in such actions as are in their own nature and upon the whole, *pleasant;* and Immorality or Vice consists in such actions as are in their own nature, and upon the whole, *painful.*"

Thus man is free when he does what he wants; that is to say, when he does all that pleases him, but as God knows everything in advance, all is fatal and predetermined. Franklin adopted this idea and put it at the head of his book, citing the verse of Dryden:

> Whatever is, is in its Causes just
> Since all Things are by fate; but purblind Man
> Sees but a part o' th' Chain, the nearest Link,
> His Eyes not carrying to the equal Beam
> That poises all above.

Then, with no further hesitation, Benjamin began, and in a hundred axioms he proved that he knew neither sin nor liberty nor personal immortality. God was only permitted to exist as a machine. Franklin wrote precisely and suavely and not without impertinence as this passage (pages 29–30) shows:

1. It is supposed that God, the Maker and Governor of the Universe, is infinitely wise, good and powerful.
2. In consequence of His infinite Wisdom and Goodness it is asserted that whatever He doth must be infinitely wise and good.
3. Unless He be interrupted and His pleasures broken by some other being, which is impossible because He is Almighty.
4. In consequence of His infinite power it is asserted that nothing can exist or be done in the Universe which is not agreeable to His Will and therefore good.
5. Evil is thereby excluded with all Merit and demerit, and likewise all preference in the Esteem of God of one part to another.

Thus God should find that the robber is as virtuous as his victim, as every one acts necessarily in accordance with the decrees of God and the nature and order of things. Benjamin did well to add with an air of assumed modesty: "I would not be understood by this to encourage or defend Theft; 'tis only for the sake of the Argument and will certainly have no *ill effect*. The Order and Course of Things will not be affected by Reasoning of this kind. . . ."

This paragraph shows to what extent the son of Josiah Franklin had emancipated himself from the time when his father had punished him for sneaking a few stones to build a little dike. These experiences in liberation, begun under the involuntary influence of his father, had now arrived at their logical development. He was touching the zenith of the curve.

Benjamin retained some of his Calvinistic beliefs, however, such as the conception of an all-powerful God, and predestination, but, above all, he was the disciple of the French Sensualists and the English Deists from whom he borrowed the mathematics of pleasure.

I. A Creature when endow'd with Life or Consciousness, is made capable of Uneasiness or Pain.
II. This Pain produces desire to be freed from it in exact proportion to itself.
III. The accompaniment of this Desire produces an equal Pleasure.
IV. Pleasure is consequently equal to Pain.

All this results in the following conclusions:

I. That every Creature has as much Pleasure as Pain.
II. That life is not preferable to insensibility; for Pleasure and Pain destroy one another: . . .
III. No state of Life can be happier than the Present, because Pleasure and Pain are inseparable.

Thus Paradise, the haven of compensation, could not exist. Even the soul was not immortal, he claimed, or at least immortal as the Christians thought, for the soul was made up of ideas, ideas come to us by our senses, and with death our senses disappear. The soul ceases to think, "And to cease to think is little different from ceasing to be."

The only survival that Franklin could conceive of was the renascence of the soul in a new body with new senses and consequently new ideas. This doctrine was always to be dear to him, and its influence is clear even in his epitaph, in which he announces he is awaiting a new *edition* of his being. But this was no Christian theory, since the soul thus resurrected no longer keeps a memory of its past, and the personality is lost.

Satisfied with his audacity, the young author concluded in affirming, "Men who like to be flattered will not like my work although it is the truth and nothing but the truth", and ended with a smile for his admirers as well, having dedicated the preface to Ralph, his companion in thought, experience and immorality.

He carefully printed a hundred copies of this thin book, with a pretty little woodcut of a boar hunt for a frontispiece. He knew it was appearing opportunely, as during the last months of 1724 and the beginning of 1725 there had been a reappearance of discussions on the subject of liberty. The *British Journal* had discussed it at length in its columns, and liberty was a timely subject.

The serious master at Palmer's spoke to Benjamin about his book, blaming him as a man, but approving of it as a publisher, for he couldn't help recognizing the crude but efficacious talent of the young man. Franklin was soon talked about in a little circle of friends. But his greatest success was with an amiable and talkative surgeon, Lyon, to whom he had shown his manuscript and who had disagreed with him.

Lyon was not contented merely to refute it, but made the young author his companion and friend. As a matter of fact, the two had many points in common: a hatred of tyranny, a tendency towards Pythagoreanism and a liking for reasoning and mathematics. Lyon had published a treatise on "The Infallibility of Human Judgment and its Dignity and Excellence, being a New Art of Reasoning and Discovering Truth by reducing all disputable Cases to General and self evident Propositions", and it had gone through three successive editions.

Lyon upheld religion but tried to make it practical, claiming that to follow it was a good habit; the wise men, he wrote, have always respected the religion of their respective countries. Chapter ten was called, "Of the religion of our Country, its rise and foundation on Natural and rational Principles. A Musical Manner of thinking on God, after the Pythagorean way, and from whence might be suppos'd to arise the notions of the Trinity . . ."

In the fourth edition of his work Lyon added some pages meant to refute Franklin. The title of the appendix was, "A Dissertation on Liberty and Necessity, occasionally wrote on the revival of their argument in some late Treaties as well as in the *British Journal*." He took up the themes of Franklin and reduced them to nothing. "Actions are produced by the will, which will is sometimes in opposition to the judgment, sometimes in opposition to the appetite, and sometimes agreeable to 'em, and is not therefore impell'd by either of 'em, or by anything else preceding itself . . ." Further he writes, "God is not the author of men's Actions Just or Unjust, by any done, mediate or immediate direction. . . . Providence is no other than an even and regular bringing of things together, to act according to their natural manner like a sagacious Politician, of the immense and Absolute Power of Man within the sphere of his senses. . . ."

After this lively discussion, the two men, despite the disparity of their ages and conditions, became good friends, and Lyon took the young workman to various taverns, showing him Mandeville haranguing his auditors at one of them. He also introduced him to Doctor Pemberton, the illustrious collaborator of Newton; in a word, he opened the doors of that curious intellectual society of brilliant, dissolute men who met in the shadowy taverns and who sometimes slipped into the salons of the great.

Franklin began to enjoy these meetings, as they reminded him of his aristocratic visits in Philadelphia and developed his mind. Later he wrote in his autobiography (erasing it immediately after), "I then made friends by every manner of means." It is easy to picture this supple and well-set boy, dressing in his best clothes, once his work was finished for the day, to go to hear the fine talkers, smile at their quips and their heresies, and reflect on their ideas. Occasionally he would amuse them with a quick sally or a popular anecdote. And at the end of the evening he would often accompany them to their homes, for they were usually drunk.

Benjamin had brought some natural curios of America over with him, as he was fond of them, and they helped him to make more friends. Thanks to a fragment of asbestos, he came to know the collector, Sir Hans Sloane. He wrote with polite audacity to attract the attention of the gentleman and ended the letter with a skillful turn in order to elicit a prompt response. Sir Sloane answered and he went to see him. He remembered this visit so well that later it seemed to him he had been invited, writing in his autobiography: "Sir Hans Sloane heard of it, came to see me, and invited me to his house in Bloomsbury Square, where he show'd me all his curiosities, and persuaded me to let him add that to the number, for which he paid me handsomely."

But these excursions into high society were infrequent for he was not ready to pay the price for them. Most of his pleasures were of another kind. It was easy for him to attend theaters and dances as he had seventeen shillings and a half to spend every week and Ralph to guide him around.

London was then very gay. Four theaters played in full swing all winter long, many dance halls were open to the public and innumerable churches were always free of entrance to pious or curious people. Operas in the French or Italian manner were often given, and at the King's Theatre in Haymarket, during these months was announced "Rodelinde, Julius Cæsar, Tamerlane, Elpidia"; The Royal Theatre in Drury Lane attracted Benjamin still more, for he liked the fine tragedies presented there better than music. Often he went to see the famous tragedians, Cibber and his son, who appeared in "Anne Bolen" (1725), "Sophonisbe" (1725), "Macbeth" (1725), "Hamlet" (1725), "Cato" (1726), or in the comedies, "The Careless Husband" (1725), "The Manners of the World", "The Tempest."

At Lincoln's Inn Field he heard the dramatic operas that were so fashionable, and the operettas, "Oroonoko", "The

Fair Quaker", "The Stratagem", "The Committee", while at the New Haymarket Theatre, an Italian troupe offered light comedies imported from France and Italy, which were then most popular, the newspapers punctually announcing, "Les Folies Amoureuses", Moliere's "Tartuffe", "Arlequin, Vicomte de Bergamotte", "La Femme Diablesse et les Epouvantes d'Arlequin", "Arlequin feint astrologue, statue, enfant et Perroquet."

The price of tickets was high enough: the gallery, a shilling and a half at the New Haymarket Theatre; orchestra, two shillings and a half; at Lincoln's Inn Field the gallery cost two shillings, the orchestra three; at the King's Theatre in Haymarket the gallery cost five shillings and the orchestra ten; but Franklin, with his good wages, didn't have much trouble in going everywhere.

He only had to be careful not to get caught in public brawls. The crowds were brutal and more than once the public dances ended in wild riots, the dancers being transported to the prison or to a hospital. For the Thursday-night dances (in winter) at Haymarket, the police announced in the newspapers: "A sufficient guard is appointed within and without the house to prevent all disorders and indecencies and to oblige persons guilty of it immediately to leave the Place."

Thus there was no end to gay and serious diversions, the newspapers often advertising the sight of "Human bodies artificially made", wax figures that had come from Paris and were on exhibition on the Strand. For more serious minds, lectures on science were given everywhere, and lords and ladies, even the Royal Family, hastened to attend them.

Sermons too attracted great crowds, for the ministers contributed to the current battle of wits, and Franklin, in all fairness, went to church to hear refutations of his Deistical principles. Ever since his boyhood in Boston he had had a liking for church meetings. He never lost this liking and it helped him to maintain his prestige as a serious man.

He heard Wollaston preach on "A Defense of the Miracle of the Thundering Legion", or the Rector of St. James preach on "The Conexion of the Prophecies and the application of them to Christ." And he attentively studied the diction of the Reverend J. Henly, who claimed he employed the ancient elocution.

But more than listening to erudite preachers or attending the elegant theaters, Benjamin enjoyed mingling with the crowd and participating in the sharp, intense, and picturesque life of the London populace.

IX

For a century which had been so filled with war, the end of George the First's reign was a rather calm and peaceful period. The alliance with France assured peace outside the borders and the vanquished Jacobites, inside England, bowed their heads under heavy fines. The King passed a good part of his time in Hanover that year (from June 21, 1725, to January 14, 1726), and no one cared, for he was not popular.

There were all kinds of fêtes to amuse the people: St. David's, March 15, when fountains of wine spilled in the public squares and crowds drank to the health of the King; Queen Anne's birthday, March 22; St. George's Day, May 4; the birthday of the King, June 21, when all the streets were lit at night and hung with flags by day; the anniversary of his coronation, August 16; and the birthday of the Prince of Wales, November 15, which was celebrated by cannonades, balls and bonfires all over the city. The year 1725 was an especially brilliant one, for in addition to these numerous fêtes were a magnificent procession across London in honor of the reëstablishment of The Order of the Bath on June 28, and a sumptuous festival for the marriage of Louis XV, September 13, given by the French Legation, when wine was freely poured out for the people and there were illuminations.

But all the noise and merrymaking could not hide the overwhelming brutality of this great city. Robberies, murders and immoralities of every kind filled the columns of the newspapers. Often the mail coaches were held up and robbed (at St. Albans in January, Farnham in February); the silver plate of the King was stolen from Windsor and Kensington in April, his pheasants in March, and the greenhouses of William Hucks were rifled in June. The newspapers recounted these outrages with exaggerated details, and for months the conventional fourth page was filled with advertisements promising high rewards to those who could deliver up the guilty ones.

Crimes were retailed at such length in print, and discussed so much in public, that interest often turned to admiration. When the famous brigand, J. Wild, was executed in May, 1725, the *London Journal* published a long account of the affair. Wild had at last been caught for stealing a bag of laces from a woman who sold them on Holborn Bridge. He told her that by giving a certain porter ten guineas she would have them back. This she did, and on asking Wild what he would have for himself, he is said to have replied, "Good woman, I desire nothing of you for my part but your Prayers." He certainly was going to have need of them.

Almost every week the newspapers mentioned the closing of various houses of ill fame where the traffic of both men and women was carried on. But sadder still were the great number of suicides, particularly those of young people. Suicides were constantly being cited in the press; on July 10 in the *Weekly Journal* appeared this characteristic paragraph: "Saturday last a poor labouring man who had 3 children to provide for and a wife big with a fourth stabbed himself in Golding Lane." The *London Journal* published this item, July 17, 1725: "A Grenadier's wife hanged herself last Tuesday in her own Room in Exeter Court in the Strand; her husband had the day before been whip'd for Desertion. The same day an Apprentice at Bridewell was drowned in the Thames."

In 1726, the *Weekly Journal* announced again: "Yesterday night a boy about 16 years old, an Apprentice to a Taylor in Bond Street near the Playhouse hang'd himself at his bed post where he was found dead and naked the next morning, he having taken off his shirt to perform the operation." A few days later the same paper printed: "A Gardiner at Hampton Court is committed for kicking a youth that was a boarder at his house so violently about the belly that he died under his feet."

Furthermore, a kind of joviality was mixed with the brutality and horror of these accounts, hiding their bitterness, the

Weekly Journal inserting such lines as these: "Also the Evening before an elderly man that carried a basket in Hungerford Market for his livelihood was drowned in an excessive Quantity of Strip and go Naked, alias Strike fire, alias Gin, at a notorious Brothel in the Strand; the poor miserable wretch expiring under a too great Dose of that stupefying Benediction."

Franklin, guided by Ralph, tasted the charm of this hard and colorful life. They were gay together, for Benjamin was not without a liking for strong liquor and lively pleasures; he was not, and would never be, a prude. However, he didn't approve of cruelty and some of the sights of London were painful to him. One had to be singularly strong, healthy and happy not to be bothered by them. England was, paradoxically, the most progressive nation of Europe and the least refined.

The two young men enjoyed their liberty very much at first and profited by it. Franklin wrote light-heartedly to Debby, his fiancée, whom he thought he would probably never see again. Ralph attempted to forget his wife by making up to the pretty milliner who lived in the same building as themselves. She was a pleasing girl, became his companion, and kept him going as long as she had money. After that, she and Ralph lived on the opulent wages of Benjamin, who found this little family a rather costly encumbrance.

It was worse when Ralph, at the end of his rope, left for the country, where he gained a niggardly livelihood by teaching the three R's. His pupils paid him sixpence each per week. However, he consoled himself by writing an epic poem, dreaming of his companion and sending long letters to Benjamin about poetry. In order not to soil the white robe of his art by pedagogy and to show his friendship for Benjamin, Ralph had adopted the name of Franklin for the length of his exile. He had also confided the care of his companion to him.

Unfortunately, Benjamin didn't like verses. His father had taught him to be disgusted with poetry and the genius of Ralph was not strong enough to change his mind. And he was too fond of women. His care of the little milliner was not disinterested and the situation soon became critical. Ralph and Benjamin did not believe in morality but they did show faith in pleasure and desire. Benjamin's conduct was nothing if not logical. He tried to satisfy his desires, that is, he tried to do good according to his fashion, and Ralph did the same.

The latter received a letter from Benjamin, saying that his verses were bad, and a letter from his sweetheart, saying that she had found Benjamin indiscreet. Ralph was furious and, taking advantage of the occasion, broke off with his importunate literary critic, rival in love, and creditor to the tune of twenty-seven pounds.

Franklin was astounded at his action. He loved Ralph and had hoped to be reimbursed. Here he was, once more in London without a sou, just as in the year preceding. He knew the pleasures of London but he now knew also its dangers for one who had no money, title, or paying vice. Ralph's gesture gave him food for reflection. It was the middle of winter, cloudbursts of cold rain flooded the city, and the streets were lugubrious, hostile and foreign.

But summoning up his strength and courage, he did not hesitate to rid himself of his past and to start a new life. Despite his adventures he had always kept his sense of discipline. He left Palmer's and went over to Watt's, a still more famous printer. Here he showed himself to be a model employee, respected by his master and admired by his fellow workmen. At first he had difficulty with them, for having been promoted from the press room to the composing room, he was asked to pay the newcomer's customary five shillings for drink. Benjamin refused, having already paid once before, but was at last forced to yield, as they played all kinds of tricks on him. He was also laughed at in the beginning, as he only drank water, but he was a handsome lad, and by showing himself so strong and prosperous and gay, he at length won over a number to his way of thinking.

Thus his moral renovation began. Like a good Bostonian, he gave moral lectures to others to cure himself. At the same time, in order to erase the incident of the milliner from his mind, and to be closer to his place of work, he changed his lodgings and came to live on Duke Street in a good widow's house. She was happy to have him, as hitherto there had been no men in the house, and, reading about the crimes in the newspapers, she had begun to fear for her life. Benjamin's solid and stocky figure pleased her, and to make sure of his protection she lowered her original rate of three and a half shillings a week for bed and board to one and a half shillings. Josiah Franklin would now have begun to recognize Benjamin as his son.

Benjamin became the darling of his landlady. She was a good soul, had turned Catholic after having been Protestant, had seen something of society life and knew a thousand anecdotes about the past which Benjamin loved to hear. Often their dinner was no more than half an anchovy and a piece of bread, but she made up for the scanty fare by conversation, and Benjamin would listen like a student.

One day the landlady introduced him to another one of her boarders, a Catholic woman who had become a sort of religious recluse. Benjamin admired this woman's serenity and superhuman frugality, often paying visits to her room which was furnished only with a mattress, a table with a crucifix and a book on it, a stool on which he sat, and over the chimney was hung a picture of St. Veronica displaying her handkerchief. He listened attentively to her explanations of miracles, and the sound of her speech was pleasing to him. It was one more bond with his past and also with the future which he began to foresee vaguely.

After a rainy spring, a warm summer set in, and Benjamin turned once more to sports. His friends were amazed to watch him dive for there were few among them who could even swim. During the torrid days of 1726 men and young men went to the river to refresh themselves but many were drowned. The newspapers mention four on June 4, two on June 18, and so it went on for the rest of the month. Once, when Franklin was coming from Chelsea on the Thames, he made the greater part of the trip by swimming and many admired his prowess. Sir William Wyndham heard of his exploit and wished to employ him as professor of swimming to his two sons.

This could have been an opportunity for him. He could still enjoy a career of adventure. Success would not have been difficult, since he had learned so much in London; the theater, dance halls and taverns had initiated him into the mysteries of a great city. He had borrowed books for a slight sum at a bookstore near his home and had read all of the works of the day. He was well informed, and his silence, his naturally reserved and dignified manners, made a good impression on every one. He had the advantage of coming from a distant land. Others have succeeded in the world with fewer attributes than these.

But he knew very well what he lacked. His master Plato and the good Tryon had instructed him to know himself. He knew he was neither pertinent nor smooth in his speech. Charlatanry repelled him and he had a desire for regular work. Literature attracted him but little. Pope had just published his translation of the Odyssey, and literature flourished in London, but Benjamin devoted little of his time or thought to it. He had nothing of the entertainer in him, either. Crowds intimidated him and he found splendor embarrassing.

London weighed on him, now that he found himself alone. He saw the misery and cruelty of the city in raw daylight. The streets were filled with famished haymakers who had no work on account of the rainy spring. They begged singly or in company, and gathered before the homes of the great lords, who sometimes gave them bread, like the Duke of Chandos. The Lord Mayor offered them charity also, but it was not enough to mend their fortunes much. Some of the men hanged themselves from trees in the gardens.

Every week in the newspapers Benjamin saw the long lists of the names of soldiers who had deserted their country and their difficult calling.

Richard Dymore, May 23, 1725, deserted from H.M. 3rd Regiment of Footguards, born near Marlborough in Wiltshire, aged 27 years, 6 foot, 2 inches high, of a fresh Complexion, high nose, hanging brows, a lusty well built man with good legs, his thumb full of warts, a labouring Man, slow of speech, and 'tis believed he went away in a white coat and a fair wig; as also from the same Company Thomas Banister, the 30th of May last, born in Kingston in Herefordshire, aged 33 years, 5 foot, 10 inches high, of a fresh complexion with a round Face with short brown Hair, walks wide with the Knees, commonly has a Chew of tobacco in his underlip, by trade a dyer, it is believed he went away in a dark brown coloured coat.

It was not hard to imagine where Dymore and Banister had fled. More than a thousand German, English, Irish and Rhinelanders had gone over to Pennsylvania in a single year.

While Benjamin was debating whether he should flee across Europe with his new-found friend, Wygate, earning his way by teaching swimming or return to his own country, his decision was suggested by the good Quaker, Denham. The friendship which had begun on board the *London Hope* had constantly increased during Benjamin's stay in London. When he had to suffer from the evil character, example and reputation of Ralph, he had always found solid support and good advice from Denham.

Denham had come back to London to liquidate many old debts, and when he paid his creditors, he offered them a banquet in honor of the occasion. Benjamin admired him greatly for his honesty. He was also very touched at Denham's interest in his future and the good Quaker merchant offered him a place as clerk in his establishment, promising to advance him later.

To take such a step was to enter the *bourgeoisie*. Instead of running the great risk which London offered, — to be a lackey to become an aristocrat, — by being a clerk he would make less, but his wages would be sure, and he would live in a milieu that he was familiar with; its simplicity would be more pleasing to him than the life of complex London.

He could not keep himself from accepting the offer. So, finally, he signed a contract with Denham, who moreover promised him fifty-two Pennsylvania pounds a year and future advancements. All Benjamin could think of now was to enter this new business and be off to America. London, smelly and warm through the long summer days, was oppressive. How he dreamed of being back in Pennsylvania! With the money that Denham had advanced, Benjamin bought a fine new cap for two shillings, and paid the ten pounds for his passage. At length, he left London, July 2, 1726, on board the *Berkshire*. Philadelphia was the destination and there were twenty-two passengers.

Benjamin wisely returned to his homeland, while the brilliant, vain, and excitable Monsieur de Voltaire (whom many still called François Marie Arouet) arrived in London, his back still sore from the blows of the Chevalier de Rohan's cane. Voltaire had wished to avenge himself for this indignity and the Rohans had had him exiled. This clever, sharp-tongued and fashionable poet had come to the English capital, filled with spleen and determined to find means of revenge.

Thus, while Benjamin Franklin was taking back the latest doctrines of the English Radicals, which he was to adapt and vulgarize to suit the taste and practical cares of the *bourgeoisie* of the New World, Voltaire had come but to study them. Voltaire, who knew how to learn so well, and how to understand even that which was not intelligible, had come to absorb the ideas and doctrines of Newton and Mandeville which were later to dominate the intellectual and aristocratic classes of Europe. He was going to furnish the aristocrats a strong arm against the kings who had begun to irritate them by over-exerting their powers. These European nobles, for whom the concept of a country did not exist, and whose fidelity to the King was often a formula, were to make up an Anglo-Franco society pervaded no more than with the philosophic spirit.

The English victories in the beginning of the century and the genius of Voltaire would be the principal causes of its growth. Voltaire was to make the audacious ideas of the English Radicals literary and elegant, while Franklin was to reduce them to common and familiar terms.

But Franklin was bringing back to Philadelphia more than a bundle of ideas. He was returning with an incomparable youthfulness of body and mind, the like of which Voltaire never possessed. London had tested Benjamin, not aged him.

While the *Berkshire*, held back by the winds, dragged along the coast of the Isle of Wight, Benjamin visited the island, and was always ready to jump into the water, to bail out a ship's boat, to help at a disembarkment, to fetch a boat anchored far from shore. . . . His radiant health encircled him like a halo and attracted every one to him; his warm optimism was more than colored by morality, it was almost a pure virtue.

The fifth of August, a fair wind sprang up and carried the *Berkshire* far from the English coast. The long but interesting voyage to America was begun and Benjamin kept an account of it. The boat was not swift but it was comfortable, and if the passengers were few, they were pleasant. Days went by in complaining of the bad winds and playing chess. Benjamin wrote in his diary, and on Saturdays, if the weather permitted, went in swimming and washed his shirt. On the nineteenth of August, a little excitement broke the monotony of the voyage. One of the passengers was caught cheating in a game. He was suspended for a while in the halyards and made to pay a fine as punishment.

But this event was soon forgotten in the new diversion of fishing for dolphins. The passengers caught a number of them and ate those which were not too bad, while the sailors explained why painters had so unjustly given hideous forms to this lovely fish in their pictures. Benjamin noted the strange reason: "As this most beautiful fish is only to be caught at sea, and that very far to the Southward, they say the painters wilfully deform it in their representations, lest pregnant women should long for what it is impossible to procure to them."

In September the *Berkshire* met up with a packet of Dublin on its way to New York and the two boats sailed in company for some days. So many visits and dinners were exchanged that life took on a city aspect. But the days were long, nevertheless, whole mornings of nervous waiting in a dead calm and long afternoons of boredom under the hazy sky. Benjamin took refuge in contemplation and in some scientific studies which his English reading had suggested. He discovered and observed some small soft-shelled crabs which he claimed were born in certain marine algæ, and finding them really curious, he preserved some of the crabs in a bottle.

But more than all this, he dreamed of his future which spread before him, vast and mysterious. Now that he had studied the Puritan and maritime civilization of Boston, the mercantile and agricultural life of Philadelphia, and the great industrial civilization of aristocratic London, he felt he could distinguish the curve that his future would take. Boston had given him the base of his education and his radicalism, Philadelphia had encouraged the development of the latter, and London had brought it to a high pitch and the final test.

The process had been interesting but its results were mediocre. Collins and Ralph were lost to him, money and time had been wasted, — to say nothing of women and worse dangers. But he had come back young, still safe and sound, and the knowledge of the dangers he had run unscathed made him all the more happy.

He promised himself he would lead a new life. It was with profound joy that he finally caught sight of America the ninth of October. Two days later he disembarked with his companions, "having happily completed so tedious and dangerous a voyage. . . ."

Benjamin had finished his education and his experiences in radicalism. Henceforward, with the aid of God, he would set himself to hard work.

BOOK TWO

THE "WAY TO WEALTH"

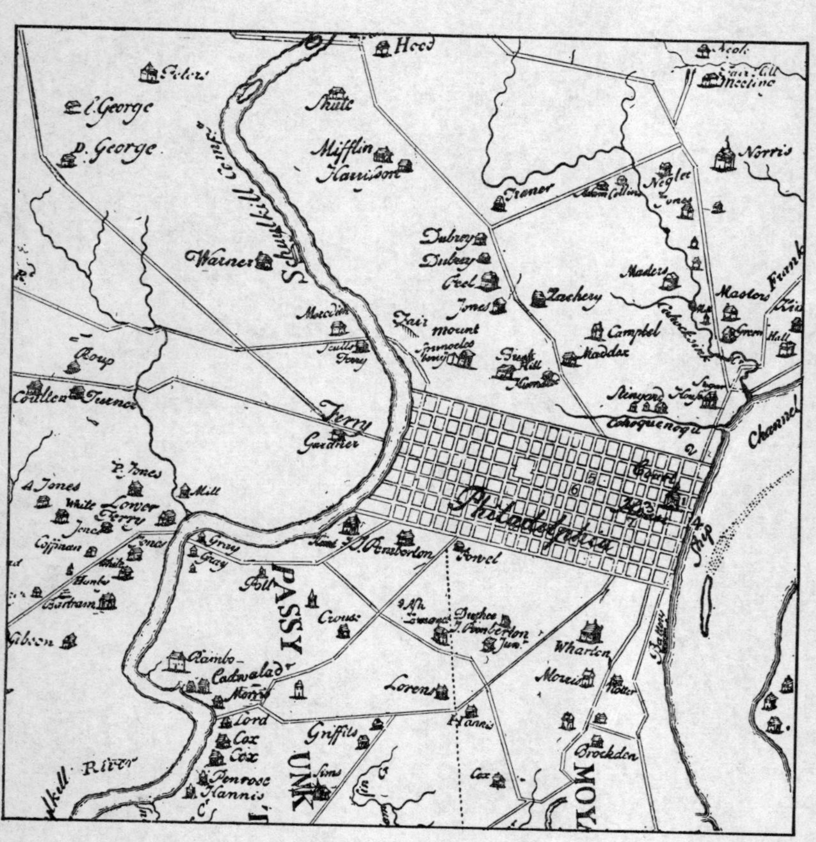

Hood
Shute
Mifflin
Harrison
D. George
Warner
Norris
Dubrey
Zachery
Campbel
Maddox
Fair mount
Ferry
Gardner
Turner
A. Jones
P. Jones
Lower Ferry
Mill
Gray
Philadelphia
Channel
PASSY
UNK
Wharton
Brockden
Lord
Cox
Penrose
Hannis
Bartram
Gibson
Griffits
Sims
River

Central section from a map in the possession of the Historical Society of Pennsylvania, entitled "Map of Philadelphia and parts adjacent, 1750, by N. Scull and G. Heap."

This map gives a clear idea of the City of Philadelphia and its surroundings at the time of Franklin: the small town surrounded with estates, where the prominent citizens spent the summers or the later years of their life, the Pembertons, the Whartons, the Norrises, the Morrises, the Coxes, etc.

The city had then 2076 houses located on nine streets perpendicular to the Delaware and the Schuylkill rivers, which were:

Vine Street, Race Street (later called Sassafras Street), Cherry Street, High Street (also called Market Street and the central axis of the city), Chestnut Street, Walnut Street, Locust Street, Spruce Street, Pine Street.

No. 1 is the first home of Franklin (1729–1748), on High Street, near the Market. The old Market was on High Street, between the Court House and the Delaware. The Court House was the place where elections were held and is shown in one of the pictures (see page 197). This early home of Franklin was in the most central and noisiest part of Philadelphia.

No. 2 is the house of Franklin from 1748 to 1763. It was on the Southeast corner of Race Street and Second Street. The garden, a long and rather narrow strip, extended to the Delaware. It was just at the outskirts of the city and much quieter than High Street, although the growth of Philadelphia tended in that direction.

No. 3. Franklin's home from 1763 to 1790. He lived there mostly after his return from France. It was in the middle of the block formed by 3d and 4th Streets, High Street and Chestnut Street. It was called "Franklin Court." The alley which led to it was on High Street.

No. 4. The Crooked Billet, the Inn where he stayed when he arrived the first time. It was on Water Street, facing the Delaware.

No. 5. The Masonic Lodge, on Filbert Street, between 8th and 9th Streets, where Franklin spent so many good hours and did so much work.

No. 6. The University of Pennsylvania, first known as the "Academy", and installed in the "New Building" (built as an auditorium for Whitefield and other itinerant preachers or speakers). It stood on 3d Street between High Street and Cherry Street. This building and the organization of the Academy were two of Franklin's most important achievements.

No. 7. The State House where Franklin spent so much of his time as clerk of the Assembly.

Central section from a map in the possession of the Historical Society of Pennsylvania, entitled "Map of Philadelphia and parts adjacent," 17[illegible], by N. Scull and G. Heap.

This map gives a clear idea of the City of Philadelphia and its surroundings at the time of Franklin: the small town surrounded with estates, where the prominent citizens spent the summers or the later years of their life, the Pembertons, the Whartons, the Norrises, the Morrises, the Coxes, etc.

The city had then [illegible] houses located on nine streets perpendicular to the Delaware and the Schuylkill rivers, which were:

Vine Street, Race Street (then called Sassafras Street), Cherry Street, High Street (also called Market Street and the central axis of the city), Chestnut Street, Walnut Street, Dock Street, Spruce Street and Pine Street.

No. 1 is the first house of Franklin (17[illegible]), on High Street near the Market. The old Market was on High Street, between the Court House and the Delaware. The Court House was the place where elections were held and is shown in one of the pictures (see page [illegible]). This early home of Franklin was in the most central and busiest part of Philadelphia.

No. 2 is the house of Franklin from 17[illegible] to 17[illegible]. It was on the Southeast corner of Race Street and Second Street. The garden, a long and rather narrow strip, extended to the Delaware. This was just at the outskirts of the city and much quieter than High Street, although the growth of Philadelphia tended in that direction.

No. 3. Franklin's home from 17[illegible] to 1790. He lived here mostly after his return from Europe. It was in the middle of the block formed by 3rd and 4th Streets, High Street and Chestnut Streets. It was called "Franklin Court." The alley which led to it was on High Street.

No. 4. The Crooked Billet, the inn where he stayed when he arrived the first time. It was on Water Street, facing the Delaware.

No. 5. The Masonic Lodge, on Filbert Street, between 3rd and 4th Streets, where Franklin spent so many good hours and did so much work.

No. 6. The University of Pennsylvania, first known as the "Academy," and installed in the "New Building" (built as an auditorium for Whitefield and other itinerant preachers or speakers). It stood on 4th Street between High Street and Cherry Street. This building and the organization of the Academy were two of Franklin's most important achievements.

No. 7. The State House where Franklin spent so much of his time as clerk of the Assembly.

I

THE fresh and vari-colored autumn welcomed the travelers to Pennsylvania. Compared to the great city they had recently left, with all its noise and brutal contrasts, this little town of Philadelphia, still shaded by reddening trees and steeped in solitude, seemed like Paradise to them. They found it almost the same as they had left it — a little grown, perhaps — with a few new houses on the banks, more men at work in the shipyards, more boats along the docks. It was October, and at the end of the month four ships arrived, crowded with Irishmen, Dutchmen, Palatines and Germans of all kinds. Philadelphia was fashionable, and the peasants of Europe, tired of misery, religious quarrels, and taxes, had come there to seek brotherly love.

The foremost thinkers of the Old World who, up to this time, had been scornful of the Quakers, began to be interested in them; the conversion of William Penn, a man of the world, had made this new sect a topic of conversation in high society. Princes and their governments perceived that the colony was a success, and that it was attracting their subjects. During this lull of twenty-five years, when the wars which had just ended were being forgotten, and those which were brooding were not foreseen, people dreamed only of making money; the Quaker doctrine, which seemed to suit commerce so well and to lead so surely to fortune, was much admired.

Monsieur de Voltaire, the forerunner of all intellectual fads, was just discovering the Anglo-Saxon world at this moment, and so hastened to make a study of the Quakers. He devoted the first four of his "Philosophical Letters" to them, — these same letters which were to make the English, their government and their philosophies, the craze of Europe. "I thought," he said in the beginning, "that the doctrine of such an extraordinary people as the Quakers merited the attention of a thinking man." Then he introduced one of these "primitives."

> This Quaker was a vigorous old man, who had never been ill because he had never known passion or intemperance. Never in my life have I seen more noble and attractive manners than his. He was dressed in the habit of his cult: a coat without pleats at the sides, and without buttons, either on the pockets or the sleeves, and he wore a large hat with a flat brim as do our churchmen.

How charming all this must have been to a man brought up in the pompous, refined and dissolute aristocracy of the Regency!

But Voltaire especially liked what he had heard of Penn's distant colony.

> In America — he wrote with admiration — Penn founded the city of Philadelphia, which is today very flourishing. He began by making a treaty with his neighboring Americans; it is the only treaty between these people and the Christians which was not sworn to and which has not been broken. The new sovereign was also the legislator of Pennsylvania. The laws he gave were very wise and have remained unchanged. The first is, to mistreat no one because of his religious belief, and to regard all those who believe in a God as brothers. . . .

It was quite new to hear a ruler being addressed by every one as "thee", to see his subjects wearing a hat in his presence, and to realize that these same subjects — excepting the judges — were all equal citizens.

Was this not a beautiful example for the King of France, and a very convenient weapon against him and his court of arrogant lords and authoritative prelates?

To Franklin, Voltaire, and all the innovators of this sturdy generation, the Quakers were a ridiculous, congenial, and convenient people. In the face of the haughty aristocrats, with their powdered wigs and stilted cult of honor, the Quakers had invented a bourgeois formula, the first in modern times. They dressed as peasants, never wore a wig, never went to war, and made love as they made money, for virtue's sake and not for pleasure. The Quaker cult was the only one in the eighteenth century which tolerated others. Its members directed their zeal in another direction; they were more interested in the art of daily living than in persecution. They sanctified commerce and agriculture, and concentrated their efforts to bring about the present happiness and virtue of man. A man's life in this crass world was their chief consideration; it was the center of their cult just as the citizen was the center of their State. God and the king remained above, but very alone.

Benjamin, on his return to Philadelphia, found himself very comfortable in this environment, which was nearer earth than heaven, to be sure, but then Benjamin was on good terms with both regions. Denham was influential and good. He instructed his disciple in virtuous conduct and in commerce. Benjamin, after all, had inclinations for both, though he had neglected the former for some time, and had not yet had the chance of trying out the second. He set himself to his task with a will, and, aided by his marvelous faculty of adaptation, he soon got into step with his neighbors. What devout Quaker could have written more like Benjamin in this letter which he sent to his beloved sister, Jane, along with a spinning wheel, in answer to an announcement of her engagement.

> Sister, farewell, and remember that modesty, as it makes the most homely virgin amiable and charming, so the want of it infallibly renders the most perfect beauty disagreeable and odious. But, when that brightest of female virtues shines among other perfections of body and mind in the same person, it makes the woman more lovely than an angel. Excuse this freedom, and use the same with me.

Thus Franklin "Quakerized" like a man of resolution. In a little time he would have become just as real a Quaker, virtuous — and rich — as the others.

But it was not fated for him to win a victory so easily. When he felt that he was really settled down in his work, when he thought he was on the highroad to a solid fortune and a comfortable career, an epidemic suddenly spread over Philadelphia, and both he and Denham caught the disease (February, 1727). His old friend passed away. Benjamin thought that he was going to die also, but narrowly escaped with a case of pleurisy.

This illness left him exhausted, jobless, penniless; he was far from his family, deprived of protection, and once more alone. The honest Denham had deluded him involuntarily just as the rascally Keith had done; Denham, after all his fine words, had neglected to make the liberal will he had promised his apprentice. Thus Franklin fell back once more among the common people, among the workmen, from which class he had scarcely risen. To succeed he could count only on himself.

Not knowing which way to turn, Benjamin took up his old craft once more. His brother-in-law, Holmes, who passed through Philadelphia at this time, advised him to do so. Franklin returned to Keimer, who was in need of a skilled workman.

Three years had been lost from the most beautiful and fruitful period of his life, and now, after his magnificent escapade and career of adventure, Benjamin had to fall back again into the squalid workshop of this eccentric printer! Here he suffered the hardest ordeal of his life, though it did teach him a lesson. What London had outlined for him, what Denham had striven to complete, now suddenly matured: Benjamin became converted.

His conversion was not like the ordinary New England kind, with visions and trembling, angelic visits and public confessions; Benjamin did not become a Puritan again, nor was he converted like Rousseau, who, on a highroad, received a violent blow from God, which taught him, in a few moments, to love men to the point of hatred, and to serve them to the point of importunity. Franklin and his Supreme Being understood each other much more simply, without any fuss, and his conversion was simply the result of all that he had lived. It had matured in a printer's workshop, at a shopkeeper's counter, and in drinking bowls of punch.

At sea he had already decided to become a thinking being and to have some order in his ideas. He set himself to four rules:

Economy: It is necessary for me to be extremely frugal for some time, till I have paid what I owe.

Perseverance: To apply myself industriously to whatever business I take in hand, and not to divert my mind from my business by any foolish project of growing suddenly rich; for industry and patience are the surest means of plenty.

Goodwill: I resolve to speak ill of no man whatever not even in a matter of truth, but rather by some means excuse the faults I hear charged upon others, and, upon proper occasions, speak all the good I know of everybody.

Loyalty: To endeavor to speak truth in every instance: to give nobody expectations that are not likely to be answered, but aim at sincerity in every word and action; the most amiable excellence in a rational being.

It is easy to see that in its beginnings, the conversion of Franklin was an act of prudence, and that it had its origin in England, where he verified the particular and general bad effects of immorality. A theory which cost him two good friends and thirty pounds could not be very good. After this observation he renounced having a code of ethics suited only to himself, and he abandoned the theory that our instincts are sufficient guides, that our pleasure makes for the best law. He ceased to consider man as a reveling animal and decided to treat him as a social being.

Finally, God, Whom he had hitherto considered as a useless and extravagant luxury, appeared useful to him, when at a crisis in his illness (March, 1727), he felt the approach of death. Then he turned towards the Supreme Being and offered him his direct personal homage. He prayed to Him as the Jews had prayed after they had destroyed the golden calf. The God that Benjamin thus adored from the bottom of his heart was not in the least like the Christian God. Rather, he resembled a Jehovah, surrounded by his cherubims, a Deity that might have been dreamed of by a disciple of Plato. Franklin's conversion made him remember all the books which had especially struck him in his childhood — those of the good Tryon, Xenophon, Shaftesbury — as well as the more recent conversations he had heard among the disciples of Sir Isaac Newton at London.

The Supreme Being of Franklin is separated from us by a series of *beings*, superior to us, inferior to him, each installed in a planet of its own, and ruling over the satellites which belong to it. As an inhabitant of the earth, Franklin thought himself obliged to worship the God who lived in the sun, and he made a liturgy for Him — a kind of abbreviation of the Anglican prayers — to which he remained faithful. Like a good Platonician, he demanded of this God, virtue, knowledge, and an after-life — probably metempsychosis — as his half-serious, half-ironical epitaph, which he composed at this time, infers:

The Body
Of
BENJAMIN FRANKLIN,
Printer,
(Like the cover of an old book,
Its contents torn out,
And stript of its lettering and gilding,)
Lies here, food for worms.
Yet the work itself shall not be lost,
For it will, as he believed, appear once more,
In a new
And more beautiful edition,
Corrected and amended
By
The Author.

He never was without this little document, and if Franklin never denied his God, he spoke but little of him, thus imitating his Deistical masters and following a Protestant tendency. He kept his personal relations with God to himself, and this mystical element did not enter into his social life. The Godhead was too high to have any need of man; prayers should be made in case of necessity, but the only real way of honoring God was by being useful to other men. The two poles of this new discipline of Franklin's were an inner, mystical, discreet and astronomical God, and an outward social code of well-doing and adaptability.

He worked, above all, to make himself virtuous. But do

not confuse the virtue of Franklin with that of St. Simeon Stylite, who spent thirty-six years on a column and ate grasshoppers, or with that of Cotton Mather, who preached at the top of his voice and hanged witches, or with the virtue of poor Jean Jacques Rousseau, who dressed like an Armenian and insulted his neighbor to improve his own morals. Here is what Franklin's perfection consisted of: "Temperance, Silence, Order, Resolution, Frugality, Industry, Sincerity, Justice, Moderation, Cleanliness, Tranquillity, Chastity, and Humility." Some of the virtues were defined thusly:

TEMPERANCE, Eat not to dullness; drink not to elevation. SILENCE, Speak not but what may benefit others or yourself; avoid trifling conversation. ORDER, Let all your things have their place; let each part of your business have its time. FRUGALITY, Make no expense but to do good to others or yourself, i.e., waste nothing. CLEANLINESS, Tolerate no uncleanliness in body, cloaths, or habitation. CHASTITY, Rarely use venery but for health or offspring, never to dulness, weakness, or the injury of your own or another's peace or reputation. HUMILITY, Imitate Jesus and Socrates.

There is no ascetism in these definitions, neither are they Christian. Rather, they recall the maxims of the good Tryon, which instructed you pell-mell how to respect the souls of sheep, how to kill bedbugs, and how to enter into communication with the angels. Franklin was only more practical; he made a little notebook for himself and ruled the pages, writing the days of the week at the top, and the virtues to practice down along the side. Each week he attacked a new virtue in particular, noting his faults and his failures, trying to avoid them, and making a clean sweep at the end of the week in order to begin the next one afresh. From week to week he went from one virtue to another until his final success.

He always carried this little notebook with him and it held a great place in his life. Franklin was very sincere and gave himself a lot of trouble to practice his thirteen virtues. He applied himself assiduously to performing all of them, but not with equal success. If it were easy for him to be resolute, frugal and industrious, as his father had taught him and as he was inclined by temperament, if he found pleasure in keeping clean (for he did not detest his body and liked to exercise it by swimming and hard work), it was more difficult for him to remain chaste and sober in an epoch that was anything but virtuous. He was scarcely more daring than his friends, but sometimes there was much gossip whispered about him.

He enhanced the performance of the other virtues by a rare ingenuity; his justice was exact, but not pitiless, permitting him to pass over the faults of others; this made him many friends and helped him to pardon his own faults, so that he was more human. He never neglected the exercise of humility, and it increased with him as he advanced in life. It became a sort of luxury to him, and as he grew older, he took more and more satisfaction in mentioning his father, the candle-maker, charming the humble people but disquieting his powerful friends. He was no less skillful in showing himself to be moderate and quiet at all times, so that he made progress in the world quickly, but without attracting too many jealous enmities.

His silence was proverbial and salutary; preferring to speak only when he would be listened to and understood, he was ordinarily taciturn; this helped him very much with the public, the voters, and ladies, who preferred a good listener to a good talker, knowing that the former is much more rare.

Admirable, too, was his use of disorder. He was never able to attain to the virtue of order, as his life was too rich and his intelligence too active. His vagabond desires were always carrying him hither and yon, and so, taking account of this deficiency, he created a system of order for himself, shrouded in mystery, which was perfectly clear to him but incomprehensible to others. It was thus that the multiplicity of his occupations was hidden from curious eyes.

His happy nature served him in every way, except in the practice of sincerity. He was an honest man, always careful to show himself frank, but the subtlety of his mind never permitted him to be simple or absolute, so that his good faith was sometimes doubted. In this theatrical century, he had the gifts of comedy and travesty, and he made use of them, shocking those who did not understand the tricks of the stage. Unfortunately, New England and Pennsylvania had no liking for plays, and his talent remained unknown for a long time. However, he made the best use of this talent that he could, for it kept up his good humor and health.

Now he was aiming at health, not sainthood; he felt amply satisfied with a code which furnished activity for him, procured success, public esteem, interior satisfaction, and the quiet atmosphere he needed to live in happily. On the whole he could be proud of the results of his method. It wasn't either sublime or absolutely new, but it served.

Nevertheless, it did not quite suffice him. He was not only converted to Virtue, but being the good son of a Puritan, he thought himself vowed to apostleship. What benefit was there in being good when the others were not? Franklin had not only reconciled himself with God, but more than this, had reconciled himself with the social order. His first act, then, was to gather his friends together in an organization, based on the two principles of morality and utility, in order that they would practice the same virtues that he did, and serve humanity without forgetting themselves too much. The ideal which this society adopted was the same that Franklin had discovered in the Masonic lodges of England: Virtue, Goodness, Knowledge.

From the little world of intelligent workmen and employees in which Franklin moved, he chose the youngest, most active and ambitious of them to make his society: Joseph Breintnall, a very literary scrivener; Thomas Godfrey, a clever mathematical glazier; N. Scull, a talented surveyor; William Maugridge, an accomplished joiner; and two respected store employees: William Coleman and Robert Grace. To these he added his comrades of the printing shop: Meredith, Potts and Webb. A large number of small tradesmen in Philadelphia also joined this modest but active club, for the sake of diversion, mutual aid and a rest from their wives. The club met every Friday evening and had a curious ritual, which Franklin put into definite form in 1728.

Though, in reality, it was Mather who had inspired this club, by his suggestions in his "Essays to Do Good", its members did not have his intention, that of saving souls and preparing them for eternal life, but rather wished to render practical services to humanity and to themselves without waiting for the hereafter. In a sense, the club was a rival to that of the merchants, the "Every Night Club" where the rich men met every evening. They nicknamed Franklin and his friends "The Leather Apron Club", but the real name was much more dignified. It was called "The Junto."

Franklin, recruiting his members from the modest classes, clearly foresaw what an advantage he would have in making use of education. At this time, the acquisition of knowledge, particularly of the sciences, was all the rage, and so Franklin insisted on this particular aspect of activity in the rules he drew up for the club. The society was at the same time a social club, a study circle, and a moral organization, resembling the Masonic lodges and Chambers of Commerce of our day. A candidate for membership had to assure the club officials that he had no enemy among the members, that he loved humanity as a whole without distinction of religion, that he believed in the freedom of conscience, and that he loved and sought liberty for its own sake.

At the meeting the men would exchange their views on the books they had read and inform each other on what they had learned; they would discuss current events and why such and such a business was a success and another a failure. Some among them would give talks on the ill consequences of intemperance and the advantages of virtue. All of them were banded together to give mutual aid and protection. They were also interested in maintaining public rights and discussed laws and their functionings.

To inculcate a little order in their investigations, without having to resort to severe regulations, they used a system of questions and answers. Franklin prepared the series which were to be used at each meeting. To give more charm to the discussions, the rules prescribed: ". . . That these queries, copied at the beginning of a book, be read distinctly at each meeting; a pause between each, while one might fill and drink a glass of wine."

As there were always twenty-four questions, the members of the Junto couldn't complain of having spent a dry evening. During the intervals they sang drinking songs, cracked jokes and told little stories, in which accomplishment Franklin was a master. Sometimes short papers on literary or moral subjects were read, which added dignity to their meetings, but as a rule they were very informal and jovial. Franklin forgot nothing in his regulations. Besides winter recreation, they included meetings for "bodily exercise" in the springtime and summer, once a month, at some discreet spot on the other side of the river.

The Junto regulations were nicely proportioned, indeed; much good was accomplished without too much effort, the men enjoyed scheming without being mean, were amused without resorting to scandal, and the conversation they exchanged was useful. More precisely than the Masons, the members of the Junto were turning towards the new morale which the century was developing: that of utility as opposed to the abstract, that of the bourgeois commoner as opposed to the priest.

Franklin saw the future of this doctrine very clearly. From 1729 on, he wrote down memoranda which read like grandiose dreams, imagining the federation of all the good men in the world, a vast laic church of formidable power. One evening, after he had dreamed over a book for a long time and felt in a quiet, contemplative and eager mood, he thought himself capable of shaking the world, and thus described his vision.

> He may travel everywhere endeavoring to promote Knowledge and Virtue; by erecting and promoting private Liberty, establishing a society of Virtuous Men in all parts, who shall have an universal correspondence, and write to support and encourage Virtue & Liberty & Knowledge by all Methods.

Franklin wanted to be the one who would perfect this doctrine and establish this society. In order to do this, he thought of writing "The Art of Virtue", which would be the moral code of the time, and he seized upon all occasions for the founding of this new knighthood. His ideas took their source from his readings, his meditations, his sufferings and ambitions, and very soon his project was as precise as a plan of battle. But to make his idea triumph was a matter of conquering the world. He needed, first of all, a group of men, organized as coherently as a political party, but without a party's weaknesses. These would have to be good men, in love with virtue, willing to accept a simple and intelligent faith, which would impose a belief in the immortality of the soul and in a creative God, the giver of all good and the avenger of all evil, worthy of adoration but desiring to be revered by the services which men would render unto one and another. United by an organization which would envelop all nations, these men would strive, above all, for the happiness of humanity. At first, the organization would be secret, and this would make it extremely powerful, as all the members would be good, wealthy and intelligent men. It would be the apotheosis of useful sainthood. The world's people would sit around a table laden with food, alternately singing hymns and drinking songs. Every one would be well dressed, well fed, comfortable, reconciled to himself and the Divine Being, and blessed by the peaceful Jehovah, who would recommend his saints to drink heartily and not to bother themselves too much about him. Thus reconciled by Benjamin Franklin, Rabelais and Cotton Mather would clink glasses in the Church of St. Francis of Assisi, who would have become like them, bourgeois.

What a beautiful dream for this young man to have! Franklin, still weak from his illness, was shivering from the cold of those long tempests which darkened the winter twilights of Philadelphia in 1727–1728. Half the people in the city were ill; those who were well did not dare go out. The Assembly held no sessions.

A torrid summer followed, with earthquakes in the autumn.

They were scarcely felt in Pennsylvania, but they upset New England, scattering fright among men and animals, attesting the wrath of God and crowding the churches. The pastors announced, from their high pulpits, that the hour of malediction, penitence and mortification had come; at every burst of thunder and rumbling of the earth, the pale and shaken crowds would press around the altars, listening in tense fear to the terrifying sounds of the elements, mingled with the voices of their ministers, who spoke to them in the name of God.

However, Benjamin Franklin, who had been converted, was determined to be happy, and listened peacefully to the thunder-claps, dreaming of a religion devoid of fear, a religion of earthly felicity.

He had to fight for it before he could possess it.

II

FRANKLIN fought. His illness had ended, his health was restored, and since he lived, he wished to live well. He neglected nothing which could aid him to success. During the three years between 1727 and 1730, he was engaged in the most arduous battle he had so far attempted, in order to make his place in the sun.

Following the advice of his brother-in-law, Holmes, he decided to return to the printing shop, where his precocious experience and his English education gave him strong advantages (Spring, 1727). Unfortunately, having no capital, he had to offer himself as a workman in one of the two printing shops of the city: at Andrew Bradford's or Samuel Keimer's. Bradford, who had been established for many years, had need of no one, and perhaps would not have taken Franklin on, anyway, being displeased, as a good settled bourgeois, with his adventurous career. Keimer, whose business had grown, was now located two doors away from Bradford on Second Street, and had five workmen under him. Three of them were young farm hands, attracted to the city by the hopes of high wages: Meredith, Potts and Harry; there were also an Irishman, bought from a captain who had taken him over in his boat from Europe, and a young Englishman, highly educated, a former scholar at Oxford, named George Webb. Webb had tired of the Old World and, hungry for adventure, had given himself up to an immigration agency, and had thence been transported to Pennsylvania where he was sold as an indentured servant on his arrival. These were all good fellows, but the ignorant Keimer had much difficulty in teaching them his trade. With such workmen, the shop was not a little picturesque; Keimer constantly indulging himself in his caprices, Meredith silently working in an alcoholic fog, and Webb indolently giving free rein to his fantastic talk.

As soon as Keimer had learned of Franklin's return he decided to hire him again. He must have known the trick Benjamin had wished to play on him when he had left for England, and he did not feel very kindly towards the vagabond, but he did see in Franklin a good chance to have his workmen well trained by an expert printer, whom he could get rid of after a while. He offered high wages to Franklin, who accepted them, finding nothing better. It was not without some repugnance that he did so, for when he had been in London he had seen some of Keimer's former friends and the wife whom Keimer had deserted, learning more than one unpleasant detail from them about the Philadelphia printer.

But Franklin had no choice and could not sacrifice the position because of nice scruples. However, he was very quick to realize what was up Keimer's sleeve and why he was being paid so well. Franklin was not without some foresight and tricks of his own. He made close friends of his comrades, thus preparing a personnel for the time when he could afford to have his own printing shop. Keimer always had a smile for Benjamin, who was always very active, in spite of the hot weather, filling the shop with his industrious energy and playing the part of a man-of-all-work. Everything went well until the workmen began to know their jobs. When that time came, Keimer seized the first occasion to get angry, insulted Benjamin, who had been innocently looking out of the window, and turned him out of doors in the winter of 1727. Thus Keimer had won the first lap.

Benjamin was without resources and thought of returning to New England when Meredith came to him with the idea of founding a new printing shop in Philadelphia. His father would furnish the money and they would be joint proprietors in the business. The idea pleased Benjamin, who, moreover, liked this big, honest, awkward fellow. It pleased Meredith's father also, for he had seen Franklin's good influence over his son and hoped it would overcome his drinking habits.

The three men entered into an agreement. The type and press would be ordered from London with the father's money, and then they would establish themselves in the spring, when young Meredith would have served his term of apprenticeship with Keimer. Thus Franklin prepared to win the second lap.

Nevertheless, he had to live, and Bradford didn't care to employ him this time, either. He went from place to place, looking for any kind of work, when Keimer came once more to him. He had had the luck to obtain an order for the paper money of New Jersey, a profitable affair, but it necessitated a conscientious and skillful workman. Franklin was indispensable. Once more the two reconciled themselves temporarily. Keimer was very pleased with his cleverness, and Franklin was not discontented with his. Both of them thought they had won this lap. It remained indecisive, for during this winter sojourn of three months in New Jersey, Keimer made enough money to be flourishing again, while Franklin, with his intelligence, culture and activity, procured precious friends for himself: Samuel Bustill, secretary of the province, several members of the Legislature, various officials and other influential men. Every one admired his industry, his ability as a printer and type-maker, and predicted he would have a fine career.

On his return to Philadelphia, Franklin found nothing to impede his project. Meredith was free, the equipment had arrived from London, and they could install themselves on High Street, near the market, in company with a glazier, Thomas Godfrey, and his family. They had made this arrangement in order to lighten the burden of the rent and to keep house together (Spring, 1728). They opened the printing shop without further delay, and George House, a friend of Franklin and a member of the Junto, brought them their first customer, a farmer, who put down five shillings for an advertisement. Joseph Breintnall, another friend and member of the Junto, secured them the clientele of the Quakers, who wanted an enormous work, relative to their society, to be printed. Here were good omens and a little money on hand; Franklin had won this lap.

Nevertheless, the men of the city, who had begun to be interested in the struggle between the three printers, were not favorable to the newcomers. They said it was foolish to found a printing establishment when every one was so worried, business so bad, and the Indians starting up again with terrifying new raids on the frontier. Some of them came to Franklin to tell what they had heard, and Franklin, in spite of his fresh acquisition of virtue, found it hard to pardon old Mr. Mickle for a proposal of this kind. He could see for himself that there were all kinds of houses for sale and rent in the city. There had been too much building, the reaction had set in and every one was suffering; a new printing shop couldn't hope to stay.

But Franklin didn't declare himself beaten so quickly as all that. He thoroughly organized his Junto, which grouped his friends around him and gave him much support; and, to utilize his experience and increase his business, he thought of printing a newspaper. There was only one in the city, Bradford's *American Mercury*. Philadelphia was large enough to support two. With this new weapon he thought he could outdo Keimer. He prepared for it quietly. He spoke to his best friends, in order to have their aid, especially to George Webb. He counted on Webb to write his articles, but he was disappointed. Webb, who was nonchalant, imprudent, and a little rascally, revealed the secret to Keimer. Without hesitation or waiting, Keimer immediately founded a newspaper, *The Universal Instructor in all Arts and Science, and Pennsylvania Gazette.* As Webb still worked at Keimer's, Franklin's project was frustrated. It was a pitiable moment for the new little printing house. Squeezed between Bradford and Keimer, it looked as though the new shop would go under. Keimer had won this lap.

But God came to the aid of His servant, and the Junto didn't abandon him. Franklin couldn't hope to demolish Bradford, who was rich, highly considered in the town, and aided by his father, the printer in New York. So he concentrated on Keimer, in order to rid himself of him as soon as possible

For this he made a temporary alliance with Bradford, who had at first scorned Keimer as an oaf, but who was now finding him troublesome. During the last three years, Keimer had disputed the rôle of official printer to the province with him, and not always to Bradford's success. In 1726, Keimer had robbed him of one of his best sources of profit, Titan Leed's "Almanac", which the people were so fond of and which sold so well. Bradford had been the publisher of this almanac for decades. He found this blow a little too hard, and when he heard that Keimer was starting up a newspaper as well, it was really too much. Franklin, who came to Bradford to offer his collaboration in killing this new venture, was welcomed with open arms.

In company with his friend and colleague of the Junto, Breintnall, Franklin wrote a series of little essays which he called, *The Busy-Body*. The public found them enticing, and their attention and favor were turned away from *The Universal Instructor*. *The Busy-Body* was not very malicious; it had neither the sharp juvenile flavor of Mrs. Dogood, nor her bold political views. Here were no attacks against the ministers, the established government or the local aristocracy. Franklin and Breintnall would joke about the craze for searching treasure, or about importunate friends, or they would censor the bad morals of the day by a noble eulogy of virtue. Nothing sarcastic was directed against Keimer, except between the lines. The authors played close; they wished to amuse, and their easy style, light joking, little allusions to local morals, and the ability with which they introduced their readers and made them speak, sufficed to guarantee success. They didn't ask for more.

During this time Keimer's business was dragging along. His *Gazette* was like a ball and chain. It had a fine title: and it had a fine program too, which Keimer took trouble to announce carefully in these choice words:

As he that intends to erect a noble and magnificent Structure, is obliged to make Use of the meanest and most contemptible Materials, in Order to begin, carry on, and perfect his Undertaking; so no Person whatever can make any true Judgment what Sort of Building it will be by only beholding the preparing of the Mortar, the digging of the Stones, the squaring the Marble, or the mixing of the Colours. The same may justly be observ'd of our UNIVERSAL INSTRUCTOR; for as Great Things are compounded of Small, we think it necessary, in Order to furnish our Paper with proper Materials deserving that Character, to introduce it with an Exposition on the Letter A, the first in the Alphabet; and as Letters were before Words, and Words only serve as so many Messengers to declare the Nature and Property of Things, it cannot be thought impertinent to begin at the lowest End first, and advance by Degrees to the highest Pitch of Knowledge we aim to arrive at.

All this explanation to announce that he was going to reprint in this paper the pages of Chamber's "Dictionary" from A to Z!

In order to keep the readers from perishing of ennui, they were also given some news of Europe and extracts from a novel by Defoe, "Religious Courtship." Webb added a few broad jokes, which he had found in other newspapers or in his own imagination. This mixed-up, unevenly written paper was sold for ten shillings a year, and the price for each advertisement was three shillings. It was, however, well printed. But there were only a few subscribers, about ninety, and Keimer didn't bring out more than two hundred and fifty copies at a time. The storekeepers and farmers were in no hurry, either, to publish their advertisements in his columns. Keimer's own natural heaviness was perhaps enough to kill the *Gazette*, but the cleverness of Franklin, who by his *Busy-Body* essays was attracting the public to the *American Mercury*, rendered the catastrophe inevitable. The *Universal Instructor*, which had begun on December 24, 1728, dragged on its miserable existence only to September, 1729.

Keimer, lost in debts, overwhelmed by fate, was now obliged to cede his newspaper at a paltry price to Franklin. Every one had abandoned the poor publisher; the people of good society, who had been shocked at his vulgarity, would have nothing to do with him, no more than the Quakers who were displeased with his hysterical mysticism, or the governor, who had not looked favorably on his publishing the pamphlets of Keith and Keith's friends, or the Aldermen who had intervened in 1728 to hinder him from organizing a lottery for a fair. In April, 1729, Keimer attempted to separate Bradford and Franklin by publishing an insulting pamphlet against the former, which had the appearance of coming from the latter's press. But everything that Keimer attempted, honest or otherwise, failed. Franklin thus won the final lap, which assured the disappearance of his rival. Keimer, who had the soul of a prophet, could, at least, have reread what he had written with solemnity and foresight on himself, a little time before.

> It certainly must be allowed somewhat strange — he said — that a Person of strict Sincerity, refin'd Justice, and universal Love to the whole Creation, should for a Series of near twenty Years, to be the constant But of Slander, as to be three Times ruin'd as a Master-Printer, to be Nine Times in Prison, one of which was Six Years together, and often reduced to the most wretched Circumstances, hunted as a Partridge upon the Mountains, and persecuted with the most abominable Lies the Devil himself could invent, or Malice utter; and yet all this while never any wise, good or even honest Man has been his Enemy, or knew any Evil of him, bating for the little Mistakes or Peccadilloes of human Nature. But so it is and has been, that the Publisher hereof has been the Subject of the most uncommon Treatment, that without Hyperbole, he may truly say, no History can parallel, or private or publick Person ever underwent the like.

After such sounding and pompous words, there was nothing for him to do but to disappear. This he did in 1729, pushed on by his creditors and aided by his apprentice, David Harry, who bought his printing shop. Keimer fled to the Barbadoes, where he spent the rest of his life in obscurity.

Franklin's success was one of intelligence over stupidity, of industry over indolence, of organization over disorder. In the person of Franklin, the Junto and its methods had triumphed. Every one had helped, some, like Breintnall, by bringing in articles, others by procuring advertisements; they had all agreed to spread his good reputation, to send customers to him, and to guarantee his credit.

But more important, it was due to the Junto that Franklin found his place in the political life of Pennsylvania. Since Keith's departure in 1727 the city had become nervous and agitated; the proprietors of the province, by leaning on the Quakers and the rich men, had been able to force Keith to flee to England and to dissolve his party, but the work of Keith had not been destroyed. This man, who with so much foresight had realized the utility of having a royal government instead of the Penns' domination, the importance of attracting German colonists, the advantage there would be in collaborating with the other English colonies, and the profits Pennsylvania would gain by having abundant paper money, had struck the popular fancy and conquered the shopkeepers. Most of Franklin's comrades were so devoted to Keith that the Quakers regarded the Junto with suspicion.

They were not so mistaken, either, for between Franklin and the Junto one of Keith's dearest projects had been brought to triumph. A quarrel on principles and an opposition of interests divided the city at this time into two factions. Philadelphia lacked ready money, and this made business difficulties; the rate of interest was high, and the impatient creditors irritated the debtors. The latter demanded an issue of paper money. But the rich men did not want this, fearing there would be a general depreciation such as had occurred in Massachusetts and the Carolinas. The poor people threatened to leave the city altogether if they couldn't have their way, while the wealthy classes predicted a catastrophe if the Government weakened on this point. The Assembly, forced by the majority of voters, demanded an issue of fifty thousand Pennsylvania pounds, but the governor put his veto to the measure and the quarrel looked as if it would become eternal.

Benjamin and his companions were extremely interested in this dispute and spoke about it a great deal at the Junto meetings. Of course, these ambitious, but far from well-to-do young men, were in favor of the issue.

Benjamin studied the question carefully and considered the various arguments in the light of what he had seen in England and what he had learned in the books of the greatest economist of the time, the head of the mercantile school, William Petty. Guided by his commercial instinct and plebeian common sense, he wrote his first pamphlet on political economy in March, 1729. This carefully written little work, lucid in spite of its difficult subject, was based on solid principles and neglected none of the conclusions. The essential theme of Franklin was that a new issue of bank notes would give prosperity to the needy classes as well as to the wealthy and the Government itself, as the State and capitalists drew direct profit from a condition of general well-being. The reasoning and the reflections in this work were exact, but the principles on which they were founded were new to the colonies. Franklin here revealed his ability to assimilate the best of a predecessor's work, making it his own by cleverly utilizing it, and by his sense of opportunity.

He attracted public favor, and as his writing was moderate and persuasive, he did not make himself objectionable to the wealthy men. Franklin was thought to be a sage, because the measure went through, and coming events were burdened with the verification of his views. With the new issue of paper money, Philadelphia had a new lease on prosperity, and this was quite to the taste of even those who had opposed the measure.

The Assembly was particularly satisfied. The representatives had regretted Keith's departure, for he had always treated them respectfully, and they had not ceased their demand for more paper money. As soon as they had won this victory over the governor, they thought of recompensing those who had aided them. Franklin's name was put in ahead by the friends he had among the representatives. Chief among these was Andrew Hamilton, the great lawyer whom he had met and served in London. It was not very difficult for the latter to secure the post of printer to the province for his protégé; this was a lucrative and honorable situation and it attracted the attention of the public. In order to facilitate the rôle of his protectors, Franklin had the votes of the Assembly printed at his own expense and sent them to each member, so that they could compare his work with Bradford's, who was holding the position at that time. It had to be admitted that he was a good printer as well as an adroit politician. Franklin had luck on his side.

But actually he had just undergone a new crisis. After having believed that the fate of his printing shop was assured, he suddenly ran the risk of being wrecked. Meredith, his partner, in spite of his friendship for Franklin, felt out of place in the city, and to console himself had taken to the bottle too often. Meredith's father, who had counted on Franklin and the printing business to convert his son, was resentful. Furthermore, he was short of money and could not fulfill the obligations he had signed for Franklin. The creditors of the business were impatient and thought of putting up everything for sale. In this extremity Franklin spoke openly to Meredith, who confessed his disgust of the city and his desire to settle in the country. They came to an agreement. Franklin would reimburse the hundred pounds his father had advanced, would pay Meredith's debts, and give him into the bargain a saddle and thirty pounds, upon which the printing shop would belong to him. To find this money Franklin solicited two of his friends and colleagues of the Junto, Coleman and Grace, who were somewhat wealthy. On the fourteenth of July, 1730, he thus became his own master, with his own printing shop on the street, and the rank of a bourgeois in the city of Philadelphia. He also owned a newspaper, was the printer for the Assembly, the center of a club, and one of the young men of the city most in the public eye.

He was even too much on view and he had to be careful. Jealous and lazy gossipers were already beginning their work. Certainly, they didn't have much to say against him, and he himself felt that his conscience was pure enough; he was gradually paying Vernon back his money and was on good terms with all his other creditors. But as to women he was not quite so blameless. No doubt, he did not bother himself much about his passing adventures with various "low women"; he had done nothing wrong. But, in the end, they could do him wrong. He almost reproached himself of treason to Miss Read, who was now leading a sad existence in her ambiguous widowhood. She had lost her first fiancé, Franklin, who had returned too late to marry her, while the man she had married, treated her brutally and then disappeared — people said he was dead — but he hadn't been careful to inform his wife about it. Thus she lived without him and couldn't live lawfully with any one else. Unhappy and solitary, she was a living reproach to Benjamin.

He was consoled and diverted, however, in observing the siege of his friend and host, Godfrey, who wished him to marry his niece. Franklin was continually invited to dinner and then left alone with the girl, until at last nothing seemed to stand in the way of making a permanent connection between the printer's shop and the glazier's. Miss Godfrey was a good girl and Franklin esteemed her, but he had so deeply imbibed of temperance and moderation, at least in regard to suitable young ladies and the virtue of economy, that love was slow in being born. However, by force of the extreme proximity and company of this particular girl, Franklin began to feel a softening change of heart, and went to confide his tender leanings to her uncle. Mr. Godfrey, who had long awaited this confession, was pleased and said so.

But, unfortunately, Godfrey was an exact mathematician, while Franklin was a wise young man given to the practice of virtuous economy. He made it understood that he would be very happy to marry Miss Godfrey along with a dowry of one hundred pounds. This sum was all that was necessary to liquidate his business debts and to furnish a home worthy of his wife. Godfrey dryly remarked that he didn't have such a sum. But this had been foreseen, and Franklin, who had a practical mind, suggested to his possible relation that it would be very easy to mortgage the house. The proposition was perfectly reasonable, but it didn't please Godfrey, who answered the young lover that printing must be a poor business, since both Keimer and his successor, Harry, had gone bankrupt one after the other. He concluded, however, by saying that Franklin could have his niece, nevertheless, but not his money. Benjamin found something shocking in this attitude, and his wisdom restrained him from taking a girl without a dowry. The Godfreys had evidently counted on his love, but that had been a misunderstanding. Marriage was a serious affair for Franklin, not a game in which he would allow his fancy to dominate.

The Godfreys forgot that Franklin had been converted to thirteen virtues, which he practiced systematically. No doubt, the star virtue for this week had been economy. Franklin told Miss Godfrey that she was free and could not consider herself as engaged to him.

The result was that the Godfreys moved away, the glazier attended the Junto less and less regularly, and gave Bradford the job of printing an almanac which, up to now, had been Franklin's work. Mrs. Godfrey tried to patch up the affair, but, when all was said and done, the two men remained separated. Franklin thought Godfrey was an awkward customer. No one will ever know what the Godfreys thought, as they were not given to writing.

Franklin found some satisfaction in having a home all to himself at last, freed from Meredith, the Godfrey family, and all the domestic complications which had hindered him in his work. However, he would have to marry. Without a wife, he felt he could not triumph over his desires. Besides, he was not rich enough to have a servant, and if he wanted to work hard, some one else would have to do the housework and the cooking in the meanwhile. How could he be a good bourgeois and not have a wife?

He dreamed of Miss Read. Since the first days of their love, both of them had been harassed by troubles and disappointments; neither of them was the same that they had been. But Deborah Read was still a robust and pleasant woman, and, in her way, she was quite superior. She talked a little sharply but was sturdy in her work, game and determined in adversity, and watchful of every penny. The preceding five years, with all their difficulties, had taken away some of her freshness, but she was far from being disheartened. She was poor, as her father had died, leaving no money. Her mother, who sold ointments, could not make both ends meet in spite of this charming advertisement;

The Widow READ, removed from the upper End of Highstreet to the new *Printing-Office* near the Market, continues to make and sell her well-known Ointment for the ITCH, with which she has cured abundance of people in and about this City for many years past. It is always effectual for that purpose, and never fails to perform the Cure speedily. It also kills or drives away all Sorts of Lice in once or twice using. It has no offensive Smell, but rather a pleasant one; and may be used without the least Apprehension of Danger, even to a sucking Infant, being perfectly innocent and safe. Price 2 s. a Gally-pot containing an Ounce; which is sufficient to remove the most inveterate Itch, and render the Skin clear and smooth.

She also continues to make and sell her excellent *Family Salve* or Ointment, for Burns and Scalds, (Price 1 s. an Ounce) and several other Sorts of Ointments and Salves as usual.

At the same Place may be had *Lockyer's Pills*, at 3 d, a Pill.

Franklin visited Deborah and her mother from time to time. He began to be intimate with them once more. He knew that they had been hurt and felt pity for them, saying that Deborah would doubtless make a model wife, simple, strong and obedient.

It was good of him to take her for his wife in September, 1730, for he thus saved her from a miserable and solitary destiny. It was good of her to accept him as a husband, for she had a breach of trust to pardon him, and an unknown little boy to accept as a son, William Franklin, whom Benjamin offered at the same time. Thus the little family was immediately completed: Franklin accepted old Mrs. Read, and she accepted the young William Franklin. The secret of his birth was so well guarded that Deborah was often taken for his mother. She neither affirmed nor denied this, and, by her treatment of the child, it was impossible to ascertain whether she was an exacting mother or a none too kind stepmother.

Franklin and she were most discreet about the whole affair, especially he, for he avoided talking about the child from the very first, even with his brothers and sisters. When a vague rumor of his marriage reached his sister, Mrs. Davenport, he wrote to her in the autumn of 1730, "I am not about to be married as you have heard. At present I am much hurried in business, but hope to make a short trip to Boston in the Spring." And this was all the news he gave to his relatives of Deborah, his wife, until three years later.

However, they loved each other. It is clear that Franklin loved her more than any one in the world, even more than his children. She called him her "Pappy", polished the furniture, swept the staircase, kept the store and went on errands; late to bed and early to rise, she could stand the solitude of the evenings Franklin spent at the Junto, as well as the crowds of customers in the shop at the time of the Fair. She was not especially distinguished, but she had lovely eyes and a good appearance. And then, she was a good fighter. Franklin learned it sometimes to his sorrow, but more often to his advantage. Through all their life and adventures, she showed herself to be strong, faithful and courageous, and as awkward in spelling and writing as she was expert in economizing a few pennies. She was at her best as a housewife. When it became necessary for her, as the wife of a great man, to receive the crowds of admirers who thronged her stairways and dirtied her floors, she fretted. She admired her "Pappy", but not as they did. Franklin knew this very well. He understood her. In his first almanac he said: "A house without Woman, and Firelight, is like a body without soul or Spirite." . . . "Never take a wife till thou hast a House (and a Fire) to put her in." He was always attached to her, always defended her, gave her her just dues and never allowed himself to leave her.

What else could he do? He had taken her in 1730 when he had need of her for his business and to become an established little shopkeeper. Later it would have been better not to have had her, when he wanted to stop being an established little shopkeeper.

For this is not only the story of his marriage, but of the most astounding social climbing the eighteenth century had seen. The campaigns of Alexander are nothing compared to the triumphs which the Supreme Being and Mercury accorded to Franklin. But Deborah Read always played her part in vain, for she never understood it very well.

III

OTHERS may have come a cropper at this game, but Franklin played it with such prudence, subtlety and boldness, it is not at all easy to follow him in the sundry paths he chose. He let people know about himself only what he wanted them to know, and to see only what it pleased him they should see. "Three may keep a secret," he said; "if two of them are dead." "Let all men know thee, but no man know thee thoroughly; men freely ford that see the shallows."

All his active life of this period thus remains hidden behind his silence, behind the obscurity of his modest life and the complexity of its circumstances. To be discreet was one of his absolute rules; it was as wise as indispensable, since it prevented men from scorning or crushing him in evil days, as it likewise kept them from being jealous or embarrassing in the times of good fortune. Besides, it suited his character. No one, even those who were closely connected with him, could oblige him to break his silence. His most intimate collaborators, the companions of the Junto, or his wife, could not or would not betray him, the former because they had as much need of secrecy as he, and were vowed by a solemn promise to keep it; the latter, because no one ever listened to what Deborah said, because Franklin didn't tell her everything, and because she would not have understood it all, even if he had.

There were many things that couldn't be said of Benjamin's life in 1730! There were so many errors and peccadillos in his short but lively past! They were enough to make him lose his standing in this little, liberal, pious city: the controversial articles in the *New England Courant*, with their air of irreligion and revolt; the story of Mr. Vernon, which looked like a theft; his rascalities, amorous adventures and atheism in London.

Franklin didn't want his family and friends in New England to hear of his English scandals, of his trivial flirtations in Pennsylvania, and of his daring marriage with his former fiancée. He liked to retain his good standing in Boston, for he was never able to detach himself completely from this city.

Fortunately, the little stories of a printer's workman were not noticed in the newspapers, and these little isolated civilizations in a vast and dissimilar world kept their secrets well. Nevertheless, a stroke of bad luck, and it would have been all over for Franklin.

That everything of his life should be known in some future time mattered little to Benjamin. What he needed now were a few peaceful years, during which he could entirely devote his energies to the preparation of his future without being hindered by his past. He needed time to create a social position of middle-class respectability. In 1730 he was still at the mercy of the slightest happening. Another printer's establishment stood next to his, stronger, older and more respected than his own; Franklin had numerous debts to pay — he still owed Vernon, Meredith, Grace and Coleman — his club was an aid to him, but it might also be a detriment, as it was not favorably regarded by many important men; finally, he had taken a wife who was not actually his, for her hidden husband could reappear some fine day and claim her back. What would the position of Benjamin be then? Absurd, troublesome, and ridiculous.

But Franklin was only twenty-three, he had luck and tenacity. Above all, he knew how to go about his business.

He was humble and worked like a slave. This was to win the favor of public opinion and the smile of fortune. He arose at five in the morning, and spent the first three hours of the day in dressing, saying his prayers, planning his program of the day, continuing the studies he had left off the night before, and then, breakfasting. At eight o'clock he began work and stayed in the printing room until noon. From twelve to two he looked over his books, wrote up his accounts and ate with his wife. From two to six he was again at the printing press. Then, at six, he set his shop in order, had supper, and took recreation in music, playing either the harp, guitar, violin or 'cello, for he handled all these instruments with agreeable skill. Sometimes, instead, with an eye to business, he would go to the tavern to chat with his neighbors, to hear about the latest political happenings, and to consider the opinions of other men. Every Friday evening he went to the Junto. Those evenings were perhaps the most active and useful of his life. Deborah spent more than one of them in solitude. It couldn't be helped. At ten o'clock Benjamin would return to her and then they would go to bed.

Thus he had seven hours for sleep, eight hours for his work in the printing shop, and nine hours to devote to what he liked: his readings, friends, God, politics and his wife. He never neglected his family. He liked to look after his children, though he let Deborah take care of the first years of their bringing up, and had recourse to his servants for their education. In 1734, when his eldest son, William, was no more than four years old, Franklin inserted this advertisement in his paper:

> Any person who has a servant to dispose of that is a scholar and can teach Children Reading, Writing, and Arithmetick, may hear of a Purchaser by enquiring of the Printer hereof.

There was no time lost in the Franklin family.

Franklin neglected nothing and was certain he had been destined to be a leader. While his son was learning to read, he himself was studying the fashionable languages of the time: French, the language of diplomacy, letters and love; Spanish, the language of honor; and Italian, the language of arts and music. He began in 1733. Later, when he had mastered the Latin languages, he took up Latin itself, which he never cared for very much, but which helped him to impress his public. In the eighteenth century a cultivated man could do without his shirt but not without his Latin quotations.

He took advantage of some of his foreign neighbors to jabber a little in German too, for the language was useful in Pennsylvania with its large Teutonic population. Other neighbors taught him a little Gaelic and repeated proverbs in this strange language. His curiosity was as inexhaustible as his patience, and as he knew how to simplify everything, he was really able to benefit from these rapid lessons.

His knowledge of foreign tongues even brought him monetary profit. The English colonies of America were at this time receiving the discontented and disinherited people of the universe, as well as the jailbirds of England. The flood of immigrants was largely directed into Pennsylvania, where the principles of religious toleration, established by Penn, permitted the devout to mingle with the disbelievers, and where the liberal policies of Keith had attracted Palatines, Rhinelanders and Germans of all kinds.

To satisfy his public, a well-informed printer had to know enough Latin to print the books of the ministers, the poets, and the erudite writers who used this language, and to republish the classics for the use of schools; he had to know enough French to keep abreast of what was happening in that country, the center of worldly culture, and to attract and supply his more fashionable customers; he had to be well enough acquainted with German to print the advertisements, Bibles and almanacs which the Germans demanded when they came to the city. As Philadelphia then kept up some commerce with the Spanish colonies, buying sugar and rum, and selling wood and cereals, the Spanish language was very useful for a merchant. Now Franklin was always a merchant; that is what gave him his superiority over the other printers.

Being a merchant gave his business a breadth of view which neither Keimer nor Bradford possessed. Franklin, who had clearly perceived the economic necessities of his country, realized that an American printer could not expect to live like a printer in Paris or London, merely by supplying books to fashionable and literary readers. He saw that one had to be a merchant in this new country, to buy and sell as many things as possible, without specializing or turning up his nose at anything. So he extended his business in all directions. As soon as he was sure of himself, Franklin founded a stationery shop and sold books. It made an annex to his printing room and it was the first store of its kind south of Boston. Up to then, customers had ordered from England.

Franklin sold the books he printed himself, as well as those he received from England, to say nothing of all kinds of printed forms: tickets, leases, bills of sale and lading, contracts for apprentices and other legal papers, which Breintnall, a scrivener for Philadelphia lawyers, helped him to write. He printed a newspaper in English and tried out one in German in 1732; he had published the votes and the minutes of the Pennsylvania Assembly since 1730, of the Delaware Assembly (as well as its paper money), and of the New Jersey Assembly since 1732.

In his shop were also found all kinds of inks at a shilling the bottle; paper, pens, fountain pens, compasses, scales, slates, and lampblack (to make ink) for five shillings a pound. He bought old rags to make paper and sold soap as he had done in his boyhood. There were also to be found in his shop: goose quills,

> . . . very good Chocolate; fine Palm Oyl, very good spermacety, choice bohea tea, the true and genuine Godfrey's Cordial; Compasses and Scales, Good Rhode Island Cheese and Codfish, Choice Mackrel to be sold by the Barrel, Quadrants, Mariners Compasses, Fine broad Scarlet Cloth, fine broad black Cloth, a new fishing net, a very neat new fashioned vehickle, or four wheel'd chaise, very convenient to carry weak or other sick persons old or young, very good iron stoves, Senaka Rattlesnake Root, with directions how to use it in the Plurishy . . .

Thus from 1733 to 1736, Benjamin Franklin could be seen hustling about in his house near the market, dressed in old leather breeches, with a big leather apron and a red flannel shirt, now busy at work in the shop behind, setting the marbles, putting the last touch on an article, now giving orders to his workman, Whitemarsh, or his apprentice, John Rose, or carving a woodcut; while in the shop Deborah Franklin, followed by her two little boys, aged respectively two and four, attended to the customers. The activity of the husband and the loquacity of the wife seemed to fill the house. When one entered into the clean rooms in back — clean, but not very well arranged, with small packs of books, almanacs, and newspapers spread about, and glue and paste pots piled pell-mell — it seemed like coming into the laboratory of a mysterious and joyful alchemist. What conversations went on within these walls about the weather and the moral value of sacrifice; about the price of goose quills and the price of slaves! . . . It was hard to determine what most to admire: the prodigious activity which reigned in this place or its amazing disorder; it seemed as though the Franklins had charmed every object and possessed a secret unknown to other mortals.

The secret of Franklin was his memory and his shrewd cleverness. It was easy for him to recall the slightest detail of even distant events, and he had a plan for everything. As a storekeeper he bought and sold all kinds of merchandise. As a printer and journalist he kept up his connections with every one; he corresponded with his friends in London, and their letters in answer made news for him. In 1733, he took a trip to New England, which permitted him to renew the intimate friendship of his family and his old friends of Boston. On his way he stopped off at Newport to visit his brother James (who had set up his business in Rhode Island), for they were reconciled now and had joined parties. New York was near by. Thanks to his friends in New Jersey, he remained the official printer to that province and was in touch with everything that was going on there. He was also the official printer to Delaware. And from September, 1731, he had been the partner of his former workman, Whitemarsh, who had founded a printing establishment in Charleston, South Carolina.

Franklin felt kindly towards every one so that every one would feel kindly towards him. He advanced his ideas cautiously, often laughingly, and always with an easy manner. Perhaps they weren't noticed sometimes, but at any rate, they couldn't offend. Franklin, himself, was never offended at anything. He gave his attention to any one freely, to the clergymen who wanted to discuss theology, to the scholars who were attracted by Virgil, to the farmers who were interested in their harvests. All he asked was that they would not engross him completely or compromise him. He wanted to be on good terms with all the world, provided he did not have to close his door on any special person. He directed the Junto along Deistical and anti-clerical lines, rented a pew in the Presbyterian Church in 1730, and tried to worm his way into Masonry.

Above all, he was careful not to cut off his political relations with any one. A period of calm had returned to Pennsylvania; the colony had become richer and larger, and the crowds of Palatines who flooded in were followed by numerous Irish immigrants. The price of ground went up, the city began to be extended, business was good; it was not the moment for intrigues. There were no distinct parties in the Assembly, and the two different groups, that of the proprietors with their allies, the rich Quakers, and that of the lower middle class, who had the majority, collaborated without a hitch. For Franklin, it was not a matter of arousing opposition, but of having his collaboration accepted by every one. In this city, dedicated to brotherly love, filled with Quakers who called themselves Friends, it was really good will and friendship which brought in profits. Franklin possessed good will to an infinite degree. He acquired as many friends as he could, and did secure more than any other man of his century. The pride of the aristocracy in this epoch was in taking a choice; Franklin, with his bourgeois wisdom, found pride in taking everything. This was his capital, his money, his method, his essential principle.

His career was the apotheosis of the solid "good fellow."

IV

To be the friend of everybody one must be pleasant and have a supple mind. But sometimes force is necessary. There are some friendships which must be taken by assault. Such was the case of Freemasonry for Franklin.

He wanted to be a Mason and he needed to be one. But at first his chances seemed slim enough. The solid bourgeois men, who made up the Lodge of Saint John of Jerusalem in Philadelphia, didn't think highly of this much traveled, adventurous, jolly little printer. He did not belong to their environment. Besides, his club, the Junto, a society of little artisans, was a kind of rival.

But Franklin wanted to belong to this circle of serious, rich, influential men, who could aid him so much in his career. In London he had seen how rapidly Masonry made its way among the important men, among the intellectuals and the most intelligent of the upper middle class. It spread over the United States with the same success. Philadelphia had its lodge in 1727, Boston in 1733, Georgia in 1734, South Carolina in 1735, etc. In Europe, Paris had its first lodge in 1725, but Florence had to wait until 1733, Hamburg till 1737, Berlin, 1740, and St. Petersburg, 1771. America wasn't behind the times.

Franklin realized what power was represented by such international affiliations and how important they could be for a journalist and printer; he knew also that all his ideas on religion, politics and the future of humanity corresponded with those of Masonry. He decided to force his way into the society and succeeded.

Franklin was not without weapons, and he was quick to see the weak point of Masonry. From its very start, Masonry had been surrounded in mystery, and this disquieted the Government and annoyed the idlers who could not join. Secrecy was the power of the Masons in business and politics, but it was also their weakness. If the newspapers were to stir up public opinion against it, the Masons risked being abolished, either by the furious crowd, or the hostile Government.

Franklin made the Masons realize that he could use his newspaper either to serve them or to harm them. In several numbers of 1730 he printed the news relative to English lodges and their functioning, and his accounts were written in an amiable tone. Then he made a sign to show that it was time he be chosen, either as a friend or an enemy. On December 8, 1730, he published a report sent from London in the *Pennsylvania Gazette* which claimed to contain a complete description of the Masonic mysteries.

By the Death of a Gentleman who was one of the Brotherhood of FREE MASONS, there has lately happen'd a Discovery of abundance of their secret Signs and Wonders, with the mysterious Manner of their Admission into that Fraternity. The following is a true copy of a Manuscript which the Deceased had written for the benefit of his own private Remembrance. . . . Their Great Secret is THAT THEY HAVE NO SECRET AT ALL; and when once a man is entered he is himself obliged, *se defendendo*, to carry on the Jest with as solemn a Face as the rest. We shall not use many Words to persuade the Publick that the following Piece is genuine; it carries all the Marks of Truth in itself; we would only refer the Reader to the Conduct of the Brotherhood upon this occasion; if they *ridicule* it or look *very grave* upon it, or if they are *very angry*; and endeavor to *decry* it, he may be satisfied it is the *real truth*.

The Masons were wiser than to discuss the matter. Some weeks later they invited the shrewd printer to join them. And Franklin, quite ready "to carry on the jest", seriously, accepted.

From the first and always he was a faithful Mason. He attended the meetings of the lodge regularly. He read some of his discourses there. He set himself to the task of beating down the numerous serious prejudices which the public held against the Masons. In the same newspaper in which he had published his impertinent report against them, he now printed, on

May 13, 1731, an extract on the subject which was taken from Chamber's "Dictionary." From time to time he inserted discreet but flattering notes on Masonic activities and ceremonies at home and abroad. But, above all, he was faithful to the spirit of Masonry, as it was then described: "It tends to promote Friendship, Society, mutual Assistance, and Good Fellowship."

It was thus that he pushed himself forward. By a master stroke he pushed the Junto forward also, so that it occupied a place in the good society of Philadelphia. He effected this by persuading his comrades of the Junto to found a public library, the first one in English America, and when this was accomplished it gave the society an opportune prestige. Books were fashionable. It was modish to be learned; people boasted of their erudition, and admired the sciences greatly, especially if they were in print. Unfortunately, books were expensive. Readers borrowed books from each other and from their ministers, but they weren't at all the books they preferred. A few rich men had fine libraries, and they were very proud of them. The only important one in Pennsylvania was that of James Logan, who had been Penn's opulent secretary, and who was now the friend and adviser of Penn's children. He was also their man-of-all-work in America, had eliminated Keith for them, and kept an eye on the governor and the Assembly.

Franklin realized what an intellectual and moral rôle the Junto would play if it became the largest center of books in the province, and also what social importance it would have. First, he attempted to organize the borrowing of books between the members. Every one was to offer all the books he didn't often need to a central library. Thus the members could enjoy the books of the whole group. The experiment did not succeed very brilliantly. Franklin soon perceived that no one was careful of the books or offered their best ones. The collection which had been composed in this way was disparate, absurd and uninteresting.

Franklin then proposed another system: to form an autonomous society, with the Junto as a center, but with its own budget, librarian, premises and collection. The books would be bought by a selected committee and placed at the disposition of the members. The idea met with favor from the start, the subscription was only forty shillings as a first payment, and ten a year, and this outlay of money was more than equaled by the profit and pleasure derived from the library.

So at one stroke the Junto won the favor of the educated and powerful men in the town; Thomas Godfrey obtained the patronage of the great Logan, who promised, moreover, to help choose the books. Another member of the club, Robert Grace, persuaded his correspondent in London, Peter Collinson, a rich Quaker merchant, to be their councilor and adviser. The two patrons were serious, pious and erudite men. They were flattered to have been chosen, and were doubly pleased because books interested them and they liked to do good. Collinson belonged to the most powerful and respected group of English Quakers. He had connections at Court and was strongly linked to the Penns.

Thus from its very beginning, the Library Company of Philadelphia was talked about in the best English and Philadelphian society. The Junto, as mother and godmother of the library, profited from the offspring, while Franklin, as father, won prestige and the opportunity of meeting intelligent, influential men, who would know how to appreciate his value. They ceased to suspect Franklin and the Junto of shady political schemes.

Franklin organized this project with system. His close friends, Breintnall and Coleman, became the treasurer and secretary. For librarian, he chose a young French immigrant, who had recently settled in Philadelphia and whom he had employed for a while in his printing shop. He was an earnest and educated lad, speaking German and English besides his native tongue, and was named Louis Timothee. Every Wednesday from two to three, and every Saturday from ten to four, Timothee was at his place in the library to attend to the readers' wants. For this work he received three pounds sterling every trimester. He was the first librarian of America.

The directors met regularly to attend to the administration and to choose new books for the library. Franklin's influence in these meetings was dominant and the choice of books clearly indicates his intellectual leanings at this time. Out of forty-five works which the directors recommended to the company in 1731, nine were devoted to science, eight to history, eight to politics and morals, six to law and philosophy, three to the English language, two to geography, five to useful arts and crafts, two to dictionaries, and two to the classics: Homer and Virgil translated into English. There were no novels, no dramas, no books of contemporary poetry or theology. The places of honor were accorded to Plutarch and Tacitus among the ancient writers, and to Sidney and Thomas Gordon among the moderns; the library was practical, but it had also an intellectual import, and this choice showed that Franklin remained a good Mason.

No one could find fault with it either, Franklin had managed the affair with such tact and discretion. Though his own ideas and interests had not been neglected, the public had been well served. Philadelphia was indebted to Franklin for this institution which added so much to her glory.

The library became a precious weapon for him. It enriched his culture, opened the doors of distinguished homes to him, propagated his ideas, and by stimulating reading among the people, increased the circulation of his newspaper. At the same time the Junto kept him as the leader of the lower middle class, the Masonic Lodge linked him to the upper society.

He had gone up another rung of the ladder. The meetings of the library directors and the evenings he spent at the Junto and the lodge enabled him to finish his political education and to prepare himself for his parliamentary career. The sessions of eighteenth-century Masonic Lodges afforded fine opportunities to learn the art of oratory. For Franklin they were all the more precious as he was neither eloquent nor fluent. To speak at his ease, he needed the cordial atmosphere of an intimate group of listeners. He found this at the Junto, the library and the lodge.

"No better relation than a Prudent and Faithful Friend," he said. Franklin's great power came from his ability to enter into any kind of an environment and his knowledge of what use to make of his friends. With Hamilton in the Assembly, Logan in the Council, Grace and Coleman in the Junto and among the merchants, Collinson in London, Franklin had the necessary nucleus of friendly connections which could shelter him from his past and enable him to grapple boldly with the future.

Franklin took account of all that could help him to success, but he was, above all, a printer. He liked this craft which demanded manual skill, intelligence and perspicacity in equal shares. To be a successful printer one had to possess the qualities of a workman, a merchant, and an intellectual; in Franklin they were all marvelously combined. Never was there such a lively brain in such a solid body! What a contrast to Voltaire's bald and scintillating intelligence, to Rousseau's burdened and eloquent heart! Franklin enjoyed his manual work as though it were an exercise. He had need of fatigue all his life, and when he no longer printed to make a living, he did so to divert himself.

Franklin enlarged his printing shop carefully. He ordered his equipment from England and he kept it in good shape, cleaning the type himself and buying new fonts when the need arose. Everything he published had such a neat and substantial appearance that his books were easily recognizable. He adopted and continued the custom, current at the beginning of the eighteenth century, of capitalizing every noun, as he thought (and very correctly) that such a practice added to the legibility and elegance of the page. He used very black inks, and paper as white as he could find. Franklin was even skillful enough to carve little woodcuts to decorate his advertisements, thus making them more attractive. One was a vessel with all sails unfurled, another a wig, another a sugar loaf, another the king's coat-of-arms. . . . He accomplished all his work with such care and exactitude that many customers came to him. His books were so well made, the texts were so accurate and readable, that even the ministers, who were the principal authors of

America in those days, gave him their work more and more. In 1733 and 1734, Bradford printed scarcely anything but almanacs, while Franklin published books of all kinds, three at least being of a religious character. These latter he printed with all due decorum. But while he was setting up the fantastic theological flights of the ministers, with their dull philosophical sequences, he amused himself by imagining all kinds of devastating replies and parodies. However, like a good merchant, he wanted to please every one, as is evident by a glance at the list of his publications.

In 1729 he published a book against slavery by Ralph Sandford, a theological work by John Thomson, and a treatise by John Meredith "proving that the Jewish or Seventh Day Sabbath is abrogated or Repealed", a translation of David's Psalms by Watts, and a mystical book by Woolverton.

In 1730 he printed a French grammar, three books in German (mystical and pious) and one in Gaelic, as well as a new attack on Slavery by Sandford.

In 1731, two poems by George Webb, one of them called "Bachelor's Hall" which was very funny, and a book on piety by Alexander Arscot came from his press.

In 1732, he issued two new editions of Arscot's book, a sermon by D. Evans, a volume of German hymns, and another book by Evans on the religious education of children: "A help for Parents and heads of families to instruct those under their care in the first Principles of Religion", and "In Honour of the Gout or a Rational Discourse demonstrating that the Gout is one of the greatest blessings which can befal Mortal Man", by Philander Misiatros, an incendiary sermon called "The Tradition of the Clergy destructive of Religion" — a sermon preached at Wakefield in Yorkshire, and a very tame essay of Joseph Morgan, "The Nature of Riches."

Thus, from year to year, he continued his care-free routine of taking anything he could find. But actually, the publishing of these books represented the most precarious and least part of his business. The almanacs, the official publications for the assemblies of Pennsylvania and New Jersey, and the various printing jobs for the proprietors represented the real source of his profits.

Nevertheless, he spent many more hours of thought and imagination and skill on his newspaper, which was one of his cherished projects. Franklin had all the gifts of the journalist; quickness of mind, and expressive simplicity of style, a sense of the comical, the ability to clarify problems and situations, the instinct for timeliness, and even the talent of speaking authoritatively on a subject he knew only superficially. His newspaper not only provided him with daily bread but with amusement as well; it was a stage on which he could play a hundred parts, and he made the most of them.

However, he didn't neglect the practical side. The subscription for his newspaper was ten shillings a year, which was sometimes paid by his subscribers and sometimes not. The paper was not very renumerative, especially as Franklin was not the postmaster and had to make underhand arrangements with the post-riders in order to have his papers delivered. He wasn't sure even then that they would reach their destinations, for Bradford, the postmaster, had no good will for Franklin, and as there was no fixed rule about the delivery of newspapers, Franklin was often embarrassed by complaints from his subscribers, saying that their papers hadn't arrived. He had to beat Bradford in some other way, and chose to do so by means of the advertisements. They furnished the largest part of the income of a newspaper in the eighteenth century, as they do now. Generally, it was three shillings for the first insertion, and two shillings apiece for the following ones. A popular newspaper in 1734 often had as many as ten.

Franklin was one of the first to solicit advertisements systematically and to give them a large space in his paper, devoting a column to advertisements on each page, whereas his rivals only gave a few lines. His friends of the Junto and the Masonic Lodge helped a great deal in finding customers. Thus his newspaper became a picturesque mirror of the life in Philadelphia. It informed the public concerning the sale of slaves, or announced that such and such a one had sold his shop, another had lost his horse, that a servant had run away, that such and such a gentleman would not pay the debts of his wife who had gone off with another gentleman. Weeping wives begged their husbands to return while others announced that they would wait no longer. And among these sad and gay, moving and indifferent advertisements, Franklin would slip in some fanciful ones. One day he published the following: "Pray let the prettiest creature in this Place know by publishing this that if it was not for her affectation she would be absolutely irresistible."

And the week after he gave the answers of the ladies of Philadelphia:

Mr. Franklin, I cannot conceive who your Correspondent means by the prettiest Creature in this Place; but I can assure either him or her, that she who is truly so, has no Affectation at all.

Sir, Since your last week's Paper I have look'd in my Glass a thousand Times, I believe, in one Day; and if it was not for the Charge of Affectation I might, without Partiality, believe myself the Person meant.

Mr. Franklin, I must own that several have told me, I am the prettiest Creature in this Place; but I believe I shou'd not have been tax'd with Affectation if I cou'd have thought as well of them as they do of themselves.

Sir, your Sex calls me pretty; my own affected. Is it from Judgment in the one, or Envy in the other?

Mr. Franklin, They that call me affected are greatly mistaken; for I don't know that I ever refus'd a kiss to any Body but a Fool.

Friend Benjamin, I am not at all displeased at being charged with Affectation. Thou know'st the vain People call Decency of Behavior by that name.

This was Franklin's art. Everything he wrote was pervaded with his good humor, and the jokes he slipped in here and there were not like those of Voltaire, sharp and sarcastic, but were filled with rich laughter. While other editors thought themselves obliged to burden their newspapers with long and monotonous accounts of the European wars, with reports of the illnesses, voyages and marriages of kings, princes and dukes, and to include no local news but that of a few crimes, of barns struck by lightning, of some Indian raids, or reprints of long sermons by zealous preachers, Benjamin peppered his pages with picturesque little stories, which were the most lively attraction of his paper then and remain so to this day. On February 10, 1730, he printed the following:

An unhappy man; one Sturgis, upon some Difference with his Wife determined to drown himself in the River, and she (Kind Wife) went with him, it seems to see it faithfully performed, and accordingly stood by silent and unconcerned during the whole transaction: he jumped near Carpenter's Wharff, but was timely taken out again before what he came about was thoroughly effected, so that they were both obliged to return home as they came and put up for that time with the disappointment.

On March 16, 1732, Franklin printed this little story:

"A servant girl near Christine Bridge hanged herself lately with a design, as 'tis thought, to haunt a young fellow who refused to marry her."

And on February 27, 1734, he wrote:

"On Tuesday last a widow of this town was married in her shift without any other apparel, upon a supposition that such a procedure would secure her husband in the law from being sued for any debt of his predecessor."

But Franklin's news was no fresher than that of his rivals and he didn't even look for different sources. Like every one, he borrowed largely from the English papers and shamelessly lifted columns from the other American papers (Boston, New York and Maryland); he included the accounts of captains whom he had met in the taverns, various official communications, and sometimes a letter from a friend or a commercial correspondent in a foreign land. But to all these items of news he gave a turn of style which was peculiarly his own. Later, owing to his numerous business and Masonic connections, he was able to secure fresher news, but this was scarcely felt until 1739.

Up to this date, his newspaper had the same appearance as the others: the first page taken up with European news in the summer and autumn — that is to say, when the European boats could arrive easily in Philadelphia — and the second with local news and letters from the readers. When he had a third or fourth page, which occurred only in summer, he published the proceedings of the Assembly, advertisements, the arrival and departure of boats, rates of money exchange, etc. Such was the typical distribution of the pages, which the editor, of course, was free to change. Franklin often took advantage of this liberty to insert an amusing essay, a sharp discussion, or a sensational piece of news from Europe, — anything to liven up his newspaper.

The letters of the readers were his triumph. Readers never tired of writing to him, and he never tired of publishing them; it is easy to imagine that he often wrote the letters for them. In 1729 there appeared "An Excellent Piece of Satire" against the tribe of commentators, annotators and critics. In 1730 there were two letters, one in answer to the other. A merchant affirms in the first that his customers force him to lie, while in the second, a customer answers that the merchant has robbed him, thanks to his lies. In 1731 there was printed the sorry letter of Anthony Afterwit, who had been ruined by his wife. She was a shrew, who wished to play the grand lady, and so gave teas and indulged in other extravagances. Then there was the letter of Celia Single in which she scolds the editor for being too partial to men and attempts to readjust the balance, and the letter of Alice Addertongue, who has organized a bureau for the sale and exchange of calumnies, slanders and other feminine wares; and finally, the best of all (June 26, 1732), the letter in which a worried reader propounds this question: "Suppose A discovers that his neighbour B has corrupted his wife and injured his bed; now if 'tis probable that by A's acquainting B's wife with it and using proper sollicitations he can prevail with her to consent that her husband be used in the same manner, *is he justified in doing it?*" The answer was supplied by another reader on July 3, 1732, and was short and to the point: "If an Ass kicks me, should I kick him again?"

In order to please all his readers, Franklin carefully balanced the grave and gay in his columns; at the same time he printed these bantering letters from the readers, he included serious letters from ministers on religious topics as well, and letters from Palatine immigrants, who complained that the captain of their boat had treated them atrociously. But Franklin always gave more room to the jovial items. Even if he accepted everything from his public, he wasn't going to allow himself to employ a correctly banal or distinguished tone all the time. On August 8, 1734, he inserted this little notice: "By being too nice in the choice of little pieces sent me by my correspondants to be printed I had almost discouraged them from writing to me any more. For the time to come and that my paper may become still more generally agreeable I have resolved not to regard my own honour so much in what I print."

This permitted him to pass over some paragraphs, which his more ecclesiastical readers must have found a little off-color. But after Franklin's adroit professional remark, to what could they object? For those who could read and understand, the newspaper included a number of serious articles outside of those on theology, and now and then a pleasantry in which much was written between the lines. Franklin was careful, however, to keep out of open campaigns. He knew from his *Courant* experience how much they might cost. To have a correct idea of the breadth of his plan one must know his whole life, his strategies, his work in the Junto and the lodge, and above all to study the ideas he slipped into his almanac.

His almanac was the pivot of his commercial success and of his popularity in America. The lodge, the Junto, the library, had only a local influence, but the almanac was sent all over the country. Although a very few persons owned libraries in the eighteenth-century America, every one possessed two books; the Bible and the almanac. The former told you what to worship and what to do and the latter, when and how. The almanac was the guide to both the country and the city people.

Neither poor nor rich could do without it. It was a complete calendar, noting the holidays, the quarters of the moon, the changes in season, the length of days and tides, the dates of fairs, and the days when the courts opened and closed. As Franklin said of it in verse:

> Here I sit naked like some fairy Elf
> My seat a pumpkin; I grudge no man's Pelf,
> Tho' I have no bread nor cheese upon myself;
> I'll tell thee gratis, when safe it is,
> To purge, to breed, to cut thy Cattle or — thyself.

Besides, the almanac had a mysterious and magical character. It predicted the weather, foretold the future, and gave information on the constellations, their courses and influences. It portended catastrophes. If these successors of Merlin, who wrote the almanacs, thought themselves to be something of enchanters, it was probably due to the desire of the public. Astrology was very much in vogue and even a famous writer like Swift had made fun of it in vain (1708). It occupied an important place in business, agriculture and private life. Astrology was employed in determining the future of newly born children, the date to choose for a hunt, the propitious period for sowing seed and gathering grapes, the opportune moment for the departure of boats. The slave-traders were particularly superstitious in this respect, and before weighing anchor, would always have a horoscope of the voyage made. Wise, serious and pious people also believed in astrology, for as late as 1728, candidates for a degree at Harvard discussed such topics as these: "Do medicinal herbs operate by planetary power?" or, "That the heavenly bodies produce changes in the bodies of animals." And on the eve of the Revolution in 1770 the Faculty proposed such subjects as these: "Is a comet which only appears after many years more a foreshadowing of divine wrath than a planet which rises daily?"

Everybody turned to the astrologers, and the publisher of almanacs had an immense public. These little books were faithful mirrors of the preoccupations of the times. There were High Church almanacs which listed the saints; Tory almanacs like Gadbury's, which mentioned the "Martyr", Charles I; ardent Whig almanacs like the one called "The Protestant Almanack", in which were enumerated "the Bloody Aspects, Fatal Oppositions, Diabolical Conjunctions and Pernicious Revolutions of the Papacy against the Lord and his annointed."

There were serious and literary ones, like "The English Apollo", by Richard Saunders. There were jovial ones like "Poor Robin Almanack", which, in the place of saints, printed droll maxims and burlesque advice, and intermingled the chronicle of English kings with such fantastic dates as:

> Since young maids were as cold as cow-cumbers, Bands were abolished, and there was no cuckolds: 1057; Since J. W. found out the invention to know a Leicester man, viz, taking him by the shoulder and shaking him as you would shake a Pear tree, and if the Beans rattle in his Belly; then he is a Leicestershire man, else not, 4; Since E. C. found out the Perpetual motion was in women's tongues, 7.

The dates of national, religious and profane events were heaped together pell-mell: the creation of the world, 3948; the Flood, 2293; the destruction of Sodom and Gomorrah, 1902; the Fall of Troy, 1182; the founding of London, 1107; the founding of York, 996.

The almanac writers, knowing the extent of the empire that they exerted over their simple readers, sought to influence them by inserting maxims and pieces of good advice. Finding it so easy to fool the public, the English almanac authors gave their imaginations free rein. The American almanacs were perhaps more serious and uniform. They were relied upon to such an extent that the authors didn't dare take too many liberties. Sooner or later they would lose by such a procedure. Their customers would turn against them, as was actually the case with Sower in Philadelphia.

One day a German farmer came into Sower's shop, his clothes streaming in rivulets. He was furious and demanded reparation for his damages. Early that morning the simple farmer had set off for the city with his produce and some woolen goods his wife had knitted. Before leaving, he conscientiously looked in his almanac and found there would be "good weather." Thus encouraged, he left without putting a hood over his wagon or wearing a coat. Towards noon it began to rain in torrents and he began to have his doubts. But in the evening, when he finally arrived in Philadelphia, after having been in the rain all day, his clothes soaked, his merchandise spoiled, words could not do justice to his fury, and he went to the printer's shop and menaced Sower for having sold him a false almanac. But Sower piously answered him: "O Friend, Friend, be not thus angry, for although It was I that made the almanac, the Lord God made the weather."

In London, Franklin had noticed these little books which sold so well, had even thumbed the pages of "Poor Robin", which amused him with its quaint wit, and the "Almanac of Richard Saunder", which pleased him because of its wise maxims. When Franklin founded his own printing shop he had his colleague, Godfrey, write an almanac which he published in 1729, 1730, and 1731. At the same time he published the almanac of J. Jermann, and imported the "Poor Robin" from England. Now to economize on the expense of a writer — thirty pounds sterling was the price in general — he decided to write one himself, thus adding the material and moral profits of an author to the gains of a printer.

He had all the qualities necessary to succeed in such an enterprise. He had to make a few calculations which were simple enough, have some notions of history, which he could easily extract from other almanacs, to secure some local information on the exact days of the openings of fairs and law courts, and to sprinkle the whole with humor, pathos, wisdom and caprice. He did not plume himself on originality. Since the almanac of Titan Leeds (whose father, Daniel, had also written almanacs) had succeeded in Pennsylvania, Franklin adopted exactly the same formula, the same classifications, the same format. As for his maxims, he took them a little from everywhere, — from his chance readings, his memory, and his reflections, but mostly from the almanacs of his predecessors.

Whenever he found one which pleased him he rewrote it in several ways. For his jokes he sought his inspiration mainly from the two English almanacs which had impressed him "Poor Robin" and "Richard Saunder" — and combining the first words of these two titles he created his own "Poor Richard." He also borrowed some sarcastic witticisms from Swift.

The full title of his great work was:

Poor Richard 1733. An Almanack for the year of Christ 1733, being the first after Leapyear, wherein is contained the Lunations, Eclipses, Judgment of the Weather, Spring Tides, Planets Motions and Mutual Aspects, Sun and Moon's Rising and Setting, Length of Days, Times of High Water, Fairs, Courts and observable Days. Fitted to the Latitude of forty degrees and a meridian of five hours West from London, but may without sensible Error serve all the adjacent places, even from Newfoundland to South Carolina. By Richard Saunders, Philom, Philadelphia. Printed and sold by Benjamin Franklin at the New Printing Office near the Market.

And as a sensational novelty, he announced in his *Gazette:*

Just published for 1733: *POOR RICHARD:* An ALMANACK containing the Lunations, Eclipses, Planets Motions and Aspects, Weather, Sun and Moon's Rising and Setting, Highwater, etc, besides many pleasant and witty Verses, Jests, and Sayings, Author's Motive of Writing, Prediction of the Death of his Friend Mr. Titan Leeds, Moon no Cuckold, Batchelor's Folly, Parson's Wine and Baker's Pudding, Short Visits, Kings and Bears, New Fashions, Game for Kisses, Katherine's Love, Different Sentiments, Signs of a Tempest, Death a Fisherman, Conjugal Debate, Men and Melons, H. the Prodigal, Breakfast in Bed, Oyster lawsuit, etc. By Richard SAUNDERS, Philomat. Printed and Sold by B. Franklin Price 3s 6d per Dozen.

The start was promising and what followed was no less good. Franklin gave his verve free rein. Rude, picturesque, and rich in humor, his almanac described the life and preoccupations of the American colonies in raw colors and bold strokes. It was an adequate expression of this country where the people worked hard and economized penny by penny, where the great happenings of the year were the snow in December, the freezing weather in January, the harvests of September, and an occasional daring joke on the minister when his back was turned. Franklin's personal faults of taste appear also; he never tires of laughing at the expense of the American girl, who, because she has eaten too many candied apples has bad teeth, and who is the source of so much work (and some pleasure) to men. He is inexhaustible in his attacks against bores, complaining, like the busy man he was, against the persons who bothered him. He speaks of cider, of debtors, of women, of priests, of the great and small, of God, and, in short, of everything:

After three days men grow weary of a wench, a guest and weather rainy.

Men and melons are hard to know. (1733)

Onions can make ev'n heirs and widows weep. (1734)

A ship under sail and a big bellied woman are the handsomest things that can be seen common. (1735)

Three things are men most likely to be cheated in, a horse, a wig and a wife.

Marry your daughter and eat fresh fish betimes. (1736)

Such an almanac had to succeed. Franklin hastened its success by an opportune discussion. He amused himself in his first almanac by continuing a witticism Swift had employed in his "Predictions for 1708 by Isaac Bickerstaff, Esquire", who had violently and quaintly denounced the makers of almanacs by predicting the death of one of them, a man named Partridge. A grotesque discussion in the newspapers followed, which stirred up much amusement in England, and which did not escape Franklin's notice. So he announced boldly and with suavity (the element he added to Swift, who was more roughshod in his attack) the death of his friend and colleague, Titan Leeds. The stars had made it known to him beyond a doubt, and Titan Leeds knew it very well too. This was the reason why Richard, who was not rich and had to make his living, had taken up the pen. Leeds was furious at this gruesome maneuver. He answered, stirring up a fine battle, to the great joy of Franklin, who needed just this advertisement to launch his book successfully. The quarrel lasted eight years, and ended by the clear triumph of Poor Richard, as Titan Leeds really died.

This almanac carried the name and ideas of Franklin everywhere. He had expressly written this book to present his ideas in a bold and lively manner, the same ideas he expressed secretly at the lodge or the Junto, or slipped into his newspaper in phrases of double meaning. Three great ideas preoccupied him then: the social and Deistical morale he wished to preach in order to repair former wrongs and to prepare a glorious future for Humanity; the propagation of knowledge, which he insisted on like a good Mason; and the most daring Whig program, to which he always adhered, and which his affiliation with Masonry had clarified: the equality of men, the rights of the people, the danger of kings, and the public menace of the Clergy.

One of his first concerns was to repair the evil caused by his brochure, "A Dissertation on Liberty and Necessity", in which he had denied the existence of Providence, the distinct reality of good and evil, the personality of God, and his rôle of rewarder and avenger, in order to base living on pure instinct and the code of pleasure. He addressed his comrades at the Junto, entitling his speech, "A Lecture of The Providence of God in the Government of the World." He said to them,

> . . . I am particularly discouraged when I reflect that you are all my intimate pot-companions, who have heard me say a thousand silly things in conversation, and therefore have not that laudable partiality and veneration for whatever I shall deliver, that good people commonly have for their spiritual guides.

He spoke very seriously and eloquently on the existence of Providence and the omnipotence of God, which is exercised over men directly and indirectly, for, as he said, it was impossible not to believe in God, as a first premise, and if there were a God, he could not be inert or stupid. He finished his discourse with;

> . . . I conclude that believing in Providence we have the foundation of all true religion; for we should love and revere the Deity for

his goodness, and thank him for his benefits; we should adore him for his wisdom, fear him for his power, and pray to him for his favor and protection. And this religion will be a powerful regulator of our actions, give us peace and tranquility within our own minds and render us benevolent, useful and beneficial to others.

But he did not think that his work was ended here. In June and July of 1730 he inserted in his *Gazette* a series of "Dialogues between Philoctes and Horatio, meeting accidentally in the fields, concerning virtue and pleasure", where he took up in detail all his former arguments and reduced the code of pleasure to nothing. Numerous maxims were distilled from this new wisdom in his almanac:

Relation without friendship, friendship without power, power without will, will without effect, effect without profit, and profit without virtue are not worth a farto. . . .

He is ill clothed that is bare of virtue. (1733)

Nothing brings more pain than too much pleasure, nothing more bondage than too much liberty (or libertinism).

Finally, in 1738, he concluded by this bit of advice, which was also a disclosure:

Each year one vicious habit rooted out,
In time might make the worst man good throughout.

Thus he preached without tiring, by written word and word of mouth, making an example of all his acts. He did not preach the Christianity of Boston or Rome, but a rationalistic doctrine which "extended" them, though supressing at the same time the mystical element and revelation. Thus, too, he wrote for his own use, a Pater, analogous to the one of Christ, but more brief and "reasonable." He had eliminated its effusions and archaic phrases.

All this he replaced by a social and utilitarian morale; he put his faith in science, in the future of humanity and in progress. Learned societies, newspapers, books, and almanacs, all served to spread his doctrine.

At the lodge he read a paper, "Self Denial Not the Essence of Virtue", which he published in his *Gazette*, February 18,

1735. It advanced the idea that a horse is no less valuable if it had been born a naturally good pacer, and that a man should receive no less merit because he could do good without effort. He concluded in these terms:

> The truth is, that temperance, justice, charity etc. are virtues whether practised with or against our inclinations, and the man who practises them, merits our love and esteem; and self denial is neither good nor bad, but as it is applied. He that denies a vicious inclination is virtuous in proportion to his resolution; but the most perfect virtue is above all temptations; such as the virtue of the saints in heaven; and he who does a foolish, indecent or wicked thing, merely because it is contrary to his inclination (like some mad enthusiasts I have read of, who ran about naked, under the notion of taking the cross) is not practising the *reasonable science of virtue* but is a lunatic.

It would be hard to deny the old ascetic morale of Christianity more downrightly than this, in order to replace it by the "reasonable science of virtue." Furthermore, he expressed these same precepts as precisely in another lecture published in his *Gazette* of November 20, 1735, "On True Happiness." Here he argued that the satisfaction of natural desires should be guided by reason, and recommended the practice of virtue as the best way of securing a stable happiness in this world here below and in the world hereafter. Likewise, in the "Poor Richard" almanac he wrote: "Sin is not hurtful because it is forbidden, but it is forbidden because it is hurtful." "Nor is a duty beneficial because it is commanded, but it is commanded because it is beneficial", and he commended economy and unremitting hard work, which is hard on the body but pleasant to the heart and purse. "Deny self, for self's sake." (1735) "If you know how to spend less than you get, you have the philosopher's stone."

At this same time he announced the reign of reason, knowledge, and wisdom, in the lodge and in his *Gazette* for October 3, 1735, in which he praised the "Usefulness of Mathematics" finding in them a new and strict logic which destroyed the ancient scholastic logic dominated by the religion of the past. He predicted that the empire of reason would stretch out far beyond purely mathematical realms, but wished that every one could study mathematics. He was certain of a magnificent future for man, and showed by striking contrast the ignorance and misery of the past, weighted down by suffering, with the radiant hopes for the future.

> All our knowledge of mathematics, of nature, of the brightest part of human wisdom had their admission among us within the two last centuries. . . . The world is daily increasing in experimental knowledge, and let no man flatter the age with pretending we have arrived at a perfection of our discoveries.[1]

These were new and bold ideas for a century still turned towards the classic and Christian past, but Franklin quietly propagated them in the crowds by his almanac and was careful not to frighten them by murmuring, "Read much, but not too many books." . . . "Reading makes a full man; — meditation a profound man — Discourse a clear man."

All this was calm and pleasant, but Franklin was also a fighter. His doctrine demanded sacrifice and struggle. He had inscribed the defense of civilian liberties as one of the ideals of the Junto, with the inference that the encroachment of the clergy must be fought. At the secret meetings of the lodge and the Junto, Franklin gave more than one carefully worded speech on this subject. In his publications he slyly inserted such incendiary books as the sermon printed by him in 1732, "The Traditions of the Clergy destructive of Religion", or this little book announced in his newspaper, "Every man his own Priest."

His tendency was even more clearly revealed by an incident which upset Philadelphia in 1731. On the order of a captain, Franklin printed an advertisement which announced the departure of a boat, and that passengers were welcome, but not ministers. To make the idea more striking, the author of the advertisement had added a *post scriptum:* "No Sea Hens nor Black Gowns will be admitted on any terms."

Of course, this advertisement shocked a good number of Franklin's subscribers. Franklin had to defend himself and did so, adroitly and warmly. At first he protested his good will to

[1] "On Discoveries", *Pennsylvania Gazette,* October 14, 1736.

the ministers, but touched on the question of principle at the same time, and made it clear to every one how printers should be treated.

"Printers," he said, "are educated in the Belief that when Men differ in Opinion, both Sides ought equally to have the Advantage of being heard by the Publick; and that when Truth and Error have fair Play the former is always an over-match for the latter." And he added: "I got Five Shillings by it. . . . None who are angry with me would have given me so much to let it alone." Naturally they would not, and Franklin scored.

This trenchant response showed the clergy of what metal Franklin was made. If they had taken the trouble to read "Poor Richard" they would have found out better still. "Never spare the Parson's Wine, nor the Baker's Pudding" (1733), he said cunningly, and "Lawyers, preachers, and tomtit's eggs, there are more of them hatched than come to perfection." (1734) In a more serious tone he warned, "Eyes and Priests bear no jests" (1735), and,

> Certainly three things agree, the priest, the lawyer and
> death, all three;
> Death takes both the weak and the strong,
> The lawyer takes from both right and wrong,
> And the priest from the living and dead has his fee. (1737)

And the better to prove that these audacities were not written by chance, Benjamin, who ordinarily never repeated a joke, had rewritten them in several ways.

Moreover, great personages and kings were no better treated than the clergy. "Kings and bears often worry their keepers." (Published in 1733, repeated in 1739.) "The King's cheese is half wasted in parings; but no matter, 'tis made of the people's milk." He even employed his muse to express his republican zeal:

> For's country CODRUS suffer'd by the sword,
> And, by his death, his country's fame restor'd:
> Caesar into his mother's bosom bare
> Fire, Sword, and all the ills of civil war;

Codrus confirm'd his country's wholesome laws;
Caesar in blood still justified his cause:
Yet following kings ne'er 'dopted Codrus' name,
But Caesar still, and emperors are the same. (1739)

And opposite these rude attacks, Benjamin wrote, like a good democrat: "An innocent plowman is more worthy than a vicious prince." (1736) . . . "Let our fathers and grandfathers be valued for their goodness, ourselves for our own" (1739), thus making a frontal attack on the most cherished characteristics of the old social order and the basis of European monarchies; he also added Masonic maxims. In his "Constitution of the Free Masons", published in 1734, he wrote, "All Preferment among Masons is grounded upon real Worth and personal Merit only."

Thus his discipline was neither monarchistic, nor, properly speaking, Christian. If it were presented to the middle class of Philadelphia with a calm and debonair exterior, it was none the less radical. What Franklin didn't dare say, the good fellow, poor Richard, said for him. His argumentative instinct, which dominated his newspaper, was so obvious that it would have been dangerous to publish biting criticism on institutions and the Church, but he gave it free rein in his almanac. Poor Richard was the real successor of the *New England Courant.* Here, in this vulgar environment, under the cloak of joking and ribaldry, the good man could speak his mind. The international vogue of this little book cannot be attributed to any other thing. No doubt, Franklin introduced new and original elements which prolonged the favor of the public, but in the beginning, it was the bold tone he assumed which won him the approbation of the shrewd American farmers, scattered over their solitary farms and on the borders of virgin forests.

Once more he succeeded marvelously in this comedy which had been such a success with Mrs. Dogood. Titan Leeds was an indistinct person, not to be identified in his book, while the titles of other almanacs, if they did not include the real name of the author, employed a transparent pseudonym. Poor Richard, on the contrary, was a very live person indeed, a distinct and concrete creation of Franklin's brain, expressing, like a character in a play, all the feelings, ideas and instincts which Franklin could not express in public himself.

Through all the several editions of his almanac, Poor Richard fights with his colleagues, quarrels with his wife and makes up with her, this faithful and insupportable Bridget, "his duchess", as he dubbed her. She plays tricks on him, changes his weather predictions to give more sunlight and fewer storms to his customers, slyly adds some verses against men, and shortens or suppresses her husband's prefaces when she finds them indiscreet. She is grateful for the new kettle, new slippers, new shifts, and the warm winter dress which she owes to the work of her husband and the munificence of the public, but she is also offended because he speaks too much of her, and inserts too many jokes at the expense of her sex.

Poor Richard improves his fortunes, becomes refined, buys a suit to wear in town and raises his position in society. What struggles he has with his enemies and his wife, and how clever is his retort to the calumniators who assert that he does not exist!

> They say in short that there is no such a man as I am. . . . I make this publick and serious declaration, which I desire may be believed, to wit: That *what I have written heretofore, and do now write, neither was, nor is written by any other man or men, person or persons, whatsoever.* Those who are not satisfied with this must needs be very unreasonable.

How could one doubt the existence of Richard Saunders? He so pervaded the life of Benjamin Franklin that he imposed not only an attitude on Franklin, but finally forced him to play a rôle. Franklin, in spite of his intelligence, wisdom and ability, never attained the perfect degree of bourgeois prudence, peasant cunning and moral prestige by which the impeccable Richard Saunders conquered the world. Still, people ended by seeing Franklin through Saunders and thought that they were both one and the same person. The printer benefited by all the virtues of his hero.

This was the loveliest comedy of the century, because it remained serious to the very end; although it began its conquest among the lowly and humble, it ended by conquering the educated world — a unique fact in the eighteenth century. Then, too, it presented a character for whom the world had been waiting, a character difficult to define: a straightforward man who could do good without being embarrassed or forced, and who at the same time could yet make a bargain.

V

A LIFE filled to the brim with activity, yet silent and regular, cradled by the rhythm of the seasons — such was the existence of Benjamin Franklin between 1730 and 1738. There were no other noises than the bustle of the near-by market place, where the farmers crowded every year in increasing numbers, the clear voices of the apprentices in the workshop, the joyous cries of the children in the house, the drinking songs and laughter with his cheerful comrades at the Junto. His family increased, the city grew larger, and happiness recompensed him for his efforts. Every year meant a step ahead in the midst of fatiguing efforts and the joys of success.

During the year 1732, Franklin not only constructed the rules for his lodge and became an officer therein, but wrote his first "Poor Richard's Almanac" as well, and firmly established his library company. His cherished son, Francis Folger, was born in this year also, the only legitimate son he was destined to have. This little blond-haired child, with sweet and lively ways, was an infinite joy to Benjamin and Deborah. It consecrated their marriage and seemed like a benediction of God to them. Several epidemics swept over the city, in particular smallpox, which had been most severe in 1731 and which returned periodically, but the child escaped them all.

The city, profiting from the peace and prosperity, was filled with joyful clamor; the young proprietors visited their province, and Thomas Penn, in company with the good men of Pennsylvania at banquets, on horseback, and in public meetings, did his best to please them It was not long before he heard of Franklin — from Logan and many others — and he showed his good will and approval by giving him some printing jobs. He praised the library company highly, and promised his patronage. Thus the year passed gayly, in spite of the fright stirred up one fine morning in August when the river ran blood red, and in spite of the terribly cold winter. Many complained of having caught colds, or of not having enough wood, but the wise Poor Richard said with satisfaction: "Snowy winter, a plentiful harvest."

The thawing along the banks of the Schuylkill in February, 1733, led to a series of catastrophes, but nothing could daunt the vigorous spirit of Philadelphia or Franklin. The printer seemed to radiate activity. His visit to Boston in the spring enabled him to renew all his connections in the North, while in the South, he set up a shop for Timothee in Charleston, to succeed Whitemarsh who had died. At the same time he began to study languages; profited by the excitement of the proprietors' visit, which aroused much civic zeal, to suggest a hundred useful projects: deepening the rivers to make them navigable, stocking them with fish, and ways and means of keeping people from falling and breaking their noses on the slippery city streets. Whenever a storekeeper strewed ashes on the snow and ice in front of his door, Franklin publicly complimented him in the columns of his newspaper.

There was everything to be done in Philadelphia, for although there were houses, trees, human beings, and cows, there were no police, no firemen, no lighting, no paving, no sanitary service or energetic administration. Franklin took upon himself the burden of setting forth these useful ideas. For every season and circumstance his practical mind furnished suggestions, and thanks to the Junto, the lodge, and his newspaper, he made them heard by the public. There were four points which he especially stressed: the reorganization of the police department, which had fallen to nothing; the propagation of inoculation (he was now an enthusiastic convert to the theory); the fight against fire — what could be more dangerous than fire for this little city built of wood? — and the preparation for military defense; Philadelphia was already wealthy, and at the mercy of any bold enemy. (Franklin often harped on this subject.) The torrid summer of 1734, with its many electrical storms and consequent fires, served him with strong arguments, and since he had just been elected Worshipful Master of the Masons, his prestige had increased, and he was in a good position to persuade his fellow citizens. In 1736, he had the pleasure of seeing the first corps of firemen organized in Philadelphia. The Junto was behind the project, and Benjamin was its guardian angel. This was the first of those half-civil, half-military groups he was to form, and which were to aid him so much in his career. The Fire Department was a sensation in Philadelphia, and rendered great services, which the newspaper never neglected to underline, thus fulfilling its civic duty without harming its publisher.

So much zeal had its reward: the Assembly, urged on by Andrew Hamilton, chose him as secretary in 1736. This was a discreet function, but very advantageous for a journalist. It placed him at the source of local news, and he could watch over all that was happening without sharing in the responsibility. Nevertheless, he could forewarn his friends, and even influence the Assembly, thanks to his close connections with some of the members.

He was filled with joy at his success. But it did not last long. While the whole city, including Franklin, were being amused at the picturesque spectacle furnished by the delegates of six Indian nations, who had come to sign a treaty with the province, smallpox once more reared its ugly head. The epidemic spread over the region with rapidity, and was so violent that the Indians, merchants and travelers all fled. The farmers were so frightened they would no longer bring their provisions to market. Every one was depressed but Franklin, who calmly continued to work without worrying, until the disease descended on his own home. His son, Francis, who had been poor in health for some days past, and who had therefore not been inoculated, was stricken, and died in a few days. There is no doubt that his death was Franklin's greatest sorrow. It was an irreparable grief which the years did not dissipate. But he was not romantic and did not dwell on his sadness. He forced himself to diminish it, so that he would not suffer too much, and to benefit from it, like the wise man that he wished to be. With great courage, he continued his service to society during these melancholy days, and soon after the death of his son he published this word (December 13, 1737):

UNDERSTANDING 'tis a current Report, that my Son Francis, who died lately of the Small Pox had it by Inoculation; and being desired to satisfy the Publick in that Particular: inasmuch as some People are, by that Report (join'd with others of the like and perhaps equally groundless) deter'd from having that Operation perform'd on their Children, I do hereby sincerely declare that he was not inoculated, but receiv'd the Distemper in the common way of Infection: and I suppose the Report could only arise from its being my known Opinion, that Inoculation was a safe and beneficial Practice; and from my having said among my Acquaintance, that I intended to have my Child inoculated, as soon as he should have recovered sufficient Strength from a Flux with which he had been long afflicted.

B. FRANKLIN.

And "Poor Richard" took up the same story in verse:

God offer'd to the Jews salvation;
And 'twas refus'd by half the nation:
Thus (tho 'tis life's great preservation),
Many oppose *inoculation*.
We're told by one of the black robe,
The devil inoculated Job:
Suppose 'tis true, what he does tell;
Pray, neighbours, *did not Job do well?*

This cruel courage of moralizing on the death of his son to ameliorate the fate of others didn't appease his suffering. To console himself a little more he wrote ("Poor Richard", 1737):

The Thracian infant, entering into life,
Both parents mourn for, both receive with grief,
The Thracian infant snatched by Death away,
Both parents to the grave with joy convey.
This Greece and Rome you with derision view,
This is mere Thracian ignorance to you;
But if you weigh the custom you despise,
This Thracian ignorance may teach the wise.

And to see his misfortune from its best side, he said, "After crosses and losses men grow humbler and wiser."

Then he continued on his way. He had no time to stop, and he had come from a hardy breed. Besides, he never allowed a feeling to take up too much room in his life.

He needed all his attention for an imminent struggle which was of essential importance. Since Keimer had left, Bradford had looked on him with no good will. At first there had been no hostility. Bradford was more powerful, and belonged to another class than Franklin. Besides, Franklin had helped him to evict Keimer by writing good articles for his *Mercury*. In July, 1733, Bradford, hard pressed by too much work, had even confided to Franklin the care of publishing, "A New Version of the Psalm of David by N. Brady." But after this, some strain entered into their relations. When Franklin had become not only a member of the lodge but the printer to the Assembly, Bradford began to sit up and take notice, and when he saw the publications of his rival increase, while his own diminished in a disquieting fashion, he set to work energetically. In 1731, Franklin issued about nine, Bradford, five; in 1732, Franklin seventeen, Bradford, eight; in 1733, Franklin twelve, Bradford, five. And, as a matter of fact, these latter five publications were only his almanacs and his newspaper. Bradford began to criticize Franklin, and Franklin thereupon began a direct attack. At first, it was only a newspaper fight.

They copied from each other and changed the dates of the stolen news items in order to make the other look like a thief. Each one made fun of the poems and essays the other had published. One day, for example, Franklin printed the letter of a worthy *litterateur*, who declared:

Mr. FRANKLIN, I am the Author of a Copy of Verses on the last Mercury. It was my real Intention to appear open, and not basely with my Vizard on, attack a Man who had fairly unmasked. Accordingly I subscribed my Name, at full Length, in my Manuscript sent to my Brother B. . . d, but he, for some incomprehensible Reason, inserted the two initial Letters only viz BL. 'Tis true every Syllable of the Performance discovers me to be the Author, but as I meet with much Censure on the Occasion, I request you to inform the Publick that I did not desire my Name should be conceal'd, and that the remaining Letters are O, C, K, H, E, A, D.

It was more serious when Bradford pilfered a letter from Franklin. The letter had been given to Franklin by a group of Palatine immigrants, who complained that they had been exploited by their captain on their voyage. Franklin had the letter translated, but finding it to be a little too severe, had put it to one side. Bradford heard of this, obtained a copy of the translation and inserted it in his newspaper. Franklin was furious and protested. He edited and inserted another translation. But there was no doubt that he had been fooled this time (1732).

The next time it was Bradford. On November 11, Franklin printed a very sharp letter from one of his readers, complaining that he published only stale news. The reader quoted dreadful examples. Franklin printed the letter in seeming good faith but he appended a little note to the effect that he could say nothing to justify himself, as the letter had been sent to the wrong address, it should have been delivered at the offices of the *Mercury*. . . . Franklin scored.

Just a year later, the two men and the two newspapers were at close quarters in a political quarrel. Franklin was decidedly on the side of the people, Bradford was for the Proprietors. The discussion was brief, Bradford evidently disdaining to prolong it. But Franklin had no great desire to play the gentleman, and in August, 1734, he printed a letter from a reader who remarked on the strange news in the *Mercury:* notably a cannon shot which was supposed to have killed both Berwick and the Duke of Savoy, when one was at the moment in Rhineland, and the other in Italy Bradford had to swallow the bitter pill again.

Another one was reserved for him. After having taken away the official publications of Pennsylvania, Delaware, and New Jersey, Franklin was going to strip him of his last official position. Spottswood, the former governor of Virginia, and the former close friend of Keith, was now Director-General of the Posts in the American colonies, and he was not at all satisfied with his official in Philadelphia. Bradford felt himself to be superior to his work, was careless, and did not send in his accounts. Spottswood thought of Franklin, of whom he had heard so much, and offered him the post. It was poorly paid, but Franklin kept himself from appearing displeased. The appointment was a considerable one in view of the distribution of his newspaper, and his general business.

But this time his triumph was too much. Bradford declared war and started a lively attack. Benjamin was a worker, a good business man, an honest printer, a good citizen, and a good Whig. On all these sides he was impervious to attack. His two weak points were his religion and his morals. In the *Gazette* several articles hostile to the clergy had already been noticed. A clerical reader had complained in 1729, and in 1731, Franklin had printed the advertisement against the "sea hens and the black gowns" which stirred up still more animosity. He was more careful in the years following, and regularly attended the Presbyterian church. After hearing many sermons which displeased him because they were dogmatic, theological and desultory, he had the good, or rather, the bad fortune, to hear the preaching of a young minister, Mr. Hemphill, who, instead of devoting himself to dogma, talked rather on morals and natural religion. He was eloquent and it was a pleasure to listen to him. He soon had many listeners in the city, and Franklin was one of his most faithful admirers, for he liked his eloquence and was pleased with his moral discourses.

Unfortunately, the most pious and affluent Presbyterians did not approve of the young preacher's doctrine at all, and the more aged ministers joined their side. Hemphill didn't want to give in, and as he was hired by the church, he swaggered. Franklin wrote two pamphlets to defend him and took his part in the *Gazette*. But Hemphill was condemned by the Synod, and had the worse luck to be forced to confess that he had stolen his sermons — one of them having been recognized by an enemy as being by a Doctor Foster. Hemphill had to admit that he had more memory than invention, and although Benjamin continued to defend him and affirm that he "rather approv'd his giving us good sermons compos'd by others, than bad ones of his own manufacture", Hemphill had to leave Philadelphia. Benjamin, annoyed and unhappy at his defeat, forsook the Presbyterian congregation. He chose the Church of England, to which he sent his wife, daughter and even his apprentices, when they hadn't hidden their shoes as an excuse to lie a-bed. He scrupulously paid his tithes and was a solid member of the parish, if he were not a fervent church-goer. He always had much work to do on Sunday mornings.

This Hemphill affair made a good deal of stir and roused animosity. Franklin, a layman, and a Freemason, had gone too far in his ecclesiastical quarrel. He had shown his ideas and feelings a little too obviously. He had attracted enmities.

They ripened during the year 1736 and added to the jealousy which his new position caused. Between the *Mercury* and the *Gazette* there was bitter war. The *Gazette* reproached Bradford for having mistranslated French quotations, for having no idea of liberty, etc. The *Gazette* also attacked William Bradford of New York for having spread perfidious rumors about Franklin and the paper money of New Jersey, which he had printed the year preceding: it also defended Robert Morris against the accusations of this same Bradford, thus always keeping the breach open and waging war as well on the clergy, absolutism, papism, heredity, etc. Franklin felt strongly and gave free rein to his feelings.

The winter was spent in this atmosphere of struggle, and no one was bothered by the earthquake which broke some pots on December 6, or by the Aurora Borealis, which frightened only a few devout souls. In 1737, the winter was intensely cold, there was skating on the Delaware, people crossed the river on horseback or in their carriages, and built snow houses on it. But this same cold which froze imprudent drunkards to death at night gave vitality to honest men. Bradford was one of them. He was not without weapons against Franklin. He and his father in New York made a solid group; they had their friends throughout the colonies, and were known and respected. The authorities of New York, where William Bradford was the official printer, protected them, as well as the majority of Quakers in Pennsylvania. And though they were less sensational journalists than Franklin, they had an exact sense of opportunity. They knew when to strike.

Throughout the world in these years of 1736–1738, Freemasonry began to have a bad reputation. It had grown so quickly, it had attracted so many men, and had succeeded so well in keeping its mystery, that a strong opposition group sprang up, believing it dishonest and being jealous of its secrets. Masonry was opposed by the three greatest forces of the century, — the Kings, the Clergy, and the Women.

The kings saw, grouped in these associations, the influential and ordinarily dissatisfied elements which they could not control: the ambitious lords, the avid intellectuals, and the grumbling bourgeois. The clergy saw that they were often attacked by the Masons, who were always attempting to replace them, as they were jealous of the clergy's political influence. The Mason took the priest's place as a professor of morals, and the lodge took the place of the church. But Masonry was human and not divine, it was a layman's philosophy and not inspired dogma.

Masonry had its own history, seasoned to taste, its own dogmas and moral principles, which closely resembled those of Christianity and were usually derived from them, but which were sufficiently different to be oriented towards man and earth, instead of God and eternity. In general, Masonry was a human, utilitarian and rationalistic application of Christian ideas and discipline. Some considered it a direct and logical extension of Christianity. Others thought it a disloyal and blasphemous extension of the Christian belief. The clergy were inclined to the latter attitude, for the success of Masonry signified the end of their social rôle.

As to the women, it was displeasing for them to see the men going off alone to these mysterious meetings, where, according to some accounts, they indulged in philosophic discussions, or, according to others, gave themselves up to all kinds of orgies. The women were jealous of this organization, as they did not possess its counterpart, and were naturally offended at being excluded from it and its pleasures.

Here were the three powerful enemies of Masonry. The women were perhaps the most powerful, due to their enormous influence over the feelings of men, and over the licentious but refined society of the century. Masonry also suffered from the danger of internal schisms, for it had grown so quickly that its chiefs could not control the spirit of it, or regulate its development. Europe swarmed with dissenting, irregular, fantastic lodges which were Masonic only in name. These "Masons" practiced all kinds of bizarre, and sometimes shocking rites which had nothing in common with the central organization, the Grand Lodge of London.

Even in England the situation was delicate, because of the conflict between the Hanoverian and Jacobite lodges. The latter were still very active and worked for the Pretender. Every catastrophe which happened in England was laid to the lodges. The people, who understood nothing about Masonry, were annoyed on this account and felt that it was only a fantastic and superfluous society.

The storm first broke in Holland, where the Protestant clergy and the crowd made violent demonstrations against Masonry (1735–1740). From Holland the counter-movement spread to France, where the most Christian king forbade the meetings of the Masons as being immoral. His command was the topic of popular discussion. Late at night you would hear young men stamping down the crooked streets and singing lustily:

Oh, the free, free Masons!
Let's sing to their honor and glory!
Oh, the free, free Masons!
What handsome fellows they are!
They get together just to drink,
What other mystery could you think?
Oh, the free, free Masons!

In Rome an investigation was made in 1737, and in 1738 Pope Clement XII excommunicated any Catholic who became a Mason. The Grand Duke of Tuscany closed the Masonic Lodge of Florence in 1737. In Sweden the Government watched over the Masonic activities, while in Lisbon the Masons were sent to the Inquisition. The storm was thundering everywhere at the same time. The *London Magazine* for April, 1737, published a long article, full of hidden insults and direct attacks. "Upon the whole this mysterious Society hath too much the Air of an Inquisition." And to this was added, "I wish it may not be somewhat like *Horrid Obligation* which *Catiline* administered to his *Fellow Conspirators*." It compared the Masons to the Jesuits and concluded by saying that in England this society was ordinarily considered as "a Parcel of idle People, who meet together only to make merry and play some ridiculous Pranks."

All this clamor was not long in being heard in America. The clergy and their devout followers, who had already defied Masonry, now concluded that there was real danger. The uneasy crowd began to murmur. A group of journalists got together to stiffen the opposition with the two Bradfords at their head, the father with his *New York Gazette*, and the son with his Philadelphia *Mercury*. They reprinted the attacks on Masonry which had appeared in the *London Magazine*. They even invented new forms of Masonry and denounced various associations of highwaymen, hoodlums, and Negro rowdies as being Masonic. The discussion spread at a great rate in the American colonies, one group of American newspapers keeping up a violent attack, while the other, realizing that the excitement of the crowd had been stirred, attempted a cautious defense of Masonry. But the opposition was strongly aided by a deplorable and horrible event which happened at Philadelphia in 1737.

A druggist, Evan Jones, who was fond of good living and notorious for his pranks, had a young apprentice in his shop, a pretty but stupid boy named Daniel Reeves. The boy had heard of Masonry, and thinking it might offer a short cut to the highway of fortune decided he would enter it. He asked his master how to go about it, and Jones, seeing an opportunity here for playing a good trick, told him he would arrange everything. With the aid of some neighbors and friends, Jones prepared a ridiculous ceremony of initiation. Reeves was forced to swear to an oath which was rather obscene and blasphemous, to swallow a laxative, and to kiss something which was not at all sacred. The company laughed all the more heartily, as the boy didn't doubt a thing. Jones was so amused he could not stop here, and knowing Franklin's taste for the burlesque and that he was a famous Mason, the druggist told him what he had done and read the oath to him. He took Reeves along with him and had him make supposedly Masonic signs. Franklin laughed. The joke was broad but it amused him. People were not so fastidious in those days. But Franklin was imprudent enough to ask for a copy of the oath, and worse, read it to his intimate friends. His shop was shortly besieged by all sorts of persons who were curious to see this extraordinary document. Thus Franklin was compromised. Nevertheless, when he heard that Jones was going to continue his joke, he didn't want to be mixed up in the affair any longer, and he even thought of warning the boy. At least, he stayed away from the second ceremony of initiation.

It was well that he did so, for this time the conspirators, wishing to add some mystery to their former operations, came to grief. They led the young man blindfolded into a dark cellar and then, thinking to terrify him, they suddenly took off the blindfold, while one of the band, disguised as the Devil, danced in front of the blue flames of a bowl of rum. Unfortunately, Daniel Reeves wasn't afraid. The initiators, out of spite (or perhaps pure awkwardness), threw the bowl of burning rum at him. In an instant the boy was bathed in flames. He screamed with pain. The persecutors, panic-stricken in their turn, threw themselves upon him to put out the fire, but they were too late, and when they carried the young man to his home he was in agony. He died a few days later (June 16, 1737).

All the people of the city, who for the last months had been reading the incendiary attacks on the Masons, and who had followed Jones' prank from the beginning, were furiously excited by this tragedy. The Masons were quick to disown any part in the initiation, and affirmed that not one of the guilty was a Mason.

However, the affair had its consequences. After the inquest, the guilty were arraigned for willful murder; acquitted of this at the first hearing, the case was carried to the criminal jury. The sessions of this court were held the first week of January, 1738. A crowd gathered such as had never been seen in Philadelphia. Thousands of people assembled around the courthouse and waited fifteen hours to hear the verdict. Finally, at two o'clock in the morning, the jury pronounced Doctor Evans guilty, and he was punished for his offense by being "burned in the hand."

The affair would have been finished then, had not Bradford printed a venomous letter against Franklin in the *Mercury* for February 14, 1738. Bradford claimed that Franklin was guilty of having known, approved and encouraged the infamous initiation, of having taken a copy of the fake oath and of having read it to several persons. The attack was direct and very dangerous, on account of the excited state of public opinion at this time, and because of Franklin's other indiscretions. Franklin freely acknowledged in his *Gazette* that he had been aware of the joke, that he had seen Daniel Reeves, heard the oath, and received a copy of it. He confessed even to have carried this copy about, and to have read it to several of his friends, but he insisted that he had disapproved of the persecutors and had tried to dissuade them from their plans. To end his defense, he gave two favorable testimonies of his character from two of the most respected persons in the city. And as his friend and protector, James Logan, was the president of the province at this time, he found shelter.

The *Mercury* was obliged to close the discussion, but in doing so, Bradford shot a Parthian arrow. How, said he, was Mr. Franklin able to have taken pleasure in reading this improper oath to all his friends, if he disapproved of it as much as he claims to now? There was no answer to this question.

The affair had unpleasant echoes all over the colonies. The newspapers which were on Bradford's side published the accounts of the story as they had appeared in the *Mercury*, of February, 1738. The *Boston News Letter* was one of them. But the newspapers which were well disposed to Franklin and the Masons kept quiet (the *Virginia Gazette* and *The New York Journal*).

There was gossiping in Boston too. Franklin's parents heard the horrible tale, and all their fears for the eternal salvation of their son returned. They wrote him anxious letters. Once more he had to justify himself, and he did so in a tender, warm, and respectful letter. In part, he wrote:

> My mother grieves that one of her sons is an Arian, another an Arminian. What an Arminian or an Arian is, I cannot say that I very well know. The truth is; I make such distinctions very little my study. I think vital religion has always suffered, when orthodoxy is more regarded than virtue; and the Scriptures assure me that on the last day we shall not be examined [as to] what we thought, but what we *did;* and our recommendation will not be that we said *Lord! Lord!* but that we did good to our fellow creatures. See Math. XXV.
>
> As to the freemasons, I know no way of giving my mother a better account of them than she seems to have at present, since it is not allowed that women should be admitted into that secret society. She has, I must confess; on that account some reason to be displeased with it; but for anything else, I must entreat her to suspend her judgment till she is better informed, unless she will believe me, when I assure her that they are in general a very harmless sort of people, and have no principles or practices that are inconsistent with religion and good manners.

Then he talked about the heavy rains and the thaws which were flooding the country, breaking down the bridges and slowing up the mails (April, 1738). And Mrs. Franklin, who was too proud of her Benjamin not to believe what he said, was persuaded, and in answer to his letter, sent her benediction.

Thus the storm passed over, passed as all storms do, with

much noise and fracas, destroying all who could not bow their heads or hide themselves. But in 1737, Franklin had known how to stoop a little, just enough, and his roots were sufficiently numerous and deep in the soil of Pennsylvania so that the first tempest had only shaken him, not destroyed him.

Besides, Freemasonry in America was neither persecuted nor thwarted. It remained strong enough to recompense those who had suffered for it as had Brother Franklin.

VI

Never was the docility of the populace, the authority of the Church, the splendor of the monarchies, greater than in 1738. All England cherished its king, France had named Louis XV "Louis the Beloved", and no one raised a voice against the established order. Watched over by his wise and homely mistress, Voltaire studied science in his retreat of Cirey, and amused himself with a theater of marionettes; Rousseau studied botany at Madame de Warren's, who had converted him to Catholicism and made him attend Mass regularly, as well as keeping him busy with trifling occupations; while Franklin kept his shop on Market Street in Philadelphia, aided by his good Debby, selling his goose quills, lampblack, almanacs and bibles.

However, a storm was brooding. In France and in England, an internal struggle was dividing the Church, and the kings were soon to engage in a murderous war which was to give the philosophers, the masses and the Masons a chance to make themselves heard.

In France, for some time past, the Jesuits and the Jansenists had been upsetting the Catholic Church by their quarrels. Their conflict, which was at first a rather subtle theological dispute, had turned poisonous and then became an intense battle. On the whole, the Jesuits represented the tendency to reform Catholicism in order to meet the needs of the day, to make it rational, human and agreeable, while the Jansenists insisted on keeping Catholicism as it always had been, with all its antique and mystical severity. Condemned by Rome, the greater number of Jansenists had recourse to an ambiguous submission, but continued their intense struggle with the Jesuits. The former were very popular and highly respected, as their gravity and mysticism had won the admiration of the crowd, while a large part of the middle classes were shocked at the elegant and worldly tone of the Jesuits.

There was even a party of the aristocracy, in whom the Puritanical tendencies were still uppermost, who took the side of the Jansenists. Unfortunately, the zeal and enthusiasm of the Jansenists, which had been so admirable in the beginning, at the time of Pascal and Racine, had finished by degenerating into a somber fervor which could often turn into madness. Deprived of their leaders, they nevertheless defied the bishops and broke into full revolt. Pushed on by mystical needs, the Jansenists committed all kinds of extravagances. Once they were seen to rush in a crowd to the tombs of one of their "saints" and there go through a thousand fantastic rites. They claimed to be inspired, that they possessed the divine spirit, and then under some miraculous influence, they would have convulsions. An eyewitness describes some of their activities in this vivid paragraph:

> A multitude of girls, women, invalids, and persons of all ages, were wrangling for the privilege of standing in Saint Medard Cemetery or in the neighboring streets. They vied with each other in having violent convulsions. Here were men struggling on the ground in the throes of actual epileptic fits, and a little farther off, others were swallowing pebbles, splinters of glass, and even hot coals. Women stood on their heads with as much decency or indecency as such a proceeding permitted. Elsewhere, other women stretched out full length on the ground and invited the spectators to hit them on their stomachs. They weren't happy until ten or a dozen men fell upon their bodies. Still others would crawl between the legs of boys and then would stand up with them astride their shoulders. Everybody wriggled and writhed in a thousand extravagant ways. And in the midst of all this, all you could hear was moaning, singing, shouting, whistling, declaiming, prophetising, yowling. . . .

Such madness is only explained by the deep need of the poor people for mysticism, which the formal and rationalistic religion of the century did not supply to any satisfactory degree.

This degradation of French Jansenism gave the Jesuits a stronger position and made them more bold. With the support of the king they were able to extinguish the sect completely, but they could neither destroy the political party nor the Jansenistic tendencies, and had to submit to occasional reprisals. In 1775 the conquering Jesuits were in their turn practically destroyed. The kings of France and Spain closed the colleges and expelled the members of them from their countries. Rome officially dissolved the order. Thus, in the course of a long struggle, the two most solid groups of French Catholicism were practically destroyed, the one by the other. They left the field free to the philosophers, who would now support the Jansenists, now the Jesuits, thereby gaining the independent position of arbiters.

The situation in England and America was analogous. The Deists, as a school and social group, had been vanquished. Towards 1738, they had ceased to be dangerous for English Christianity. But there still existed many unbelievers, and these had taken refuge for the most part in the English clergy, in order to be tranquil, to have leisure and to work at their ease. Though the Church of England conserved its strong armor, it had an internal weakness which the pious and zealous worshipers felt keenly. It was still capable of maintaining the social and spiritual order, but it could not supply the spiritual nourishment, the ardent faith, or the mystical satisfaction, which every one, and above all, the crowd, had need of in this contradictory century.

The Protestant Dissenters realized the danger and tried to awaken the Christian zeal of the faithful, tried to electrify them. They hardly succeeded as is proved by all the vain efforts made in New England, and by the discouragement of the ministers between 1715 and 1735. America, which had formerly been the refuge of saints, was now becoming the domain of perdition. In vain God attested His wrath by hurling bolts of lightning which destroyed barns and farmhouses, by loosing floods and earthquakes which turned cities and villages upside down. The people would be frightened and religious for a while, but soon would take up their dissolute life again. The young people played cards, danced and amused themselves on the very eve of the Sabbath. They had invented those dreadful occasions called "frolicks", when boys and girls, without distinction of family, ate, drank, danced, and kissed far into the night, while the despairing ministers didn't know what to do. The churches were deserted and the taverns full, drunken women zigzagged down the streets and the printers published unhealthy and irreligious books. Philadelphia was a center of corruption. The Quakers with their tolerance had let every one in: the English and German mystics who tried to outdo each other in fanaticism: the Moravians, Mennonites, Dunkards, Schwenkfelders, etc., as well as the unbelievers who were occupied only with eating, drinking, and doing what they wanted.

But all this changed both in England and America between 1736 and 1740, when the first Methodist apostles went forth among the crowds, stirring up a fanatic and mystic delirium analogous to that of the Jansenists, by their brutal, terrifying, and compelling eloquence. Beginning in 1736, Jonathan Edwards had begun to arouse the crowds by his preaching, but it was only in 1739 when the Reverend George Whitefield began chasing the Devil over two hemispheres that the people were actually conquered.

This very young minister — he was only twenty-three — was gifted with extraordinary eloquence and had the soul of an apostle. He knew how to move his audience to tears and laughter and how to convert them. When he spoke of hell his listeners "were melted down, were drowned in tears." His piercing eyes, powerful, melodious voice and sweeping gestures, dominated the people, who did not notice at the same time his little pointed nose and jovial chin, or his rounded belly.

He and his imitators had an overwhelming success. Here is how one of them proceeded:

At length, he turned his Discourse to others, and with the *utmost Strength* of his Lungs addrest himself to the Congregation, under these and such like expressions; viz. You poor unconverted Creatures, in the Seats, in the Pews, in the Galleries, I wonder you don't drop into Hell! It would not surprise me, I should not wonder at it, if I should see you drop down *now, this Minute* into Hell! You Pharisees, Hypocrites, *now, now, now*, you are going right into the Bottom of Hell. I wonder you don't drop into Hell by *Scores*, by *Hundreds*, etc.

He would make a brief prayer for all the souls in distress and before he had hardly finished twenty persons would be crowding about him. Then he would jump from the pulpit, throw off his robes, leap upon the benches, screaming from right to left:

> The War goes on the Fight goes on, the Devil goes down, the Devil goes down!

And as he did so his face would turn red and he would stamp his feet "most dreadfully."

One can imagine the result:

> This frequently frights the *little children* and sets them a Screaming; and that frights their *tender Mothers*, and sets them a Screaming and by Degrees spreads over a great Part of the Congregation: and forty, fifty, or an hundred of them screaming all together, makes such an awful and hideous Noise as will make a Man's hair stand on End. Some will faint away, fall down upon the Floor, wallow and foam. Some Women will rend off their Caps, Handkerchiefs, and other Clothes, tear their Hair down about their Ears, and seem perfectly bereft of their Reason.

The intelligent people in the city objected to these delirious exhibitions, but there was only a handful of them (then, as now) and Tennent, Davenport, and Whitefield were the most popular men of America from 1739 to 1760.

Whitefield arrived in Philadelphia for the first time on November 5, 1739. He imposed himself on the city immediately and several churches were opened to him. Both the middle class and poor people thronged to hear the new minister and filled the pews. The newspapers published such flaming verses about him as these:

> Whitefield that great, that pleasing Name,
> Has all my Soul possesst:
> For sure some seraphin from above
> Inspires his Godlike breast . . .

While Whitefield to thy sacred strain
Surpris'd we listen still.
Immortal heights we seem to reach,
Celestial transports feel . . .

Whitefield could even say that the people in Philadelphia were half-animal, half-devil, could empty their purses and carry off their good money to spend in Georgia, could make them scream with horror and sweat from fear just because he talked about hell. Everything was forgiven him, because he brought with him enthusiasm, faith and life. Franklin was among his first auditors. All that had life attracted him, and he was interested in every form of success. He, who had ceased attending church, went to hear all of Whitefield's sermons. He gave his money like the others, and like them, too, he testified to having felt a profound enthusiasm. But he did much more for Whitefield than the others. He gave him the support of his newspaper, of his printing shop, of his Junto, and his wisdom. In short, he became his temporal manager. Three weeks after Whitefield's arrival — November 28th — Franklin announced that he was going to publish the minister's sermons, and that subscribers had better hurry. In his *Gazette* he noted even the most trifling facts and gestures of the apostle.

Nevertheless, he didn't rally to his principles. Whitefield was a Calvinist and believed in the doctrine of predestination, which Franklin refused to admit. But he admired Whitefield for his soul-stirring powers, his oratory, and his ability of organization. He was attracted to him as to any good, honest man, but he worked for him, above all, because that served his own ideas, the ideas of Benjamin Franklin. Poor Richard said in 1742:

When Knaves fall out, honest Men get their goods,
When Priests dispute, we come at the Truth.

Whitefield and his disciples renewed the popular fervor in the English colonies in America, but they did more to divide and diminish the power of the churches than all the discussions and books of the Masons and Deists combined.

This was accomplished by the demoralizing effects of these wandering ministers. One of them would arrive some fine morning in a town which was still peaceful. He would begin to convert the people, turn their minds topsy-turvy, and then, after having established a personal clientele and having taken up the offering, would leave for other districts, with the inference that the Spirit of the Lord was leaving with him also. One after another, these wandering evangelists would pass by, leaving their listeners behind them in a profound spiritual disorder, still enthusiastic, but avid and disappointed. The poor curate of the parish, who had his work still before him, would be bereft of his former power and unable to cope with the situation. The Church authorities and the conservative churchgoers rapidly united against these insatiable and disorderly vagabonds.

Whitefield saw the doors of the church close. It didn't matter much to him. He started preaching in the market place from a balcony, and even in the streets. The clerical opposition, far from harming him, increased his reputation and attracted new listeners. The street meetings were moving and picturesque, Whitefield spoke as often as twice a day, and it was an immense crowd which formed his audiences. A Philadelphia correspondent sent the following note which appeared in the *Boston News Letter* for December 6, 1739: "On Sunday at Whiteclay Creek he preach'd twice, resting about half an hour between the sermons to about 8000 people: of whom about 3000 'tis computed came on horseback. It rain'd most of the time, and yet he stood in the open air."

One can imagine the vivid sight: Whitefield, addressing the people, some who sat or stood on the turf, some mounted on horseback, some leaning from their buggies, his eloquence carrying above the monotonous beat of the rain, compelling attention and beaking down the opposition of his listeners by saying they were made of clay and that to clay they would return. Another time, when Whitefield preached at Philadelphia, the occasion was no less picturesque. With a porch for a pulpit, he expounded on the damnation of sinners until night fell, and a little child was placed near him to hold a torch for light. But Whitefield preached in such a beautiful and terrible fashion that the child wept and then fainted, while the fallen torch threw a thousand red sparks, lighting up his gaunt face. The listeners moaned and twisted with anguish.

In spite of their enthusiasm, however, the bourgeois friends of Franklin, and Franklin himself, were afraid of catching cold while they were being converted out-of-doors. Therefore, they decided to erect a beautiful building for Reverend Whitefield, not only to show their enthusiasm for him, but to give a lesson in tolerance to the local clergy as well. Franklin said:

> The design in building not being to accommodate any particular sect, but the inhabitants in general; so that even if the Mufti of Constantinople were to send a missionary to preach Mohammedanism to us he would find a pulpit at his service.

In this way Franklin could help Mr. Whitefield without renouncing his Masonic ideas, and at the same time render service to the "vital" religion and tease the orthodox ministers. Moreover, this church was consecrated to the inhabitants and not to a precise God or religion, thus being in accord with the philosophic spirit; in the Middle Ages temples had been built to provide a habitation for God, but now they were erected to provide a meeting place for men. Finally, there was also the advantage that the building would stay; Mr. Whitefield couldn't carry it with him, as he could take away their money, their enthusiasm, and spiritual peace (Spring, 1740).

Much as Franklin disapproved of Whitefield's idea of founding an orphanage in Georgia — Franklin felt that Georgia was not ready to undertake such a vast enterprise and that Philadelphia had more need of it —he promised to aid his pious friend in every way He set his accounts in order, printed his sermons in his newspaper, and took his part in the incessant quarrels which the churches stirred up. And he advertised him. Whitefield couldn't dine, move, preach, or travel, but what the *Pennsylvania Gazette* announced it. The columns were always open to letters which were written in defense of Whitefield or to poems which rhapsodized on the new saint.

Franklin only reserved the right to moderate the reforming zeal of Whitefield's disciples. For the city had been transformed. Every one had been gathered into the fold and walked the streets with a devout air. No one spoke any more except about God, and Salvation, and Virtue. No books were bought, except the religious ones. Franklin sold many of them — and thirty-six prayer societies were formed during one year. The churches had two public prayers every week day, and as many as four services on Sunday. Psalms and canticles were the only songs you would hear sung in the city, for Frivolity, Luxury, and Diversion, had been banished in disgrace.

But the people were human still. In 1737, a certain pious "Pythagorean Cynical-Christian Philosopher", Benjamin Lay, placed all his dear wife's "large parcel of valuable china" on the street, saying that he wished to make a sacrifice of it in order to show God his scorn of luxury. He invited every one who passed to break a cup and then convert himself. The passers by soon became numerous and ran off with the dishes intact, for a cup was a cup and could always be of use. Poor Richard's lessons in economy had more weight that day than his mystic enthusiasm. But in 1740, some time before the second visit of Mr. Whitefield, his most fervent admirers closed the Dance Hall the better to sanctify the city. They published this note in the *Gazette* as well:

> Since Mr. Whitefield's preaching here the Dancing School Assembly and Concert Room have been shut up as inconsistent with the Doctrine of the Gospels: and though the Gentlemen concerned caused the Door to be broke open again, we are informed that no company came to the last Assembly night.

This was too much. People of good society and of the rich middle class attended these concerts and assemblies. They did not partake of the general enthusiasm for Whitefield and protested. Franklin saw that there were troubles ahead and the next week published a letter of rectification from the organizers of the dances and concerts. They affirmed that everything was going on as usual. To this letter Franklin affixed a personal note in which he defended himself concerning his promise to Whitefield not to publish any attacks. Franklin declared himself always ready to publish anything that was sent to him on the subject.

I have often said that if any person thinks himself injured in a publick newspaper he has a right to have his vindication made as publick as the Aspersion. (*Pennsylvania Gazette*, May 8, 1740).

In fact, he was faithful to Whitefield. During all his visits of 1740, 1745, 1746, and 1747, he entertained him, guided and defended him. In 1742, when the churches of New England were making an energetic campaign against the wandering preachers (among them, Tennent, the friend of Whitefield), Franklin published a defense of them. However, his case was bad, for Davenport, one of Whitefield's converts, had let himself go to deplorable extremes of language against the established ministers. As bold as Whitefield, but less a master of his tongue, Davenport had put himself into such a false position that he had to retract. This was the principal danger for these evangelists: as long as they preached and held the crowd under the spell of their eloquence, all went well, but when they published their sermons their colleagues found the reading highly unpleasant. These printed sermons were an endless source of quarrels. In 1740, when Whitefield attacked the venerable archbishop Tillotson, claiming that he "knew no more of true Christianity than Mahomet", he was ensnared in newspaper discussions and became the object of many pamphlets. Franklin followed him faithfully, even though his adversaries had the better of him. He continued to lend his support in the great combat between Whitefield and the professors of Harvard (1744), who had turned against him furiously for all that he had dared to say against the established ministers. In these theological combats Whitefield received many a blow, and his faithful Franklin also. But their answering pamphlets sold well, and this was some consolation.

So much courage and devotion on the part of Franklin, who seemed so realistic and matter-of-fact, touched Whitefield to the heart. One day when Franklin had offered him his hospitality, Whitefield asked him if he made the offer "for Christ's sake", for then he would "not miss of a reward." Franklin answered, "Don't let it be mistaken; it was not for Christ's sake but for your sake."

He could have added that he was losing nothing by doing so. Whitefield was a popular author. He increased the number of library readers, furnished news for the *Gazette*, and added to the list of Franklin's customers. He helped Benjamin to efface all memory of the scandal of 1737, and gave him the means for satisfying his taste for religious mattters, morality and apostleship. All this was agreeable since Franklin could still conserve his radical ideas and continue his patient and methodical assault on the established churches. "The Church, the State and the Poor are three daughters which we should maintain, but not portion off."

To a wise and tender observer of the human heart, such as Benjamin Franklin, it was charming to hear the eloquent and saintly Whitefield uplift the crowds with his holy enthusiasm, and leave them thirsting for the vague exaltation they had experienced. From 1739 to 1748, the American people began by being drunk on devotion, and then went to the opposite extreme and did everything that could excite them. This period, after the long calm of 1715–1730, gripped the people suddenly, like a sharp attack of fever.

The long peace between England and the Bourbons had ended. Walpole was pushed towards war in spite of himself, for behind him was the compelling combination of a commercial bourgeois class leagued with an opulent aristocracy. In France, under the peaceful and adroit government of Cardinal Fleury, commerce had developed, the country had become rich, and men had vast ambitions. Every one believed in commerce and wanted to have monopolies. All those interminable wars, with Spain and France on one side and England on the other, had their origins in commercial disputes, although there was also a rivalry of civilizations. But the wars took place when the business men, tired of peaceful competition, had recourse to violence. They were intense wars, which only came to an end by the conquest of a market. The first of these long wrangles (1740–1748), the war of the Austrian Succession, was a violent struggle between the Bourbons and England for the market of America and the Indies.

The Franco-Spaniards, with their great superiority of numbers, could have been certain of success had the English not had the superiority of internal organization. England was a modern nation with a central government, with its own language and religion, and with well-defined frontiers. In France, the frontiers were still uncertain, and while it was conducting a commercial war on the sea, it was waging a dynastic and territorial war on the continent.

The struggle began in 1740 by a naval conflict between Spain and England. According to the Treaty of Utrecht, England had the right to carry on commerce with the Spanish colonies within certain limits, and under the control of the Spanish government. But this friendly compromise was, as almost always happens with compromises, the origin and occasion of a new war.

The Spanish control over the English vessels gave place to constant quarrels. The English traders, and, above all, the seamen of the North American colonies, were unscrupulous, and continually went beyond their rights, while, on the other hand, the Spanish authorities didn't hesitate to exercise their supervision by the most harsh and exaggerated means. In time, menaces were succeeded by negotiations, and negotiations by actual fighting. Finally, on April 12, 1740, at noon, the governor of the Province of Pennsylvania, in company with his corporation, and surrounded by a great, cheering multitude, read a proclamation from the King of England which declared war on Spain. Salvos were shot from Society Hill, and drinks were freely distributed all over the city. The people clinked glasses and drank to the health of the King, of the Royal Family, and of the Royal English Navy. All day long the crowds surged in the streets, and in the evening there were bonfires and much dancing. The war that the people had wanted and waited for so long had come at last.

CARTOON OF 1764 DESCRIBING FAMOUS ELECTION IN WHICH FRANKLIN WAS DEFEATED

And for forty-three years, almost without interruption, the city of brotherly love was going to live in the excitement of struggle and in the fever of danger.

The different classes of people in the city held opposite beliefs. For the rich, peaceful Quakers, obliged by their convictions to eschew war, and obliged by the size of their plantations to have many workers, this period was one of endless calamity. The little farmers lost also, for they had difficulty in exporting their produce. They tried to keep out of the war as much as possible and to live by themselves. The poorest classes in the city thought the war might bring suffering, but there was a bigger chance that they would make money. The servants and Negroes, hoping to escape their servitude, enrolled in the army or simply fled, thanks to the general disorder. The storekeepers counted on the garrisons, on the coming and going of recruits to make their fortunes. They and the non-Quaker merchants knew that a privateer in the harbor meant good business and they set to work with might and main.

The governor was now busy with the defense of the colony, and obeying the orders of the King, who wanted troops. Unfortunately, the Quakers refused to serve, refused moreover to force others to serve or to vote appropriations for the army. Now, thanks to the German farmers, they had the majority in the Assembly, for while the number of original Quakers had diminished, the Germans had increased in number till they represented a third of the Pennsylvania population. The Government tried to win the support of the middle class in the city, but it was an unorganized minority, while the non-Quaker merchants were egoistic and individualistic. The governor was in a cruel and comical position: his salary depended on the good will of the Assembly; if they were not disposed to pay him, he could die of hunger. If he ceded to them, the discontented Penns and the angry king would recall him. So he was between the devil and the deep blue sea, without any resource save his dignity. He took refuge in this but, of course, no one can live on sheer dignity.

In the streets, however, men were recruited for the King, who wished to send an expedition against Havana; then, too, there were the "Gentlemen Sailors" who were enrolled in the crews of the privateers for the merchants of Philadelphia. Later these vessels returned, towing their rich Spanish prizes with them: galleons laden with sugar from the West Indies, with woven stuffs of Peru, gold from Carthagene, and precious stones of Mexico. The first one of these privateers to leave was the sloop *George* with ten cannon and ten swivels. It left in November, 1739, and returned on July 1,1740.

Benjamin Franklin observed people and objects carefully. At the Junto, the lodge, the library, and the Assembly, he lent an attentive ear to all that was said, persuaded that this political imbroglio could not last forever. Gradually, indeed, the situation became strained. In 1740 the war was seriously begun, and in 1741 was a hard year for the poor city. The winter was rigorous and severe on the poor people, the irregularity of money exchange made all business difficult, and there were violent riots in the streets when the storekeepers counted four and a half Pennsylvania pennies as being equal to five English pennies. The crowds pillaged the shops. A civil guard had to be organized to keep the Negroes from circulating in the streets after sunset. Finally, the height of misfortune was reached, when the poorly paid quarantine doctor was careless in his examinations, and one of the boats brought the yellow fever; seven hundred and eighty-five persons died in Philadelphia, an increase of five hundred over the normal figure of the year preceding, two hundred and eighty-nine. Poor Richard, always prompt to seize an opportunity, gave in his Almanac of 1742: "Rules of Health and long life, and to preserve from Malignant fevers, and sickness in general."

VII

Franklin wisely contented himself by being a philanthropist. He didn't intervene in the quarrel between the Assembly and the governor. Wasn't he dependent on the Assembly as a printer? Wasn't he protected by the Quakers? Wasn't he connected with the people of the middle class, who supported the governor and put their shoulder to the wheel? Was he not the friend and protector of that fiery patriot Whitefield, who, in his prayers, never failed to invoke the aid of God for his king? Thus being the friend of every one, his hands were tied, at least for the moment. Nevertheless, he thought about the war a good deal, for he was a son of New England, a good Whig, and a good fighter. With his precise mind, he detested disorder. Not being able to do anything else, he urged his fellow citizens on to patriotism and made fun of their quarrels. In his Poor Richard of 1743 he wrote:

A Year of Wonders now behold!
Britons despising *Gallic* Gold!
A Year that stops the *Spanish* Plunders!
A Year that they must be Refunders!
A Year that sets our Troop marching!
A Year secures our Ships from Searching!
A Year that Charity's extended!
A Year that Whig and Tory's blended!
Amazing Year! that we're defended!

And then, less poetic, but more precise, he said in this Fable:

A Town fear'd a Siege and held Consultation,
What was the best Method of Fortification:
A grave skilful Mason declar'd his Opinion,
That nothing but Stone could secure the Dominion.
A Carpenter said Tho' that was well spoke
Yet he'd rather advise to defend it with Oak.
A Tanner much wiser than both these together,
Cry'd *Try what you please, but nothing's like Leather.*

The various factions were distinguished by those who depended on the grace of God to safeguard Philadelphia, others who wanted cannons, and others who thought the distant situation of the colony was a sufficient protection. Franklin wisely took his time, tried to satisfy his customers as usual, but had his own thoughts on the matter. Hadn't he suggested since March, 1734, that the colony take military precautions and prepare for war? Franklin had a feeling for the British Empire. He, who, properly speaking was neither a sentimentalist nor a mystic, nor an artist, had perceived the grandeur and beauty of this huge organization. He took pleasure in it and loved it.

His faith in God was not the same brand as that of those who thought action superfluous and hateful. Besides, he had his fortune to make, and his family and craft took too much time for him to throw himself body and soul into these disputes, to risk his situation in such a manner. He could only prepare for himself and for the future of the British Empire. He saw with a genius-like clarity what he had to do: develop the national sentiment of America, group the lower middle class and give them intelligent chiefs with broad views. He set himself to his task with ardor, knowing that when it was once accomplished, the hour for great action would come.

He let the various factions fight among themselves and use up their forces. The first sign of his cunning was his passivity. All the others, as a matter of fact, only covered themselves with ridicule. There was even a fist fight at the elections of 1742. The partisans of the Assembly occupied the entire stairway of the City Hall where the voting was done, and they thus held the vote at their mercy, for the voters deposited their ballots only when leaving the building. Some of the governor's devotees agreed that the voting was unfair, and, after a little while, there came a compact group of sailors from the port, claiming their right to cast a ballot. They asserted that they should be accepted as voters, inasmuch as Germans and other foreigners were admitted, and to prove that they were good voters, they fell with might and main upon the men massed on the stairway.

They seized the City Hall but they could not hold it long. The partisans of the Assembly, determined on peace even if it meant their death, gave the sailors such a bad time of it that all of them who were not carried off to the hospital, bleeding and unconscious, or who did not remain on the ground, forever freed from political cares, were thrown into prison. Thus the Assembly men, the Quakers and the cause of peace had a landslide at the election.

Franklin didn't like this fighting, and thought it proved nothing. He had abstained from taking part in the fray. But he was active. First, he spread his influence far and wide, to make it national. After his venture in South Carolina — with his workman Timothee and Timothee's widow — had prospered, he aided the widow of his brother James, who lived in Newport, and in 1741, he established a printing shop in New York. He put another one of his workmen, whom he had hired in 1733, in charge, one James Parker, who had fled from his master, William Bradford. When Franklin had taught him, he sent him back to struggle against his former employer.

Thus Franklin's influence radiated from the south to the north, and throughout the central regions of the colonies. It was most brilliant, of course, in Pennsylvania. His printing shop was very well equipped and comprised an important personnel, five or six workmen at least: Parker up to 1741; a German, J. H Miller, who had come to America with Zinendorff; a Swede, Olav Mälander; the young John Rose; his nephew, James Franklin of Newport, whom he had taken on in 1740 as his apprentice. With such a group of workmen, Franklin could print in German, Swedish, and English, and thus satisfy all the elements of the population.

This swelled his profits, and, also, during these war-time years, there were crowds of customers in the shop to hear the latest news. It became the center for the solid middle-class people of the city and for the farmers, who came to know what had happened, what was happening, and what was going to happen. Even if they pestered Franklin, he made money on them. Various distinguished strangers also paid him visits:

Virginians, who had come up on business to Pennsylvania, and Bostonians who would consult him about this and that. His position as mediator was a considerable advantage at this time, when the war was stimulating national zeal and a more intimate coöperation among the colonies.

The better to work for this union, and to give the people a sense of the British Empire, Franklin decided to found a political and historical review on the model of those he had read in England. This monthly periodical would be written to inform and guide the bourgeois, Whig and patriot elements of the population. He thought of giving the management of this magazine to John Webbe, one of his tavern companions and a former collaborator. Webbe had been a soldier under Marlborough, was a strong radical, a patriot and clever speaker, who occasionally wrote flamboyant but dull articles for the *Gazette*. Franklin came to an agreement with him, and then, when all was ready, Webbe, wishing to make more money, and not caring much about honesty, betrayed Franklin's plans to Bradford and promised to edit a review for him.

This was the last great battle between Bradford and Franklin. The scandal of the apprentice's Masonic initiation had given Bradford courage, and had caused some falling off in Franklin's business as is shown by figures. In 1733–1734, Bradford had published respectively five and eight works, while Franklin had come out with sixteen and fifteen. In 1737, 1738, 1739 Bradford went up from eight to ten to twelve, while Franklin fell from fifteen to eight and nine. The struggle was sharp, and Benjamin didn't regret closing the post to Bradford's newspapers by the order of the postmaster-general of Pennsylvania, whom Bradford had irritated by his negligence.

Bradford was only too happy to have overheard Benjamin's secret, and announced the publication of his *American Magazine* ahead of Franklin, who, nevertheless, hastened to advertise his *General Magazine and Historical Chronicle for all the British Plantations in America*. Bradford got ahead of him again by bringing out the first number of his periodical February 14, 1741, while Franklin's appeared three days later. This was the last victory for Bradford; his review disappeared at the end of three numbers, while Franklin's, which was more lively, went blithely on through six. Though Franklin also had to give up his project, he found some consolation in collaborating with a printer of Boston, who brought out a review of the same kind, the existence of which was more durable. But these magazines, which contained only economic and political documents, newspaper clippings and official communications, did not pay. Bradford almost ruined himself with his, and when he died, a few years later, he left the field free to Franklin. Bradford's son and widow spoiled what possibilities were left in the business by their quarrels.

From then on, sure of himself and instructed by his setback, Franklin tried to arrive at the same goal by other means. Gradually he changed his *Gazette* into an important financial and political newspaper. News and advertisements took up almost all the columns. The letters from readers and jokes were more rare, and when he inserted them he tried to give them a useful character. In a word, the *Gazette* was made serious and official. And its publisher, without denying the lower middle class to which he owed his splendid career, appeared as one of the "great personages" of America.

All his life was tinged with this ambiguity. He was still a bourgeois, because of his family, which he didn't abandon, and because of his good Debby, who made the neighbors smile a little — the way she called Mr. Franklin "Pappy" all the time! — and then those awful quarrels with her son William. . . . And the Franklins were bourgeois, though William might think what he would. Fat, shrewd and willful, he indulged a gentleman's whims, and cantered down the streets on the pretty little bay mare his good-natured father had given him, with a grand air. He ran away one day for a cruise on a privateer, and then would only return to fret and fume about the house. His little sister, Sarah, who had been born in 1744, was of quite a different disposition, and mildly accepted being her mother's companion, consolation, and helpmate in domestic activities.

Franklin remained affectionate with all his humble family of Boston. He visited them in 1743, the year which preceded the death of his good old father. And he didn't tire of helping them. He kept James Franklin, his nephew, at home with him, and sent the pleasant and fantastic Benjamin Mecom, the son of his beloved sister, to Parker, his partner in New York. In his shop at Philadelphia he sold the ointments of his mother-in-law, the Widow Read, and the "Crown" soaps of his brothers, John and Peter, who had succeeded to their father's business. A little later he established his brother-in-law, Davenport, the widower, as a butcher and grocer in Philadelphia, and gave him much aid in his business of sugar, biscuits, preserved oysters, etc. He didn't forget any one of his family, often offered proofs of his devotion, and was haughty with none of them. Nothing disturbed his relatives except the vague feeling of religious disagreement and the increasing impression that he was not of the same environment.

With his old friends of Philadelphia he remained a faithful comrade, a good-natured middle-class printer. At the Junto, which had grown and flourished, he still went to drink and sing with the men. He would repeat the catches he had written for them:

> Of their Chloes and Phyllises poets may prate,
> I sing my plain Country Joan,
> These twelve years my wife, still the joy of my life,
> Blest day that I made her my own.

This one was less pure:

> Fair Venus calls; her voice obey,
> In beauty's arms spend night and day.
> The joys of love all joys excell,
> And loving's certainly doing well.

Chorus:

> Oh no!
> Not so!
> For honest souls know,
> Friends and a bottle still bear the bell.

Then toss off your glasses, and scorn the dull asses,
Who, missing the kernel, still gnaw the shell;
What's love, rule or riches? Wise Solomon teaches
They're vanity, vanity, vanity still.

Chorus:
That's true;
He knew;
He'd tried them all through;
Friends and a bottle still bore the bell.

He had some broad stories for them also, which he sometimes printed, as the two letters on marriage, published by him in 1746 with this delicious title: "Reflections on Courtship and Marriage; In Two Letters to a Friend. Where in a Practicable Plan is laid down for Obtaining and Securing Conjugal Felicity."

This little work had so much success that Franklin saw three editions of it in his own lifetime, one of them appearing in Edinburgh. It was also imitated by William Bradford who published in 1747: "Observations upon Beauty, Coquetry, Jilting, Jealousy, etc., with some reflections on a married state."

But this imitation had neither the force nor the savor of Franklin's little book.

To answer the pleasantries of his Junto friends, he also published in the *Gazette* the now famous plea of Polly Baker, the young woman of Boston who had five natural children. Accused of her crime, she put her case so well, that the judges absolved her, and one of them married her the next day, to whom later she gave fifteen legitimate children. In her peroration, the good girl said:

Take into your wise consideration the great and growing number of bachelors in the country, many of whom, from the mean fear of the expences of a family, have never sincerely and honourably courted a woman in their lives; and by their manner of living leave unproduced (which is little better than murder) hundreds of their posterity to the thousandth generation. Is not this a greater offense against the publick good than mine? Compel them, then, by law, either to marriage, or to pay double the fine of fornication every year. What must poor young women do, whom customs and nature forbid to solicit the men, and who cannot force themselves upon husbands, when the laws take no care to provide them any, and yet severely punish them if they do their duty without them; the duty of the first and great command of nature and nature's God, *encrease and multiply*; a duty from the steady performance of which nothing has been able to deter me, but for its sake I have hasarded the loss of the publick esteem, and have frequently endured publick disgrace and punishment; and therefore ought, in my humble opinion, instead of a whipping, to have a statue erected to my memory.

By these joking paragraphs, Franklin excused himself of the stories people whispered about him, retained his good footing with his old friends, and kept the Junto alive. Franklin did not want to see it die, as it was too useful for him, and he knew that only joviality could develop and keep up the confidence of the bourgeois mind.

However, his reading, study, and observation had refined his always active mind, and he kept looking farther and with better results, for its nourishment. His ambition to be a leader attracted him to the environments where he found men of a quicker and more subtle intelligence. He knew that America had need of an aristocracy and he wished that this might be an aristocracy of mind. To develop it, he planned a college and a learned society. His tentative efforts to form a college in 1744 were rebuffed, but he was more happy in his attempt to create an academy. The American Philosophical Society open to all the learned men in the English colonies was designed to encourage the sciences and scientific works, and, above all, to promote useful discoveries. To form the kernel of it, he chose the most intelligent men he knew at the Junto and some distinguished men from other places. His work was facilitated by the great vogue for science at this epoch. Every one wished to study science and learned societies began to spring up everywhere. The people had heard of Newton and his theories, and they were eager to learn about them. Every American city, besides its magic lanterns and pantomimes, had its scientific lectures and experiments. At Boston, in 1739, Mr. Isaac

Greenwald gave a course of lectures including various experiments, Mr. Spencer did the same in New York in November, 1743, and in Philadelphia in 1744. Franklin was only following a prevailing tendency, but prompt to seize upon currents of opinion and to utilize them cleverly, he immediately suggested the most proper means of transforming this vain mode into something useful. With the support of his Quaker correspondent of London, Collinson, who was also a botanist and philanthropist, and who had been the means of introducing Franklin to the famous and worthy Bertram, the best botanist in the New World; by making the most of his connections with his mathematician friend, Godfrey, who had, at last, pardoned his marriage; and with the aid of the famous engineer, Cadwallader Colden of New York, Franklin launched his project (May, 1743).

That the subjects of the correspondence be; all new discovered plants, herbs, trees, roots, their virtues, uses, etc.; methods of propagating them, and making such as are useful, but particular to some plantations, more general; improvements of vegetable juices, as ciders, wines, etc.; new methods of curing or preventing diseases; all new-discovered fossils in different countries, as mines, minerals and quarries; new and useful improvements in any branch of mathematics; new discoveries in chemistry, such as improvements in distillation, brewing, and assaying of ores, new mechanical inventions for saving labour, as mills and carriages, and for raising and conveying of water, draining of meadows, etc.; all new arts in trades and manufactures . . . and all philosophical experiments that let light into the nature of things, tend to increase the power of man over matter and multiply the conveniences or pleasures of life.

This was a fine plan, analogous to the program of the French Encyclopedists, though its tendencies were more bourgeois than intellectual. Franklin was attracted by the practical and realistic side of civilization. He was not interested in being a mere thinker, he wanted to be a producer. He showed this desire then and there, and set an example to his colleagues by publishing, "An Account of the New-Invented Pennsylvania Fire-places", one of the inventions which did more for his glory than anything else; people living in the chilly eighteenth century thought it was no less than a discovery of genius. Franklin's chief principles had been to avoid the smoke, diminish the expense and utilize the most heat, and for the rest he had followed the experiments of Desaguliers and the Frenchman, Gauger, without claiming to be original. He had just perfected their discoveries and made them of practical use. But how grateful were the old maids, and the shivering families, who had kept poking their dying fires in winters hitherto without really getting warm!

Franklin knew what rôle he was playing, and didn't deceive any one. He did not even want to take any personal profit from his work. All the money that was made on the invention went to his old friend of the Junto, Robert Grace, to whom he had given the plans. But the society he was fostering suddenly received much prestige; it was spoken about in Europe, and the people in the colonies realized that it was not a useless association of pedants.

Thus encouraged, Franklin devoted all his time and voyages (Boston, 1745, New York, 1744) to this great work. He had difficulty in succeeding, for the distances between the colonies was enormous, the means of communication were bad, and the men were absorbed by the war, or preferred to sit drinking in the taverns. He himself had to make an effort to escape such attractions and to give up his mugs of cider. It was a kind of apprenticeship at which some men smiled. But one cannot become a great lord of the intellect without work. Franklin knew how to work. And while he was doing so, he was conscious that he was serving humanity, the British Empire, and himself.

Franklin remained calm, but every one was thinking about war. Since France had come to the aid of Spain, the situation had become serious. June 14, 1744, the governor made a proclamation to the effect that critical times were at hand. Tired of quarreling between themselves, the Assembly and the governor had at last come to an agreement, and each made concessions to the others. Governor Thomas signed the laws which the Assembly wished to pass, and authorized a new issue of paper money, by means of which the Assembly immediately voted to pay him all his back salary, amounting to some fifteen hundred pounds. Thanks to the new money, the Assembly even agreed to quarter the troops of Her Majesty, and to supply them with all the "grain" they needed. If the governor chose to buy powder "and other grain", the Quakers did not object.

The merchants of Philadelphia, excited over the profits that some among them had made, by arming their vessels — and being perfectly sure that more money could be made, as no one had yet suffered any huge losses — multiplied the number of privateers. After the *George*, there was the *Joseph and Mary*, which on one cruise in 1742 brought back a prize of one hundred thousand pounds sterling; then, in 1743, the *Trembleur*, with fourteen cannon, the *Tartar* with thirty-six cannon, which sank directly after having been launched in the Delaware with all its sailors and stockholders on board: then the *Wilmington*, which was a beautiful ship, built to replace the *George*, and which weighed three hundred tons; finally, in 1744, there were built the *Marlborough*, two hundred and thirty tons, eighteen fixed cannons, fourteen swivels; the *Cruiser*, two hundred tons, fourteen fixed cannons, fourteen swivels; the *Warren*, two hundred and twenty tons, 16 fixed cannons, eighteen swivels. This little navy was very profitable to the stockholders, for the French West Indies were rich, and not at all ready for war.

However, as the years went by the hardships of war began to make themselves felt. The French built armed privateers also, which bothered Philadelphia commerce. The city began to feel the effects of five years of constant excitement. Immorality had made great inroads, as was recognized by a special jury in a report which Franklin wrote. It mentioned more than one hundred houses out of nine hundred which had received cabaret licenses. A certain district was even known as "The Devil's Corner." Vice was rampant everywhere and there were no means to hinder it!

In all this confusion, the city grew larger. A new market place was built. The population was so large that four companies were recruited for service in the West Indies and the North, including more than six hundred men. The privateers had plenty of work. The *New George* had an epical and indecisive battle with a privateer of Saint Malo, *Louis Joseph* (Captain Piednoir), which was sunk shortly thereafter by the *Warren*. The taking of Louisburg from the French was celebrated by festivals and illuminations (1745). Mr. Whitefield was received in triumph and every one exulted in the excitement of the moment. Franklin's shop was filled with men coming in to hear the news, and when the post arrived, there were always crowds of people to ask questions. He laughed and didn't complain.

The year 1746 taught some rude lessons. The disembarkment of the Pretender in Scotland kept the Americans in suspense for two months. The French had learned how to hide themselves and how to fight. The sea was swept clean of prizes and covered with privateers; often the vessels of Philadelphia returned with empty holds and chagrined crews. One of them was taken by the Spanish. Moreover, a deadly epidemic spread over the colonies, a kind of diphtheria inexactly called "putrid sore-throat."

Franklin then sent William to the army in the north, thinking that war was less dangerous than the disease, and less unhealthy than the incessant quarrels he had with his mother. He himself went to Boston to see his friends, his aged mother, and his customers. On his return he found Philadelphia turned upside down.

The French began to learn the channel of the Delaware. Towards the end of May, 1747, twelve Philadelphia vessels were seized. Franklin and his friends were trying in vain to raise a subscription among the rich men, to arm the *Warren* for coastal guard service — there was nothing to be done about it. In this kind of war it was much easier to attack than to defend. Pennsylvania learned this to her sorrow. On July 12, 1747, a French privateer, flying the English colors, arrived at the mouth of the Delaware. A pilot went out to it, was hoisted on board, made a prisoner and forced to guide the boat up the river. The privateer pillaged two plantations and seized a vessel bound for London with rich cargoes. Excitement and fear reached its height in Pennsylvania. But once more the Assembly, in which the Quakers formed the majority, refused to do any thing, refused even to be bothered. They had confidence in God. The French knew of this confidence, but they were sure that God would not listen to the prayers of heretics, and didn't hesitate to send three more of their privateers up the Delaware. They seized three merchant vessels and spread disorder along the banks. This was too much for the people, who could no longer support this inactivity, and as the governor had resigned, yielding his place to the president of the council, Palmer, who was likewise helpless, there were murmurings in the streets that they wouldn't wait much longer.

Franklin's hour had come. As secretary of the Assembly, he had attended the regular sessions for eight years, as well as the secret meetings, and he had noted all that had passed. He had seen how intensely the members desired peace, and with what increasing embarrassment they maintained this policy in the face of the manifest danger which menaced the colony. He had watched the group of men who were hostile to the Quakers develop into a party, and he had read the violent letters against the Quakers which had been printed in the newspapers of both England and America. These letters inveighed against the Quakers for their inertia and their hypocrisy, and the following quotation gives an idea of what they were like:

INSTRUCTIONS HOW TO MAKE A PERFECT QUAKER

First take a handful of the Herb of Deceit, and a few leaves of Folly, and a little of the Rose of Vain Glory, with some of the Buds of Envy, and a few Blossoms of Malice, with a few Formality Flowers and a Sprig or two of idle Conceit; take some of the Seeds of Pride, and some of the Seeds of Hypocrisy, and some Seeds of forbidden Pleasure, and some of the Bark of Self Will, and put them all together into a Mortar of Defiance, and pound them with a Pestle of Headstrong Wood: Also take an Ounce of Ill-Manners, and Three Quarters of an Ounce of Cheat Seed, a good Quantity of the Roots of Ambition, and the Pith of Self Conceit, together with some Plums that grow on Runagate Hill, and some of the Grapes that grow in the Suburbs of Sodom, and some of the Spices of Babylon; and then take these twenty Sorts, and stew them together in a stonyhearted Jugg; over the fire of Cold Zeal, and pour in a little of the Water of Wild fountain, and when they are all simmed and soaked together enough, grate in a little Folly Powder, and strain it through a Cloth of Vanity, and spuck every Morning thro' a Spout of Ignorance, and in a little time it will raise the spirit and you will quake and shake and smite on your Breast and so you will become a perfect Quaker.

The Quakers now formed a rich and conservative aristocracy in the province, which did not enjoy the favor of either the jealous Anglo-Saxon public, or of the governor. (The Penns, some time before, had given up the faith of their father to join the Church of England.) The aged Logan was no longer active enough to serve as intermediary between the Quakers and the proprietors; the former were angry at having been betrayed, the latter were annoyed with the pacificism which the Quakers showed. Logan, moreover, believed in the legitimacy of defensive wars. If the Quakers were ever abandoned by the Germans, they would find that they were in the minority and cursed by every one. This troubled them.

Franklin had a bird's-eye view of the situation, and following his quick political intuition, he put himself forward as a mediator between the parties, managing the Quakers with much care. He began by attracting the undecided Quakers to his side by publishing in his *Gazette* the pages of the great Quaker, Barclay, who approved of defensive war (November 5, 1747), and he returned to this subject three different times. Then, aided by some friends, members of the Junto, the lodge and the library, he wrote: "Plain Truth; or, Serious Considerations on the Present State of the City of Philadelphia and Province of Pennsylvania. By a Tradesman of Philadelphia."

He wrote this pamphlet with great precaution and much skill, adopting a devout air, and taking examples from the Bible, which he presented in Mr. Whitefield's manner. He drew a

CARTOON OF 1764 DESCRIBING FRANKLIN AND THE PENNSYLVANIA POLITICIANS

hideous and striking picture of the horrors of war, telling of the atrocities inflicted on a city taken by assault and pillaged by pirates. But he displayed the greatest skill in saying that the scrupulous Quakers were not the only ones to blame; that the rich merchants, who were called gentlemen, were just as guilty, and less excusable, with their refusal to act unless all the people acted with them. He did not scold the Quakers, but tried to help them out of their difficulty with amiable words for their religious faith. He ended his pamphlet by making an appeal to the middle-class farmers, shopkeepers and business men, who had everything to lose by the ruin of the city, but who were not hindered by religious convictions from taking arms. He strongly urged them to save themselves and their province, showed them how strong they were, and what resources were at their disposition, "60,000 fighting men, acquainted with Fire Arms, many of them Hunters and Marksmen, hardy and bold. All we want is Order, Discipline, and a few Cannons." He finished by a pious invocation to "The God of Wisdom, Strength, and Power, the Lord of the Armies of Israel."

This pamphlet was sober, suave and persuasive. It was well received by the public which Franklin had prepared, thanks to his *Gazette* and the Junto. Without waiting any longer, Franklin gathered a group of faithful shopkeepers around him who applauded his project. He thanked them, but he did not yet want them to sign anything. Indeed, only two days later, on a Monday, there was a new gathering at a coffeehouse, and a number of the distinguished and important men of the city attended it. Views were exchanged, Franklin gave a speech and said that his *Gazette* and press were entirely at the disposition of the national cause. He then submitted a plan of association, which was accepted, and a meeting was scheduled for the next day at the New Building (the temple which had been erected for Whitefield). Over three hundred persons attended and signed their names to the document in the midst of great enthusiasm. The Municipal Council approved of the initiative shown, and made an appeal for aid to the proprietors on behalf of this association. The Provincial Council fell in step, and asked the Board of Trade in England to send a warship to protect the Delaware. The wealthy merchants, seeing the success of the movement, rallied to Franklin, in addition to a good number of Quakers, among them Logan, who supported the martial printer with all their strength.

Then all Philadelphia played at war, and Franklin went through his first drill. The association increased with lightning-like rapidity. Volunteers were grouped in companies, and companies in regiments. Franklin was elected colonel, but refused to accept the appointment and proposed Lawrence. He also encouraged the Germans to fight, and they rapidly got a regiment together, as the raid of the French privateers had really frightened them. The ladies of Philadelphia made beautiful flags and richly colored symbolic standards. These were offered to the regiments with solemn ceremonies, and a great military parade was held, the first in the City of Friends. Franklin then went to New York (March, 1748), and by a skillful maneuver with Governor Clinton (after a few glasses of Madeira), procured eighteen cannons for the association. They were mounted on a battery which overlooked the Delaware; a permanent guard was organized, and Franklin, as one of its members, spent more than one night in patient watching for the privateers. He was not lacking in work by day, either, what with drills, reviews, meetings, and the financial labor which the association entailed.

Franklin had his opponents too; some ardent Quakers attacked him, claiming that he was tempting God by his lack of confidence in Him, and that, to their notion, the author of "Plain Truth" must be a hypocrite, for if he had as much faith in God as he claimed to have, he would not be so troubled, nor would he be spreading this unchristian, warlike agitation among the inhabitants of Pennsylvania. This last objection was not without some justice, but in the excitement of the moment, and considering the difficult circumstance of the province, they could not have had much weight. Many Quakers, who were frightened at the responsibility their sect undertook by hindering the colony from military preparation, were discreetly on

Franklin's side; the wealthy merchants, although a little hurt at his language, couldn't resist the current of popular feeling; and the governor put his shoulder to the wheel and worked skillfully.

Then, in order to obtain the support of the religious groups, Franklin, like a good son of New England, suggested "A Day of Fast and Humiliation", a custom which had been practiced a long time in Boston, but which had never been seen in Pennsylvania. This innovation was well received, and offered an opportunity to Gilbert Tennent and other Methodists to support Franklin and his friends in eloquent speeches. Throughout Philadelphia they proclaimed that the God of Israel was certainly the Lord of Hosts, and that He would protect the English armies, as He had protected His chosen people. Thus the wandering preachers paid their debt to Franklin.

The new year of 1748 had begun, and Franklin, the printer near the market place, walked in the streets, wearing the uniform of a private, but everybody looked at him as the one man who had stirred the province to action and saved it by breaking the stupefying charm that the Quakers had cast over Philadelphia. He was considered to be the real arbiter of the situation, and his enemies murmured that he was preparing a *coup d'etat.*

They couldn't understand his calm bearing, or guess that he was planning very much more than a simple *coup d'etat.* He was always ahead of those around him, and now that he was the leading politican of the colony, he was going to become its greatest mind. He worked steadily for this end, thanks to the leisure that the reorganizing of his shop had offered him.

There was scarcely any competition against him in Philadelphia. Although two new German printers had established themselves, and William Bradford had made strong efforts, Franklin's position was impregnable. By good luck, Franklin had found an excellent workman, David Hall, who took care of the heaviest part of his professional work. He owed this good fortune to one of his relatives, Jimmy Read, who was connected in a business way with a great printer of London, William

Strahan. Read showed Franklin one of Strahan's letters, in which he mentioned his workman, Hall, who wanted a place in America. Franklin seized the opportunity, had Hall come, and by 1747 the two were close friends. Franklin began to let him take care of the business, in 1748 he took him on as his partner, and they remained so until 1766. Hall busied himself with the printing and took charge of the bookshop, while Franklin continued to edit his newspaper and to write his almanac, furnished the capital and directed the general policy of the house. The profits were divided, and Franklin, who had made about two thousand pounds sterling a year, received at least a half of this yearly after 1748.

Without losing interest, Franklin slowly broke away from his business. His newspaper took on a more and more impersonal tone. It contained almost no propaganda, although he did use it to help his political career, at least up to 1757. But Hall didn't like politics and detested discussions.

In the almanac Franklin remained more himself, although there was a change here too. He became a gentleman and an official, his former broad jokes now embarrassed him. "If I now and then insert a Joke or two that seem to have little in them," he wrote, "my Apology is, that such may have their Use, since perhaps for their Sake light airy Minds peruse the rest and so are struck by somewhat of more Weight and Moment." "Poor Richard" was a too useful publication, and a too precious means of doing good to be abandoned to sheer gayety. Nevertheless, Franklin kept as much humor as he could, and up to the very end put the best of himself into it, but the tone seemed to have become more and more elegant, it was called from then on "Poor Richard Improved", and was decorated with pretty woodcuts. After 1747, it included thirty-six pages instead of twenty-four, and as the price was not raised, it defied all competition; no other almanac could approach its volume and intellectual richness. That Franklin sold ten thousand copies a year was not at all surprising.

Franklin, who had now sufficiently mastered French, Italian, Spanish and Latin, to read in these languages, enriched his almanac with the new treasures he found in his foreign readings. But this was not enough for him, and, in accordance with the tendencies of his time, he turned his attention to science, especially natural science; on this virgin continent it was Nature which most attracted the bold thinkers. Many of them studied botany like the worthy Bertram, but Franklin was dreaming of more useful and picturesque sciences.

Now he saw that the entire universe, in trying to divert itself from war and from the classical tragedies of war (which were beginning to tire the ladies also), was passionately interested in electricity. Musschoenbroek of Leyden had succeeded for the first time, thanks to the famous bottle, in condensing electricity, and could produce long sparks by applying a conductor to the two sides of the bottle. These sparks, which every one could see, and the shocks, which every one could feel, seemed like magic, and were very delightful. Every one talked about electricity, ladies doted on it, and there were all kinds of experiments in the salons, universities, coffeehouses and fairs. There wasn't a single woman, from a duchess to a dairymaid, who didn't want to feel an electric shock. Wandering charlatans went from village to village, selling an electric shock for a chicken or a turkey. In Madrid, the Abbé Nollet electrified an entire regiment of guards simultaneously. In Italy some scientists hurriedly caught up with the fashion and endeavored to cure (or kill) people by giving them electric shocks against paralysis. Some of them became very skillful. But there was the great vagueness as to the nature of the mysterious "fluid" and of its more mysterious cause.

It was at Boston, in 1746, that Franklin first met an experimenter who talked with him at length on this subject, — a man named Spence. Franklin was struck with wonder, like every one else, and when, some months later, Collinson sent him a tube by which he could make electrical experiments, he was all ready to fling himself headlong into this science, forgetting the printing shop, war, Deborah and Sarah.

After he received this tube, he bought the instruments which Spence had used and settled down to steady work. He made excellent progress while his contemporaries of Europe were merely groping, for he was superior to them in two ways: he was a skillful manual workman and quick at seeing his way out of a fix. This he had learned from his father, and he was able to make much of his apparatus himself. When almost all the European experimenters, with their white hands and lacy cuffs, could do no more than the simplest experiments, employing workmen to manufacture their instruments and for the dirty work in general — that is to say, exposing themselves to innumerable causes of error — Franklin, thanks to his manual skill and his habit of physical labor, was able to make the most complicated experiments all by himself. Being a journalist gave him another advantage, for as he was not familiar with the technical jargon of science and had to use clear, simple English, he avoided the absurd errors of the European scholars, who used the old-fashioned expressions for their new-fashioned discoveries. Franklin, who had no other basis for his theories than his experiments, and no other way to explain them but in common everyday words, began from the beginning and remained constantly logical and intelligible. It was precisely this quality which the study of electricity demanded.

In a very short time he succeeded in some fine experiments, which were very picturesque and amusing, and which attracted his neighbors (Winter 1746–1747 and 1747–1748). While war was raging and business was bad, while Deborah inveighed against visitors, the foul weather and her son William, Benjamin Franklin closed his door, and meddling with his tubes, would produce brilliant sparks; their vivid light would flare up in the quiet laboratory, which was bathed in the clear shadow of winter. Franklin also instructed some of his neighbors and friends in the science, in order to dispense with troublesome visitors, and to obtain some collaborators. These were: Ebenezer Kinnersley, Philip Syng, Thomas Hopkinson. Kinnersley became very skillful, but none of them, not even the most shrewd, could achieve the art of understanding it like Franklin.

By 1748, he had already developed a theory. He wrote it

and sent it to Collinson in England, out of gratitude for his gift of apparatus.

The year 1748 marked the beginning of his great scientific works. It was also the year of the Peace of Aix-la-Chapelle, between France, Spain and England; this was a truce which was due to the temporary fatigue of the adversaries, for, despite the fact that France had had more than one brilliant victory, none of them could claim a definite success. Then, too, 1748 was the year when Franklin withdrew from his shop to take a house in a quiet corner of Philadelphia, beyond the noise of the market place, and out of the reach of insistent people. As they were no longer his customers, he no longer had to seek or tolerate them. Still, it was in this same year of 1748 that Franklin's fellow citizens, grateful for his public services, gave him an electoral function for the first time, and appointed him a member of the Municipal Council of Pennsylvania.

1748! The year when Franklin was very close to glory.

VIII

A GREAT personage of the eighteenth century had to possess estates, a brilliant army record, a fine mind, a way with the ladies, and to have known mistresses and adventures. It was not at all fashionable to be either a booby, an ignoramus, a coward, a clown or a pauper. Some of these styles have remained, others have disappeared, but it is very surprising that such an old-fashioned century should have demanded so insistently that men of the world know how to think, serve, command and love — or at least, to make love, a nuance which was not at all clear then.

Up to 1748, Mr. Franklin of Philadelphia had proved his aptitude for the latter activity, but for the rest he still seemed to be a novice. He didn't lose his time, however, and in some months, in his own way, he acquired all the necessary characteristics of a great personage. We have seen how he armed and fortified his city; he accomplished his other tasks still more brilliantly. In 1747 he had already begun his estate by buying three hundred acres in New Jersey near Burlington, and he didn't stop there. He was no longer poor and he knew how to manage what he had. His leisure was not a means of spending his substance, but of increasing it. If this did not place him in the nobility — to which he never belonged — it did give him a position among the chosen few of the society of his time. He forced himself among them in four years, just as he forced himself on the great thinkers of the age, without seeming to mind about it. He had a sixth sense for finding opportunities. Always a journalist, both in spirit and actuality, he now made a discovery which the whole world was waiting for.

All Europe was excited over electricity, and great discoveries were in the air. In 1749, one of the most brilliant learned societies of France, the Academy of Bordeaux, formulated the problem which preoccupied every one, and made a contest out of it, asking the question: Is there any analogy between Electricity and Thunder. The prize was won by Monsieur Barberette, a doctor of Dijon, who made a fine dissertation on the analogy between the "Thundering Matter" and the "Electrical Matter," as they said then.

But during this time, Mr. Franklin of Pennsylvania, who didn't know about the Academy of Bordeaux, or Monsieur Barberette, had done better: he had *demonstrated* the identity of lightning with electricity. He had even found the means of proving it scientifically. Such was the result of three winters of work.

Aided by his three good neighbors and friends, Ebenezer Kinnersley, Philip Syng, and Thomas Hopkinson, Franklin had put body and soul into his task. The first year they studied the electrical property of metallic points, which was still unknown, and discovered that they attracted and emitted electricity. They repeated all the experiments of Musschoenbroek and those which Wilson had written in his books. As they were not used to scientific jargon, and thought in a simple way, they had to invent their own language, that is to say, to present a new hypothesis on the nature of this curious, invisible and brutal force. Renouncing the ambiguous terminology of Dufay, which was then employed, and which distinguished two kinds of electricity, resinous and glazed, Franklin named them instead, positive and negative. He expressed them by plus and minus signs, and this was really a flash of genius, for all that was known on this subject was immediately made clear and simple. Franklin and his friends amused themselves with all kinds of little tricks, playing with this new force like children who have discovered a new toy. They would strip the gilding off a book by using the volume as a conductor and shooting electricity along the edge, and they delighted in electrifying a little metallic crown which surmounted an engraving of the King of England, because whoever would touch it would receive a shock, and thus electricity would show its loyalty to the dynasty.

These toys were not useless, as they appealed to the imagination of the people and diverted the wise. But they would have been worth nothing at all, had it not been for the great work of Franklin. After having proved that metallic points could attract or emit electricity, Franklin demonstrated the identity of lightning with electricity, and his method was one of extreme rigor and simplicity: he showed by experiments that electricity had all the characteristics of lightning, and that lightning had all the characteristics of electricity. He suggested a proof which rendered the theory irrefutable: to erect a pointed iron rod on the top of a hill or tower, when storm clouds were low, and then, by means of a regular experiment with the conductor, determine whether it were electrified or not.

Franklin was so sure of his observations and conclusions that he did not wait to make this proof, but, pushed on by his genius which forced him to be useful, he invented the lightning rod, called in the eighteenth century an "electrical conductor." In his "Poor Richard for 1753", he wrote a detailed description of his discovery, so that every one could understand it and make use of it. It was like Franklin to do this, and it showed him to be different from his European colleagues. While they studied their complicated formulas intensely, and manipulated their terrifying machines in solitary laboratories, Franklin invented these sublimely simple and clear theories in playing with objects which he knew how to handle, and verified his discoveries by utilizing them, and not by giving subtle discourses about them in the academies, as was done in Europe. While other learned men, huddled in dusty rooms, bitterly fought over principles, Franklin invited his collaborators to an "electrical picnic" on the banks of the Schuylkill.

> Spirits . . . are to be fired by a spark sent from side to side through the river, without any other conductor than the water; an experiment which we some time since performed to the amazement of many. A turkey is to be killed for our dinner by the electrical shock and roasted by the *electrical jack*, before a fire kindled by the *electrical bottle;* when the healths of all the famous electricians in England,

Holland, France, and Germany are to be drank in *electrified bumpers*, under the discharge of guns from the *electrical battery*.

No wall, diploma or theory existed between Franklin and nature, between Franklin and the public. Also, as his discoveries had been clear and rapid, they quickly spread over the civilized world. Mitchell and Collinson both sent the papers of their friend, Franklin, to the Royal Society of Science, and they were received, after some sarcastic observations, with esteem. Collinson published them, and they enjoyed a great success, especially in France, where the scientists were prompt to become enthusiastic, seeing the consequences of his discovery more quickly. The famous Buffon, who had learned of Franklin's work from his English friends, hurried to translate these exciting papers, and, what was better still for Franklin, to verify them.

On May 10, 1752, at Marly, the French scholar, Dalibard, succeeded in the experiment which Franklin had suggested. He set up a high pole of metal on the top of a hill during a storm, and soon found that it was charged, just as Franklin had predicted. A few days later, the experiment was performed again by another scholar, DeLor, in the presence of his most Christian Majesty, King Louis XV, with equal success. Lightning had become a plaything for men, and Jupiter, empty-handed, had nothing to do but to return to Olympus and make love with Juno. He could no longer frighten human beings.

King Louis XV was so impressed by the experiment that he immediately sent his compliments to Franklin. This was the first letter that a king ever wrote to a candle-maker's son. Naturally, such a brilliant token of admiration soon caused jealousy, especially among electrical technicians. Abbé Nollet, one of the greatest experimenters in Europe, was particularly chagrined, and though he was a brilliant man, he was confused by his own subtlety. He thought that the discoveries of the Philadelphia School (as it was then called) were over-estimated, and proceeded to say so in a series of scientific pamphlets, which were bitter against Franklin. Franklin was nettled at first, but after reflection, decided not to answer.

His French disciples, who were numerous by now, would answer for him and the great Italian scholar, Father Baccaria, took it upon himself to reduce Nollet's arguments to nothing. Nollet, however, was strongly established in the academies and universities of France, and, up to his death, he succeeded in preventing them from offering public homage to Franklin. Benjamin had to be satisfied for the moment with the royal letter and the adoration of his faithful French friends.

All this enthusiasm, which the learned newspapers of France freely reported and increased, had its repercussion in England. The Royal Society in London did not want to seem any less well-informed than Louis XV, and so presented Franklin with one of their highest awards, the Copley Medal, in 1753, while the Society for the Encouragement of Art elected him as one of their members.

It was during this time, in June, 1752, that Franklin, by a decisive experiment which crowned his theories with success, added another cubit to his glory. Going out during a storm, with his son, Franklin flew a kite, to see if he could draw electricity from the clouds. He could have killed himself by this experiment, but luck was with him, no accident happened, and to his inexpressible joy, he found that the key attached to the end of the kite string was charged with electricity. It was in this way that the most brilliant discovery of the century was achieved. Franklin set up a lightning rod on his roof, which, by a pretty little system, would ring a bell whenever it was charged. People wrote to him from all over the country about storms and the effects of lightning. He was himself insatiable for facts on the subject and published the following request in his newspaper (October 19, 1752):

Those of our readers in this and the neighboring provinces who may have an opportunity of observing, during the present summer any of the effects of Lightning on houses, ships, trees, etc, are requested to take particular notice of its course, and deviation from a strait line in the walls or other matter affected by it, its different operation or effects on wood, stone, bricks, glass, metals, Animal bodies, etc and every other circumstance that may tend to discover the nature and complete the history of that terrible meteor. Such observations being put in writing and communicated to Benjamin Franklin in Philadelphia will be very thankfully accepted and acknowledged.

About the same time this was printed, he wrote a descriptive and practical essay on the subject: "How to Secure Houses &c. from Lightning." Thus, without losing a single year, he had perfected his discovery by making an invention out of it which was useful for all mankind. The effect was overwhelming. Lightning rods shot up from Boston to Charleston. And in the largest scientific periodical of France there appeared this paragraph:

Most of the Physicians in Europe have been interested a long time in knowing what electricity corresponded with. They have seemed to care less for new experimenting than to make researches for the causes of the phenomena they have observed, and to study the application that could be made of electricity. But a Quaker, immured in a corner of America, has just demonstrated to all the scholars of our hemisphere that they had failed to notice the most striking and beautiful phenomena of electricity, and that they had not observed enough to offer theories. It is very surprising that a matter which has been worked over so much, should appear so new in his hands. Mr. Franklin is not satisfied with publishing his experiments and his detached observations but gives such grandiose and extended views on the subject that there is hope the mystery will some day be unveiled, and that it will be more useful to us than is generally imagined.

Philosophers and leading thinkers, without any further delay, became enthusiastic about this invention which made fun of the gods. Science had invented something practical and exciting for the first time: it had made progress which all could see, appreciate and utilize. By this brilliant invention, Science had reduced the realms of religion and annexed those provinces which had hitherto belonged to Faith and Prayer. In all countries and in all religions, but especially in America, where man appeared so weak before the overwhelming forces of Nature, earthquakes and electrical storms seemed to be direct and wrathful manifestations of God. The doctrines of the New England clergymen were clear on this point. Every time a thunderstorm occurred in their parish, they would quote the verses from the Bible which mention thunderbolts as being the weapons of an angry Jehovah. The most liberal of them admitted that there might be natural secondary causes, but that thunder had only the primary cause of God and his wrath. Then, the explanations of Franklin could still be supported, as they only touched on secondary causes; but his efforts to restrain the avenging hand of God were clearly impious.

The lightning rod, which was invented just at the end of the religious renascence in America, became an object of attack for many churchmen. Franklin had to defend himself. He asked his neighbor, friend, and collaborator, Ebenezer Kinnersley, to help him. Kinnersley had had a hard time in business, and had lately turned to electricity, as it was so successful, for his livelihood. So Kinnersley gave lectures on his subject which Franklin helped him to prepare. He spoke at Boston in the autumn of 1751, in the West Indies in 1753, and held some public experiments when he returned to Philadelphia in 1754. One of them was to prove "The Lawfulness of endeavouring to guard against lightning." The conflict was serious. The New England ministers knew only too well what deep and fortunate influences the atmospheric phenomena had over their congregations. It would be dangerous to diminish this ancient faith of the fervent population. And year after year, they took up their cudgels to show that Franklin had mistaken himself, that he had been sacrilegious to continue his efforts, and that his proceedings were not at all certain. In 1755 there was a sharp discussion between the Reverend Th. Prince and Doctor J. Winthrop, a professor of Harvard. Following an earthquake, one of Reverend Prince's dissertations on this natural phenomena was published and he wrote as a postscript to it:

> The more points of iron are erected round the Earth, to draw the Electrical substance out of the air, the more the Earth must needs be charged with it. And therefore it seems worthy of consideration, whether any part of the Earth being fuller of this terrible substance may not be more exposed to more shocking Earthquakes. In Boston

are more erected than anywhere else in New England; and Boston seems to be more dreadfully shaken. O! There is no getting out of the mighty Hand of God! If we think to avoid it in the air, we cannot in the Earth: Yea it may grow more fatal; and there is no safety anywhere, but in His Almighty Friendship through Christ the Mediator, and by heartily repenting of every sin and heartily embracing the Savior in all his Offices and uprightly Living to him.

This fine homily, which incriminated Franklin by attributing the origin of earthquakes to lightning rods, angered J. Winthrop, who was a great friend and scientific disciple of Franklin. He gave a lecture in the Chapel of Harvard to refute Prince, saying at first that he was surprised to see so many errors of logic and science in the sermon of the Reverend Minister; he then went on to show how thunder and electricity had nothing in common, so that it was absurd to imagine that lightning rods, by attracting electricity, could engender earthquakes. Finally, going to the bottom of the question, he affirmed that without offending God it could be claimed that earthquakes did not express his anger; far from being harmful, they were really very useful. "Even Thunder and lightning, which, next to earthquakes, are the most terrible phenomena of nature, are yet universally allowed to be necessary to free the atmosphere from a certain unwholesome sultriness, which often infects it." This is how a scholar, in the name of Science and Holy Script, stood up for Franklin, lightning rods, and storms! An identical discussion was taking place at the same time in Charleston, between Doctor Lining, one of Franklin's partisans, and some devout souls; to quiet these latter persons, the *Gazette of South Carolina* suggested raising lightning rods to the glory of God.

In general, the strict religious people of Europe regarded this new invention with the same horror, despite the fact that it seemed so innocent. Moreover, they had the most advanced scientists for allies, for these men thought that lightning rods were more dangerous than helpful. The discussion was prolonged.

Franklin's enemies among the scientists were those who

were more interested in theory than in its practical application. This was only Franklin's due, for his practical mind did not help him much in grappling with abstract ideas, and he was only at his ease before facts and theories which could be verified by experiment. In 1727 he believed that tiny crabs were born in seaweeds; in 1737 he explained again to the readers of his *Gazette* that earthquakes and thunder were produced by sulphuric vapors, either in the air or the bowels of the earth, which tried to free themselves. He even said, "Why there may not be thunder and lightning underground in some vast repositories there I see no reason. . . ."

Neither his technical vocabulary nor his faculty of intellectual criticism permitted Franklin to show himself at his best in his theories. He used such awkward formulæ as these: "Electrical fire loves water, is strongly attracted by it, and they can subsist together." "The particles of air are said to be hard, round, separate, and distant from each other; every particle strongly repelling every other particle, whereby they recede from each other, as far as common gravity will permit." Although he wrote these definitions at a time when the scientific language was still in a state of flux, they could not have been very satisfactory to men of exact and methodical minds. However, though this laxness harmed Franklin in his theoretical discussions, it was advantageous in that he was obliged to use everyday language, and to turn to experimenting for his results.

Here he was superior, for he had his own exactitude and method; he could take hold of any subject immediately, and understand its connection with current ideas. In all the fields of science which touched on actuality, and where he could make use of his good common sense, he showed a genius-like precision and rapidity. His observation was always keen; by reading about storms in the newspapers and following their progress over the country, he discovered that the northeastern storms came from the southwest; and once galloping through a tiny whirlwind of leaves in Maryland (1747) he noticed that they turned in a clockwise motion. From this he concluded a general theory on whirlwinds and quickly deduced what direction a vessel should take to escape cyclones and tornadoes.

Franklin was not a mere experimenter, but derived a disciplinary pleasure from science and mathematics, fully realizing the empire they could exert over the mind. He wanted their methods to be adopted for the rules of thought and criticism, but here again he insisted on the concrete and came to some bizarre conclusions. For example, in attempting to make his old enemy, Heredity, bite the dust, he employed a species of Voltairian reasoning, which was convincing but not correct. Now that he was a scholar, he wasn't satisfied with the maxims in "Poor Richard" such as, "Tis a shame that your family is an Honour to you. You ought to be an Honour to your Family", and he affixed a long essay to them in 1752 to demonstrate mathematically that every person receives but half of his father's blood, half of his mother's, a quarter of the blood of his grandfather, and a quarter of his grandmother's, etc., so that by going back several generations, a descendant has only an infinitesimal strain of the blood of his ancestors. Counting back twenty-one generations, a gentleman would then have 1,048,576 ancestors.

> Here are only computed 21 generations, which allowing three generations to a hundred years carry us back no farther than the Norman Conquest, at which time each present nobleman to exclude all ignoble blood from his veins ought to have had one million forty-eight thousand, Five hundred and seventy-six noble ancestors. Carry the reckoning back 300 years farther and the number amounts to about 500 millions which are more than exist at any one time upon Earth and shows the impossibility of preserving blood free from such mixture, and that the pretention of such purity of blood in ancient families is a mere Joke . . .

Now this fine reasoning omits the possibility of intermarriage in a family and supposes that blood is something purely material, comparable to coconut milk. Franklin didn't doubt but what the laws of biology were identical with the laws of mathematics, and that procreation was nothing else than an addition. "Take half of a man and half of woman and you have a child", Franklin thought to himself. This notion seemed so evident to him that he returned to it with satisfaction again and again. Franklin was intoxicated by calculation and good sense, the same way Voltaire became drunk on logic and irony. Both of them used logic so well that they employed it on every possible occasion, and sometimes on impossible ones.

However, between 1749 and 1757 Franklin was still prudent, though he was more strong and skillful than he had ever been. In "Poor Richard", Religion and Morals took a preponderant place. He filled his calendar with pious, Deistical, and laic verses, excused himself for his jokes, and when he made an attack on established ideas he did it under the cloak of morality. He was already in full possession of that technique which Voltaire was to employ later in his pamphlets and little philosophic essays. If Franklin's art were less finished than that of the Frenchman, he had more tact and a more persuasive good nature. Here is how he denounces prayer in the name of Morality: "Serving God is doing good to man, but praying is thought an easier service, and therefore more generally chosen" (1733). Then he gave advice, analogous to that of Voltaire: "In the Affairs of this World Men are saved not by Faith but by the Want of it." And he returned to his old attacks: "Sound, etc., sound Doctrine, may pass through a Ram's horn and a Preacher, without straightening the one, or amending the other." "Children and Princes will quarrel for trifles." "Many princes sin with David, but few repent with him."

His morale remained spirited but utilitarian and deviated from Christianity. His politics were still for equal rights and were clearly anti-monarchial. Nevertheless, he relied on human wisdom, and not on the crowd, for, as he said, "A Mob's a Monster, Heads enough, but no brains" (1747). He did not wish to let it loose. "Talking against Religion is unchaining a Tyger; the Beast let loose may worry his deliverer" (1751). And in his collection of thoughts, which he published in the beginning of "Poor Richard" for 1758 (later known as

"The Way to Wealth" or "Father Abraham's Speech"), one finds nothing but advice on moderation, morality, and frugality. It was based on a human and material wisdom, outside of Christianity, though it was never directed against the Faith; nor did it attack the established government, or the existing social order.

In his *Gazette* he was still more discreet. From 1749 to 1757 it contained scarcely anything but articles and essays taken from the English reviews and contemporary newspapers. He printed fewer and fewer articles. Thus, when Hall would take up the newspaper, there would be no sharp contrast. Franklin still used the *Gazette*, however, for his philanthropic and patriotic campaigns: the hospital, military preparation, the academy. But the burning questions of domestic politics, and the great philosophical problems were omitted from then on in the newspaper.

He watched his step, and climbed up in the world as his genius expanded, and became imposing. And he was careful of every trifle, because he knew, "For want of a Nail, the Shoe is lost, for want of a shoe, the Horse is lost, for want of a Horse, the Rider is lost."

He pushed himself ahead with consummate skill, never losing contact with the middle class, never losing sight of the goal he wished to attain. He remained in the middle class, but he became the Leading Bourgeois of America.

In his pretty new house, with its long gardens stretching to the Delaware, he spent many hours working over his electrical problems, among his bottles, wires, bells, test tubes and pieces of wax. There, too, he wrote his letters, welcomed his friends and the distinguished foreigners who came to visit him, like the young Swede, Kalm, sent by Linné to study America, and received as well the innumerable curiosity seekers, who all but besieged him.

He wanted his family to rise with him, especially his son William. This was not easy, for under the influence of military life the boy had changed into a haughty and ambitious young man. He had become handsome too, with delicate features, a long pointed chin, and cold eyes. William thought he was a gentleman, was surprised to find that his father was not, but dismissed the matter easily with an exquisite shrug. Benjamin Franklin boasted to his friends that he had made William knuckle under, but his lessons could not have been very severe. When the war was over, William began to study law. His father quietly introduced him into the House of Representatives where he became secretary. He thought of sending him to London to put the finishing touches on his education and to prepare him for a brilliant career. William made no effort against being helped, any more than he objected to being courted by the fashionable young ladies of Philadelphia at the "Assembly", to which he belonged. This was an aristocratic place where not every one was allowed to enter. The rules prescribed that the sons of artisans be excluded, but Benjamin Franklin is said to have asked then, if they would exclude Jesus Christ, who had been the son of a carpenter. The members gave in to him, but it was arranged, nevertheless, that the Assembly would be exclusive. There they danced minuets in the light of candles, drank rum, wine and beer, and flirted under the mocking eyes of a flunkey paid seven shillings six a season. Miss Graeme, the poetess, turned her sweet eyes on William Franklin, and he did not hurry to withdraw from her gaze. Gossip followed. But Benjamin Franklin didn't bother about the matter, remembering the advice of "Poor Richard": "Marry your son when you will, but your daughter when you can" (November, 1734).

Benjamin instructed his son in political, administrative and financial affairs, had him help him with his experiments, and sent him on trips to Boston and New York, to develop his mind by travel. Benjamin was proud of his son, although he felt him to be very different from himself, and he did not have complete confidence in him. He was careful to keep him separated from his mother, who could not "understand" him. In order to avoid scenes, he sent him to live elsewhere than at home.

His good Debby did what she could to please "her master", she tried not to quarrel with William too often, nor to cause too much gossip among the neighbors. On Sunday she put on fine clothes, and when she left for church, wearing her double necklace of golden beads, her long scarlet cloak with its double cape, accompanied by her pretty little blonde-haired girl, and followed by two Negro slaves, she cut a good figure, and the neighbors had to admit that she looked like the wife of somebody.

She kept her house in good order, now that it had become important, and besides her old servant "Goody Smith", she had several Negro slaves, who were lazy and difficult to watch over. Fortunately, Sarah was pleasant, sweet, and faithful; she diverted and consoled her mother, whose tempestuous nature hadn't exactly been calmed down by the years. She remained what she had formerly been, a good, courageous, hard-working housewife, who spoke loudly, and who was more made for use than for show. Franklin also had remained a shopkeeper in becoming a great man. While Hall stayed at the press and sold books, Franklin kept up their business connections with buyers and tradesmen, wrote his "Poor Richard", and many papers for the *Gazette*, and especially tried to increase the scope of their affairs. He had invested in paper factories and sold paper in Jamaica. He installed Benny Mecom in Antigua, to take the place of one of his deceased partners, he kept Jemmy Franklin at Newport, Parker in New York, Dunlap at Lancaster. He placed Armbruster and J. Bohm in his German printing house at Philadelphia, and after them, Miller and Samuel Hoffman (1753). He was going to found another in New Haven. He still had William Smith under him in the Dominican Islands, and kept up his connections with South Carolina, Georgia, and Kingston, Jamaica, where Daniell was his partner. His business was good; "Poor Richard" sold annually more than ten thousand copies. Hall had an established clientele, but it was no longer the same as heretofore, and as a sign of the new times, a newcomer, Chattin, announced "The Newest Printing House." When Hall put the same imprint on his books that Franklin had used — "New Printing" — it seemed to be an anachronism.

Each one of his enterprises was in the hands of an earnest employee who had been carefully chosen, and, in general, Franklin had little trouble with them. As he wrote to his aged mother, "For my own part, at present, I pass my time agreeably enough. I enjoy, thro' Mercy, a tolerable Share of Health. I read a great deal, ride a little, do a little Business for myself, more for others, retire when I can, and go into Company when I please, so the Years roll round, and the last will come when I would rather have it said, He lived Usefully, than He died Rich."

He serenely accepted the inevitable sorrows which Time brought: the death of his good mother, which summed up her full life in May, 1752, and he made her funeral oration in a single line: "She has lived a good life, as well as a long one, and is happy." He refused to take his inheritance, just as he had refused his father's bequests, and left it all to his poorer relatives.

Soon after this, his worthy and helpful friend Logan passed away; Logan, who had aided him so much by his influence, erudition, skill and goodness; his old companion, Hopkinson, whose advice had often guided him, also died. At every death, Franklin felt a chill, but he was wise and did not pity his friends too much, for he knew that his own turn was coming; he was not afraid, for he was virtuous and on good terms with God.

He continued to serve Him by serving his neighbor, and this did not hinder him from serving himself. He knew how to reconcile all these three duties, and did so, admirably, between 1750 and 1757 in Philadelphia. He deserved praise for he was in an inextricable position.

Peace had been made but every one felt it was precarious. The patriot newspapers were against it and the *Gazette of Philadelphia* joined the chorus of the English Whig papers to denounce it. Another fatal war was close at hand, and it created a sharp and hidden conflict among the different political parties in Pennsylvania.

The Quakers didn't want to fight or to prepare for war.

The Penns, who were the proprietors of the colony, and their friends, wanted the colony to take arms, but they did not want to pay anything; they also refused to allow their estates to be taxed for war appropriations.

The Anglo-Saxon artisans wanted to go to war, but thought that every one should join in paying the costs, — the Quakers, proprietors, etc.

The "Gentlemen" — rich merchants and non-Quaker planters — who were jealous of the Quakers, wanted to profit by the occasion and take away their power; thus they confused the situation as much as possible and refused to pay for the war unless the Quakers contributed.

The Germans did not like war and liked still less to pay. They would have voluntarily stayed out of the discussion altogether had not the Indian raids in the west of Pennsylvania frightened them into action.

Besides this question, there were other discussions hanging fire, which united or separated these groups in different combinations: the artisans, farmers, and the majority of the Assembly didn't stop asking for more paper money, but the Penns and the Royal Government opposed them; the Anglo-Saxons, the governor, and the rich merchants regarded the Germans with mixed hate, scorn and suspicion, and had they felt strong enough, there is no telling what they might have done against them. At least, they obliged them to talk English. The Quakers and the Penns had stopped being on good terms ever since the proprietors had renounced the religion of their great ancestor. And, finally, the governor had a permanent quarrel with the Assembly on the subject of their prerogatives, his salary, etc.

In the midst of all this confusion, the Court of England — from 1752 on — constantly urged the parties to unite and prepare for war. At last the differing parties agreed that they would make the British Government pay as much as possible.

Franklin's situation was delicate but favorable. He had put himself in the lead of those who wanted to arm the province and so had compromised himself. He had taken this position in a critical moment, and no one seriously begrudged him it. He made an effort to remain as mediator between the differing factions. In recognition of his brilliant and fruitful services he received the following offices, one after the other: Alderman of Philadelphia, Justice of the Peace (1749) and Member of the Assembly (1750). With his lodge, Junto, and library (which he never lost track of), his fire department, his *Gazette* and almanac, his partners and friends, his extensive correspondences in the colonies and his English connections, Franklin had many powerful agencies in hand. But he wanted to use them only for the good of the community, and for a project which would rally every one around him.

There was a great deal to be done in Philadelphia. The city had grown enormously during the eight years of war, but being poorly administered and without discipline, it was in extreme disorder. The quarantine regulations were insufficient and loosely followed, letting by floods of unhealthy immigrants who spread deadly epidemics. Because of the war, all the men had learned the use of firearms, and now, under the stress of enthusiasm or nervousness, they shot off their guns on the slightest provocation. The streets were dark and filthy, infested with slinking alley curs, runaway Negroes, and licentious soldiers who would rob you while you were out walking in the night, or during the day when you were at home. In 1750 Franklin had his home burglarized with the connivance of his Negro slaves, but he recovered nearly all that had been stolen.

Then, too, there was the sad story of the good man who entered Philadelphia just at nightfall. A couple of blackguards thrust a pistol under his nose and demanded his money. Unfortunately, he didn't have enough, and so to punish him and amuse themselves, they made him take off his clothes. The poor man wept so much and was so pathetic that the robbers felt some remorse, and at last only took his shoe and knee buckles.

Franklin set himself to remedy these evils. He insisted that the streets be bettered, for he was a business man, and he knew how important a matter this was. He participated in the work of the Assembly, which finally put a restraint on the use of firearms, forbidding them especially to Negroes and servants; passed new measures to improve the quarantine, and enforced severe regulations for the muzzling of dogs. Thus, order was once more established.

It was only a first step. The city was rich and huge now. It included more than seven thousand taxable citizens. From a point of view of culture and commerce, it was the center of the English colonies in America. It was only right that they should make the most of it and fulfill their civic duties. Franklin took up his great idea of founding a college in Philadelphia once more. No doubt, his New England heritage pushed him in this direction. But his plan was very original. What Franklin demanded was a college adapted to the city and the times. He didn't want a new Harvard, to prepare young Puritans for the holy ministry, nor a new William and Mary to instruct the young aristocrats of Virginia in the art of commanding. He wanted an academy which would develop the young Philadelphians, and teach them how to become active, hard-working, economical, rich, and virtuous merchants and artisans of the eighteenth century. There would be no classical languages taught, only English; no indulging in scholastic fancies, only good, practical, common-sense education. Franklin had had this idea for a long time, and he had written about it in his *Gazette* ever since 1733. He was no enthusiast over ancient languages; he had studied them slightly and had often made fun of them. In the middle of this century, whose ideal of culture was Greco-Latin, Franklin's suggestion was exceptionally bold. A liberal education, a gentleman's education, in all countries of the world, was then based on classical studies. Franklin wanted to found a cultivated bourgeois class, oriented to the present time, and he knew very well that he would meet with obstacles. Nevertheless, he proceeded with method, skill, and rapidity.

He spoke of it to his friends, to the members of the Junto, and to the cultivated people that he knew. He prepared his public by various articles and letters in his *Gazette*. His most striking article (August 24, 1749) reproduced a letter of Plinius the Younger to Tacitus, in which all the advantages of bringing up children in a neighborhood school were enumerated and emphasized. He made use of his brothers of the lodge and his companions of the Junto, and distributed among them a brochure in which his project was explained. It described the plan and included a subscription blank. A little later, in a second pamphlet, Franklin summed up his ideas in these words:

> Thus instructed, youth will come out of this school fitted for learning any Business, Calling or Profession except such wherein Languages are required; and tho' unacquainted with any ancient Tongue they will be Masters of their own, which is of more immediate and general Use; and withal will have attain'd many other valuable Accomplishments; the Time usually spent in acquiring those Languages, often without Success, being here employ'd in laying such a Foundation of Knowledge and Ability, as, properly improv'd may qualify them to pass thro and execute the several Offices of civil Life, with Advantage and Reputation to themselves and Country.

Such an appeal conquered the public opinion; the subscriptions flowed in. The administrators were named immediately, and among them, of course, were Logan, Allen, Inglis, Shippen, Hopkinson and Franklin. Being the soul of the enterprise, Franklin promised to give ten pounds sterling a year for five years, Inglis and Shippen promised as much, while Hamilton gave fifty and Allen seventy-five. Then Franklin drew up the constitution for the academy, submitted it to the administrators, who approved it and appointed him president (November 13, 1749). Thus the social leaders of the city chose him to organize this school where all the young generations of Philadelphia would go, or rather, they were willing to rally around him in this work which promised so brightly for the future. Franklin gave himself body and soul to his duties, attending all the meetings of the administrators, except when he was kept away by absolute necessity. He found the money (four thousand pounds sterling), premises and professors for this new academy. The premises were acquired by a pretty little negotiation between Mr. Franklin, President of the Council of Administrators of the Academy of Philadelphia, and Mr. Franklin, Member of the Council of the New Building, which had been erected for the Reverend Whitefield in 1740. People were a little weary of Whitefield now, and more reassured of their salvation. It was easy to bring the two councils to an agreement.

The choice of professors was more difficult. Up to now, the only teachers in America had been churchmen and some dubious refugees, who, of course, could not be considered. Franklin started looking for a wise and highly educated minister, who would be sufficiently pious and yet not too clerical. First he had negotiations with the Reverend Samuel Johnson, the minister of the Church of England, in Connecticut, a philosopher of some talent, and a man of easy-going ways. But this worthy gentleman didn't want to come to such an agitated and quarrelsome city as Philadelphia. Later he became the president of the College of the King in New York (to-day Columbia). A Mr. Martin was chosen at last, who did very well from the start, and who pleased Franklin moreover, as he was an excellent chess player. But he died in December, 1752, and Franklin had to look elsewhere. Unfortunately, his troubles put him on the track of a brilliant Scotch clergyman, William Smith, a man of rigid character, unswerving honesty, profound thought, and great talent. But Smith was also without delicacy, had a total lack of judgment, and was very obstinate and vain. He was as skillful in a social way as Franklin, but while Franklin always tried to accomplish his work in the most quiet and discreet manner, Smith used his skill to make as much noise and hurly-burly as possible. However, they got along together very well at first, for Smith, who was cultivated and had a lively mind, was deeply interested in education; for two years they exchanged compliments.

In the beginning, Smith bowed down, like every one, before the glory of Franklin, not so much for the brilliant reputation of being the world's greatest scholar which Europeans were making for him, but for the no less enviable fact that Franklin was a man who knew best how to make a difficult enterprise succeed, and how to secure money from his neighbors. He had already rendered this service to Whitefield, and he did as much for the academy. He was asked to help found a hospital, to establish a fire insurance company, to help the Reverend Tennent erect a new church, and to send a boat to look for the Northwest Passage.

It was Franklin's assistance which made every one of these projects succeed. To gain money for the hospital he employed a system which was new then in America: he obtained the promise of a subsidy from the Assembly if an equal amount could be raised among the citizens of Philadelphia. First, he had asked the Assembly for a subsidy outright, but met with objection among the representatives of the countryside, who thought the hospital would not be of any use to their voters. Then Franklin offered the measure again, with the conditional clause that the Assembly would pay two thousand pounds sterling if the people of Philadelphia would give a like amount. None of the representatives thought that Franklin could secure such a huge sum from the people of Philadelphia, and they passed the bill, not reckoning on the force of their promise. Franklin and his friends went all about the city, saying that they must have the two thousand pounds so that the Assembly would help them. To the surprise of every one the scheme succeeded; the hospital was constructed and opened in 1755. For the insurance company, it was easier, and likewise for the vessel *Argo*, which made two voyages in vain (1753–1754). Franklin had become such a technician in this art of extracting money from other people's pockets, that nothing was done in the city without him. In spite of his habit of not going to church, he was appointed churchwarden and asked to organize a lottery which would procure the funds necessary to purchase bells and erect a bell tower for the Church of Christ (1752). And finally, Gilbert Tennent asked him for help. Franklin refused, saying that he could ask no more from his fellow citizens, but he gave his receipt to Tennent: "In the first place I advise you to apply to all those whom you know will give something; next to those whom you are uncertain whether they will give anything or not, and show them the list of those who have given; and, lastly, do not neglect those who you are sure will give nothing, for in some of them you may be mistaken." Tennent, who knew how to work, did even better; he asked every one immediately — and succeeded.

Such were the good works and great happenings in Philadelphia during those years. Franklin was mixed up with everything. He took trips from right to left, going to Connecticut in 1749 for the affairs of the academy, to Trenton to see a copper mine, and visiting the coast in 1750. During the hot and dry summer of 1750 he also worked on his farm. In 1751 he went to western Pennsylvania and stayed awhile there with his friends, the Wrights, at Hempfield. His business affairs and politics kept him in Philadelphia in 1752, even during the simmering summer months. He suffered from this, because his health, diversion, and advancement demanded much travel. Nevertheless, he couldn't complain of being indispensable.

About this time, one of the discreet negotiations which he had begun in the month of May, 1751, came to fruition, and engaged him in a new line of activity. He had heard that the postmaster-general of America, Benger, was very ill, and not likely to get well. Now, this was a position which suited Franklin to a T; it was lucrative, apt to become more so, respectable, and required much travel in order to keep up connections between the colonies; it was useful for a politician, a scholar, a man of the world, and especially so for a journalist. Franklin, not without some hesitation, decided to try for the position, and asked his friend and Masonic brother, William Allen, as well as his London friend, Collinson, to help him. Allen was the most distinguished, most influential and richest man in Philadelphia, and Collinson, too, had a large fortune and much influence. Franklin wrote that they should not consider the cost. In two years the negotiations succeeded;

Benger died and Franklin was named Postmaster-general of America conjointly with Colonel Hunter of Virginia, the publisher of the *Virginia Gazette*.

The importance of this position was considerable, for it was one of the very rare civil functions which concerned all of the colonies. In times of peace, the business of the whole continent depended on it; in times of war, it was an essential factor in the defense of the country. At all times it enjoyed the exercise of extraordinary rights and prerogatives, as the privacy of letters was not then very scrupulously respected. The officials of the government did not hesitate to read them if they were interested in their contents, while people thought that letters offered an easy and perfectly decent manner of informing themselves on their neighbor's affairs. One has only to remember the way Franklin sent to Hamilton letters which were destined for other correspondents. Here is a typical scene described in the *Virginia Gazette* (1751):

> Some time ago calling at a Public House a box of letters came from on board a Ship arrived from England; they were no sooner spread upon the table but the busy Crowd, anxious for themselves and friends, made a Circle round it; having no concern myself (from the misfortune of outliving my Friends) I took my Place in a corner of the room, when of a sudden a Person snatches up a letter, reads the subscription. To ——. "Egad," says he, "I must know the Contents of it, and made off."

As the postmaster-general of America, Franklin held the fate of all newspaper publishers in his hands, could regard the American merchants from a superior plane, and was on equal footing with the English officials. Moreover, he had a mine of jobs at his disposal: twelve postmaster's places at a hundred pounds each, for his hungry family and eager friends. He began by appointing William the postmaster of Philadelphia (1753), then he named him the comptroller of American posts (1765). He made his brother, John, the postmaster of Boston, gave a position to Parker, and to various cousins, such as W. Dunlap.

However, he didn't think only of himself and his family. He was a remarkable Postmaster-general, and improved the service, which had been hitherto rather mediocre, until it became a highly perfected organization. The English Government, which was used to standing an annual deficit, wished to rectify this, and promised Franklin three hundred pounds sterling a year if he could make profits above this sum. He knew the country well and guessed what its future would be, so he accepted the proposition without dilly-dallying, and set to work immediately. He made a survey trip through all the colonies, excepting the Southern ones, to see how the post-offices functioned and how to better them.

This hard work was a pleasure. He was especially happy to visit New England again. His father and mother were dead, his brothers were old men, his pretty sister now had pretty daughters, and Franklin returned an important and respected man to the city where he had been an untidy and disgraceful apprentice. Harvard and Yale, some months later (summer, 1753), conferred an honorary degree of Master of Arts upon him, and distinguished people sought after him and held him in high esteem. Franklin felt strong. He talked amiably with important merchants and procured them the best possible postal service. He chatted about science with the Harvard professors. He was at home everywhere.

This feeling became so strong in him that it accentuated his desire to have the colonies united in a federation. He returned to Philadelphia, his mind bursting with this great idea which had haunted him a long time. Years ago he had wanted to establish coöperation between the English colonies of America. At this critical moment, when a new war was brooding and disquieting rumors arrived from England, he felt that his hour had come.

He published articles, urging a union, in his *Gazette*, and used his influence to have them reprinted in other newspapers of the colonies. He even drew a little symbol: a serpent cut in segments, each representing one of the colonies (North Carolina, South Carolina, Virginia, Maryland, Pennsylvania,

New Jersey, New York, New England) with this device inscribed: "Join or Die." Through Franklin's efforts, nearly all of the newspapers of the colonies reprinted this emblem (1754–1755).

When this preparatory work was accomplished, he went to Albany as one of the commissioners of the Government of Pennsylvania, to negotiate with the Six Indian Nations, in coöperation with the other colonies, and to study the means of defense in case of French attack. Franklin believed that efficacious defense could only be realized by a union of the colonies under the guiding protection of England, and asked his Masonic, professional and official friends to support this plan. In time of peace, a union would guarantee growth and prosperity. Franklin proposed a compound system, by which a military governor-general appointed by the king would be sent from England to take care of the country's defense, while other domestic affairs would be handled by a kind of intercolonial Parliament, composed of representatives from each colony; the number of these representatives would be proportioned to the sum which the colony would pay to the national treasury, and taxes would be levied on alcoholic beverages. This governor and this council would attend to relations with the Indians, the management of the frontiers, and the development of a Federal army and navy. The governor would also have the colonization of the West under his charge. Franklin considered this colonization urgent and indispensable, not only to keep the French from surrounding them, but to give the colonies an opportunity for their complete development.

This simple, clear and judicious plan met with a favorable welcome by all those who had a sense of government, but they were few. It could not please the men of the Assemblies, who clung to their rights tenaciously, and were afraid of being dominated by a governor-general or a central Parliament, any more than the Royal Government, which found these little isolated colonies already quite difficult to manage, and did not want them to be strengthened by a federation. Thus, in spite of Franklin's desire, in spite of the enthusiasm of William Shirley,

Governor of Massachusetts, who also thought a union was needed, and in spite of the wish of the Congress which had submitted the scheme to London and various local Assemblies, both England and the majorities in the colonies were against the project. England was afraid that under the pretense of making this union against France, it would be made against her: the intuition was a good one, but it didn't go far enough.

This was a cruel disillusion for Franklin. He was wise enough to have foreseen the obstacles and to guess the objections that the various factions would have for such a federation, but he had counted on the fear and hate of France to overcome them. He believed that the national union was necessary, but that it could be brought about only at the expense of some enemy. He had wished that this nation were France, but Destiny had decided otherwise.

He didn't tire yet. With the silence and supple intensity which made his strength, he at least tried to establish a practical coöperation between the colonies. While his *Gazette* was thoroughly approving of the patriotic efforts of the Virginians to push back the French from the western frontiers, praising the gallant conduct of the young Colonel Washington in particular, Franklin left his wife and daughter, the Assembly and its quarrels, to make an inspection trip, with his colleague, Hunter, of the post-offices in the eastern and northern colonies. For six months he went from city to city, stopping most of the time in New England, where he could dwell in the memories of his childhood; there he saw his dear sister, Jean Mecom, surrounded by her children, visited his scholarly friend, Bowdoin, and organized the postal service, so that in lieu of two deliveries throughout the months of winter for the western regions, there was a regular weekly service. Then, through the storms and cold blasts of this winter, 1754–1755, which was very severe, he went to New Haven and stayed a while at Yale. There he was received by his old friend, President Clapp, and by Professor Jared Eliot, with whom he passed long hours, discussing science and telling good stories, in the warmth and flickering light of a bright fire.

But of all the persons he met, the sweetest and most radiant was Miss Catherine Ray. She came of a distinguished Connecticut family which Franklin had become acquainted with on his former trip. Miss Ray very soon occupied a tender place in Franklin's heart. She was young, lively, naïve, witty, practical, and sentimental, a charming lady of the world. Franklin put his family behind him and lived again in his past, in the oblivion of his old dreams and new desires; he forgot Deborah and the loud, vulgar atmosphere of his home, to abandon himself to this unusual feeling, to this smiling and effulgent tenderness which slowly rose and expanded in him. While Katy Ray prepared sugarplums for him, telling him all the while of a handsome Spaniard who had stirred her heart, Franklin dreamed, — Franklin, who for so long a time had only thought and acted.

This young girl of New England gave him that sweet melancholy, that elegant tenderness, half-libertine, half-paternal, which was so fashionable at the time, and which Monsieur Rousseau de Genève had begun explaining in his immortal works. Mr. Franklin, who had not wept a tear for the death of his parents, as he was certain of their eternal happiness, who had steeled his heart to sentiment and left off reading poetry years before, felt a strange mist over his eyes one night, when he bade farewell to Katy. It was an evening in winter, and she left on a little boat to visit her mother who lived on an island; Franklin stood on the bank a long time to watch the boat, and as it faded from his sight he felt deliciously disconsolate. And on his long trip home, while the horse slipped and stumbled on the icy roads of New England, Benjamin Franklin, Esquire, Postmaster-General of His Majesty the King of England, in America, instead of thinking about his accounts and paying attention to his horse, lost himself in visions of his New England childhood, and saw through the snow which fell lightly a flattering young face, which turned towards him with a radiant smile. He wrote to Katy: "Your favours come mixed with the snowy fleeces, which are pure as your virgin innocence, white as your lovely bosom, and — as cold."

Franklin was a great personage. He had acquired one of the most precious luxuries that the eighteenth century could offer, one which he had never known, and one which he would never have known, had it not been for the gracious instruction of a young girl of New England. It wasn't without some repugnance that he returned to his noisy home, to his quarrelsome Assembly and to his good, tiresome neighbors. Certainly, he was an American, and more ardently so than he had ever been, but nevertheless he began to detach himself from Pennsylvania. He had dreamed of going to London ever since 1749, and now this desire became more strong in him.

To escape! Oh, to play on a stage which was more noble and huge, where he could make a better use of his gifts, where he would not be ceaselessly struggling against niggardly odds! Thus, as Franklin's mind and heart and dreams expanded, he constantly looked and longed for more light, glory, and love.

IX

A VERY sweet feeling, however, still retained him in Pennsylvania. After years of effort, he had disarmed his enemies. It seemed that he had become the pivot of all the political life in the colony, that nothing could be done without him, and that he alone made harmony. Between the Junto and the lodge, the Quakers and the Penns, the artisans and the rich bourgeois, he moved easily, the friend of all, the only one who could avoid being jostled, and who succeeded in reconciliations. Franklin reveled profoundly in this rôle of arbiter, which he had always dreamed of playing and which made him so powerful.

To put a finishing touch to his triumph, he tried to bring the Germans over to his side. He owned a German printing shop in order to oppose the anti-patriot, Christian Sower, whose writings and publications influenced the Germans almost to revolt.

Franklin was seconded in his efforts very shortly by two societies organized among the Anglo-Saxons, Masons, and patriots, to instruct the Palatines gratuitously in English, and to evangelize them, in English. Unfortunately, the Palatines didn't care about schools at all. They were ignorant and thought that ignorance was bliss. Their own Christianity suited them very well, and they did not care what Franklin or William Smith believed (these men were partners in the great work). The pious Catholic and Lutheran Germans thought they were farther along on the road to heaven than the Masons who mixed their Christianity with Deism. Sower, who was heavy-handed, was rough to his opponents, and Franklin didn't have good business in his German printing shop. He finished by selling it at a low price to the Society for the Evangelization of the Germans, and retired discreetly from the dire combat.

He devoted his efforts to the double political struggle then going on in the Assembly: the small business men joined with the Penns against the Quakers, saying that the colony must prepare for war; and the Quakers against the Penns, demanding the right to tax their domains. Each party had an excellent comeback: the Quakers said that the Penns were destroying the liberty of the colony by refusing the Assembly the right to tax and by sending tyrannical instructions to their governors; the Penns answered: the Quakers are traitors to their country, if they don't want to serve in the army, they should leave the Assembly, and if they want to remain in the Assembly, they should serve their country faithfully.

Franklin was a faithful auxiliary of both parties. He worked with the Penn partisans to oblige the Quakers to pay for the war and to permit military preparations. He worked with the Quakers to oblige the Penns to cede the right of taxation. His position was delicately balanced, but valuable. He needed a remarkable sense of orientation and equilibrium to keep his place. But Franklin knew how. He was the mainspring of the Assembly, and the new Governor Denny, following the advice of both Collinson and the Penns, put himself closely in touch with him immediately.

Once more he was the indispensable man; during the summer of 1755, England and France had not officially declared war, but were engaged in it already; England took as many French boats as possible, which was convenient and practical, as the French merchant vessels had not yet been warned to look out; there were also sharp disputes over the territories in the center of America (Ohio, Mississippi). The Treaty of Aix-la-Chapelle had been so well written that England judged herself perfectly right to occupy the regions which France attributed to herself without hesitation.

After some unfortunate attempts on the part of the Virginians to check the French in the West, the British Government decided to send over some regular troops, headed by a trained officer, General Braddock, and a brilliant English staff. All these fine men were to dislodge the French and make war in earnest, even if it were not official.

These expeditionary forces had scarcely landed before they began fighting with the colonies, and especially with the Pennsylvanians. The Quakers continued to think that war was impious and refused to stir. As to the other provinces, excepting New England, they all thought that money was hard to come by, and that the King had better pay for this little war of his fancy himself. In the midst of all this, General Braddock stormed and raved, and vowed that he would treat the Pennsylvanians so that they would know what war really meant. He threatened to quarter his soldiers on the citizens, seizing their houses by force, etc. The general was courageously ready for anything, and his troops would gladly have followed him in this offensive against the Quakers and the German farmers.

But Franklin was there and watched. He knew that if Braddock should do anything against the inhabitants, the English Government risked losing all their sympathy, and yet, to refuse all aid to Braddock, leaned too much to the Quaker's side and seemed an extreme attitude. Franklin intervened then and presented himself boldly but modestly before Braddock. He asked him for the list of things he needed and promised to supply him with wagons and carriages which were absolutely needed to transport the troops to the frontier. Braddock was skeptical but accepted the offer on the chance that it might work. Franklin immediately went to William Allen, his Masonic brother and fellow-trustee of the academy, and talked over the matter with him. Then he printed posters which offered a large sum to the farmers who would loan their wagons, harnesses, horses and mules, to the troops of His Majesty. The poster further announced that in the contrary case, the troops of His Majesty would take measures to procure the vehicles and animals without paying. These strong words, accompanied by the exhortations of Allen and the financial guaranty of Franklin that all would be paid, decided the farmers. After some weeks, Braddock's cavalcade was formed, and the people thronged the streets to see the redcoats leave. There were American soldiers too, with their flags snapping in the wind, and fife and drum sounding; and Indian guides, marching ahead and behind. And as the long file slowly wound its dusty way to the horizon, the people in Philadelphia prepared fireworks to celebrate the imminent victory.

But on July 18, 1755, tne news spread in the city that Braddock had been surprised with his men in the forest, by three hundred Indians and two hundred Frenchmen, that he had died of his wounds, that his men had been practically massacred, his officers killed or wounded, his wagons taken by the enemy, and that his vanguard had fled in terror, in order to save a few Englishmen for His Majesty.

The impression produced on the colonies was disastrous. It was unthinkable that this brisk and ostentatious troop, whose insolence the people had borne because it was the flower of the English army, had fought so stupidly and shown the white feather. All the western frontier of Pennsylvania was left to the mercy of the enemy by the cowardly flight of the redcoats. The few that were left were commanded by Colonel Dunbar and only stopped at Philadelphia, where the ladies charitably gave them apple pies and rice cakes to console them.

But their husbands were not so tender-hearted. If the Frenchmen, who knew very well the attitude of the Germans and the Indians, wanted to concentrate on Pennsylvania, the colony would have a hard time of it. All along the frontier the Indians stole cattle, burned down the houses, scalped the inhabitants or burned them at the stake. The refugees who arrived in Philadelphia shook with fear, and the Germans said that the Indian raids could be worse than war. Under these conditions, the struggle between the governor and the Assembly was somehow absurd and repugnant. The Assembly refused to do anything to avert the horrors of war just in order to wrangle over an abstract principle of liberty, while the governor, trying to obey his egoistic instructions, failed as a leader and was just as much to blame. Thus Franklin saw the situation. He was just as unquiet and unhappy as they, for at the same moment he was beset with all kinds of difficulties. All the farmers who had lost their wagons and horses came to him to be reimbursed of the loss as he had guaranteed. The persons who had been irritated by his intelligent conduct with Braddock turned against him. His friend, William Smith, the president of the academy, added injury to insult in this tragi-comic imbroglio, by becoming a violent advocate for the Penns and making a brutal attack on the Quakers in a pamphlet called, "A brief View of the Conduct of Pennsylvania for the year 1755." The pamphlet threw all the responsibility, past, present and future on the Quakers. Meanwhile, the frontier farms were burning, the population was panic-stricken, and the English officers fumed to no avail.

Fortunately, Franklin had his electricity, which consoled and diverted him. He kept his outward calm, but he was coldly furious against the Penns. He never forgave them the anguish they caused that summer, when he thought he was ruined and dishonored, and that the province was lost. General Shirley, who was a great friend of Franklin and the commander-in-chief of the troops of His Majesty, since the death of Braddock, saved the situation by ordering that the wagons be paid for out of the army funds.

Some months later, Sir William Johnson beat General Dieskau, the commander-in-chief of the French forces, and this calmed the colony somewhat. However, the future was so uncertain that the governor appointed Franklin to take charge of the defense of the western frontier.

A measure to create a militia was hastily passed by the Assembly, and Franklin left at the end of December. The Assembly and the governor were still wrangling, and Benjamin was glad to escape. He led a troop of the Pennsylvania militia, and their first stop was at Bethlehem, in the valley of the Lehigh. The weather was severely cold, and they were careful not to walk into an ambush as Braddock had done; Franklin had good guides and went slowly. They stayed for a few days among the good Moravians of Bethlehem, whom the Indians had harassed. The Moravians were very cordial to Franklin, offered him a huge dinner with music, and then one of their ministers gave a long sermon, to which Franklin listened attentively. He was particularly struck by the wisdom of the Moravians in that they never put their creed down in writing; they could thus constantly better it, and they would never be embarrassed in later years by its rigidity.

After a pleasant halt, Franklin and the soldiers left again, and now they went very slowly indeed, for they were in dangerous territory. At the slightest stir of a bush they were ready to fire. The country they passed through had been laid waste by the Indians, the farmhouses had been burnt, and here and there were the charred remains of farmers and their wives and children, all of them scalped — horrible evidence of the Indians' cruelty. The company finally arrived at Gnadenhutten, which had just been pillaged, as the fresh tracks of the Indians showed. Without losing a moment, Colonel Franklin had a fort of earth and wood constructed. The men worked day and night. Now and then Franklin received a letter from Philadelphia or a message from his good Debby, which would be accompanied by a generous slice of smoked beef, apples, and syrup in case of a cold. It rained in torrents, and the country was not gay, but there was not much time to think about it, as there was so much work, and the danger was so imminent. Colonel Franklin conducted himself very well; he held his men together like a real chief, and didn't neglect anything, not even their souls. He made them work hard, to divert them from their cares; and, by the simple expedient of giving the daily allowance of gin just after prayers, all his men attended the morning worship. Though Franklin may not have succeeded so well as Napoleon, and may not be considered as a rival of Cæsar, he certainly could have ranked among the leaders at the siege of Troy.

When his fort was constructed, and affectionately named "Fort Allen", Franklin returned to Philadelphia without any trouble. Once more he found his good Debby, his tender Sally, his handsome William, and his quarrelsome Assembly. But he was tired of all this and didn't stay long in Philadelphia. People called him "Colonel" now, and he had his own regiment, just like the great personages in the Old World. His was no mediocre career. And even if he did have too much work, it was at least interesting and new.

When he left for Virginia to see his colleague Hunter and regulate his accounts, the officers of his regiment, in full dress and with drawn swords, escorted him to the frontier of Pennsylvania. He said later he had been very much annoyed at this demonstration of affection, and no doubt all those young men, prancing and cantering about his joggling horse, as he bounced and jounced in the saddle, kept his mind off serious thought.

The trip to Virginia was pleasant and useful. The University of William and Mary conferred the degree of Master of Arts upon him, he was named an honorary citizen of the city of Norfolk, and the leading men and officials of the region came to flatter him, for they thought his star was in the ascendant. On his return to Philadelphia, new honors awaited him: Governor Denny, lately arrived from Europe, presented him with a diploma of Member of the Royal Society of Science in London. Life was difficult, but not too bad.

However, the storm was still raging in Pennsylvania; Denny, like his predecessors, was bound by his instructions, and he could not consent to the taxation of the Penn dominions. The Assembly would not give in to them, and so both parties turned to Franklin, the mediator. He knew that if he kept up this rôle he would lose everything in the end, and he thought again of leaving. Clouds began to gather around him in Pennsylvania; the Penns, for the first time, showed their disapprobation; they could not pardon the rank and importance he had taken. To see him as master of the situation had wounded their pride to the quick, and when they heard of the officers' escort they were furious. Had they ever been so honored? What did it all mean? The Penns were not particularly intelligent; they began to fear a *coup d'état*, and thought that Franklin was the lowest kind of an intriguing politician. When this became known in Philadelphia, the influential bourgeois were obliged to choose between him and Penn; naturally, they had black looks for Franklin, tried to keep away from him, and spread a number of stories about him in whispers. His old friend and protector, Allen, and a number of his comrades at the lodge turned against him. William Smith was in a fair way to become his principal opponent. Neither at the academy nor at the lodge could Franklin find peace. It was war everywhere.

But it was the last straw when, near the end of July, 1755, a pompous and funereal gentleman, who called himself the Earl of Loudoun, arrived from London. He had been sent by the Prime Minister, Newcastle, to be the commander-in-chief of all the forces of His Majesty in America. This conscientious nobleman, who was slow-thinking, suspicious, and what was worse, honest, had come to this strange circus of America, where every one wanted war but wanted it fought by his neighbor, where every one wanted to spend the least money possible and, moreover, have it spent by some one else. He had brought along his writing desk, which he used in writing innumerable methodical and illegible notes, on innumerable little pieces of paper. He noted all that was told to him, all that one ought to have told him, all that had happened, all that ought to happen, and all that which would never happen. One of the first persons he saw was Franklin, as he had been instructed to do. He asked a thousand questions; what was being done in Pennsylvania; did they pay; did they enroll men; did they lodge them; and lastly (he was very unquiet about this) were there any spies; was this young Colonel Washington a spy? Franklin, like a good Whig and a good son of a Puritan, chose to denounce, instead, a certain Catholic. But Loudoun didn't let him go at that, because he wanted him to accomplish the very delicate task of making the Assembly execute the will of His Majesty. Franklin answered that he would do everything the Earl of Loudoun desired — providing it was in his power.

There was no doubt that his power was very great, even a little dangerous. The Quakers, who were tired of quarreling, had left the Assembly, but they were as stubborn as ever, and had designated Franklin and his friends in such a way that Franklin became the leader of a party which depended on them and their advice. Thus, Franklin was invested with vast authority. The quarrel simplified itself; it was no longer a maelstrom of the people, Quakers, Germans, gentlemen, and the Penns, swirling about the central Franklin, but a definite two-sided affair: the people and the Quakers had joined hands to fight against the Penns and the gentlemen. Franklin had ceased being an arbiter; he was the leader of the first group and received the brickbats of the second.

All summer long, Franklin and the governor tried to find a solution, while Loudoun, the Penns, and the voters harassed them. They made negotiations with the Indians, who claimed they had been robbed in the various sales of their grounds to Pennsylvania. A treaty was made with them, but to no great effect. The frontiers continued to be pillaged, the French had new successes in the north. The situation was painfully difficult. Loudoun was too busy filling up his notebooks to do anything worth while, and Franklin didn't want to remain in Pennsylvania for fear of becoming a scapegoat. He was an excellent diplomatic politician, but a poor champion.

So when the Assembly decided to make a bold move and voted to send Franklin to England, to find some basis of agreement with the Penns, he was highly satisfied. The Assembly had attempted to get along with the Penns' representatives in vain; now the Penns would have to meet one of their representatives. The wise printer found the plan very much to his taste and prepared for his departure at once.

Loudoun, who had not understood the functioning of democratic institutions, continued to beleaguer Franklin, saying he must make the Assembly yield. Franklin, who counted on Loudoun to reimburse him for the remainder of the sum due on Braddock's wagons, didn't want to treat him too roughly. But the noble earl annoyed him. When he first touched discreetly on the subject of the famous wagons, Loudoun was very amiable, desired to see the figures, noted them, and then thought on the matter. He found the price to be colossal, and felt that even if Braddock had lost everything, it was not so much as Franklin figured. He put down this unpleasant detail in his

CARTOON ILLUSTRATING THE OPPOSITION OF POLITICAL PARTIES IN PENNSYLVANIA FROM 1755 TO 1775

notebooks and his memory; his will became as rigid as a pole, and as his thought was not very flexible, it was as far as he could go; Franklin could not obtain a penny from him. Franklin realized what Loudoun thought, and conceived a profound disgust for this gentleman, whom he had first judged serious and conscientious. During March in Philadelphia, and during April in New York, where Franklin was waiting to leave, they indefinitely discussed the postal service, the question of Pennsylvania servants enrolled in the English army, why Pennsylvania didn't want to pay her masters, the impossibility of immediate reimbursement, what was wrong with the governor and the quarrels of the Court. The two men agreed perfectly, as long as it was nothing more serious than drinking or eating together, or talking on general principles, but though they treated each other courteously, each of them scorned the other a little more every day. The Earl of Loudoun was convinced, by what Franklin had said, that the colonies wanted the English Government to make war and pay for it, while Franklin insisted that the English Government merely wanted to fleece the colonies by profiting from the war. He was all the more annoyed when he saw that there was no way of touching the Penns, except through the Royal Government. He decided to please the King if he could.

In the midst of these laborious negotiations, Benjamin made affectionate farewells to his good Debby, his tender Sally, his dear Katy, and to all his old friends. All he dreamed of was getting away. But this was not easy with a man like the Earl of Loudoun. He had put an embargo on all vessels, as he was preparing an expedition against Canada. As long as his communications were not written, he refused to let a vessel leave, and alas, they never were written. Franklin and William remained eight weeks in New York, waiting impatiently. Three times Franklin sat down to write farewell letters; what could be more fatiguing than that?

The summer came in with warm days, and the season was beautiful. His Excellence, the Earl of Loudoun, didn't stop writing his interminable notes, the calm sea invited the exasperated Franklin to leave New York, and Debby organized her way of living so as to be quiet and to take a rest from all the excitement her great husband caused her. She had everything to do during his absence: manage the posts, make the accounts, keep an eye on his political friends, put impertinent gentlemen in their places, and bring up Sally. She found time to accomplish all this, to say nothing of writing long letters to "her Pappy", making jam for him, and sending him apples and squirrels for his English friends.

But would she ever see him again? She knew it was not at all sure. That was why he had been in such a hurry to leave. He had achieved the most beautiful bourgeois career in the world, but what was it worth in this narrow-minded country? London and his youthful adventures were no doubt over for him, but there are also adventures for older and more experienced men; with a little money, genius, and skill, many things could happen. As he wrote to his dear friend, Whitefield:

> Life like a dramatic Piece should not only be conducted with Regularity, but methinks it should finish handsomely. Being now in the last act I begin to cast about for something fit to end with. Or if mine be more properly compar'd to an Epigram, as some of its few Lines are but barely tolerable, I am very desirous of concluding with a bright Point.

"The bright Point" was to be an epic poem.

BOOK THREE

DR. FRANKLIN BUILDS AN EMPIRE

HIGH HOLBOURN
HOLBOURN
BROAD ST GILES'S
Lincolns Inn Fields
Newmans Row
Portugal Row
Holbourn Hill
Chick Lane
WEST SMITH FIELD
ALDERSGATE STREET
Grub Street
London Wall
Middle Moor Fields
Bedlam Hospital
Covent Garden Market
THE STRAND
Somerset House
the Savoy
Temple Bar
FLEET STREET
FLEET MARKET
FLEET DITCH
Fleet Lane
Church Yard
Threadneedle Street
CORNHILL
Thames Street
Church Street
Charing Cross
Parade
White Hall St.
Kings Arms St.
Privy Garden Stairs
Manchester St.
WESTMINSTER
R I V E R
T
LONDON BRIDGE
THE BOROUGH
Vine St.
Angel Street
Narrow Wall
the Upper Ground
Willow St.
the Bank Side
Maid Lane
Bridge St.

Central portion of a map in the possession of the British Museum, entitled, "Map of London, by J. Ellis, 1767", and made during Franklin's sojourn in England.

From a Franklinian point of view, the points of interest are (left to right, and bottom to top) as follows:

Left angle, lower part, facing Whitehall, the Cockpit Tavern, where Franklin had his great triumph in 1772 and his downfall in 1774. The Privy Council of the King held their meetings here. A little above Haymarket were the two theatres Franklin visited so often during his first stay (1724–25): (*a*) The Opera House, (*b*) The New Theatre.

To the right, Craven Street, between the Thames and the Strand, where Franklin lived from 1757 to 1775 in the home of Mrs. Margaret Stevenson; (first at No. 7; Mrs. Stevenson moved later to a larger house on the same street).

Above the Strand are Covent Garden and Drury Lane, with their two theatres, both called "Theatre Royal" (*v* and *w*). Franklin often frequented them during his first stay in London.

Just to the left of Drury Lane is Duke Court, where Franklin lived in 1725, "opposite the Romish Chapel", when he was working at Watt's printing house, near Lincoln's Inn Field (to the right of Drury Lane).

Beyond Lincoln's Inn Field, between the Strand and the Thames, is Essex Street. It was here Franklin went in November, 1774, to hear the first sermons of Theophilus Lindsay, the great Unitarian preacher.

In the center of the map is the Temple, where William Franklin studied law between 1757–62. Near by is Fleet Street and the little lane, Crane Court. The Royal Society of Science met in a building located here (1). Above Fleet Street is Ludgate Hill, where Franklin went to talk and drink at the London Coffee House. This was the first meeting place of his club, the Whig Club. In the same portion of the map, but a little more to the right, is Garlick Hill. Franklin frequented the Dog's Tavern which stood here.

Above Saint Paul's Church Yard is Little Britain, where Franklin lived in 1724, and Bartholomew Close, where he worked at Palmer's Printing House.

On the right-hand side of the map, a little above the Thames, is the Post Office (*h*) on Lombard Street. Franklin often went here to see the Postal Officials.

Central portion of a map in the possession of the British Museum, entitled "Map of London, by J. Ellis, 1767," and made during Franklin's sojourn in England.

From a Franklinian point of view, the points of interest are (left to right, and bottom to top) as follows:

Left angle, lower part, facing Whitehall, the Cockpit Tavern, where Franklin had his great triumph in 1778 and his downfall in 1774. The Privy Council of the King held their meetings here. A little above Haymarket with the two theatres Franklin visited so often during his first stay (1724-5): (1) The Opera House, (2) The New Theatre.

To the right, Craven Street, between the Thames and the Strand, where Franklin lived from 1757 to 1775, in the home of Mrs. Margaret Stevenson (first at No. 7; Mrs. Stevenson moved later to a larger house on the same street).

Above the Strand are Covent Garden and Drury Lane, with their two theatres, both called "Theatre Royal" (9 and 10). Franklin often frequented them during his first stay in London.

Just to the left of Drury Lane is Duke Court, where Franklin lived in 1725 (opposite the Romish Chapel), when he was working at Watt's printing house, near Lincoln's Inn Fields (to the right of Drury Lane).

Beyond Lincoln's Inn Field, between the Strand and the Thames, is Essex Street. It was here Franklin went in November, 1774, to hear the first sermons of Theophilus Lindsey, the great Unitarian preacher.

In the center of the map is the Temple, where William Franklin studied law between 1751-[illegible]. Near by is Fleet Street and the little lane, Crane Court. The Royal Society [illegible] in a building located here [illegible]. Above Fleet Street is Ludgate Hill, where Franklin went to talk and drink at the London Coffee House. This was the [illegible] meeting place of his club, the Whig Club. In the same portion of the map, but a little more to the right, is Garlick Hill. Franklin frequented the Dog's Tavern which stood here.

Above Saint Paul's Church Yard is Little Britain, where Franklin lived in 1725, and Bartholomew Close, where he worked at Palmer's Printing House.

On the right-hand side of the map, a little above the Thames, is the Post Office (7) on Lombard Street. Franklin often went here to see the Postal Officials.

I

LONDON bound! A gallant company of young men crowded the vessel which had the honor of carrying Mr. Benjamin Franklin, Postmaster-general of the American Colonies for His Majesty, the King of England, Member of the Legislative Assembly of the Parliament of Pennsylvania, and Envoy, intrusted with a confidential mission by this Assembly to the Honorable Proprietors of the Province and the Royal Government.

Of all his fellow passengers, the most brilliant was, no doubt, the young Mr. Abercrombie, the son of Major General James Abercrombie, Vice Commander of the British Forces in America. This charming boy was so talented for mimicry that it is said he contracted consumption by imitating the coughing of his friends. However, on board, he kept every one in a gale of laughter. Then there was a young Irish beau, who sported florid waistcoats, while two young officers of the Royal Navy, Captain Kennedy and Mr. John Temple, paraded on the deck in their most showy uniforms. A gentleman of Rhode Island completed the party, which did not, however, eclipse the picturesque figure of the captain, an old sea dog, who was always swearing a blue streak when he wasn't coughing, spitting or gulping down a glass of gin. But he knew the ways of the sea.

William Franklin liked especially to chat with John Temple, whose fine features, distinguished manners, and excellent connections interested him. He belonged to the noble family of the Temples, which was the most influential and powerful in the Whig aristocracy; three ministers were counted among its members, — Lord Temple, the head of the house, Lord Grenville, and William Pitt, the greatest Englishman of his century. John Temple, who had been born in America, where one branch of this family flourished, was on his way to England to resume relations with his powerful cousins and to make the most of his lively intelligence, his sincere zeal for public welfare, and the general esteem which his family enjoyed.

Both he and William had the same ambitions, which, moreover, were going to be gratified. Their aristocratic conversations helped the young Philadelphian to forget the crass bourgeois atmosphere of his native city and the chagrin of his disappointed love. For Doctor Graeme, a Member of the Provincial Council, was an enthusiastic adherent of the Penns, distrusted William and forbade his daughter to marry him. Mrs. Graeme, who was very pious, had heard some little stories about young Franklin which upset her. Miss Graeme, like the dutiful daughter she was, suppressed her love, and she and William bade farewell to each other, swearing eternal faithfulness. She spent her time in weeping, wrote verses to her absent one, and unburdened her heart to her intimate friends. William went sailing off, his heart touched to the quick at leaving his love, but not too unhappy at the prospect of a vacation and new sights. The memory of his beautiful poetess who spoke so wisely, lifting her graceful eyebrows as she said good-by, was mingled agreeably with the pleasures and incidents of his voyage.

Though William's father was less light-hearted, he was none the less touched at leaving Philadelphia — for always, perhaps — this city where he had made his fortune and where he had achieved the finest bourgeois career that had ever been seen. He was leaving behind him a distressed Pennsylvania, a colony ravaged by war and torn by internal quarrels; he was leaving his good wife, his little girl, his old friends, and the taverns where he had tossed off many a glass and planned many an adventure.

On board, he smilingly observed the games of the young men and listened intently to the technical explanations of Captain Kennedy; he watched the sea, the winds, the waves, and the sea-birds, but most of the time he was dreaming of the great work he wanted to accomplish, the creation of the British Empire. "The foundation of British grandeur is in America," he said to himself, over and over again. America was the paradise of Anglo-Saxons to him, a vast, rich, uncultivated land, which only awaited the hand of man to make it fruitful. He believed in America and did not fear, like the philosophers of the Old World, that it would absorb thousands of people without benefit to humanity. He thought that the immigrants would prosper and multiply, that the empty places they left in Europe would be easily filled, and that Great Britain, without being enfeebled in Europe, would win immense domains in the West, insuring her worldly supremacy.

Franklin was born a Whig, reared as one, and now, pervaded with the spirit of English Masonry, he held to the hegemony of British civilization, with its ideal of liberty and Protestantism. It seemed right to him that the center of this empire should be located some day in the New World, to which England would owe her fortune, but after the Albany Convention, he lost hope in the colonies organizing an Anglo-Saxon empire themselves. They were too occupied with their own little jealousies and their little internal quarrels. He turned towards England, from which country alone the empire should spring. Only England could make his plan real, by giving it to the colonies in the form of a command. He had applied all his subtle wisdom to this plan, and all his vast experience as a politician. His program was to enlarge the British domains by the immediate constitution of the colonies, which would insure the execution of British law on the continent and prepare for the future; to establish an Anglo-Saxon confederation with its capital, king, and Federal Parliament in London, the latter conserving the rights of the Magna Charta, and sending representatives to the Imperial Parliament. Pennsylvania, in his plan, was to set an example and be the kernel of the confederation. And himself—But he was too wise to tempt Fate by those dreams of personal ambition which are so bitter when they are dissipated. It was enough for him to know his program and to realize that it could not be effected unless he were the mainspring. And he also knew that every good workman was worthy of his hire.

For some days Franklin's packet boat followed the flotilla of Lord Loudoun which was sailing to Canada, but finally, the

General sent them the communications he had been working on so long, and the vessel got under way for England at last. The captain was skillful, and by shifting the ballast, increased the speed of the vessel so materially that they easily outstripped all the French privateers which gave chase. They were favored by fair winds and escaped storms; the Falmouth lighthouse saved them from being wrecked the night before they reached port. The voyage had taken thirty days and the spectacle of the animated town of Falmouth, with its surrounding green fields, was most welcome to the passengers.

They all set off for London; the Franklins took a calash and drove through the beautiful east country which was green and sunny. For the sake of William, Benjamin stopped at Stonehenge and the superb estate of Lord Pembroke at Wilton, with its collection of pictures. William liked the collection as it was in good taste, but Benjamin preferred the Druid ruins, which recalled the eager discussions of the old days, when, as a poor young apprentice, he had investigated the origins of religion and talked about virtue with the elderly gentlemen of London. He realized that the times had changed more than he.

They arrived at the capital on July 26, in the evening. Franklin was being eagerly awaited. While he looked out curiously at the great city, which had not changed, but which seemed more smoky, black, populous, miserable and luxurious than ever before, his correspondents crowded about him, anxious to become his friends: Peter Collinson, the good merchant and Quaker botanist, with whom he stayed the first few days; Fothergill, the noted Quaker doctor, to whom Franklin had been recommended by the Pennsylvania Friends, and who became the intermediary between him and the Penns; William Strahan, the stout, cordial printer, who fell into Franklin's arms (this was the first time they had met, but they had loved each other fraternally for the past ten years, as often happens between men who help each other to make money); James Ralph, his boyhood friend, who had been attracted to Franklin by the memories of their intimacy and Franklin's new glory (the little milliner, debts and poetic dreams had been forgotten); and lastly Charles, the agent for Pennsylvania in England, who had prepared lodgings in a suitable quarter, the Strand, in the home of a poor but distinguished widow, Mrs. Margaret Stevenson, at Number 7 Craven Street, by the Thames.

Franklin didn't lose any time; the province was paying him to settle their differences with the Penns, and he felt that a meeting with them would be the proper beginning of his English career. So Fothergill took him to the Penns immediately.

He found them ensconced in virtue and prudence, and so suspicious of his every word that there was little left to hope for. Their heavy wigs were less weighty and bothersome than their prejudices. They wanted more authority but no change, and they refused any project which seemed in the least risky. Though in England they were bourgeois, they considered themselves as the kings of Pennsylvania, and so showed themselves to be as imperious as kings, but as fearsome as cheap little capitalists. They had been very distrustful of Franklin ever since they had heard of the famous cavalcade. And what was worse, their chief counselor was Ferdinand John Paris, a haughty, artful and unbending lawyer, who could not pardon Franklin's mercantile spirit, and who had a grudge against him for his irreverent speeches in the Assembly. It was obvious that between the lawyer and the business man this discussion could not come to an end. There was no solution to be looked for from the Penns, who were virtuous, hypocritical, unintelligent, and above all, obstinate.

They received the agent of their tenants with distant politeness, and with profuse protestations of good will which boded ill for the future. They didn't want anything but what was reasonable, they affirmed, and Franklin said that was all he desired. But what was reasonable to Franklin was most unreasonable to the Penns; and the moment they wanted to be practical they clashed. The Penns would roll up like hedgehogs, showing only their quills and refusing to stir. Franklin had hoped for a broad-minded bargaining between them, in which he would have excelled, but he saw that even this was impossible. He promised to send them a written memorandum, which they asked of him out of distrust, and Franklin retired from the scene, discouraged.

He was to have a still more discouraging experience. The great Anglo-Virginian merchant, John Hanbury, took him to see Lord Grenville, the president of the King's Council, who had expressed a desire to talk to him. Grenville was one of those rare English parliamentarians who worked seriously, and he welcomed this Pennsylvania commoner with great civility. He had heard of Franklin's devotion to the Crown and the services he had rendered to Braddock. Grenville asked him some questions about the American situation and then lectured him solemnly:

> You Americans have wrong ideas of the nature of your constitution; you contend that the king's instructions to his governors are not laws, and think yourselves at liberty to regard or disregard them at your own discretion. But those instructions are not like the pocket instructions given to a minister going abroad, for regulating his conduct in some trifling point of ceremony. They are first drawn up by judges learned in the laws; they are then considered, debated, and perhaps amended in Council, after which they are signed by the king. They are then, so far as they relate to you, *the law of the land*, for the king is the *legislator of the colonies*.

Franklin was astonished and shocked; he protested that the colonists were free Englishmen, like the others, who made their laws with the approval of the king, but did not receive them without a word to say. Lord Grenville shook his wig gently, answered that the law was not otherwise than he had explained, and ushered Franklin very politely to the door.

Franklin was dejected by these hard blows and wanted to see if anything could be done through the Great Pitt. Pitt had just been named Prime Minister, and in the midst of the disasters which were overwhelming England — the taking of Minorca, the American defeats — every one looked to him as the hope of the country. Franklin tried to see him, but in vain; a strict and discreet order forbade him all access to Pitt and kept the door closed to him for eighteen years. He could see only the secretaries.

The Prime Minister and the king washed their hands of the affair. The administration and the English aristocracy had only black looks for Franklin. The Americans were suspected of ambitious designs, and the English had a grudge against them. They wanted colonies, counting-houses, subjects, but not fellow citizens. The English aristocracy distrusted the American middle class; they wanted an empire after the London pattern, not according to the pattern of Philadelphia. It was a struggle of classes.

About this time Franklin suddenly underwent a very serious physical crisis. The air of London was so unhealthy that doctors had to send their patients to the bridges of the Thames, where they could breathe freely. This condition, plus the change of diet, change of routine, extra fatigue and disappointments all had their effect on Franklin.

He caught cold, but indomitably continued his intense work until he had a rising fever which produced violent headaches. The top of his head seemed to burn, he claimed, and for a while he was delirious. These crises endured from twelve to thirty-six hours and left the scalp tender and sore. He weakened. Filled with compassion, the good Mrs. Stevenson and Doctor Fothergill, helped by William, the Negro servant, Peter, and the maids, did all they could for Franklin. They cupped him, gave him quinine, and administered so many laxatives that he could no longer stand the taste of them. He did not dare take emetics for fear of seriously endangering his head. In spite of the doctor's efforts, his condition went from bad to worse, until one fine day, for no reason whatsoever, his stomach reacted violently, as strong eighteenth-century stomachs often did, and in a short while he was out of danger.

His pains lessened from day to day, but he remained feeble, tired and changed. He was always at the mercy of colds during the years he lived in England (in September, 1758, February, 1760, December, 1764, April-May, 1766, Spring, 1767).

Instead of a robust, brisk young man, ready to lavish his energy, he felt like an aging man who has to husband his strength and organize his life carefully. He was no longer the strange youth who ran about the dark streets of Boston, visiting the squalid taverns of the sailors, nor the young man who displayed his well-turned leg to the girls at a Haymarket ball or won the admiration of his companions when he plunged nude into the Thames. His face was now a little too large for his body, and his huge wig shadowed his serious eyes and thin lips. He looked like an enigmatic personage of deep wisdom who could command both reverence and fear.

Towards the end of November, 1757, when he felt better, he reorganized his life. He knew that a long struggle awaited him in England and he had to settle down to prepare himself for it; he needed comfort too, as he was getting old.

Fortunately, the excellent Mrs. Stevenson all but worshiped him and furnished him with all he needed; during his illness she had been most assiduous, respectful, maternal and tender in her care of him, and she had no idea of neglecting him now. When Mrs. Stevenson suffered from rheumatism, Franklin gave her a remedy, and he advised her in the education of her charming daughter, Marie. In return they pampered him, piled his newspapers — which were always scattered all over the room — in orderly heaps, arranged his clothes, and made him little presents like the Chinese ivory back-scratcher, when he suffered from the itch. Mrs. Stevenson aired and warmed his shirts before he put them on, avoided serving boiled or roast beef, as he found these meats injurious, furnished him with long-sleeved cotton nightgowns, flannel trousers and warm slippers so that he could sleep snugly. She trained her servants, the maid, and the cook, Nanny, — even the cat — to respect his mannerisms. There was no doubt but what he was well cared for in this comfortable little home, where he occupied four rooms and ruled over all.

A solid bourgeois respectability enveloped the Franklins; they had rented a handsome coach to go riding about London, and when they left their house accompanied by their Negro servant, Peter, and the little Negro lackey (who ran away soon after their arrival) they looked like people of consequence. Franklin bought a pretty sword to go to court with, a silver dinner service to use when he had guests; he always received company in such a way as to impress them.

He believed in the worth of public favor, and had a right to do so. Wasn't he a rich bourgeois? His printing shop in Philadelphia brought in a thousand pounds a year, the post-office, three hundred, and his houses in Philadelphia, one hundred and fifty. At his departure, the Assembly had given him one thousand five hundred pounds, and they were to give him more on his return. He still had his farm at Burlington, his estates at Germantown, his properties in Boston, the revenues which came from his partnerships with printers all over America, and the interest of various other investments. Franklin was well off and didn't neglect to increase his fortune by sure little speculations which were easy to make in London, the center of news and influential people. But he also knew how to be generous; after the great fire of Boston he subscribed a large sum for the refugees, he continued to aid his incorrigible nephew and partner, B. Mecom, and he never refused to give a shilling here or a shilling there to people who needed it. The effects of his goodness were spread far and wide.

But, above all, he was a perfect friend, cheerful and fond of good living, a hearty drinker and a good story teller. Excepting those persons who were blinded by their snobbishness, every one was obliged to love him. He adapted himself without effort to the rich and cultivated middle-class society of London, who liked, as he did, strong beer, broad stories, clever turns of business and useful sciences. He was the delight of Collinson and Fothergill, and through them exerted his charm over the entire society of Friends and many wealthy men of London. His frank gayety met a cordial response in Strahan, and the two of them, clinking glasses, talked over the military tactics of Frederick the Great and planned to have their children engaged: Sally Franklin aged thirteen, and William Strahan, Junior, aged seventeen. This friendship was useful, for Strahan was one of the foremost printers of London and knew all the authors, many actors and influential people; both Doctor Johnson and Garrick were among his debtors. Moreover, he edited the *London Chronicle* and published whatever idea Franklin suggested.

Even his old friend, Ralph, had become useful to him. They had forgiven each other, and Franklin served as intermediary between the first wife of Ralph, remarried to Mr. Garrigues, and Ralph, who had also married again and was the father of a little girl. Franklin very tactfully gave him the news of his children and grandchildren, while the unfortunate bigamist, who cared for his first wife when it was too late, sent back most touching messages. Just as Benjamin had predicted, Ralph had spoiled his life; his marriages had tired him, his poetry had led to nothing, he had never been anything but a salaried political writer, and the periodical pamphlet he wrote for the Duke of Bedford, the Protestor, was still another deception. Ralph was a moral spectacle, for he was a living proof of the commercial bankruptcy of immorality and poetry. Nevertheless, he was useful, as he could be intrusted with discreet missions. He had too much need of Franklin's assistance not to be faithful and sure.

Thus Franklin was solidly established among the publishers, printers and journalists; he was still connected with Cave, the director of the *Gentleman's Magazine*, and he made the gracious gesture of returning to his old workshop, where he offered drinks to every one, showing himself to be a generous, cheerful and simple companion.

In parliamentary circles he had found a precious friend, William Jackson, an eminent lawyer, who was called "Omniscient Jackson", owing to the extent of his erudition and understanding. Franklin realized his value even before the English saw it, and made use of him immediately.

He was still more firmly established among his erudite friends. Being a fellow of the Royal Society in London and considered as the greatest physicist of the world, Franklin basked in the admiration of all English scholars. He was per-

FRANKLIN AS A MIDDLE-AGED MAN

sonally connected with Wilson, Canton, and Doctor Pringle, who consulted him on electrical medicine. Pringle especially attracted him with his amiable smile, enormous stomach, fine spirit and good heart: he was one of the most popular men in high society and because of his knowledge of science and his brilliant service in the army, he was going to become the physician to the King and Queen. Franklin met many of the city gentry at his home, and what was more important, politicians who enjoyed the favor of the King.

Pringle became his intimate friend, and Franklin faithfully attended the meetings of both the lodge and the academy. But the taverns and the newspapers were his favorite means of spreading his ideas among the public. He needed them also to keep in touch with the political situation and to find his bearings. In the taverns he was sure he would not be misunderstood or betrayed, and often went there to talk with journalists and writers and — to drink. He went first to the Philadelphia Coffeehouse, where the men of the colony met, then he enlarged his circle and was seen at the Paul's Head Tavern, at the King's Arms Tavern, the New England Coffeehouse, the New York Coffeehouse, the Pennsylvania Coffeehouse, the St. Paul's Coffeehouse in Birchen Lane, the Dog Tavern on Garlick Hill, the George and Vulture Coffeehouse, where he indulged in fish and brandy. He was frequently seen, too, at the Queen's Head Coffeehouse, at St. Paul's Churchyard, and at the London Coffeehouse (Ludgate Hill), where he attended, every Thursday fortnight, the meetings of the Whig Club. This club was made up of intelligent, even cultivated, middle-class men, who drank their whisky straight and made no bones about it: Fothergill, Collinson, Watson, Priestley, Price, Maty, Doctor Hawkesworth, Doctor Kippis, John Lee, Stanley, etc. The club was held in a private room, which was connected with the barroom, but partitioned off from it so that the men could feel at home, talk freely, and still keep up their drinking with zest.

Now that Franklin was well settled in this bourgeois environment, which diverted and rested him, he could begin his crusade. He had a great deal to do and his good American friends counted on him as though he were a magician. He wanted the King to ratify all the laws which had been passed by the Pennsylvania Assembly, to secure the reimbursement for servants enrolled in the British army, and he wanted the Penns to permit them to tax their property and to treat them as equals. He also wanted to be indemnified for the money he had spent to make good Braddock's losses. Lastly, he had a thousand private errands to accomplish for his friends, — some wanted books, others sought business information, and some like Norris, gave him money to invest. A village peddler did not have so many different tasks, but Franklin didn't mind, as he was a Jack-of-all-trades both by nature and taste.

Of course, he had his son to aid him, and William accomplished his tasks intelligently, albeit in a high and mighty manner. He admired his father greatly, but he admired himself even more, and he approved of his handsome and distinguished appearance. He had no desire to fall back into the middle class, and though he helped his father in politics, he did so after his own fashion.

He was glad to be his father's intermediary to Galloway, the young Pennsylvania politician, who was just beginning to be known, and who was stirring up the enthusiasm of the people; he was perfectly willing to write political articles under his name, such as the long defense of the Quakers which appeared in the English newspapers (September, 1757) and which was immediately reprinted in the *Gentleman's Magazine*, but he did not like to do any scraping and bowing, and thought that his father was far too modest.

Benjamin Franklin was so busily engaged in his struggle that he did not notice how much secret opposition had sprung up against him. William's letter, and the prudent energetic manner of Benjamin Franklin had irritated the Penns extremely; they dropped their simulated kindness for the moment and began attacking the father and son in every way they could. They employed various pretexts in order not to answer his memorandum, claiming that it had been written disrespectfully (Franklin had omitted using their full titles) and that the

Assembly had not intrusted Franklin with enough power to deal with them; they asked Franklin to submit a typical law to them, such as the Assembly might frame, but Franklin was wise enough to decline, seeing the danger. They clashed on all these points, and the Penns were all the more offended by what Franklin didn't dare to say. Even before Franklin's arrival, the Penns had complained a great deal about him, saying that he was too fond of power, and that he was crafty and ostentatious. They did not stop spreading evil reports which could injure his reputation and harm William. Wasn't his son illegitimate?

Franklin soon learned to hate them. After a particularly oily and fractious conversation with them he wrote: "I conceived at that moment a more cordial and thorough contempt for him (Thomas Penn) than I ever before felt for any man living, a contempt that I cannot express in words, but I believe my countenance expressed it strongly, and that his brother who was looking at me must have observed it."

In the same letter, he compared Thomas Penn with "A low Jockey who triumphed with insolence when a purchaser complained of being cheated in a Horse", and he prophesied that "The Proprietors will be gibbeted up as they deserve, to rot and stink in the nostrils of Posterity."

He expressed these energetic feelings in his letters to Galloway, who sympathized with him. Unfortunately, the terms Franklin had used concerning the Penns leaked out. The Penns took umbrage at this, decided to have nothing more to do with Franklin, and answered the Assembly directly, thus insulting Franklin and the Assembly. Franklin was furious but asked in vain to be recalled: his stay in England signified that the Assembly wished an open fight against the Penns.

This suited Franklin perfectly; one of the essential points of his program was to have the King take back Pennsylvania under the Royal Government. His chances of success were good, for he knew that Pitt was hostile to the principle of private colonies. The great minister disapproved of this system which uselessly complicated the government machinery, and as it savored of feudalism it was all the more displeasing to him, the leader of the Whigs. Unfortunately, the war occupied all his attention; the various other offices of the government were suspicious of the Americans and did not favor any change suggested by them. Method was needed for success. Franklin suggested an infallible one to his colleagues of the Assembly — discreetly, not saying he approved of it — a revolt against the Penns which would be a brilliant proof of their inability to govern, followed by a sabotage of all the laws, which would make a solution imperative. But while he dreamed of such heroic proceedings, he prepared for a long war. It took him all winter, all spring, and a part of the summer.

In the midst of various changes — the taking of Louisburg by the English, Montcalm's victory at Ticonderoga, Frederick the Great's heroic exploits — the war continued in its disquieting way.

Franklin took a trip into the country to calm his nerves and to restore his health, which the life of smoky London had somewhat impaired. He also wanted to renew some of his family connections, and his trip was in the nature of a genealogical expedition. In the beginning of May he went to Cambridge where he conducted some interesting experiments on evaporation with Hadley; evaporation was a great mystery then, and no one knew why it had a cooling effect. Then he traveled through Huntingshire, Northumberlandshire, and Wellsborough to reach Ecton. He followed up all the traces he could find of his family: the Franklins, Folgiers and the Reeds. At Wellsborough he found two old cousins, Mr. and Miss Walker, who were humble but happy, and who had kept many of the family souvenirs. At Ecton, the curate showed him the chimes which Thomas Franklin had erected, while his wife told him the village stories about this Franklin who had been a skillful and influential man in his time. At Birmingham, which was the next stop in their itinerary, the Franklins visited the factories, talked with the local scholars, and discovered the Cashes and Flints, who were cousins of Deborah, all honestly working as turners, buttoners, etc.

Thus they rendered their homage to the past, offered and gave aid to their poor cousins, noted a thousand touching and pleasing scenes on their way. To the great satisfaction of William, Benjamin finished up the trip by going to the fashionable watering place, Tunbridge Wells. William Jackson and Hunter were also there and they all had a long and agreeable vacation together; the season was brilliant and there were many London society people. However, Benjamin returned to the capital sooner than most, for he had much work and a long fight ahead of him.

The year 1759 was a memorable one for the world. It marked the definite breaking down of French domination in the West Indies and Canada. Quebec, Guadeloupe, Marie Galante were taken, and French flotillas were defeated on both the Mediterranean and the Caribbean. Havre was bombarded, Brest and Dunkerque blocked. In Germany, the victory of Minden saved Frederick the Great, and proved the weakness of the allies, who could not obtain a definite success. Pitt, who was more popular than a Roman dictator, led the English people to the very summit of glory. Meanwhile Voltaire, quietly living in Ferney, published his great sarcastic pamphlet, "Candide", which tolled the knell of the French aristocracy, and Monsieur Rousseau de Genève announced a new evangelism, based on equality and democracy.

England was drunk with success and Franklin felt the effects of her exaltation. Pitt had definitely established the British Empire on the universe, and the time was ripe for the wise man of Philadelphia to bring forth his great ideas. The first obstacle in his path was the Penn family, and he tried to break it down with all his might. The struggle was epical for Franklin was the most astute politician in the world, and the Penns were the greatest blockheads imaginable.

There were three principal points to the quarrel: the taxation of Pennsylvania, the William Smith scandal, and the Indian affairs.

On the subject of taxation no conclusion was reached in 1759. Governor Denny, who was weary of fighting with the Assembly, and more desirous of being on good terms with the people he was governing than with the absent proprietors, ratified a law which permitted an issue of one hundred thousand pounds sterling in paper money. This sum was to pay for the maintenance of the King's army and was guaranteed by a land tax, which included the estates of the Penns. Naturally, the Penns were furious, decided to make the law null and void, and to recall Denny immediately, but the year went by in preparatory maneuvers, for the struggle promised to be a decisive one, and neither side wished to begin without being sure it possessed all the weapons possible.

Moreover, the William Smith scandal was enough to keep Franklin and the Penns busy. In 1756–1757, a certain Pennsylvania judge, Moore, had been denounced in the Assembly as a grafter. Now he was one of the Penns' chosen men, and the Assembly was only too glad of the opportunity to order him to appear before them. Moore refused to do so, saying the Assembly had no jurisdiction over him. The more obstinate he was, the more the Assembly fumed. William Smith, the president of the academy, was too fond of a quarrel to miss such a good one as this, and intervened for Moore. The Assembly was furious, and ignoring Governor Denny's objurgations, thrust Moore and Smith into prison to teach them how to respect the Assembly and the rights of British citizens.

Smith did not take the lesson in good part, and as soon as he got out of prison he left for England to complain to the Royal Government. He was swollen with hate and anger against the Assembly, and soon won over to his side many of his Scotch compatriots, his colleagues in the Church of England, and some suspicious government officials who thought that the American Assemblies arrogated too many privileges to themselves. It was a fine quarrel, for Smith argued well, and the money of the Penns was working for him.

At the same time this was going on, a very delicate Indian problem was being discussed. In 1737, Thomas Penn had played a trick on the Delaware Indians which merited hanging. In order to make more room for the immigrants, Penn had bought a strip of ground from them which extended westward to the distance of a day and a half march. This was the way the Indians measured and it was as clear to them as a mile is to us. A day and a half march meant about twenty-five miles to them. But Thomas Penn had too sharp a sense of reality not to make the most out of his bargaining. By a little underhand dealing, he procured three young white athletes who were known for their endurance and rapidity in walking, and after instructing them, presented them as the surveyors for this grant of land. They walked sixty-six miles in the allotted time, but the Indians were soon exhausted and refused to follow them.

The Indians and the Penns had quarreled over this affair ever since, but in times of peace it did not matter much, for a few long speeches, some money and a little rum sufficed to make the negotiations agreeable to both parties. However, in war time, it was different, for even if the Indians had rum and had become conscientiously drunk, they would return and burn down the plantations. The Assembly stood up for the Indians, and in 1757–1758 was particularly desirous of seeing justice done to them.

The Assembly was also in intimate relations with an Indian chief named Teedyuscum, the most foxy and tricky of them all, and one of the greatest drinkers that has ever been known. He served as a benevolent intermediary between Pennsylvania and the Delaware tribes, being at various times a salaried spy, a paid traitor and a pure hero. In 1759, he signed a new treaty with the Penns at Euston; it was very effusive, and the word "brothers" was used in every line. But at length, Teedyuscum felt he had been duped once more, and complained, half-whining, half-menacing. He brought up the 1737 affair again, and the Assembly instructed Franklin to carry on his suit before the English authorities. Even if it failed to succeed, it wouldn't bring Thomas Penn any honor.

The Indian quarrel was important, as it had such a bearing on the solution of the Western problem (in which Franklin was so interested), and the Smith matter was equally significant since it would serve to define the rights of the colonial Assemblies. Franklin had to take precautions.

He neglected none of them. He prepared public opinion carefully by giving from time to time, notes, news and essays to the *London Chronicle*, Strahan's newspaper, and to the *Gentleman's Magazine*. He also began to bring out pamphlets. His son William and Jackson wrote for him, Strahan and Ralph took care of the printing, and thus he was sure of having his work done well and discreetly.

He first published, "An Inquiry into the Causes of the Alienation of the Shawanese and Delaware Indians." This was a resumé of the Penn-Teedyuscum quarrel, written by one Charles Thompson, and very bitter against the Penns. Franklin, who had found the reading of it difficult, had added some picturesque and touching stories of the missionary, Post, and his trips to the Indians. Thus he transformed a heavy and quarrelsome pamphlet into an interesting book which stimulated the imagination. And it must not be forgotten that during these years Monsieur Rousseau de Genève and the lovely ladies of Paris had made the Indians very popular.

This "Inquiry" was published at the expense of the province, and shortly after there appeared a large book of four hundred and forty-four pages entitled, "Historical Review of the Constitution and Government of Pennsylvania." It was not signed, and the publisher was obscure. But it was dedicated to Arthur Onslow, Speaker of the House of Commons, and aimed to show all the Penns in an unfavorable light, even the great founder of Pennsylvania. No one doubted that the book came from Franklin, for it was so definitely an attack on the Penns. Franklin had "ordered" it and prepared the material, which William and Richard Jackson had written up into book form. Every chapter was loaded with irrefutable facts, and written with such earnestness that the book was highly interesting to men of this witty century, who had so much leisure and such violent tempers. Franklin distributed copies right and left and tried to increase the sales by having favorable comments of the book inserted in his friends newspapers, while the Penns paid other periodicals to criticize it adversely.

With the ground thus prepared for him, Franklin began his first skirmish. He went to all the ministers, visited Lord Halifax and Lord Grenville, whom the Penns had also tried to influence, showing the danger of angering the Indians at such a time, and talked as well about other rascalities of the Penns. Finally, he came before the Lords of the Council on Plantations to defend Teedyuscum directly and to attack Thomas Penn. Teedyuscum wanted the council to reprimand the Penns and oblige them to refund him for the land they had stolen; the Penns wanted the Council simply to dismiss the case and to confirm their rights to the grounds they possessed. The discussion began with great dignity, and the Penns were sure of themselves. They knew that to prove anything, all the property titles would have to be examined and these were not to be found. On the occasions of these treaties, when titles were established, the Indians always held great bacchanalian celebrations which kept them dead drunk for a week afterwards. During this time the copies of the deeds which had been given to them disappeared, while the originals were put away and were well hidden.

Franklin surprised the Penns by asking them to show their property titles. They protested, saying that it was not up to them to show their documents, that he should produce his own. Then there was a silence while Franklin took a big sheaf of papers from his pocket and shook them saying, "I have copies of them; here they are." The Penns had forgotten that at the last treaty Teedyuscum had a white man for his secretary, as the drunkenness of the whites was less profound than that of the redskins (May, 1759).

After some confusion and further protestations from Penn's lawyers, the council recognized the validity of the documents and Franklin scored. But knowing better than to attempt putting the tangled situation in order, the council referred the matter to Sir William Johnson, the governor of the western territories for the king. This decision was not a success for Teedyuscum, who had formerly refused this solution, but it was for Franklin, who knew Johnson, and who knew how to guide the latter's judgment.

The agent for Pennsylvania could be proud of this victory, which had been won solely on his own ability, but he could not be happy, as it had been compensated by a sudden serious setback.

William Smith had been in England since January, making a great fuss all the while to secure justice, and to be avenged on the Assembly of Pennsylvania. He was a good fighter, but he had a preference for the big stick, whereas Franklin liked to proceed diplomatically and discreetly. They were both rude antagonists after their own fashion. Smith had prepared his attack by getting on good terms with the ecclesiastical authorities, the Bishop of London, the Penns, and various conservative politicians. Then, to the great joy of Franklin's enemies, he wrote an article in which he endeavored to prove that Franklin had stolen his scientific discoveries from his neighbors, particularly Kinnersley. This article was printed in the *American Magazine*, which belonged to the Bradfords, the old enemies of Franklin. Franklin's strength in England was based on the esteem which scholars accorded him; few accusations could do more harm than this, and none could hurt him so much. Whenever he or William spoke of Smith, he was always mentioned as "that parson."

Smith presented himself before the attorney-general on April 17, 1759. He attacked the Assembly directly, saying it had exercised rights which belonged only to the Parliament of Great Britain, and that all the intrigues against him were managed by the Quakers who were jealous of his influence. He cleverly stirred up the prejudices of the Anglicans against the Friends, and roused the anger of the English parliamentarians against the colonial Assemblies. Franklin had foreseen the danger and had sought to parry it by dedicating his "Historical Review of the Constitution and Government of Pennsylvania" to the President of the House of Commons, but now, driven into a corner, he could only take refuge in a technical defense, alleging that some laws passed in the time of Queen Anne gave power to the Assembly which was now denied it.

But Franklin fought for a hopeless cause. Every one was against the Assembly of Pennsylvania: the King, the Parliament, where Moore had a brother, the Episcopate and the Ministry. On June 26, 1759, the Private Council of the King handed down a peremptory and insulting decision against the Assembly, signifying "His Majesty's high Displeasure at the unwarrantable Behaviour of the said Assembly, in assuming to themselves Powers which did not belong to them and invading both His Majesty's Royal Prerogative, and the Liberties of the People." And to be even more humiliating, the Privy Council intrusted the delivery of this reprimand to the Penns and their governor. The only ironic note was the insistence of the Privy Council in advising the Penns not to be too gracious in the treatment of their colony. Some time later the Royal Council on Plantations scolded them for being too good-natured to the Assembly.

Thomas Penn, who had no sense of the ridiculous, found this criticism very unjust, and Franklin was too sad to be amused by it. The first year of his struggle had ended in overwhelming defeat. This decision of 1759 made it clear that the Parliament, the aristocracy and the Ministry considered the Americans as their subjects. The dream of an Anglo-American empire began to fade from Franklin's mind.

But his health had returned and he had many friends to divert him in London. Life in the great city pleased him with its chatter over tankards of ale, its comfort and luxury, and he preferred not to be unhappy. He would not say that he was beaten but laughed at his bad luck. He took his setback as a useful lesson, and to give himself time to reflect he decided to take a pleasant trip to the country.

Summer had come, Parliament was on a vacation, and the streets of London were empty. England was joyous and throughout the country fireworks were shot off to celebrate her victories. Franklin and his son took a coach to visit the North. They went first to Liverpool, then Glasgow, then Edinburgh. On their way they studied the farms, learned about industries, and observed the different customs of the people. At Edinburgh they were cordially welcomed by the scholars of the city. Most of them were doctors, as the Department of Medicine was the principal one of the university. They became intimately connected with Sir Alexander Dick, the famous doctor, and Lord Kames, an illustrious judge and lawmaker who enjoyed considerable prestige throughout Great Britain. He was a tall, lanky, lively old man who wrote huge tomes on law, and long books, which were highly praised but rarely read, on morals, theology, philosophy. He was known chiefly for the balance of his decisions, and for his exaggerated taste of practical jokes. He played them on his friends, his family and his colleagues of the Bench.

Franklin was taken with Kames at first sight. They both had so many tastes in common, they enjoyed discussing but hated disputes, they loved liberty but they knew its dangers, and they liked to use a joking tone when they spoke of serious things. They also liked to be surrounded by pretty girls, although they knew the risks of such a proceeding and the dangers that might ensue.

They passed long hours together at Kames' home in Berwickshire, discussing science, morality, religion and playing tricks on each other. One fine day Franklin remarked to Lord Kames that there was a sensational passage in the Bible, which the clergy never noticed or explained, in which the God of the Hebrews ordered his disciples to be tolerant. Lord Kames was very surprised and brought his Bible to Franklin, who read aloud to him the beautiful story of the reprimand which God addressed to Abraham, when the latter had refused his hospitality to an infidel. "And God said, Have I borne with him these hundred ninety and eight years, and nourished him and clothed him, notwithstanding his rebellion against Me; and could'st not thou, that art thyself a sinner, bear with him one night." Kames was very impressed, saying that he thought he knew his Bible, but that this verse had certainly escaped him. A few days later he tried to find the passage, but failing to do so, brought the Bible back to Franklin, who discovered the page without any hesitation and read the verse once more to him. Then Franklin began to laugh. The verse was of his own writing and he had recited it by heart.

Like most of his "inventions" it was only an adaptation. The story was a very old one; it had been known even before the seventeenth century and appeared in the "Historia Judaica" of Gentius in 1651. Jeremy Taylor had translated it and inserted it in his "Discourse on the Liberty of Prophesying." From then on it had been taken up by one journalist after another, in quest of copy. But Franklin gave it a fixed and agreeable form, and the little scenario he employed in presenting it had so much success that his friends never forgot it. He printed a limited edition of the story in 1760 to please them.

Thus he enjoyed himself in Scotland, overwhelmed by the friendship of his scholarly friends and by the gracious attentions of the ladies. At Edinburgh, David Hume, Robertson, and Alexander Carlyle were everywhere to receive him, the city named him an honorary citizen, the University of St. Andrews presented him with a doctor's diploma, and Lady Dick sent him a purse she had embroidered with her own white hands. Some time later when a Society of Sciences was established in Edinburgh, Franklin was one of the first men to be admitted. Every one wanted to show that they loved and esteemed him.

His son William was even better liked, for William spoke wittily and subtly, while Benjamin was more wont to listen than to talk, in this eloquent and erudite company. When he did say something it was almost always a little too wise or a little too heavy. People found Benjamin to be middle-class but judged William to be a gentleman.

When he returned to London, William took back an unforgettable memory of Edinburgh, Franklin of Kames. Franklin had also secured a more correct view of British opinion outside of London; he had formed valuable connections between

America and Scotland, and the pleasures of friendship and conversation had been excellent tonics for his mind and health. But, above all, he brought away that precious gift of a doctor's diploma, which crowned his self-taught career so appropriately. All the world was to know him as Doctor Franklin. He found a particular pleasure in being addressed as Doctor, and it was the only title he ever accepted willingly. He wisely knew how ridiculous a title made a middle-class man, but he also realized how much it could do for a man in this century of etiquette. This title did not separate him from his environment, but conferred a distinction on him which he needed, for he was an official personage, and the vivacity of his youth had been replaced by the importance of his position.

François Marie Arouet had himself called Monsieur de Voltaire, Comte de Tournay, and Monsieur Rousseau made himself known as Citoyen de Genève; both these titles were local and imbued with human frailty. Benjamin Franklin was Doctor Franklin, and the word doctor in Latin means "he who teaches."

He left Scotland very late in the season and very happy, to celebrate Christmas in London.

II

During the gay holiday months, England was really a merry England. It had never been so great, and strong, and proud. Austria had been vanquished on land, and France, beaten at sea, was gasping. Moreover, the joy of victory was heightened in London by the delightful promise of a speedy and lucrative peace. This was worth more even than a glorious war. Pitt was a great minister, who managed affairs with a high hand and didn't hesitate before sacrifices and expenses. The merchants of London also began to dream of peace by 1760, for French commerce had been destroyed, there wasn't much left to gain and the expenses of the war began to tell on them. Peace became a delicate and delightful subject of conversation; the terms could be dictated, it seemed, and there would be huge profits. All this had to be managed carefully. The English pamphlets in the first months of 1760 discussed the subject gloatingly and greedily.

Europe interested them scarcely at all. Of course, Frederick the Great would have to be well provided for, but he looked out for himself very well; Dunkerque would have to be dismantled, but that would go on by itself. The West Indies and Canada were the attractive prizes. England had taken both, and the question rose as to which one she should keep. Some said the West Indies, for Guadeloupe, with its vast sugar plantations, would make fine booty for the English merchants. The planters of the British West Indies begged for Guadeloupe too, as they wanted to share the spoils, and the Ministry, knowing that the people of this island were docile, saw an advantage in acquiring a possession which would be easy to govern.

But the Patriots, many of the Whigs, and all of the Americans, without rejecting Guadeloupe, insisted that Canada be annexed. Wasn't it the origin of the present war? Wouldn't it be the keystone of the English empire in America? Wasn't it the basis of a tremendous fur trade which had been, up to now, in the hands of the French? And finally, wouldn't it be a fine guarantee of understanding, friendship, and gratitude between England and the American colonies?

A third group wanted to keep both Canada and Guadeloupe, since they had seized both of them in the war.

The discussion proceeded apace; the Earl of Bath wrote an agreeable pamphlet, "Letter to Two Great Men", which was in favor of a definite occupation of Canada. William Burke answered forthwith in his "Remarks on the Letter to Two Great Men", which enjoyed a lively success, partly because of the personality of the author, who was the secretary of Guadeloupe and the cousin and friend of Edmund Burke, and partly because of his judicious arguments and graceful style. He explained how Canada and all North America could become the possible rivals of England, since their produce was similar, but that Guadeloupe was a fruitful source of colonial wares which England needed. Then he contrasted the Americans who stayed at home, always close-fisted, while the good planters of the West Indies went to London to spend their money. He warned his readers to beware of the Americans, for he said that as soon as they had no more need of protection they would turn their backs on England.

Many people were of this opinion, both in the public and in high places. The English newspapers had mentioned the danger of American independence since 1748. The idea haunted English statesmen and was strengthened by the quarrelsome attitude of certain colonies. Massachusetts and Pennsylvania had furnished nothing but trouble for the past ten years! Such was the trend of gossip in London.

Of all the Americans living in the capital, Doctor Franklin was the most in the public eye. It seemed to him that his duty was to say something, and his wisdom impelled him to do so. For the past three years in London he had devoted his time to bitter quarrels which were not interesting, however, to the great English public, and which brought him no particular glory. Now he had an opportunity to express an opinion which would impress all the British people. All his connections with the newspapers, the mercantile middle class and the cultivated people, gave him the opportunity to make himself heard. He had just received a new proof of the esteem in which he was held and it encouraged him. The DeBray Associates, who were a distinguished group of liberal men, organized to aid the education of Negroes, invited him to become a member of their council. This designated him as one of the leading philanthropists of England. He was listened to whenever he spoke, by an enlightened audience, and this power could be put to use for England, America, Pennsylvania, and himself. In a few weeks he wrote and published a brochure entitled, "The Interest of Great Britain considered with regard to her colonies . . ." in which he examined the Canada-Guadeloupe question from a national and practical point of view.

Here were no theories, but only straight facts and statistics. His arguments were simple and direct, presented in a lucid, occasionally ironical, but always good-natured style. He compared the immense future of America with the insignificance of Guadeloupe, and asked whether England was a business house or an empire. Even in the former case there was more to be gained in America than in the West Indies, for it presented an unlimited market for English industrial products. The pamphlet was as convincing as a bank statement, but it was not at all tiresome.

He devoted a large part of it to show that there was nothing to fear from the Americans, — were they not all Anglo-Saxons, Whigs and Protestants? He made fun of the "imaginary danger of American Independence." Didn't persecuted Holland have all the trouble in the world to separate herself from Spain, with whom she had nothing in common? His defense was all the more skillful as he never dropped his calm manner.

He wrote with so much tact, appropriateness, and liveliness that his pamphlet spread all over the English world in a very short time. In spite of the attacks of the *Critical Review* which were instigated by the Penns and by Tucker, Dean of Gloucester, it was heartily welcomed. Two editions appeared, one after the other, in London; in Philadelphia, one; in Boston, two; and one in Dublin. The Americans understood very well that behind this plea for the annexation of Canada there was really another plea in favor of the colonies and of an Anglo-American empire. Many Englishmen saw this too, and not without alarm, as the contemporary pamphlets proved. Franklin insisted that Canada be acquired in order to assure the future of the American colonies and of the new empire. His opponents answered that by taking Canada, they would be giving immense power to the colonies, and by displacing the axis of the Empire, threaten the bankruptcy of England. Both of these propositions were true.

But England was finally convinced by Franklin's imperialistic arguments and prepared to annex Canada as though it were an islet in the Bois de Boulogne. The glory of Franklin was infinitely increased and his political importance became tenfold greater. People listened to him as though Pitt himself were speaking, and Franklin had spoken as the great minister thought. To the Americans he had rendered the inestimable service of extending their territory, and he had given Englishmen a great imperial vision and the most perfect understanding of Anglo-Saxon interests which had ever been reached. His prestige was at its zenith, and it had attained its height not a moment too soon.

The serious hour of a final decision was at hand. A series of Pennsylvania laws had been submitted to the King for his approbation. They first had to pass before the Council on Plantations, which would then report to the Privy Council, and this body of men, presided over by the King, would definitely decide on the laws. The greater part of them were attacked by the Penns, especially the one which permitted the issue of one hundred thousand pounds sterling in paper money. This issue was "for the King's use" and was guaranteed by a land tax on all Pennsylvania properties without exception. Governor Denny had ratified it, but the Penns had punished him and demanded the repeal of the law vociferously.

Franklin listened to every rumor during the whole spring. Pennsylvania had a bad press. There was a public grudge against the colony because of its stubbornness. The paper money was not liked, and people thought the Penns should be supported, for they seemed stupid, inoffensive, and rather pitiable.

In the early days of June, 1760, the committee appointed by the Council of the Lords of Plantations finally decided to report unfavorably on the financial law of Pennsylvania. They asked for its repeal and enumerated seven reasons for finding it unjust, dangerous, and corrupting. Franklin was downhearted at hearing this news. It meant the final condemnation of his party, his work and his mission.

But he was not a man to give in without a fight. He harassed the members of the Council on Plantations and made them realize that if this law were repealed, the one hundred thousand pounds already issued would become worthless, financial anarchy would rule over the province and the King would eventually lose this great sum, without any compensation. How would that please the great Prime Minister?

It was enough to make any lord, who knew Pitt's character, take a second thought. Franklin pushed his idea with an audacity he was never to equal again, and sent a letter of supplication to the Prime Minister, whom he had never been able to see, but who remained his only hope. To this respectful and urgent epistle he added this postscript:

> Between you and I it is said that we may look upon them all to be a pack of d . . . d R . . . ls, and that unless we bribe them all higher than our Adversaries can do and condescend to do every Piece of dirty work they require we shall never be able to attain common justice at their hands.

To make this statement less bold, Franklin ran his pen through this postscript with two big crosses, which did not hide what was written, but which saved Pitt the duty of answering. Then he waited a few days.

Following this, he went to find Lord Mansfield, one of the members of the Council on Plantations, and suggested that the law be condemned in principle, but he begged him not to repeal it, as that would only throw disorder into the colony and provoke war. He said he would be glad to receive the reprimand in the name of the colony and would promise to make all the modifications necessary, but that by all means the law should stand. Lord Mansfield, who had also passed some difficult hours over this question, nodded his head and the bargaining was done.

The Great Defeat was avoided. Now it had to be transformed into a victory. A few weeks were all that was needed to play this game of pass-the-button. Franklin signed a paper promising the modifications that the Lords of the Council on Plantations desired.

The Penns, frightened by the looming shadow of Pitt, withdrew their veto.

The report of the council declared that the financial law of Pennsylvania was "fundamentally wrong and unjust and ought to be repealed", unless radically changed. But as these changes had been promised by Franklin, the Lords concluded to let this law go by as it had been originally framed (August, 28, 1760).

On September second, the Privy Council of the King listened sleepily to the reading of the report from the Council on Plantations and approved of the financial law with the promised changes.

As soon as Franklin knew that the law had been approved, he wrote to his political friends in Pennsylvania to let them know that the promise was neither regular nor legal and could not bind them. He advised them to be moderate in their taxation of the Penn grounds and then kept quiet.

They followed his counsel and the famous financial law was never amended; Franklin's promise remained a scrap of paper, and the meeting of the Privy Council on September 2, 1760, was transformed by his care and skill into a complete victory for the Pennsylvania Assembly. The estates of the Penns were no longer immune from taxation and both the Penns and the King admitted it.

The King's Privy Council, bothered by a hundred other matters, rapidly forgot the affair, but the Penns did not; and this tangible proof of Franklin's duplicity was only a left-handed consolation for them.

Englishmen who were well informed on the situation, but impartial, thought like Edmund Burke who wrote: "From this and many other instances, I conclude that this able man is more anxious in general for the temporary accommodation than the permanent credit of government."

But this splendid victory had been tiring. Franklin longed to take a rest. He needed it, for a thousand other worries were besieging him. Since his colleague Hunter had come to England for his health, he had had to direct the American posts through Deborah and Parker, and it was no easy task. Deborah had a mind of her own and accomplished her tasks with a vehemence that often created difficulties. She would not let any one walk on her toes and when some one wrote to her complaining of the service, she would answer asking how that person had the impertinence to complain. Then Franklin would have to straighten the tangled affair from England. Deborah wrote him long, formless, badly spelled letters, telling him the twaddle of the town and begging him to return as soon as he could.

To calm her, Franklin sent her presents: shawls from India taken from French boats, porcelain ware made according to the latest methods, rugs, tablecloths, bedcovers, prayer books printed in expressly large type for her — and he sent her good advice. He begged her not to get mixed up in politics, to be calm and happy, to watch over Sally's French, piano lessons, and piety, to be kindly with her neighbors and friends; and to sugarcoat all these instructions he added compliments:

I send you . . . a large fine Jugg for Beer, to stand in the Cooler. I fell in Love with it at first sight; for I thought it look'd like a fat jolly Dame, clean and tidy, good-natur'd and lovely, and put me in mind of — Somebody.

But nothing he did for her was appreciated. She wanted him. Deborah was ill at ease; her house was too solitary and the city was too big. She would hide under the sheets at night when she heard the ringing of the bells which Franklin had connected with his lightning rods to know when the atmosphere was charged. The bells frightened her all the more in 1760, when her mother died.

Strahan had tried in vain to persuade her to come over, saying that London was charming, the crossing easy, and that her husband was faithful, even if he were entertained. Nothing could move her, not even this last argument.

And Franklin did not wholly regret her obstinacy. What would he have done with his charming, subtle Mrs. Stevenson? How could William have supported Deborah? That would have been a problem indeed, for William was not easy to handle. He had broken off with Miss Graeme, which was fortunate, although he had done so in too emphatic a manner. Then he had deceived his father in not giving all his attention to Marie Stevenson, called "Polly" for short, whom Benjamin and Mrs. Stevenson had thought would make such a good wife for him. Nevertheless, the affair was finally arranged, it seemed, and Polly, sweet as always, cast smiles on the good-looking William, in a way that said a great deal. But the romance had an abrupt end.

William had courted Polly while he studied law, and while he was supposed to be serving Pennsylvania, but in the meantime, he was also engaged in other amorous affairs. And so it happened one morning in 1760 that Doctor Franklin was presented with his first grandson, William Temple, who had been born in a secluded quarter of London and whose father and mother were unknown.

This marked the end of the Polly-William idyll. Polly took refuge in the country at the home of an old aunt, where she consoled herself by study, while Benjamin Franklin wrote her instructive and tender letters. He kept up a kind of discreet courtship for some time, but — what can one know about it?

To give William some diversion and to take a rest himself, Franklin took his son on a little trip through England, visiting Coventry, Bristol, Bath, Liverpool and even going into Wales. They investigated the factories and mines, and Franklin tried

— not very successfully — to penetrate into the intimate life of his son.

He really didn't succeed at all. The father and son understood each other less and less. William wanted to have a fixed place in the English aristocracy, even if it were secondary; but his father was too fine-grained and too great to accept such a belittling promotion. He wanted a high post, above the aristocracy, or nothing.

He waited for it all the winter of 1760. He had been proposed as a Member of the House of Commons but had refused. He accepted being entertained as a scholar and both Pringle and Wilson treated him as a superior master. At their homes he met various distinguished travelers, such as the good Jesuit, Boskovitch, who liked Franklin immensely and said that he had the profile of a Roman medal head. It was flattering to hear such things, but Franklin felt he was not leading a real life. He still busied himself with Assembly matters, although the great problems had been temporarily settled. He invested money for the Assembly which the Ministry had given to the colonies as reimbursement for the war expenses. This was an infinite bother, for the Assembly, trying to be clever, began speculations in England, tangled up everything and finished by losing many of the investments.

Franklin published serious or sardonic articles against a premature peace, which he did not sign, in order to keep in touch with national politics. He was still a great, sturdy patriot and a faithful imperialist. But all this writing was a mere groping about and could not satisfy a man of action.

Then Fate offered him a chance once more.

On September 25, 1760, George II suddenly and discreetly died. George III mounted on the throne and the English middle class rejoiced everywhere. He was known to be hostile to elegance, suspicious of nobility, and desirous of cultivating strict, simple and religious customs in his court. The newspapers said of him:

Perhaps very few Princes in the world have ever [had] so many virtues, or much wisdom as his present Majesty King George the third. His religious duty to God in public is a truly good example to all subjects of what rank soever. His piety, duty, and affection, are worthy of imitation. His Majesty riseth at five o'clock every morning, lights his own candle from the lamp which burneth all night in his room, dresseth himself, then calleth a servant to bring him bread, butter and chocolate. At six he goeth to chapel, where he hath morning prayers in the most religious manner. At his return he readeth petitions and letters; after which he rideth on horseback for two or three hours for exercise, and air; then readeth some religious or moral book, until his ministers of state come to consult on the affairs of the nation, at which he is very ready to give directions and answers, knowing the constitution of all his dominions exceedingly well. His dinner consisteth but of four dishes, dressed up plain, eateth temperately of them, and drinketh but a small quantity of weak Rhenish wine mixed with water. His supper is a crust of bread and a glass of water. He is remarkably respectful and loving to his mother the princess of Wales. . . . He is also very affectionate and generous to his brothers and sisters and sheweth the greatest respect and esteem to his uncle the duke of Cumberland (*Boston News-Letter* May 21, 1761).

It is said that he drove courtiers from his presence because they spent their time playing cards, and he lectured one great lady very severely because her Sunday parties were too gay. She had to accede to His Majesty's wishes, and promised that people would be as bored at her house on Sunday as they were throughout England.

George III was going to be the middle-class king, the delight of England, and Poor Richard had a brotherly feeling for him. Disgusted by the corruption in Parliament, and the arrogance of the aristocrats, Franklin wrote:

You now fear for our virtuous young King, that the Faction forming will overpower him and render his reign uncomfortable. On the contrary, I am of Opinion that his Virtue and the Consciousness of his sincere Intentions to make his People happy will give him Firmness and Steadiness in his Measures and in the Support of the honest Friends he has chosen to serve him; and when that Firmness is full perceiv'd, Faction will dissolve and be dissipated like a Morning Fog before the rising Sun, leaving the rest of the Day clear with a Sky serene and cloudless.

This prediction of the virtues and the obstinacy of George III was excellent and really prophetic. It was to be remarkably verified. Franklin had all the more confidence in the virtue of George III since he was then guided by his honest friend, Lord Bute, a Scotchman who was connected with all the Scottish Clan that Franklin knew. He was also one of Pringle's friends, and a great patron of scholars.

Franklin was careful not to stay away too long from London, but made a little tour of Flanders and Holland with William and Jackson (August–September, 1761). They visited Ghent and Bruges, where the churches amazed them; Brussels, where Prince Charles of Lorraine welcomed them cordially, showing them his physics laboratory; the Hague, where they dined fashionably with Sir Joseph York; Leyden, where Musschenbroek received them affectionately; finally, Amsterdam, where the stout merchants outdid themselves to make their stay agreeable. Franklin, William and Jackson liked the people's gayety, the Dutchman's love for his pipe, and, for a while, they allowed themselves to be lulled by the compliments that were offered them on every side. But a nasty voyage back to England made them sea-sick and awoke them to reality once more. They returned in time for the coronation.

The winter was another period of waiting, filled with activity. Franklin hoped for victories, for peace, for a sign of Fate — but Fate was in no hurry.

He frequented the taverns where all one heard was feverish talk of conquests and of peace. Franklin went from shop to shop to secure the parts of an harmonica which he constructed and improved. The tinkling sound of the water-filled glasses pleased him and pleased his friends, the ladies. He lectured Polly and took care of Mrs. Stevenson's rheumatism; wrote long scholarly letters to philosophers who consulted him; went to Oxford in April to receive the degree of Doctor of Laws which the university conferred on him at the same time it honored William with the degree of Master of Arts. He became friends again with William Smith, who had spread such calumnies about him, but who promised to retract them in writing. Mr.

Hume, the most profound philosopher of England, hearing that he was going to leave the country sent him a beautiful letter in which he said: "America has sent us many good things, gold, silver, sugar, tobacco, indigo, etc.; but you are the first philosopher, and indeed the first great man of letters for whom we are beholden to her. It is our own fault that we have not kept him."

But so it was. Franklin had wanted to stay but he could not continue this existence of doing nothing. And neither Parliament, nor the honest Ministry, nor the virtuous young king made an effort to retain him.

Franklin must have decided to leave, not without some melancholy. He wrote to Polly: "I fancy I feel a little like dying Saints, who in parting with those they love in this world are only comforted with the Hope of more perfect Happiness in the next."

However, he left. He embarked from Spithead alone, for William stayed behind to continue his courtship of a young lady from the West Indies and was negotiating with Bute, who liked him. The father and son had come to crossroads.

Franklin returned to America victorious and vanquished. He had succeeded in many details, but he had failed in his great enterprise. He had humiliated, duped and humbled the Penns but the Anglo-American empire remained a dream. He needed the stimulus of America to begin all over again. He had been frozen by the coldness of the Ministry and abashed at the hostility of the English aristocracy, but he refused to admit he was beaten. Such a beautiful project as this empire demanded much effort, and the King, who had not been sounded on the subject, remained a buoyant hope.

Franklin would doubtless have suffered from melancholy on this long sea voyage, in this vessel which was taking him from his future to the past, from his young friends to his old wife, had it not been for the inexhaustible ingenuity of his mind. It was his intellectual curiosity which kept him from being too sad and which caused him to remark the cabin lamp, — how the water underneath the surface of oil was in great commotion though the oil remained tranquil.

He drew scientific and philosophical conclusions from this observation. It was even pertinent to his own life, for his ambitions goaded him to constant action, while his wisdom always maintained his serene equilibrium and was a source of light.

III

Franklin had a slow and gentle voyage. The sea was calm, the weather agreeable, and his vessel the *Carolina*, Captain Friend, was in company with nine others, all of them under the protection of the war frigate, *Scarborough*, so that there was nothing to fear. The passengers were pleasant company, and Franklin, always interested in men, enjoyed the visits and dinners that were exchanged between the different boats. The wind sped the boats to Madeira, where they landed for a few days, and Franklin had an even more interesting time studying the island. Autumn was at the height of its glory, the peasants were gathering their grapes, and the sun-bathed scene of the vineyards was restful and encouraging to the travelers. They left, taking with them enormous clusters of grapes, which they suspended from the ceiling in their cabins, as a reminder of the goodness of God. Whenever they ate the grapes they would thank Him for the good weather and the navy of His Majesty.

Doctor Franklin profited by his stay in observing the country and writing down economic, scientific, philosophic and political remarks, which he sent back to his friends in London. He wrote to Pringle, telling him the best way to preserve gunpowder, and the best method to insure the hygiene of the Senegal garrison, both of which were suggestions for Lord Bute, and he sent an essay on paper money to Lord Shelbourne. The notes he wrote on Madeira he mailed to R. Jackson, and they were passed around in the English Parliament. And he sent some pretty shells to Lady Bute.

Thus he expressed his gratitude to the country which had given him so much. He had left England, burdened with charming presents: a harp from his neighbor Caleb Whiteford, a book of Scotch melodies from Lady Dick, and a hundred nice things got together by Mrs. Stevenson. But the most precious presents of England were the memories of the pleasant, erudite conversations he had enjoyed in London and Edinburgh, and which had so stimulated his intelligence. They made him realize the value of wisdom, which served him so much more usefully than his shrewdness, and brought back all the dreams of his youth. Just as in 1732, he wanted again to write "The Art of Virtue", which would guide all good men to human perfection, with him as their leader. He owed this beautiful dream to Great Britain and was thankful to her.

But Franklin had to turn towards America, though he could not do so without some fear. What a contrast! Smith and the Penn party had fought bitterly against him in America and he knew it. There were rumors in England that he had lost his American popularity, and he didn't doubt but that he had many enemies. Before leaving in 1757, he had instructed Galloway to keep his thumb on them, but he knew that the absentee is always in the wrong. His enemies had taken advantage of his long stay in England to spread reports that he was going to be named Baronet and Governor of Pennsylvania, that he lived in London in great style, spent the money of the province right and left, and danced attendance on people in high places. They also added that by his obsequiousness and rascality he had turned several ministers against him. Thomas Penn took pleasure in spreading these rumors in England and seeing to it that they reached America.

Franklin wondered if they had succeeded in exciting the crowd against him. He was too wise not to know that this was always possible, and too human not to suffer from it. When the boat entered the port of Philadelphia he was torn by anxiety. But a moment later his trouble was dissipated and turned into deep joy; for the docks were black with cheering people and bright with waving flags. When he landed, an imposing company of five hundred men on horse was waiting to escort him home. He returned like a Roman emperor, in the midst of the people's benedictions and the cheers of the children.

His faithful Deboy and his charming Sally, who was now a graceful young lady of eighteen, welcomed him tenderly. His large house was filled with visitors, all the while he was distributing presents to his family and friends. Both enemies and old acquaintances came to see him, some out of curiosity, others out of affection; to have arrived from London was a rare distinction in the distant colonies, and Franklin, moreover, had lived there as a great personage. The members of the old Junto came to hear the new stories he had to tell, the scholars from the Philosophical Society questioned him on the new discoveries of Europe, while Galloway, Norris, Pemberton, and various other politicians came to learn of English current events. Young ladies also arrived in throngs, curious to see if Franklin had aged and what gowns he had brought back for Sally. The young men of the university came to offer their respects and presented him with several odes.

He gazed half-smiling at them all, sparing his words, but cheered by a glass of cider. Then, when he had spoken of London, enough to make him homesick for the city, he would sit down at his harmonica and charm his listeners with touching little melodies. One of them sent him this little poem:

Hark! the soft warblings, sounding smooth and clear,
Strike with celestial ravishment the ear,
Conveying inward, as they sweetly roll,
A tide of melting music to the soul;
And sure if aught of mortal moving strain,
Can touch with joy the high angelic train,
'Tis this enchanting instrument of thine,
Which speaks in accents more than half divine.

It was thus he could evoke the exquisite shadow of Marie Stevenson and the memories of the precious moments he had spent talking lightly with her. He thought of having her come to America, or of leaving soon to join her. Then he shook his head and resumed the serene line of his life.

He was busy at first with the arrival of William and his wife (February 19, 1763). This same William who had left America as a handsome young lad, but nothing more, returned as His

Excellency William Franklin, Governor for His Majesty of the Province of New Jersey. He owed this important place to the private protection of Lord Bute; "the high and mighty William", said his enemies sneeringly, but they didn't dare talk too loudly, for William was well backed. He and his father had returned with the double glory of having served the people's interests without stint and of having gained the esteem of men in power. Thus, in spite of the hard times, the snow, mud, wind and ice, a crowd gathered to greet William. It was made up of his loves of yesteryear, who were wrapped in furs and accompanied by their husbands; inquisitive people of one sort and another; and his father, mother, and sister, their faces shining with pride as the boat neared. William's dignified and beautiful wife was much admired, and the whole city gave parties to this family which had risen so high in less than forty years.

After the festivities of welcome were over, Franklin accompanied William to New Brunswick and to Perth Amboy. In spite of the storms they were followed by a long escort of gentlemen in sleighs and a squad of the cavalry regiment of Middlesex. His predecessor welcomed him solemnly and William took his oath before the Provincial Council, called together for the occasion. The troops paraded before him to render their respects, and the crowd cheered him. Then the doctor departed, leaving his son and daughter-in-law to their duties. William devoted himself to his work and began to acquire a portly figure.

Benjamin had returned to America to work. He found conditions more favorable than he had hoped. He didn't lose any time, but threw himself headlong into an active life: he attended to his business affairs, had a new house built, stirred up his partners, Hall in Philadelphia, Parker in New York and Mecom in Boston. He took his place in the Assembly once more, where he had been elected every autumn during his absence, served as one of the commissioners on Indian affairs, and apportioned the taxes which had just been voted, as an Indian revolt had broken out again in the West. But he was mostly interested in putting the post office on a firm footing.

The war ended by the taking of Cuba, the occupation of Martinique and the conquest of the West Indies; Russia had joined in an alliance with Prussia, the French and Spanish navies had been annihilated, and the treaty guaranteed to England the domination of the sea, the control of the West Indies, of North America and the African coast, and of all maritime commerce. England had carved an empire around the Atlantic, which was comparable to the empire the Romans had built around the Mediterranean, but she wondered how best to manage it. There were grumblings, complaints, recriminations from all sides. Some complained of the financial difficulties which followed the war, others of the territories returned to France and Spain. Pitt, the great war prime minister, enfeebled by illness and restricted by his parliamentary habits, was powerless to remedy the situation. The King was virtuous but dull, the Whig aristocracy was verbose and greedy, and the country got nowhere. No one seemed to understand that once having conquered an empire, it had to be organized. The overwhelming success of the war, the compliments of Montesquieu, the hundred millions sterling which had been taken in spoils, and the luxury which flourished in England seemed to have blinded its leaders. A kind of sottishness, due to the stupefying effects of happiness, pervaded the country, and there was no great writer, brilliant diplomat, or superior philosopher to disperse it.

Franklin was the only one who seemed to understand what had happened, and he guessed what was going to happen. He started to build up the Imperial Post Office of America in earnest, for that was practical, at least. Afterwards he would busy himself with politics which were more delicate.

Without waiting for instructions from London, he took up connections with his new colleague, Foxcroft, who had succeeded to the office at Hunter's death in October, 1761. They saw each other in Virginia in May, 1763, and succeeded in establishing postal service between Quebec and the colonies. They also cleared up the accounts and prepared a great campaign of postal reform, planning a trip all around the colonies to see their agents and carriers, and to examine the roads. They wanted to increase, regulate and speed up the service as much as possible.

The importance of the post office was understood in London, but no one knew how to manage it well. The new directors, Lord Hillsborough and Lord Le Despenser, and the new secretary-general, Anthony Todd, begged Franklin and Foxcroft to make their service active and productive. Wasn't it the vital artery of the dominion, the great resource of the Government and the police of His Majesty when they wanted information? Business, armies, navies, diplomacy, all these needed the post office. The King needed it still more. The King's Councillor, S. Conway, wrote to the postmasters in December, 1766, reminding them to open, copy, and send to the First Secretary of the King, "all letters directed to or sent by any Foreign Minister of what Rank soever, residing at their court." The rôle of the Director of Posts was thus delicate and important. Franklin filled it to the satisfaction of every one. By the end of spring in 1763, he had firmly established the postal service between Quebec and the colonies, suggested a practical system to regulate the correspondence with the West Indies, and to build a central office in New York. He also demanded a law to forbid hotel keepers and tavern men to grab the mail on its arrival from the packet boats. Then he made his trip and stirred up the service with such success that from this year on, the time for a letter to travel between Philadelphia and New York was reduced from a week to two days, between Philadelphia and Boston from three weeks to six days, between Boston and New York, from fifteen to four days. He obtained these results, thanks to a bold innovation: for the first time in America, the carriers traveled day and night. These reforms and the development of business made the post office very prosperous; in 1757 it had stood a deficit of 265 pounds sterling (1416, expenses; 1151, receipts), but in 1764 the figures were radically reversed: 1747, expenses, 3818, receipts.

This achievement had required much work and trouble, which were compensated by the pleasures of traveling. Franklin enjoyed his long trip of sixteen hundred miles across the colonies. He left in June with Sally. First they went to Woodbridge, then they visited Elizabethtown and New York. In the latter city a great dinner was given in honor of Franklin by the Corporation, and was attended by the most fashionable people of the city. They were even invited to another dinner with Lord Stirling, who didn't like them at all. Franklin attended the splendid funeral of his old friend, Kennedy, and had a magnificent supper with General Amherst. At New Haven there were other pleasures; and he talked once more with his friends, the professors of Yale. In Rhode Island, they visited Katy, who had become Mrs. Greene, but who was as tender, pleasant and gay as ever. Fortunately, or unfortunately, Franklin fell down, and had to be cared for by his friends. He fell again in Boston and was forced to rest for two months, as he had dislocated his shoulder. But he was well taken care of by his sister, Mrs. Mecom, and his cousins, the Williamses. It wasn't so disagreeable to be the powerful Doctor Franklin, a royal officer, and an American lawmaker, in this city where he had been a little apprentice, cursed at by every one and ashamed of himself.

Franklin thought he was on the right road. If he could only manage politics the same way he managed the post office, how fortunate it would be for his country and himself! But the horizon remained black. England was a hotbed of quarrels. In America a new storm burst.

The situation had come to a head suddenly. All summer and autumn an Indian war had raged on the western frontiers; it was the last guttering flare of their long struggle against the white invasion. The revolt of Pontiac had been bloody and brutal. It had not menaced the center of the English colonies, for the measures taken to suppress it were prompt and efficacious. However, thousands of white refugees flooded Philadelphia. They had to be taken care of, and the terrible tales they told about scalping, tortures, and the hideous slavery the women had to suffer spread through all the towns and farms of Pennsylvania. At first the excitement didn't have bad results. The people were glad of their victory, glad of the reconciliation with the Penns, and glad to receive the nephew of the family, John Penn, as their new governor. He seemed to possess all the desirable qualities of an executive: he was distinguished in appearance and manners, he had a good heart and was pleasant to deal with, and he was moderate in everything, even in the use of his intelligence. The ovation he was given on his arrival was equal to those offered Benjamin and William, and was one more manifestation of reconciliation. The old quarrels had been forgotten; collaboration was to be the new policy, and every one agreed to love his neighbor as himself.

This state of affairs lasted about six weeks, up to December 14. At this date, the Scotch-Irish Presbyterian farmers, excited by the rumors of the Indian War and aflame with religious zeal, were inspired to convert the Indians even if it were by the baptism of fire. They attacked a little group of submissive and civilized Indians who lived near Lancaster, and killed six of them in their homes. Some days later they returned and massacred fourteen others, who had taken refuge in the prison and were living there under the protection of the Magistrates of the County. All the other civilized Indians, especially the numerous families converted by the Moravians, fled to Philadelphia.

The Moravians and the Quakers were angry at the farmers for this stupid butchery; the Episcopalians said absolutely nothing, and the Presbyterians seemed to approve of it as a pious act.

Franklin was too closely connected with the Quakers and, moreover, too human, to approve of such cruelty. He had many business friends trading with the Indians, and one of his cherished projects was to found a new colony beyond the frontiers. So in a few weeks he had written an eloquent pamphlet, "A Narrative of the Late Massacres in Lancaster County", denouncing this act, and demanding justice according to the measures the governor had taken to protect the Indians. It was straight from the shoulder, vehement and just; perhaps the best piece of controversial writing Franklin ever did. Clear-thinking people applauded it.

But the people, and especially those who lived on the frontiers, hated the Indians, and could not follow the reasoning of either Franklin or the governor. The killers were known as "The Paxton Boys" and became popular heroes. Numerous men joined them, and forming an armed troop, set off on a march to Philadelphia. They were going to demand the governor and the Assembly to give up the unfortunate Indians who had taken refuge in the city. As they approached, Philadelphia was all confusion; there were no police or soldiers to maintain order. The governor was beside himself with worry and could do nothing better than to throw himself into the arms of Franklin. He begged for advice and took refuge in his home. Franklin, who was always a good journalist and an expert in organization, didn't have much trouble in getting together a troop of a thousand decided men. The members of the Junto, the Fire Department, and the Military Association all came to his aid; and the new association was known as the "Hearts of Oaks." At the moment the Paxton Boys were about to enter the city, Franklin met them, followed by his thousand men and authorized by John Penn to act as he saw fit. He did not fight, but made a speech, and persuaded the "brave boys" that they were in the wrong. They returned to their homes without killing any one, not even an Indian, and pillaged the white men's farms here and there to have some fun on the way.

But it was a fatal victory for Franklin. The governor, furious for having appeared so weak and for having appealed to Franklin, turned against him. He did nothing in the way of serious punishment to the Paxton Boys. He preferred to fight with the Assembly, taking up the eternal question of taxing the Penns' domains from the beginning all over again. He refused to ratify the laws if the people would not guarantee their loyalty and deference. He blocked the law to establish a militia, as it gave too much power to the soldiers in the choice of their officers. It was the old story of mutual opposition, and the two parties began exchanging the same old insults. Franklin was criticized again for having lost the Assembly's money in bad investments, for not having kept the promises he made in writing in 1760 to the Penns and the King, for having spent the people's money — in short, he was tricky, insincere and covetous. The governor denounced the men of the Assembly as being arrogant usurpers and they returned the insult with interest. They saw that it was sometimes worse to have a stupid enemy than an intelligent one. John Penn, with his blind and awkward violence, was much more dangerous than the intelligent governors they had had hitherto.

At last the time for a decisive battle arrived. The Assembly voted a petition, written by Franklin, which begged the King to take back the government of the province from the Penns. As soon as this grave measure was adopted, the Assembly broke up, and the members went to consult their constituents. Franklin wrote, printed and distributed a vehement pamphlet: "Cool Thoughts on the Present Situation of our Public Affairs." With his great journalistic talent, he showed how anarchy was ruling in Pennsylvania and all the benefits which would result from direct Royal Government. Both parties made violent campaign efforts for six weeks. Then the Assembly met again with three thousand names signed to the petition. The Proprietor's Party was able to secure only three hundred names for a counterpetition (May 14).

The spring session of the Assembly was stormy. There were great debates. Franklin was elected president to succeed Isaac Norris, an aged man who was frightened by all this tumult. Under Franklin's leadership, the Assembly voted to send the petition to the king by an overwhelming majority. Then it separated.

The elections came in October. The two camps prepared for the struggle with excitement and bitter remarks were exchanged between them. Franklin and Galloway handled the party called the "Old Ticket", which wanted a definite revolt against the Penns. The "New Ticket" was made up of the officials, the distinguished men, the old merchants, and — owing to Franklin's Indian pamphlet — the Presbyterians, as well as a large number of people who detested the Indians.

They had had enough of the Quakers and of the Assembly, which was devoted to Quaker interests. The Episcopalians were divided on the question, but the Dutch Calvinists followed the Presbyterians. Franklin went everywhere, despite the danger, and published two brochures, one after the other: "A Preface to the Speech of Joseph Galloway", which was a brutal personal attack against J. Dickinson, the leader of the other party, and "Remarks on a Particular Militia Bill", in which Franklin appealed to the democratic feelings of the population. The newspapers were filled with articles pro and con, families were divided on the question, and the city seemed on the eve of civil war.

At last came the fatal day. The voting began at three in the afternoon. There was such a crowd around the city hall where the election was held, the voters jostled each other an hour before they could put their ballot in the box. At eleven o'clock there was still a crowd around the building. At three o'clock in the morning, the "Old Ticket" proposed to prolong the voting until five in the afternoon. They had a whole collection of feeble, tottering old codgers in reserve, who would vote if they were only given time. The men of the "New Ticket" accepted the proposition and sent their cavalry — the Scotch-Irish farmers — to scour the countryside for voters. They galloped here and there on their dray horses and went to the distant farms to search out the fat Dutchmen or the heavy-footed Germans who had not taken the trouble to vote. If they refused to go, they were threatened by a whip. Once in the city, they were made to vote twice. Some of them slipped several ballots at a time into the boxes and many of the boxes had been filled in advance. At last the elections were closed and — *the Old Ticket was beaten*. Franklin and Galloway lost by less than twenty-five votes out of four thousand. The victors formed in bands, and went shouting and singing across the city, menacing their enemies.

When Franklin heard the news he smiled and went to bed. At least, he pretended to sleep, for he was a wise man. But Galloway couldn't hide his rage. He had been beaten by his own guns. The democracy of Pennsylvania had turned against him.

But later on, the two defeated candidates found some consolation. The "Old Ticket" still kept the majority in the Assembly — thanks to the Quakers and Germans whom Franklin knew — for the "New Ticket" had taken only the city of Philadelphia. Franklin's followers were somewhat diminished in number, but they were still the masters of the situation and gathered around their leader, eager for vengeance. The Assembly convened without delay. It solemnly passed the petition which prayed the King to take over the government of Pennsylvania, and in spite of the clamor and eloquent protests, Franklin was appointed to be its agent in England (October 26, 1764). As there was no ready money in the treasury, the merchants of the city pooled a sum of eleven hundred pounds sterling to pay the expenses of his voyage.

The adherents of the Penn party quivered under the insult and showed their teeth. Without delay, the minority in the Assembly and a goodly number of the most distinguished men in the city signed a petition in which they explained in detail their antipathy, scorn and hate of Franklin. He was touched to the quick of his pride. There were the signatures of some of his old friends on this list, old comrades of the lodge, collaborators in the academy and hospital projects, men he had known for thirty years and who had no right to defame him. He answered harshly, in "Remarks on a Recent Protest." He defended his honor in this pamphlet and upheld his financial integrity which had been attacked. He had lashing words for the Penns, who were capable only of foul and infamous thoughts, and cited Allen as saying, "The King's little Finger we should find heavier than the Proprietor's whole Loins . . ." For every insult that had been hurled at him, he had another to hurl back, and he spared no one.

The press was flooded with abusive language. Obscene, insulting and defaming pamphlets were exchanged by both parties. Franklin's life was searched for scandal, the illegitimacy of William's birth was held up before the world again, and he was imputed to have had a whole series of like adventures. Franklin's adherents answered by publishing the story of Allen's Negro mistress and all her sorrows.

Thus, while little court intrigues and long dreary discussions took up the time of the English Parliament, the Pennsylvania democracy indulged in a mud fight.

Franklin dreamed only of fleeing; the idea had been in his head for some time, and it was a wise one. The political storm had burst in all its fury, every man had lost his head, and there was no use in remaining. He wanted Deborah to come with him, but she refused. She was afraid of the sea, liked Pennsylvania, and knew that if they ever left together they would never return. So Deborah stayed at home to take care of the new house. Then Franklin wanted to take Sally with him, but Debby would not hear of it. At last, he resignedly decided to go alone, and gave his friends a great farewell dinner with turtle soup.

On November 7, 1764, Franklin went to Chester to embark for England. He was escorted by an immense crowd of people on foot and men on horseback, all shouting at the top of their voices: "Hurrah for the 'Old Ticket!' Hurrah for the King! Hurrah for Franklin!"

His boat was named *The King of Prussia* and Galloway, Wharton and James came up on the deck with him to shake hands for a last time. Franklin swore that he would not return without a royal charter.

He would construct an Anglo-Saxon empire in spite of the Penns, their governors, and the blindness of the people.

The King of Prussia weighed anchor, and a storm swept Franklin and the vessel out to sea.

IV

Captain Robinson was very careful of his illustrious passenger, but he could not hinder the storm from shaking him violently; when Franklin arrived at Portsmouth on Sunday, December 9, after a hard, rapid crossing, he was jaded from fatigue. He hastened to land, took a post chaise, and reached London on Tuesday, the eleventh. It was high time that the good Mrs. Stevenson should be taking care of him.

She was happy to see him return so unexpectedly, and she resolved not to let him go again. It was clear to her that he was tired of America. In spite of the pleasure he had experienced in seeing his old American friends again, and of resuming life with his family, his last impression of America was a bitter one. He hid it as well as he could, even to his most intimate friends, but it was revealed in certain accents of his voice, when he spoke of American politics, and in certain brief allusions which he could not avoid. It was easy to see that he was tired and disgusted with brutal fighting. He became sad more frequently, remembered his little Francis, who had died thirty years before, spoke of God, and sent others to church, even if he didn't go himself.

The pamphlet war was prolonged in Philadelphia. Franklin's enemies printed insults against him in the newspapers, and the worst of them were written by his old friends: William Allen, William Smith and the professors of the academy. This was a bitter change. He was glad to see his friends as violent and foul-mouthed as his enemies, however. John Hughes distinguished himself by promising, in a vulgar letter, a large sum of money to any one who could sustain and prove the accusations made against Franklin. This letter threw a wet blanket over the Penns' activities. Then, too, the hatred for Franklin made him many new friends, particularly among the students of the academy, who defended him as strongly as their professors attacked him. When it was learned in Philadelphia that Franklin had arrived safe and sound in London, there were demonstrations of joy in the streets, bells were rung, and the ships in the harbor flew flags. But Franklin had dreamed of another popularity, based on love and not on hatred.

While this battle continued noisily without, another was going on in the new house where Deborah was establishing herself with difficulty. She found the workmen impertinent, thought that the contractors bore her ill will, and she quarreled with all the purveyors. She sent for her "Pappy", and they sent for the Great Doctor Franklin.

The rains and storms of winter darkened the calm lodgings at Number 7 Craven Street, but they did not trouble Benjamin Franklin, who warmed himself by the fire in the corner and talked to Polly and Mrs. Stevenson about his struggles and adventures, adding some good stories to make his conversation gay. These women were delicate-minded and sweet, they openly admired him and always said that he was right. The cat, purring in the shadow, added to the peace of the place.

Parliament was not in session, most of Franklin's friends were absent, and this gave him time to reflect.

He found England turned upside down. The great Whig leaders agreed to hinder the king from assuming the power, but they could not agree to govern together. Between Lord Chatham, the Marquis of Rockingham, Lord Grenville, Lord Temple and the Duke of Bedford, it was a game of hide-and-go-seek, for none of them could hold a majority in the House except by having a coalition cabinet which would break up in a few weeks. During the winter of 1764–1765, Grenville was still in power, but no one thought he could keep it for long, because the Tories and Pitt's adherents were leagued against him. The situation was precarious, and the government continued by sheer momentum, while the workmen shouted in the streets, complaining of unemployment, low wages and the high cost of living. Newsboys, on the corners, cried pamphlets for or against Wilkes.

These last months had taught Franklin that the American colonies were powerless to unite and organize. They were proud and strong, but they didn't know what they wanted, and no group had formed to lead them. The initiative had to come from England. But England was busy with insignificant disputes, and the politicians had no time to think of America. A very few enlightened men realized that England and America needed to change their political systems. Thomas Pownall, a great friend of Franklin, was one of these exceptions, and they often spoke together. The several editions of Pownall's great work "The Administration of the Colonies" all carried traces of Franklin's ideas. The book was widely read and then forgotten for other more absorbing matters.

The different political groups could scarcely understand what was going on in America. It was so far off, and the problem was so vague. Besides, they had no general ideas, only tendencies: some were straight Royalists, considering the King as the real and only sovereign, who should rule, with the Parliament acting as his councilor; others considered the Parliament as the supreme authority, while the King was merely the symbol of national unity and should rule without governing. The people did not count, except when they made a racket in the streets, and then the politicians merely cursed them. America had a bad press. Too many sacrifices had been made for her during the last war. She was noisy, bothersome, and always asking favors. Many politicians considered her future independence as certain, and wanted to get as much money out of America as they could, before it was too late.

Lord George Grenville was the most formidable of all the great English parliamentarians — from the American point of view — for he was pompous both in the way he thought and acted. He strictly believed in the supremacy of the King, even more in the rights of Parliament, and his own judgment was law. He worked seriously, and according to himself, never made a mistake. But he accomplished his work with an obstinacy that was worthy of a better cause.

There was little chance that the cabinet he led in 1764–1765 could stand, and it was certain to fall the moment it could no longer raise money. It seemed natural to demand money from America. As America had no representation in Parliament, the honorable members could tax it without fearing the wrath of their voters. Moreover, the Americans were unpopular, and taxing them would bring them into line. The Ministry wanted to levy about one hundred thousand pounds sterling to begin with.

Grenville wished to accomplish this without any wailing or gnashing of teeth. He looked up in the files of the government and found an old project which had been suggested since 1739 by such American Royalists as William Keith: a stamp tax which would be levied on the newspapers, law deeds, and various other official documents. In England the same tax was already in force, and several politicians had suggested that it be levied in America. It had the advantage of being relatively easy to collect, and entailed lucrative positions which could be given away to friends. But it had the disadvantage of weighing heavily on the journalists and lawyers, who formed a quarrelsome body of men, hard to fight. England, however, felt strong, and was not afraid of a few lawyers or half-civilized scribblers on the other side of the Atlantic.

Grenville proceeded with method, nevertheless. In 1764, he informed the agents of America in England of his intentions, and politely asked them to notify the colonies, in order that they could tell him if they preferred to pay the sum in another way. The Pennsylvania Assembly answered that it was overburdened with taxes, debts, and necessary expenses, that it did not believe the English Parliament possessed the authority to tax the colonies, but that if the King would kindly ask them for aid, they would contribute according to their funds.

There was nothing practical here, and Lord Grenville concluded that one tax was as good as another. After a year's delay, he proposed this measure to the House of Commons. Always considerate and polite, Lord Grenville gathered the agents of the colonies together again and offered them the choice of this tax or any other. The only important point was that the colonies had to pay. The agents looked at him shrewdly;

they were certain that the Americans wanted to pay nothing at all, and they had no idea in what manner the Americans preferred to pay, if they were forced. The most obsequious of the agents said they were sorry not to give an answer to the obliging Lord Grenville, but the wisest of them simply went off without saying a word. A deep silence was the only answer to the minister's offers; the agents had made a clean escape, and Franklin shuddered later when he thought of that quarter of an hour.

The Stamp Law was then proposed in Parliament. It was passed without any discussion one fine evening when the House of Commons was empty. The agents, still frightened from their upsetting interview, had not been able to do much; Franklin had the gout, did not feel like fighting, and had done less against the law than any one. He thought the law was absurd, but that it might be a blessing in disguise. It would force the Americans and the English to examine the principles on which their relations were based. They would have to open their eyes to the fact that a catastrophe was imminent. There would be a frank discussion under the best possible conditions, for the English Whigs would join the American cause, and the Americans would be forced to forget their petty quarrels. Thus, though Franklin disapproved of Grenville's idea, he accepted it as one of the inexorable moves of Destiny. He merely managed, with the aid of his colleagues and friends in Parliament to attack certain clauses which would have permitted the English troops to be quartered in American homes: such a proceeding would surely have resulted in a civil war. The clauses were suppressed and the law, thus lightened, was passed by the Lords. It received a prompt and cordial sanction from the King on March 22, 1765, and was made public on that day. Starting on November 1, 1765, the loyal colonies of America would have the honor of participating in the budget of Great Britain, and paying their share of the national expenses by the stamp tax.

Grenville, who was kindly and tactful to the very end, announced that the money collected from this tax would be applied to public works in America and the maintenance of British troops there. Let no one be excited; the money would stay in the country, and it was all going to be calm and pleasant. To be extremely obliging, Grenville told the agents that they could choose the tax receivers themselves, and that these men should be native Americans. Urbanity couldn't be pushed farther than this.

Franklin had suffered from the bad manners of his compatriots and appreciated this gesture. He quietly let matters go on as they would, suggested Hughes, his old friend, as the tax receiver of Pennsylvania, and took steps to make the best of a bad law.

He bargained for himself and Pennsylvania, trying to secure, in the way of compensation, a good financial law which would create American money; and pushing the petition of Pennsylvania. He sent Hall new supplies of paper which were sized so as to cost less to stamp, thus giving him an advantage over his competitors. He hastily sent the text of the law to his friends, and without expressing any particular exasperation, told Hall to insert it in the "Poor Richard" for 1766. It was printed without any critical commentaries, next to the calendar of fairs, and took up half the pages.

He wrote to his correspondents that the law was absurd, annoying, and all the rest, but there was nothing to be done about it, and England seemed decided to make the colonies pay. He advised them to bear up under the load and wait, for America was not strong enough to protest yet — one and a half millions against six — but that in time the affair would be smoothed out and the measure repealed. The law would have the advantage of joining the colonies together and making them industrious and frugal.

Franklin was not worried. He played his harmonica and talked about science to his English friends, traced magic circles for Canton, performed errands for his American friends, and went to the taverns. Life was not a tragedy for one who knew how to think clearly, drink gayly, and practice wisdom.

His great friend and adviser, R. Jackson, had told him that

his work was a matter of time. The important thing was to mold public opinion to his way of thinking. Franklin tried to accomplish this, and from time to time sent a sardonic letter to the newspapers in which he affirmed, for example, that the sheep of America had such long woolly tails they were forced to have them carried in little wagons behind them when they went to graze. Thus he taught a lesson to the professors of history and political economy who held forth in the taverns and applied all his wisdom and patience to the great Anglo-American problem.

A thunderclap frightened him out of his quiet routine. There was a formidable clamor on both sides of the Atlantic. All the journalists, lawyers and politicians of America protested violently, when they heard the Stamp Act had been passed. The crowd, still nervous from the excitement of the war, joined them, and the merchants followed them soon after. Never had there been such a hue and cry raised against England. It was loudest in New England and Virginia. Around the great ports of Massachusetts, a radical spirit began to develop. In Virginia, an independent and impatient aristocracy rose up against the haughty airs of the English lords. Their attitude found utterance in Patrick Henry, who made an impassioned speech at the Virginia Assembly. He invoked Cromwell in words which echoed all over the world, shocking England, and making the French Minister prick up his ears.

Franklin's American enemies took time by the forelock, for if the Pennsylvania Assembly was the least violent in all the colonies, it was not the least discontented, and it was in an odd situation. The "Old Ticket" which had formerly included all the liberal, popular and democratic ideas in its campaign against the Penns, found itself compromised in its turn. Its partisans had become reactionary and conservative, since they had to remain on good terms with the King — the only one who could help them against the Penns. On the contrary, the Penn enthusiasts took all the credit for democratic and liberal zeal. It was not Thomas Penn, but the Prime Minister, who was oppressing the colonies. And Franklin was his accomplice!

This was clearly borne out by his letters and advice, by the supplies of paper he sent to Hall, by the fact that he was in close touch with Grenville and the Prime Minister's secretary, Whately, and finally, by the brazen appointment of his friend, Hughes. This last bit of news spread all over the province and the neighboring colonies, much to Franklin's detriment. William Allen publicly announced that Franklin was in favor of the Stamp Act, that it was he who had framed it, suggested it and had it approved by the Royal Family, by using the chaplain to the Queen. This was nothing, if not precise. The Dutch ministers declared several times from their pulpits that Franklin was completely responsible for this criminal Act, and that he had even been mean enough to have books published in German taxed more heavily. Letters telling the same story were sent to all of Franklin's faithful supporters, the solid German farmers. It was certain that Franklin and his son had sold themselves to the ministry, that Grenville had promised advancement to him, and that Thomas Ringold had given Franklin money in order to be appointed tax receiver for Maryland. A vulgar drawing of Franklin was hawked about everywhere. It showed him listening attentively to the Devil, who was whispering in his ear: "Thou shall be Agent B E N for all my Realms."

Thus public opinion was roused against Franklin. On the streets of Philadelphia people gave Deborah the cold shoulder. There was some talk about setting fire to Franklin's new house. Deborah was advised to take refuge at Burlington with her son, as no one knew what might happen to her. But Deborah was courageous and firm; she got together arms and munitions enough to defend herself, and provisions for a siege, much preferring that to the hospitality of William. Her cousin Davenport came to her aid, but when she was ready for combat, no one came. The people knew her too well.

But the anger of the crowd turned against Hughes. The stamps arrived in the first part of October and as soon as this was known, Hughes was bothered by continual manifestations in front of his house. They yelled that if he didn't resign they would lynch him. He was menaced with hanging, drowning, or being burnt alive with all his furniture; but Hughes was a hard-headed fighter, and as he did not have much money he wanted to hold on to this lucrative appointment. He had the luck to be very ill at the time, in danger of death, and this not only reduced his risk, but diminished the pleasure of his attackers. But the crowd berated him to such an extent, nevertheless, that he finally gave in, signing a paper by which he promised not to perform his duties unless the Stamp Act was put in force throughout America. Then he published indignant letters, both in America and England, protesting against the violent treatment he had suffered.

The crowd who had besieged him had been led by one of the Bradfords and the son of William Allen: grudges were lasting in Philadelphia and the turning of tables must have been disagreeable to Franklin. There was worse in store for him. David Hall followed the crowd. Galloway tried to struggle against it in vain. All that his influence could accomplish was to have the protestations and recriminations of the Assembly couched in moderate, almost polite terms, which contrasted with those of the North and South. What a misfortune that the Stamp Act was passed just when the Patriots needed to be on good terms with the king! And what luck for the stupid Penns! Franklin was overwhelmed with letters from all parts of America. People were horrified, irritated, shocked, disapproving!

It was all the worse, since he was in poor health. But he saw the extent of his danger. The reputation he had so carefully built, year by year, was falling about him like a house of cards. He realized his peril all the more keenly when he read the London newspapers. They were violently against America, and daily published letters from readers which insulted and denounced the colonists as being rich misers who would do nothing for their country. The quarrel became a national struggle. Franklin took advantage of his connections with English journalists to have published important, grave, burlesque or eloquent answers to these attacks. (Series of letters to the *Public Advertiser* and to the *Gazetteer*, January, 1766.)

He made the best of his circumstances by some adroit maneuvering. After England had been led to the very brink of rupture with America by her parliamentarians, Franklin saved her from the danger by his fantastic politics. Shortly after the passing of the Stamp Act, the Grenville cabinet fell. Another cabinet was formed under the protection of Pitt, composed of eminent Whigs and in particular, Rockingham. Franklin had friends among them, thanks to Lord Shelburne and Sir Grey Cooper, Secretary of the Treasury. He made new ones, spoke with Rockingham and Dartmouth, and, in a word, besieged the ministers about the Stamp Act. Like good parliamentarians they all thought that the measures and gestures of their predecessors were absurd. The Stamp Tax had been one of Grenville's inventions. Now Rockingham was a sincere Whig and an idealist: it pleased him to play the rôle of peacemaker.

As for the King, he approved of the Stamp Tax. But he was young, honest, virtuous and proud of his popularity. He didn't want civil war. Moreover, he held Grenville in holy horror, for the pompous Prime Minister had bored him hours on end, with his interminable explanations of his interminable doctrines. The Stamp Tax suffered from all the personal unpopularity of Grenville. To repeal it was complicated but not impossible, and the parliamentary machine was set in motion. It was more difficult to persuade public opinion and the English aristocracy that it was wise to repeal the measure. Most politicians thought it to be a proof of weakness towards America and a dangerous precedent; it was simply a means of temporarily escaping a crisis which had to come.

Franklin and the other agents contributed articles to all the newspapers which were written to persuade the masses that the Stamp Act was the *only* obstacle to Anglo-American understanding, that if it were only overcome, the Americans would be only too glad to do all they could for England, that England had immense business opportunities in America, and that to ruin America was to ruin that part of England which depended on colonial trade. Finally, it would be unwise, they pointed out, to push America to the wall, for that would break the

THE FAMOUS CARTOON WHICH FRANKLIN HAD MADE AT THE TIME OF THE STAMP ACT

British unity, just at the moment the enemies of England were signing a family pact of revenge, uniting all the Bourbon powers of France and Spain.

They enrolled the English merchants, who did business with America, in the campaign, and made use of their money, influence and connections. They harassed the Members of Parliament and the Lords, following in their footsteps everywhere and filling their ears with facts on America. In order to impress them still more, Franklin had a little drawing printed: it depicted a woman, cut in pieces, with only her head intact. Her face had an imploring expression. The woman represented England, when she should have succeeded in ruining the colonies and alienating them forever. The drawing was printed on a little card which Franklin used for correspondence.

The discussion reached its height in January, 1766. Franklin fought off his fatigue and held his place by sheer will power. There seemed to be no end of articles to write, of visits to make to ministers and important members of Parliament. But the news he received from America, where popular hatred had reached such a point that his poor friend Hughes had been hung in effigy, stimulated him. If he failed, he risked losing everything.

He had his great day. He was summoned before Parliament to answer questions of Members of the House of Commons on the probable effects of the Stamp Act in America. Franklin sat calmly before the eager agitated men, his words a little heavy, his voice a little tired, his spectacles a little crooked on his nose. For three hours he answered their questions in a staid tone of voice, always prudent and carefully frank. Everything went along marvelously. He had prepared most of the questions beforehand himself, with the aid of his friends in Parliament, and they gave him the occasion to prove that Americans loved England, that they were poor but loyal, and so impassioned for liberty that they would never accept the Stamp Act. This was the limit of his previsions and no one dared to question him further. But it was enough to make some of the men on the benches do some hard thinking. The play had been rehearsed between Franklin and his friends and there had been no prompting. When Grenville and his faction wanted to intervene, and tried to make Franklin contradict himself — suggesting that he denounce certain colonies as being too violent, or that he confess there was no exact distinction between the internal taxation which the Americans refused to have dictated by Parliament and the external taxation they accepted, — he Socratically reduced them to nothing, and fortified himself in such a persuasive and imposing silence that the questioners seemed like buffoons. All this questioning, which was so loaded with facts, and prudently sugar-coated with statements on the traditional rights of Parliament and English liberty, was a triumphal success for Franklin. It was an extremely valuable precedent for the numerous friends of America, and a deadly blow to Grenville and his few followers.

Thanks to this parliamentary struggle and the efforts of Pitt, and in spite of the violence of the Americans which caused such stinging animosity, the Stamp Act was repealed on February 22, 1766. Franklin slept that evening as he had not slept for two years. He had saved his country, saved the future of the British Empire, and he had saved himself. There was to be no civil war, after all, and the rôle he had played was so prominent that every one in the world had to applaud his skill.

Once again he was the father of his country.

All the newspapers of America repeated the fact. They could not refuse it to the postmaster-general. The victory was celebrated throughout the colonies, and Franklin's name was linked with that of the king, of Parliament, and Pitt. After the long bitter weeks of fighting, the triumph was sweet.

Thus one of the greatest misunderstandings of the century was covered over but not cleared up. Of course, the Americans did not believe in the sovereignty of Parliament — Franklin was one of them — but they let people believe that they recognized its authority in every matter except internal taxation. It was by such a belief that they obtained the aid of the Whigs and hence the majority.

The Whigs, who considered Parliament as the supreme factor of government, had denied its power of imposing domestic taxes on the colonies, in order to rally them around Great Britain and their own party. An alliance had been formed on a diverging point of view.

On March 18, 1766, the King sanctioned the repeal of the Stamp Act, though on March 7 Parliament had voted a solemn text, which proclaimed the universal, complete, and legitimate authority of the King and Parliament over the British colonies.

The Americans, who were busy celebrating, did not care about the principle, as long as they enjoyed the fact. But it was more than a principle to the English parliamentarians; it was a deep-rooted feeling with them, that had to show itself.

The Americans celebrated their great parliamentary victory over the English as they had celebrated their great military victory over the French; their friends in Great Britain tried not to see the insulting side, and excused it as being an effusion of liberalism. But the Americans never forgot this triumph or how they had bluffed the English.

They had come to an agreement only by closing their eyes to the facts. The danger of rupture had really increased. One more lie stood in the way of the necessary solution, and a sincere understanding became impossible. The Stamp Act had announced the crisis, and its repeal had made the Revolutionary War inevitable.

V

THE battle of the Stamp Act had been won. But the atmosphere was still tainted with politics and Franklin felt he had a right to some rest. A little traveling was the diversion he preferred, and accordingly he set off with Sir John Pringle for the waters of Pyrmont.

This little city in the principality of Waldeck had been fashionable for a century. Great men went there to rest, rich people to be cured of anemia, and beautiful ladies to soothe their nerves. Both Peter the Great and Frederick the Great had visited it. In 1681 there was the extraordinary sight of twenty-seven Highnesses on the main street at once, with all their servants. When Franklin arrived, the shopkeepers were still talking about it.

Pyrmont attracted Sir John Pringle because he wanted to take the waters, but Franklin wanted to go there for a change of scene. The two scholars left London on June fourteenth. They were both fond of good living and made joyful companions. They were not bored a moment in their travels and were highly amused in Germany. There were celebrations for them everywhere. The news of Franklin's brilliant parliamentary victory had spread far and wide, and every one was enthusiastic over his electrical discoveries.

After some weeks of rest at Pyrmont they went to Göttingen to see the University of the Royal Society of Science there. They were received like kings, and there was no end to the questions their hosts addressed them. Franklin spoke with Herr Achenwall, Professor and Councillor to the Court, and gave him some details of the quarrel between England and America. Achenwall made a book out of the information he had received; it was the first on the subject to be published in Germany and was widely read. Franklin also spoke to a lead-

A TYPICAL ENGLISH CARTOON MADE BY THE WHIGS AND THE FRIENDS OF THE AMERICANS TO CELEBRATE THE REPEAL OF THE STAMP ACT

ing scholar, Herr Johann David Michaelis, Honorary Professor of Philosophy and Royal Councillor, telling him about the Patagonian giants, of which he had just heard from Commodore Byron, lately returned from a cruise. Byron had told Franklin that they were twice as tall as a man and Michaelis wrote to his correspondents throughout the world concerning these Patagonian monsters who were as huge as a pyramid of men. A group of scholars questioned Franklin on the destiny of America one night, and then they talked about it for twenty years.

From Göttingen the two travelers went to Hanover. There they met the same warm reception. The well-known scholar, Hartmann, showed Franklin his marvelous electrical apparatus and eagerly listened to the words of the great man. The Prince of Schwartsburg-Rudolstadt sent an ambassador to pay his respects to Franklin and to find out how lightning rods were made, but the ambassador mistook the day, the road and the person, so that he was unable to bring back a response.

Finally, after having visited Cassel, Frankfort and Mainz, Franklin and Pringle crossed over Holland again and arrived in London on August 13, 1766.

This trip had been extremely agreeable for Franklin and had rested him. All his memories of it were satisfactory except he regretted he had spoken about the Patagonian giants, as he was not sure of his information. Some time later he had to smile, in reading the German newspapers, for he found that the giants had become still taller, and that his conversations with Achenwall had been much elaborated upon. It was his first experience in international propaganda but it was conclusive. By using some method, he could say what he wanted and it would be repeated throughout the world. On the continent he found that he met neither the brutal opposition he found with in America, nor the dull resistance he was offered in England. He told Pringle to please write their German friends and inform them that the Patagonian giants were not so tall.

When he returned to London he found a bundle of letters waiting for him and a heavy political task to accomplish.

At home everything was going wrong: his brother Peter had died and his wife had followed him soon after. Of all the "Franklin children of Boston", only he and his dear sister Jane (Mrs. Mecom) remained. If he had had more time he would have been sad, but all he could do was to write affectionate letters to Jane and Debby. Debby was grumbling, for the house was not yet finished and a continual state of war existed between her and the contractors. She refused to pay the bills and they were then sent on to the doctor. William, who had always been displeased by the middle-class side of his father's life, had had a rash quarrel with David Hall, because of the latter's revolutionary tendencies. He had broken off with him completely, and with the aid of Galloway established a new printing shop in Philadelphia. A man named Goddard did the work and brought out a new newspaper, the *Pennsylvania Chronicle*, which promulgated a Royalist-Patriot, anti-Penn and pacifist doctrine. The shop was located in the same place where Benjamin Franklin had begun. Hall was annoyed, of course, and this made more difficulties. Benjamin thought sadly of his long partnership with him, which had been so pleasant and lucrative, and which was now ending disagreeably, owing to William's hot-headedness. Benjamin was all the more vexed, as it would complicate the accounts. But he had not finished his letters. Parker, his representative and man-of-all-work, and comptroller-general of the posts, sent several pages of lamentations: the summer had been so rainy that every one was ill, he had the gout himself, his wife was not well, and his son was sowing his wild oats indiscreetly; all of Franklin's various partners and friends were having poor business, especially his nephew, Benjamin Mecom, now set up in New Haven. Parker concluded philosophically that he had never enjoyed any rest in his life, but that death could not be far off and he hoped to have some then.

As to the political letters, there was such a heap of them that Franklin hesitated to begin.

Fortunately, Mrs. Stevenson was on hand, always taking care of her illustrious boarder and always adroit. She knew what was needed. After all, Benjamin Franklin was a solid middle-class gentleman, belonging to his time, and as warm-hearted as men were then. He needed a family and had an instinct for gallantry. Mrs. Stevenson knew all the pleasure that Franklin took in the company of her dear Polly, but she also knew that Polly was getting older and would probably marry. So she was wise enough to invite Sally Franklin, the daughter of Thomas Franklin, the dyer of Lutterworth, to come and live with them. Franklin was kind to her, as he was kind to all his relations, but she was an ignorant country girl and not very tempting. But while Franklin was away in Germany, Mrs. Stevenson secretly instructed Sally, teaching her how to dress and wear her clothes, how to put up her hair more attractively, how to come down a staircase and walk in a drawing-room . . . She succeeded so well that Franklin scarcely recognized his niece when he returned, she was so charming. Sally continued to live with them and kept a youthful atmosphere in the house which was very pleasant for the two elderly people. Then, too, Mrs. Stevenson took care of the little Temple, because his grandfather didn't want to abandon him, and she invited her country cousins to come and make company. Whenever a young Philadelphian passed through the city she had him dine with Franklin, or sent both of them off in the boat on the Thames. They would have a good dinner at some riverside restaurant, and then return in the moonlight, talking about far-off places. Franklin had his scientific friends, drinking comrades among the merchants and printers, aristocratic connections in the political world, but Number 7 Craven Street was a little family oasis for him, where Mrs. Stevenson was always careful to provide the atmosphere he needed. It was there he was admired and petted, and taken care of when he suffered from dizziness in his head, gout in his feet, pains in his stomach or itching all over. At Number 7 Craven Street, Franklin was the great man at home.

Thus he habituated himself to life in London. He constantly spoke about returning to America, but that was more out of habit than conviction. He could scarcely do otherwise: it would not be very kindly to Deborah to stay on indefinitely and he would have risked losing his position as postmaster-general of America. He was even now supposed to be living in New York to fulfill his duties, and he trembled to think they might be taken away from him. Franklin was beginning to lack for money, and he spent more than one painful evening poring over his accounts. After 1767 he would no longer have the income of his printing house, as his contract with Hall expired then (a loss of a thousand pounds a year). Benny Mecom was a blockhead, Parker was earnest but long-faced, Holt of New York paid poorly; his old friend, Hugh Hughes, was bankrupt, his friends, Baynton, Morgan and Wharton, a leading Philadelphia firm, were in financial difficulties, Deborah spent more than five hundred pounds yearly without counting the pennies and had even borrowed money from her friends, London was costly, he needed some ready money for some real-estate speculations he had undertaken in America, and he had to think of marrying Sally.

Politics could help him but that was a delicate game.

In 1766–1767 his friends were in power, Lord Shelburne, particularly. In spite of his heavy face, Shelburne was perhaps the only one of all the English politicians who was intelligent enough to recognize Franklin's genius. He would have liked to have helped him and given him a place. But Shelburne was exact and careful, and had to understand a problem thoroughly before tackling it. In political life he was constantly being beaten by speed; no sooner had he assimilated a question and was ready to decide, than his ministry fell. Thus, Franklin's most beautiful projects were never realized, and he never became a minister.

However, he hoped to make the best of Shelburne. The legislative bodies of America and England were so balanced — neither one wanted to give up a tittle of its power — that the only way anything could be accomplished was by a single man, if he were backed by the King.

Franklin sounded out Shelburne on two matters which were close to his heart: the issuing of American paper money and the formation of new colonies in the center of America.

One of Franklin's great and judicious ideas was that England would fare much better with the colonies if she adopted a creative policy, in place of acting like a stepmother. Instead of restraining business and hindering the colonies from printing paper money, England should issue standard American money and administer it from her own mints. Thus the colonies would be enriched, they would be more united, and the money would be another tie to bind them to England. Franklin was so taken with this idea that he had his friend Thomas Pownall insert it in the fourth edition of his great work, "The Administration of the Colonies", and he submitted a detailed plan of his project to Shelburne. Shelburne appraised it, and was just beginning to like it, when he left the ministry. No one else in England who read Pownall's book perceived that this imperial idea was one of great value.

The fall of Shelburne put an end to another one of Franklin's ideas. For fifteen years he had repeatedly suggested to the English ministers the establishment of new colonies, and said that if the colonists were busy clearing the forest and enriching the land, they would have less time to quarrel with their mother country, they would use more of England's industrial products, they would be happier and so would the English merchants. Though these arguments sounded convincing, many politicians were not of the same mind. They protested that further colonization would depopulate Great Britain, the colonies would become too powerful, even dangerous, and that English business would not profit as the center of America was too distant. Shelburne consulted Franklin on this subject, and after long conversations, he understood it and decided to apply Franklin's ideas.

Franklin had suggested the foundation of two new colonies in the west, which would protect and further the development of the old colonies. He had even drawn the boundaries. But this was only a patriotic dream. Shortly after the war he had been solicited by the heirs of a certain Cox, who had planned a western colony in the seventeenth century. They offered to go into partnership with him if he could push the plan through.

Franklin was pleased with the idea, took some trouble about it, and had R. Jackson make a search in the government archives for the documents. This resulted in nothing and the affair fell to pieces.

In 1762 Franklin began to be interested in a Newfoundland speculation, as well as some other Philadelphia merchants, particularly Hillegas. He became so enamored of the project that he wanted to visit the region and planned a voyage to Newfoundland in 1767. Some of the ground there was very good for agricultural purposes. But the country was too cold and developed slowly.

At last, in 1766–1767, he had his great chance. His friends Baynton, Morgan and Wharton of Philadelphia, who did business with the Indians, had been so fortunate or so unfortunate as to have sustained heavy losses in the last Indian war, but they were clever enough to take advantage of them. They were on good terms with the governor of the West, Sir William Johnson, who was a friend of Franklin's also, and used as their agent the explorer and former soldier, Croghan. Samuel Wharton was the youngest of them all and perhaps the shrewdest. He went to Fort Stanwix where a treaty between the "six nations" and Johnson was negotiated. When this business was in progress, there was a good deal of rum drunk, many presents given away, and Wharton quietly began to work on his own little project. With a few well chosen words he persuaded the Indians to sign a little private agreement with him by which they ceded an immense territory in the west of Pennsylvania and Virginia as recompense for their losses and those of all the other merchants who had been likewise wronged. As a matter of fact, their present was not so generous; the ground might belong as well to other tribes, to the King of England or to anybody. But it was a valuable document, if one knew how to use it.

Once started in this direction, the Whartons did not stop, but bought the rights to the Illinois territory from French speculators. They organized a company to exploit this concession as quickly as possible and among its members were

Galloway, William Franklin, Sir William Johnson, and J. Hughes. Benjamin Franklin was added to this list and instructed to secure the double authorization, necessary to make the most of these papers, from the Royal Government.

Nothing should have been easier, as Shelburne let Franklin guide him in these matters. But the affair fell through, as Franklin was too wise and Shelburne too exact. At first, Shelburne needed several months to comprehend the fundamental principles which Franklin had explained, and then he needed several weeks more to persuade himself that the Illinois Company — as the enterprise was called — would be faithful to its principles. To be more certain of success, Franklin took Jackson into his confidence, and the lawyer succeeded in interesting Conway, another minister, in the project. Then Shelburne, thoroughly imbued with Franklin's enthusiasm, presented the enterprise to his colleagues, along with the complete plans for the establishment of two new colonies in the West. They found this idea very new and said it sounded too intelligent to be practical. Shelburne reported this to Franklin and said they would first have to prove the practicability of the plan to the cabinet, and then they could proceed to authorize it. He and Franklin went to a lot of trouble to convince the ministers that the company was feasible, and were just on the point of succeeding when Shelburne left the ministry. The colony of Illinois disappeared into the thin air without ever having existed.

The Whartons thought that Franklin had been too easy-going and too idealistic. They didn't trust him to make anything out of the Indian treaty, and sent young Samuel Wharton to negotiate with the Government. This young man had principles, and the one that was clearest to him was that if you wanted men, you had to *buy* them. At Fort Stanwix he had been ready to buy the Indians, Johnson and Croghan. He is not mentioned in histories as having failed. On December 30, 1768, he arrived in London with the same intentions. Franklin was to be his technical adviser and was not to be consulted except on the prices of men and the rates of exchange. Naturally, Franklin was a little offended, but he took the interest of the public so much to heart that he did not want to abandon such a useful enterprise for a mere difference in method.

But he saw that Shelburne had disappointed him twice on matters of essential importance. He began to think that nothing would happen, neither solution nor crisis, but that things would go on from bad to worse without ever reaching a catastrophe.

Parliamentary factions controlled everything in London. There were no longer any great parties with doctrines, but just little groups which had tendencies one way and another and private interests to satisfy. The great Pitt was no longer on the scene, due to ill health, and a crop of cheap politicians had sprung up behind him. The worst of it was that these men were not complete fools, and did not suffer from their stupidity enough to see the need of any change. They were pompous, noisy, narrow-minded; the victories of England and the grandeur of Parliament had made them overweening, and they were extremely irritated with the Americans who were always begging for something when they weren't insulting them. They refused to admit that their sovereignty might not extend over all the English territories. They were ready to give up all the material profit they could take from America, if it were absolutely necessary, but they would not sacrifice their prestige or the "parliamentary rights."

Unfortunately, the Americans were equally proud of their strength, their liberty and their success of 1766. They had celebrated the repeal of the Stamp Act with a gayety which had fooled many people, but not the wisest of them. Their joy was one of victory, not of reconciliation. The excitement and animosity remained, as well as most of their grievances.

The English parliamentary aristocracy did not understand that it had to recognize another parliamentary aristocracy which was being developed in the colonies. The latter was ready to come to an agreement if a place were given it, but it was just as ready to go to extremes, with the aid of a rising democracy, at any attempt of suppression. This was a new fact. It was not enough to maintain the traditional rights; a new formula had to be invented; but the English Parliament admired itself too much to make any important changes. Now it would menace the Americans, now laugh lightly at them, not knowing which policy to pursue, while the Americans varied, now being white with fury, but silent, and now exploding in an anger that knew no bounds. Such was the state of the colonies from 1767 to 1775.

Franklin, as agent for the Pennsylvania Assembly, had a delicate part to play: he had to satisfy a personal vengeance against the Penns; by joining Pennsylvania to the Royal Government he hoped to build an Anglo-American empire, which no one wanted in England; and he had to safeguard the sovereignty of the Pennsylvania Assembly which the Prime Minister and Parliament had attempted to keep in subjection ever since the judgment of 1759.

From a practical and official point of view he had a triple mission:

1. To have the King accept the petition of the Pennsylvania Assembly, and take over the government of the Province.

2. To persuade the ministry and Parliament to authorize Americans to print and issue paper money.

3. To influence Parliament to renounce taxing Pennsylvania. To persuade it to recognize the Pennsylvania Assembly as the legislative authority of the province.

Besides this, he had to secure the ratification of the laws passed by the Pennsylvania Assembly and to keep its members informed on what was going on in England.

On any of these three points, Franklin was powerless to do anything. The ministry and the King were too irritated and too embarrassed by the American situation to dare make it more complicated by another change — even if the change were for the better. Their great idea was to save time, but they only succeeded in losing it. And Franklin walked from one anteroom to another, with his eternal petition in his hand, hearing nothing but words which were more and more vague, and receiving invitations to dinner which were more and more cordial. The American question had been rehashed so many times that people ended by not thinking any more about it.

Paper money was a still more burning question and quite as inextricable. The English Parliament and the ministry claimed that paper money was bad in principle and should be forbidden in America, lest the English merchants should lose by it, which God forbid! The Pennsylvania Assembly claimed that paper money was a panacea, without which the colony would decline. Franklin could do nothing about the discussion at all, except to leave some excellent writings about it to posterity. American paper money remained a dream, a wearisome chimæra.

As to taxation, the opposition of the two illustrious legislatures was so notorious and radical that it was better not to talk about it in London. Benjamin held his peace.

Thus, the scope of his creative activity was reduced, but he still had an enormous amount of work. He had to make the legislative life of Pennsylvania a practical certainty by securing the ratification of the laws passed in the Assembly as they were not applicable until they had received the royal sanction. As the ministry and the King became more and more distrustful of anything the Americans wanted, Franklin had an incalculable number of visits, and an increasing number of setbacks.

His other great work was to watch Parliament, in order to have laws which were harmful to American business repealed, and to hinder the approval of new measures which would be unfavorable. The reconciliation of 1766 contained the germs of many violent quarrels. While the Americans exulted, Parliament was in a bad humor, and not at all satisfied with its magnanimity. A law which permitted the quartering of English troops in American homes, to "protect" the colonies, was thus hailed with joy in 1767. The colonies considered it as a criminal attack on their rights as Anglo-Saxons, and as a portent of more serious incursions against their liberties. When the soldiers came to live with the Americans, the latter saw to it that they were annoyed in a thousand ways and eventually exasperated.

This was a new subject of petition for Franklin.

In 1767 Charles Townshend furnished him another. This minister thought America should be taxed on her importations. Thus the Americans could not complain of internal or direct taxes. Only tea, paper, glass and paints would be taxed when imported; and Parliament, delighted with this skillful solution, celebrated the passing of the measure. The Americans were deeply hurt and irritated. They found this tax just as offensive and more hypocritical than the Stamp Tax, and excitedly banded together, refusing to import anything from England (1768). However, they insisted that these taxes be abolished. And Franklin petitioned!

The men of New England who had developed a great maritime commerce, objected strongly to the restrictions which England imposed on their business. They refused to buy molasses from the British West Indies when they could buy it cheaper from the French. And the French West Indies formed a capital market for their exportations. Even if they were deprived of the right to trade with them they continued to deliver contraband goods with a pious obstinacy. The English knew it and their immoderate anger was displayed in the means they took for suppression. The other colonies were shocked. Thus, all the agents petitioned in favor of Boston.

All these petitions suffered the same fate. They collected dust on the tables in the House of Commons or, at the Privy Council of the King, quietly slid off on to the floor. It was even worse in the House of Lords. The Americans had no chance to win the day except when a ministry fell or a minister was changed. In such a case, the successor always wanted to show the imbecility of his predecessor and his own sagacity, and so would unmake all that had been made before him. Thus in April, 1770, all the importation taxes, except the one on tea, were abolished. But, naturally, just keeping on this one was enough to keep up the American discontent.

The struggle became more and more bitter and confused. No one saw clearly any longer, and nothing was understood. Both antagonists instinctively decided not to give in an inch.

As soon as Franklin heard of an unfavorable measure which had been proposed in Parliament he hurriedly got into his coach, rode about the city to visit all his friends and enemies, and, in a few days, would have killed the law before it had been voted. He soon had perfected his technique to such a point that he killed laws before they had been proposed or even thought of. Then he would return home, exhausted but satisfied.

But he was paid back in his own coin. Whenever he wanted to present a petition, no one came near him. He could find no one to defend or present it in Parliament. Then he would go for long walks across the city, his lips compressed, and the petition in his pocket. When the paper became too torn he put it among his archives, wrote to Galloway that he had done all that was possible for the moment and that he would continue to watch for a favorable occasion. Then he rested until it was time for another petition.

Days and weeks passed, and the heap of wrecked laws and torn petitions became higher and higher. Instead of coming closer together, the English and American peoples drifted farther apart. Their respective rights had been so much discussed that they became as obscure and tiring as ancient mythology with its hundred thousand gods. With the exception of a few politicians, every one was surfeited of the subject, and no one understood anything any more. Intelligent people gave up the task and let events take their course. Franklin, who was a wise man and a Mason, would not admit of such weakness and patiently set to work to clarify the problem. The most prominent item of his expenses for the province was for propaganda articles published in the *Gazetteer*, the *London Chronicle*, etc.

He tried to maintain some clear principles in the minds of his fellow citizens and contemporaries: every one would lose in an Anglo-American war, the Americans were capable of fighting and even of conquering, and they were sure to win in the long run, as their population doubled every twenty-five years while that of England varied but slightly. Franklin hired a number of English writers to keep up a running fire of facts and rumors favorable to the American cause in the newspapers; Massie, a skillful hack writer and formerly anti-American, was among them, and Richard Jackson, now a member of the House of Commons, was the star contributor. Lastly, he made use of the English merchants, who did business with America, to see that these writings were distributed, to bring pressure to bear upon the rich, and to launch and back the petitions.

In spite of his optimism, Franklin was too wise to believe in rapid progress. He was now the one who knew both countries better than any one else, the one who pulled almost all the wires, the one who had the greatest number of admiring, affectionate or paid friends. This was attested not only by his interior satisfaction but by the facts: in 1767 he was one of the thirteen commissioners named to fix the boundaries between New York and New Jersey; in 1768, he was appointed agent for the Georgia Assembly, and, in 1770, for the Massachusetts Assembly, though he had many enemies there; in 1769, both the governor and the Assembly of New Jersey named him as their agent also. He had become such a specialist in this craft that every one wanted him to be his agent, even his enemies and his son, which made the situation rather curious and complex.

It wasn't because they loved him; of that he was sure. He was one of the most heartily hated and suspected men on two continents. In spite of his part in repealing the Stamp Act, many American patriots had their suspicions, and wrote to Almon, the leading Whig printer in London, to supply them with the *real* text of Franklin's answers in Parliament. Allen continued to affirm that Franklin had invented the Stamp Act. At New York, the same rumors were current. Franklin had a letter which Fothergill had written, exonerating him from all complicity with the partisans of the Stamp Act, and distributed it among all the little German villages in western Pennsylvania for his defense. But an essay he had published in the *London Chronicle*, "Causes of American Discontent", was used by his enemies against him. He had defended the American theme in it with much moderation and with a polite phrase for

Parliament. This was enough to make him cursed. He was calumniated everywhere; some of his colleagues among the other agents for the American colonies said that his attitude in 1765 had been ambiguous, and Dean Tucker, the pamphleteer, repeated the statement. The rumors even reached London, where notorious liberals like Thomas Hollis, the great merchant, considered Franklin to be a "trimmer." The Royalist attitude of William, the Toryism of some of his friends, in particular Pringle and Strahan, and of some of his protectors, among them Lord LeDespenser, gave strength to these accusations.

Nevertheless, the loyal subjects of the King, both in America and London, distrusted him. Franklin had noticed this, and as far back as 1764 had Colonel Bouquet write a letter in which the brave soldier testified at length to Franklin's devotion to the King, and enumerated all his many services. He had a few friends like this everywhere, who could protect him and turn the storm in another direction. But they couldn't suppress the danger; they could only put it off.

Franklin felt that he was spied on: in 1768 his enemies wanted to deprive him of his situation as postmaster-general, and they had a good reason, as he didn't live in America, but he defended himself savagely, and thanks to his persistence and the protection of Lord LeDespenser, he kept his office. Nevertheless, he had no guaranty on it. He knew that his enemies had sneaked the letters he had written to Galloway, and that they had been read in public. Even Deborah's letters had been taken and ridiculed openly in the taverns. Galloway warned him to be prudent when he wrote to the Committee on Correspondence of the Pennsylvania Assembly, for his letters were seen by every one, and one of them would have been printed, except for the timely intervention of his friends. The battle was in ambush, and the more a man was clever, subtle and complex, the more his conduct was judged suspicious, and the more danger he ran in case his secrets were discovered. Now Franklin was more clever, subtle and complex than any Englishman of his time.

This heavy atmosphere of doubt and uncertain waiting would have been unpleasant if he had not known how to react to it. His circle of friends became constantly larger, and his scientific studies, which spread his fame farther and farther, were relaxing exercises for his mind. He no longer busied himself in original research, and abandoned his tentative experiments in phonetic writing (1768), but he was interested in the inventions of others and worked for the practical perfection of his own. He was more and more consulted concerning his lightning rod and tried to improve it. Priestley's big book on "The History of Electricity" spread his glory to the four corners of the world.

Religion attracted him again, and it was even a pleasure. When Whitefield came to London Franklin often went to visit him. He also became acquainted with the first group of Unitarian ministers, whose liberalism pleased him. He was soon on good terms with them, and this was useful, as these virtuous ministers — Price, Priestley, and Th. Lindsay — had such strong protectors as the Earl of Huntington and Lord Dartmouth. But here also the complex attitude of Franklin troubled his friends. Was he not intimately connected with Lord LeDespenser, who was the greatest libertine of the century, and who, at the same time he protected the curate of his village, held Black Masses in the ruins of an old abbey? There were many stories about these Medmenham Monks who had profane drinking orgies and made strange sacrifices to love. Men did not understand that Franklin, as he grew older, needed piety more and more, but that his profound knowledge of English society forced him to turn away from the Church of England. This attitude caused just a shade of embarrassment between him and some of those he loved most: Whitefield, Priestley, and even his dear sister, Jane.

But even outside of politics, his life was not always gay or easy. Travel was the one pleasure for him which was not alloyed with sadness or danger. He took an increasing joy in it each year. The more the Anglo-American situation rankled and festered, the more Franklin left England to visit foreign lands.

After he had visited Germany (1766), where he kept his connections all his life, and Holland (1762), which was always one of his centers of correspondence, he established his position in Italy, where a whole school of electricians, and especially the Father Beccaria and the Jesuit, Boskovitch, formed a veritable Franklin cult. The great Dutch savant, Ingenhousz, during a visit to London, became Franklin's friend, and later, spread his fame in Austria when he served in that country as physician to the Empress-Queen. Then, of course, there was the King of Denmark, who dined with Franklin on his visit to London in 1768. The son of the candle-maker was very proud of this, but it didn't influence either his social life or his intellectual career. The King carried away an excellent impression. There was something very attractive in Franklin's dignified and cheerful companionship which never failed of its effect on the good-hearted, sentimental Germans.

But his triumph was in France. As far back as 1762 his translators and admirers, Dalibard and LeRoy, wanted him to come to Paris. But Franklin had too much tact to visit the traditional enemy so soon. When the quarrel was over, the Stamp Act repealed, and the difficulty over importation taxes seemed to be permanent, Franklin felt a glow from his triumphs and decided to visit Paris. He knew that it was the capital of enlightened public opinion, and that it was essential both for himself and his party that he be well considered there.

He left on August 28, 1767, in company with Pringle. They took the post chaise to Dover, where they spent the night, and late the next morning they embarked, wisely having foregone their breakfasts. The crowd of passengers on the deck, who had not done likewise, were soon upset by the relentless oscillation of the sea, affording a grotesque sight to the two philosophers. It was at Calais that Doctor Franklin first stepped on the soil of France. The first Frenchmen he knew were the porters, valets and coachmen. He found that they robbed him right and left, the same as in England, but that they were more polite. This was his first impression and the most vivid one of all his journey. As his coach rolled rapidly down the great highways, bordered by stately trees, he admired the rich country of Northern France that met his eyes, and the busy city of Abbeville, where there were a few fair-skinned women. Franklin had an Anglo-Saxon taste and brunettes repelled him.

At first, Paris was a surprise, with all its hubbub in the narrow streets. Then he acquired a taste for the foreign city, admired the sewerage system which was much more modern than that of London, the way of filtering water, and the fad of always going out walking with an umbrella. He was amazed at the ladies and their more amazing dresses, but he was shocked at the way they wore rouge — in great round splotches. He wrote to Polly about it with humorous disapproval:

> As to Rouge, they don't pretend to imitate Nature in laying it on . . . Cut a hoop of 3 Inches Diameter in a Piece of Paper; place it on the Side of your Face in such a Manner as that the Top of the Hoop may be just under your Eye; then with a Brush dipt in the Colour, paint Face and Paper together; so when the Paper is taken off there will remain a round Patch of Red exactly the Form of the Hole. This is the Mode, from the actresses on the Stage upwards thro' all Ranks of Ladies to the Princesses of the Blood. . . .

He visited Versailles and was overwhelmed by its magnificence. He attended a supper of the King, who spoke to him amiably, and whose presence, distinction and grace of manner struck him with admiration. He saw an illumination at Notre Dame to commemorate the death of the Dauphine, as well as the painting gallery and all kinds of curious sights. He was welcomed with great politeness everywhere, and when people knew who he was, he was treated with every mark of honor and respect. England was a hateful country, but it was fashionable, and America still more so. Weren't the Americans related to the redskins, so beloved of Monsieur Rousseau de Genève and the fashionable world? As to Franklin, every one had heard of his scientific discoveries and of his stand before Parliament. There was much bowing and scraping before him and Franklin was mildly pleased by it all. He tried to please others, too, dressed like a Frenchman, and gave up his heavy English wig in favor of a light French one, which was fashionable at the time and which left his ears free. It made him look twenty years younger and he felt very dapper.

He felt even younger after a visit to Monsieur Quesnay.

This venerable old man was the doctor to Madame Pompadour, the King's mistress; he was also the founder of a philosophic sect, the Physiocrats, and was considered to be the most virtuous and philanthropic man of Europe. In his home, Franklin found what interested and pleased him most: a gay, intimate, erudite and philosophical society. There he heard of the latest scientific discoveries and the newest literary fads. Franklin was all but bowled over with delight.

The group of Quesnay's followers was the first to react against the mercantile theory and English influences. Quesnay, the Marquis de Mirabeau and their disciples were Continentals and owners of estates. They were interested in the well-being of the people and claimed that agriculture was more important than commerce. The rural life seemed the only normal one to them. The only fortune, they claimed, was in the produce of the earth. All the rest was superfluity, mere expenditure and not investment. The laborer was the only producer, and the soil the only creator. They used emphatic language to exalt the farmer and country life; the farmer should be the center of the State, according to them, and they demanded that he have free trade, free exchange and reasonable taxes. The Physiocrats were generous and practical in small things, but foolishly idealistic in matters of importance. When they were appointed governors of some province they managed to build good roads, plant trees, and keep up the best breeds of swine, but when they came to Paris they spoke disparagingly of big cities and industries. Besides, they knew that humanity is stupid and wanted to better the fate of the people by using reason and despotism.

After Quesnay, the most illustrious in the group was the Marquis of Mirabeau. This spirited gentleman was called "The Friend of Men" because of a book he had written with that title. He wanted to be so good to people, and so good to his family, that he didn't stop quarreling with them: he put his son into prison when he wouldn't do as he wanted and forbade him to use his name. He had a strong character, but his son had an even stronger one. Like the rest, the Marquis de Mirabeau was fascinated by Franklin, and Franklin, in his turn, was fascinated by all of them. He had come from America, which was an essentially agricultural country, he was a great scholar and famous for his wisdom, and he confirmed all their theories. Small wonder they adopted him and paid him homage!

His most enthusiastic admirer was a good doctor, Jacques Barbeu Dubourg, a man of some notoriety and warm feeling. He made Franklin his idol and devoted himself to him, heart and soul. He took care of all the translations of Franklin's works in French and for ten years was at Franklin's beck and call. He pledged all his fortune and energy to the Philadelphian, for his faith in him was infinite, and if he did not have much critical keenness, he had enough enthusiasm to make up for it.

Franklin saw more scholars at the home of Dalibard, who pampered him, and still others in the reception halls of the Marquis de Courtenvaux who, like other great lords, was fond of science. But in this short trip of six weeks his real discovery was the Physiocrat Party.

Franklin realized immediately how important their ideas could be to him. He reduced them to their simplest elements, saw how they could be utilized in the Anglo-American discussion, and to what point they supported the claims of the American farmers against the English merchants. He realized the power of this group even if it were restrained, and how solidly constructed it was. It was strengthened by a magazine *The Citizen's Calendar*, which was read by all the leading minds of the world, and which kept up a correspondence with all the enlightened rulers of Europe. Franklin subscribed to the review and sent the editors some translations of his writings. Then he sent them news on the American situation and made the magazine an organ for American propaganda.

This was a real revolution in his mind. The old English

Whig system of Thomas Gordon, and the mercantile theories of William Petty, by which he had been guided since 1720, suddenly seemed old-fashioned. The constitutional discussion between England and America had already tired him, and he thought it was missing the main issue. His rich intelligence, made sharp by these new principles, worked more briskly. He adopted the principle that only agriculture is productive, believed that trade should be free for all, and that indirect taxation was absurd. The discussion with England had already turned his mind practically in this direction, and the Physiocrats furnished him with a doctrine, which he made use of in his writings of these stormy years.

To keep in touch and to watch over the publication of his works, Franklin returned to France in 1769. He wanted to go again in 1770 but was hindered from doing so by his duties. His correspondence with France became enormous, and more than two thirds of it was devoted to the Physiocrat group. His French friends loved him deeply and sometimes saw him in London. This adoration was new to Franklin, who was used to living among Anglo-Saxons and in the midst of political quarrels. He found it very pleasant and tried to turn it to good account on the behalf of his country.

He kept up his connections in Ireland and Scotland for the same reason, and took a vacation in Scotland in 1771. He was received everywhere with respectful and flattering hospitality. In Ireland he was surprised at the sympathy which the Parliament and the popular party had for him and America. The Parliament especially honored him, and at receptions given in his honor by the "courtiers" he noted the force and the weakness of the two groups. In Scotland he saw his old friends, the Dicks, Kames, and Hume, and all the Edinburgh scholars. The good long talks he had with them gave him peace and serenity.

It was easy for him then, on his return, to solve a prickly problem which had been hanging fire for three years. In 1767 Sally had married Richard Bache, a merchant of Philadelphia. She was deeply in love with him and Deborah approved, but

William found the match hardly distinguished, and too middle-class. Both Debby and William had written the doctor to decide. He was too wise to do anything about it. No doubt, he wanted another kind of son-in-law, and was not enthusiastic about his daughter marrying a man who had just gone bankrupt and who was considerably older than she. But he knew better than to thwart the mother and daughter if they were in agreement. Besides, Mrs. Stevenson advised him to yield. Franklin then imposed silence on William, who was all ready to stir up a family mix-up, and the marriage was celebrated in great pomp, with the bells of Philadelphia clanging in Sally's honor and the vessels flying flags. But there was no celebration in Burlington or in London.

From 1767 to 1771 Richard Bache worked hard to put his business on a firm footing again. He had some success, and in any case, proved that he could make Sally happy. So he risked coming to England in 1771 to see his father-in-law and to ask him for an official position. It was a delicate business, as Franklin was tired to death of requests, and had no great affection for this son-in-law whom Debby had chosen.

Fortunately for Bache, he arrived in London when Franklin was in Scotland. He found only Mrs. Stevenson, and as she had decided in advance to like Bache, she was very agreeably impressed by him. She wrote many wise letters to Franklin to calm and prepare him. Bache, himself, wrote and invited Franklin to stop at his parents' home in Prestonfield on his return from Scotland. Franklin accepted, and was surprised to find how pleasant this halt on the road was. The trip had tired him and he was received with such respectful affection. He embraced his son-in-law, and when, a little later, he was able to persuade him that he had better stick to business, his respect for him visibly increased. Both of them returned to London to celebrate the family reconciliation with Mrs. Stevenson — who had prepared it all so well.

However, Franklin had yielded all the more easily as he was tired. For the first time, a trip, instead of resting him, had left him more exhausted than before. He felt age coming on and wished to end his life tranquilly, taking his pleasure in the study of science and philosophy. Politics seemed like something very vain to him. He only continued in the political world because he was caught in its harness, and because of his irresistible fighting instinct which would not let him give in to his enemies.

His enemies were increasing, however, and he did not want to retire from the scene until he had won some brilliant battle. Massachusetts had appointed an assistant agent, Arthur Lee, ostensibly to help him but really to keep an eye on him. Arthur Lee was a radical and thus the patriots showed their distrust of Franklin's liberalism. The ministry at London were also suspicious. Lord Hillsborough, who was in charge of American affairs, arranged his office routine so as never to see Franklin, and indirectly made William realize what it cost to be the son of the doctor. He also efficaciously thwarted Franklin's plans but Franklin succeeded in giving him a lot of bother. The two men neutralized each other. The petitions accumulated at the minister's door without any hope of consideration. Franklin's friends were now all in the Opposition, and if any one said something about giving him a post, it was to compromise him.

Franklin could only think of the future with fear. He avoided doing so, hoping that the present difficulties and troubles would not break out too violently before he died. "After me, the Deluge," Louis XV is quoted as saying, but Franklin was too philanthropic and too wary of the Bible to express himself likewise. Just the same, he hoped to die peacefully, but thought that his grandchildren would have a hard time of it.

He really didn't know where he should go. He liked to stay in England, on account of the good Mrs. Stevenson, his comfortable lodgings, his pleasures, but he was also attracted to America by his old memories, his friends, his aged wife who was now very ill — she had had an attack in the winter of 1770–1771 — and his grandchildren. His duty lay perhaps on the other side of the Atlantic, but the pleasure of living was in England. Influenced by the nonchalance that comes with old age, Doctor Franklin decided to stay on in England until some incident should force him to leave — or cause him to stay there forever.

But his mind retained its liveliness behind this mask of fatigue. Both his friends and his enemies were deceived by it, just when he would be preparing a sly trick. The best was the one he played on Hillsborough. It was very characteristic of the long period of guerilla warfare in Parliament between the repeal of the Stamp Act and the crisis of 1774.

Lord Hillsborough was a tall, florid and vain man, who had a groping mind. He had been one of those most favorable to the establishment of a new western colony, and had then become one of the worst enemies to the idea. This imposing gentleman may have changed his mind because of his antipathy for the Americans who were behind the enterprise, or, using his brutal, illogical intelligence, he may have come to this conclusion by a simple taste for contradiction. He stubbornly refused to answer the petition of the Ohio Company which was anxious to receive recognition of the gift the Indians had made to the Whartons, and to utilize it for the establishment of a huge colony.

Hillsborough had begun by tricking the two agents of the company, Franklin and Samuel Wharton, saying to them that they would have a greater chance of success if they would ask for an extension of ground sufficient for the establishment of a colony. The petition was changed to read in this wise, and then Hillsborough said the matter was too grave for him to decide alone, that he would have to ask the advice of his fellow ministers. Now these men were not much interested in this enterprise and didn't desire the responsibility at all — it belonged naturally to Hillsborough — and so they failed to attend his meeting. The petition moldered in a corner.

This wasn't very satisfactory to Samuel Wharton who had come to England expressly to shake up Franklin and to persuade the ministers. He then took Franklin's advice and distributed shares of the company among politicians. Thus he conciliated the "Pittites" and the "Grenvillites." Once this was done, he offered the direction of the affair to Thomas Walpole, a notorious politician, influential banker, and brother of the famous Horace Walpole. By this maneuver Wharton was secure in Parliament.

This was not yet enough to oust Hillsborough. Through Strahan, who was intimate with Lord Hertford, the King's chamberlain, Franklin obtained the protection of His Majesty. The King was favorable to any enterprise which would extend the boundaries of the British realms.

By a master stroke, Wharton persuaded two ministers to enter the company: Lord Rochfort and Lord Gower, neither of whom were fond of Lord North, and both of whom were in need of money. They saw the company as a good chance to take revenge and to become rich, and were glad to take it. The ambush was then ready.

Discreet but clear hints from the palace obliged Hillsborough to prepare his report on the project, and to submit it to the Lords of the Board of Trade. He did this on March 25, 1772, and it was a complete and brutal condemnation of the plan: the boundaries were poorly defined, he claimed, the territory extended too far to the west, and the idea of founding a new colony in the center of America was dangerous and liable to depopulate England. Thus Hillsborough was forced to break his silence. He was compromised and had exposed himself. He felt the effects of it immediately. His report was to go before the Privy Council of the King, which was filled with his enemies and stockholders of the company. The Council wanted to appear impartial, but not being able to change the report of a minister into a public trial, asked Hillsborough to publish it, and convoked the stockholders of the company to appear before them on June 5, 1772, to *inform* them about the project. In reality, this was just to organize a discussion in which Hillsborough couldn't answer.

It took place in the Cockpit Tavern. All the members of the Council were present and very attentive. Walpole, Wharton, Franklin, Trent and Mercer spoke for the company. But the best speech and the most insinuating one was made by Wharton.

When he finished, the auditors nodded their heads pleasantly and felt that the affair was settled. Urged on by Rochfort and Gower, the Privy Council presented a definite report to His Majesty which was entirely favorable to the company, on July 1, 1772. All that was left to Hillsborough was to swallow his humiliation and yield, or to retire. He made visit after visit to his friend, North, the Prime Minister, to obtain his support, but his efforts were all in vain. North was no hero. He felt that Parliament and the King were favorable to the company and he didn't want to compromise himself. If he couldn't save one of his ministers, he wanted to save his ministry. He quietly ushered Hillsborough to the door, and made haste to suggest a successor, so that the conspirators would not take further advantage of their trickery. Thus Rochfort and Gower ousted Hillsborough, who was a friend of North, but his successor was his cousin, Lord Dartmouth.

The petition was approved. Such a miracle roused the enthusiasm of the stockholders and of the directors of the company. Samuel Wharton walked the streets like a hero and his praises were sung everywhere. In London and Philadelphia he was celebrated as being the only American who had succeeded in stirring up the inertia of the ministry. He was contrasted with Franklin, who seemed to be so soft.

But Franklin rejoiced nevertheless. His great enemy, Hillsborough, had fallen by Wharton's hard work, but also by his scholarly snare: the withering pamphlet he had written in answer to the Hillsborough report. Then before Dartmouth was named, Franklin had been consulted as to the choice. Finally the company was going to get rich at last, if it succeeded.

He was a little annoyed by all this praise of Wharton. But like a wise man, he knew how to console himself. He wrote to William and Galloway that Wharton had succeeded but only in a preliminary step. He advised them to wait.

They waited, and for two years nothing happened. The Department of the Colonies was in complete disorder, and owing to Lord Dartmouth's attempts at reform nothing was accomplished. Besides, the document had to be submitted to the attorney general and the solicitor general to see that it contained no illegal clause. For some unknown, mysterious and inexplicable reason — the most plausible being that these two men had no especial *cause* to be interested — they put a brazen face on the affair and arrested all progress. Cunning as Wharton had been, he had made no more headway than Franklin. You could no more make a river run uphill than oblige a British ministry in 1772 to take a positive and creative decision on an American question.

Franklin knew this, and that was why he aged comfortably, without security, without leaving London, and without really settling there, from 1770 to 1774.

VI

Nothing happened.

The passing years seemed only to prolong the Anglo-American quarrel; the newspapers were filled with monotonous phases of its development and the people were tired of reading about it.

Franklin was even more weary than they. For nearly ten years he had been in England, trying to present the petition of Pennsylvania which asked for royal government, and he was still wondering to what minister he could present it and what chance it would have of being favorably received.

His stay had certainly not been a success. His enemies had the game in their hands and could smile at his efforts.

However, when he considered his position, he felt he had to thank the Supreme Being for all his blessings. Besides all the various official appointments he enjoyed, he was the political adviser of Lord Shelburne, and one of the most active Whigs in London. If his political career were to end here, it would not be without some glory.

His name shone with an incomparable luster for other reasons than political. He had become the most illustrious scholar of the world. Since 1756 he had been a Fellow of the Royal Society of Science in London and of the Society for the Encouragement of Arts and Manufactures; in 1773 he was made a member of the Society of Antiquaries. He had been unanimously elected president of the American Philosophical Society in 1769, for both his friends and his enemies realized that the vigor of the society depended upon his prestige. He belonged to many foreign groups as well: the literary, scientific and artistic Society of Göttingen (1767), the Society of Experimental Science of Leyden, and the Royal Academy of Sciences of Paris (1772). His works were translated everywhere, and a complete edition of them appeared in Paris later making his fame a certainty in all parts of the civilized world.

He held the place that Newton had formerly occupied, and perhaps his reputation extended still farther. He was popularly known as the "Thunder-Master" and ladies of the French court repeated the verse Turgot had written: "*Eripuit cælo fulmen sceptrumque tyrannis*." (He has snatched the lightning from the heavens and the tyrant's scepter.) Princes and scholars erected lightning rods everywhere to protect people from the blind brutality of the elements, and wherever they were raised the name of Franklin was celebrated. The petty princes of Germany rivalled each other in their enthusiasm. The Grand Duke of Tuscany, the most enlightened ruler of his time, as well as the Chief of the Republic of Venice, put up lightning rods on all their public buildings; the Academy of Sciences recommended them in France, and throughout England, manors and powder magazines were equipped with them; His Most Christian Majesty supplied all his vessels with lightning rods, and an especially large one surmounted the rooftree of the Queen's palace in London, a convincing emblem of the triumph of science.

Many people didn't understand how lightning rods were a protection, and the more Franklin's invention was adopted, the more the doctor appeared to the masses as a benevolent magician. In this sceptical and bored century people were willing to lose their religion, but they demanded picturesque diversions; thus Franklin, the wise scholar of Philadelphia, was ranked among the host of famous enchanters: with St. Germain, who had spoken with Solomon and who could enlarge diamonds as others fattened pigs; Casanova, who seduced women and dominated the Devil; Swedenborg, who was interrupted in eating a steak, by a blow from God, in order that the existence of angels should be revealed to him, and Cagliostro, who had chatted with Jesus Christ and cured humanity by establishing an Egyptian Freemasonry.

All these men, whether mad or wise, were adored by fashionable people and venerated by the masses. The scholars were jealous but bowed down before them like the rest. However, Doctor Franklin was both a great scholar and one of these strange apostles, for, like their magic exhibitions, his inventions fascinated the imagination, and he knew how to juggle with the passions of men.

The scholars and philosophers who visited England at this time never forgot the spectacle which Franklin presented one autumn afternoon at Bowood. Lord Shelburne was entertaining quite a large party at his castle; there were a number of scholars from both the Continent and England, some able ministers who succeeded in purifying God, such as Priestley and Price; other churchmen who were expert in avoiding God, like the Abbé Morellet of France who ministered to courtesans and atheists; and some lords and ladies. Franklin seemed to be a little detached from all this group, his face seamed with age and lined with wisdom. He walked slowly down the wide alleys of the park, which were colored by the fallen leaves, and leaning heavily on his stout cane as he progressed, he conversed with Abbé Morellet. They talked about the Bible and science, and Franklin, half-smiling, said that the Biblical miracles no longer seemed like miracles to him, that he could calm the waters quite as easily as Jesus Christ. The Abbé was too polite to contradict him but too educated to believe the statement. He looked at a pond that gleamed near by through the trees and thought that he could soon prove that Franklin was exaggerating.

Franklin sensed what was going on in his mind, and calling the company together, they went to the pond. A slight breeze was ruffling its surface with a thousand tiny ripples, and Franklin slowly encircled it while the party waited in a curious silence. Then, raising his staff abruptly, Franklin whirled it three times above the water and inscribed some magic hieroglyph in the air. With a wave of his hand, Franklin then turned to the company and showed that the water was calming down.

In a few moments the pond was as glassy as a mirror and a vague light glimmered over the immobile watery surface.

The spectators stared at each other without knowing what to think. Then they surrounded the doctor, overwhelming him with compliments and adulation, but he escaped from them and disappeared down a shady walk, still conversing with Morellet. He leaned on his cane heavily and laughed softly.

The Abbé was frankly mystified, so Franklin then showed him that his staff was hollow and that he had filled it with oil. It was this oil, spread over the water, which had stilled it. A hedge fortunately hid them from the others, for the Abbé burst into a clear peal of laughter which was joined by Franklin. They laughed all the more when they saw through the twigs that the party was still standing by the pond, fearfully exclaiming over the event.

Franklin's miracles were the delight of the crowd, and deeply appreciated by the philosophers and the Masons, for they enlightened humanity and made for progress. All the lodges of France and England sang the praises of their illustrious brother.

It was no small advantage to have them on his side. The lodges began to exercise a profound influence over the social and political life of Europe. In England Freemasonry was already deeply rooted; in Prussia, Frederick the Great was a Brother and Patron; in Tuscany, the virtuous Grand Duke encouraged the Masons in every way, and in France they had conquered the most vigorous groups of the clergy, nobility, and the middle class, and were becoming increasingly important. The Masons wanted to spread their "new light" (as the "philosophers" defined it) everywhere; they constantly attacked the Established Church and its political domination, and they preached liberty and equality. Franklin and his career was the best example of their ideals.

Even up to this period of his busy old age, Franklin was faithful to Masonic principles. He printed the Deistical pamphlet of his friend, Doctor Barbeu Dubourg, first in English at London, and then in French, for Dubourg was afraid to bring it out in his own country. Then to further rationalize Deism in Great Britain, he revised the prayer book of the

Church of England. He was aided in this work by Lord Le-Despenser, who was an expert in blasphemy, and who knew how to make religion suit the taste of those who didn't like it.

This was all a part of the fantastic preparation for the overwhelming of the world. In the beautiful white and gold salons, the scholars pronounced the words which the people were later to shout in the streets, brandishing their pikes on which were fixed the heads of their enemies, — their friends.

Doctor Franklin dreamed only of peace, of a gentle and glorious disappearance from the world. He felt that his hour was coming; his admirers were increasing, but all his old friends were leaving and their departure was a warning to him. He had to accept the decline of age. His good old Debby was very ill; no doubt he would never see her again. His comrades of the Junto disappeared one after the other, and the young people began to take on responsibilities: Polly Stevenson married a doctor and left her mother's home, though she returned frequently; Sally Franklin married a farmer who lived near London; his nephews, the Williamses, after a short stay (1770–1772), returned to Boston, and the house on Craven Street, which was always comfortable, became as peaceful as a harbor at a low ebb.

Franklin often went to Twyford to have a change. Jonathan Shipley, who was the Bishop of St. Asaph, and one of the most ardent Whigs among the high clergy, was his friend there. He had several charming daughters, and Franklin always found affection and veneration awaiting him in Shipley's home. He was especially fond of Georgiana, who was a young girl then, with fine features — the chin was perhaps a little sharp — and childish but delicate ways. Franklin gave her presents and she recounted her troubles to him. One of his gifts was a Pennsylvania squirrel, which she fondled and petted, but the little animal did not live long, and when it died the whole house was in mourning. Franklin wrote two epitaphs, one of them sad and pompous, the other gay and realistic, and he promised another squirrel, asking Deborah to send it. He gave good advice to these charming daughters, telling them to marry well and to work hard; and in return he received their confidence with that youthful smile which encouraged him to enjoy the last pleasures the world could offer him.

He chose Twyford as the place where he would write his autobiography. He had begun it in 1770, for the purpose of justifying himself to his son, who had been separated from him by politics and circumstances. He wrote also to guide his descendants, for Franklin never gave up the idea of founding a dynasty. William and William Temple were to be the ones to realize his dream, and his memoirs should be passed on to them as the will of the founder of their race. He felt a melancholy pleasure and some pride in reviewing the humble scenes of his childhood, the disturbing memories of his first adventures in London, where every one loved him and no one menaced him. While Georgiana and her sisters played under his study window, Franklin wrote line after line saturated with youth and dedicated — without his knowing it — to the invincible youth of the world.

It seemed to him that he was making a farewell to the future before leaving this world, and he did not delay. Every spring he made his preparations. In 1773 he wrote to his friends that he was going to return to America in autumn, and that he would renounce all political activity in order to have a good rest. William and he were in political disagreement, for the Governor of New Jersey believed that England was the legitimate sovereign of America, while Benjamin recognized only the supremacy of the King. His old friend Strahan was no longer intimate with him either. He had become the printer to the King, and he was worried to see Franklin engaged in such mad adventures. He had gently closed his newspaper to him, *The London Chronicle*, and Franklin now had to make his propaganda in the *Public Advertiser*. Alarming news arrived from Boston; the Assembly censured him for his negligence in keeping them informed; both the friends of the former agent and of Arthur Lee, his new assistant, attacked him, the former out of vengeance, the latter to make a clear place for the newcomer. Franklin had published in London the "Letters of a Pennsylvania farmer" (Dickinson), which he didn't quite approve of. Nevertheless, it didn't stop Allen, his son-in-law, Dickinson, and they continued to assert that Franklin had invented the Stamp Tax. His old friends, the Whartons, thought that by his trickery and jealousy the Ohio Company was kept from succeeding. They suspected him of intrigues. The British Government spied on him and considered him so unfavorably that the members of the Ohio Company were afraid their concession would be refused just because the name of Franklin was found on its papers. Lord North avoided Franklin, and Lord Dartmouth, who was always polite, good and Christian, took refuge in his virtue in order to keep from making any hostile gesture.

Franklin's position had become delicate and false. He continued to serve with Foxcroft as the postmaster-general of America, which was a royal office; he was agent for the Pennsylvania Assembly which was very moderate, for the New Jersey government of his son, which was very Tory, and for the Massachusetts Assembly, which was very radical. The Massachusetts parliamentarians were especially eager to badger all royal officers, and they would not acknowledge England's right to take a revenue from America. Now the post office furnished a very pretty little revenue to England and Franklin had his share of it. After the reprimand which had come from Boston, people thought that at the next difficulty, the Massachusetts Assembly would recall Franklin without thanking him.

He could count only on a party of liberal patriots who lost ground every day, and on a few influential but not highly respected politicians such as LeDespenser, who had a shady past, and Shelburne, whom every one hated. Shelburne was the real patron of Franklin at this moment, when every one, in Parliament and out, were unanimous in their dislike. He was ordinarily called "Malagrida"; Fox said that he was "a perfidious and infamous liar"; Burke and Horace Walpole saw in him "a Catalina and a Borgia"; the King, who was in agreement with his subjects but more moderate, called him "the Jesuit of Berkeley Square." The worst was that Shelburne could not count on any party. He was rich enough not to be bothered by financial cares, but he was not solid enough to make a good support.

Strahan, Hutton, and some gentlemen close to the King continued to serve Franklin, nevertheless. And the doctor felt protected. He thought that he was loved by the virtuous young monarch. Pains had been taken to assure the King of Franklin's honesty. But Franklin didn't know how often his letters had been opened, and how their contents had shocked the simple mind of His Majesty.

However, he guessed the danger, and though he continued to petition and make visits, he prepared for his departure. Irritation and indignation inspired him and he published the most brilliant attacks on the British administration he had ever written: in June, 1772, an article on "Tolerance in Massachusetts and England", in September, 1773, the famous "Edict by the King of Prussia" and the "Rules for Reducing a Great Empire to a Small One."

In the former pamphlet, Franklin imagined the King of Prussia as claiming to impose upon England — a country which had been colonized long before by Prussian emigrants — the same duties which England was trying to impose on America. Thus Frederick the Great taxed England's trade and hindered its development. The "Edict" was written in a burlesque, pompous style which seemed so real that many readers were deceived by it. Franklin had written it in a few hours. The other pamphlet, more serious and more incisive, was a summing up of all the main faults England had committed. Like a good chess player, Franklin revealed all the methods by which the British Government could ruin the situation. Neither of these pamphlets were signed, but well-informed people knew where they came from. They dissipated Franklin's spleen.

But he needed more than this. He dreamed of returning to America with the relations between the two countries on a firm footing, and all shadow of suspicion removed from his character. By ousting the enemy of America, Hillsborough, Franklin and his friends paved the way to a reconciliation, and the appointment of Lord Dartmouth as minister of the colonies had given them a thousand hopes. They wanted to push their success still farther, and get rid of all the other officials of the administration who were anti-American. The most brilliant among them was also an inveterate enemy of Franklin, Thomas Hutchinson, the distinguished Governor of Massachusetts. He considered Franklin as a low middle-class politician, a revolutionist and a none too scrupulous journalist, and hindered his recognition as the agent for the Massachusetts Assembly. Franklin was thus deprived of his salary. Hutchinson had also spied on him and copied his correspondence. He harmed him in every way, direct or indirect, that was in his power.

The inviolability of letters was not much respected in the eighteenth century, and the wall of privacy was not impervious to political passions. Without making any expenditure, the ministry had copied all of Franklin's letters to his son and Galloway. The result was a little portfolio which would be very convenient, if they wanted Franklin to be hanged. Of course, this was a game which could be played by two, and Franklin bought up everything in sight that interested him in the way of letters and documents. Lackeys sold him the old papers of their masters, and the clerks of the ministry copied all the communications of the governors and of the ministers for him. The most precious of these acquisitions was a bundle of letters written by Hutchinson, Oliver and Bernard, all royal officers of Massachusetts. These private letters concerned public events and had been addressed to William Whately, Secretary to Lord Grenville, at Grenville's request. They were in the nature of political reports for the Great Parliamentarian, who was then a member of the Privy Council, and they were very hard on the Americans. Hutchinson, Bernard and company recommended that force be employed to down the rebel element in Massachusetts. Grenville read and studied these reports and then showed them to his friends, collaborators and partisans: Lord Temple, Richard Jackson, William Fitzherbert, etc. There was a lot of gossip about them in London.

John Temple mentioned them to Franklin. Since he had crossed the Atlantic with Franklin in 1757, he had had a brilliant and stormy career. Owing to his high family connections, he had obtained the posts of surveyor-general of the customs for the Northern District of America, and of lieutenant-governor of New Hampshire. Because of his handsome face he won the daughter of the rich and illustrious Bostonian, James Bowdoin, for his wife. And thanks to his Whig convictions, he enjoyed great popularity among the Bostonians but was extremely unpopular among the Tory officials of America. He had engaged in a sharp struggle with Hutchinson, who thereupon denounced him in London and almost succeeded in ruining his career. He lost his position as surveyor-general of the Customs, and had come to England to justify himself. His family saved him once more. Lord Temple protected him stoutly, and all the Temple parliamentary clan: Grenville and even Pitt defended him. He was presented as a martyr of Whigism, and at length he secured a still better position than he had held before. He was appointed the joint surveyor-general of the customs in England. Thus his administrative and parliamentarian situation was very strong. In America, he was the adviser, correspondent, secret agent and spy of the Patriot Party. Consequently, he desired the punishment of the traitor, Hutchinson, and he proposed a plan to Franklin which seemed very attractive to the wise philosopher.

Hutchinson and the others were Americans, not English, and yet they had proposed violent measures against their own compatriots. Temple felt that the pillory was the best place for them, and that putting them there would be the best possible initiative for either country. It would be one of the rare, efficacious means of stopping the slowly rising tide of Revolution in America. Hutchinson and Oliver had claimed in their letters that the struggle was only of two parties and not of two nations. If the Americans knew how to use this, and the English Government only took the opportunity, their mutual grievances might be easily adjusted.

Franklin had always wanted to have the King as arbiter. It was in him alone that he saw the possibility of conserving the Anglo-American union. The King was the logical center of the empire he had in mind. To denounce Hutchinson in order to whitewash George III, and then to obtain Hutchinson's recall from the King, would be an impressive maneuver that could easily lead to an Anglo-American understanding, and the rational organization of the empire.

The operation was dangerous but it might succeed, as Hutchinson had powerful enemies. Even Dartmouth did not like him, and Franklin saw that by uniting all the Whig forces, his friends, and the Temple clan, they would form an imposing opposition. But the affair had to to be handled discreetly and prudently, in order that a party of the accomplices would not become frightened and desert them at a critical moment.

Grenville, who had passed these letters about, died in 1770, and the letters were not returned. Copies were in the hands of Fitzherbert, who committed suicide on account of his money troubles in January, 1772. Whately, who had received the originals, died in June, 1772. Franklin found copies of these letters all about, and decided that the moment was propitious. The dead could neither accuse him nor defend themselves, and the danger of spreading these compromising letters seemed at a minimum. In December, 1772, he sent them to the Committee of Correspondence in Boston, and asked them to use the letters to enlighten public opinion but not to publish them.

Massachusetts was then far from calm. Since 1768 the government had been in a critical state. The Massachusetts Assembly had protested violently against the Townshend laws, which established custom taxes, and had been broken up as a punishment. Boston was placed under military government on September 1, 1768. Following this, there were nothing but brawls between the troops and the populace. In March, 1770, the soldiers fired on the civilians, and the indignation of the Bostonians became intense. Then they read the letters of Hutchinson and shook with rage. At first, they were read furtively, then passed about and copied. Finally, some one printed them. Franklin had not expected it would be otherwise; he was no child, but he had vaguely wished to remain in the shadow. His wish was granted at first, for no one knew where the letters came from.

The tumult they stirred up gained rapid headway, and the Assembly of Massachusetts decided to send a petition to the King. It was almost amiable in tone to the British Government, but insulting to Hutchinson (June, 1773). Franklin seemed to have succeeded in turning the course of the popular indignation into another channel. The Boston parliamentarians alleged in their petition that after such treason, Hutchinson could not be maintained as the governor of Massachusetts. It was strong, and differed from most American petitions, in that it was clear and direct.

The copies and the pamphlet which gave the text of the letters stirred up profound feeling in England. Every one asked who had stolen them and who had sent them to America. Franklin rested quietly in his corner and didn't breathe a word. People were still groping for an answer when a deplorable incident forced Franklin to admit he was the one.

Thomas Whately, the brother of Grenville's late secretary, was a confident, hot-headed, simple, fat banker. He worked for the government also, with much ministerial zeal, to the fullest extent of his mediocre intelligence. He had a remarkably middle-class mind, and he now thought that his situation was menaced and that the honor of his family was in jeopardy. He started to inquire, and found out that Hutchinson's worst enemy was John Temple. He remembered that shortly after the death of his brother, Temple had wanted to see Whately's papers, and had been authorized to take some of them (October, 1773).

Without hesitation, Thomas Whately concluded that Temple had stolen these Hutchinson letters and attacked Temple in some conversations with his friends. The newspapers took

AN ENGLISH CARTOON OF 1770

up the story (September 4, 1773). Hutchinson's friends quietly began a campaign for the governor in September and October. On November 29, the *Public Advertiser* formally denounced Temple. He protested on December 8 and begged Whately to rectify his error. Whately, who was furious over the affair and determined to find the guilty one, published an ambiguous and half-insulting answer to Temple's request (December 9, 1773). John Temple was hot-headed too. He immediately sent one of his friends, Izard, to challenge Whately to a duel, and they fought on the same day at four o'clock. Whately was pot-bellied and awkward, Temple was tall, deaf as a wall, and prematurely old. Both men were so irritated that they didn't take the trouble to wait for their seconds. First they used pistols, without any result. Whately didn't know how to use any arms. They continued the duel with swords. Whately didn't know anything about them either, whirled his sword around like a brush, and was so furious that he shortly had Temple at his mercy. Temple knew how to fence, but he didn't want to massacre Whately, and when Whately asked him to acknowledge he was beaten, Temple didn't hear but fought straight on. Rain began to fall and twilight darkened the field. The men stamped in the mud and fought like tramps, losing all consciousness of how they were acting. At last Whately received a wound, and he slipped, panting. Temple wounded him a second time in the back. Whately thought that he was lost and cried for mercy. Temple was too deaf to hear him and would certainly have killed him, had not some men, coachmen and innkeepers, run up and stopped the fighting. When Temple finally understood that Whately had yielded, he knelt down with tardy gallantry and helped his adversary to stand. The seconds arrived just in time to witness this touching scene, the conclusion of an odious and ridiculous duel in which two men of the world had behaved like scoundrels.

All London spoke about the duel. Both Temple and Whately were ridiculed, and the latter, who thought that his honor had been washed clean by the shedding of his blood, saw that he had to begin all over again. His friends affirmed that Temple had acted like a brute. There was talk of a new duel, which could only be more absurd and more bloody.

Benjamin Franklin was then staying at the Shipley's in Twyford. The rumors of this stupid and disagreeable story soon reached him. He was annoyed and saw the danger. Whether Whately killed Temple, or Temple killed Whately, there would be an enormous scandal. If he kept his silence, the "Grenvillites" and the friends of Temple would never pardon him. So on Christmas Day, 1773, Franklin sent a letter to the *Public Advertiser* in which he affirmed that he was the only one who had been responsible for the sending of the letters to America. The stupidity of the two duellists had forced him to compromise himself — something his enemies had never succeeded in doing. Since the preceding November 25, Franklin had tried to have this duel avoided by sending letters to the *Public Advertiser* which were signed, "A Member of Parliament", and which entirely exonerated Temple without revealing the real culprit. But now he was denouncing himself under his own signature. He was no longer the Franklin who was cunningly preparing an ambush for Hutchinson and the Ministry, but an unfortunate man, exposed to the wrath of those in power and the indignation of the crowd.

For, after all, he was a royal dignitary, and by this act he had betrayed another royal official to the detriment of their mutual administration. He could allege that he was only doing his duty as agent of the Massachusetts Assembly, but he certainly was not respecting the conventions as the postmaster-general for His Majesty in America.

If these two functions were incompatible he was certainly wrong to keep both of them. As postmaster-general he was supposed to be particularly respectful of the privacy of letters, but here he had procured these compromising documents in a manner he refused to reveal. Even if the proceeding were honest, the action was not. He had no right to spread abroad the letters of a citizen without that person's permission, nor to denounce another official without consulting their mutual chiefs.

In the face of these accusations, Franklin could allege that these Hutchinson letters were of a public character, that they had passed through all kind of hands before coming to his, and that by sending them to Massachusetts he was really rendering the ministry a service as he diminished their responsibility.

These arguments were listened to favorably in America, but not in England, where Franklin was above all a royal officer. And Franklin was in England. That was what alarmed his friends. Franklin counted on the inertia of the administration, the numerous enemies of Hutchinson, Lord Dartmouth's friendship, and the good will of the King. But all this was a *mistake!*

He had presented the petition of the Massachusetts Assembly for the recall of Hutchinson to the Privy Council of the King. The petition cited the letters. It was delayed and delayed, and Franklin, who had first hoped for a solution, despaired, thinking that it would be buried under the papers of the ministers just as the others. So he was rather surprised on Saturday, January 8, to be summoned to appear before the Privy Council on the Tuesday following, in order to discuss the petition. Franklin went there with Bolan, the other agent of Massachusetts, and obtained a delay of three weeks without much trouble, in order to put his papers in order and to instruct his lawyer. He was told that he would have to explain how he came by the Hutchinson letters.

All London discussed the affair. The ministers and their employees seemed furious concerning the loss of the letters and accused one man and another. John Temple didn't appear at all innocent, as he had announced the letters to his friends in America just at the time Franklin sent them over; Richard Jackson, the tricky agent for the Americans, who had enjoyed the confidence of Grenville for so long, was also mentioned; but William Fitzherbert of Tissington, Member of Parliament, and Commissioner for the Board of Trade and Plantations, was especially blamed. In the midst of the financial difficulties which preceded his suicide, Fitzherbert had been forced to make money any way he could. Franklin's letter had cleared Temple, although the latter remained suspected of complicity; Jackson's innocence was recognized by the Government as he enjoyed such high favor; and as for Fitzherbert he was dead, and his eldest son was held in such esteem by the King that these attacks could not seriously hurt him. The English newspapers made Fitzherbert the scapegoat.

But the vengeance of the Government fell on Franklin.

The meeting of the Privy Council, presided over by Lord North, was to take place on January 29, 1774. Hutchinson was to be represented by an American named Mauduit, and a fiery Scotch lawyer, Wedderburn, the solicitor-general who was accused of being mercenary, as he was always trimming his sails to be on the side of the majority. Franklin employed one of the most cunning and homely lawyers of England, Dunning.

On the morning of the twenty-ninth, he dressed carefully in his fine suit of "spotted" somber Manchester velvet. Then he put on his largest wig and took his magic staff. The meeting was held in the Cockpit Tavern, the room in which Franklin and Wharton had formerly triumphed over Hillsborough. To-day another group of elegant men were pushing at the door. Thirty-five members of the Privy Council sat around the table, all in full dress and wearing their decorations. Owing to the smallness of the room the number of spectators was limited, but it was very distinguished. There were Lee, Burke, Bancroft, Jeremy Bentham, Priestley and several others.

Franklin sat near the chimey place, and assumed his most serene and immobile expression. The fire crackled softly beside him. Dunning spoke first. He presented the letters and the petition, taking care to show that it was only the humble demand of the people of Massachusetts and nothing more. His discourse was brief but excellent, judicious and cold. Then Wedderburn stood up to speak and the execution of Franklin began. Wedderburn spoke for an hour, denouncing Massachusetts and insulting Franklin to his face. He pounded the table with his fist as he ranted on, calling Franklin a "thief" and comparing him to Zanga, the African murderer in Young's poem. In short, he gave Franklin a merciless drubbing.

Wedderburn was not much respected. This little scene, no matter how disagreable it was, would not have been serious if the members of the council had not shown that they were highly pleased with it. They nudged each other, snickered when Wedderburn said something particularly vulgar, and stared at Franklin as if he were a curiosity. Franklin had frequented the homes of these polite noblemen for seventeen years, but to-day was the first time he knew the extent of their scorn. Shelburne, Priestley, and Burke were furious, but they could do nothing. The pitiless meeting seemed to be interminable. It was also useless, as it could give no legal or administrative result. It came to an end only when the solicitor-general for Great Britain had vented all his spleen and was applauded by the most fashionable men of the kingdom.

During this time, Franklin lost all the illusions he had on England, her aristocracy, and all the hopes which turned on the future of the Anglo-American empire. His face remained immobile, but in two hours his mind had changed its orientation. He left the room calmly, shaking hands with some of his friends silently at the door, and then went off alone, a stranger.

Two days later (Monday, January 31, 1774) he received a letter from the postmaster-general, which informed him that his position had been taken away from him. He understood what this signified. The King had rejected him. The British Government and the King had thus eliminated the one American who could still have directed the evolution of his country towards England.

They also made an end to the moderate Patriot Party in America and put the colonies into the hands of those who wanted war.

By this master stroke the British Government gave a

popular leader to the Americans, a man who was respected throughout the world, and they made the uncertain union of Massachusetts and Pennsylvania a certainty.

Franklin, who had never been in favor of violence, and who found resistance by force to be odious, was carried away by the current of events. The insults of Wedderburn and the lords had awakened all his middle-class hatred for the nobility, and the loss of his post turned him definitely to revolt. He was thirsty for vengeance. He sent the plan of a private post office to his friends in Pennsylvania and Massachusetts, which would permit the merchants to do without the British post and which would soon ruin the latter. At the same time he wrote to his son:

> This line is just to acquaint you that I am well, and that my Office of Deputy Postmaster is taken from me. As there is no Prospect of your being ever promoted to a better Government, and that you hold has never defray'd its Expense, I wish you were well settled in your farm. 'Tis an honester and a more honourable, because a more independent employment. You will hear from others the Treatment I have receiv'd. I leave you to your own Reflections and Determinations upon it. . . .

William's reflections were profound, and he decided at length that he was a royal officer. And as such, he remained faithful to the principle that the King could do no wrong. He wrote very politely to his father, urging him to return to America and to spend a peaceful old age among his friends, who admired him, and his family, who loved him. To their mutual friends in England he wrote that he did not share the political views of his father. Thus their paths separated.

The height of the crisis was held in abeyance for several months. At the moment when Wedderburn insulted Franklin, to the delight of all England, the people of Massachusetts lost patience. Some brave Bostonians, disguised as Indians, boarded a boat of the East India Company and dumped its cargo of tea into the harbor. The captain had paid the customs tax on it which the Americans refused to recognize. Secret societies and revolutionary organizations dominated all the cities and villages of New England. If a British official resisted them, he was tarred and feathered and had to ride a rail through the town. The lukewarm Royalists were treated in the same way. The Revolution had begun.

This news arrived in England at the same time as Wedderburn's triumph. It stirred up great agitation in governmental circles and among the people; measures to repress the rebels were immediately voted. The most serious of them was to close the port of Boston. Of course, the people put the two events together, and concluded that Franklin was the cause of everything; Matthew Robinson Morris, second Baron of Rokeby, one of the most mediocre pamphleteers of the time, and so one of the best mirrors of public opinion, wrote in his pamphlet, "Considerations on the Measures Taken in Regard to the American Colonies" (1774): "Our colonies might be well enough were it not for Dr. Franklin, who has with a brand lighted from the clouds set fire to all America."

Up to now, Franklin had been considered as a sly, malignant man, who had his price; since 1763 he had been suspected by the American public, for he had been too subtle, and used methods which they could only interpret incorrectly. But now, having been solemnly condemned by the British Government, Franklin found he possessed an incomparable popularity. Scorn had changed into a respectful hate. He became a symbol.

He was no longer the tricky negotiator; he was a hero, who, whether guilty or wise, had risked his life for a sublime cause. The Americans went into transports of enthusiasm. In Philadelphia, Wedderburn and Hutchinson were burned in effigy, and to make the fire all the merrier, they kindled it by an electric spark. The Bostonian Patriots sent Franklin their congratulations and their best wishes.

Even though some of the English newspapers insulted him, and others, like the *London Chronicle* of his old friend Strahan, gave him the cold shoulder, he had ardent defenders also. The *General Evening Post*, and the *Public Advertiser* wrote many articles of praise and printed many letters from readers which covered Wedderburn with insults. Franklin was far from being isolated. Chatham, Shelburne, LeDespenser, Lord Stanhope, Hartley, all his old and new friends, showed him their esteem.

For the first time since he had arrived in England, Franklin was fashionable in high society. Up to now he had appeared as an intelligent, boring and suspicious personage. The scandal had suddenly simplified the situation and made him glorious. He was the creator of the American Revolution and its symbol. Dinner engagements flooded his mail, and ladies begged him to visit them. They would shiver as they listened to him talk and were utterly delighted. Even such a blue-stocking as Mrs. Montagu was only too happy to welcome him, and there was no end to the messages and presents he received from the continent. England had made him a world hero, in spite of himself.

He didn't tire of the sudden change, and once more his departure was postponed. Deborah was slowly dying in Philadelphia, and decisive events were being prepared there, only awaiting the magic presence of Franklin to make them real. He remained in England, however, to revel a little more in his glorious catastrophe and to wait.

It always seemed to him as if something were going to happen, and not much was needed to have made this protracted stay in England cost him dearly. Lord Dartmouth was very angry at him, all the more since he had formerly esteemed Franklin so highly; and the King was also opposed to him on account of his duplicity. They decided to set a trap. They had some of the letters Franklin had written in 1773 to the Massachusetts Assembly, and they considered them as evidence of high treason. However, they did not press the matter, as they had heard of other letters still more compromising and more recent, which they were trying to secure. Dartmouth had written to Gage, instructing him to send them, and they were now waiting for them from one mail to another. Should they arrive at the same time as tidings of bloody brawls in New England, Franklin ran the risk of being sent to prison — or worse.

Franklin knew this, but stayed on just the same, coddled by Mrs. Stevenson and flattered by English ladies who wanted to be kissed by him, and who always found him obliging. In the meantime he was meditating an important step.

Then he received a signal honor, — a note from Lord Chatham, who wanted to see him. It was as much a surprise as the humiliation he had received at the Privy Council. Lord Chatham, the greatest Englishman of his time, had at last been attracted to Franklin, by his magnificent catastrophe, and invited him to come to Hayes, his country house, where they could talk over a plan of Anglo-American reconciliation. He thought that with Franklin's aid he could swing a parliamentary group which would influence the King to repeal all laws disagreeable to the Americans; he dreamed that there would at length be a British Empire extending from the North Sea to the Pacific.

From August to December, Franklin made countless visits: to Shelburne, at Bowood, to LeDespenser at West Wycombe, to Mr. Sargent at Halsted, to Lord Stanhope at Chevening, and to Lord Chatham at Hayes. People bowed to him everywhere, and statesmen were glad to ally themselves with him. They wanted to prepare a *coup d'état* in Parliament similar to the repeal of the Stamp Act.

Franklin had his hands free; his enormous new American popularity permitted him to act as he wanted, while his jealous colleague, Arthur Lee, always in advance of events, had just made a dangerous voyage in Continental Europe. Since Chatham's letter, Franklin thought such haste was not necessary. He did not want to precipitate events. It still seemed possible to him to turn the American troubles into a purely political conflict, and have this conflict succeed in a triumph for the Whigs. A ministry with Chatham, Shelburne and Franklin was much more attractive than a civil war. And during the autumn months of 1774, it seemed that it would be possible to come to this triumphant result.

Every one came to ask him his good offices. Chatham had asked to see him, and then asked him the preliminary question: Does America want to be independent? Franklin answered with an emphatic negative. Chatham was then reassured and promised to promote a plan of reconciliation which would be satisfactory to both countries, at least to the Whigs. When Franklin knew all the details of this plan, he was not completely satisfied, for Chatham, always a stickler for parliamentary doctrine, had insisted on the theoretical sovereignty of Parliament, which the Americans refused to admit. But if a new misunderstanding would effect a successful reconciliation, Franklin was only too ready to consent.

He was all the more flattered when he received solicitations from the Quakers and the illustrious Howe family to prevent war. His old friend Fothergill, and the great merchant Barclay, prepared a program of reconciliation during the month of November, and undertook to present it to the ministers. Lord Howe had his sister invite Franklin, and then passed by at her house to talk with him as they played chess. Howe, who was virtuous, liberal, and beloved by the King, was popular in America because of the military renown of his family, and he wanted to appear as a peace-maker in the New World.

For both Howe and Fothergill, Franklin drew up the plans which were shown to the ministers. In these critical hours, his idea was that an understanding was still possible, if the King would forbid violent measures against America, and if the Parliament would give up its claim to suzerainty. He wanted to make the reconciliation a permanent one, by establishing a New Congress for all the colonies, in Philadelphia. If the King would use this Congress to govern America, there would be no doubts about the colonists' loyalty and everything would go smoothly. Thus he returned to his great idea of an Anglo-Saxon empire, governed in Europe by the King and the British Parliament, and in America by the King and the American Parliament. The two bodies would cease to be rivals under such circumstances and would collaborate. Franklin was so taken with this idea that he was willing to reimburse the East India Company out of his own pocket for the tea which had been thrown overboard.

Franklin was listened to with pleasurable attention. The King, Lord North and Lord Dartmouth all abhorred the idea of a civil war. They were ready to make great sacrifices to escape it. Franklin worked night and day, almost drunk with hope. After a short period of illness in the spring, he recovered his energy and spent his strength heedlessly.

The suit which Whately had started against Franklin, in order to clear the memory of his brother, continued slowly, as the British Government was not anxious to extend this scandal; Franklin did not have to worry about it. He concentrated his efforts on influencing the public. The publisher, Almon, printed pamphlets for him which the people were always eager to read. The most important of them was written by Arthur Lee. It was a methodical and calm summing up of the quarrel. At the same time, Franklin had printed a speech and a sermon of his friend, the Bishop of St. Asaph, in order to impress the liberal Anglicans, as well as publishing a pamphlet of Priestley which was written to reach the Unitarians, and other liberal Protestants. In February, Franklin himself wrote a series of articles which were printed in the *Public Advertiser*, and in November, still another. He also prepared a pamphlet to dissipate the bad impression of the Hutchinson affair. In all of these writings he emphasized the horrors of civil war. The most audacious of them was, "The Intended Speech for the Opening of the First Session of the Present Parliament", in which the King is made to declare, "Now, Gentlemen of the House of Commons, I give you this fair notice for yourselves and your constituents. If you undertake this job, it will cost you at the last farthing a good round sum of 40 to 50 millons; 40 to 50 thousands of your Constituents will get knocked on the head and then you are to consider what the rest of you will be gainers by the bargain even if you succeed!" This was not a writing that could be printed; it was passed about in manuscript secretly. Oh, if the King had only spoken in this wise! The Anglo-Saxon empire would have been saved and the English Parliament would have received the most useful lesson ever given to a constitutional body!

But it was precisely this that neither the King, nor the people, nor Chatham wanted; Franklin could deceive himself on the subject if he wanted, but even the most ardent enthusiasts for America were forced to confess it. The Bishop of St. Asaph said in 1773: "The only point in which the Administration seems to have the People on their side is in asserting the sovereignty of the Mother Country."

And Burke in September, 1774, said the same thing. "I agree with your Lordship entirely; the American and foreign affairs will not come to any crisis sufficient to rouse the public from its present stupefaction during the course of the next session . . . the insensibility of the Merchants of London is of a degree and kind scarcely to be conceived!"

However, Franklin still counted on them and worked steadily. He had petitions written which were favorable to the Americans, and had them sent from all the industrial cities of England which were touched by the crisis. He fired the zeal of the London merchants. During the autumn elections he encouraged the boldest Whigs to put an American plank in their platforms, and in the environs of London there was much strong speechifying. There were all kinds of war rumors, not only with America but with Spain, and Franklin hoped they would influence the people and the King to put an end to the internal quarrels, and that Parliament would let American matters alone.

His hope was only an illusion. The people didn't follow the Whig leaders who wanted to reorganize their party and to come into power again on the strength of an American reconciliation. The English people, especially the farmers and the Londoners, were extremely annoyed with the Americans, and enjoyed listening to the virulent speeches made against them by the Tories. Johnson, with his skillful pamphlet, "Taxation No Tyranny!" and Wesley, who appealed to the Methodists in favor of obedience to Parliament and the King, had much more success with the public than Franklin.

Chatham didn't want to humiliate Parliament. And the King didn't dare to pose as judge between America and England. After all, he was the King of England, and though he would be generous and pardon America, if America asked pardon, he could not place himself between her and England. Could he have done so? The idea would have seemed pure blasphemy to him. It was hazardous at least, even if it were brilliant.

Thus, eacn party had to resort to trickery. Dartmouth was trying to secure the letters which would incriminate Franklin, as he wanted to divide the Americans between themselves. They made Howe promise Franklin a substantial post if he would guarantee peace. Dean Tucker was heard from again in a pamphlet, reiterating the old story that Franklin had invented the Stamp Act and that he had promised tax receiverships to his friends. Franklin protested against this attack in vain. All during the summer rumors were spread in Massachusetts that Franklin was allied to the Royalists by means of a big bribe. In autumn, Strahan passed around a letter of William Franklin, which was filled with expressions of strong royalism, and which was very compromising for its author. Naturally this little scandal reflected on the father. Thus, in trying to make the most of Franklin's influence they were attempting to destroy it in America.

At first, he didn't pay any attention to these attacks. He was too busy. His activity had excited and rejuvenated him, and he undertook all kinds of work. He published a pamphlet on how to calm the sea with oil, aided George Whately to revise his book on the principles of trade, brought out a fifth edition of his scientific works in English, and the first Italian one, wrote innumerable letters to encourage trade, industry and agriculture in America, took up a work he had abandoned ten years past — the culture of silkworms in the New World — and recommended Bache to some English farmers who wanted to settle in Pennsylvania. He also sent over an adventurer, who was a Quaker, a Mason, an employee, a vagabond, and who wanted to establish himself in America. He was a self-taught and eloquent man, named Thomas Paine. Thus, while Franklin was preparing for peace, he had sent a man to America who was to unloose the most violent revolutionary passions of the people. But of course, Franklin hadn't realized the scope of his charity.

Nothing could turn him away from his great work; neither the death of his poor old wife (December, 1774) nor the misunderstandings which increased daily. He knew he was strong and cunning enough to win the liberty and happiness of America, by twenty years of bargaining, if he were only allowed to go his own way. He said to J. Quincy Jr. the young patriot, who had come from Massachusetts as an ambassador for the Revolutionists, that they were sure of winning over England without violence, if they would only be patient. There was no need to seek alliances with Spain or France, he claimed; the colonies had only to band together, refuse to buy English goods, and the laws hostile to America would be repealed within the year. His conviction was so profound that Josiah Quincy, who had arrived full of suspicion, was convinced that he was right. He believed in Franklin and returned to America. In these first months of 1775, a solution by violence seemed absurd to Franklin, and he would have staked his entire fortune on the probability of an Anglo-American reconciliation.

The only precaution he took was to keep in touch with his Dutch friends, the Physiocrat group, the French Chargé d'Affaires, Garnier, and some big French merchants, such as Holker, the founder of the Normandy textile industry. He even sent his nephew, J. Williams, on a business trip to France. But he refused to have correspondence with any official at Versailles or Paris. He remained a faithful subject to his British Majesty.

It was in vain. Chatham failed piteously in trying to persuade the Lords. In vain Franklin and Lee presented the moderate petition of Congress demanding justice. Neither the King nor the House of Commons paid any attention to it. The two agents received nothing but insults. One of the orators in the House of Lords even slandered Franklin. Chatham rebuked him sharply and the vaulted room resounded, as the greatest Englishman made a speech praising for the greatest American.

Howe insisted on his friendship and his desire to collaborate. Fothergill told Franklin time and again that he wanted to help him in his great work of peace-making. The Constitutional Society gave him a hundred pounds for the Boston refugees. But all of them must have seen that for the moment, at least, they were failing. They even had to confess that Franklin's liberty was in danger if he remained in England.

The most bizarre rumors about Franklin circulated in London: at the court they said he had gone to Switzerland, while others said he had left for France. Hutchinson said he had been arrested and put in prison. This rumor was the most popular one.

Franklin had to depart once more. He had delayed his departure for fourteen months, giving as an excuse the absence of Lee, the petition of Congress, and the projects of Chatham. Now, there was nothing to hold him. He was powerless in London, and had he stayed much longer in England, he would have been quite as weak in America.

Franklin went to see Burke and they talked about England and America. Franklin said, "America has achieved many happy days under her rule previous to this unhappy dispute and might possibly never see such again."

He sat for several hours at Mrs. Stevenson's fireplace and talked with her and Polly. Polly's husband had died six months past and the two women were rather sad. Franklin tried to be optimistic and said they would all see each other again. But he could not smile.

He received Priestley and they talked about science, as if they were to meet again the next day. But it was no use, and they found no pleasure in their conversation. The newspaper on the table was filled with the miseries of Massachusetts, now occupied by the British army. Together they read the warlike declarations of the other colonies which had been sent to Boston to encourage the revolutionists. Then they looked at each other, their eyes filled with tears. Of what use was intelligence — patience? The time for bargaining was over. Franklin had to go.

On March 25, 1775, he embarked furtively with his little grandson, William Temple, on the *Pennsylvania Packet* (Captain Osborne). The wind blew wildly and the waves were turbulent. The ship was soon pitching in the open sea, already far from England, far from the Kingdom of Great Britain, making slow headway to the empire which Franklin had dreamed about.

Its birth terrified him. He seemed to have lost everything, but behind the winds and the storm, his Empire was waiting for him.

BOOK FOUR

HIS EXCELLENCY, DOCTOR FRANKLIN, THE PATRIARCH

I

Doctor Franklin, a tired and vanquished old widower, slowly paced the deck of the *Pennsylvania Packet* as it sped over the waves to America. As he walked, he leaned on the arm of his slender, supple grandson, who looked with lively interest at the horizon. His fine features bore the imprint of William Franklin — he had the same slightly heavy chin — but he was called William Temple. The old man had lost everything in England and the young man owned nothing at all — not even a father.

All that Franklin had was his wisdom, and all that William Temple possessed were his hopes. Franklin now knew that the "virtuous young King" was a blockhead who had forsaken his duties as sovereign in order to remain a good Englishman, and consequently, to make the Americans pay. He knew the stupid vanity of that heavy, traitorous machine — the British Parliament; it was good only for fattening the sly aristocrats and for lining the pockets of the unscrupulous democrats. He knew, too, the baseness of the English crowd, which, when led by a Wilkes, threw mud at the lords and went shrieking through the streets, but which was incapable of realizing its own duties and true interests. Six months had passed since Franklin had lost all his illusions and almost all his faith. Masonry alone had not been a deception; in his worst moments it had befriended him, and its maxims had been a guide. He still counted on it.

He counted above all on life. The King, Parliament, and the crowd were hostile, and the fate of arms was always doubtful, but the God of Nature showed Franklin the way to victory. America could conquer England by the very simple means of increasing her population. It was not a matter of cannon but of birth statistics. America's birth rate doubled every twenty-five years, while that of Great Britain remained nearly stable. The colonists would only have to wait for fifty years when England would have to bow down before their gigantic numbers. And Franklin, the Patriarch, stroked the forehead of William Temple and dreamed of the victory that his grandson's children would have, when they would sweep away the enemy by the sheer force of their multitudes.

But here he had to temporize. Of what use was it to despoil and kill? He had spoken with Garnier, the French Chargé d'Affaires, before his departure, and said that America would neither submit nor attack. He wanted to establish a federal union between the colonies, in order to prepare for the future, to have the ports opened to foreign countries in order to stimulate the development of their commerce, and to make an offer of financial coöperation with England, in order to gain time and to make one last attempt at reconciliation. Such were the three points of his political program. His national program was also limited to three heads and they were phrased in the imperative form: Make money, Be economical, and, Have children.

He was a little too aged to set an example himself, but he was going to force his son, William, to recognize the illegitimate William Temple. As to the Baches, he had nothing to say; they had just had their second son and foresaw others.

Thus Franklin dreamed like a good Patriarch and a good Mason. But he was active too, and took the temperature of the sea with a thermometer, making the first discoveries relative to the Gulf Stream. William Temple held him company and talked about his future. He wanted to be a painter or a doctor, rather than a lawyer. The old man would hear none of it. He looked at William's slender, nervous hands and his lovely proud eyes, but in spite of them he decided that William should not be an artist, but an established middle-class lawyer, for when every one spoke of justice and enjoyed quarreling, a lawyer's profession was the best.

They were in the midst of their discussions when the tide and the strong wind brought them straight to Philadelphia, during the evening of Friday, May 5. They landed immediately. The sea behind them was less turbulent than the country they were entering.

The war had begun. Blood had been spilled. A royal troop, marching across the country, had been surprised by the American volunteers at Concord and Lexington on April 19. They had been forced to retreat and left behind them two hundred and seventy-three dead and wounded; the glory of Old England suffered a setback. This news inflamed the colonies with excitement, and the Congress met in Philadelphia in the midst of great stir. Delegations came from all parts of the country, by horse, wagon and boat; the Virginians and Carolinians were dressed in beautifully embroidered uniforms and were attended by their Negro slaves, fitted out in green and red; the monied New Yorkers wore rich velvet habits; and the Yankees of New England arrived in long overcoats, dusty from their tiresome journey, but speaking excitedly about it with glowing eyes.

Crowds flocked in front of Franklin; every one was anxious to be the first to tell the great man what had happened in America, to learn what was going on in England, and to show their veneration for him. His house was besieged for a week. Franklin was certainly a father who had returned to his children. He was acknowledged to be the Martyr of American Liberty, the Apostle of its Rights, and the Patriarch of the New World. The welcome he received made him twenty years younger.

But he didn't allow himself to be carried away by all this adulation. He listened carefully to everything that was said to him. All America was stirred up and vibrant; the people wanted no more of the English. The Patriots were unanimous on this point, and those who didn't rally to them, suffered. Thus Franklin's old friend and right-hand man, Galloway, was suspected of being a spy for the enemy, and he protested in vain that he was innocent (*Pennsylvania Gazette*, May 17). He was known to be a royalist and had to disappear. He retired to his estate at Trevose, weary and disgusted. Occasionally a letter from William Franklin encouraged him in his stand. William was still the governor of New Jersey, and as zealous a Royalist as ever, but his situation was becoming increasingly precarious. Franklin's old national-radical-royalist party had been ruined. He was famous because of the Wedderburn scandal, not for the numerous services he had rendered in the past.

To have no more of the English, however, was the one and only point on which the Patriots agreed. The people held enthusiastic demonstrations, not knowing what they wanted, and every political chief had his own program. The newspapers of Pennsylvania were filled with the praises of Thomas Penn, who had died in March at London, and the partisans of the Penns took up the wall once more. They profited by Galloway's fall and by the eloquent liberalism of their chief, Dickinson. But their leaders didn't agree among themselves. Dickinson wanted to go back to the old constitution of William Penn: a loose connection with England. The Quakers thought it was all right, so long as it did not entail war or expenses, to which they were formally opposed; the Presbyterians, on the contrary, preferred the use of force. Their leader, James Wilson, was a determined revolutionist. The Episcopalians were ordinarily Royalists. The rich merchants of Philadelphia were afraid of disorder. The German farmers, who didn't know what was happening, voted with the Quakers, as their wide hats and dignified manners seemed serious to them. If submission was mentioned every one rose up in protest. If independence was suggested, every one was shocked. The election of 1764 and Franklin's absence had their effect on Pennsylvania: internal politics were confused, and the leaders weak: Galloway was cunning but not very foresighted, Dickinson was honest, but long-winded and narrow-minded.

The other States were more firmly governed. In Massachusetts, the Masonic lodges and revolutionary committees led the dance. They had established a central group, which was determined on revolution, and capable of realizing it. It was the same in Virginia, where the aristocrats were ready to wield power and were tired of British rebuffs. The other little States followed them with enthusiasm but a little fearfully. They were definitely against England, but they were afraid of being swallowed up in a nation under the protectorate of Virginia, Massachusetts or Pennsylvania. Compared to Virginia and Massachusetts, which were well run, Pennsylvania had no influence at all, and her great leader, Franklin, was powerless. In local politics, he did not count except as a man with a famous name, and in national politics he was considered as a veteran of another age.

Everything proved it to him. On May 6, the day after his arrival, Franklin was unanimously elected by the Pennsylvania Assembly to be one of its representatives to Congress, but his point of view was shared by no one else in the delegation, which voted as a whole, so his influence was practically nil. Only his advice could be worth something, but he did not like to make long speeches, and many young politicians were yearning to make themselves heard. He was embarrassed also on account of his son and Galloway. In spite of his personal popularity, Franklin felt that he was suspected. On May 7, he wrote to William and urged him to give up his royal post, in favor of agriculture which was much more lucrative and much more respectable in revolutionary times. William did not think so. The two men did not understand the word "honor" in the same way. William understood it like a gentleman who has sworn allegiance to his King, Benjamin as a middle-class patriot who had faith in his country. The father remained affectionate, the son respectful. But it was a cruel sorrow for the old man. He sent a letter to Galloway, on May 8, begging him to return to public life as a revolutionist, but his plea was not very successful. All Franklin's political past went up in smoke.

Franklin then took his place at the Congress, and listened, silent and attentive. Sometimes he made a ten-minute speech on a question of principle or some important practical point. He urged religious toleration, defended the Moravian pacifists against the harsh measures of the Congress, protected the Royalist Episcopalians from the brutal persecution of the mob, and tried to develop a favorable attitude towards the Catholics. He protected the arts also. He saw to it that the embargo on

English goods was not applicable to scientific instruments. Franklin maintained an understanding among all these excited and enthusiastic men, by his good fellowship, serenity, and a few well-placed jokes.

To comfort some of his colleagues who were discouraged by all the internal quarrels, he told them the story of the two keepers of the Eddystone lighthouse. These men spent all winter together, their lighthouse perched on a solitary rock in the midst of storms, without seeing a soul. In autumn, all their winter provisions were brought to them but when spring came they were supplied regularly. One spring the visitors found only one man there. They asked him where his comrade was, and he answered that he must be up above; it was six months since he had seen him. The men were ready to arrest him as a murderer, when they found out that he was right. The two keepers had quarreled, shortly after the former visit, and had amiably divided the lighthouse in order not to bother each other. Thus they had spent the winter in *peace*.

Franklin liked this story because it illustrated for him the mood of parliaments in general and the value of peace. He loved peace, and although he was a good revolutionist he didn't stop working for the former but quietly tried to put his program forward. On July 21, he proposed a plan of federal union for all the English colonies of America, including Canada, the West Indies, and Ireland. This very curious plan showed Franklin's state of mind at that time. It included a weak legislative body (a Congress) which was elected annually, and annually changed its residence; an executive body which was still weaker, consisting of a council which was elected for three years by and in the Congress, a third of it being changed every year. This Assembly would have possessed very limited powers only: war, navy, trade, commerce, currency, and Indian affairs. If England had accepted this plan it could have become the basis of an imperial parliament and included peers. Franklin had foreseen all this also. At the same time, he suggested that the American ports be opened to foreign trade, and, as compensation to the British Government, one hundred thousand pounds should be contributed annually for the amortization of the national debt. This suggestion was inserted in the form of a clause in the response that Congress proposed sending to Parliament (June, 1773). It was discussed at length in Congress but nothing came out of it. The Liberals were too frightened of independence to accept the plan of union, and the Revolutionists were too anxious to have a strong government to approve of it. It was not voted on, and was not even entered in the Congressional Record, but was laid on the table for the future disposition of the members. The same fear was shown concerning the commercial plan. The conciliatory proposition was not sent off either, owing to the bad news from England and the hostile attitude of Parliament. Franklin had failed all along the line. For all his triumphal return, he had been only a figurehead in the Congress. Of course, he had been elected to several committees — ten, in all — but his practical initiative had not been followed. Franklin opposed in vain the new petition they wanted to send the King; in vain he struggled against a new issue of paper money which Congress was preparing. Parliamentary activity was not Franklin's specialty.

He was happier in his practical life: Congress elected him to be the postmaster-general of the American posts for a year, and this was a source of great joy to him (July 26, 1775). He was given a salary of a thousand dollars, plus the enormous power of naming all his employees. These included a secretary at three hundred forty dollars a year, local postmasters at divers salaries, and a large number of carriers; Franklin enjoyed choosing them. He imposed the new service on the inhabitants by his skill and strength, despite the fact that the British post office was still functioning. He didn't lose any time, and knew how to make use of the system which a journalist, Goddard, had started to elude the official service. After August 30, the American post office published its routes, and some months later it was fully organized: three deliveries a week for New York, two for the North, and two for the South.

He succeeded still better with the Provincial Committee of

Safety. This was a kind of revolutionary committee, formed of twenty-five patriots, and loosely connected with the Assembly. It grew stronger and stronger and gradually usurped the Assembly's authority. Franklin was the soul of this organization, and he knit it together with much skill. His scientific knowledge helped in arming the men, and in procuring saltpeter, gunpowder, etc., while his classical erudition stimulated his imagination. After having strung *chevaux de frise* across the Delaware and having prepared the forts on the banks, he considered establishing a fleet of rowboats, similar to the Roman galleys, and since there was not enough powder, he constructed a plan of arming the Americans with bows and arrows! Hadn't England won Agincourt because of them? And arrows did their work so silently and cleanly!

II

THE Patriarch had come from England as a peacemaker, fully expecting to return rejoicing to London in the autumn, and now he was deeply engrossed in warfare. There was a tense atmosphere of battle in all the colonies. At home, Franklin saw the little Bache boys marching with their toy guns and whistling by way of a fife. It was a touching homage to the War God. Then, too, there was his struggle with his only son. Benjamin's relationship with William was too delicate to continue; either William would have to renounce his policies or break off his connections. When Congress dispersed in August, 1775, Franklin took advantage of his leisure to visit William at his home in Perth Amboy. Both father and son passed some moving hours together, but all of Franklin's arguments came to naught. The two men did not speak the same language and so could not come to an understanding. William held to his standpoint rigidly and almost commanded his father to leave off his dangerous activities. They constituted treason in William's eyes. Franklin answered him with some feeling, talking about America as America, and reminding him of his filial duties. Elizabeth only wept. She was incapable of resisting Franklin or of helping her husband, and she could not keep from suffering. Young Temple looked at the scene feverishly, wondering what kind of a man this new grandfather was, and why he was breaking up the family when he had just joined them together. After some days, Franklin had to leave. He was beaten. King George had a faithful servant in William but Franklin had lost a son. Since the death of Francis, no sorrow had touched Franklin so profoundly.

Fortunately, there was much work waiting for him in Philadelphia. His books and furniture had just arrived from

London. He was able to have them landed by an authorization of Congress, and arranged them in his home where the Baches were living also. Congress met again, just at this time. More and more committees were formed, and Franklin was elected to the most important of them: Committee for Powder Manufacture (September 18), Committee for the Development of American Commerce (September 22).

At last he had to help Washington create an American army. The troops that had been gathered in Boston were courageous but undisciplined. A national army which would be solid, well-trained and respectful of its superiors was needed for the long war before them. It was also necessary that the army should not cost too much. In May, Congress had been swept with patriotic ardor which resulted in Washington's being appointed commander in chief, but since that time, months had been lost in aimless discussions, and now Congress wanted to rectify her errors and felt the need of action. Franklin was chosen to inspect the army at Cambridge. It was a difficult mission, but one which was suited to his practical mind, and he was aided by two other men, T. Lynch and B. Harris. The three left on October 4.

All New England was colored by the brilliant foliage of autumn, and the muffled excitement of war was in the air. Franklin stopped here and there to visit the postmasters, to stir up the patriotic zeal of the journalists and printers, and rested at the homes of his friends. On October 17, the delegates arrived at the headquarters, where they were received with much honor: the soldiers cheered them lustily, and the generals Washington and Mifflin offered great dinners with turtle soup. The most charming ladies of Boston acted as their hostesses, and the wise Doctor Franklin, whose appearance was so imposing, was much admired. Mrs. John Adams was deeply impressed by him and wrote:

> I found him social but not talkative; and when he spoke something useful dropped from his tongue. He was grave, yet pleasant and affable. You know I make some pretensions to physiognomy, and I thought I could read in his countenance the virtues of his heart,

among which patriotism shone in its full luster; and with that is blended every virtue of a Christian.

Mrs. Adams was a useful person to know, for she was talkative, educated — though Molière shocked her — and influential. Franklin had still livelier pleasures than these; he went to visit his dear friends, the Greens, saw Katy once more, and his sister Jane Mecom, who had taken up her home with them. He spent some days here, rejuvenated by the affection of these people, and when he went away he took their young son, Ray Green, with him as a talisman of youth. This brief vacation, his conversations with Washington and the invigorating atmosphere of the camp had given him much energy. He felt he had accomplished some good work; the big Council of War on October 18 marked the real beginning of the American military power. There it had been decided to create an army of thirty-six regiments, the main army rules had been drawn, a basis of collaboration with the Indians had been planned as well as the provisioning of the troops and the system of recruiting. The presence of the delegates from Congress was a convincing proof of the solidarity of the colonies, and the New England revolutionists could be certain that they were struggling for a new country, and not simply against an ancient tyrant. On their return to Congress, the delegates could testify to the loyalty of New England and the entire army without any overstatement.

After this charming military interlude, Franklin took up his tiring parliamentary work once more. On November 9, he was elected to the Assembly of Pennsylvania, along with a majority of his enemies and Liberals who were against independence. Following this, the Assembly elected him to the Provincial Committee of Safety. Since the preceding August he had been an Alderman of Philadelphia, and on January 26, the Philosophical Society of America once more elected him to be their president. In reality, these were all vain honors, and though they were pleasant, the Patriarch realized their vanity, — and their danger. He did not feel at his ease at all, for example, in the Assembly. It was like a prison to him, under the domination of Dickinson and the timid majority, and he felt that its lukewarm attitude would only result in making all of them, as well as himself unpopular. He avoided attending, and did not take part in the voting or discussions in which the principle of independence was severely condemned. He did not join the Assembly in swearing an oath to the King. Finally, he took advantage of his age and weariness to beg the Assembly to excuse him from his functions (February, 1776). The Assembly consented without too much ill grace, and that was the end to their relations. At the same time, he resigned his place as Alderman.

Once rid of these burdens, Franklin was ready for the great struggle of 1776. The beginning was hard. William had nothing but catastrophes. Lord Stirling, who had been watching him for twelve years, took the first occasion at hand to ruin him. This noble Lord was a member of the Council of New Jersey, and had accepted a military position at the Congress. William Franklin heard of it and immediately deprived him of his functions. The New Jersey Assembly was furious, and when Stirling succeeded in securing one of William's letters to Lord Dartmouth, in which the governor expressed his inalterable devotion to the King, it was too much altogether. The Assembly, once having read the document, considered William as a traitor and decided to treat him likewise. He was placed under a guard of soldiers to keep him from serving the King too well, or from fleeing. Benjamin Franklin knew all about it but he would not budge. Many thought he was like Brutus, others thought his political instincts stifled his paternal feelings. Still others, who were wiser, avoided talking about the subject and pitied him.

But Franklin had really no time to ask questions of himself or to suffer. After November 29, new duties piled on him in an ever-increasing load. A Committee of Secret Correspondence had been formed in Congress to establish connections between the Friends of America in England, and *outside* of England. Franklin took part in it even though it were high treason. If the revolution failed, it was certain he would be hung, anyway.

He was bound to the cause, body and soul. He worked for it without flinching. At first, he sought to establish diplomatic connections with foreign countries. A beautiful edition of Sallustius, which had been sent to him as a present from Don Gabriel de Bourbon, Infante of Spain, gave him the occasion not only to thank the prince but to inform him that America would be interested in an alliance. Dumas, who sent him a set of Vatel's works from Holland, was also a disciple and friend of Franklin. This permitted Franklin to answer at length, begging Dumas to sound out the diplomatic corps, to spread propaganda in the newspapers, to procure arms and munitions, and to send over two engineers for the next campaign. For all this service, Franklin enclosed his compliments and one hundred pounds. Propaganda was not so costly then! The instructions were sent through an American merchant, Thomas Story, and at the same time, a French dealer of Nantes, Penet, took over another one of Franklin's letters to the good Dubourg. Franklin wanted to make the most out of this latter connection. The West Indies were adopted as the center of this compromising correspondence.

All this was well and good, but Franklin knew that foreign nations would not come to their aid, unless the people made some definite display of patriotism; the army would have to gain a great victory and Congress would have to be active, before France or Spain could be expected to help them.

Pennsylvania was the pivot State, and Franklin first wished to stir up its people against the inert Assembly, against the verbose Dickinson faction which refused independence. He used a mortal weapon against them. Thomas Paine, his disciple and protégé, had felt his ire rising ever since he had stepped foot in America. He was ready for a great outburst, and in January, 1776, he published his pamphlet, "Common Sense", at Robert Bell's. No newspaper had dared accept it, for Paine had not restrained his audacity in writing it: the pamphlet was a most terrific denunciation of monarchy, heredity, and all that formed the basis of the contemporary civilization. The book spread like wildfire, and four editions were sold out in a single month. It was distributed throughout the colonies and crystallized the revolutionary sentiment. Franklin had just forced the British post office to relinquish its service, and so the book had a more devastating effect than ever. December, 1775, had been the last month for the English mail carriers, and now that the Revolutionary service was in full power, Franklin saw to it that only patriotic newspapers and pamphlets were distributed. By this victory, Franklin secured the domination of public opinion for Congress, and Paine took the profits.

In this new atmosphere of freedom, the newspapers of Pennsylvania were filled with articles on independence and commentaries on "Common Sense." Heretofore, they had not even dared mention the subject, but once they began, other colonies imitated them, as Philadelphia was the economic center. Rumors of the change arrived in Europe, and many people there attributed "Common Sense" to Franklin. They were almost right.

Franklin rallied the most energetic group in Congress about him: the Adamses and the other Yankee delegates, who wanted independence and union as much as he. In the early part of 1776 he worked with them to influence the Assembly to their way of thinking, but they met with so much resistance that at one time they thought of making a limited confederation for the States which wanted to enter. But finally, they decided to wait a little longer before taking such a serious decision, hoping for a great military victory to impress their voters and the diplomats of Europe.

The Revolutionary Army, after some success, had failed before Quebec; General Montgomery had been killed, and the troops had been forced to retreat. If energetic measures were not taken immediately, it was clear that Canada would slip through their fingers. Then Franklin, Samuel Chase and Charles Carroll of Carrollton were sent to Canada. They were accompanied by the good priest, John Carroll, and their mission was to persuade the Canadians to join them. The delegates left with their chaplain at the end of March, and made haste. They went through New York City which had been abandoned by the gentry, and continued their journey up the Hudson in a boat, studying the positions of natural defense and admiring the Palisades. At Albany they were received by General Schuyler, who treated them with portly Dutch magnificence, and then conducted them to Saratoga in his own calash. There it was bitterly cold and Franklin thought he would die from the exposure. He warmed himself as best he could and wrote farewell letters to his friends. Still, he had the courage to go on, and after fourteen days of severe trial, now sleeping under tents, now on boats, now in deserted taverns where there were no doors or windows, Franklin and his companions arrived in Montreal on April 29. They were received in a noble fashion by the commander in chief, Arnold, and the ladies of the town offered them a suitable dinner and a pretty little song recital. But from the very beginning, everything was lost. The French Canadians did not at all approve of the passages in the "Address to the People of Great Britain" in which Congress denounced Catholicism; their clergy had even been very shocked. And they had been disagreeably impressed by the brutality of the American soldiers too, all the more since the English regiments were held in such strict order in Canada. Had the Americans been conquerors, or well supplied with ready money, the Canadians might have accepted them. But they watched them retreating, and complained they had not seen the color of their dollars. Franklin tried to have the Canadians paid in proclamations, which he had printed by Mesplet, a good fellow, but only the priests knew how to read, and they were not anxious to inform the people about the ideas of Congress. The Americans soon realized that it was a matter of military strength and financial backing. They had neither one nor the other at their disposition. The cold climate and exposure had weakened Franklin and he knew that by persisting he could only secure an honorable death for himself which he thought premature and useless. On May 11, he left hastily to inform Congress of the situation. Father Carroll treated him as though he were his son, and Franklin's strong constitution carried him through. They still rode in the calash which Schuyler had lent them, and arrived in New York in the evening of May 26. He was at Philadelphia before the month was over, but a sharp attack of gout kept him in his room for three weeks, once he had arrived. It was only what was due him, and Franklin learned that a Patriarch had no business going to war. Adventurous life closed before him, just as his parliamentary activity had ceased.

But he still found a way of serving his country, — by being an independent Great Man. After the Canadian setback, it was absolutely necessary to stir up the enthusiasm of the country and make its revolutionary spirit felt in foreign countries. The Declaration of Independence, which Congress was then discussing, was the best way of accomplishing this, but it was blocked by the constantly temporizing Pennsylvania Delegation. Naturally, Pennsylvania was essential to the scheme, and Franklin decided to force her hand. Despite the revolutionary campaign and the numerous editions of "Common Sense", the people had elected a large majority of the lukewarm Liberals (May, 1776). This party held the colony in its power, and it could not be broken up by parliamentary tactics. Franklin and his friends made use of the Masonic lodges which were then propagating a liberal doctrine among the upper middle-classes, and also of the "Associators", the association of volunteers, shopkeepers and workmen which Franklin had formed in 1749 to establish a voluntary militia. They were the only armed and trained men in the population, and they were patriots too. The Tories, who had been too free in their language, had been severely punished by them in the preceding autumn. Two or three would be kidnapped at a time, tied hand and foot, set up on a wagon, with an insulting poster hung upon them, and paraded through the streets bareheaded. At every crossways the wagons were stopped and one of the victims would have to make a confession. Meanwhile the crowd jeered, threw mud and stones . . . and if the Tory were impertinent enough to show spirit, the crowd shrieked and menaced lynching. No person was spared, and Franklin saw some of his old friends treated in this brutal way. He suffered from it, but he knew it was useful. An impression of enormous power was produced, and the streets belonged to the revolutionists. There was even a rumor to the effect that the "Associators" were preparing a *coup d'état* (October, 1775). They denied it but that did not lessen the fear they inspired. Now they made no attempt to quiet these rumors, and, on the contrary, showed they wanted to be respected. Given an impetus by their old master, Franklin, they organized meetings to protest against the attitude of the Pennsylvania Assembly (May, June, 1776) and of their delegation to the Congress. A "Preconvention" was assembled by their efforts (June 19) which prepared for an election and then actually held it (July 8). All the members of the association, no matter who they were, were eligible to vote, while the other citizens had to give guarantees, declare their "patriotism" and prove that they owned a considerable fortune. Thus they had satisfactory elections.

The Provincial Convention, which was elected in this manner, held session immediately and began its work (July 15). This consisted of administering the province and of drawing up a constitution. Its first act was to choose Franklin as the president and then to send him to Congress as a representative of Pennsylvania with a strong patriot delegation. Thus the difficulty had been surmounted. The Assembly had received a mortal blow. The members protested eloquently, struggled nobly, but their power died of inanition.

Thanks to this maneuver, Congress was at last able to approve of the Declaration of Independence. The text of the document was written by Jefferson, corrected by Franklin, and it gave the Americans a symbol for which they could fight. It was the war cry of the New Republic and spread like fire over the world. Primarily, it was a document of propaganda, and this is why it was so curious and ambiguous in character. Up to now the Americans had directed their fury against the Ministry and Parliament, considering the King as innocent and as their last resource. Now, suddenly, they turned against him with invective.

For a long time every one had agreed in cursing Parliament, but in 1776 there were many who still had faith in the King and the empire — Washington was one of them. These had to take a step ahead. The Declaration of Independence imposed unity of action in America. Foreign nations had to be solicited for much-needed aid. As the Americans were rebels, they could no longer count on the churches and monarchies to help them. But they could count on the philosophers, who were immensely powerful; and the great middle-class movement which was in progress throughout the world was another definite factor of assistance. Their quarrel, which had begun as a dispute between the local Assemblies and the central Parliament, had developed into a crusade against a tyrant, against all tyrants. Franklin perceived this, and by helping Jefferson to correct the Declaration of Independence, he had skillfully made the text more precise and more solemn. He knew very well how to make it appeal to the European public.

Congress was not of much help. The members nearly put Jefferson out of his wits by their changes. But Franklin calmed his susceptible friend. He told him again and again how foolish men were when they got together, and advised him to accept their criticism with a shrug of his shoulders. Then he recounted the apt and pleasant story of the hatter and his signboard, which he later wrote down in these words:

When I was a journeyman printer, one of my companions, an apprenticed hatter, having served out his time, was about to open shop for himself. His first concern was to have a handsome signboard with a proper inscription. He composed it in these words: "John Thompson, Hatter, makes and sells Hats for ready Money", with a figure of a hat subjoined. But he thought he would submit it to his friends for their amendments. The first he showed it to thought the word hatter tautologous, because followed by the words makes hats, which showed he was a hatter. It was struck out. The next observed that the word makes might as well be omitted because his customers would not care who made the hats; if good and to their mind they would buy, by whomsoever made. He struck it out. A third said he thought the words for ready money were useless as it was not the custom of the place to sell on credit. Every one who purchased expected to pay. They were parted with; and the inscription now stood, "John Thompson sells hats." "Sells Hats," says his next friend, "Why nobody will expect you to give them away. What then is the use of that word?" It was stricken out and hats followed, the rather as there was one painted on the board. So his inscription was reduced ultimately to John Thompson, with the figure of a hat subjoined.

Franklin knew this foolish proceeding in legislative bodies so well that he was careful not to be brilliant in Congress or to play an important rôle there. Congress was dominated by John and Samuel Adams, and Franklin spoke but little. He was satisfied to defend a few principles, especially proportional representation. The smaller States were frightened and demanded an equal number of representatives for all States, despite the size of their populations. Otherwise, they claimed, their situation would be like poor Jonah before the whale. Franklin reminded them that this comparison had already been made when Scotland had joined England. In 1760, Lord Bute brought so many of his countrymen into his administration that throughout England it was said, "Jonah had swallowed the whale." Thus Franklin tried to head off the bad measures proposed in Congress and succeeded in doing so without making the representatives angry.

On July 12, while Philadelphia was celebrating the Declaration of Independence with fireworks, balls, and drinking parties, Howe arrived with his huge navy in the harbor of New York. He had come with a peace proposal but he was just a week too late. However, he didn't give up his enterprise, and immediately wrote his "worthy friend", Franklin, an amiable note, filled with pacifist phrases, which he signed as his "sincere and faithful humble servant." At the same time he issued a proclamation which was considered to be generous by the English but which the Americans found provoking. Franklin knew that the moment for compliments had passed. He submitted the matter to Congress, and with its permission, sent an answer to Howe in which he spoke of England's "fondness for conquest", "lust of dominion", and "thirst for a gainful monopoly." However, he seasoned it with some personal compliments, intended for Howe, but no longer used the tone of 1774. Congress was pleased with the letter but Howe was surprised. His "old friend" had apparently changed. Later, though, when Howe had defeated Washington on Long Island and taken New York, he thought that Congress and Franklin might have reflected. He wrote again to Franklin, and sent General Sullivan, whom he had just taken as prisoner of war, and whose services he had bought, to Congress. The representatives did reflect and discussed the matter for two days. Then, in order not to displease the moderates and not to irritate the irreconcilables, a delegation of three was chosen to see Howe: John Adams, Franklin and Rutledge. Thus, everybody was satisfied, the gesture was made, and it was certain that it would not have any consequences.

Franklin and Rutledge rode in a postchaise, and Adams followed on horseback (September 9). In two days the delegates had crossed Pennsylvania and New Jersey, which were filled with disbanded and undisciplined troops. They slept in a squalid, crowded lodging house where Franklin and John Adams shared a cubbyhole of a room with a single bed. This gave the Philadelphia sage the opportunity of informing the Boston leader how good fresh air was for the health. He didn't convince him but he did put him to sleep. The next day they met Howe at Staten Island.

After polite greetings and a pleasant light repast, they started to talk. The first point in Howe's instructions was to have the Americans recognize the suzerainty of George III, while the first point in the congressional instructions was to refuse any such recognition. The delegates finally agreed that an understanding was impossible. They were graceful about it, and Franklin was even facetious, reminding Howe of America's cumulative birth statistics. Howe was courteous to the end, though his suavity was touched with sadness, and the men parted with polite bows. They were good friends and sincere enemies.

The delegates then reported the meeting to Congress, which highly approved of their having conformed so closely to the prearranged scenario. Then the representatives went ahead with their business, for according to the happy formula of Franklin: "If they did not all hang together, they would be hung separately."

Since the defeats on Long Island, Congress had more clearly perceived the weakness of the American army, and the second hypothesis did not seem so very improbable. The representatives looked to Europe for aid, with an interest that amounted to anxiety.

Europe remained very quiet! In April the Committee of Correspondence had sent a Mr. Deane to France to make negotiations for a commercial treaty and to secure the assistance they needed so greatly. Deane was a showy merchant of Connecticut and had been a member of Congress. As yet, nothing had been heard from him. The only favorable signs were the number of French merchants who had arrived in America during the last six months, and the flood of adventurers from the West Indies and France, who besieged Congress to accept their services. Some of them were even very distinguished and brought promising letters, such as the Chevalier de Kermorvan, who landed in June with secret messages for Franklin. But these were only glimmers of hope, and Congress eagerly awaited answers to the appeals Franklin had made in December. At last, an enormous letter from the good Dubourg arrived in September. After expressing his pleasure at hearing from his venerable master, Dubourg went on to describe France, saying it was on fire with enthusiasm for America, and he added that his time, influence and connections were completely at the disposal of the Americans. He would obtain anything they wanted: powder, cannons, officers, generals — all they had to do was to ask him.

The Americans who had ardently wanted such a letter, without daring to hope for it too much, were almost drunk with joy. They decided that they must not lose this chance. On September 26, Congress elected Franklin, Deane and Lee to represent America in France. Franklin accepted. He was touched and said, "I am old and good for nothing; but, as the storekeepers say of their remnants of cloth, 'I am but a fag end, and you may have me for what you please.'" He knew this journey might mean his death, if the vessel were caught by the English — and, of course, his embarking could not be hidden — but if it were a success he was certain to win universal glory. By leaving, he escaped the thick heavy atmosphere of Congress and launched out in the most beautiful adventure of the world.

Before going, he left a brilliant political last will.

He had broken off with his son who was now in prison. He punished him, moreover, by taking William Temple with him as secretary and companion. The lad protested he wanted to stay by his father and serve him instead, but Franklin had the upper hand and broke off the relationship he had just made.

He gathered together all his ready money and put it at the disposition of Congress in the form of a loan, showing that he was willing to play high stakes for the independence of his country.

Finally, at the Convention of Pennsylvania, he cast his vote for a strange constitution, one which was no more parliamentary than royalist, and which consisted in an Assembly, annually elected by universal suffrage and under the constant control of the people; a body of executives drawn from this Assembly, elected for a term of three years and not immediately eligible for reëlection; a council of censors, which would verify the functioning of this constitution every seven years and suggest improvements. These were the principal characteristics of the Constitution; it had clearly taken its source in Franklin's plan for federal union, and Franklin's influence was evident in every line. His contemporaries acknowledged it, despite the fact that the constitution was supposed to be the result of mere circumstances, by quoting one of Franklin's remarks. Franklin was against a parliamentary system of two houses, and compared it to a wagon, hitched up with two pairs of steers, one in front

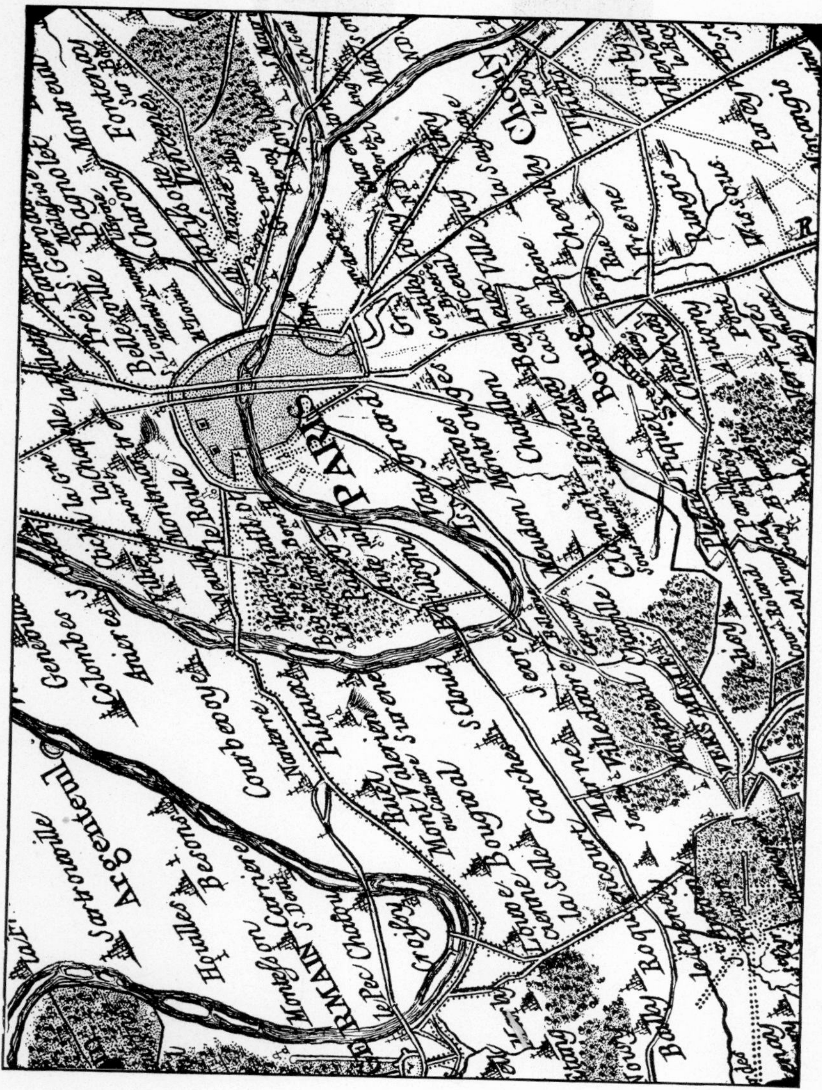

Central section from a map in the possession of the Bibliothèque Nationale (Paris), entitled, "Carte de Paris et de ses environs, 1781." It shows the location of Passy, near Paris, but in the direction of Versailles. The wooded country all about was healthful and restful for the Patriarch. The King hunted in all these forests. On the left-hand side of the map is Marly, where Court was held now and then, and where Franklin went to visit the Château Royal, and Madame DuBarry's beautiful estate, as well as St. Germain, where his friends, the Alexanders, lived.

and one behind, under the pretext that, so arranged, the descent from a mountain would be easier.

The whole world discussed this constitution, and the principle of tolerance it upheld was much admired. Franklin meant to give his country a lesson in enthusiasm and skepticism by this document. It inferred a deep distrust of all royal or parliamentary forms of government and stressed the importance of life itself, by its simplicity and malleability. The two years of work in America had confirmed the ideas Franklin had brought back from England.

Among all the lawmakers, who were so fond of formulas, Franklin remained a Patriarch.

His compatriots, who were so anxious to play a parliamentary rôle, laughed at him, and his colleagues were troubled. His skepticism and the French ideas he had picked up among the Economists, seemed like nothing worth while to them. He felt their disapproval so keenly that he still considered his best friend to be Galloway, and after Galloway made some vague promises of loyalty to Congress, Franklin intrusted all his papers to him. All his papers in the hands of a Tory! All his money in the hands of Congress! Franklin's destiny was strange, and he stood, a solitary and contradictory figure, in the midst of all his glory.

He shivered from fear in these hours of torment, and felt such a deep need for support that besides William Temple, he took along with him his exquisite little grandson, Benjamin Franklin Bache. The little Benjamin was the image of his son Francis, who had died forty years ago, and so it seemed that an angel was guiding him.

Just as Abraham, at the age of seventy-five, left for Egypt, the wise old Franklin, now turned sixty-nine, prepared to leave for France.

III

A STEADY autumnal gale sped Franklin's boat to France for thirty days. It stirred up the sea so violently that both he and his young companions suffered disagreeably, but it also saved their lives, as it kept them at a safe distance from the English cruisers. The wind was bitterly cold, freezing the two fearful boys, but it did not daunt the spirit of the Doctor, even when it caused him physical discomfort.

He continued to study the course of the Gulf Stream, for this great warm river which crossed the ocean and kept its current unimpaired fascinated his imagination. Then, too, he meditated on another river which had a still more mysterious course: public opinion in Europe. It was a dark river to him but he was going to learn all its windings and sound all its depths as he worked for the salvation of his country. The first year of war had proved that America could not triumph over British navies, armies, or British money. America had to be supported by some other country; the governments of Europe were suspicious and yet they had to be persuaded to help. Perhaps by persuading the people first, the governments would be forced to comply.

Franklin had no other weapons than his skill and many promises. What was he, himself? An old man of seventy, who had fled from his country when the enemies were ravaging it. He no longer had a home, since his old wife had died, no son, since William had betrayed him, no money, since he had loaned it all to Congress, no party, since his party had not followed him. Jealousy was rampant in the States he had left, the little were against the big, the South against the North, etc. Congress was divided, the Radicals against the Liberals, the Parliamentarians against the Democrats, and he, himself, was suspected by every one. There was nothing to hang on to.

France, with its monarchy and Catholicism, was an unknown country to him; he had fought against it for twenty years, and now he was pinning all his hopes upon it. At seventy, he had to begin a new life. He was throwing his past away, and to symbolize it, he threw his wig into the sea.

He replaced it with a fur cap in order to keep his head warm and to give his hair a chance to grow. The good Brittany peasants saw him land at nightfall on December 3, 1776, and were amazed at his appearance. The boat had not reached Nantes, its destination, but the Bay of Quiberon, and Franklin had waited there four days for a favorable wind. Then he decided to go by land the rest of the way, and disembarked, leaning on a tall slender boy of seventeen, accompanied by a smaller lad, with fair hair and a delicate beautiful face. Doctor Franklin, William Temple and Benjamin Franklin Bache were surprised, in their turn, at these hairy peasants, with their huge wide-brimmed hats, short vests, baggy pantaloons and small gaiters, who eyed them curiously, uttering gibberish among themselves. The *Reprisal*, on which Franklin had crossed, remained in the harbor, accompanied by two prizes it had captured on the coasts of France: the *Success*, a brigantine from Cork, laden with a cargo of wood and wine, and *La Vigne*, a brig from Hull, carrying flaxseed and alcohol. As Franklin's calash rolled away, the *Reprisal* fired a last farewell salute.

Franklin turned in for the night at Auray and took just time enough to write to Barbeu Dubourg, Deane and Thomas Morris, who was the commercial agent for the United States at Nantes. Then he hurried on his way. The roads of Brittany were broken up and muddy. There were only old calashes, without springs, at Auray and Vannes; Franklin had to buy a cabriolet. The days were short and sombre. Now and then the travellers met the strange peasants on the roads. They looked like wild men to them, and the wives looked stranger still, perched grotesquely on the plodding horses. The great solitary forests they passed through were sad and dark with autumn. And when they could understand the peasants they only heard murky tales of brigands. The old man and the two boys trembled from weariness, and did not dare to look in front of them.

When they arrived at Nantes (December 7), life changed its hue. For two days the inhabitants had been talking about Franklin's imminent arrival. In Europe, no one yet knew that Congress had sent Franklin to France. He fell out of a clear sky and there was something miraculous about his coming.

The news spread as fast as a lighted fuse. Paris received the good tidings on the seventh, and, on the fifteenth, the announcement of Franklin's arrival in the capital was already made. On the thirteenth, all Bordeaux was talking about it; Leyden heard the news on the sixteenth, and before the end of the month it was in all the newspapers of Geneva, Brussels, Avignon, etc. The news reached England, too, at the same time, and Horace Walpole wrote: "Dr. Franklin at the age of 72 or 74 and at the risk of his head had bravely embarked on board an American frigate and, with two prizes, taken on the way, had landed at Nantes in France and was to be at Paris the 14th where the highest admiration and expectation of him were raised."

Franklin had hoped to rest at Nantes. He took his lodgings a little outside of the city, at the home of Monsieur Gruet, the partner of Penet, whom he had seen in America concerning some American business affairs. He counted on recovering his strength at this pleasant estate, with its pretty little grove, but he had to sing another tune very quickly. The country house of Monsieur Gruet became the object of pilgrimage for all the inhabitants of Nantes — especially the fashionable ones. They hurried to see the great man and his companions. Merchants came to talk business to him, officers to ask questions on the war and to find out their chances of winning stripes, magistrates offered their homage with great oratorical tirades on liberty, and the ladies arrived in crowds, their faces alight with admiration. He won all their hearts by the dignified and tired expression on his face, the silence that he wisely kept because of his imperfect French and the rapid fire of questions, by his strange appearance with a fur cap

BENJAMIN FRANKLIN
Né à Boston dans la Nouvelle Angleterre,
le 17 Janvier 1706.

PORTRAIT OF FRANKLIN MADE IN FRANCE

for headgear instead of a wig, and because of his two handsome companions. The ladies gave him the greatest honor they could give to any man: they created a "Coiffure à la Franklin", dressing their hair in a high curly mass which imitated his famous beaver.

The French had met him more than halfway. Franklin, who was always so silent, had the time to perceive this fact, while William Temple, taking the advantage of his age, was quite satisfied just to enjoy it.

France of 1776 was like the England of 1763. It had just won a great commercial war, as England had won a great military war. The commerce of France, which had been cut in pieces between 1756–1763 had been firmly reëstablished. It had gone beyond anything known up to then, beyond all that had been hoped. The navy, which had been practically annihilated, started up again so brilliantly that the sea was covered with active French boats. Industries had sprung up in all the cities, the farms were prosperous, and the West Indies were so opulent that they furnished all Central Europe with sugar. "The virtuous young King" gave his people the most delightful hopes No more recriminations, no more despotism, no more spites or severe punishments; reconciliation was the keynote of the new monarchy, the patriotic young King was going to give his country the unanimity that had been vainly desired ever since the death of Louis XIV. Such was the dream of Louis XVI. He had called the most popular men of France to aid him: Turgot, who was dear to the philosophers and the financiers; the old Comte de Maurepas, who was beloved by the crowd because of his long disgrace under the preceding reign; Malesherbes, who was the most enlightened magistrate of Europe; Vergennes, a skillful diplomat, who had reëstablished the prestige of France in Northern Europe, thanks to *his* revolution in Sweden, and who consorted with broad-minded people. The French liked to call Maurepas "Mentor", with the understanding that Louis XVI was his "Telemachus."

France was again supreme in Mediterranean Europe, owing

to the "Family Pact" which joined all the Bourbons together. The marriage of Louis XVI to Marie Antoinette of Austria, and the ageing of the King of Prussia, made the position of France firm also in Central Europe. The country was once more an equal of England. However, it was peaceful to the point of pacificism, for its grandeur was based on commerce, its prosperity depended on peace, and the party of enlightened men who influenced the King were not favorably disposed to war.

Franklin had been struck by all this, even at Nantes. He noted the extreme popularity which the United States enjoyed, but also the high esteem for England, "The Mother of Liberty." He found a great desire for national unity everywhere and noted that the Government was anxious to maintain peace.

He felt refreshed after a fortnight, more from his enthusiastic welcome than from actual rest, and after having organized the American commercial and maritime service at Nantes, he left for Paris, and many hearts went with him.

His carriage rolled along the royal highways of France, and the hoofs of the horses clattered on the pavement. The boys leaned out, curious, as always, to watch the changing countryside. The nearer they came to the capital, the more rich the country became, and at every stop there were more and more messengers. Barbeu Dubourg had spread circulars all through Paris, announcing Franklin's arrival. Every morning and evening Paris was filled with rumors that he was in the city. His coming was the most popular topic in the cafés. Monsieur le Comte de Vergennes had instructed the police to forbid all talk of Franklin in the cafés, in order to avoid the reproaches of the British Ambassador, but the result was easy to imagine.

In the evening of December 20, Franklin discreetly arrived at Versailles. He took a room at the Auberge de la Belle Image, as he was too tired to go any farther. Nevertheless, he sent a word to Deane, telling him of his intention to arrive in Paris the following afternoon. Deane didn't wait to be told twice. He jumped into his carriage, dashed to Versailles as fast as his horses could carry him, and then met Franklin with open arms and a beaming face. The arrival of his illustrious colleague was an immense relief for Deane, who was a sturdy patriot but fond of comfort and good living. He had a commanding appearance, but his career of schoolmaster and Connecticut merchant had been a poor preparation for the life he had to lead in Paris. He spoke English only and had no imagination. He knew nothing about the French, although he got along with them on account of his good fellowship. Even though the American situation was only so-so, he had the sympathy of the French just by being an "Insurgent", and because of the florid waistcoats he sported over his very respectable waist line. But there were clashes no end, nevertheless. Deane obtained permission from the French Government to buy and send the provisions which Congress needed for the war. He sent them through Franklin's old friend, the good Doctor Dubourg, who was the first Americanophile of Europe. Dubourg was a fairly good doctor too, an excellent friend, a mediocre writer, and a very poor business man. He often made blunders, was almost always in an upset state of mind, and was not very favorably considered at Versailles. Vergennes treated him haughtily, and made Deane accept Caron de Beaumarchais as commercial agent in his place. The famous and fantastic comic author, in quest of adventure and enthusiasm, took it into his head to discover the Americans. Then he preached on the present virtues and future grandeur of America with such charm that both the King and Vergennes were persuaded and rewarded him with this brilliant situation. He received a million francs from the French Government, a like sum from Spain, and with this money founded the firm of Roderigue Hortalez and Company which dealt in contraband with America on a grand scale. The Government helped him to procure arms, munitions, uniforms, etc., but with the understanding that he alone was responsible. His transactions had to have the air of serious business, though in reality they were high politics for Vergennes, and good theater for Beaumarchais. He was a whole *dramatis personæ* in himself: a diplomat, a spy, a business man, a privateer, and a recruiting agent, and his manifold cues delighted him. He rushed from one end of

France to the other to keep up the interest of his audience, but poor Deane and the English were quite bewildered by his zeal. Beaumarchais certainly played this tragic comedy with passion and sincerity, but played it so well that his acting became noticeable. The British Ambassador, Lord Stormont, set spies on him, and then started a racket of protest. His vigorous objections, abetted by the bad news from America, made Vergennes decide to stop all boats leaving for America.

Thus Franklin arrived at a good moment — the worst one. Deane felt quite lost in the midst of all these spies, mysteries and dangers. Nothing was sure to him, except the fact that he didn't know what was going on. When Franklin fell out of the clear sky, with a comforting message from Congress and new hopes, Deane felt new life. His joy was doubled at seeing the change in Vergennes' attitude. The French minister was very grave, but a little greedy too, and said that Mr. Franklin would have to act very discreetly; the philosopher should claim he had come to France for his health, and for the education of his grandchildren, and he should not visit Versailles, except under strict incognito. By using such means he would be most welcome and the minister would be glad to see him. A child who hides his treasures could not have taken more precautions. But Franklin and Deane found all this trouble to be a good sign. The hours at the Auberge de la Belle Image were filled with contentment; their hopes were as vague as happiness and as shimmering as a first love.

Towards noon, they left for Paris and when they arrived, Franklin rubbed his eyes in astonishment; it was certainly like a first love. He couldn't make a step without being surrounded by an enthusiastic crowd. The people thought that they had caught glimpses of him for the past two weeks, but now they really saw him, and they were overjoyed to find him so simple and dignified. They were delighted he should wear a plain brown suit without ribbons, that he should do without a wig; his august features and unaffected republican manners won much admiration. He was so different from any one else they had seen, up to then. Americans had already been noticed in Paris but they were like the English. Franklin was a real insurgent, a real Quaker. Just by looking at him the people were able to envisage all America, a charming and exotic country. His foreign simplicity won over all the beautiful souls at a time when persons plumed themselves on having beautiful souls. They doted on Quakers, whom they called "primitives," and this rage went so far that in the police records there is recounted the story of a young unscrupulous blade, who dressed as a Quaker and then secured all he wanted from his mistress. She felt that it was impossible for her to refuse anything to one of that sect. Franklin was too old and too wise to go as far as this, but he was also too old and wise not to take advantage of being thought a Quaker, if that added to the enthusiasm of the French, for it was his country which would benefit from this harmless error.

At first, Deane and Franklin took rooms at the Hotel d'Entrague, and curious crowds gathered in front of the building. Then the two Americans established their quarters at the Hotel d'Hambourg, Rue de l'Université, and this place became famous throughout France and Europe.

Deane was delighted and embarrassed. But all the fuss was perfectly clear to Franklin. The French were quick witted, and as eager for new styles as they were clever at launching them. Franklin was the last word in intellectual fashions. Monsieur de Voltaire was venerated by the crowd for his sparkling intelligence, but he had already been talked about too much, and no one ever saw him any more. The forgetful people still had an indifferent admiration for him *but* fastidious society criticized him. They might have been more touched by the splendid genius of Monsieur Rousseau de Genève, who was superior to Monsieur de Voltaire in that he did not have that philosopher's vain futility, mannerisms, or barren heart. But Rousseau only wanted to be one of the masses in Paris; he succeeded in effacing himself, and the fame he enjoyed among the intellectuals did not extend to the people he lived with. Moreover, the quarrel between Rousseau and Voltaire had greatly weakened the philosophic group by cutting it in two. The ironic Voltairians and the lyrical Rousseauists were constantly insulting each other in the salons, lodges and learned societies. Their disputes were not pleasant to hear, and it would not have taken much to make Catholicism fashionable once more, the people were so tired of listening to these quarreling philosophers.

But Franklin appeared among them with a double halo: he was a rational sage like Monsieur de Voltaire, and a child of nature like Monsieur Rousseau. The Rousseauists were very fond of the sayings of Poor Richard which expressed the moral good-fellowship they practiced; while the Voltairians, after a brief and discreet inquiry, were certain that Mr. Franklin was more deistical than Christian, and this pleased them very much. All the philosophers had to love him, and as it was fashionable to love, they did so to their hearts' content. There was no paucity of reasons to venerate Franklin either; had he not been the first to explain electricity, and to disarm the gods with his lightning rod? The English said he had organized the American Revolution, and they had to be believed. Moreover he was thought to be the author of the Declaration of Independence, "Common Sense", the Constitution of Pennsylvania, and all the other American documents that were known. Franklin was the only famous American who had come to Europe, and he received all the enthusiasm the people felt for his country.

Le Comte de Vergennes couldn't fail to be impressed. This serious minister had surrounded himself with the "philosophers", and was under their influence. He wanted France to regain the high position she had held under Louis XIV, but by means of commerce, not by war. However, he was not absolutely against a war if it would not cost too much, or be too long and bloody. He especially desired to efface the humiliation of the Seven Years' War, to restore the prestige and world importance of France. However, like the modern intellectual he was, he wished to make use of the moral forces which dominated the epoch. Vergennes wanted France to set a good example for Europe, to give England a good lesson and America a good lift, but he could not succeed without the support of public opinion. He was ready to have recourse to war, even to urge his countrymen to it, but not to impose it on them. Unfortunately, public opinion was divided on the question. The philosophers sang the praises of the United States, but they didn't want war at all; the conservatives, the country gentlemen, and the solid middle-class merchants, who all hated the English, would have been glad to declare war, but they were distrustful of the American revolutionary ideas. The King was on their side, while the young courtiers, infatuated with modern ideas, followed the philosophers. Vergennes could do nothing in the face of such contradictory tendencies, except to wait, and to have interviews with Franklin.

Fortunately for the United States, Franklin took account of the situation immediately by his divine intuitiveness, and didn't waste a moment. After he had embraced his faithful Barbeu Dubourg, hired a coach and some servants, among them the faithful Champagne, he made three important visits: one to Monsieur le Comte de Vergennes, one to Monsieur le Marquis de Mirabeau, the Friend of Men, and one to Madame la Marquise du Deffand, the greatest Enemy of Men.

On December 28, at Versailles, Monsieur le Comte de Vergennes received Messrs. Deane and Franklin. Imposing speeches were exchanged between the great minister and the great philosopher, although there were eloquent silences as well. Franklin discreetly testified to his good will and spoke of the offers of Congress. Vergennes, who wanted to be a serious and good minister, was made to feel that Franklin had succeeded in being serious and good for a long time. He narrowed his eyes and made a vague but friendly response: Franklin could be sure of the King's protection as long as he stayed in France. Then Franklin saw the Head Secretary, Gérard, who promised him 2,000,000 francs in the name of the King, a few days later. This was the first victory of the Patriarch over European diplomacy.

His second triumph was held at the home of Madame du Deffand. Her salon was the greatest information bureau of

Europe; all the wit and tittle-tattle of the time was known there, and it was violently pro-English. The aged Marquise, who had once been fresh and gay and mocking, now had a leathery face and a hard, calculating mind. She had become so foresighted that she could anticipate, by her dislikes, all the enthusiasms and satieties of her grandnephews. When every one doted on republics in 1776, she was a Royalist. Her bizarre tastes were exemplified in her strange late love — one might say heroic — of Horace Walpole. After having many lovers she had not loved, she adored this man who was not her lover. Naturally, she defended England staunchly, and was faithful to the English Ambassador, Lord Stormont. The Americans were not attractive to her, and she was very desirous of finding Franklin a simpleton.

He went there after dinner on December 29, and a brilliant company was gathered in the redoutable salon: the Vicomte de Beaune, the Chevalier de Boutteville, the Abbé de Barthélemy, who was librarian to the King, the Comte de Guines, who had been the ambassador of France at London, the Duc de Choiseul, a former prime minister, and the young Elliott. The habitués knew the bad news which had just arrived from America and the pointed remarks which the mistress of the house held in store for Franklin. They smacked their lips in advance, thinking of the drubbing he would receive from her if he tried to swagger. But they smacked their lips in vain. Franklin surprised them all. Had he used compliments he would have been considered frivolous; had he bragged he would have been ridiculed; humble airs would have seemed low, and a proud attitude would have been called arrogance. All this had been foreseen, as it was the ordinary game of diplomats. But it had not been foreseen, that, like a Patriarch, Franklin would smile silently while he waited for others to talk, and then that he would listen with interest, even if it were a lady who spoke. Such unprecedented conduct floored everybody. Not one person dared to be impertinent to him, or even to mention his country's misfortunes. Franklin left the salon like a conqueror. He had spontaneously discovered the only way to fascinate and intimidate the fashionable world.

His visit to the Marquis de Mirabeau, on December 30. was no less important. The Marquis was the head of the Economist School, which was then in vogue, especially among the rich bankers and officials. Now, these were precisely the people which the United States needed most, for they could furnish credit and be of financial aid. Unfortunately, the Economists were as devoted to peace as they were passionately fond of the Americans. They claimed that since the "Insurgents" were fighting for true principles, they would certainly conquer in the end, for Truth always had the final triumph. Thus, it was useless for the French to give military aid, and besides, they needed all their money for the restoration of France's financial power. Such was the point of view of Monsieur Turgot, who next to Mirabeau, was the most influential of all the Economists. But he was also the friend of Franklin. When Turgot was alone he gave his pacifism free rein, but when Franklin was on the scene, his love for America took the upper hand. Thus, Franklin counterbalanced the pacifist theories of the Economists and other philosophers, which might have been dangerous for America, simply by his presence. More than this, he turned the enormous influence of this famous school in the favor of America, which was a big step towards the control of public opinion.

Now that he knew the lay of the land, and had swept it clear of obstacles, Franklin developed his plan of action. His two colleagues advised him oppositely: Arthur Lee was for finesse and a thousand intrigues, Deane for shaking the big stick. Franklin shook his head. By such procedures they would be beaten in advance; England had much more cunning diplomats than they, and her merchants were more forceful and better armed. But England had no patriarch in Paris, who could maneuver public opinion as he could. Franklin knew that his original and unforeseen method would disconcert his adversaries, who were expecting much finesse, but not much simplicity.

Franklin adopted a deferential and loyal attitude to the

ministry. The Duc de Choiseul, who was eager to get back into power again, fawned on him, and posed as the leader of the war party. He was quite ready to back Franklin and to exploit him. But Franklin did not play into his hand, and remained completely faithful to Vergennes, whose heart was touched by this loyalty. He finally won over Vergennes by his majestic suppleness. Versailles wanted to aid America by plotting, so Franklin plotted. Others would have found it humiliating to be received always at the back door. Franklin knew it was just as flattering as any other door and was quite pleased to plot since it was with Monsieur de Vergennes and against the King of England. He made the most of these meetings, and by his charming company and affectionate conversations won the hearts of Gerard, Hennin, and all the men he met there. Thus, friendship and his great fame as a savant put him above the ambassadors.

He did not suffer from his ambiguous situation at all. It simply added a little piquancy to his glory, which was based on solid foundations. Starting on January 15, Franklin regularly attended the meetings of the Academy of Sciences. And his illustrious colleagues were so proud of this, that, contrary to custom, his name was inscribed in the minutes. He went among them often, with LeRoy and LeVeillard, who introduced him and acted as his bodyguard. By showing himself first as a savant, he was certain of pleasing Vergennes and winning public approval. In January he spent much time visiting the great libraries of Paris: the Library of the King, the Library of St. Geneviève, the Mazarine Library, etc., where he was also received with veneration. The Academy of Sciences and all the renowned scholars held a position of great prestige in the world and this reflected on Franklin too. As a savant, he kept in touch with the social and intellectual elect of the entire world. In Paris, the Duc de Croÿ, the Duc de Chaulnes, and Comte de Lauragais, all great noblemen who plumed themselves on their erudition, hurried to visit Franklin and to talk on scientific subjects with him. Prince Gallitzin, Minister of Russia at The Hague, and a faithful Mason, treated him like a master; Ingenhousz, his old friend, was now doctor to Maria Theresa, the Empress of Austria, and kept up a scientific and political correspondence with him which was read by Her Imperial Majesty; Baron Blome, Minister of Denmark to Paris, the shrewdest diplomat of Europe, had also this worthy pretext for visiting Franklin, and Monsieur d'Eyck, Minister of Bavaria, imitated him.

Franklin knew how to add the advantage of snobbishness to these precious connections. The high French nobility, pervaded with Rousseauism and the encyclopedic spirit, were looking for an idol; Franklin, with his bare head, large glasses, and Quakerish air, fitted the pedestal perfectly. His first worshipers were the La Rochefoucaulds. They had an enormous fortune, a family tree with ancient roots, and were not only philosophers, but adherents to the Economist creed. From the very beginning, the young duke treated Franklin like a prophet, and agreed to work for him as a secretary. He immediately set to work, translating the American State constitutions into French.

Following this powerful family, there came another which was no less influential, the Noailles, which included three dukes, various cardinals, generals, and ambassadors — one was the ambassador to England — and an infinite number of court dignitaries. One of the most brilliant of them, the young and rich Marquis de La Fayette, who was son-in-law to the Duc d'Ayen, took it into his head to go to America. He besieged Franklin to obtain his support — and succeeded. In spite of the King, the ministers, winds and tides, La Fayette left for America in May. His departure was the occasion for universal excitement. While he was gone, his wife and relatives adopted Franklin and the Americans. The Patriarch also came in touch with the famous French general, the Comte de Broglie, who had some ideas on America where he hoped to become a military dictator. His project did not come to a head, but it connected the Broglies to Franklin. With these three great families behind him, Franklin had all the fashionable society at his feet. Some of them came to venerate him as a sage, others to ask him for letters of recommendation to the American army. These latter counted on becoming generals point-blank. It was difficult for Franklin to satisfy them, and impossible to send them back empty-handed, so he finally wrote a standard letter to meet his purposes:

The bearer of this, who is going to America, presses me to give him a letter of recommendation, though I know nothing of him, not even his name. This may seem extraordinary, but I assure you it is not uncommon here. Sometimes, indeed, one unknown person brings you another equally unknown to recommend him; and sometimes they recommend one another! As to this Gentleman, I must refer you to himself for his character and merits, with which he is certainly better acquainted than I can possibly be. I recommend him however to those civilities, which every stranger, of whom one knows no harm, has a right to; and I request you will do him all the good offices, and show him all the favor, that on further acquaintance you shall find him to deserve.

The bearers did not feel at all slighted by this letter, but on the contrary, found Franklin's attitude charming. The further Franklin retired the more he was besieged by visitors. He had gone to live on a pretty hill in Passy, near Paris, in an attempt to satisfy his taste for leisure and to be close to his grandson, Benjamin Franklin Bache, whom he had placed in a boarding school near by. Vergennes was pleased by this move, and so was Monsieur Le Ray de Chaumont, who had arranged the affair. Franklin inhabited the *basse cour* (servant's quarters) of the Chaumont property, in a house which was called the "Petit Hôtel de Valentinois", while his proprietor lived at the other end of the garden in the "Grand Hôtel de Valentinois." Passy had many charms for the Patriarch: the clear air refreshed him, the hot mineral baths he took three times a week were invigorating, and the society of his neighbors was charming. In the spring and summer, Passy was a popular resort for fashionable people, satisfying both those who came to have a good time and those who wanted a rest.

Passy was also the center of a philosophic, Economist, and Masonic group. The lodges were active there, working outside of the great city and yet near enough to enjoy its advantages. French Free Masonry was experiencing a period of rebirth. The Orléans family had given it a strong impetus and the society was being reorganized and established everywhere. As a philosopher and Deist, Franklin entered the Masonic groups immediately, and they were of great aid to him. Through the Masons he had access to the newspapers which were officially controlled by the Government, but which were really written by the Masons and the philosophers, such as Morellet, Suard, De la Dixmerie, who were all Franklin's friends. Practically all of the French newspapers published outside of France were in the hands of the Masons also. Franklin had his writings accepted without any trouble by the *Gazette de France*, the *Mercure de France*, the *Affaires de l'Angleterre et de l'Amerique*, a magazine of propaganda published by the French ministry to bother the English; he inserted anything he wanted in the *Courrier de l'Europe* and the *Gazette de Leyde*, which was supposed to be the best on the Continent, as well as in the *Gazette Française d'Amsterdam* and the *Courrier du Bas Rhin*. He had illustrious collaborators in this work: the Duc de La Rochefoucauld, the Abbé Raynal, who was the most talked of French philosopher in his time, a certain Abbé Niccoli, who was Minister to France for the Grand Duke of Tuscany, and Courtney Melmoth, an English actor and writer whom he had in his employ. But Franklin did most of the work by himself. In February, 1777, two little pamphlets were furtively circulated in manuscript and quoted in the newspapers. Their origin was unknown, but their style revealed the author. One was "Comparison of Great Britain and the United States in regard to the basis of credit in the two countries", and the other was entitled, "A Letter from the Count de Schaumbergh to the Baron Hohendorf commanding the Hessian Troops in America." The first of these pamphlets showed with simple but blinding clarity how much more worthy America was to receive money than England, and why an investment in the new country, with its immense resources and frugal population, was more certain to be fruitful. The French public, the government, and the *fermiers généraux* could not fail to be impressed by this skillful plea.

The second piece of writing was a masterpiece. It was the letter of a petty German prince who, with paternal solicitude for the brilliance of his court, recommended his general in America not to take care of his men, since England gave him thirty guineas apiece for each soldier killed, and he needed the money to pay for his last trip to Italy and for his coming season of Italian Opera. The letter even had grandeur.

> . . . I am about to send to you some new recruits, — wrote the prince, — Don't economize them. Remember glory before all things. Glory is true wealth. There is nothing degrades the soldier like the love of money. He must care only for honour and reputation, but this reputation must be acquired in the midst of dangers. A battle gained without costing the conquerer any blood is an inglorious success, while the conquered cover themselves with glory by perishing with their arms in their hands. Do you remember that of the 300 Lacedæmonians who defended the defile of Thermopylæ, not one returned? How happy should I be could I say the same of my brave Hessians!

This pamphlet appeared at an appropriate time. All Europe was furious over this sale of men to England; Mirabeau published a vehement protest in Holland, but the cunning Frederick the Great, who kept one eye on public opinion and the other on his coffers, continued to tax the petty princes for every mercenary soldier who passed through his States, at the same rate he used for cattle. Franklin's cutting irony was much appreciated, and the Masons, who claimed to defend "The Dignity of Man" above anything else, were most active in distributing his pamphlet. It was not the only service that they rendered him in this time, when many officials in the Department of Foreign Affairs were Masons, as well as the King himself.

Franklin had a strong backing: the Masons, the fashionable world, and the learned societies. But more than this, the great unofficial society of women stood by him and adored him. His serious air and glancing wit, priestly unction and journalistic unconstraint, his delicacy and brusqueness, his grave and manly appearance, all made him seem exquisite and exotic to them. They surrounded him and overwhelmed him with questions which he seldom answered, except by smiles or an occasional kiss. He knew they had much to tell him, and that they preferred the homage of silent courtesy to the voluble gallantry so common in France. His position might appear frivolous now, but not in his time, when the salons were the real news agencies. When an American traveler could not decide whether France was a monarchy, an aristocracy, or just a plain petticoat government, the support of the women was not to be scorned.

Besides all this power, Franklin had still the advantage of the connections he had made during his travels: his English friends, Shelburne, Price, Priestley, Strahan, Thomas Walpole, and S. Wharton, who continued to correspond, and some others like the good Mrs. Patience Wright, an eighteenth-century Madame Tussaud, who did some discreet spying for him. She was his principal source of information in England, and Dumas told him what was going on in Holland.

What could Lord Stormont do in the face of all this? No doubt he was a handsome man and high-spirited; he even had a kind of spontaneous impertinence which could have helped him in this century. But in 1777 France was really the arbiter of the situation. There were a few old ladies who liked Stormont for his well-turned legs and his haughty airs, but the public found him irritating. In spite of the conciliatory policy of his government, he was very arrogant with the French ministers, just as if nothing had happened since 1763, and they were exasperated. He helped Franklin more than any other Parisian of his time, and America owes him a statue. His rôle was difficult, but he persisted in playing Cæsar, even in this comic opera. It was not surprising that at the last curtain he had to be put to the door, or that he seemed awkward and out of place opposite the Patriarch.

However, he fought as best he could. He had begun the battle even before Franklin's arrival in Paris. Up to then the

English had the gazettes in their own hands, and kept up the tone they wanted, because Deane, who didn't speak French, was not strong enough to defend himself. But Franklin had no sooner landed than he began to spread hopeful news about America which he succeeded in having printed everywhere.

He even took the offensive. At an inn between Nantes and Paris, Franklin stopped to dine and heard that the famous historian, Gibbon, had just arrived and was upstairs. Franklin courteously asked him to spend the evening with him, but Gibbon refused, writing that he could not hold any conversation with a "revolted subject." Franklin replied, saying that when "the decline and fall of the British Empire should come to be his subject . . ." — which could be soon expected — he "would be happy to furnish him with ample material which was in his possession."

Paris and Versailles were soon buzzing with stories about Franklin, and Stormont was quick to see the danger. He made a swift counterstroke by taking advantage of Franklin's attitude. Franklin was quiet for prudence's sake and because Vergennes forced him to be, but Stormont claimed he was only a poor deserter, who had had a dreadful quarrel with Congress, and who was very desirous of humbly submitting to England if that were still possible. Stormont was believed by a part of the public. Even such well-informed people as the Duc de Croÿ took up the story, as it was so pleasant to slight a famous man.

But Stormont's maneuvers didn't have any effect on the ministers who were acquainted with the real situation of Franklin. Stormont tried to influence them by predicting that Franklin would lie, promise, cajole, and use all the subtlety he was master of. Stormont thought he had persuaded Monsieur de Sartines, Minister of the French Navy, who was supposed to have told his intimate friends that Franklin was a *master rascal.* The English ambassador also informed Maurepas and Vergennes of Choiseul's intrigues, showing Franklin as the accomplice. Stormont's spies then brought him news that both these French dignitaries had spoken harshly of Franklin;

and the British Minister rubbed his hands. But, unfortunately, the English spies had not read a letter that Vergennes had sent to Monsieur le Noailles, Ambassador of France in London:

> Mr. Franklin lives very modestly in Paris. He made me a visit and I returned it. His conversation is gentle and truthful; he seems to be a rather witty man. Lord Stormont says he will hoodwink us as he hoodwinked three British ministers. I don't know if he has such a project in mind, but at any rate, he has not yet made any effort to execute it. . . .

Later, Vergennes said that Stormont had "the talent of attaching much importance to trifles."

Franklin's silent dignity made Stormont look like a pygmy, and the latter's slanders, which did not have the virtue of wit, seemed merely disgusting. The English ambassador tried to ridicule the fur cap but no one would join him.

In January and February, the American privateers, Wickes, Nicholson, etc., were well established in the French ports, and did no end of damage to British commerce. They succeeded in capturing one of the mail packet boats which plied between Holland and England, and insurance taxes in London climbed ten per cent., causing a panic. Then Stormont gave vent to all his fury and Vergennes had to calm him by putting some fictitious prohibitions in force. Some officers of the American navy were imprisoned, treated to champagne and then released. Monsieur de Vergennes hadn't failed to issue some very strict orders, quite to the liking of the British ambassador, but the strictest one was not to execute them.

As a result, a good number of British sailors were taken prisoners, though they were ordinarily released, as the Americans had no place to intern them. But Franklin wanted to take advantage of the situation, and as some of his compatriots were interned in England, he sent a letter to Stormont, proposing an exchange of prisoners. At first he received no answer, so he insisted on one, and this time Stormont wrote on a scrap of official notepaper:

"The King's ambassador receives no applications from rebels unless they come to implore his Majesty's mercy."

He thought this was a good answer, but unfortunately, the rebels were already affectionately called, "The Insurgents", in France, and Stormont was considered a lout.

Nevertheless, America was in a bad way. Washington was retreating, and Howe was pressing him harder and harder. Franklin, Deane, Lee, and their agents went visiting everywhere to counteract the bad impression and to spread encouraging news. The old lady admirers of Stormont asked him if he weren't going to answer these impertinent reports, but he responded lightly that General Howe would take care of that. When Franklin heard this remark he bit his lips.

Not long afterwards, however, he had his revenge. Stormont, excited about the British successes, started rumors of a thousand victories, and exaggerated Howe's achievements. Franklin's faithful friends came weeping to him and asked him if this bad report were a truth or a lie.

"No," answered the Patriarch, "it is not a truth, it is only a Stormont." This time the British ambassador bit his lips, for all over Paris one heard the word "stormont" used in place of "lie", and "stormontades" for rodomontades.

But Fate was against the Americans. Philadelphia was taken in September, and when the news reached Paris, an Englishman, with stinging politeness, asked Franklin if Howe had really taken Philadelphia. Franklin shook his head and said, "Philadelphia has taken Howe."

But, alas, the English did hold the city, Congress was in flight, and the friends of the rebels were profoundly discouraged. Only Franklin held firm. His calm smile never left him and he often repeated his famous phrase, "It will go."

The French loved the steady heroism of this man, who continued to struggle and hope though his house and lands, fortune and papers were in the hands of the enemy, his son in prison, and his family in flight. No matter what would happen to him, he would have the public on his side.

Nevertheless, his genius was not strong enough to change the course of events. Howe occupied Philadelphia, and Burgoyne was coming down from Canada with a superb army to separate the northern and central colonies. There was little news from Congress, though it did not cease to ask for money, arms, and aid. Franklin was sorry but he could send nothing except hope; the French were intimidated by the British successes and didn't want to join in the war. France was still interested, however, to the extent of loaning another three million francs, and Spain gave a like amount also, though the Spanish Government refused to receive the American envoy, Arthur Lee. Frederick the Great followed their example of exclusion; frontiers and pocketbooks, outside of France, were closed everywhere.

It could hardly be otherwise, when nothing could be returned for their help. And what was worse, the delegates from Congress did not get along together. Deane and Franklin were from the North, Lee was from the South, and this geographical difference was enough to set up a barrier between them. Lee was a vain, suspicious scandalmonger, and his jealousy amounted to a monomania. Unfortunately, he was also intelligent — in a narrow restricted way — a fluent speaker, and he was respected for his honesty. Small wonder he was a very dangerous man! His envy of Franklin might have resulted in some unhappy consequences had not the critical circumstances forced him to have a proper sense of his duties. But collaboration was difficult. It was altogether impossible with Thomas Morris, the commercial agent of Congress at Nantes, who had all the vices which can upset a routine life: drunkenness, libertinism, dishonesty in money matters, and some others. The delegates warned Congress of his activities, but all Congress did — faithful to parliamentary habits — was to let Morris know he had been reported, without dismissing him from his office. Then Morris went up to Passy to insult Franklin and Deane (September, 1777).

But this was not the worst. At the Hôtel d'Hambourg there was a little group of Americans who were most eager to "help" Deane and to carry out his instructions. Two of them were important and distinguished personages: Doctor Bancroft and Mr. Carmichael, who both informed Lord North on everything that was going on among the delegates. They were well paid for this service, — at least, Bancroft was. Then there were a clergyman, the "Reverend" John Vardill, two supernumeraries, Cal Smith and George Lupton, who, though not especially qualified, would do anything for a little money, and finally, the most precious man for England of them all, Captain Hynson of the American navy, who kept the government of His Majesty informed on all the sailings of the American boats. By this means, all the communications intended for Congress were sure to reach London first. The work was so well done that once a captain of the American navy (Folger) arrived in Philadelphia with a packet of *blank* messages. The envelopes had been substituted between Passy and Nantes. The poor man was at a loss to explain himself, and though he was innocent, he thought he would have to forfeit his honor and his life. Hynson knew his job and the British Government was sure of him, as Stormont had bought a smart girl who could twist him around her little finger. King George III didn't like either these men or these policies, but war was war, and he wanted to win. He carefully read and noted all the spies' reports, which were written in synthetic ink. These reports were transmitted to the King in a romantic way. They were first stuffed in a bottle which was buried under a stone at the foot of a tree in the Tuileries. Then every Tuesday evening at nine-thirty, an English agent would unearth them and rush to Calais.

The English spread confusion in the American camp at Paris and every one was suspected. Vergennes didn't know whom to trust, though he instinctively believed in Franklin. The doctor's silence bothered Beaumarchais — who found all silence suspicious — and he was afraid that Franklin was going to join the English. The French knew that Franklin had secretly seen Summer, the friend and agent of Shelburne, as well as his old friend, Alexander, the regular correspondent of the prominent English parliamentarian, Pulteney, and they wondered if the subject of peace had not been broached.

They were not far from the truth. In these long agonizing summer hours of 1777, Franklin had dreamed of peace. He told his English friends that all the Americans wanted was independence, and that if this were granted, peace would be made in ten minutes. Was this betraying his country? Franklin spoke to his American friends, and even to Lee, saying that the reluctance of France to enter should not be deplored, it would only be better in the end, and that America had need of severe tests to develop herself. Then, too, it would be much better to conquer without the help of Europe. Nevertheless, Franklin urged a speedy alliance, when he spoke with his French friends. He showed them that it was to their advantage to come in while America was still weak, for he assured them that America would one day be strong and dangerous. And he warned them with a winsome, half-petulant smile, that he would leave France if they did not decide soon.

He was answered by expressions of love and admiration, but he wanted more than this. One day, a lady went into ecstasies, talking with him, about the beautiful spectacle America was giving the world. Franklin responded dryly that it was a beautiful show but that the spectators didn't pay to see it.

It wasn't because he didn't urge them to do so. Franklin continued to publish pamphlet after pamphlet, two of which were attributed to his pen: "A Catechism relative to the English National Debt", and "A dialogue between Britain, France, Spain, Holland, Saxony and America." In these writings he brought England to account, showing the overwhelming weight of her national debt, the foolhardiness of her politics, and the dangers into which she had thrown herself headlong. Franklin besieged the French ministry, demanding a definite answer. In January, 1777, the delegates had decided to risk everything, even their lives and the esteem of their constituents, to obtain this result, but now, in the fall of the same year, they were holding a council to find the best way out. They failed to discover it.

Had Franklin been less great, less confident in life, or less happy, he might have despaired. But France was a most agreeable country to live in. He was charmed with the respect he received on every hand, and the free admiration of the women was a tonic to his mind. All the great personages wished to see him. Joseph II had been hindered from meeting him the preceding summer by some slight incident, but Franklin's old, faithful friend, Ingenhousz, visited him instead. Franklin took good care of himself, the air was soft and pleasant in Passy, and he was in good health. He was well sheltered, and a police guard watched over him night and day. When a rumor spread that he had been assassinated there was sorrowing all through France, but as soon as he appeared on the streets, very much alive, the sorrowing changed to rejoicing, and every one wanted to indulge him all the more. Benjamin Franklin Bache worked conscientiously at his boarding school near by, and Temple was also happily busy at his studies. His little trips to Versailles gave him the advantage of learning court manners, which he acquired very gracefully, and during his leisure time the pretty young ladies of Passy taught him gallantry, in which he excelled very quickly. Now and then the doctor would contemplate him musingly, as he played a game of chess with some faithful friend, and if a disturbing thought came into his mind, he considered it squarely and then put it aside, saying to himself, "It will go."

He was right. One morning, just a year and a day after his landing in France, he heard that an American messenger was coming from Nantes with important messages. One after another, the Americans in Paris came to Passy, to be among the first to hear the news, and their devoted French friends came too.

At last the post-chaise of the envoy thundered into the courtyard, and a young man, Jonathan Loring Austin, jumped out. He had come all the way from Boston, having left October 31 on the Brigantine *Perch*.

Franklin was trembling with emotion and asked,

"Sir, *is* Philadelphia taken?"

"Yes, sir," replied Austin, "but, sir," he continued, "I have greater news than that! General Burgoyne and his whole army are prisoners of war!"

America was saved! The people at the Hôtel de Valentinois went drunk with joy. Beaumarchais, in a delirium of enthusiasm, leapt into his carriage and ordered his coachman to whip the horses so that he would be the first to reach Paris with the news. The coachman complied so well that Beaumarchais was thrown headlong into a ditch, and, to the great glory of the United States, dislocated his shoulder. All night long the delegates wrote bulletins which they sent everywhere, announcing the great victory. Paris was buzzing with excitement by morning. Lord Stormont arose and dressed leisurely. But just by looking out the window he realized he would soon have to be on his way. At the same moment, Monsieur de Vergennes was thinking that the time to act had come.

Franklin's prophecy was being fulfilled.

IV

FATE had at last offered him the occasion he had been awaiting for a year. He was too wise not to take advantage of it, and too good a chess player not to take that advantage immediately. Franklin acted so quickly and secretly, that no one knew what was happening but himself.

He had stirred up universal enthusiasm in Versailles and Paris by the announcement of the Saratoga victory. Since Denain, no victory had caused such pleasure. The verb, "To Burgoynize" was invented, and the people showed they would support the King in anything he might do to help the Americans. They had been well prepared by Franklin's propaganda, and it needed just such a victory as this to bring America into high favor among them.

Nevertheless, the financiers, the Turgot group, numerous diplomats and philosophers were still against war. The allies of France, too, brought heavy pressure to bear against such a proceeding. Both Austria and Spain disapproved, fearing the European coalition would be enfeebled, and that intervention would be a bad example for colonies in general. Spain had no desire to go to war, for the unpleasant memories of 1760 were still green, and she exercised an enormous influence on the foreign policies of France, due to the Family Pact which linked the Bourbons together.

Franklin knew all this, as well as the pacific intentions of the King.

Then, to the bewilderment of Stormont and the British ministry, the American propagandists announced, in the same breath that they proclaimed the Saratoga victory, that the moment for peace had come. The surprise increased, when some days later, Franklin sent Major Thornton to England. The major was sent ostensibly to see if something could be done about the American prisoners, but when he asked Lord North's permission to better their conditions he spoke of other matters as well. . . . Some weeks later he was followed by J. L. Austin, the welcome messenger, for whom Franklin had conceived a lively affection. The Patriarch had him destroy all his papers and then gave him two letters of recommendation, sending him to London to see the Whig leaders. Austin visited them all and had a good time. Parties were given for him and he ate and drank and danced. Rockingham, Shelburne, Camden, Jackson, and others, gathered around to hear him talk. He even met the Prince of Wales. Then he returned to Passy, gorged with good food but empty-handed. Had his mission been a useless one?

Certainly not. The English finally understood, though vaguely. They sent messengers over to Paris one after another. Between December fifteenth and twenty-fifth, Franklin saw Paul Wentworth, the head of the British Spy Service in Europe; a little later, Mr. Dempster and Sir Adam Ferguson paid their respects. In the beginning of January the messengers continued coming: Sir Philip Gibbs, Baronet, and "Saint Hutton", an amiable, deaf, aged man, who was a kind of "Pope" to the Moravians and an unofficial confidant of George III. All these messengers came to ask for the same thing, Franklin's peace conditions. They were quickly informed and usually left immediately, except Hutton, who was a patient old duffer. Franklin talked intimately to him for a long time at the top of his voice, but nothing came out of their meeting. In March, the most serious negotiator of all arrived, William Pulteney, member for Shrewsbury. He was the intimate friend and banker of North, and had definite offers to make to Franklin. He wanted to be sure that Franklin would consider them, and had his agent, Alexander, besiege the Patriarch during the last days of March and the first week of April. Pulteney wanted Franklin to approve of the conditions of peace and reconciliation which the English commissioners would present to America in the name of the Parliament and the King.

He failed because he did not offer independence, but he was

followed in April by still another messenger, one Hartley, a member of Parliament, the most long-winded and conscientious talker in the world. He was also an old friend of Franklin, was accompanied by a man named G. Hammond, and the two of them harassed the Patriarch with untiring obstinacy. They even went so far as to propose a three-party agreement between England, France and America. The King very rightly considered Hartley to be a hopeless blunderer and retracted all that his messenger had proposed. Nevertheless, Hartley gave Franklin no peace with his peace offers, writing him every two months, between 1778 and 1783. In June, a strange letter arrived in Passy, signed "Charles de Weissenstein", in which an Anglo-American alliance was suggested, excluding France, and with the promise of pensions and titles to the leading Americans such as Washington, Franklin, Adams. . . . The answer was to be given the following noon at Notre Dame. There were policemen waiting to meet Mr. de Weissenstein, but they could not distinguish him, and he must have gone home chagrined. Franklin always believed that this letter came from the King. A last naïve proposal was made in May, 1779, when the savant, W. Jones, suggested a "philosophic" peace between America and England.

Franklin had a dry, point-blank answer for all these proposals. Peace was easy; independence and evacuation would secure it; a reconciliation was more difficult and could only be effected by the ceding of Canada, Newfoundland and Florida. Now the King, on the other side of the Channel, thought it was his bounden duty never to sign a paper recognizing the independence of America, and that in order to "hold" America, he had to keep Newfoundland, Canada and Florida for himself. Such a definite attitude made all misunderstanding or understanding impossible.

As a matter of fact, Franklin and George III were the only two to understand each other. The King thought that Franklin was tricking him and he was right. Franklin was tricking him by telling the actual truth, which was just what the King couldn't believe. This was Franklin's method, and he kept

Vergennes informed, either directly, or by his friend, Chaumont, of all his negotiations with England. He even revealed his transactions with Pulteney which he had promised to keep secret. Due to such a frank proceeding, the project of a treaty with France made progress by leaps and bounds.

On December 6, Gérard, First Secretary of the Minister of Foreign Affairs, came to tell Franklin that the King congratulated the United States on their victory and suggested that the moment had come when they could draft an alliance to offer France. The delegates worked two days on the document. Then William Temple took it to Versailles and delivered it with his own hands to Vergennes on the eighth. Four days later, Vergennes received the three delegates secretly in a house near Versailles, and told them that the alliance would certainly be accepted, though before an official answer could be given, Spain would have to be consulted. On the fourteenth, the Government ordered that a frigate be prepared, in order to send the news of these negotiations to Congress by special boat. (The vessel left on January first.) On December seventeenth, Gérard, who had heard of Wentworth's visit, came to Passy to say that the treaties had been formally decided upon and that they would be drawn up as soon as the courier returned from Spain.

But on the eighth of January, Vergennes heard of the visits of Hutton through Grant and Chaumont, and somewhat alarmed, sent Gérard to find out what was needed to keep the delegates from joining England and to give confidence to Congress. After a little confusion, the delegates answered him that they wanted a treaty, ships and some money. Gérard told him he was authorized to make two treaties, a commercial one, and an offensive and defensive alliance, both reciprocal.

Thus Vergennes hurried the affair, frightened of an Anglo-American reconciliation which would not only have reëstablished the prestige of England at the expense of France but which would have been a direct menace to the West Indies. Of course these islands were very important to French commerce, as they were also to the American traders who bought molasses there to make rum. England could dangle these islands temptingly to the colonists who wanted to expand their territories. Considering all the aid the French West Indies had given to the Americans, there were pretexts enough for such a gesture. Vergennes was thoroughly alarmed and hastened the negotiations.

On January eighteenth, Gérard brought the treaty project to the delegates. They studied it and everything seemed satisfactory, as the reciprocality was strictly maintained throughout. The Commercial Treaty was merely a guarantee of friendly business relations with no special privileges for either party. In the War Treaty, the independence of America was taken for the chief goal, conquests were disavowed, and separate peace was forbidden. But there was the sticky question of molasses. The delegates wanted the King to promise never to levy an exportation tax on molasses, which was such a useful product for American industries. Gérard consented, but desired a counter article. Franklin proposed that the United States agree not to levy taxes on the exportations of products sent to the French West Indies. They came to an agreement with this suggestion, and the King accepted the treaty as it was. But alas! Lee was conscientious and reflected on Franklin's proposal. He did not find it to be completely reciprocal, with molasses on one side, and all kinds of products on the other. After a week of meditation, he was furious and thought they had been hoodwinked. He spoke to his colleagues about it, and though they did not share his views, for the sake of peace they decided to do something about the matter. Gérard was interviewed. But Louis XVI had already signed the treaty and it would be tempting Providence to have him sign it again. These were anxious moments. Were a few kegs of molasses to spoil everything? Then Gérard had a flash of genius, and said that if Congress refused to ratify these two clauses, the equality would not be broken anyway, and the King would willingly ratify the treaty even if the two clauses were lacking. Franklin breathed a sigh of relief; Lee was satisfied and the treaty was saved.

It was signed at Paris on February 6, 1778, in the office of the Minister of Foreign Affairs, which was located in the former Hôtel de Lautrec on the Quai des Théatins. The ceremony was simple. Some noticed that Mr. Franklin wore a rather old-fashioned suit of Manchester velvet which was too tight for him, and others recognized it as being the same costume he had worn in the Cockpit Tavern, when Wedderburn had insulted him before the tittering Privy Council of the King of England. This suave Franklin enjoyed the bitter taste of vengeance.

For the last three months, Franklin had humiliated England as well as the English King, who had sent over numerous offers and even *prayers* to persuade him. Franklin rejected them from top to bottom and frustrated all the intrigues — even the most subtle ones — which were made against him. The Economist group, though it included many of Franklin's friends, tried to hinder the extension of the conflict through Hutton and Dupont de Nemours, even at this moment, when the Government of France was negotiating an alliance with the Americans with the approval of its people. The Economists demanded free trade for France and guaranteed French neutrality in return! Turgot was the secret motivator of this suggestion, which, however, miscarried. Neither his affection for Franklin nor his devotion to the King had stopped him.

There was an attempt at suppression from the American side, too. One of the five delegates, Ralph Izard, a Carolinian patriot, who was provided with a lot of money but not much common sense, hated both France and Franklin and did everything he could to keep the treaties from being signed. On January 25, 1778, Hutton wrote from London to Germaine, Minister of the colonies:

> I am just arrived from Paris. Last Wednesday, one of the American Delegates at whose house I was, called me on one side and let me read a short paper he held in his hand which I ask'd him to give me, but he refused it, and I was interrupted in the reading it by a Continental navy officer who was just going to set out.
>
> The contents of this paper were to this strange effect: That if I meant to save England, I should procure from the King a sign manual

declaring the independency of America, *but that it must be done within ten days;* that in that case he was not unwilling if His Majesty would employ him therein, to go over to the Congress to favour such an alliance with England and America as might be very acceptable.

I thought there was an extravagance in this, which I verily believed came from a preferable love for England in comparison of France, and indeed a kind of love in itself. The thing that struck me was the time fixed. I fancy there is something brewing between France and America, but more of this when I see you. The Gentleman advised me to "have wings." I set out next morning and was only an hour and a half at Calais. I was just 73 hours from Paris to London.

Parliament and the King needed four years still to realize that independence was fatal. In February, through the efforts of Lord North, Parliament voted some laws of conciliation, which gave the Prime Minister the power of offering a generous peace, but which did not, however, include the recognition of independence. The law was at least twelve days too late, and should have been passed three years before.

It was on the twentieth of March that King Louis XVI received the American delegates at Versailles, having changed his mind about awaiting the ratification of the treaties by Congress before announcing them publicly. There was the stir and hum of preparation for the great event at Passy, Chaillot and the Hôtel d'Hambourg. Franklin's friends came to give him advice and encouragement, for he had nothing but one vexation after another when it came to dressing himself. He wanted to wear a wig again as it was the rule at court, but the wig refused to fit. Or, rather, the head refused to fit the wig. The barber fussed about with it in vain, and finally despaired. "The wig is not too little, sir," he said, "but your head is too big." The French found this remark charming, and all over Paris they repeated, "He has a big head and a great head."

There was nothing to do — the wig was out of the question. Franklin resignedly decided to make the best of it, and boldly made the style fit his taste. He carefully combed his white locks, put on a rich suit of dark brown velvet, adjusted his glasses on his nose, smoothed the knee wrinkles of his fine gray hose, slipped on his silver-buckled shoes, and taking a little hat under his arm, he threw his sword in the corner of the room, and left for the Court. The son of a tallow-chandler was going to visit the grandson of Louis XIV.

An immense crowd thronged the shady alleys, the vast courtyard, the wide stairways, and even pressed into the ante-rooms. A trembling of wonder shook all the people when they saw Franklin, and they murmured, half-fascinated, half-frightened, "He has dressed like a Quaker!" The four other delegates, Deane, Lee, Izard, and W. Lee, who followed, wore ostentatious court garb and seemed merely like lackeys to set off the Patriarch's appearance. The delegates first went to see Vergennes, and while the drums beat out of doors as a signal to lower the palace flag, and the troops presented arms, Vergennes conducted them up the great royal stairway. The monumental doors of the King's apartments swung open slowly and the Major of the Swiss Guards stepped forth and announced sonorously: "THE AMBASSADORS OF THE THIRTEEN UNITED PROVINCES." Franklin was almost overpowered by emotion, and wept. He advanced, however, leaning on Vergennes and Deane. They steadily elbowed their way through the crowd of bishops, nobles, diplomats, professors and magistrates. Ladies rose as they passed and, finally, Louis received them with ease and simplicity. He took Franklin by the hand, and, addressing all the delegates, said: "Gentlemen, I wish that you would assure Congress of my friendship. I also pray of you to make it known that I have been most satisfied with your conduct during your sojourn in my realms." Thus the youngest republic in the world was presented to all nations by the oldest and most imposing monarchy of Europe. If July 4, 1776, was the date which marked the end of the Colonial Era in America, March 20, 1778, inaugurated its national career.

The spectators of this memorable scene felt the profound sense of its grandeur as well as its picturesqueness. The courtiers of Versailles, who had seen so many reviews, masquerades and balls, had never witnessed anything like it. In former days, the Great King had thrown a veil of gauze over his robes at Carnival, in order to make his grandeur more human without disparaging himself, but to-day, Franklin had refused all finery in order to make his humanity greater, and the most elegant court of the world applauded his act. "Everything about him proclaimed the simplicity and innocence of ancient customs," a spectator wrote. "He had stripped his head of all borrowed locks. . . . To the astonished multitude he showed a bare head, worthy of Guido's brush. . . . His pride seemed that of nature."

Franklin heard a murmur of adoration on either side as he passed; the ladies and the young men were overwhelmed by his genius, the halo of his beautiful old age, and by his foreign garb. After having bowed to the King, the delegates went from room to room, paying homage to the ministers and receiving compliments in return. Whenever the people caught a glimpse of them, they shouted for joy. Vergennes offered a most sumptuous dinner in their honor, and then they went to the gaming rooms of the Queen who welcomed Franklin and paid particular attention to him.

Finally they returned home, tired but happy, and prepared for the duties of the next day, when they had to attend the levee of the Queen, and make a visit to Monsieur and Madame, (the brother-in-law and sister-in-law of the King) and to the King's sister. Their welcome was everywhere the same.

Franklin had touched the French to the heart once more. His dress might easily have been taken for an impertinence, and the English pamphlets did not fail to point this out, but the French had been delighted. The Queen had not been shocked in the least, but had been enchanted to see a real American. It was no diplomat who had saluted her, but a man, come from the country of Liberty, Reason and Nature.

All this boldness might have ruined any one but Franklin. It only made him all the more a hero. People would have thrown themselves at his feet, had he allowed them to. He scarcely resisted any more, and instead of retiring to the

WOODCUT OF LOUIS XVI GIVING TO THE AMERICANS A PAPER ON WHICH IS WRITTEN "LIBERTY"

seclusion of Passy, he accepted invitations and went out visiting every day except Sunday, when he entertained his compatriots at dinner. No matter what he did, the love of the crowd encircled him like a nimbus. On March 24, he went to hear the famous lawyer, Target make a speech, which attracted an immense audience. Franklin had only to appear, the crowd made way for him on every side, and he was ushered to his place in the midst of cheers.

His glory was solemnly consecrated by a decisive incident. Voltaire was then in Paris. He had arrived several weeks before, having decided to enjoy his popularity for the last time, and he was gorging himself on the glory from which he died. As Franklin believed that in France he should act as Frenchmen did, he went to greet Voltaire at his Hôtel de Villette. Voltaire was suffering from a burning fever and his cavernous eyes glittered. Franklin was accompanied by his colleagues and William Temple. The two great men spoke for a few moments in English, but their little audience, disappointed at being deprived of such great words, protested, and they continued to talk in French. Their interview was touching, but Franklin had too much instinct for the theater not to feel that the audience was waiting for more. He dramatically seized William Temple by the shoulders and pushed him before Voltaire, asking for his blessing. Voltaire did not hesitate, but placed his emaciated hands on the young man's fine head, and blessed him in the name of God and Liberty. None in the audience could restrain their tears, but burst into sobs. Love was such a pressing need in the eighteenth century! They had forgotten that Monsieur de Voltaire had scarcely any faith in Liberty and none at all in God, just in seeing this meeting of the boldest man in the world, Voltaire, with the wisest of them, Franklin, under the aegis of the two greatest principles: God and Liberty.

Some days later, on April 29, Franklin attended a meeting of the Academy of Science, and Voltaire came too, playing his part of the eternally dying great man. The famous D'Alembert spoke in his beautiful French, giving funeral eulogies on various scientists such as Jurieu, and Duhamel, but there began to be a distinct murmuring in the audience. The murmuring increased shortly to definite requests, and finally Voltaire and Franklin had to stand up, bow and talk together. Even this did not appease the people, and they began to shout: "You must kiss *à la française!*" Voltaire and Franklin hesitated a moment; in former times, they had known how to joke, but now they feared being ridiculous. Franklin was bulky, Voltaire was a skeleton, and their accolade might seem like one between Mardi Gras and Ash Wednesday. But the people didn't laugh and the two old men could not retreat. So they kissed each other on either cheek while the crowd applauded, wept and cried how charming it all was, this embrace between Solon and Sophocles!

Perhaps it was just a scene of marionettes on the great stage of the world, but it was a scene which filled the crowds with enthusiasm and gave them magnificent visions. Now near death, Voltaire recognized the necessity of love, of following nature, and he designated Franklin as his spiritual heir. Franklin had influenced the most skeptical of philosophers to take a positive attitude and to proclaim the union of nature with civilization. This was more than Monsieur Rousseau de Genève, with all his genius, had ever been able to accomplish. Franklin had become the leading public man of his time after his presentation at Versailles, and after Voltaire's kiss, he had really become the Patriarch of the New and Old Worlds.

The six French editions of "Poor Richard" which appeared in France between 1777–1778 and the innumerable pamphlets on his theories of heating, printed at the same time, guaranteed Franklin's fame among all classes.

It was almost too great for a man of his age. It was far too great for the envious delegates. The breadth and solidity of Franklin's glory is only understood when one knows the efforts that his enemies made to undermine it.

His American colleagues in France were his most constant detractors. Deane, of course, was a good man, neither imaginative nor sensitive. But Lee had a genius for slander, and his jealousy made him precise and inventive. The difficult months of 1777 had restrained him from following his natural bent, but the apotheosis of 1778 was intoxicating and brought him back to himself. He was spurred on by Ralph Izard and then by John Adams, who had been sent over by Congress to replace Deane.

In all America there was no man more honest, more courageous or more patriotic than Mr. Adams. It would have been hard to find a more educated or perspicacious man, but it would have been extraordinary to have met a man who was more blind to his faults and more conscious of his qualities. Mr. Adams had the instinct of self. He conceived all his interests to be rights, which made him profoundly moral and very powerful in discussion. Moreover, he was a lawyer and imposed a logical and rigorous form on his egoism so that he could believe in his own justice. Whenever he perceived the existence of some one else he was judicious and excellent, but ordinarily he was occupied only with himself. Franklin impartially said that Adams was "always an honest man, often a great man, and sometimes positively mad."

At first Adams had highly respected Mr. Franklin, whose conversation was so interesting, and who was a reflection of Mr. Adams' brilliancy in Congress. As such he was very satisfying. But when Mr. Adams arrived in Paris in the spring of 1778 and had to be a mere reflection of Doctor Franklin, who ruled over the ministers, ladies, and the learned men, he immediately thought the situation was unhealthy. Nevertheless, his instinct of "justice" made him wait for some provoking incident before he should give vent to his anger.

He did not have to wait very long. Franklin and Lee did not get along together, and Adams judged Franklin to be in the wrong, right away. Franklin did not pay rent for his pleasant house but did pay for his suitable retinue of servants. This was all wrong. He should have paid for the house, since it was humiliating for an ambassador to be lodged for nothing, but he did not need a coach or so many servants, as the United States was a poor country. Franklin associated with scholars and intellectuals; Adams discovered that this annoyed other groups of French people and he felt that they were right. Franklin was on good terms with Maurepas, Vergennes, and Sartines, who made up the leading set in the Government, but Adams found this criminal, as it was the other set which was made up of honest men. Franklin worked night and day, sometimes sleeping only two or three hours, and was more interested in the output of his work than in sticking to formalities. Adams started to put Franklin's portfolios into such order that the Patriarch could no longer find anything he wanted. Franklin also employed Alexander, Bancroft and Carmichael, who did a little spying for England but much more for America. They were sure men, now that they were certain to be paid. Adams thought that to employ spies was dabbling in treason. On every subject, he agreed with Lee, and the two of them made life difficult for Franklin.

They deprived his nephew, J. Williams, of his post as maritime agent at Nantes, under the pretext that Congress had named W. Lee as the commercial agent of that city. They made every effort to change the life of the old man and tried especially to have him recalled. Lee wrote to his brother in Congress that Franklin was a bungler, and a lazy, injudicious spendthrift, while there was an orderly man at Paris, who was economical and hard-working, and who ought to be named ambassador, namely, Arthur Lee. John Adams wrote to his cousin, Samuel Adams, who was the most influential representative of Massachusetts in Congress, that there was nothing but waste, confusion and errors in Paris, due to the plurality of envoys. Their number should be reduced to one well-chosen man. His own choice was so evident that he did not take the trouble to state it. At first his friends and Lee's adherents made good headway; the project of naming one single minister to Paris, instead of three delegates, was voted by Congress, but then the maneuver failed, because of a misunderstanding between the friends of Adams and Lee. They could not come to a compromise, and Franklin's friends, energetically supported by the French minister in Philadelphia, elected their candidate quickly, even though the Pennsylvania delegation voted against him. Lee was elected to remain in Paris as Minister to Spain, while John Adams had to return to America, where he would have time enough to slander Franklin. He had a good opening since Franklin's name was mentioned in the "Deane Affair." This was one of the Lees' creations. The brothers were convinced that Deane had dealt in graft with Beaumarchais, and persuaded their set of Virginia gentlemen in Congress of the fact. Through Adams, they managed to persuade the Northerners, who made up the other predominating group of Congress, and Deane was caught in a wedge. He was not even allowed to explain himself, and though he was in the right, he began to think he had done wrong and published an imprudent apology. This turned Congress against him, and as he felt he was lost and did not understand why, he wrote some furious letters which were seized by the English, and which sealed his fate for good. When he had died of his misery, and when his persecutors had gone to their graves with the respect of the public for their patriotism, it was discovered in 1848 that he had been in the right after all, and amends were tardily made by giving alms to his granddaughter.

Franklin had supported Deane by a commendatory letter and a loan; and he had been right to do so, in spite of Congress and appearances. This cast much discredit on him. As he had been named minister on account of Vergennes' solicitation, Franklin found that the majority of Congress accused him and his nephew Williams of making money at the expense of their country, of being infeodated to France, of associating with suspicious individuals who were doubtless devoted to the English, such as Alexander, and of being dissolute and extravagant. In 1781, Franklin held onto his post only because he had some personal friends who were clever at intrigues, and because he enjoyed the favor of the King of France. Congress didn't spare him any insults. When Louis XVI asked for a plenipotentiary to make peace, John Adams was chosen and not he. Adams returned to Paris in January, 1780. When the hopes of peace had faded, the jealous New Englander gave some lessons in politics and morals to Vergennes to divert himself. First Vergennes listened with polite interest, then he began to be irritated, and finally was exasperated. He begged Adams to hush and sent the papers to Franklin, asking him to return them to Congress. Congress was a little embarrassed, of course, but wrote a note to Adams, complimenting him on his patriotism and advising him to handle Vergennes with gloves. Adams then went to Holland to represent Congress there.

Franklin stayed on in France alone. In the beginning of 1778, T. Morris died of drunkenness, and Lee, Izard and Company left the country shortly after. But Franklin's situation was delicate. Every traveler who returned from America described his unpopularity. Franklin was told that Congress hadn't wanted him to take William Temple as his secretary. In 1782, his son-in-law Bache was unceremoniously deprived of his situation as postmaster-general. Franklin's relatives were all barred from public offices, and he, himself, was isolated.

He needed support and coöperation, however, to make the alliance of practical use. France had entered the war to make a beautiful gesture, to attract the sympathy and affection of the world for the new nation, to give a gentle lesson to the hated and admired England, and to obtain a few commercial advantages. All these results were to be attained by a short, brilliant war. Vergennes had so much confidence in the power of liberty, and had been so influenced by Franklin's guile, that he did not think the war could be otherwise. Now it was long and painful; the English evacuated Philadelphia in 1778, but the Americans could not make any serious progress, and the French naval attacks on Newport and Savannah failed. There was no important victory in 1779, despite the intervention of Spain, but the English ravaged the South of the United States and occupied it. In 1780, matters went from bad to worse, Charleston was taken by the redcoats, Virginia was overrun by cavalry raids and the establishment of a royal governor in Georgia seemed to toll the knell of Southern insurrection. Cornwallis, who was commanding the British armies in this region, was a conqueror everywhere. Bouillé's successes in the

West Indies consoled the French, though his victories were more picturesque than useful. Finally, in 1781, Arnold's treason capped the climax of the American disasters, and as an anticlimax, Cornwallis had a brilliant campaign in South Carolina. No one understood anything any more at Versailles; every one was sorry and angry. The French had thought that the Americans would have doubled their efforts, being encouraged by the alliance, but, on the contrary, they seemed to have softened. This was no illusion. Most of the Americans had thought the alliance would reduce their troubles and efforts, and that the intervention of France would draw the main English forces to Europe. They were somewhat surprised and shocked to realize that their own country was still the chief battleground, and found it quite natural to ask France for more money to continue the struggle, to demand indispensable vessels to maintain their naval supremacy on the coasts, and even — contrary to the spirit of the treaty — they asked for an army to chase the English out of their own country. Poor Monsieur de Vergennes, who had walked into the snare of his own accord, gave in only when he had to, and resisted more and more.

Congress only increased his annoyance. The less the Americans succeeded in war, the more Congress demanded in the way of peace conditions. The alliance guaranteed them independence, but the Americans had got it in their head to make a conquest of Canada (1778–79). This would have embarrassed the King of France very much, for the French Government no longer wanted this province, though a strong political party still did. The people would not have understood why Canada would not be returned to France if it were once more taken from England, and the other kings of Europe would have been furious to see France securing so much power for such a young and eager republic. The representatives of the Southern States in Congress demanded Florida, all the territory up to the Mississippi and the right to navigate on that river; these requests irritated the Spanish, who wanted to control the same regions. Finally, the representatives of New

England insisted on the right to fish off the banks of Newfoundland and to dry their fish on the Newfoundland coast, as though it were a God-given privilege. They were in opposition to the French fishermen, who were very jealous of their rights. During the negotiations, Vergennes realized he was not dealing with ethereal, modest, philosophic persons but with living human beings, who were ambitious and exacting. He should have known this before, but the legends about the Quakers and Franklin's manners had deceived him.

His awakening was disagreeable. Between 1780–1781 it took all the art of Franklin to avoid an open break between Vergennes and Congress. Two parties had been formed in Congress, one of them pro-French, the other Nationalist. The former was glad to accept the aid of France, had every confidence in her, was ready to ask her for more help or would have consented to peace on moderate terms. The Nationalists found it humiliating to ask and receive so much aid, would have liked to have avoided doing so and wanted an absolutely autonomous position in the world. They wouldn't hear of any kind of peace except a triumphant one. Naturally, the two parties were opposed, but in the voting this only resulted in a compound majority which combined their viewpoints: all that France gave they accepted willingly, but they were still resolved to have a perfect peace. This point of view did not seem very logical to Franklin, but he had to defend it before Vergennes who had less and less faith in Congress.

Franklin was saved by the impeccable method he used. He was always calm, discreet and frank with the King and Vergennes; he listened to them attentively, realized their point of view, and loyally presented it under a favorable light to the Americans. Then he waited for the right moment to expound the views of Congress to the French. Sometimes this delayed matters, but it guaranteed a suave collaboration which was very essential in times of war. Franklin never adopted a haughty manner, never discussed anything officially, but always like a man, and Vergennes was charmed, without seeing that Franklin was the one who benefited. Franklin's position as

Patriarch, his age and illnesses — which he used as a last resource when he wanted to withdraw from a blind alley — all gave him the ascendency over a minister who, from a political and social viewpoint, was his superior. Franklin avoided many annoyances due to his elaborate simplicity. In 1779, when he had been named Minister Plenipotentiary, all the accredited diplomatic body at Versailles prepared to receive his visit, as was customary, but not to return it, for their countries did not recognize the independence of America. This would have been a correct insult both to America and France. Franklin avoided it. He made no visits to any of his colleagues. They didn't interest him. He was too busy. Besides, he had foot trouble and couldn't climb up all those stairs. The courtiers found this to be a consummate piece of evasion; that "too tender feet" was an idea of genius. Vergennes was grateful for it.

He was all the more touched by the way Franklin supported French policies in his official and private correspondence with the Americans and the French. The discontented element in the French population began to increase: there were officers who had returned from America but who had not become generals, and who had neither been decorated nor paid; there were merchants who had been hurt by the fall of the dollar or ruined by the capture of their boats; ladies of the court who were weary of war, and writers who wanted to swindle the ministry. All these persons were very dangerous under the rule of a benevolent King who was anxious to please, but Franklin was able to cope with them. He knew how to handle the press and public opinion.

He collaborated with Genêt, who was the interpreter for the Minister of Foreign Affairs and Vergennes' right-hand man. They published jointly, *Les Affaires de l'Angleterre et de l'Amérique*, a periodical in which all the English slanders were refuted and the cause of the alliance ardently upheld. When it ceased to appear (December, 1779), Genêt distributed the propaganda between the *Mercure de France*, which received the larger part and the *Gazette de France*. He also planned a gazette in English in order to enlighten Americans on the situation in France. Franklin and he continued to supply news to the other publications which were friendly to America: *Courrier du Bas Rhin*, *Gazette de Leyde*, *Gazette Française d'Amsterdam*, etc. They even managed to insert propaganda items in newspapers which were less favorable, such as the curious *Courrier de l'Europe* which was sold to both the French and the English governments. Franklin also had access to such publications as the *Journal de Paris*, a fashionable leaflet, by his Masonic and philosophic affiliations. It refused to publish simple propaganda, but it was only too glad to accept all that the doctor offered. He continued to have the aid of such great nobles as the Duc de La Rochefoucauld, who translated the American State Constitutions for him (published in book form, 1778) and other revolutionary texts.

But Franklin accomplished most by the aid of the Masons. He was solidly established in French Masonry, being a member of the Nine Sisters' Lodge and its Grand Master between 1779–1781. He guided their activities. Various other lodges, philanthropic and learned societies invited him to their meetings, "to increase the sweetness of fraternal union", as they phrased it. Thanks to them, Franklin maintained zeal and respect for America among the enlightened middle classes. At the Nine Sisters' Lodge there was nothing but celebrations and special meetings in honor of the United States.

Such a brilliant rôle and such a sure method permitted Franklin to request and receive a great deal.

He obtained a total of eighteen million francs in various loans, at a time when the coffers of France were practically empty; he was able to send a French army to America in 1780 with the aid of La Fayette, and a huge French fleet in 1781. Franklin blushed when he thought of all the requests he had to make of Vergennes, but he always had the best reasons to back them and used most subtle propaganda. Thus, in February, 1780, when his need for money became urgent, he distributed his "Letter of Congress to its Constituents", in which the financial situation of America was viewed through rose-colored glasses.

But he worked in vain, for the moment had come when the French Government showed it was weary, and this attitude was exaggerated immediately by British propaganda. It was said that the King gave a cold shoulder to Franklin and that Vergennes was at the end of his friendship. The French diplomats murmured among themselves, calling Franklin an "agreeable charlatan", and in the streets one heard songs sung about "the Doctor in partibus" and "the octogenarian chameleon."

At the same time, two infamous pamphlets were covertly circulated, one called "Monsieur de Sartines' Green Box", and the other "The History of a French Louse." These were filled with slanders against Franklin, which had originated at the British Ministry and in English newspapers, claiming that the Sage was dissolute, rascally, and over fond of money. His enemies even tried to compromise him by making it known he had approved of Pulteney's peace propositions, which had been submitted to him in April, 1778. This was, of course, an absolute untruth. He was even attacked on scientific grounds. Wilson, his former collaborator, having been urged on by the King, claimed that Franklin's pointed lightning rod was not as efficient as the blunted ones. George III thereupon put blunted lightning rods on all the public buildings. Pringle refused to be convinced that they were in any way superior, and as a consequence lost his post as doctor to the Queen as well as the presidency of the Royal Society of Science. At the same time, some fanatic published a brochure to show that Franklin was just a clever nitwit, "A Letter to Mr. Franklin . . . London, 1778."

But all these attacks, coming from the four quarters of the globe, didn't disturb the Sage in the least. He scarcely ever defended himself, except when he feared that Congress might have a bad impression otherwise. George III could throw away his pointed lightning rods for all he cared, though he wrote, "If I had a wish about it, it would be that he had rejected them (conductors) altogether as ineffectual. For it is only since he thought himself and family safe from the thunder of Heaven that he dared to use his own thunder in destroying his innocent subjects." He knew very well that the entire scientific world was on his side. The innumerable letters he received from England were ample testimony that he was always loved there. He knew that even if the French made up songs about him they had not ceased to adore him. When an American merchant, one Peter Allaire, brought a suspicious bottle of Madeira to Franklin, the police arrested him immediately, and he could have ended his days in the Bastille had not Franklin somewhat reluctantly intervened.

The unpleasant side of his life, however, was not so much in the attacks of his enemies, which added spice to his glory, but in the overwhelming and tedious work which fell on his shoulders. Besides being Minister to France, he was also the American Consul, and had to secure huge funds for the United States. All the business of the American frigates, privateers and merchant vessels passed through his hands. Franklin had to act as arbiter in all kinds of disputes between French privateers and American sailors, to answer the complaints of sailors who were undernourished, of passengers who had been poorly accommodated, of ruined privateers, etc. Sometimes he had to deal with such heroes as Connyngham, or John Paul Jones, whose privateering in 1778–1779 disorganized British commerce, kept the English coast towns in a state of terror, and roused French enthusiasm to a high pitch. All this was very fine, but the negotiations to share the spoils and expenses and to exchange prisoners were fractious and interminable, even granting the highly philosophic supposition that the negotiators were honest! When Franklin had to pronounce judgment on these rough, insincere privateers, who argued at Brest, Lorient, Nantes or Bordeaux about fights which had taken place in mid-Atlantic, he could only rely on his intuition. These maritime affairs represented half of his correspondence.

Sometimes they were sufficiently picturesque to amuse him, but, for the most part, the business was dull enough. It was often complicated and annoying. Moreover, Congress had fallen into the habit of drawing bills on Franklin, his colleagues in Europe did the same, and even William Bingham, American Commissioner in the West Indies, followed their example. Bills rained on him from everywhere and they were always unexpected, for Congress knew that Franklin would refuse if he were warned ahead of time. The situation grew steadily worse, and in 1781 Franklin found himself in a semi-tragic, semi-burlesque position. The French Government had just promised him a gift of six million francs, which he needed urgently, when Colonel John Laurens arrived, authorized by Congress to ask for forty million francs. He was pledged ten million and started to spend them in a royal fashion. Franklin was delighted to watch him. Suddenly he had a cold sweat for he accidentally discovered that Laurens was spending *his* six million, for the ten other millions were only a hope. This time it was too much; Franklin put a stop to these activities, and wrote to Laurens' secretary, Jackson:

"I applaud the Zeal you have both shown in the Affair; but I see that nobody cares how much I am distressed, provided they can carry their own Points. I must therefore take what care I can of mine, theirs and mine being equally intended for the Service of the Public." Franklin was so overwhelmed under this avalanche of bills he let Vergennes know about it, and the minister, like a faithful friend, came to his aid. He had his secretary, Rayneval, write to the banker, Grand: "The financial affairs of Monsieur Franklin are as complicated as a labyrinth; if you could find the thread again, Monsieur le Comte de Vergennes begs you to come here as soon as possible." And in a few days Grand had untangled the skein.

All these complications, embarrassments, and irritating preoccupations could have killed Franklin in a few months had he not known how to take everything calmly. His passivity helped him to wait for the easier times when he could refresh himself. But it was a source of exasperation to nervous men, and his enemies made the most of it. Franklin's negligence was often cited in Congress, and the French Government, though it defended him, "acknowledged his apathy." No one realized what services this "apathy" had rendered to the alliance and to the health of Mr. Franklin. A rigorous exactitude would have meant the end of either one or the other.

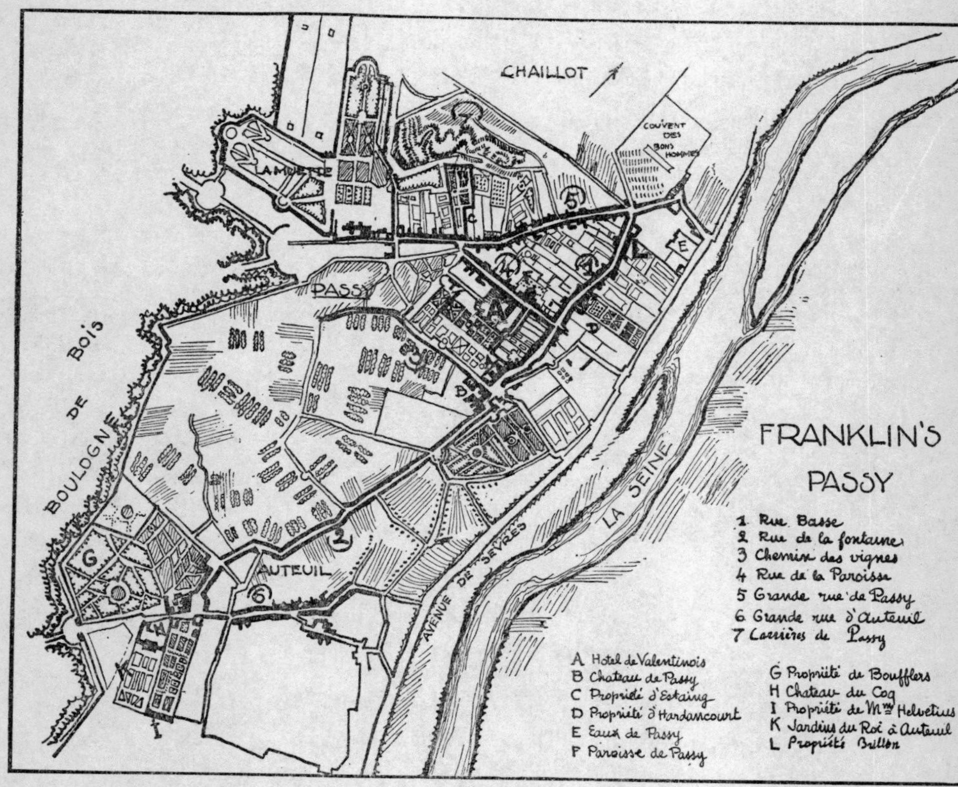
CHAILLOT
COUVENT DES BONS HOMMES
LA MUETTE
PASSY
BOIS DE BOULOGNE
AUTEUIL
AVENUE DE SEVRES
LA SEINE
FRANKLIN'S PASSY
1 Rue Basse
2 Rue de la fontaine
3 Chemin des vignes
4 Rue de la Paroisse
5 Grande rue de Passy
6 Grande rue d'Auteuil
7 Carrières de Passy
A Hotel de Valentinois
B Chateau de Passy
C Propriété d'Estaing
D Propriété d'Hardancourt
E Eaux de Passy
F Paroisse de Passy
G Propriété de Boufflers
H Chateau du Coq
I Propriété de Mme Helvetius
K Jardins du Roi à Auteuil
L Propriété Brillon

A sketch of Passy and Auteuil as they appeared in Franklin's time, made according to the map of Roussel (1751) and a Map of Paris and its suburbs during the First Empire (1800–1820). This sketch was also drawn according to the many valuable hints given in the Bulletin de la Société Historique d'Auteuil et de Passy (1792–1914).

An eighteenth-century traveler, coming from Paris, entered Passy by the "Grande Rue de Passy", now "Rue de Passy." To his left, was the "Rue Basse" (now Rue Raynouard) which ran parallel to the Seine. On the left side of this street were the mineral springs and baths of Passy (*E*) which were managed by Franklin's great friend, Le Veillard (*L*). A beautiful house with a terrace and garden extending to the Avenue de Sèvres. It belonged to M. Brillon, who lived there with his charming wife and two daughters. (Now No. 13 Rue Raynouard.) (*D*) Another fashionable estate, belonging to M. d'Hardancourt, who was a friend of Franklin and probably one of Madame Brillon's family. (Now No. 51 Rue Raynouard.)

If the traveler turned to his right, he entered the then Rue de la Paroisse, and shortly reached the Church of Passy (*F*) and the dignified entrance of the Hôtel de Valentinois, belonging to Monsieur Donatien Le Ray de Chaumont (*A*). The rear of the main building faced Rue de la Paroisse, now Rue de l'Annonciation, No. 9–13. Then there was a courtyard, with a staircase at one end, descending to a garden where there was a little pond. Beyond this were the kitchen gardens, and the whole was encircled with a rather large terrace which extended as far as Rue Basse and Chemin des Vignes. One had a lovely view from here. Several small buildings were situated on the right or upper part of the terrace: the greenhouses, and the little house where Franklin lived when he first came to Passy. It was called "le Petit Hôtel de Valentinois" or "la basse cour de Monsieur de Chaumont." Later, Franklin moved into the Grand Hôtel de Valentinois, on Rue de la Paroisse.

Continuing along the Rue Basse, the traveler would reach the Chemin des Vignes (now Rue des Vignes), where a stately castle stood, surrounded by a beautiful park (*B*). This was the Château de Passy, which belonged to the Comte de Boullainvilliers, father of Mademoiselle de Passy.

After the Château de Passy, it was clear country, with vineyards and fields. Rue Basse was changed into Rue de la Fontaine, and eventually led into Auteuil. To the right stood a dignified castle with long leafy avenues, belonging to the old wealthy family, the Boufflers. Their "intendant" was Monsieur Caillot, and it was this gentleman's daughter-in-law, a pretty young woman, who was Temple's great love (*G*).

The Rue de la Fontaine came to an end in Auteuil when it met the Grande Rue d'Auteuil, and at this junction, there were several charming houses. The first one (1) belonged to Madame Helvétius, the second one, "Château de Coq", was the property of M. Joly de Fleury, Minister of Finance from 1781 to 1783 (*K*). It had formerly been a part of the "Jardin du Roi" (King's Garden), and was sold in 1776.

Passy was on the outskirts of the Bois de Boulogne, where the fashionable people went to dance or walk or ride when Spring came. The procession on Good Friday was the most fashionable event of the year.

In one of the dance halls of the Bois de Boulogne, the Ranelagh, the Lodge of the Nine Sisters, met in 1778.

V

BUT the real salvation of Franklin was Passy. After his brief excursion into the fashionable world which followed the signing of the treaties, Franklin retired to his village, and never left it, except on official errands or to attend Academy meetings. Every Tuesday he went to Versailles, visited the ministers, paid his respects to the royal family, dined sumptuously at Vergennes' table, and then went to enjoy himself in the salon of Count d'Armanda, a cross-eyed, majestic personage whose ices were famous. Finally, he returned to Passy, suffering from his sore feet, crammed with food, but on the whole, satisfied.

Besides, he was on such good terms at court, and knew how to manage his illnesses so well, that it was often possible for him to avoid this noble task. Occasionally he attended the meetings of the Academy of Science, the Royal Society of Medicine, the Philanthropic Society, the Assembly of Scholars and Artists at Hotel Villayer, Rue St. André des Arcs; he sat at the solemn sessions of Parliament, or sometimes, more frivolously, went to the opera. But for the most part he stayed at Passy. He held his chancellery there with Temple, Laire de la Motte, his secretary, and a clerk. All his portfolios were arranged in the Petit Hôtel de Valentinois, and it was there he took care of his correspondence, negotiated business affairs, amused himself and rested. He had even installed a little press so that he could "play at printing", and publish the charming little writings he made for his friends. He printed twenty-three of them between 1778 and 1785, and the most famous were the "bagatelles": "Dialogue with Gout", "The Whistle", "Ephemères", "Les Mouches", "A Parable against Persecution", etc. They were written in the French style of the time, with humor and feeling, and were intended for his friends, especially for the charming ladies he knew. These latter directed the course of his life in Passy and were the sweetness of his existence.

He stole only the morning hours from them. As long as Benny was there, he took him to the banks of the Seine and taught him how to swim by swimming with him. When Benny left, he found he was too old for these exercises and took sun baths, or rather, air baths, all alone in his room, and claimed they were very refreshing. When he was not gouty he took long walks, either in his garden or to his neighbors. On Sundays he walked in the Bois de Boulogne and in Bagatelle, the new estate of the Comte d'Artois.

The whole region of Passy was filled with gardens, terraces and shady alleys of leafy trees. It harmonized with the peaceful, wealthy, fine society of people it sheltered. Franklin could enjoy all the advantages of the country without dispensing with the pleasures of society. Moreover, with his coach, he could go wherever he wanted; Paris was only a mile away and Versailles but seven. He liked staying at home, though, best of all. It was well furnished and managed by Monsieur Finck, the *maître d'hôtel* of whom Franklin said later: "As to Finck . . . he was continually saying of himself, *Je suis honnête homme, je suis honnête homme*. But I always suspected he was mistaken; and so it proves." Under Finck were Coinet, the cook, Joseph Rogey, the kitchen boy, François, the coachman (who was succeeded by Arbelot), Brunel, the footman, etc. All this little world of servants was meagerly paid: the cook received three hundred francs a year, and the coachman the same, plus wine, powder and breeches; the kitchen boy earned two hundred and four francs a year. Franklin spent about fifteen hundred francs a month, though sometimes he spent a little more, as in July, 1778, when his bill came to two thousand three hundred forty-six francs because of the Independence Day celebration (six hundred francs).

The pantry was always well supplied with hams, meat pies, tarts, and custards; the cellar, stocked by the Chevalier O'Gorman, the son-in-law of the Chevalier d'Eon, was also

VIEW OF THE SEINE AND PARIS FROM FRANKLIN'S TERRACE AT PASSY

worthy of passing notice. In 1778, Franklin's wine list included 1040 bottles: 258 of red and white Bordeaux, 15 of old Bordeaux, 21 bottles of Champagne, 326 bottles of white Mousseux, 113 bottles of red Burgundy, and 148 bottles of Xeres, for Franklin was very fond of Spanish wines, and his friends often sent him some bottles to please him. For the five masters and the nine servants, he paid 1360 francs a month to his *maître d'hôtel:* 730 for the masters, 240 for the servants, 400 for guests.

This gave him also the right to a breakfast, about ten o'clock, of bread, butter and honey, coffee or chocolate; a dinner at two o'clock, consisting of two meat courses: beef, veal or mutton, followed by hare or fowl in season, then two side dishes, two vegetable courses, a pastry course — of course, *hors d'œuvres* of butter, pickles, radishes, etc., was understood — two fruit courses in winter, and four in summer, two fruit stews, a plate of mixed cheeses, wine biscuits, candies, and ices twice a week in summer, once in winter. Franklin's coach cost him five thousand eighteen francs a year, and between his coach and his pantry he lived a comfortable life. When occasionally it was not so comfortable, he had recourse to a medicine chest which was well stocked with quinine, Peruvian bark, Spanish licorice, anise seed, alkali, gargles, manna. Franklin could have withstood a siege without suffering.

He had gained the devotion of every one, from his opulent neighbors, the Comtes de Boullainvilliers, to his unassuming purveyors: Brunel, the cabinet maker, and the woodman, Chocanne. He returned all their favors with expansive generosity, as his account books prove. He loaned the use of his coach to a charming lady, he gave a Polish priest twenty-four francs, a young German six, a poor author fifteen, etc. Franklin received an almost uninterrupted procession of American prisoners, beggars, hard-up poets, officers about to sail, convicts out of bounds, monks who had lost in gambling, Masons who wanted positions. Even the Duc de Bourbon arrived one day, begging him to procure some dogs and horses which he "needed" from England, as the war had made it difficult. But the most surprising request came from a gentleman of Perche. Franklin showed the letter to Cabanis. The good man had written that it was clear to him America couldn't get along without a king, and that he, of an antique line which went back to William the Conqueror, had all the qualities necessary to govern well, that he offered his services and if he couldn't persuade Congress to accept them, he would be satisfied with the title of King and an income of fifteen thousand francs, remaining all the while in his own country, and allowing the Americans to govern themselves as they pleased! Such letters as these arrived constantly with propositions of perpetual peace, advice to Congress by Swiss judges, campaign suggestions by various officers, complimentary odes from poets, and requests from grocery boys who wanted to go to America. Franklin would glance them over, and then pass them on to the ladies he knew for their amusement.

He owed them at least this. Franklin was their idol; he was adored from the highest ladies of the court to the lowest of chambermaids. Marie Antoinette had him explain the mysteries of physics to her, the Duchesse de Bourbon played chess with him, Madame Bertin, niece of the Chancellor, took him for rides in her coach, the Comtesse Golofkin sang, "O God of Love!" for him, and they all wanted to kiss him and to call him "Papa." He must have conceded this privilege to a number of them, Madame Conway, Madame de Flainville, Madame Brillon, Madame Dutartre, and others. He was generous with his kisses, and explained this propensity to his friends on the other side of the Atlantic in one of his letters:

> You mention the Kindness of the French Ladies to me. I must explain that matter. This is the civilest nation upon Earth. Your first Acquaintances endeavour to find out what you like, and they tell others. If 'tis understood that you like Mutton, dine where you will, you find Mutton. Somebody, it seems, gave it out that I lov'd Ladies; and then everybody presented me their Ladies (or the Ladies presented themselves) to be *embraced*, that is to have their Necks kissed. For as to kissing of Lips or Cheeks it is not the Mode here; the first is reckon'd rude, and the other may rub off the Paint.

He could not appear in any salon but what he was immediately surrounded by several beauties, and if he sat down, they sat down too — on the arms of his chair. Such eagerness at times caused him some difficulty, for each one wanted to be the most beloved. But like a sage, he had foreseen the possibility and turned it to advantage. When one of them would ask if he didn't love her the most, he would always answer: "Yes, when you are the nearest to me, on account of the force of attraction."

However, this force was not always of the same strength. One of his most intimate friends was Madame la Comtesse de Forbach, Duchesse douairière de Deux Ponts, a picturesque old lady with a lively mind, who had been a dancer. She kept her prettiness despite the years and gave Franklin beautiful presents: a pair of scissors, a gold-headed cane — but it was her admiration which he found the most precious. Then there was Mademoiselle de Passy, the daughter of the Comte de Boullainvilliers, who owned almost all the hill and a splendid château on its slopes. Franklin often went there to visit his little friend. He was so fond of kissing her and she was so indulgent in her embraces that there was some joking when she married the Comte de Tonnerre (Count of Thunder). "How is it, Doctor Franklin," his friends waggishly asked him, "that with all your lightning rods you couldn't keep Thunder from hitting on Mademoiselle de Passy?"

But there were plenty of others who were only too willing to replace her, such as the princesses Sapieha and Sangusko, who wrote him a clever little note to remind him they were awaiting his coming with impatience. They promised him that he would not have to go to sleep like Alain Chartier[1] "to enjoy privileges of mistletoe" and that they had "no officers to propose." Alas, they couldn't have had as many attractions as Mademoiselle de Passy, for in spite of all his guarantees, he forgot the dinner!

[1] A fourteenth-century poet who was kissed as he slept by Marguerite d'Écosse. She explained her action by saying she had not kissed the man, but the lips "from whence had issued so many golden words."

But he always accepted the invitations of Madame d'Houdetot, who gave country festivals in his honor at her estate in Sanoy. The most charming of them took place on April 12, 1781. Even Rousseau would not have declined it. The company walked in advance to meet Franklin, who was to arrive in his coach. They met him about a mile away from the château. Then, as he alighted, they sang songs on liberty, and conducted him across the park which was hung with festoons, to a table burdened with food. The meat was excellent and wine flowed copiously. After every bumper the guests sang heartily:

Here's to the mem'ry of Benjamin,
The good he has done is no story,
In America he will have altars,
While in Sanoy we sing to his glory.

As the number of empty bottles increased, the guests made impromptu verses in his honor, and the Countess succeeded so well she was suspected of having thought up hers beforehand:

He gave his laws to human kind
And freed them with his lightning rod,
Virtue borrowed his face to find
The adoration given to God.

The men were not to be outstripped and the Vicomte d'Houdetot won applause for his couplet:

Though America's destiny lies in his hand,
Like a true sage, he drinks with our band.

After dinner, the Countess begged Franklin to plant a Virginia locust tree in her garden. She had even prepared a pretty marble inscription in honor of the happy tree so Franklin could not refuse. When this ceremony was over, the cool spring twilight had already fallen, and the guests returned to the château in a stately procession. Some musicians preceded them, and as they walked, they sang one last song:

Oh, may this fair Virginia tree,
Which his own hand has planted,
Be great as his nobility.

And may it cast a happy shade
Over the hamlet and the glade.

Lightning will not dare to strike it,
Thunder will be forced to like it,
Franklin's blessing is on this tree,
Insuring immortality.

Night had fallen, dark and fragrant, when Franklin's horses were finally harnessed. As they champed at their bits and pawed the dusty road, Franklin bade his hostess farewell and she answered him in verse:

Solon of one land, beloved of two,
Man in all ages owes thee praise,
But now, I pray, accept from me,
The debt of all my enduring days.

But so much admiration was nothing compared to the daily delights of his two dearest companions: Madame Helvétius and Madame Brillon de Jouy. Madame Helvétius was no longer young, though she didn't know it, and her charm was so pervasive that her guests were not aware of it. She had been so remarkably beautiful, an effulgent halo of loveliness still remained. Her family was one of the oldest of Lorraine — the Lignivilles — but it was also one of the poorest. They had not been able to educate her and she always spelled like a scrub-woman, although she had spent her youth in Paris with one of her aunts, Madame de Graffigny, who was a writer of some repute and noted for her tact. People thought she would know how to marry off her niece, who quite independently thought she could manage very well by herself. There was a young student who danced constant attendance on her and gave her every encouragement. His manners were a little heavy, but he had a brilliant, sensitive mind and he was of distinguished birth. The two young people loved each other very much and finally told Madame de Graffigny. She was not indignant, but merely said they were mad: Mademoiselle de Ligniville didn't have any dowry and Monsieur Turgot was without a sou. Monsieur Turgot who was a philosopher and Mademoiselle de Ligniville, who was intelligent, realized that the aunt was right. They swore eternal friendship and saw each other almost every day. Some years later, Mademoiselle de Ligniville married Helvétius, the son of a noted financier-doctor. He, himself, was a famous financier and was very rich, as he could boast of an income of three hundred thousand francs a year. She loved him very much; he was worthy of her love and adored her in return. All of their friends were delighted in their happiness and elaborated on the extraordinary virtues of her husband — all, excepting Turgot, who thought Helvetius was a rather unpleasant man. It was the only point on which he disagreed with Madame Helvetius, whom he continued to see every day, except when she was living at her country estate.

At length, Helvétius passed away, and Turgot paid his visit of condolence, offering his services once more, now that he was rich and famous. But Madame Helvétius, who lived in luxury, and who was surrounded by friends who coddled her, answered, "Why change, my dear Turgot? Hasn't our friendship always been perfect?" and she spoke of her debt to Helvetius too. He had to agree that all she said was true. Consequently, he was her most assiduous guest at Auteuil, where she retired after the death of her husband. There she lived in rustic magnificence, surrounded by her eighteen cats, ten dogs, various birds, philosophers, monks, and Masons. The entire Nine Sisters' Lodge, which had been founded at the suggestion of her late husband, often met at her home. Ever since Franklin had established himself at Passy he had become hers by right of conquest, and she belonged to him by the same tokens. Madame Helvétius had seen the whole world pass in review before her in her salon, she knew all the peculiarities of her century, she had love for every one she met, except for women who were always her pet aversion, and she thought there was no more novelty in life left for her. But she had not counted on Franklin. The novelty of this man, who was so serious and ironic, so rustic and exquisite, so reserved and so audacious, was unbelievably delightful. She was mad about Franklin and showed her fondness for him in a hundred ways. When he entered the room she would hold out her slender hand to be kissed, indicate the most comfortable armchair to sit in, and then she would flatter and tease him. If he stayed to luncheon she would gorge him with that thick whipped cream Abbé Morellet liked so much. She had moles and wrinkles and didn't wash her face every day; her salon with all the dogs and cats was more like a stable than anything else; and she had such little regard for her furniture that she let the abbés drive nails into the chairs to make experiments. She was constantly kissing her favorite little dog, Poupou, whether Poupou merited kissing or not, and she kissed Franklin almost as often, not only on the cheek but on his forehead too. She would press his hands as she did so, or put her arm around his neck, and then, when she was tired, she would indolently lie on the sofa, and with the hem of her petticoat negligently wipe up the traces of Poupou.

Although she had the manners of a peasant she kept the air of a queen. And queens are always young, especially to gallants of eighty years. Franklin loved her and wrote one little story after another for her amusement. It was so lovely to visit "Our Lady of Auteuil", to hear her "little stars" of girls sing, to be chided and petted by her. For Madame Helvétius had a strong, clearly marked character, a precise brain and sharp wit, and a robust body. When he was near her, he felt like a little boy, who is always protected even when he is whipped, and his need of affection made itself felt once more. This clever energetic woman reminded him of his good Debby, who had also been so energetic and so agreeable in her rusticity.

He dreamed of Madame Helvétius so much that one fine day he proposed to her (1780). She was overwhelmed and weakly leaned against the mantlepiece, unable at first to answer. She almost knocked over the little plaster model of Helvétius' tomb — a woman weeping over a funeral urn — and taking it in her hands she mutely showed it to Franklin in sweet reproach. He was wise enough not to accept this as a refusal, and after vainly insisting for another answer, he took his leave, and they bade each other farewell with more than usual tenderness. During the feverish night that followed he wrote a charming apology: his "Descent to Hell." According to the tale, he met with Helvétius, who was glad to see him in the infernal place, and happy at being married again on the other side of the tomb. But his wife was no other than the late Mrs. Franklin, and when Franklin had reproached her gently, she answered with a flash of her old spirit: "I was your wife for almost half a century; be content with that." Then came the moral, or rather the conclusion to Franklin's fable: "Here I am. Let us have our revenge!"

The heart of Madame Helvétius, which should have been calm after all these years, suddenly beat with delicious violence. Such a great force seemed to push her to Franklin. The next day, however, she left in her coach for the same place she visited every day, though she alighted more dreamily than was her wont. Then she climbed the stairs of her old friend's house slowly, in a tender reverie. She told Monsieur Turgot of Franklin's proposal, how surprised she had been, and of all her trouble and hesitation. Her old friend leapt up in consternation. This fine marriage of a gallant of eighty with a shepherdess of sixty-five seemed like a caprice of second childhood to him. Madame Helvétius was almost shocked at his intense opposition, but she blushed when he warned her of the consequences. He told her she should do as she liked, but that if she did marry Franklin she was certain to lose her salon. Madame Helvétius left, still somewhat troubled, and took a long ride in her coach. When she had returned in the evening she was calm and decided: she never could do without her friends. Franklin could talk of love as much as he wanted and she would always answer with a gentle smile — and give him an extra helping of whipped cream.

But, at length, too much whipped cream became tiresome. France had roused all of Franklin's ardor, it had developed tastes in him that he had never known he possessed, and he was eager to satisfy them. He was eighty when he finally met the woman who was not only to give him the most love, but the most tender love.

Madame Brillon de Jouy was young. She was beautiful in a frail, delicate way and a mere word could wound her deeply. Her mind was clear and exquisite and she was eager for affection. She had come of a distinguished family — the Hardancourts — and without consulting her, they had married her to an intelligent financier, Brillon, Treasurer of the Parliament of Paris, who was a man of low upbringing and twenty-four years older than she. He was very generous and good-hearted, though given to chaffing, and his manners were as simple as his tastes. He was an excellent husband to his wife, and an indulgent father to his two beautiful daughters. Though he and Madame Brillon were rich, happy, and respected — even envied in the high society they frequented — they both felt there was something lacking in their conjugal life. Unfortunately, this "something" was not the same for both of them; it was physical for Monsieur Brillon and psychical for his wife. She would have needed the tears of St. Preux to console her, and he, a pretty little tavern maid of twenty.

When Franklin came to live at Passy he seemed like the God of Wisdom and Goodness to Madame Brillon.

> I began by worshipping you with the respect that every one owes to a great man — she wrote to him — then I was curious to see you, and to flatter my self-respect by receiving you in my home. After your visit I could remember only your sensitive friendliness, your simplicity and goodness. I said to myself, this man is so good he will love me, and I have since begun to love you deeply, hoping you would return my affection.

She was drawn instinctively to Franklin, and let him caress her, with the same touching confidence that a sick little girl has in the family doctor. Franklin called her "My daughter", and she answered with "Papa." As she was nowhere near forty, Franklin found this appellation singularly sweet. He spent long evenings with her every Saturday and Wednesday in the summer, and after they had played a few long games of chess, she gave a little recital on the clavecin. She was a competent musician and even composed for the instrument. When she tired of playing, Franklin would take her on his knees and kiss her tenderly on the back of her fresh young neck. They prolonged their infinite conversations far into the night, and she never grew weary of his stories, even when he kept her sitting two or three hours in her covered bathtub. Occasionally she would correct his French, which was always imperfect, as Franklin often mixed his genders. She sympathized with him when he said:

"*Il y a bien 60 ans que les choses masculines et feminines (hors des modes et des temps) m'ont donné beaucoup d'embarras. J'espérais autrefois qu'à 80 je pouvois en être delivré. Me voici à 4 fois 19 ce qui est bien près. Néanmoins ces féminins françaises me tracassent encore. Cela me doit rendre plus content d'aller en Paradis, où l'on dit que ces distinctions seront abolies.*"

She comforted him and said that his mistakes didn't matter, feminines or not, his style was always exquisite, and she warned him not to let himself be corrected by pedants. She always had some charming little stories to tell him, and was careful not to have Monsieur Brillon hear them first, for he was fond of them, too, and would have stolen them. Then she wrote little fables in verse for him, and on the evenings when he was very tired and wanted to meditate, she would quietly sit down to her clavecin and play the simple little tunes he loved: a Christmas carol, a popular minuet, or the "March of the Insurgents" which she had composed especially for him. In return, he would play on his harmonica such pieces as "The Little Birdies", or more poetically, he would write a little tale for her such as the "Ephemères" which he composed in her honor one evening when they had visited Watelet's garden. It was called "Moulin Joli" and was one of the first English gardens in France, an island in the Seine with lovely shady walks and winding streams. As they walked there, Franklin especially noticed the shimmering little insects, their wings glinting in the last rays of the sun, and he was reminded of life's brevity. He wrote his "Ephemères" as though it were a monologue by one of them on this theme, and concluded:

"To me, after all my eager pursuits, no solid pleasures now remain, but the reflection of a long life, spent in meaning well, the sensible conversation of a few good lady ephemerae, and now and then a kind smile and a tune from the ever amiable *Brillante.*"

She thanked him with more kisses, and more of those tender confidences which are so sweet to the suffering, love-burdened heart. It was an infinite pleasure for her to weep on his shoulder and he would stroke her hair with gentle melancholy.

There was as much charm in protecting Madame Brillon as there was in being protected by Madame Helvetius. And the role of "Papa" lent itself as easily to virtue as to delicious errors.

Monsieur Brillon was quite happy. Franklin had simplified his life and he was delighted to see his wife satisfied once more. Besides, he was fond of the good old Franklin who was as much a peasant as himself.

As the months passed, their intimacy deepened. Madame Brillon was wretched with chagrin and told Franklin all the little artifices that her daughters' governess, Mademoiselle Jupin, employed to keep Brillon from his duties. Mademoiselle Jupin even wanted to leave the Brillons and take refuge at Franklin's. But the good "Papa" intervened, gave his daughter some advice and sent Mademoiselle Jupin packing. Then he arranged a reconciliation between Monsieur and Madame and had the half-sad, half-dissolute pleasure of teasing Madame Brillon and asking her for some recompense. She overwhelmed him with letters to ease her heart:

I was too happy on Saturday, Sunday and Monday. Yes, dearest Papa, I was too happy and my present chagrin is a proof of it. I have not yet wanted to go and arrange your rooms, for everything reminds me so sharply of your absence. I went out to the fields instead, but everywhere I saw the traces of your footsteps; the trees seemed colored a sadder green and the river seemed to flow more slowly. . . .

People praise sensitivity so much, and yet it wreaks so much harm . . . still it makes for so much pleasure . . . without it I should never have been able to estimate your tenderness, dear, dear Papa, nor would I have been capable of returning it. Let us rather suffer and love, if one cannot love without suffering . . . I look on the beautiful sky and think that my friends can be enjoying it too, at the same moment; if I stretch out to rest on a lawn I love, I regret that those I love are not with me; the very air seems to breathe of liberty, and though this should fill my cup to overflowing it rather awakens in me a sweet melancholy — the price of a truly sensitive heart. It is in this state of melancholy that I spend my days here. . . .

Franklin answered her, speaking a little of the flesh. He said there were two more commandments not generally known: "Increase and multiply. Love one another." And to prove that she didn't live up to the last, concerning him, he recounted the tale of the Bishop and the Beggar.

A Beggar asked a rich Bishop for Charity, demanding a pound. — "A Pound to a beggar! That would be extravagant." — "A Shilling then!" — "Oh, it's still too much!" — "A twopence then or your Benediction." — "Of course, I will give you my Benediction." — "I don't want it, for if it were worth a twopence, you wouldn't give it me."

That is how the Bishop loved his neighbor, that was the extent of his Charity. If I examine yours I find that it isn't much more. I was hungry and you did not give me food, I was a foreigner and almost as ill as the Colin in your song, still you didn't either receive me or cure me — you did not even comfort me. You were as rich as an Archbishop in all the Christian and moral virtues, yet you couldn't sacrifice even a small portion of them without feeling that you would be losing too much.

Madame Brillon knew very well how to answer all these impertinent compliments, saying that the Bishop was a Miser, the Beggar a rascal and Franklin a mere Sophist. But he kept on persisting and wrote that "his love had been so under-nourished it had become a perfect skeleton since it had nothing to live on but a nutriment made of sound, which was nothing more than air", and, threatening its very imminent death, he demanded, "some solid nourishment."

She answered with a dissertation on Platonic and carnal love: "The one demands a love of flesh and bones, demands to be petted and spoiled. The other — the woman considers these little gentlemen to be airy little creatures, who are very pretty and amusing at times, but she always tries to blunt their arrows."

The gallant dispute continued all during his absence. He informed her that he would like to be the Angel Gabriel so that he could come to see her and carry her away on his wings. She wrote back that she would be distrustful of an angel Gabriel who was Franklin at the same time. Such a miraculous combination could only be dangerous for a lady.

Thus the bantering went on, in letters, and then in visits, chess games, long walks through the Tuileries, or in Madame d'Hardancourt's garden (Madame Brillon's mother) and even in Madame Brillon's own garden, where a great staircase of a hundred shallow steps led down to a wide lawn. The rococo setting alone was enough to make hearts and inkwells overflow with idyls, madrigals, and peaceful pastorals.

In spite of appearances, Franklin's heart, always eager and wise, was not deceived by such illusions. He had never ceased being a home-loving man. He had never been able to do without Debby in America, or the good Mrs. Stevenson in England. Now when he cast his eyes over his disorderly room, with his papers scattered everywhere and his coats and shirts inelegantly draping the stately chairs, he sighed. Perhaps it had been no vain chimera of love when he asked Madame Helvétius to marry him, but just a good bourgeois instinct. The desire to have a real home made him request Madame Brillon to marry her eldest daughter to William Temple. Temple was nice-looking and well-bred. He found favor in most feminine eyes and especially pleased the Brillon girls. Because of her friendship for Franklin, Madame Brillon had been maternal with William, and had allowed him to play with her girls and to kiss them surreptitiously now and then. She had helped him choose a fine pair of hose and taken care of him when he was ill. As William was the heir of his grandfather and protected by him, he could have been sure of a brilliant diplomatic career in Europe. And for Franklin the marriage would have been a gentle culmination of his too active life.

Monsieur Brillon was surprised by the offer and Madame Brillon was touched. She even wept. Then they thought the matter over for some days and finally answered Benjamin with a polite refusal. The difference in religion, the possibility of Temple returning to live in America, and the necessity of Monsieur Brillon passing on his post to his son-in-law, all made the match inadvisable. Franklin protested in vain that their religion was at bottom the same; they admitted it but insisted that formalities were important for a young household, and besides, there were other objections. Madame Brillon's letter was no less tender than the others, but it was extraordinarily precise and wise. She added that Brillon thought as she did, which was probable, though it was certain he had been influenced by her. She had a pretty clear idea of what men were (April, 1781).

Temple left for a change of scene to visit the Chaumonts in Touraine, the Brillons departed for Nice to rest after all this emotion, and Franklin remained alone at Passy to dream on the chimerical events of his past life.

Were all these exquisite flatteries and autumnal tendernesses merely the counters of some sophisticated game? There is a story told which has all the perfume of these artificial flowers. Either Madame Brillon or Madame Helvetius invited the Sage to come and spend the day with her, and he answered, saying that he had spent so many days at her home that he thought it was high time to spend a night with her.

The answer was quite as immediate: "Come this evening."

This was an unexpected embarrassment for the Patriarch, who was far from being a lively blade of twenty, and who yet did not wish to offend his friend. But he had become witty with the years and saved himself by answering: "It's not worth while to trouble you on these summer evenings; let us wait for a winter night."

Alas, the long night of winter which ends all human life was already lowering. Franklin was spending the sweetest hours of his old age now, dividing his time between his Voltairian and his Rousseau Muses, which were different but both equally exquisite and equally deceptive.

In February–March, 1779, he had a violent attack of gout, another still more serious in October–November, 1780, and all during the August of the same year he had been indisposed. His old friend, Barbeu Dubourg, died in December, 1780, and the Comtesse de Forbach was very ill. And as they disappeared, others began to take their places: Benny was studying at Geneva and had become an adolescent, J. Williams had married Alexander's daughter, and William Temple was a proud young man, very difficult to manage. The doctor felt tired and handed in his resignation which was refused. The war continued interminably, exhausting the finances of France and the patience of the people. Poor Monsieur de Vergennes turned a little more yellow every day. Franklin thought he would never see the end.

VI

Then, suddenly, on November 20, 1781, the news arrived in Paris that Cornwallis and all his army — the best in the New World — had been captured on the Chesapeake near Yorktown by the Franco-Americans. Fireworks blazed against the French sky and the joy was intense. The old song of "Malbrouk s'en va-t-en guerre", which had been forgotten since Denain's time, became popular once more. At the court and in the city people babbled incoherent praises of Louis XVI, Washington and Franklin. In London, when the disaster was affirmed, every one thought it meant peace.

Lord North had dreamed about peace for a long time. This solemn defeat was almost a comfort to him and he lost no time in finding out Franklin's stand on the matter. But the bad luck he had had all during the war stuck to him. The three men he employed for these negotiations were the last three he should have chosen: Digges, who was a notorious crook, Alexander, whose situation was ambiguous, and Hartley, who carried misfortune wherever he went. Both Franklin and Vergennes rejected England's respective offers of a separate peace.

Fortunately, North fell from power in March, and the Shelburne-Rockingham-Fox ministry which followed was determined to put an end to the war. At the same time, Lord Cholmondeley returned from Nice where he had often visited the Brillons, and went to Passy to pay his respects to Franklin. The Patriarch begged his visitor to congratulate Shelburne on his nomination and to communicate his desires of peace to him.

Thus the work of peace was in hand, beginning with April. Shelburne, Minister of the Colonies, sent over Oswald to deal with Franklin, while Fox, Minister of Foreign Affairs, sent Grenville to deal with Vergennes.

The prospects were bright. The three principal characters of this great play were all philosophers who admired each other and who venerated peace: Franklin, Vergennes and Shelburne. They wanted a treaty which would not only put an end to the fighting, but which would be an actual reconciliation. All three of them spoke the same language of philosophy and idealism.

Alas, they had to navigate on a Sargasso sea, for never was a peace negotiated with more dignity and more rascality. On account of their wisdom and virtue they all blindly tricked each other. It was a comedy of dupes, just as the long period of 1763–1775 had been a comedy of delays for England and America, and just as the interminable war with tiny navies scouring the immense sea and tiny armies pursuing each other over infinite territories had been a comedy of errors.

King George III was the only one who was not deceived. From the beginning to the end he thought that the entire American affair was suspicious and incoherent. In 1782 he wrote to Shelburne: "I am sorry to say it but from the beginning of the American troubles to the retreat of Mr. Fox this country has not taken any but precipitate steps whilst caution and system have been those of Dr. Franklin, which is explanation enough of the causes of the present difference of situation." Consequently, this time His Majesty did all he could to hinder the peace negotiations from proceeding too rapidly. He succeeded so well that he thought he would drive all his ministers mad.

One can imagine the nervous effect this method produced on the British ministry, whose days were numbered; on the French ministry, whose treasury was quite empty; and on the American delegates, who depended on reëlection. When the peace was final'y signed the negotiators were unanimous in their exasperation.

It had been nothing but a cyclone of suspicions!

England suspected France as an old, treacherous and cunning enemy, and considered America as a young, emancipated daughter who wanted to turn against her mother. George III judged Vergennes to be a dangerous hypocrite, Franklin an intriguer of the lowest class, and Adams a fanatic. He had no more confidence in his own ministers either; Shelburne was a Jesuit to him and he rated Fox much lower than Shelburne. A thriving hate existed between these two ministers, moreover, to add to the complications of the situation. They wanted peace with the enemy but they had declared war between themselves. The French and Americans who did not know this fact were disconcerted. They attached profound reasons to gestures which were merely the outcome of disorder.

France distrusted England, as she had been her rival for six centuries, and distrusted America, as the war had lasted too long. Vergennes distrusted Shelburne because he knew him; Jay because he didn't, Adams because of the unpleasant scene he was reminded of, and Franklin because he got along altogether too well with him.

America distrusted England because of the events of the past twenty years, and distrusted France because it had been her habit to do so for over a century. Franklin had no faith in George III, Adams had none in Vergennes, who had offended him, and Jay distrusted all the French ministers on general principles, being of Huguenot origin. Laurens distrusted every one, because his long prison term had soured his disposition. Adams thought that Franklin was an atheist of no morality, and Franklin thought that Adams was a madman, who was all the more dangerous as he was honest.

And the members of this interesting group each judged themselves to be upright men and spoke highly of virtue on every occasion.

France wanted independence for America, Gibraltar and Florida for Spain, and a few West Indian islands with much prestige for herself.

England wanted to make peace on the best terms, to divide the Americans and French if possible, and to prepare for a revenge. Shelburne dreamed of an economic and political reconciliation with the United States, and of an economic collaboration with France.

The American delegates wanted independence, territory up to the Mississippi, and the right to fish off the Newfoundland Banks. They thought these conditions would be pleasing to France and were satisfied with them themselves. They would not have minded playing a dirty trick on Spain, and Spain returned their good will with interest.

George III was absolute in his demands for compensation to the American "Loyalists", and up to the very end he wanted to refuse independence. He was constantly ready to leave for Hanover, and to retire there as a sign of his disapproval.

The most delicate matter for France was the necessity of making the American demands dovetail with those of Spain. The two countries were her allies, but they were far from being allied among themselves. By trying to moderate the demands of the United States and Spain, France looked like a poor friend to both of them.

The negotiations began under all these happy auspices. Shelburne began to feel his way without any further delay. He knew that Henry Laurens, the American plenipotentiary, who had been taken by an English privateer and imprisoned in the Tower of London, hated France. So Laurens was sent to The Hague, to visit Adams, and see what he could do there. An elderly and respected merchant, Richard Oswald, who was candid and intelligent as well, was sent to see Franklin with instructions to go ahead. He was accompanied by Caleb Whiteford, Franklin's former neighbor in London. They settled in Passy, talked with Franklin and were presented to Vergennes. Franklin repeated what he had been saying for four years, that if England wanted peace she had only to recognize the independence of America; if she wanted a reconciliation she should offer Canada. Oswald found this judicious and returned to report to Shelburne and the King. These latter did not agree with him, although they approved of Oswald personally. The King thought Franklin was tricking him again.

Unfortunately, Fox was jealous of Shelburne's fame and wanted to steal the glory of the peace for himself. He sent

Grenville to Passy to negotiate with both Vergennes and Franklin. As Franklin wasn't aware of the Fox-Shelburne quarrel he didn't understand, and all kinds of suspicions rose up between them. Grenville promised independence forthwith, not in order to please the Americans, but to cut out Shelburne, who, as minister of the colonies, would have nothing to do with a peace between free States. This initiative surprised every one, especially George III. The situation became more complicated.

The naval victory of the English over the French in the West Indies, the fall of the Rockingham ministry which entailed Fox's disappearance, and which was succeeded by a Shelburne ministry, plus Franklin's gout, were all contributing factors to more delay.

At last the negotiations were started once more under the direction of Shelburne, who was eager to have them over. The King wanted to hold them back, and the plenipotentiaries, who didn't know what the negotiations were all about. Fitzherbert replaced Grenville but this was the only change. At the same time, Jay arrived from Madrid and joined Franklin. The first step was to make England recognize the independence of America. The King did not want to, and a stiff struggle went on for three months. Finally, George III gave in, permitting Oswald to deal with the "United States." This was the first American victory.

In September, Oswald tried to separate the French and the Americans: a project dear to the British. He told the Americans that Gérard de Rayneval, the French First Secretary of Foreign Affairs, had left on a secret mission to London. Thus he raised their suspicions and most unjustly too, for Rayneval was only going to deal with French questions. He had gone to London to calm Vergennes' fears, for the French minister doubted Shelburne's sincerity. Oswald increased the American's uneasiness by showing them a letter of Marbois, the French envoy in Philadelphia, who severely criticized the American peace program and advised his Government to block it. (Which the Government didn't do, of course.) At this time, Jay and Adams had just returned from Holland, and Oswald went to see them. He did not have any difficulty in persuading them of French duplicity, and since the two of them formed a majority in the American delegation, it was decided, despite Franklin's protests and the instructions from Congress, to negotiate a peace treaty without consulting Vergennes. Oswald rubbed his hands, for he did not see that he was a cat's-paw, and that England would have to pay dearly for this reconciliation. The only British success was to have divided the French and the Americans temporarily by these deceitful maneuvers. To keep the breach open, England was obliged to hurry as much as possible in order not to upset the applecart, in which case France would have taken the ascendant. But Shelburne had so little trust in the Americans that he let Rayneval know by innuendo what had happened. The French didn't understand. Oswald made haste, and by doing so, put himself at the mercy of the Americans, for in negotiating it is always the hurried man who has to give in first. Thus from the end of September to November 30, 1782, the British defense fell bit by bit. Jay would reason, Adams would fume and thunder, Franklin would tell a story, and Oswald would give up another point. The United States obtained all the territory up to the Mississippi and the entire province of Maine, as well as the right to fish off the Newfoundland Banks. On the last day, the British were even satisfied with a vague clause in favor of the "Loyalists." Congress was not bound to do anything definite for them, merely to advise the States to treat them humanely. When this was decided, Oswald was delighted to sign (November 30).

On the next day, Franklin took the document to Vergennes with a request for another twenty million francs. Vergennes made a grimace and for the first time he treated the doctor rather dryly. But Franklin calmed him by suggesting that the British would be only too glad to discover a disagreement between France and America. He argued also that the American preliminaries included a clause which prevented their being effective until the Franco-British preliminaries should be signed. These latter dragged on for several weeks (January 18, 1783). All the preliminaries were finally signed at Versailles on January 20, 1783.

The British ministry sent Hartley to draft the final treaty and to end this work of reconciliation which had been so well begun. He worked zealously from April to September without success. The Fox ministry, which had in turn upset the Shelburne ministry, wanted to take advantage of the division between the allies, but public opinion and the King were both against giving a part of British commerce to the revolted subjects. Hartley was powerless, and after a thousand fine projects had been considered and rejected, the British had to sign the same text of the preliminary negotiations. There was no commercial treaty as no basis of commercial reconciliation could be found. The British had been the dupes throughout; they had paid very dearly for an Anglo-Saxon understanding without deriving any immediate benefits. The French had been deceived, for they had hoped for commercial privileges and worldly prestige which were not guaranteed by the peace. As to triumphant America, she had known how to get the better of her enemies and allies, but not of herself. Jay and Adams, by their patriotism and exacting demands, had probably deprived their country of Canada, which Franklin, by dangling his bait of reconciliation and taking his time, might have acquired. Such was the verdict of the wise, but the people were too eager for peace. They wanted their stores, taverns and theaters filled once more, and they wanted a chance to set off fireworks and drink.

The peace satisfied Adams, since he had modeled it according to his own will. Franklin, he thought, had played a decent rôle, for ever since the Congress of 1776, the Patriarch had been content to say "Amen." Franklin was in accord with the attitude of the delegates, except on one point: he was much more intensely opposed to the "Loyalists" than they. Whether he was thinking of the King, of his guilty son, or just basing his opinion on general principles, Franklin was refractory on this subject. During the peace negotiations he continued his opposition and he increased it by a masterpiece of propaganda. In April, 1782, all Europe was shocked by reprints of a copy of the *Boston Independent Chronicle*, which had really been written and printed by Franklin. It contained apparently authentic and stupefying evidence against the British: a letter from J. P. Jones to Sir J. York, British Minister in Holland, which was a violent indictment of George III, and two other letters, one from a captain of the American Militia, the other from an Indian chief to the Governor of Canada, in which were detailed the number of scalps the Indians had secured on the American frontiers for England, and which they sent as proof of their devotion, hoping for the promised payment. There were eight packs of the scalps of soldiers killed in battle, of poor farmers assassinated or burned alive, of their wives, sons and daughters. Franklin devised this piece of propaganda at Passy and sent it on to Holland; from that country it spread everywhere and succeeded in its purpose. The most curious thing was that the British could not be truly accused of this barbarism, which had, however, already been employed by the Pennsylvanians against the French, during the Seven Years' War. But thanks to this fake newspaper, Franklin maintained the European indignation against the British and the "Loyalists." The other delegates disputed over the terms of the treaty but Franklin was the real spirit behind it.

VII

Life was pleasant at this time and as picturesque as a Watteau painting. The peace had been signed, a Dauphin had been born, and the Monarchy, supported by this new glory, seemed destined for centuries of grandeur. The City of Paris held masked balls and set off fireworks in honor of the King (January, 1783), and Louis XVI with Marie Antoinette witnessed the love of their people among the Pierrots and Harlequins. Cagliostro ruled over the court and city in his splendid canary waistcoats and plumed headgear, practicing his Egyptian Free Masonry and holding mysterious initiations; the Cardinal de Rohan was his patron, and Comte de Vergennes his protector. For ten thousand francs he would initiate you into the mysteries of wisdom — or even of love. Monsieur Mesmer suddenly arrived from Vienna with his precious secret of "animal magnetism." Fine lords and ladies gathered around his magic bucket, filled with scrap iron, to cure themselves of their illnesses and to experience delicious thrills. Everybody visited him, and the Government even thought of buying his secret for some hundreds of thousands of francs. The most brilliant gentlemen of the land formed a society, called the "Lodge of Harmony", which had an entry fee of ten thousand francs and Mesmer for its instructor. His most ardent disciple was the richest and most famous noble of France, the young La Fayette. Mesmer had his poor followers as well, and electrified one of the trees near his house so that the crowds could benefit from his scientific labors, and tell how good-hearted and generous he was. Maids, lackeys, water-carriers, any one in fact, could come to the magic tree and be cured of their ills.

Monsieur Rousseau had died, but his glory and sensitivity emanated from his tomb in Ermenoville. Masonry spread its branches everywhere; there was nothing but secret meetings, lodge sessions and strange convents, all occupied with the most unsubstantial fads of the day or with the most ancient ideas of the Orient. A typical manifestation was the Congrès des Philadelphes, organized in 1784, which included Martinists, Swedenborgians, Égyptian Masons à la Cagliostro, Mesmerians, Scotch Masons and regular Masons, all looking for a formula of union. Paris was crowded with foreign travelers. The young English cosmopolitans took promenades once more all along the Champs Élysées to the Bois de Boulogne. These same young gentlemen were called "macaronis" in London. They set the styles and rigged themselves out in enormous hats, similar to the gigantic coiffures the women had adopted. The first balloons ascended, elegant and strange, their baskets festooned with flowers and decorated with the King's arms, their nacelles wound with gold and silver, and they floated lazily in the sky, the dream of an epoch in love with love.

The sky had never seemed so blue or the trees so leafy; the thick lawns of Auteuil and Passy had never been trod upon by such loving people.

The most splendid of all the styles was Doctor Franklin. The French who had welcomed him as a refugee-envoy of a feeble and persecuted people now admired him as the ambassador of a powerful republic. French and foreign visitors besieged him night and day at his fine home. Franklin had changed his quarters and was now living in the most elegant wing of the Grand Hôtel de Valentinois. The Duc de Croÿ arrived one day to kiss him formally and to present his little grandson. He made Franklin talk about America and when he left he was dumbstruck with admiration. "That country has come about like a dream," he murmured (February, 1783).

All was quite as glimmering as a dream then. Sweden, Denmark, Portugal and Prussia all sent their ministers to Passy to negotiate commercial treaties with the new country. The Pope dispatched his Nuncio to talk with Franklin about the organization of Catholics in the United States and the establishment of hierarchy there. Such were the beginnings of the Baltimore diocese. Such illustrious persons as the

Italian savant, Filangieri, the Spanish Comte de Campomanes, the famous Czech professor, Steinsky, sent their books to Franklin; the Duke of Dorset, the Comte Castiglioni, Lord Fitzmaurice, the son of Lord Shelburne, a flood of young Englishmen, Poles, Germans, etc., came to pay their respects; Romilly, Baynes, Polish bishops, Prince Henry of Prussia, the King of Sweden and the Bishop of Bordeaux, were still other distinguished visitors to Franklin's brilliant salon. Passy had become the Versailles of Philosophy, and the illustrious men of all lands came to bow before the Patriarch of Wisdom.

His presence was felt throughout the realm. Franklin's portraits were innumerable; Cochin, Duplessis, Greuze, Fragonard, Madame Lavoisier, Van Loo, Madame Filleul, Carmontelle, were artists who had had Franklin sit for them at some time or other, and there were engravings of these portraits by the hundred. Nini had made a little medallion of Franklin in terra cotta, Caffièri, a bust, and Mrs. Patience Wright, a head in wax. There were bronze statuettes of Franklin being handed the peace treaty by Louis XVI, Franklins in faïence made by Monsieur de Chaumont's potters, "Franklin dolls" writing down the Pennsylvania laws, experimenting, etc. Louis XVI presented a splendid chamber pot, with Franklin's spectacled face painted on the bottom, to the charming Comtesse Diane de Polignac, who was very fond of the Sage. Franklin wrote to his daughter:

> The clay medallion of me you say you gave to Mr. Hopkinson was the first of the kind made in France. A variety of others have been made since of different sizes; some to be set in the lids of snuffboxes, and some so small as to be worn in rings; and the numbers sold are incredible. These, with the pictures, busts, and prints (of which copies upon copies are spread everywhere), have made your father's face as well known as that of the moon. . . . It is said by learned etymologists, that the name *doll*, for the images children play with, is derived from the word IDOL. From the number of *dolls* now made of him, he may be truly said, *in that sense*, to be *i-doll-ized* in this country.

The French artists had good reasons for not tiring of painting him. The best one was that the portraits sold so well. But there were others: Franklin was an excellent customer for the French painters, sculptors and engravers. He was continually ordering works of art for Congress: a monument for General Montgomery, who had been killed at Quebec, a sword of honor for La Fayette, a commemorative peace medal, etc. He employed artists for still more discreet purposes, such as making symbolic engravings and emblems for the United States, cartoons and caricatures to ridicule England and her politicians. He made so much use of the artists that a "Franklin genre" is clearly distinguishable in French engraving from 1775 to 1790. It was only natural that he should be so popular among the men he supplied with so much work.

Franklin enjoyed the same kind of fame in the learned world. His influence among the scientists was so great that his name was venerated by many ambitious young writers and scholars. They never lost their enthusiasm for translating and adapting Turgot's famous verse: "*Eripuit cælo fulmen, sceptrum que tyrannis.*"

Their elders were no less fond of praising him. Not a day passed but what some new society showed their appreciation by naming him an honorary member. Some of these societies were the Grand Lodge of Carcassonne, the Manchester Literary and Philosophic Society, the Royal Academy of Arts and Sciences of Padua (1782), as well as the corresponding Academy in Turin (1783), the Royal Academy of History of Madrid, the Royal Society of Physics, Natural History and Art of Orléans (1785), the Academy of Lyon (1785), the Parnassus Society of Marseilles, which held a special festival to crown his portrait, the Patriotic Society of Milan (1786) and the Imperial Academy of Sciences of St. Petersburg (1789).

The Society of Sciences of London, through the medium of its president, implored Franklin not to let himself be absorbed by politics. It was jealous of the Academy of Science in Paris, which had had the honor of listening to Franklin's lecture on the Aurora Borealis on April 14, 1779. To console his English friends, Franklin sent several reports on the Paris balloon ascensions to the London Society. He also sent the

Manchester Academy some reflections on the severe cold spell of 1783–1784, which had originated, he claimed, in the persistent fogs of the preceding summer. He kept up his correspondence with Ingenhousz on the subject of electricity, studied geology with Abbé Soulavie, and fascinated his Passy friends with his "Account of Toads Found Enclosed in Solid Stone" (1782). The Sage wrote:

> If these Animals have remain'd in that Confinement since the Formation of the Rock, they are probably some thousands of Years old. . . . One of them was quite dead, and appear'd very lean; the other was plump and still living. . . . Toads shut up in solid Stone, which prevents their losing any thing of their Substance, may perhaps for that reason need no Supply; and being guarded against all Accidents, and all the Inclemencies of the air and Changes of the Seasons, are, it seems, subject to no Diseases, and become as it were immortal.

Such were the scientific mysteries which Franklin never tired of studying.

Outside of these interesting researches and useful discoveries, Franklin's scientific prestige had been greatly increased by the attitude he took regarding the famous Captain Cook. Either at the instigation of the Duc de Croy or by his own volition, Franklin gave instructions to American privateers not to molest the famous explorer, if they should meet with him on his return. King George III was touched, in spite of his cordial hate, and he authorized Howe to send the works of Cook to Franklin as a token of his gratitude; the Royal Society struck off a gold medal to honor him. Franklin's manifold activities bewildered the savants; he was interested in the pirogues of Otahiti, proposed daylight saving time, invented a new kind of wheel and had them manufactured for him by Viny in London, as well as a new kind of spectacles with bifocal lenses; planned a new model of a stove which was being perfected for him in Paris, and an original modification of the harmonica which was built for him at Versailles. He experimented with lighting at Passy, constructing new lamps, and studied the projects and inventions which were sent to him from all over the world. A German alchemist sent him instructions how to make gold and silver, Le Roy submitted the plans of a river boat, the *Naupotame* which Franklin elaborated; his late friend, Barbeu Dubourg, willed him his lightning-rod-umbrella, which was so convenient for fearful people in a storm, — provided they did not get entangled in the ground wire.

Franklin was the arbiter of inventions. He never missed a balloon ascension and was often consulted on the future of this new means of transportation. He was enthusiastic about it, and did more than any one else to interest England in the subject. But his sovereign position was best illustrated by the part he took in the Mesmer investigation. The French Government, Louis XVI, and Marie Antoinette, were not favorable to Mesmerism and suspected that it was only a cloak of some reprehensible activity. The ministry thereupon requested the Academy of Sciences to name a committee of investigation to examine the Mesmer processes. It was formed with Bailly as president but Franklin was the real authority. Both Mesme and Ledru (called Comus), the two principal exponents of animal magnetism, declined to perform for the scientists, but Deslon, their leading disciple, consented. Divers experiments were conducted in Paris, but as gout and gall stones confined Franklin to Passy, the committee came to his home and held the experiments in his garden. Doctor Deslon had seven sick people to practice on, and used the trees. The subject was blindfolded and then sent out walking in the garden, having been instructed that some of the trees were electrified. This information had a radical effect: at the first tree the subject shuddered; at the second, he foamed at the mouth; at the third he gave a death rattle, and at the fourth, fell down electrocuted. Of course, none of these trees had been electrified. Franklin submitted himself to an experiment which was quite thorough. Knowing a good deal about electricity and other things, Franklin did not hesitate a moment to write a devastating report (August, 1784). Nothing was left of animal magnetism when he got through, and there was one telling paragraph written for the French Government only, which was kept secret, as it exposed the relationship between Mesmerism and eroticism. Poor Mesmer had played the harmonica at Passy in vain, and his protector, La Fayette, could write all he wanted — the cause was lost. Marie Antoinette's antipathy, plus Franklin's condemnation, had ruined Mesmer's system. He had to flee.

Franklin's spiritual dictatorship in France would not have varied much from other French eighteenth-century fads had he not been the champion of Masonry and its living symbol.

The Nine Sisters' Lodge had grown speedily and included among its members the boldest men of France. Lalande sat next to Greuze, Lacépède with H. Vernet, Franklin with Voltaire. Voltaire had been initiated on April 7, 1778, and had entered, leaning on the arm of Franklin. He was the beloved son of the lodge. When he died the Royal Government forbade all celebrations in his honor, but the lodge would not hold its peace. More pious than prudent, it commemorated his apotheosis on November 28, 1778. Diderot, D'Alembert and Condorcet did not *dare* attend this session, which ended by a banquet and a toast to America.

The King, who was also a Mason, was deeply irritated by it. He was too closely linked to the Order to set his police against the Masons, but within the organization he exerted influence against the Nine Sisters' Lodge and tried to have it closed. He did not succeed at first, but finally the lodge, by a new imprudence, greatly endangered its position. It gave a fête in honor of Madame to which even the uninitiated ladies were invited. Generally, on such occasions, tableaux were given, portraying the evolution of humanity according to the Book of Genesis, the Talmud and Masonry. Ordinarily the first tableau showed Adam and Eve, the apple and the serpent. This time, the Nine Sisters' Lodge, always bold and literary, made an innovation. In place of the vulgar apple and the ugly serpent, there stood an Eve-Venus, tempted by Cupid, and pierced by his arrows. The result was a dreadful scandal. Some of the ladies bustled out in anger, others protested loudly, still others silently fainted away. The Masons were very embarrassed and the Nine Sisters' Lodge was ordered to close.

Threatened by such a great danger, the brothers banded together to combat the bad impression. Lalande went to beg the authorities for clemency. Then some one had a flash of genius and Franklin was elected as the Grand Master (1779). With such a great leader they thought they would be protected against every one, even the King, and they were not mistaken. Between 1779 and 1781, while Franklin officiated, the lodge was sheltered from all persecution and enjoyed a period of great vigor. A large number of illustrious men entered the lodge, among them the privateer, John Paul Jones.

But more important, the lodge developed the first institution of higher laic instruction. Of course, Franklin was the spirit behind it. The new society, made up of a committee in the lodge, was called the Apollonian Society and met once a week to listen to lectures on literary, philosophic and scientific subjects. After 1781 it was called the Musée de Paris and its meetings had such great success that when a branch was formed under the direction of Pilatre de Rozier, Monsieur did not hesitate to accord his protection. The association continued to prosper and by 1782 was rich enough to construct a building for itself which was inaugurated November 21, 1782. On March 6, 1783, a great celebration was held there in honor of Franklin, whose bust was solemnly crowned with myrtle and laurel, and honored by speeches, songs and canticles.

Monsieur, the Comte d'Artois and the Duc d'Orléans patronized and subsidized these institutions, in which La Harpe gave his famous course in literature. Between 1783 and 1790 they were the meeting places of the intellectual youth of France, from the young William Temple Franklin to the young Benjamin Constant de Rebecque.

Franklin's influence was vivifying and stimulating. At the same time he was developing the Musée, he undertook a great campaign for judiciary reform and the lightening of punishments which was brilliantly carried on by President Dupaty.

He was still more clever and mysterious in propagating his "great principles." His "Poor Richard" made him the legislator of the layman's morale in France. "Intendants" and bishops recommended this little book to schoolmasters and priests as a useful complement to the Catechism, and the provincial newspapers echoed their opinions. The philosophers rather broadly hinted that "Poor Richard" could replace the Catechism, and thus this little book found its way into the most humble cottages of France, and was the first literary success which ever started with the masses. It invaded the domain of the morale, which had been held hitherto by Catholic and other churches and it lessened the fear of God. Another result was the general distribution of lightning rods. Franklin's correspondence bears faithful witness of this. He received letters from England, Ireland, Germany, Italy and especially France, requesting instructions for setting up these precious instruments. Now, wherever they were erected, they were a symbol of philosophy. "You may distinguish the learned and the superstitious man when it thunders," wrote Rivarol; "one seeks protection in sacred relics, the other in a lightning rod." In some places, however, the devout people revolted against lightning rods. Such was the case of Saint Omer, where a certain Monsieur Vissery de Bois Valé had erected a lightning rod on a house he had rented from a canon. The frightened neighbors thought that Heaven would punish this blasphemy and filed a suit against him which they won. But Monsieur Vissery de Bois Valé appealed the case to the Conseil d'Artois, the Superior Court of the Province. The great legal struggle which followed roused intense excitement, and for the first time the public heard the name of the young lawyer who defended the lightning rod: *Maximilian de Robespierre.* He made an excellent plea, and though he lost his case, he was proud of having been able to pay his homage to His Excellency, Doctor Franklin (1782).

Franklin was the center of all kinds of audacious projects, and his contemporaries guessed more than they knew about them. They would have been frightened had they known the details of his campaign against the "Cincinnati." This was a society of the American veterans of the War of Independence. The soldiers had been poorly paid and were not much respected by Congress; they had returned to their homes discontented, and in order to make their strength felt, they organized this society. It was a society of mutual aid, and a military order which was to be carried on by the male descendants of the veterans, to keep the memory of their glory intact. In spite of the high patronage of Washington, Congress regarded this institution with ill favor. Perhaps this was on account of a guilty conscience, or the suspicion of monarchical intrigues which were actually going on, or just the ordinary jealousy of the civilian for the military.

Franklin received information relative to the Cincinnati in the first months of 1784. His democratic instinct roused him to opposition immediately. On January 26 he wrote a long letter to Mrs. Bache, severely condemning the "Cincinnati" by a repetition of his arguments against heredity, which he had formerly published in "Poor Richard" (1751). He even wrote a pamphlet on the subject which he sent to Morellet to translate. The Abbé read it with interest and enthusiasm, but the pamphlet also frightened him. He translated it, however, and wrote to his famous friend:

"This paper is excellent, but would you allow me to suggest that it might anger some persons whose enmity you might not like to incur? I think you should show it only to those readers who are sufficiently philosophical to realize the absurdity of the principles you have opposed so brilliantly."

Franklin answered with thanks for the translation and the good advice, saying that the paper would never be printed in his lifetime.

However, Monsieur de Mirabeau, the son of the Friend of Men, — he, himself, the Friend of Women — was at that moment in great distress After a long stay in a dungeon of Vincennes — for having eloped with his neighbor's wife — and after difficult, dishonorable lawsuits, Mirabeau had at last been freed from his wife and released from prison, but he did not have a penny to his name. He was in love once more, with an exquisite woman, Madame de Nehra, and was looking for glory — at least, notoriety — and for money. Franklin invited him to come to Passy and talked over the Cincinnati matter with him, showing a violent pamphlet printed in America, which a certain Ædanus Burke had written against the society, and his own suave pages with their hidden barbs. Mirabeau realized that something might be made out of them, and accepted the papers along with some money and Franklin's benediction. Thus armed, Mirabeau left for London accompanied by Madame Nehra and a rascally servant. He had procured some other documents — how, no one knew — which he hoped would bring him some money also. He finished writing his pamphlet on the Cincinnati at London, and, thanks to the letters of recommendation which Franklin had given him, he found a publisher. Mirabeau was also received by Shelburne, Price, Priestley and practically all the friends of virtue and liberty. The pamphlet was entitled, "Considerations on the Order of Cincinnatus." It was ardent and eloquent, the first thorough attack on heredity, and one of the first portents of the French Revolution. Mirabeau signed it in his own name, the first time he had ever done such a thing, saying, "I think I owe it to myself to publish nothing from now on but my own acknowledged writings." This pamphlet was a mixture of Burke's ideas, Franklin's phrases, and his own flaring eloquence. Before publishing it, he returned to France to read it to Franklin, who had given him such practical, moral and material aid in the meanwhile. The famous occasion of the reading took place in July, 1784, and Chamfort attended it. Then Mirabeau offered the pamphlet to the public, and the excitement it stirred could scarcely be estimated. The part of the pamphlet which criticized the principle of heredity, however, caused the most discussion. This was Franklin's contribution, and was a repetition, almost word for word, of his article in the *New England Courant* for February 18, 1723, and his article of 1751. There were the same calculations on the portioning out of ancestral blood according to the generations. Mirabeau had even attacked Washington and La Fayette to stiffen his pamphlet. No piece of writing could have been more certain to rouse public opinion. Mirabeau won an immense success, even though some perspicacious readers saw the telltale traces of Franklin's thought.

Their collaboration did not stop here. Mirabeau thought of founding, in conjunction with Franklin, an important Anglo-French review, *Le Conservateur*. His project did not come to fruition, but in 1788 he translated and published one of Franklin's letters against capital punishment — already published anonymously in England in 1786 — along with his "Observations d'un Voyageur Anglais sur . . . Bicetre." Mirabeau and Franklin understood each other perfectly, and although their characters were opposite, a deep intimacy sprang up between them.

It was extraordinary that Franklin's ideas should have been received with such eagerness and welcome, but the fact was that France was the true country of his mind. He had fought against her for so long in the name of Whig principles, that his success was nothing less than a miracle. He had arrived in France as an utter stranger, bringing with him all the ideas that had resulted from his radical education in Boston and London. His principles on the church, divinity, liberty and equality had not changed since 1723, but he could now express them openly, and found that they were marvelously adapted to his aristocratic environment.

It did not embarrass him in the least to talk about the Bible and he even suggested a new version of the Book of Job. The verse, "Now there was a day when the sons of God came to present themselves before the Lord, and Satan came also amongst them," was changed to "And it being *levée* day in heaven, all God's nobility came to court, to present themselves before him; and Satan also appeared in the circle, as one of the ministry." This might be considered as droll, but it was blasphemy as well. It delighted the readers whom Voltaire had accustomed to this tone. No one in Passy was surprised to hear Franklin made such proposals as these:

"There are several Things in the Old Testament, impossible to be given by *divine* Inspiration, such as the Approbation ascribed to the Angel of the Lord, of that abominably wicked and detestable Action of Jael, the wife of Heber, the Kenite. If the rest of the Book were like that, I should rather suppose it given by Inspiration from another Quarter, and renounce the whole."

A group of young Episcopalian seminarists in America vainly tried to be ordained through the Church of England, and, writing Franklin for advice, the Patriarch suggested they address the Papal Nuncio, who would doubtless be only too glad to give a proof of Roman liberalism. He pretended to be very surprised when he heard the Pope could not ordain Protestant ministers. He took up the proceedings he had used against the Mathers in 1723–1724, and which Voltaire had popularized in France. In their youth, Voltaire and Franklin had both drunk at the same spring: the English radicalism of Gordon, Collins, and Shaftesbury. But Voltaire had developed it into a witty, dry and sharp-tongued philosophy, while Franklin had expanded it with good fellowship and sentimentality. France was saturated with Voltairianism; but Rousseauism, which taught men how to love, also wielded much influence. Franklin, who combined the two philosophies, was the man all France was waiting for. The ideas which had forced Franklin to flee from Boston made him the ruler of intellectual Paris.

He talked about pastors as his friend D'Holbach did. He refused to have any of them around him, and this caused some surprise, as all the diplomats had their private chaplains. Franklin rejected the offers of various churchmen, claiming that he could say his prayers himself. He praised the Quakers who had no ordained ministers and who did not pay their preachers. He considered the Church of Rome to be like raw sugar, the American churches like refined sugar, for they were less influenced by hierarchical systems or mysticism. He saw a certain advantage in the multiplicity of churches in the world, as that made for competition and competition made for trade, but he didn't think churches were of any importance in heaven, as is proved by his story of the officer, Montresor. This good fellow arrived at the gates of Paradise, and, as St. Peter asked what religion he professed, he was obliged to answer that he had none. This was puzzling as all the blessed ones lived together according to their denominations. The Celestial Porter thought a moment, and then told him to go on in and stay where he wanted.

Franklin spoke about miracles with the same levity, and enjoyed recounting an anecdote about an incredulous English farmer. The farmer did not believe Franklin could calm water with oil, and when the Sage had accomplished the experiment, much to his stupefaction, the farmer threw himself at Franklin's feet and asked him what he should believe. "What you have seen and nothing else," answered the doctor testily. "This man," he said later, "had witnessed something extraordinary and was quite ready to believe the most absurd ideas. Such is the logic of three-fourths of all men!"

He did not want to preach morality, except when it was useful, and his attitude was summed up in these words: "If rascals knew the advantages of virtue they would become honest through sheer rascality."

His faith in the existence of God, however, had other foundations than simple utility. He retained a pious belief in Deism, oriented towards the future of humanity and science, and mixed with Pythagoreanism. To his most intimate friends he confided: "I cannot suspect the annihilation of Souls or believe that He will suffer the daily waste of millions of minds ready made that now exist and put Himself to the continual trouble of making new ones. Thus finding myself to exist in the world, I believe I shall in some shape or other always exist." Science seemed to reveal an order in things and a directing hand, he thought, if it were studied deeply enough. It seemed also to him that science foretold a happier day for humanity. For example, he believed in balloons. When some one asked him, "What good are they?" [1] he answered, "Of what good is a new born babe?" and he elaborated this witticism in speaking on the subject to the Duc de Croÿ. "It is a child; perhaps it won't amount to much, perhaps it will be very brilliant. We will have to see its education completed first." And Franklin contributed to the expenses of aëronautic experiments.

[1] Originally in French.

He was no less free and bold in politics. Concerning kings, he had a little story:

> A Spanish writer of certain visions of Hell relates that a certain devil, who was civil and well bred, showed him all the apartments in the place, among others, that of deceased kings. The Spaniard was much pleased at so illustrious a sight, and after reviewing them for some time, said he should be glad to see the rest of them. "The rest?" said the demon, "Here are all the kings that ever reigned upon earth from the creation to this day. What the devil would the man have?"

Once Franklin was playing chess with the Duchesse de Bourbon and at the end of the game he took her king. She protested that this wasn't the custom in France. Franklin shocked her very much by answering that in America the kings were always taken.

He condemned nobility still more severely:

> The *descending Honour*, to Posterity who could have no Share in obtaining it, is not only groundless and absurd, but often hurtful to that Posterity, since it is apt to make them proud, disdaining to be employ'd in useful Arts, and thence falling into Poverty, and all the Meanesses, Servility and Wretchedness attending it, which is the present case with much of what is called the *Noblesse* in Europe.

He was almost as hard on the parliamentarians, for he had seen too much of them in England. He objected indignantly to high-salaried political posts, seeing in them the source of all political corruption, and the cause of the possible future decadence of the British Empire. Universal suffrage attracted him, but he did not consider it to be very important. His dream was not of such and such a form of government, but of a vast liberty, with the least possible amount of laws and government, under the most simple and direct popular control. He wrote these audacious phrases:

> Superfluous Property is the creature of Society. Simple and mild laws were sufficient to guard the Property that was merely necessary. The Savage's Bow, his Hatchet, and his Coat of Skins, were sufficiently

secured, without Law, by the Fear of personal Resentment and Retaliation. When, by virtue of the first Laws, Part of the Society accumulated Wealth and grew powerful they enacted others more severe, and would protest their Property at the Expence of Humanity. This was abusing their Power, and commencing a Tyranny.

These bold lines recall Rousseau, and indeed, the life of simple occupations and simple pleasures attracted Benjamin as it had attracted Jean-Jacques. The entire society of Passy was pervaded with Rousseauism and it reminded Franklin of his childhood, when he had been happy to swim in the Charles River, work hard all day, and in the evening, court some Boston lass under the dark trees of the Common.

The same tendencies, which were encouraged by the Economists, gave Franklin his hatred for all restriction of trade, or limitation of the freedom of the press.

However, all this did not form a philosophical system, but rather, a picture. Franklin was not rigorously logical, for despite his rustic tastes, he admired luxury as a stimulant. Nevertheless, there was a certain unity to the mirage which persisted in his mind. It gave him the energy to write his pamphlets against heredity and capital punishment, to urge the English negotiators to adopt a clause in the final treaty which would forbid privateering in times of war, and to devise general protection for the sailors and laborers. He proclaimed that there was "never a good War or a bad Peace", and he dreamed of universal peace. He had gladly welcomed the strange letters of a Masonic prisoner, one "Pierre Gargaz, called Fransé", who, as soon as he had been liberated, submitted a plan of world peace to Franklin, a kind of brotherly contract between the principal kings of Europe, a Holy Philosophic Alliance in 1783! Franklin printed the work on his press and sent it to Vergennes. ("Le Conciliateur de toutes les nations de l'Europe ou Projet de Paix perpétuelle" par P. A. G. . . . 1782.) Franklin even wanted to procure "letters of rehabilitation" to help the poor Gargaz. At the same time he urged the idea of a pact between France, England and America. He succeeded in inserting a clause in a Prusso-

American commercial treaty of 1785 which forbade privateering in war time. Any weapon against war seemed good to him. He sighed as he thought of the idea he had once had, of buying up the British Parliament. He sighed, for it would have avoided spilling the blood of thousands of young Revolutionists.

But Franklin obliterated this cruel vision by the splendid hope of a progressive betterment of the world. "The Multitude," he thought, "are more effectually set right by experience than kept from going wrong by reasoning them. And I think we are daily more and more enlightened." He prepared for this idyllic future of the universe and his country by various pamphlets he published at this time: "To Such as Would Remove to America" (English, German and French editions in 1784), and his fine praise of the savages, "Remarks concerning the Savages of North America."

This optimism did not make him hostile to his own time. He knew how to render justice to his contemporaries. When some one spoke to him about Louis XVI he declared: "Perhaps no sovereign ever born to rule had more goodness in his heart, or possessed more of the milk of human kindness than Louis XVI," and he assured the revolutionary abbés that there could be no revolution in France. "It is a strongly constituted state," he affirmed. "I do not doubt but what it will resist for a long time the spirit of change which ruins all our states. I think that neither you nor I will ever see all the upheavals you predict. . . ." France was dear to Franklin and he hoped it would undergo a slow and profound intellectual transformation, resulting in a gradual political renovation.

Franklin's friend, the Comte de Vergennes, without having his audacities or suspecting the half of them, was attracted by the same ideas. He protected Cagliostro and Mirabeau and encouraged the efforts to liberate the French Protestants, by giving them a normal standing in society. But he was overrun by the crowd of idealistic young nobles who surrounded Franklin, and who listened to his words as though he were an oracle.

How could a Frenchman have refused to be fond of a man who was so fond himself of Frenchmen? Franklin said of them:

> I am exceedingly pleased with your Account of the French Politeness and Civility, as it appeared among the Officers and People of their Fleet. They have certainly advanced in those Respects many degrees beyond the English. I find them here a most amiable Nation to live with. The Spaniards are by common Opinion suppos'd to be cruel, the English proud, the Scotch insolent, the Dutch Avaricious, &c., but I think the French have no national Vice ascrib'd to them. They have some Frivolities, but they are harmless. To dress their Heads so that a Hat cannot be put on them, and then wear their Hats under their Arms, and to fill their Noses with Tobacco, may be called Follies, perhaps, but they are not Vices. They are only the effects of the tyranny of Custom. In short, there is nothing wanting in the Character of a Frenchman, that belongs to that of an agreeable and worthy Man. There are only some Trifles surplus, or which might be spared.

Franklin had attempted to enjoy the French seriously and discreetly, but without sacrificing anything of his own personality or of their qualities. Thus he achieved the miracle of being loved for his similarities with French character, and venerated for his originalities.

When his French friends saw him dreaming or meditating for long spaces at a time, they silently respected his detachment. They were touched to tears when he broke his silence, saying: "At your age, the soul is outside, but mine is inside of me, and quietly regards the noisy passersby without participating in their quarrels." [1] They understood why the Sage spoke so infrequently; the spectacle of the world alone satisfied him and he was absorbed by his work. He no longer read much, but merely reflected on past events, and calmly enjoyed the last caresses of life.

They were many, and even God himself seemed to want to honor the Patriarch. During the terrible winter of 1784–1785, an eagle was beaten down by the wind into his garden

[1] Originally in French.

and allowed itself to be captured. Some one quickly wrote this quatrain:

> The eagle has honored your garden so fair,
> Oh, Envoy of Lightning, and Lord of the Air,
> His oath to Jove he thinks but a blunder,
> And wants to pay court to the True King of Thunder!

Nothing could have been more pleasant; the love of the crowd is intoxicating but the love of cultivated people is a voluptuous treasure. What joy could equal that of being the intellectual arbiter of the most intelligent people in the world?

But no one's path is always smooth and easy, and although Franklin was powerful and happy, he had to follow Mather's advice and "stoop" when he was at the topmost point of happiness and glory. His authority was uncontested in Europe but it remained feeble in America. He could neither cement Franco-American friendship, due to the systematic opposition of Jay, Lee and Adams, nor could he succeed in bringing about an Anglo-American reconciliation, due to the hesitation of the English ministers and the hostility of the British people. His two great ideas remained chimeras.

Every letter he received proved to him that his situation across the sea was tottering. Calumnies increased and multiplied; he was accused of having speculated with his nephew, J. Williams, on supplies; of having helped France to make criminal demands for the reimbursement of French merchants, who had suffered from the depreciation of American money; of having been an unsatisfactory, nonchalant and pro-French negotiator, of having been ready to sacrifice the Newfoundland fisheries. This last accusation was too much for Franklin, and he asked Jay and Adams to testify to the honorable part he had played in the peace negotiations, in order to combat it. They came to his aid, of course, but it was very humiliating to have had to ask them. He was forced to, however, as his old friend and protector, the Reverend S. Cooper, had died. The Adams ruled over Massachusetts without any opposition. The Dickinson faction in Pennsylvania continued to attack him, and the unpopularity of his cherished offspring, the Constitution of Pennsylvania, was also detrimental. Bache, who had become a merchant once more, had no longer any influence. Franklin did his best to defend himself from his great distance, but no one listened to him. He urgently requested an appointment for Temple, but Congress did not take the trouble to answer him, having even the cruelty to dispatch a new Secretary of the Legation, Colonel Humphrey, who could not talk French. So much injustice roused all the ire of the old fighter, and he decided to return to America, to justify himself, crush his enemies, and save his family.

He had other reasons for wanting to leave. Since neither Madame Helvetius nor Madame Brillon had helped him to make a home, he felt unsettled in France. And though the country pleased him, his relations found it difficult to live there. Williams was in bankruptcy. Franklin had to ask Vergennes to order a postponement which would prevent the creditors from putting Williams in jail. He obtained it, but it was not very pleasant to have had to ask for it.

Temple could have been a comfort — he was charming, and Franklin loved him deeply, but unfortunately, Temple's affairs with the Brillon girls had embittered him, and the exaggerated flatteries of Franklin's fashionable friends had spoiled him. He imitated his grandfather, put on important airs, affected long silences, and occasionally told droll stories in his grandfather's inimitable manner. He also made fun of the Americans in Paris. In short, Temple was a fop, and he did not hear the undertone of ridicule in his nickname, "Franklinet." People applauded his stories because he was the grandson of the Patriarch, and he did not notice their amused glances at his vermillion heels, embroidered coats, the Angora cat he paraded with, or his little dog, Boulet, which barked at every one. On the contrary, Temple thought he was superior to Franklin. He thought his grandfather was a little vulgar, and let him know that he thought so. He was weak enough to have agreed with Arthur Lee that Franklin was lazy, and to negotiate directly with Adams over his grandfather's head. Visitors to Passy were surprised at the unceremonious way he treated the great man.

Perhaps at the bottom of his heart he felt revengeful. Perhaps he had a grudge against Franklin for having stolen his father from him. Before the peace preliminaries had been signed, he had hurriedly sent a plea for his father to Shelburne, without Franklin's consent. His request was transmitted to the English minister through B. Vaughn, and Shelburne paid close attention to it. At the very moment when Franklin was trying to prevent a clause in the peace treaty conceding anything to the Tories, his grandson was asking the British Government to give a good post to his father, who was one of the most notorious Tories in America. Then Temple hastened to London, where he stayed with his father, and he did not send a letter to Franklin for a long time.

When he returned, he refused a position which Brillon offered him and led a most frivolous kind of life. He drove to the balls of Paris in his pretty cabriolet, spent his evenings at the Vauxhall or went to music halls (Les Grands Danseurs du Roi). He would parade on the boulevards too, with his friends, the young Le Veillard, Le Ray de Chaumont, Chevalier de Sainte Olympe, Chevalier de La Neuville, and the Chevalier de Keralio. He accepted their flatteries. In the evening he returned to Passy and furtively glided under the huge dark trees to see his "Blanchette", the wife of one of their neighbors, Monsieur Caillot. Thus in 1785, Franklin had a great-grandson, who was the illegitimate son of the illegitimate son of his illegitimate son. The babe only lived a few months. Blanchette wept, but the tears in her lovely blue eyes no longer moved the haughty Temple. The Patriarch felt as though a tide of sadness had risen and isolated his house; Blanchette's plaintive letters seemed like a dolorous commentary on his own innocent love affairs.

He needed a family's care. In 1784, his gout became more serious and he suffered from gallstones. He could no longer visit Versailles; every movement pained him, and the coach became impossible. His friends vainly coddled him at Passy, which had now become a prison of verdure and tenderness. One after another, his old friends of France and England disappeared. Mrs. Stevenson was dead, as well as Pringle, Canton and Fothergill; Vergennes was ill, and his probable disgrace was a common topic of conversation; Le Ray de Chaumont, constantly threatened with bankruptcy, had become nervous and exacting. The only support that was left to Franklin was his charming Benny, who had returned from Geneva, a handsome, shy, good-hearted youth. Temple had been a lesson to Franklin and he decided not to make Benny a diplomat. Instead, he sent him to Didot, one of the best printers of the time in Paris, to prepare him for an artisan's life. But Franklin was thus often deprived of Benny's society, and in order to escape the solitude of long winter evenings he invited the good Polly Hewson (the former Polly Stevenson) to come with her children (1784). The gleeful band filled the huge house with noise that warmed his heart; Polly made tea for him in the English way, and in the evening he played cards with the little family.

However, he did not cease harassing Congress to obtain his recall. He was afraid that if he waited many more months he would be too ill ever to leave. Madame Helvétius invited him to come and spend his last days at her home in vain, for that was not to his way of thinking. Once he had wanted to marry her, but now he wanted to go away.

At last, on May 2, he received the summons from Congress which made him free once more. He welcomed it almost gayly, in spite of the connections he would have to break, and the tears that glittered in beloved eyes whenever he mentioned his departure. With Benny's aid, he began packing immediately, and despite the hurry there seemed to be no end to the boxes. Finally, on July 12, Franklin departed in a litter His Majesty had loaned him so that he could make his journey with the least suffering possible. An adoring procession followed the slowly advancing mules, as they wound across the Bois de Boulogne. People lined the road to cheer and to join the procession, while women wept. Franklin knew that behind him in Passy, in an exquisite white and gold salon, there were two women in particular who were dabbing their burning eyes with lacy handkerchiefs. "Oh, Franklin, Franklin, why did you go?" cried Madame Helvétius over and over again, while Madame Brillon answered with a trace of bitterness, "His staying depended only on you." But Madame Helvétius, who was wiser, could have answered that there was much to say on that subject, and that they were both of them equally responsible.

The royal litter went from Passy to St. Germain, from St. Germain to Mantes, Gaillon and Rouen, where the Cardinal de la Rochefoucauld welcomed Franklin splendidly. Then Franklin began the last stretch of his journey in France, across the lovely Normandy country, dark and green in the sumptuous summer twilights. It was days before they reached Havre, and they had ample time to taste the voluptuous sorrow of a long-drawn-out departure.

They sailed from Havre on July 22, and reached Southampton two days later. William came there to greet his father formally. They had pardoned each other, but the love between them was dead. William made a gift of his American lands to his son, and then they separated politely. But the true friends, B. Vaughn and the Shipleys, had hurried to Southampton and spent four days there while the boat was loading. They had given Franklin great joy and great glory, and now he bade them an eternal farewell. Then without warning, the boat set sail at five in the morning, so that the sharpest moments of their separation were avoided.

In eight years, Franklin had achieved one of the most brilliant of all careers, and he had so touched human hearts that some one even dared to compare him with Christ. Now he was returning to his own country, torn by the very sweetness of the friendships he had made.

Fortunately, there were flying fish, a hurricane, and the Gulf Stream to distract his active mind. He began to take the temperature of the sea once more, and his studies soon made him forget his gallstones, politics, Temple, who was seasick, Madame Brillon's tears, America, France, glory, and life itself, which cannot be enjoyed unless it is forgotten.

VIII

THIS voyage, which he had feared might end his life, gave him back much of his old energy. Captain Truxton had handled his boat very carefully in order to avoid as much fatigue and suffering as possible for his illustrious passenger. The food was excellent: during the trip half a dozen sheep were consumed, a like number of swine, and several hundred chickens, pigeons, ducks, geese and turkey. Punch, porter and claret flowed copiously and kept up a general good humor aboard. The doctor felt so hale and hearty he worked as he had not worked for years, and instead of writing about the past, as his friends in France had begged him, he turned towards the future, and filled innumerable pages with maritime observations, wrote a treatise on "*The Causes and Cures of Smoky Chimneys*", and another, "*Description of a New Stove for Burning of Pitcoal and Consuming All Its Smoke.*" Thus, diverted by his philanthropy, Franklin was not bored by his voyage and felt quite fresh when the *London Packet* hove in view of Philadelphia on September 13.

Franklin was lively and ready to fight, but he somewhat anxiously wondered if the current would not be too strong for such an old man as he. A pleasant surprise was in store for him. As soon as the boat had been sighted from the city, the bells were set ringing, and the citizens crowded to the docks. When the doctor landed there was an enthusiastic throng to welcome him. He was taken to his home in the midst of fervid cheers which continued until late in the night. The next day the President of the Congress, Richard Henry Lee, was the first to visit him, and he was shortly followed by the Pennsylvania Assembly, which welcomed him with a majestic complimentary address, part of which ran as follows:

We are confident, Sir, that we speak the sentiments of this whole country, when we say that your services in the public councils and negotiations have not only merited the thanks of the present generation, but will be recorded in history to your immortal honor.

On the next day, September 15, the University and the Philosophical Society joined in the unanimous chorus of praise. Franklin's unpopularity had been rumored in Europe and his friends expected he would be received with sticks and stones. Before they heard the contrary, there was another frightful rumor that the *London Packet* had been captured by the Algerian pirates. His friends were relieved to learn that he had received the welcome that was due him and concluded that he would be the arbiter of the political situation in America just as he had been in Europe. Franklin thought so too, for he was not only elected Councilor, but on October 26 was chosen to be the president of the Executive Council of Pennsylvania, the highest office of the State.

There was no doubt that, after all this acclamation, Franklin ranked with Washington as the most popular man of the United States, but their positions were not identical. Franklin was adored by the working classes and the farmers, but the clergy, the established middle classes, the former officers and the rich merchants distrusted him. The parliamentary aristocracy was especially hostile to him; it had come into existence during the years he had lived in England, and had been strengthened and established while he stayed in France. It consisted mainly of men from the very pious and conventional New England middle class, and of Southern plantation owners; the deistical printer's devil who had become a philosopher meant nothing to them. They were ready to bow to him, to make use of him, but not to treat him as though he belonged to their class.

Compared to the masses, who had no organization, this aristocracy was strongly united and had the power in their control. They allowed Franklin to govern Pennsylvania, but they kept him and his family outside of the real official world; the last years of his life were taken up in making vain efforts to please them, or by obliging them to give him a place.

From 1785 to 1788, as president of Pennsylvania Executive

Council, Franklin played a rôle of primary importance in the administration of his country. During a troubled period he was a peaceful influence, and he succeeded in calming the political parties and avoiding breaks between them. But he struggled in vain to keep up the Constitution. A popular majority and almost the entire middle class were opposed to this complex and awkward régime with a single house and a multiple executive body. Its democratic qualities didn't compensate for its heaviness and faulty service. The people wanted a constitution similar to the British, which would establish a true parliamentarism, create a ruling class with stable power. Such a constitution was framed in 1790, and one of Franklin's most cherished projects did not outlive him.

His illustrious companions of the struggle — Washington, Jay and Adams — somewhat ironically watched the political life the Patriarch had taken up once more. At Mount Vernon, Washington amused his visitors by talking about the doctor's efforts to keep his balance on the "slippery ground." Others more unceremoniously called him "the Old Fulmen Eripuit", and could not pardon his French popularity. Even his devoted sister, Jane Mecom, was troubled, and warned him tenderly and timidly.

It would not have been so bad had Franklin's work amounted to something, but it was all in vain; he could neither make his ideas prevail nor establish a family. He felt his failure keenly, and sometimes reproached himself for his public zeal. But it was too late; struggle had become an instinct for him and was essential to his daily life. When he was past eighty he wrote to his friends abroad like a young politician: "You will therefore not wonder if you should hear that I do not finish my political Career with the same Eclat that I began it."

The Constitutional Convention of 1788 was a clear proof for him of the vanity of his popularity. It consisted of all the illustrious citizens of the United States who were determined to find a remedy for the anarchy which menaced the country. They were directly opposed to Franklin's philosophical tendency, which might be summed up in this formula: the least government possible is the greatest possible good. The Convention wanted to organize a strong central government, as it was clear the people could not enjoy an unlimited liberty without abusing it. The members of the Convention were to meet in Philadelphia, Monday, May 2, but they were slow in coming together, and when Franklin held a welcome dinner on Wednesday, May 16, he had only a few guests. Gossips were quick to claim that he had given the dinner ahead of time, before the arrival of all the delegates, in order to avoid the expense. This was the way the fashionable world of America judged "Poor Richard."

Throughout the session of the Convention, Franklin advocated lost causes and praised the French liberalism in which no one was interested. Three theories were particularly dear to him: the danger of paying government officials high salaries; the necessity of establishing a feeble, plural executive body; and the justice of representation which was proportioned to the population and the State's wealth.

He was beaten on all these three points. In spite of his speech on June 2, liberal salaries were attached to all Federal appointments; in spite of his address on June 11, which urged that the smaller States accept equal taxation if they demanded equal representation, the smaller States won out. He had to propose a compromise himself, to the effect that the equal representation should be maintained except on financial measures. But this was not enough; the Convention agreed to establish a Federal Senate, to which each State would send an equal number of representatives. Franklin had no success, either, in his proposition for a multiple executive body (June 30).

The Convention did not talk the same language as he did. On June 28, after hours of vain discussion on this question of representation, Franklin suggested they have recourse to prayer and ask heaven for assistance. His discourse, which was brief but moving, and filled with Biblical piety, would have made the ladies of Passy weep, but it had no effect whatsoever on the American delegates. One of them answered with a crushing objection: the Convention did not have the money to pay for a minister! There was a short discussion and Franklin was forced to realize that "*the convention, except three or four persons, thought prayers unnecessary!*"

This was a lesson to him. He no longer participated in the session except to propose or support compromises: on balloting, slavery, the extension of suffrage, and on the measures by which Congress could exert a direct control over the President. Franklin was no longer deeply interested in the Convention. No matter how dear certain ideas were to him, he preferred his instinct for life — his principles — to Fate.

In his final speech he explained his attitude:

> I confess that I do not entirely approve of this Constitution, at present. . . . In these sentiments, Sir, I agree to this Constitution, with all its faults, — if they are such; because I think a general Government necessary for us and there is no *form* of Government but what may be a blessing to the people, if well administered; and I believe, farther, that this is likely to be well administered for a course of years and can only end in despotism, as other forms have done before it, when the people shall become so corrupted as to need despotic Government, being incapable of any other.

Thanks to this speech, the plan of the Convention was adopted unanimously and became the Constitution of the United States. From the standpoint of public opinion, his intervention was decisive, for the people were rather hostile to this new project, and would have probably rejected it if a leader such as Franklin had denounced it. Thus, he had played an important rôle at the Convention but it was political suicide; he had helped to organize a régime which was different from what he wanted, from what he had been recommending for thirty years, and he had put a group of men in power who had no confidence in him.

He knew it and they made him feel it keenly. Congress was not very generous to him: he was allowed to keep a portrait of Louis XVI, mounted with magnificent diamonds, which the King had given him at his departure, but he received no reward for his services, not even an address of thanks, and Congress arranged it so that the accounts were not settled. A deaf ear was turned to all of Franklin's requests for an appointment for Temple. The latter was forced to take up farming on the grounds his father had given him. But farming was not to the taste of the elegant young diplomat, nor was he attracted to the law, which Franklin suggested he study in 1784–1785. In 1788, the Patriarch knew he had rendered valuable service to the Convention and repeated his requests. Washington opposed them politely but rigidly, and he turned down Bache's petition to be postmaster-general.

When the American Federal Constitution began to function there was no descendant or relation of Benjamin Franklin in the service of the United States. Such was the end of his political career.

Of course, his scientific and philosophical career was left to him, but they did not offer sufficient consolation. He suffered bitterly from his political and dynastic setback, for in the midst of all the triumphs of his life, his family had been his great care. He had never been consoled for the death of Francis, and he could not forget William's abandoning him. He was sorry to see Temple adrift and took his failure to be a personal defeat. The Baches were his only joy; his devoted daughter took care of him affectionately, and the eight happy healthy children were very fond of their grandfather. Benny, who was a handsome young man by now, seemed to be his spiritual heir. Franklin never tired of talking to him about morality, religion and philosophy; in every way possible he prepared him for a social, political and intellectual struggle. He even set up a printing press and type foundry for him, and Benny became a young workman just as Benjamin had been, strong, humble, pious and deistical, believing in progress and Masonry.

Then, for himself and the Baches, Franklin had his three houses on Market Street built over into two, with a passage between leading to the garden and to his old home which had been built in 1763. It had been much altered in 1786, when he had added a huge library on a level with his room, the best in the house.

This library seemed fantastic to visitors, not only for the number and quality of books, such as were seen nowhere else in America, but because of Franklin's decorative inventions: the long mechanical arm which took books off the topmost shelves, the machine which illustrated blood circulation, his marvelous letter copier, his armchair with its mechanical fan, etc. This fine room was the center of Franklin's life, during the last three years of his existence. Up to 1787 he had still hoped to travel, and before he had left Europe he had dreamed of making a trip through Austria and Italy, or of spending a farewell vacation in England. In 1787 he went to Lancaster, to attend the inauguration of a German University. But in the last month of the same year, he fell down a flight of steps in his home, and this was the end of his physical activity. He kept to his bed, or a corner by the fire; occasionally he would timidly venture into the garden, but he no longer risked going any farther.

He no longer looked like the illustrious, brilliant philosopher, who had dazzled the exquisite ladies of Passy, but rather, as a realistic American visitor described him: "A short, fat, trunched old man, in a plain Quaker dress, bald pate and short white locks, sitting without his hat under the tree. . . . A very gross and rather homely lady watched the children . . . over whom she seemed to have no kind of command but who appeared to be excessively fond of their grandpapa."

It was thus he received the learned societies which met at his house after his retirement: The American Philosophical Society and the Society of Political Research, and though his appearance was no longer brilliant, his mind was as vigorous and lucid as ever, as the list of the several pamphlets he wrote during the last months of his life testifies: in 1786, "The Art of Procuring Pleasant Dreams", "The Retort Courteous" (a bitter answer to England), "The Internal State of America; being a true description of the Interest and policy of that vast Continent", which was in reality a clever advertisement for his country; in 1787, a letter "To the Printer of the Evening Herald", to defend Massachusetts against those who accused her of having established the Stamp Act; another letter "To the Editor of the Pennsylvania Gazette", on the abuse of the press, and still another to the same newspaper "On Sending Felons to America", which suggested that the English boats should take back all the criminals they had brought over; in 1788, "A Letter to the Editor of the Federal Gazette; a Comparison of the Conduct of the Ancient Jews and of the Anti-Federalists in the United States of America"; in 1789, "Observations relative to the Intentions of the Original Founders of the Academy in Philadelphia", a lengthy study which he showed only to his friends, and in which he bitterly reproached the administrators of this association for having sacrificed the study of English to Latin, contrary to the will of the founders and the needs of the nation; two letters to the *Federal Gazette*, one to defend the Constitution of Pennsylvania with its single legislature and plural executive body, the other to criticize the abuse of the freedom of the press. Finally, in 1790, his last writing, "An address to the Public, from the Pennsylvania Society for promoting the Abolition of Slavery, and the Relief of Free Negroes unlawfully held in Bondage", which was a sharp satire in the form of a parody of slavery theories.

Such a creative mind and such an ardent fighter could not be expected to give up life easily; these last pages have all the vehemence of a final appeal to his contemporaries and of an invocation of posterity. All his cherished themes were repeated in this address: his scorn for the unjust and brutal England, his confidence in the future of America, his desire to see men govern themselves with the least amount of parliamentary mechanism, his respect for human dignity, especially in the case of slaves exploited by their masters, or in the case of public men defamed by the newspapers, and finally, his hatred of violence in all its forms. This last, along with scientific subjects, was the theme of his daily conversations with his friends. He talked more and more openly of his ideal of a society which would be based on reason and virtue, which would be hostile to all use of violence and all superfluous governmental routine. It would be a society of wise men, who would be Christian because of their goodness, pagan because of their belief in a universal Deism, and modern because of their faith in practical common sense. He developed these theories picturesquely and serenely, chiefly by using anecdotes; he was bitter only when he talked about doctors, who made him suffer so much he could not keep silent about them; Congress, which would neither give justice to him nor settle its accounts, and finally, the teaching of Greek and Latin,—"literary quackery" which tended to create a lazy and useless aristocracy in America.

When he spoke of God he was as vague as he was tender, and far from reproaching Him for the evils he had received, he thanked him for having sent so few. As the days passed he seemed more and more inclined to take up this subject.

The secret connections between his fine subtle ideas were not understood, and his Masonic doctrine, which he had cherished since he was twenty, confused his friends more than it drew them to him. A large number of men admired Franklin, but for different reasons, and they did not form a homogeneous party around him. They were only his friends, and the best among them were women: the good Polly Hewson, who had come to stay with him in Passy and who followed him to America; his faithful sister, Jane Mecom, who wrote only to bless him; or his charming Katy, who was now a grandmother—her tenderness was still as sweet, however, and she sent Franklin fine ears of sweet corn and some delicately candied plums which he had been so fond of in the old days. And though these presents may have been mixed with those from Catherine Shipley (a purse), Mrs. Mecom (dried fish), or Madame Helvétius (a cloak in the newest style for Mrs. Bache), it was Katy's praise which touched him the most deeply: "I impute a great part of the happiness of my life to the pleasing lessons you gave me in that journey."

Up to the last minute of his life he kept the "chains" of his friendship clear and shining, according to a favorite Indian proverb, and his heart was filled with solicitude for all the persons he had met and loved, and who had loved him in return.

It was not surprising that he kept the deepest and most constant affection for his French friends, as they had given him the most exquisite love. He could not forget them and dreamed of them at night. Whenever he gave receptions he served not only Pennsylvania cider, but three kinds of European waters: Seidlitz, Seine and Passy, and the philosopher felt they were not his least luxury. His mail from the other side of the sea delighted him and he continued a scientific, philosophic and political correspondence.

Of course he had to take notice of the French Revolution. In public he affected a complete confidence in this new conquest of liberty, but when he sat down to write to his most intimate French friends he expressed the true feelings of his heart and all his chagrin. He had expected there would be gentle reforms in France, perfect in their gradation, and this outburst of violence in a land he loved so dearly, surprised him. He no longer recognized his lessons, his friends or his hopes, and wrote: "A great part of the news we have had from Paris, for near a year past has been very afflicting. I sincerely wish and pray it may all end well and happy, both for the King and the Nation. The voice of Philosophy, I apprehend, can hardly be heard among those tumults."

On November 13, he wrote to Le Veillard: "The troubles you have had in Paris have afflicted me a great deal. I hope by this Time they are over, and everything settled as it should be, to the Advantage both of the King and Nation."

These thoughts darkened the long reveries that had become habitual with him now, and the letters he had written were imprudently shown about by his French friends, arousing the hostility of the Revolutionists.

Cursed by the Federalists and the American conservatives, Franklin began to have a bad press among the European democrats. He had become a solitary old man, whose carefully distinguishing mind was no longer able to cope with the brutal demands of life, and whose friendships, flung over the wide world, made him vulnerable to attack in a hundred places at once. Now that night was falling, and his suffering become acute, Franklin felt he had been cruelly abandoned. The cries of the children in the garden and the familiar clamor of the street no longer comforted him; every move he made as he lay in bed was a torture to him, and was all the more sharp since he retained the clearness of his mind. He realized perfectly he was dying and that he was alone. He could no longer turn to the past, with all its gayety and all its sorrow, and decided not to finish his autobiography. As to the future, he felt he had no longer the energy to work or even to dream: his day was over.

He closed his eyes.

During the autumn of 1789 he lost weight and became increasingly weak. In the beginning of the following spring, an improvement was noticeable: he tried to write once more. But April had scarcely begun when he was seized by pleurisy, and a terrible fever set in, showing that the disease was gaining on him. He felt the approach of death and welcomed it as a deliverance from pain. He said to one of his friends: "These pains will soon be over. They are for my good; and, besides, what are the pains of a moment in comparison with the pleasures of eternity?" He asked his daughter to put fresh sheets on his bed, so that he could "die in a decent manner." When she protested and said she expected to see him live for many years more, he answered, "I hope not." Towards the same evening, he began to sink noticeably. One of the bedside watchers advised him to turn on his side, so he could breathe more easily. "A dying man can do nothing easy," he answered, and then his last agony began.

The long hours of the April evening ebbed with the passing of his strength. There was no other sound in the chamber but the heavy rise and fall of his breathing; Benny and Temple awaited immobile at opposite sides of the bed; occasionally a tear would silently steal down Benny's cheek. Franklin gropingly fluttered his fingers over the counterpane and eagerly grasped their proffered hands. He held them for a long time with pitiful tenacity, and when, at length, the young men gently extricated them from the stiffened grip, the arm of

Doctor Franklin fell inertly on the bed, inactive for the first time, and forever (April 17, 1790, at eleven P.M.).

The house was filled then with the dolorous sound of sorrow, though Franklin's death had been long awaited and came as a relief. The sad tidings spread throughout Philadelphia, throughout America, and then pervaded the entire civilized world, plunging France into deep mourning. There were superb funeral ceremonies in Philadelphia, the Government, the University, the workmen, the Masons and the churches all joining to pay him honor. By some ironical twist of fate, the man chosen to pronounce the funeral oration was none other than his former enemy, William Smith, whom Franklin had sincerely hated. However, Smith accomplished his task as well as a friend might have, and the crowd beneath his pulpit — friends, enemies and spectators — wept at his words.

Though vague rumors of Franklin's disapproval of the Revolution had reached France, the National Assembly forgot their misunderstandings and proclaimed a period of national mourning for three months. Mirabeau made a splendid oration, and funeral services in honor of Franklin were held by the Jacobins, the Friends of the Constitution, the Academy of Science, the Royal Society of Medicine, the National Guard, the Masonic Lodges, and the printers. The mourning extended throughout all the provinces of France. One contractor became rich by selling statuettes of Franklin made from the stone blocks of the Bastille. Franklin's face, simplified by death, was venerated everywhere.

There was a great deal of weeping but it did not last for long; the men were hindered by the exigencies of revolutionary activity; the women because Franklin had left them five years before; Madame Brillon because she had a superb son-in-law, Paris d'Illins; Madame Helvétius, because her abbés and her cats did not like to see her sad.

In Philadelphia, Franklin's will was being discussed. During the last three years of his life, Franklin had collected his debts and set his affairs in order. He divided his money into quarters, two for the Baches, and one for Benny and Temple

EMBLEMATICAL PORTRAIT OF FRANKLIN

respectively. He left his furniture to the Baches too, and his books and papers to Temple. Benny received the printing press and type foundry, William his lands in Newfoundland. Outside of the family there were few bequests. Franklin willed the cane of Madame de Forbach to Washington, his court sword to Cabanis, all the money owing to him to the Pennsylvania Hospital, and a thousand pounds to Boston and Philadelphia each, which was to serve as a loan fund for artisans. The loans were to be made at an interest of five per cent., and at the end of a hundred years, one hundred thousand pounds were to be contributed to some public work. The remaining thirty-one thousand was to be reinvested, and at the end of another century the capital of over four millions, gained by the interest, should be disposed as the State or city saw fit.

But this will, which was so noble and so full of moral intentions, was not destined to spread the happiness Franklin had hoped for in writing it; the Baches had too many children to be appreciably enriched, Temple had acquired luxurious tastes by living in France, which could not be satisfied by the money he received, and he became more and more needy as the years went by. Benny might have lived happily with his bequest, but he died at the age of thirty from an attack of yellow fever and the fatigue of the political struggle in which he was engaged. The artisans of Philadelphia and Boston objected to the high interest on the loans, it became almost impossible to handle the money, and the administrators, by some unwise decisions, reduced the piquant philanthropic project of the doctor to very little.

Franklin's true legacy to the world was not these perishable riches, but his genius.

He had been a great scholar, the most prominent if not the most original, of his century. All that he invented was current supposition at the time; his work lay rather in confirming and defining the scientific notions of others, but he did it so perfectly that he succeeded in presenting a modern idea of electricity out of vague clouds of speculation, and of giving concrete form to hazy abstractions on the subject.

His activity in other realms was analogous. His greatest literary work, "Poor Richard", was a collection of thoughts gleaned from everywhere. None of them were original, but they were grouped in such a way as to form a whole and give expression to a solid and practical doctrine. His precise, direct and dignified style enhanced his sayings with that majestic good fellowship his century demanded.

It was of aid to him also in politics. Though he was never a great orator he had great ideas: the union of the American colonies, the British Empire, a universal moral federation, a Franco-American *entente*. All of these projects were wise and feasible, but they were ahead of their time, and Franklin presented them too intelligently to have them understood by the crowd. His profundity and prudence roused suspicion, and his thought, which had been perfectly developed by Whig ideas, Masonic principles, and French philosophical notions, was beyond the understanding even of his admirers. They believed he was proffering a chimerical and original philosophy, when, as a matter of fact, it was the quintessence of good common sense.

His moral and religious theories frightened the century and environment he lived in. He was accused alternately of atheism and bigotry, for though his God resembled its parent, the Christian Divinity, it had distinct differences. When, at length, Franklin had many adherents, it was because of a double misunderstanding; in America, he was followed because he was believed to be a Christian, in France, because he was classed with the atheists. But Franklin had been a disciple of Pythagoras, he had adapted Christianity to his own ideas, and first and last, he had been a Mason.

All these misunderstandings made him the most accessible and the most mysterious public figure of the eighteenth century; he was the bantering *bourgeois* whose smile was never understood. However, Franklin had done more to develop Philadelphia and Pennsylvania than any other person; he was the first to give his country a sense of its national unity, to help it achieve its final victory, though in the meanwhile others knew how to take more glory from the great happenings in which he ranked among the leaders.

But this did not matter. His fame shone all the more brilliantly behind these clouds, as on the spring evenings at Passy, the sun set all the more gorgeously because of its storm halo.

In the eighteenth century, no one cared a great deal if Franklin had invented scientific or philosophical theories, a religion, or political principles. It was he, himself, they loved; it was the magnificent rôle he had created for himself, he the most gifted actor of his time, that attracted people. No one had ever been able before to play the *bourgeois*, but he had known how. Voltaire, Comte de Ferney, had aimed too high; Jean-Jacques Rousseau, the solitary walker, had aimed too low; neither belonged to any particular class, and Frederick the Great had been a king. Franklin had become a *bourgeois* and knew how to hold his rank. He had found that the balance of all his ideas and of all his scientific moral and artistic concepts centered in the principle of utility. He had known how to discard absolute beauty, absolute truth, absolute good, as well as evil, voluptuousness, frivolity and elegance; he had only kept hold of the practical and had given it a human, attractive and picturesque form.

Humanity could not forget him.

Benjamin Franklin Bache, "Benny", who fostered his spirit, did not forget him either. Soon after his grandfather had passed away, Benny took a notebook of his school days, and, turning over the pages till he found a blank one, he began to draw the sturdy, fine profile of his grandfather. As Benny looked at it, it seemed dearer to him than all the legacy of genius Franklin had willed to the world. Lovingly he considered the features, modeled by experience and work and success; then, momentarily displeased with his drawing, he took up his pen and firmly traced the lines of the mouth once more, emphasizing the firm lips, which in the darkest moments had known how to say: "It will go."

BIBLIOGRAPHY

Every sentence of this book is based upon a document, — and generally upon several of them. Were I to give my complete bibliography, I would need a special volume of several hundred pages; had I used footnotes, they would have taken up more space than the text.

I shall furnish only a summary bibliography here, which will give the general reader an idea of my work and enable the scholar to trace my statements to their principal sources.

MANUSCRIPT SOURCES

PUBLIC COLLECTIONS

The American Philosophical Society (Philadelphia). Probably the richest Franklinian Collection. Many letters of Franklin, but particularly good unpublished letters to Franklin. Best for the 1750–1790 period.

The Historical Society of Pennsylvania (Philadelphia). Very comprehensive. Has some fine unpublished documents on Franklin's early life, but is particularly rich for the Philadelphia period, 1727–1757, and the last years of his life: 1785–1790.

The University of Pennsylvania. Good collection; covering mostly the 1765–1790 period.

The Library of Congress (Washington). Large Franklin collection with an original manuscript of the "Autobiography." Particularly rich for the 1757–1790 period.

The Huntington Library (Pasadena, California). A most interesting collection of Franklin documents, including the original of the "Autobiography" and some very valuable papers on the 1740–1775 period. The Loudoun papers, and the Abercrombie papers are filled with good Franklin material.

The Clements Library, at the University of Michigan (Ann Arbor). A good collection of letters to and from Franklin, mostly for the 1770–1780 period. The Germain papers, and the Clinton papers are of value to the Franklinian scholar.

Bibliothèque Nationale, Département des Manuscrits (Paris). Some interesting Franklin letters. A good many letters addressed to him, and a great many letters, documents, manuscript newspapers, etc., about him. Interesting for the 1775–1790 period.

Archives du Ministère des Affaires Etrangères (Paris). Filled with valuable information, especially for the 1773–1790 period. The most interesting documents are in the Correspondance Diplomatique, Etats Unis, years 1778–1790, Angleterre, years 1773–1785, Mémoires et Documents, Volumes 1 to 10, 14, 17, etc.

Bibliothèque de l'Institut de France (Paris). A very interesting collection containing the papers of many of Franklin's French friends: Condorcet, l'Abbé de la Roche, Mme. Helvétius, etc. The Doniol papers also. Interesting for the 1775–1790 period.

Archives de l'Académie des Sciences (Paris). Very interesting accounts of the lightning rod dispute, and the growth of Franklin's influence.

The Public Record office, in London, the Reichsbibliothek in Berlin, the Royal Library in Stockholm, the Royal Archives in Copenhagen contain also a good deal of interesting material, and some unpublished letters of Franklin.

PRIVATE COLLECTIONS

The W. S. Mason Collection (Evanston, Illinois). A real treasure of Franklinian manuscripts, documents, prints, books of reference, etc. Particularly rich for the 1750–1790 period. It contains the Franklin-Galloway letters, which are indispensable if one wishes to understand the political life of Franklin in Pennsylvania and England from 1750 to 1775. See description in the Proceedings of the American Antiquarian Society, October, 1924. It possesses also three volumes of the Archives of the French Legation in Philadelphia from 1778 to 1790, filled with curious and rare information.

The Franklin Bache Collection (Philadelphia). No less valuable. Letters, accounts, registers of Franklin, letters addressed to Franklin, papers of Mrs. Bache, Mr. Bache, Benjamin Franklin Bache, William Franklin and William Temple Franklin, etc. It gives innumerable details on the last thirty years of Franklin's life.

Dr. Rosenbach's Collection (New York). A very good collection of Franklin's letters. The two gems of these archives are the series of letters from Franklin to his beloved sister, Jane Mecom, and the famous letter of Franklin to Jimmy Read concerning the proper use of women.

The collection of Mr. J. P. Morgan, New York. It contains a very interesting group of Franklin's letters, and letters about him, in particular, The Temple-LeVeillard correspondence, 1785–1790.

Mr. Roelker's Collection (Providence, Rhode Island). It includes the charming letters of Franklin to Mrs. Greene — Katy Ray, 1750–1790.

The De Mun family (in Paris) has some very interesting letters and documents, coming from one of their ancestors, Mme. Helvétius; the De Chazelle family, also (papers of Lavoisier, an ancestor). M. le Duc de Duras has some very curious Franklin letters, coming from the Chastellus family; M. de Guestiers and his family have the letters of Franklin to Mme. Brillon, who was one of their ancestry.

PRINTED SOURCES

NEWSPAPERS

At the New York Public Library, the Massachusetts Historical Society, the Pennsylvania Historical Society, the Huntington Library the following files have been read:

Boston News Letter, 1706–1767
Boston Gazette, 1721–1760
New England Courant 1721–1727
New York Gazette, 1725–1738
New York Weekly Journal, 1735–1750
New York Evening Post, 1745–1750
American Mercury, 1725–1740
Pennsylvania Gazette, 1728–1790
Pennsylvania Packet, 1775–1777
Pennsylvania Evening Post, 1775–1777
Pennsylvania Mercury, 1775
Pennsylvania Ledger, 1775–1776
Maryland Gazette, 1728–1735
Virginia Gazette, 1737–1752, 1766–1767
North Carolina Gazette, 1751–1778, etc.

At the British Museum:

London Weekly Journal, 1725–1727
London Daily Courant, 1725–1727
London Gazette, 1725–1727

London Chronicle, 1757–1775
Gentleman's Magazine, 1757–1775
Lloyd's Evening Post, 1780–1785

At the Bibliothèque Nationale:
Gazette de France, 1706–1790
Mercure de France, 1750–1790
Mercure de Trévoux, 1750–1760
Journal des Savants, 1750–1790
Journal Encyclopédique, 1756–1767
Journal Etranger, 1754–1760
Journal de Paris, 1777–1790
Ephémérides du Citoyen, 1765–1769
Gazette de Leyde, 1775–1790
Affaires de l'Angleterre et de l'Amérique, 1775–1778
Gazette de Deux Ponts, 1770–1786
Courrier d'Avignon, 1775–1788
Courrier de l'Europe, 1776–1790, etc.

At the Bibliothèque Nationale and at the Reichsbibliothek in Berlin:
Vossiche Zeitung, 1750–1787
Frankfurter Gelehrte Anzeigen, 1772–1784
Hallische Gelehrte Anzeigen, 1766–1788
Teutsche Merkur, 1773–1778, etc.

The proceedings of the learned societies or Academies of Lyon, Dijon, Bordeaux, Göttingen, Turin, Bologne, etc.

FILES OF PROCEEDINGS OR COLLECTIONS OF CONTEMPORARY HISTORICAL SOCIETIES

The Massachusetts Historical Society (Proceedings and Collections).
The American Antiquarian Society
The Colonial Society of Massachusetts
The New York Historical Society
The Pennsylvania Archives
The New Jersey Archives
Bulletin de la Société historique d'Auteuil et de Passy, etc.

FILES OF MAGAZINES DEVOTED TO HISTORY

Pennsylvania Magazine of History
American Historical Review

Atlantic Monthly

Revue de Littérature Comparée, etc.

All the books of Franklin, and all the books on Franklin available in New York, Paris, and London. (For a complete list, see the Catalogues of the New York Public Library, the Bibliothèque Nationale and the British Museum.)

Among them the following were found of especial value: "Franklin Bibliography." Paul Leicester Ford, Brooklyn, 1889. An old book of surprising accuracy.

"The Works of Benjamin Franklin." Edited by Jared Sparks, Boston, 1840. 10 vols.

"The Complete Works of Benjamin Franklin." Edited by John Bigelow, New York and London, 1887. 10 vols.

"The Writings of Benjamin Franklin." Edited by Albert Henry Smyth, New York, 1907. 10 vols.

Each of these three sets has its value. Smyth is the most complete and the most accurate, but he has suppressed some very interesting essays of Franklin, and does not give the letters addressed to Franklin, which were published by Sparks and Bigelow.

"Calendar of the Papers of Benjamin Franklin in the Library of the American Philosophical Society." Edited by I. Minis Hays, Philadelphia, 1908. 5 vols.

Of all the innumerable books published on Franklin, two can be singled out and put aside for their lasting value:

"The Life and Times of Benjamin Franklin." James Parton, Boston and New York, 1864 and 1892. 2 vols.

"The Many-sided Franklin." Paul Leicester Ford, New York, 1898 and 1921.

BIBLIOGRAPHIES FOR THIS VOLUME

BOOK I

On Boston and the life in New England during the period 1706–1725.

Samuel A. Drake. "The History and Antiquities of Boston." 1856.

Justin Windsor. "The Memorial History of Boston." 4 vols. 1881.

I. S. Homans. "Sketches of Boston Past and Present." 1851.

Edward H. Savage. "Police Records and Recollections." 1873.

M. Farwell Ayer. "Early Days on Boston Common." 1910.

Carl Holliday. "Women's Life in Colonial Days."

(See also the above-mentioned newspapers published in Boston and Philadelphia at that time.)

On the political life of the American Colonies during that period.

H. L. Osgood. "American Colonies in the XVIIIth Century." 4 vols. 1919.

J. T. Adams. "The Founding of New England." 1920.

J. T. Adams. "Revolutionary New England." 1923.

On the intellectual movement in England and New England during that period.

Leslie Stephen. "English Thought in the XVIIIth Century." 2 vols. 1901.

Harold J. Laski. "Political Thought in England from Locke to Bentham."

J. Hunt. "Religious Thought in England." 3 vols. 1873.

Vernon Parrington. "The Colonial Mind." 1927.

Th. G. Wright. "Literary Culture in Early New England." 1920.

An Article of Max Attenborough in the *Westminster Review* (1901) on the Deists in England.

On Inoculation.

P. Delaunay. "Le Monde médical parisien au XVIIIe siècle."

On Douglass.

G. H. Weaver. "Life and Writings of William Douglass." (In the Collection of the Society of Medical History of Chicago. Vol. IV. 1921.)

On Cotton Mather.

Barrett Wendell. "Cotton Mather."

Kittredge. "Cotton Mather." (In Publications of the Colonial Society of Massachusetts. Vol. XIV.)

On William Keith.

Charles P. Keith. "William Keith." (In *Pennsylvania Magazine of History*. Vol. XII.)

On London and the life in London at that time.

"England and the English in the XVIIIth Century." 1892.

(See mostly the above-mentioned English newspapers of that period.)

On Thomas Tryon.

Alexander Gordon. "A Pythagorean of the XVIIIth Century." 1871.

The quotations on pages 31–32 are taken from "The Way to save Wealth." Thomas Tryon, London, 1697. P. 12.

The quotations on page 33 from "Wisdom's Dictates." Thomas Tryon, London, 1691. Pp. 1, 31, 90, 107, 110, 111, etc.

The article of the *New England Courant* quoted on pages 36–37 was published in the issue of 28, I–4, II 1723.

The quotation on pages 42–43 comes from "Wisdom's Dictates." Thomas Tryon. P. 506.

The anecdote on page 79 is taken from the "Writings of B. Franklin." Smyth Edition, Vol. IX, p. 209.

The quotation on page 84 is taken from "A Collection of all the humorous Letters in the London Journal." Thomas Gordon, London, 1720. Pp. 40–49.

Page 16. These hitherto unknown details on the quarrels between Josiah and Benjamin Franklin are given in an unpublished letter of Franklin to Mrs. Mecom (July 17, 1771) in the possession of Dr. Rosenbach.

Page 106. These details on Denham's loan of money to Franklin and the price of the new cap are given in an unpublished document of the Pennsylvania Historical Society: the account books of Denham.

BOOK II

On Philadelphia and the life in Pennsylvania from 1725 to 1757.

Watson. "Annals of Philadelphia."

J. Th. Scharff and Th. Westcott. "History of Philadelphia." 1884. Vol. I.

T. W. Balch. "The Philadelphia Assemblies." 1916.

J. T. Adams. "A History of American Life. Provincial Society." 1927.

(See also the above-mentioned newspapers published in Philadelphia and the other colonial cities at that time, and the excellent collection of the Logan papers at the Pennsylvania Historical Society.)

On the political life of Pennsylvania at that time.

H. L. Osgood. "American Colonies in the XVIIIth Century." Vol. II.

Jesse L. Rosenberger. "The Pennsylvania Germans."

Votes and proceedings of the House of Representatives of the Province of Pennsylvania.

B. A. Konkle. "Georges Bryan and the Constitution of Pennsylvania." 1922.

(See also the Collection of the "Pennsylvania Archives" and of the *Pennsylvania Magazine of History*, etc.)

On the printing business and the almanacs in Philadelphia at that time.

Isaiah Thomas. "The History of Printing in America." 1810.

Charles R. Hildeburn. "Issues of the Press in Pennsylvania."

William J. Campbell. "Collection of Franklin imprints."

P. L. Ford. "Franklin Bibliography." 1889.

J. C. Oswald. "Benjamin Franklin, Printer." 1917.

G. L. Kittredge. "The Old Farmer and his Almanack." Boston, 1904.

C. S. Brigham. "An Account of American Almanacks." 1925.

(See also in the *Historical Magazine*, January, 1861, the article on Poor Richard's Proverbs, and the collection of Almanacs at the British Museum or the Huntington Library.)

On Freemasonry in the XVIIIth Century.

M. M. Johnson. "The Beginnings of Freemasonry in America." 1924.

A. G. Mackey. "The History of Freemasonry." 3 vols.

Bertrand Van der Schelden. "La Franc Maconnerie belge." 1923.

G. Bord. "La Franc Maconnerie en France."

Julius F. Sachse. "Benjamin Franklin as a Freemason." 1916.

Historical Magazine. Vol. V. 1861.

On sciences in America during that period.

Michael Kraus. "Intercolonial Aspects of American Culture on the Eve of the Revolution." 1928.

William Darlington. "Memorials of John Bartram and Humphrey Marshall." 1848.

W. A. Durgin. "Electricity and Its Development." 1912.

(See also the very interesting collection of the Cadwalader Colden papers in the Collections of the New York Historical Society and in the archives of this society.)

On James Logan.

Mina Jane. "The Life and Public Service of J. Logan."

On William Smith.

H. W. Smith. "Life and Correspondence of the Reverend William Smith."

On Franklin's religion.

Essay of Charles Lyttle in *Meadville Theological School Quarterly Bulletin.* I. 1928.

On Franklin and the Post Office.

R. L. Butler. "Dr. Franklin, Postmaster General." 1928.

Wm. Smith. "The Colonial Post Office." (*American Historical Review.* Vol. 21.)

(See also the Loudoun and Abercrombie manuscripts in the archives of the Huntington Library.)

On Franklin and the Library Company.

E. M. Abbott. "A short History of the Library Company." 1913.

On Franklin and the University of Pennsylvania.

Th. H. Montgomery. "A History of the University of Pennsylvania." 1900.

On Franklin and his ideas.

The very excellent book of Lewis J. Carey. "Franklin's Economic Views." 1928.

Th. Diller. "Franklin's Contribution to Medicine." 1912.

W. Pepper. "The Medical Side of Benjamin Franklin." 1911.

On Franklin's business and printing house.

The most interesting and enlightening book of Mr. G. S. Eddy. "Account books kept by Benjamin Franklin." 1928.

The quotation on pages 114–115 is taken from J. F. Sachse, "Franklin as a Freemason." P. 15.

The list of wares for sale, page 142, is taken from advertisements published by Franklin in the *Pennsylvania Gazette* in 1732–1733, etc.

The quotation on page 185 is taken from Figuier, *Histoire du Merveilleux.* Vol. I, pp. 368–369.

The quotation on page 189 is taken from Charles Chauncey, "Seasonable Thought on the State of Religion in New England." 1743. Pp. 105–106.

The verses on pages 189–190 are taken from the *Pennsylvania Gazette*, 29, XI, 1739.

Pages 211–212. The instructions how to make a perfect Quaker are taken from the *Virginia Gazette*, 24, XI, 1738.

The quotations of Prince and J. Winthrop are taken from "Earthquakes the Works of God . . . Being a Discourse on that Subject", by Th. Prince. Boston, 1755.

"A lecture on Earthquakes, read in the Chapel of Harvard College." John Winthrop. Boston, 1755.

The unpublished papers of James Logan at the Pennsylvania Historical Society have enabled me to describe the political situation in Pennsylvania and the attitude of the Junto, as I have done on pages 21 and 22.

In the unpublished correspondence of Franklin and Katy Ray, in the possession of Mr. Roelker, I have found the facts on the friendship of Franklin for Katy, which I relate on pages 246–247.

The pages 248–258 are based upon the Loudoun papers and especially the diary of Loudoun, which is kept at the Huntington Library.

BOOK III

On London and the life in London from 1757 to 1775.

H. B. Wheatley. "Hogarth's London." 1909.

W. C. Sydney. "England and the English XVIIIth Century." 1892.

J. Nichols. "Literary Anecdotes of the XVIIIth Century." 9 vols. 1813. (Entertaining, not very reliable.)

The best sources are the contemporary newspapers. See list above.

On the political life in England from 1757 to 1775.

Lecky. "History of England in the XVIIIth Century." 7 vols. 1892.

Cl. W. Alvord. "The Mississippi Valley in British Politics." 2 vols. Collection of the Illinois State Historical Library. Vols. X and XI.

W. S. Mason. "Franklin and Galloway." 1925.

(The contemporary newspapers and the Reports of the Royal Commission on Historical Manuscripts are the most interesting and enlightening sources.)

On the Stamp Act and Franklin's enemies.

J. H. Jesse. "Memoirs of the Life and Reign of George the III." 1861. 3 vols.

W. M. Reed. "Life of Esther de Berdt." 1853. (Especially pp. 107, 210, etc.)

J. Almon. "Memoirs of a Late Eminent Bookseller." 1790. (Especially pp. 32, 33, 47, 48, etc.)

J. Almon. "Biographical, Literary, and Political Anecdotes." 3 vols. 1797.

Thomas Hollis. "Memoirs." 1780.

Josiah Quincy. "Memoirs of the Life of Josiah Quincy." 1825.

(See also the Reports of the Royal Commission on Historical Manuscripts, 14th Report, Appendix 10, Vol. 55; the Galloway-Franklin letters at the Mason Library and the articles published in the *Pennsylvania Magazine of History*, Vol. 25, pp. 309–322; the Publications of the Colonial Society of Massachusetts, Vol. 13, pp. 306–310, etc.)

On the Hillsborough affair.

The best document is the 14th Report of the Royal Commission on Historical Manuscripts. Appendix 10, Vol. 55, pp. 252–255. See also the Galloway-Franklin letters at the Mason Library.

On the Hutchinson affair.

Thomas Hutchinson. "Diary and Letters." Vol. I.

Thomas Hutchinson. "History of Massachusetts." Vol. III.

Lord Mahon. "History of England." 1850. Vol. V, pp. 270–290.

Bowdoin-Temple letters. Collections of the Massachusetts Historical Society. 6th Series, Vol. IX.

(See also the above-mentioned works of Almon, the 14th report of the Royal Commission on Royal Manuscripts, the contemporary newspapers, and the Proceedings of the Massachusetts Historical Society, 1st Series, Vols. 15 and 16; 2nd Series, Vols. 5 and 6, etc. The amount of literature published on this episode is enormous, and I mention here only the most important documents.)

On the intellectual movement in England from 1757 to 1775. See Book I.

On Franklin's English Friends.

Memoirs of Dr. Priestley. 1806.

N. G. Brett James. "The Life of Peter Collinson." 1917.

A. F. Tytler. "Memoirs of the Life of Henry Home of Kames." 1814.

"The story of a printing house, being an account of the Strahans." 1922.

J. C. Lettson. "Memoirs of Fothergill." 1786.

H. Fox. "Dr. J. Fothergill and His Friends."

J. H. Burton. "Life and Correspondence of D. Hume." 1846. Vol. II.

J. L. Peyton. "Rambling Reminiscences." 1888. (On Jonathan Shipley and Franklin.)

Lord Edmond Fitzmaurice. "The Life of William Earl of Shelburne." 1875. 3 vols.

The story of Miss Graeme and William Franklin, on pages 262, 292, etc., is taken from the *Pennsylvania Magazine of History*, 1911, pp. 415–462. Vol. 35, and Vol. 39, pp. 259–270.

The quotation on page 291 is taken from "Works and Correspondence of the Rt. Hon. E. Burke." I, 220.

The praise of George III on pages 293–294 is taken from the *Boston News Letters*, 21, V, 1761.

The verses on page 300 are taken from Nathaniel Evans. "Poems on several occasions." Philadelphia, 1772. Pp. 108–109.

The tale of Franklin's trip through Germany is based upon "Benjamin Franklin and Germany." Beatrice Victory. 1915. A very interesting book, although not always reliable.

On Franklin and the French Economists, see Carey's "Franklin's Economic Views." Pp. 134–167.

The anecdote of Franklin calming the pond on pages 353 and 354 is told by Abbé Morellet in his Memoirs, 1821. Vol. I, p. 197.

Page 374. The quotation from Burke is taken from his "Works and Correspondence." Vol. I, p. 235.

The unpublished Franklin-Galloway correspondence kept in the Mason Library has furnished me with many unknown facts.

For instance, the quotation on page 273 is taken from these archives, letter of Franklin to Galloway, 14, I, 1758; the very bold and important letter of Franklin to Pitt (page 289) is only known to us by a letter of William Franklin to Galloway, 26, VIII, 1760, in the same archives.

The quotation from a letter of Bishop Shipley to Franklin in 1773 (page 374) is taken from the same archives.

The description I give of Franklin's attitude towards England and the British Empire is based largely on the marginal notes he wrote on many pamphlets of the time. These are unpublished, but due to Mr. G. S. Eddy's great kindness I possess accurate copies of them.

The description I give of Franklin's trip in the Netherlands in 1762 is based on a letter of William Franklin in the possession of Dr. Rosenbach. It is the only document we have on this journey, and it has never been published.

BOOK IV

On the political situation in America in 1775–1776.

Journals of the Continental Congress (Ford Edition). **Vols. II** to VI.

Pennsylvania Archives. 3rd Series, Vol. X, 1896.

Charles Francis Adams. "Familiar Letters of John Adams and Abigail Adams." 1876.

Wm. Duane. "Passages from the diary of Christopher Marshall." 1838.

B. A. Konkle. "G. Bryan and the Constitution of Pennsylvania." 1922.

W. B. Reed. "Life and Correspondence of Joseph Reed." 1847. 2 vols.

S. B. Harding. "Party struggles over the First Pennsylvania Constitution." (Report of the American Historical Association, 1894.)

Votes and Proceedings of the House of Representatives of the Province of Pennsylvania. Vol. VI.

On Franklin's trip in Canada.

Brantz Mayer. "Journal of Charles Carroll of Carrolton in 1776." Maryland Historical Society, 1876.

W. R. Riddell. "B. Franklin and Canada." (*Pennsylvania Magazine of History*. P. 48.)

On Franklin's share in writing the Declaration of Independence.

J. C. Fitzpatrick. "The Spirit of the Revolution." 1924.

On the relations between Franklin, William and Temple, the best and only complete source is the Franklin-Bache collection of manuscripts.

On Paris, Versailles and the life in France between 1775 and 1785.

A. Mercier. "Tableau de Paris." 12 vols. 1782–1788.

Hale. "Franklin in France." 2 vols.

Mes Loisirs . . . Journal . . . de Hardy. (Manuscript diary at the Bibliothèque Nationale.)

"Mémoires secrets." 36 vols. 1791.

"Correspondence secrète, de Métra." 18 vols. 1787.

"Lettres de M. de Kageneck." 1884.

"Correspondence de Grimm." Vols. 12, 13, 14, 15, 16. 1880.

(See also the newspapers mentioned before and the memoirs listed in the bibliography of B. Faÿ, "L'Esprit Révolutionnaire en France et aux Etats Unis à la fin du XVIIIe siècle.")

On the diplomatic activities during 1776–1785.

Doniol. "Participation de la France à l'Etablissement des Etats Unis." 5 vols. 1899.

B. Faÿ. "L'Esprit Révolutionnaire en France et aux Etats Unis à la fin du XVIIIe siècle." 1923.

F. Wharton. "The Revolutionary Diplomatic Correspondence." 3 vols. 1889.

Deane Papers. Published by C. Isham. 1886–1890.

Reports of the Royal Commission on Historical Manuscripts. Passim and especially Reports 8, 9 (2d part), 10 (6th part), Vols. 47, 49, 55.

Stevens. "Facsimiles of Manuscripts in European Archives, relating to America. 1773–1783." 1889. Vols. 1 to 24.

Fortescue. "Correspondence of King George III." 6 vols. 1927.

Benjamin Vaughan's letters (Massachusetts Historical Society proceedings. 3rd Series. Vol. 17.)

John Adams. "Life and Works." 10 vols. 1855.

Thomas Jefferson. "Writings." Monticello Edition. 20 vols. 1904.

J. B. Waller. "Reminiscences of B. Franklin as a Diplomatist." 1879.

On Franklin and Freemasonry.

L. Amable. "Une loge Maconnique d'avant 1789."

See also the books mentioned previously for Book II, and the archives of the American Philosophical Society where Franklin's correspondence of this time is preserved. It contains full evidence of Franklin's Masonic activities.

On Franklin and the physiocrats.

G. Weulersse. "Le mouvement physiocratique en France." 1910. 2 vols.

(See also the book of L. J. Carey mentioned previously. "Franklin's Economic Views.")

On Franklin, Turgot and Madame Helvétius.

Turgot. "Oeuvres, publieés par Schelle." 5 vols. 1913.

Dupont de Nemours. "Mémoires sur la vie et les œuvres de M. Turgot." 1782.

Morellet. "Mémoirs." Vols. 1 and 2. 1821.

Gilbert Stenger. "La Société de Madame Helvétius à Auteuil." (*Nouvelle Revue.* T. 26.)

Guillois. "Le Salon de Madame Helvétius."

Cabanis. "Oeuvres posthumes." 1825. Vol. V.

(See also the papers of Cabanis and of the Abbé de la Roche at the Bibliothèque de l'Institut de France.)

On Franklin, Mirabeau and the Cincinnati.

Bernard Faÿ. "Franklin et Mirabeau collaborateurs." *Revue de Littérature Comparée.* Jan.–Mar. No. 1928.

On Franklin and Mesmer.

Dr. Morand. "Le magnétisme animal." 1889.

On Franklin and Robespierre.

Charles Vellay. "Franklin et le procès du paratonnerre." *Revue historique de la Revolution française et de l'Empire.* 1914.

On Franklin and his press at Passy.

L. S. Livingston. "Franklin and his Press at Passy." 1914.

On Franklin and his life in Philadelphia from 1785 to 1790.

Collection of the *American Museum.* 1788–1790.

"Reminiscences of Dr. Franklin." Colonel Robert Carr. (Contribution to the Great Sanitary Fair.)

Pennsylvania Magazine of History. T. 12, pp. 110–113. ("Journal of Manasseh Cutler.")

T. 29. Excerpts from the papers of Dr. B. Rush.

(See also the papers in the Morgan Library, the Mason Library and the Bache Collection. See the archives of the American Philosophical Society.)

The quotation of Garnier on page 382 is taken from a letter of Garnier to Vergennes, Archives du Ministère des Affaires Etrangères; Correspondance politique, Angleterre, Vol. 508. 5 V 1775. (Unpublished.) The quotation of Mrs. Adams, pages 390–391, is taken from "Familiar letters of John Adams and his wife, Abigail Adams. 1876." Pp. 113–126.

The letter of J. Hutton quoted on pages 435–436 is taken from the Reports of the Royal Commission on Historical Manuscripts. Vol. 49, 2d Tome, p. 91. The secret dealings of the French Economists, and especially of Dupont de Nemours with Hutton are mentioned and explained in a report of Hutton to Dartmouth, 14th Report, Appendix 10, Vol. 20, 2d part, page 418.

Pages 436–438. These details on the reception of Franklin are given by the Danish Minister Baron Otto Blome to his King. See Royal Danish Archives, Diplomatic Correspondence, 1778.

The verses given on pages 458–459 are taken from "La Comtesse d'Houdetot, par Hippolyte Buffenoir." 1901. Pp. 44–47.

The quotations from the letters of Mme. Brillon to Franklin are taken from the originals deposited at the American Philosophical Society.

The anecdote of Duc de Croÿ, page 479, is taken from his "Journal du duc de Croÿ." 1907. Vol. 4, p. 272.

The story of Gargaz (pages 493–494) is to be found in the excellent book of G. S. Eddy: "A project of Universal Peace." New York. 1922.

The conservative sayings of Franklin (page 494) are to be found in "Memoires historique et Politiques du Règne de Louis XVI." J. L. Soulavie. Paris, 1801. Vol. V, p. 183. Also in the publications of the Massachusetts Historical Society, 1st Series, Vol. 19, pp. 311, 312.

Page 495. This anecdote of Franklin is taken from Guillois, "Le salon de Madame Helvétius." P. 60.

Page 503. The expression used by Washington concerning Franklin's political career is reported by John Hunter in the *Pennsylvania Magazine of History*, Vol. XVII, p. 79. The nickname "Old Fulmen Eripuit" for Franklin is to be found in a letter of Belknap to Hazard, 9, III, 1786, published in the Collections of the Massachusetts Historical Society. 5th Series, Vol. II, p 432.

The details on Franklin's life in Passy are given in the unpublished manuscripts of the American Philosophical Society and of the Bache Collection. For instance, the letter of Princesse Sapieha (page 457) belongs to the Bache Collection.

The details on Franklin's life in Philadelphia (pages 509–510) and on his homeward voyage are taken from several unpublished letters of William Temple Franklin to Le Veillard, preserved in the Morgan Library.

The description of Franklin's death is written according to a beautiful unpublished letter of Benjamin Franklin Bache, in the Bache Collection.

Several quotations in this last book were originally in French, notably Franklin's phrase "Ça ira." Notice is given here in order to obviate the bother of footnotes.

INDEX